THE FIRST SOLDIER

THE FIRST SOLDIER

SOLDIER

Hitler as Military Leader

STEPHEN G. FRITZ

YALE UNIVERSITY PRESS
NEW HAVEN AND LONDON

For information about this and other Yale University Press publications, please contact:
U.S. Office: sales.press@yale.edu   yalebooks.com
Europe Office: sales@yaleup.co.uk   yalebooks.co.uk

Set in Minion Pro by IDSUK (DataConnection) Ltd
Printed in Great Britain by TJ International Ltd, Padstow, Cornwall

Library of Congress Control Number: 2017963161

ISBN 978-0-300-20598-5 (hbk)

A catalogue record for this book is available from the British Library.

10 9 8 7 6 5 4 3 2 1

I now wish to be nothing other than the first soldier of the German Reich. Therefore I have put on that tunic which has always been the most holy and dear to me. I shall not take it off again until victory is ours, or – I shall not live to see the day!

Adolf Hitler, speech of 1 September 1939
announcing war with Poland

Contents

Maps

Plates

1. Hitler with comrades from the 16th Bavarian Reserve Infantry Regiment. BArch, Bild 146-1974-082-44/o.Ang.
2. Hitler speaking to an enthusiastic crowd gathered at the Heldenplatz, Vienna, 15 March 1938. BArch, Bild 183-1987-0922-500/o.Ang.
3. Neville Chamberlain's return from Munich on 30 September 1938. BArch, Bild 183-S61353/o.Ang.
4. German troops crossing the Meuse River, France, 14 May 1940. Ullstein Bild Dt./Contributor/Ullstein Bild/Getty Images.
5. British prisoners at Dunkirk, France, June 1940. NARA 242-EB-7-35.
6. Hitler at the Eiffel Tower with Albert Speer and the sculptor Arno Breker. NARA 242-HLB-5073-20.
7. Hitler at a situation conference with Keitel, Brauchitsch and Halder, c. 1940–1. BArch, Bild 146-1971-070-61/o.Ang.
8. German troops from the Infantry Regiment "Großdeutschland" attack a village in Russia, summer 1941. BArch Bild 146-1974-099-19/Kempe.
9. A German soldier saluting Colonel-General Heinz Guderian, Russia, c. July–August 1941. BArch Bild 101I-139-1112-17/Ludwig Knobloch.
10. German troops pulling a stuck vehicle out of the mud, November 1941. BArch Bild 146-1981-149-34A/o.Ang.
11. A German supply column struggles through the cold and snow during the advance toward Moscow, 21 November 1941. BArch Bild 101I-140-1226-06/Albert Cusian.
12. Hitler at a situation conference at Army Group South headquarters, June 1942. BArch Bild 183-B24543/o.Ang.

Preface

Life is normally characterized by irony, paradox, ambiguity, and ambivalence, but Adolf Hitler saw it with a startling (and frightening) clarity. Beginning early in his career as an orator and political rabble-rouser, he habitually used history as an explanation and justification for his actions. He had, indeed, read a great deal of history, and was as confident in treating his public audiences to lengthy expositions as he was in repeatedly invoking historical analogies in talks with his generals. In many respects, then, his ideas and actions were largely derivative and rarely original. He often acted (or tried to act) as others had, but more often than not failed to consider the respective historical contexts. To a considerable extent, based as it was on his "reading" of history, he valued his own understanding of Germany's historical destiny more than the stability and economic well-being of the country. Moreover, he had the ability to discern what many Germans wanted, to describe a vision of the future that was his but persuade them it was theirs as well. Although certainly stylized, he also created an image of himself – one he came to believe was real – as a leader with a historic mission, one consumed by the task of restoring the broken body of Germany. Like Napoleon, he had a sense that he was acting out history in deciding the fate of his people.

His reading of past events had convinced Hitler that Germany had been cheated by history. The horribly destructive Thirty Years War – fought in German lands but for largely non-German reasons by primarily non-German armies – had devastated the country and, Hitler believed, deprived it of its rightful dominant position in Europe and the world. This role had then been usurped by France and Britain, which proceeded over the following centuries to keep Germany weak and divided. The First World War, to Hitler, had been an attempt to redress this mistake, but Germany failed because its leaders lacked a clear notion of what they were trying to achieve. Ideas matter, and, for good or (mostly) ill, Hitler then developed a set of ideas based on his own (and Germany's) ordeal of the Great War. The experience of national humiliation in 1918, in particular, was deeply ingrained in the minds of Hitler and the German people. He was not alone in believing that their past had been taken from them, that their struggle and sacrifices had been rendered meaningless. If nothing of value had been achieved by the enormous loss of life in the Great War, then what had been the point? This nihilistic thought tormented Hitler in the days and months following Germany's defeat. In his early speeches, and then in his later actions, he moved to restore meaning to a national life he thought scarred by the haunting fear that it had all been in vain. His goal was thus not merely to revise the Versailles settlement, but to expunge the national shame, and this required war.

Once in power, Hitler set about implementing his ideas and, within his frame of reference, made decisions that were logical and rational (or at least not irrational), in the sense that they were taken with a calculated consideration of external circumstances and behind them there existed a logically coherent pattern. It is also critical to understand the importance, for Hitler, of hatred, as well as his obsessive need for revenge against those groups and countries that had ruined Germany. Although there would have to be another war, this was not to be just any war, but a conflict that would punish those held responsible for Germany's humiliation, as well as ensure that such a national disgrace did not happen again in the future. The Second World War, then, would be a radically transformative war, the next, and final, attempt to set things right; not for nothing did Hitler think and speak in apocalyptic terms. Germany, he insisted, faced one of two options: world power or destruction. To Hitler, it would be nothing less than a war for survival, one in which Germany's mortal enemies had to be defeated and the nation given the means to exist. He chronically thought in terms of grand schemes, but this vision was a sort of "apocalyptic utopianism" in which everything was black and white. He saw himself and his nation as being in a struggle for its very survival, and he was certain that defeat meant the end of Germany. The searing experience of the Allied "hunger blockade" of the First World War had convinced him of that. He had, he thought, drawn the proper lesson: in the next war, it would be others who starved, a "lesson" that eventually doomed millions to death. His was an all-or-nothing, social Darwinist view, but it was also fueled by his reading of history. After all, he believed the Roman Empire had expanded, survived, and thrived because it had annihilated those who opposed it.

In the liberal imagination evil is a failure of reason, so the tendency is to see Hitler as irrational. Hitler, though, tended to think and operate according to his own logic, instinct, and intuition, his very dynamism and pernicious creative mind fashioning a compelling narrative from history that was difficult to refute. The problem, then, lies in the failure to understand that "reason," as such, is not necessarily the key focus of political loyalty or action, and that it provides scant emotional comfort in times of crisis. Far more than an appeal to reason, nationalism or group or ethnic loyalties have allowed states to mobilize and demand sacrifices from citizens, and then to construct stirring accounts of suffering and martyrdom. Sacrifice, in particular, entails a shared, sacred experience that provides collective meaning, something that the notion of progress struggles to comprehend. Hitler's lack of humanity thus might be seen as being driven by his "larger" historical concerns: avenging the alleged insults done to Germany and pursuing its proper hegemonic status in order to restore meaning to history. Hitler thus raised his political-ideological goal to one of existential significance. In willing the ends, though, one also has to possess the means to achieve them, and in this Hitler clearly understood Germany to be deficient: it had to gain *Lebensraum* (living space) to secure its future existence, but in the present it lacked the economic resources to do so. He hoped to solve this conundrum through political-military cooperation in a war that – since it was one waged for his nation's very existence – would be absolute and allow for no compromise. The very harshness of the war that Hitler unleashed, in turn, affected both his decisions and the determination of his enemies to fight on. Carl von Clausewitz warned about mistaking one type of conflict for another, but, if anything, it was Hitler's generals who fell victim to this fallacy, for he himself had a clear awareness of the nature of his war, what it was meant to accomplish, and by what means. He also came to understand better than his generals that his war would so harden attitudes that his opponents would be little inclined to negotiation or compromise; for them, as well, it would be all or nothing.

Hitler generally had a sound grasp of strategic and economic realities through the first half of the war, although he never had a clear understanding of how to convince the British – or was it Churchill? – to abandon the conflict, a fact that increased the time pressure he faced. Despite claims to the contrary in their memoirs, his generals were no better either as strategists or (arguably) even in operational conceptions. To a considerable extent, he also deferred to his commanders and military advisors, as long as they proved successful. Hitler tended to be wary of any plan that did not originate with him, but, at least in the beginning, it was possible to reason with him. The trick, though, was to carefully pick when and where to do it: it was always better to pose alternatives indirectly, to allow him an avenue of escape in any dispute, and to be the last one to speak with him. Even when he issued a seemingly final military pronouncement, he not infrequently bowed to the wishes of his generals if they provided a convincing explanation for their course of action. Hitler did, indeed, come to distrust his generals, whom he regarded as cautious, conservative, and forming a secretive clique, and often for good reason. General Franz Halder, especially, persistently circumvented Hitler's wishes. As Führer and Feldherr (commander-in-chief), Hitler demanded that his power be respected, but, perhaps equally important, he wanted to be told that he was right. When things went wrong, he was not in error – others had made mistakes or had deceived him with false information.

Still, his generals commonly expressed admiration for his political skills and support for his expansionist goals. Hitler began to founder only when the war turned against Germany, when he believed his military leaders had failed – or were deliberately obstructionist – when he became increasingly impatient at what he saw as a rapidly closing strategic window, and thus when he tried to micro-manage all affairs. Having made such vast territorial gains, and been tantalizingly close to achieving the Lebensraum that was, for him, the goal of the war, he could not envision giving any of it back voluntarily. From at least the second half of 1942, he immersed himself in the details of the war, an enormous effort that affected him in terms of both his health and his ability (or willingness) to see the larger picture. It was as if the very act of immersion in details shielded him from having to admit the grim strategic truth; occasionally this broke through, then he would flee back into the realm of details. This, perhaps, also accounted for his characteristic leadership style, which seemed to consist of equal parts of indecision and stubbornness. He undoubtedly possessed a powerful force of will, which, of course, is not to be confused with wisdom.

In the later stages of the war, too, there was the question of his increasing use of drugs such as Pervitin, a methamphetamine, which probably resulted in over-stimulation and heightened self-confidence (as well as anxiety and paranoia), and the likelihood that he had advanced Parkinson's disease, which perhaps deprived him of some mental acuity and flexibility. Still, it would be unwise to make too much of his declining health as a key factor in his decision-making. In crisis situations, people tend to revert to what they know how to do, what has been done in the past, and here, too, Hitler's knowledge of history played its part. Until the very end of the Great War, his first war, German forces had virtually always mastered and resolved crises, and restored the situation, when military and political leaders recovered their nerve and stood firm. Now that he, Adolf Hitler, combined both offices in his person, it seemed a doubly important lesson for him to embrace. Further comparison with the earlier war is intriguing as well. During the second half of 1918, General Ludendorff refused to retreat to the more defensible Hindenburg Line, was unwilling to give up territory, and envisaged a stubborn foot-by-foot defense. Reverses on the Western Front eventually forced a retreat, which caused Ludendorff to become nervous and agitated, lose self-control, blame those around him, and immerse himself in detail, a pattern of behavior similar to that of Hitler in 1944–5.

From mid-1943, at the latest, Hitler also knew that victory of any sort was unlikely. If not yet this early, then certainly following the failure in Normandy, historians usually locate his descent into irrationality, arguing that he fought on senselessly. But from his perspective, was it, in fact, senseless? With whom was he going to negotiate? Could he have negotiated peace and survived – not in power but physically? If his regime was going to be destroyed and he was going to die in any case, why not a *Heldentod* (hero's death) in a struggle to the finish? Driven by his resolve to prevent and expunge the humiliation of 1918, he came to believe that an apocalypse was preferable to any effort at negotiating a way out, that a heroic death had a redemptive quality to it, that the courage to fight to the end, to the death, without hope of victory or even survival, laid the basis for national regeneration. In this sense even his suicide could be seen as a form of revenge. His potent sense of threatened national identity stiffened and prolonged German resistance as well, to the point that there seemed among many almost a perverse pride in their ability to take punishment and stay standing. This was a lasting response and rebuke to the failure of 1918. To the end, though, beneath this apocalypticism, Hitler remained insightful on the larger political issues. One cannot, however, make a disjuncture between the political leadership and the purposes of politics; one cannot admire political skill independently of the aims of policy. To a great extent, Hitler willed his life, from obscure artist to unknown soldier to rabble-rousing politician to Führer and then, ultimately, to Feldherr. But his will could not overturn physical reality: Germany did not possess the material means or power to attain Lebensraum or overturn the outcome of the First World War. In his efforts to reverse history, to set things right, though, Hitler became perhaps the most extraordinary figure of the twentieth century; the Second World War, the worst conflict in human history, was inconceivable and remains inexplicable without him.

1

Clausewitz, Hitler, and Absolute War

Sweating profusely from nervousness and clearly uncomfortable in a dark-blue suit, late on the evening of 1 February 1933 Adolf Hitler addressed the German people by radio for the first time as Reich Chancellor. Uncharacteristically hesitant, and speaking in a flat monotone, Hitler denounced the Marxist-induced "spiritual, political, and cultural nihilism" of the past fourteen years that had brought Germany to ruin. The task ahead, he stressed, was difficult, with the immediate goal the elimination of unemployment. In foreign policy, the new regime, the Chancellor emphasized, regarded its crucial mission as safeguarding "the rights of existence" of the German people, although he was quick to emphasize that the key to this national resurgence was overcoming internal class divisions and the creation of a unified national community (*Volksgemeinschaft*), not military force. Fully aware of Germany's feeble international position, Hitler posed as a man of peace, stressing his desire for a disarmed, peaceful world.[1]

If his initial appearance as Reich Chancellor was notable primarily for its banality, a few days later Hitler faced a much more formidable challenge. While offering the upstart corporal an opportunity to stabilize Germany's perilous domestic situation, President Paul von Hindenburg nonetheless gave a clear signal that he intended to keep the Reichswehr out of his direct control: General Werner von Blomberg had been named defense minister by the aged field marshal a few days before Hitler's appointment, and the general now called together the leading figures in the military for a first meeting with the ambitious new political leader. On the evening of 3 February, accompanied only by his personal adjutant, Friedrich Brückner, Hitler arrived at the home of army chief General Kurt Freiherr von

Hammerstein-Equord, where two dozen top army and navy commanders in the Reichswehr had gathered, ostensibly to mark the sixtieth birthday of Foreign Minister Konstantin von Neurath. If not exactly a hostile gathering, it certainly represented a more skeptical audience than the one Hitler had addressed over the airwaves two days before. Although those present engaged in pleasant small talk during dinner, the overall mood turned noticeably cool and reserved as Hitler began his presentation. It had, in fact, the look of a job interview, as both Hitler and his audience sought to feel each other out, to get a sense of their respective aims and intentions. Although Blomberg and his deputy, Colonel Walter von Reichenau, were both known Nazi sympathizers who wanted to bring the army closer to the Nazi Party, the new defense minister's top priorities were to ensure that the Reichswehr maintain its political neutrality and not be drawn into any possible domestic political strife. Since Blomberg believed that the new government provided the basis for national and military renewal, he was also seeking to arrive at some suitable division of labor in the task of rebuilding German power. For his part, Hitler clearly sought to curry favor with the military leaders. He intended, as well, to outline his ambitious plans for the future – possibly to elicit support but perhaps also to gauge opposition.[2]

Both during the dinner conversation and in his talk the new Chancellor succeeded, to a considerable extent, in allaying the most pressing misgivings of his listeners. In presenting himself as a humble corporal from the World War, for whom it was almost a dream to be addressing the assembled generals and admirals, Hitler played astutely on the prejudices and self-perceptions of the officer caste. There then followed a typical, for him, recitation of the difficulties facing Germany, foremost among them the danger posed by Bolshevism, and the need to eradicate Marxist influences in Germany. More importantly for the assembled military leaders, though, Hitler stressed that this was a task for the political leadership. "I have created my own weapons for the inner struggle," he noted, none too subtly; "the army is only for foreign political conflicts." In an instant, Hitler had reassured the officers that the military would not be dragged into internal conflicts, but could concentrate on rearmament. Uprooting Marxism and educating German youth once again with the will to fight would, he thought, take about eight years. By that time, as well, the army would be capable of supporting an active foreign policy.[3]

Hitler also made it clear to those present that his vision of military expansion had little to do with the disarmament discussions then taking place in Geneva. Over the past fourteen years, Reichswehr leaders had proposed endless expedients to overcome the crippling weakness imposed on Germany by the Treaty of Versailles. Despite their efforts, Germany remained vulnerable to invasion not only from France, but from Poland and Czechoslovakia as well. Ultimately, the generals came to understand, no strategy, however clever, could turn weakness into strength. For that, they needed more arms and more soldiers. In this connection, Hitler's observations could not fail to appeal to them. In order to achieve the Lebensraum on which Germany's existence depended, he stressed, the rapid buildup of the armed forces, the most important institution of the state, was vital. To that end, conscription must be reintroduced and the army strengthened.

Rebuilding the army, Hitler observed, was not without risk, as he raised the possibility of a French preventive strike. "We will see what kind of statesmen they have," he remarked; "if they do [have any perceptive leaders], they will not allow us any time, but will attack us, presumably with their eastern satellites." Hitler also left little doubt that this new power would be used for the conquest of living space in the east. "But," he stressed, in a remark pregnant with future significance, "a Germanization of the population of the annexed or conquered territories is not possible. One can only Germanize soil." Given his still insecure relationship with the military, revealing the full extent of his ambitions in the east was a rather risky move, one he must have thought necessary in order to gauge the mood of the officers present. In the event, few seemed to have comprehended fully the implications of this statement, or they simply dismissed it as naive ranting. In closing, Hitler again made it clear that he envisioned a cooperative relationship with the military. "We will stand on the side of the army," he emphasized, "and work for the army. The glorious German Army, in the same spirit that ruled it during the heroic time of the World War, will freely carry out its tasks." Then, as if to remind the assembled officers that he and they shared a common aim and a unique historic moment, he closed, "You will not again find a man who will work with his entire strength for his goal, the salvation of Germany, as I will. And if you say to me, 'The attainment of the goal depends on you!', I will reply, 'Good, take advantage of my life.' "[4]

Hitler's aim, facilitated by Blomberg, had clearly been to win over doubting generals and ensure army support for his government. Hitler had long courted Reichswehr leaders, but often had an uneasy relationship with the aristocratic generals, many of whom could barely disguise their contempt for the upstart corporal from the wrong social class. Still, despite a few dismissive comments from his audience, none opposed Hitler's ideas and some embraced them wholeheartedly. While his remarks were generally deemed "very logical and good in theory," most supported his immediate vision of a rebuilt army. Despite some reservations, primarily from Werner von Fritsch and Friedrich Fromm, who grumbled about his limitless intentions, Hitler largely succeeded in his task. This was hardly surprising, since he held out the prospect of restoring army strength, removing it from internal political restraint, and establishing the armed forces as the key pillar of a restored German nation. For a brief moment, in fact, military leaders seemed to be in the ascendancy, with an apparently subordinate National Socialist government ready to provide the financial, material, and personnel resources needed to rebuild the army. Blomberg's deputy, Reichenau, an ambitious Nazi sympathizer, went so far as to claim that never before in German history had the military and the state been so identical. In agreeing to provide resources for restoring the army, though, Hitler had ensured that the same Reichswehr that had opposed his coup attempt in November 1923 would now be working with him ten years later – a minor curiosity at the time, perhaps, but an irony that the self-satisfied generals failed adequately to ponder. Hitler's speech on 3 February 1933 not only initiated a partnership between the Chancellor and the army, but also marked the beginning of the latter's active complicity in his policy.[5]

This episode also showed that for all of his authority within the Nazi Party, and for all of the talk of his potential role as Führer, Hitler still faced a challenging situation in defining his relationship with the generals, and in asserting his dominance and the primacy of his ideas. Thus, although the goals of Hitler and the military leadership overlapped to a considerable degree, from the beginning there also existed a fundamental divergence about the nature and timing of any future war, a disagreement perhaps masked by the seeming triumph of the generals' enhanced status in early 1933. While Hitler willingly provided the resources necessary for military action, he never accepted the generals' assumption that in this war the political leadership would be subordinated to the imperatives of the military. Certainly, as the would-be and, after August 1934, actual Führer, Hitler expected to exercise control over the clearly political functions of defining war aims and determining strategy, which included the mobilization of political, economic, diplomatic, military, and psychological resources. Additionally, though, Hitler evinced an interest in military matters, understanding as he did from Germany's experience during the First World War the crucial connection between overall goals and the military means to achieve them. Given his own personal knowledge of war, he also inclined toward involvement in the purely military aspects of fighting a war, such as operational concerns involving the management and movement of troops, as well as the tactical handling of armies and formations in actual battles.

This resulted in inevitable tension with the military high command, a renewal of an ongoing conflict in Prussian/German history. In this struggle, Hitler frequently asserted a position that might be termed neo-Clausewitzian, for he often seemed more in tune with ideas articulated by Carl von Clausewitz, while the generals, not surprisingly, clung to arguments made – in opposition to the great Prussian theorist of war – by men such as Helmuth von Moltke, Alfred Schlieffen, and Erich Ludendorff. Given its geographical position in the center of Europe and its economic and military inferiority in the likely event of a multi-front war, the Prussian custom from Frederick William I to Frederick the Great had evolved from a concept of limited war for limited aims to one that emphasized rapid, all-out wars, not necessarily to destroy the enemy absolutely so much as to encourage the negotiation of a lasting peace. The goal was the attainable rather than the ideal. War, to Frederick the Great, was thus a means to an end, with victories in battles establishing the conditions for peace. Moreover, it seemed self-evident that these triumphs had to be accomplished quickly, in order to limit the direct impact of war on the citizens of the state. Hitler thought this too, although he also believed, as a strict social Darwinist, that war was an inevitable phenomenon in itself. In any case, he would readily have agreed with the novel and bold ideas on war introduced by Clausewitz following the Napoleonic Wars.[6]

Writing as a theorist, or more accurately, a philosopher of war (in the spirit of the German Idealist philosophy dominant at the time), Clausewitz aimed to explain the phenomenon of war, unlike his prominent Swiss rival Baron Antoine-Henri Jomini, who sought to make war into a precise geometric exercise in order to prescribe guidelines for its successful prosecution. Clausewitz, of course, famously described war as "a continuation of politics by other means," a statement now so familiar that it has lost any clear meaning. Part of the problem, as Christopher Bassford has pointed out, is that the German word *Politik* can, in English, mean both policy and politics, with the former implying rational action and the latter the interplay of conflicting forces. War, Clausewitz recognized, tended to absolute violence, but precisely for that reason it could not be allowed to exist as an independent phenomenon. War as an act of violence must be restrained by policy, in that a nation going to war must have a clear idea of what it intends to accomplish and how, so strategy of necessity had to be political in nature. If the political objective set the goal, with war merely the means of attaining it, then the military had to be subordinated to political leadership, and strategy had to be subsidiary to policy. Even once war had erupted, though, politics must retain its sovereignty, Clausewitz stressed, since war was merely the instrument, albeit a powerful one, by which to accomplish the political goal. This meant, in practice, that the main lines of all strategy, even military strategy, were to a considerable degree political in nature. The political element thus found itself inevitably entangled down to the details of a specific military campaign, so it was impossible to speak of a purely military assessment of a situation or proposal for a strategic decision. Not only could political insights not be separated from the conduct of war, but the notion of subordinating the political viewpoint to the military was absurd, since it was politics that had produced the war. It was the intelligence, the military the mere instrument. The political authority represented the interests of the entire society; only the head of state had a comprehensive view of the situation, so the subordination of the military commander to the political leader was a logical necessity. For their part, though, political leaders had to understand the limitations of their military force, and not attempt to use it to achieve purposes for which it was unsuited.[7]

Military strategy, which Clausewitz defined as "the use of battles for the purposes of the war," thus proved an elastic concept whose borders were fluid. If strategy aimed to accomplish the goals of the war, and tactics were employed to win the necessary battles, then the operational level was the connective tissue between the two. The constant interplay of war aims, strategy, operations, and tactics, though, meant that the political leadership inevitably had to have a broad input into the military conduct of the war. "An apolitical war," Clausewitz noted, "is not so much impossible as stupid and wrong." That reality framed the basic dilemma: clarity in the division of competencies between the political and the military leadership was a precondition of a harmonious conduct of a war, and with it, success. As a German Idealist, Clausewitz regarded politics as the articulation of the essential interests of society, so without a fundamental understanding of the political goals of a war, no military strategy, however clever, could be successful. The military commander, for Clausewitz, thus functioned as a bridge between the political concept and its military implementation, and he was required to understand both spheres of activity. Just as importantly, the political leadership had constantly to transmit its notions to its military leaders, to show them the way, as it were. Clausewitz famously stressed the importance of "friction" in war, the unpredictability stemming from chance, confusion, fear, exhaustion, poor intelligence, misunderstandings, or simply the moral shock of violence. Overcoming this friction required decisive individual action, often revolving around willpower, or the ability to impose order over the chaos. Clausewitz identified the "military genius" as someone possessing a powerful sense of purpose and an iron will. The political leader who saw himself as a military commander, such as Hitler, complicated the already ambiguous boundary between the political and the military, standing as he did at the border of conception and execution – and needing to be competent at both to ensure that strategy and war goals were in accordance. This Feldherr, as Hitler styled himself, would coordinate military and political objectives, fusing war and policy in one man's hands. Through his will and understanding, the Feldherr would become a statesman who retained the ability to conduct war.[8]

Clausewitz, of course, has often been cited (most often, and disapprovingly, by B. H. Liddell Hart) as an apostle of "absolute war," and he did indeed frequently scorn the notion of the use of limited force. Still, Clausewitz was anything but dogmatic, stressing as he did that the character of each war was shaped by the conditions of its own times, and that the soldier should not be bound by abstract theory. Destruction of the enemy army was not always the fixed aim, as political leaders needed to choose a form of war consistent with their goals and the overall situation; if necessary, since wars often take on a logic of their own, the ends should be adapted to the means. At the tactical level, in fact, Clausewitz asserted that the defense often conferred the greatest relative advantage, given the defender's ability to choose his own ground and build powerful entrenchments. Still, decisive victories could not be won by a passive defense, for it was only in the pursuit, when one side broke, that disproportionate losses could be inflicted and a major triumph attained. As always with Clausewitz, though, nothing was ever final or definitive. He also warned that an offensive inevitably weakens as it advances from its original base, while the defender falls back on its sources of strength. Every offensive, no matter how successful, thus has a "culminating point" at which it outruns its military capability and has to turn to the defense. If the attack has continued beyond an equilibrium point, the momentum will shift and the defender might well seek decisive victory by going on the offensive. In drawing on the example of the Napoleonic Wars, in fact, Clausewitz seemed to be pessimistic about the prospects for success in an aggressive war in which the aggressor faces an aroused population and in which his very triumphs have created countervailing forces determined to defeat him.[9]

The key point here, though, is that the logic of "decisive battle," an idea deemed central to Clausewitz's concept of the conduct of war, flowed from the primary assumption of the political nature of war. If the object of a war was to impose your will on the enemy's by use of force, the most effective means to do that was by destroying his principal means of resistance, his army. The most efficient way to accomplish this, in turn, would be the destruction of the enemy's armed forces in a decisive battle. But aiming at a swift triumph through a *battle* of annihilation, which did not necessarily mean the physical extinction of an army, but rather its elimination as a factor of military power, was not synonymous with a *war* of annihilation. The very speed of the victory produced by a decisive battle would tend to limit war; and, in any case, absolute war, for Clausewitz, remained largely a philosophical concept, an ideal type rather than a reality. Politics, once again, acted as the restraining force. Since the political goal of a war could never be absolute, once the cost of a war exceeded its political value, Clausewitz logically concluded that the political leadership would then renounce the object of the war and seek peace. In this, he believed that reason would triumph over passion.[10]

Still, as a product of his era, Clausewitz recognized that Revolutionary France and Napoleon had introduced something fundamentally new and dangerous, the notion of a people's war. The advent of these ideologically mobilized citizen armies threatened the return of war "in all its elemental fury," a reversion to "absolute war," a war of extermination. The stronger the motives, the more deeply the people were involved in all aspects of the war, the greater the risk that popular passions would break loose and the war would become an existential clash for survival between nations. In such a situation, then, policy would be less likely to constrain than to escalate a war's violence. The idea of a decisive battle depended on the assumption that the destruction of its army would cause a state to surrender. The Napoleonic Wars had shown, though, that the clash of arms could spread beyond regular armies and involve the people at large. In such a case, war might well lose its political logic and descend into senseless violence, a fearful possibility that Clausewitz could never quite dismiss or reconcile with his essential rationality. "As politics becomes greater and weightier," he wrote, "so does war; this can continue to the point at which war attains its absolute form." Indeed, he admitted, the more war became a "question of 'to be or not to be'," the more it became a matter of "simple violence and destruction." In a battle for sheer existence, Clausewitz seemed to be suggesting, perhaps with the example of the German historical experience in mind, politics can lose its restraining influence and war can take on a life of its own.[11]

For Hitler, as we shall see, the very purpose of war was to acquire Lebensraum and secure Germany's existence as a nation and people, so no expenditure of effort could exceed the value of the political object, and thus there could be no peace short of achieving the absolute goal. Hitler, then, redefined the nature of politics and war and turned Clausewitz's formulae upside down, not so much in the sense that politics became a continuation of war by other means, as that the political goal now required total war and the absolute destruction of the enemy. His war would be resolutely political, a fanatical, uncompromising battle, "the execution of the nation's struggle for existence." As such, it would be savage and brutal to an extent inconceivable to Clausewitz. In *Mein Kampf*, Hitler had already asserted the "right to apply even the most brutal weapons . . . in the necessity of victory of a revolutionary new order on this earth." As Führer, he raised the political-ideological goal to one of life-or-death existential importance. Germany had to acquire Lebensraum (and deal with the alleged Jewish-Bolshevik threat) in order to survive, so it had to wage war, even if the means were insufficient. Politics (both domestic and diplomatic) and military operations (new methods) were thus meant to complement each other and enable an objectively weaker Germany to prevail. Politics, for Hitler, no longer proved a restraining force, but acted as an impetus to radicalization. In a war for existence, the logic was clear. In the fight against Bolshevism, he asserted as early as 1922, there could only be two possibilities: "Either victory for the Aryan side or their extermination and victory for the Jews." In the next war, then, one side would lose absolutely; there could be no compromise. But in asserting the primacy of the political goal, however extreme, over military concerns, Hitler essentially embraced the Clausewitzian view of the proper relationship between the political leader and his military commanders.[12]

German military commanders, though, had never been comfortable with Clausewitz's insistence that war, as an essentially political act, should be dominated by the political leadership. The Prussian answer to this dilemma had been to use all-out force in pursuit of a quick victory for limited aims. Although seemingly in agreement with the Clausewitzian notion of decisive battle, it also implied that war, as a complex activity, could best be pursued by a specially trained group of professional soldiers acting independently of the political leadership. Even the new threat of a people's war, with the prospect of limitless violence making a quick victory problematic, seemed to confirm the critical role of an autonomous military. Precisely because of his fear that a limited war could spin out of control into a war of annihilation, Helmuth von Moltke (the Elder), the military leader who had delivered the victories that led to German unification, argued that war had become far too serious and technical a business to be left to the politicians. Moltke readily accepted political predominance in determining the origins and goals of a war, but once the order had been given to fight, the military should be given a free hand to win the battles that would provide the preconditions for a favorable peace. At that point, military commanders would again withdraw in favor of the statesman, whose task it now was to translate military into political success.[13]

Ever a realist, Moltke clearly recognized that the allegedly decisive victories of the wars of unification had not only been very close-run things, but
that they also frequently failed to deliver the desired results. The victories
over France in 1870 had been complete by any military standard, but had
not convinced the French to stop fighting and sue for peace. For Moltke,
and the German military in general, the period after the triumphs at Sedan
and Metz had been a nightmare, with inconclusive fighting, costly partisan
war, a popular uprising in Paris that left no government with which to
negotiate, and the sinking realization that German forces were too weak to
successfully capture the capital and enforce a peace. In a foretaste of things
to come, the German army had proved adept at winning battles, but at a
high price and with its triumphs threatening to ruin it. The underlying flaw
in Clausewitz's rational calculations had been laid bare by the French.
Although their armies had been destroyed at Sedan and Metz, the French
people did not accept defeat nor did their resistance weaken. The full horror
of a people's war had been revealed, with neither German political nor military leaders having a clear idea of how to respond. Although originally
viewing the destruction of the enemy army as the main goal of war, Moltke
grew less convinced of its actual decisiveness. "We want to believe," he later
told the Reichstag, "that neither the Thirty Years War nor Seven Years War
will recur, but when millions of individuals are engaged in a bitter struggle
for national existence, we cannot expect that the matter will be decided
with a few victorious battles."[14]

To Moltke, the lesson of 1870–1 seemed clear, and foreboding: govern-
ments might initiate wars, but citizens sustained them, often to unacceptable extremes. In reflecting on the meaning of the Franco-Prussian War,
Moltke initially embraced the idea of taking a people's war to its logical
conclusion with no regard for the political consequences. In deviating from
Clausewitz, Moltke also demanded autonomy for the military to fight to the
end for the goal of total victory. In his view, the political objective of the war
could no longer be allowed to influence military operations. Once war
began, the military should remain independent, even at the risk of subordinating policy to strategic thinking and making war an end in itself. As
Moltke continued to ponder the new nature of war, however, and especially
the ever-present nightmare of a two-front war, he concluded that absolute
war would only threaten the very existence of the newly unified German
nation. His thoughts then turned to the notion of preventive war to forestall
any French or Russian aggression against Germany. Again, though, the
more he reflected, the more he concluded that preventive war would not
solve the dilemma facing Germany, so made no sense. The experience of

the recent war against France led him to conclude that Germany "could not hope to rid itself quickly of one enemy by a rapid and successful offensive, leaving itself free to deal with the other enemy." Having dismissed the essence of what later became the Schlieffen Plan as unworkable, Moltke eventually concluded that deterrence was the only feasible alternative to a people's war. As he grew older, in fact, Moltke became ever more pessimistic. In his famous Reichstag speech of 14 May 1890, he declared prophetically, "The age of cabinet wars is behind us – all we have now is people's war . . . with all its incalculable consequences . . . If this war breaks out, then its duration and its end will not be foreseeable . . . Not one of [the great powers] can be crushed so completely in one or two campaigns that it will admit defeat . . . It may be a war of seven years or of thirty years [*sic*] duration – and woe to him who sets Europe ablaze."[15]

Moltke's warnings revealed a clear realization of the key question facing Germany: how could the new nation, given its geo-strategic position, wage a future war that in all likelihood would be a two-front struggle for its very existence? Moltke, the arch-military man, concluded that the idea of a short war was obsolete; strategy could no longer provide a way out of the dead end of a people's war. Moltke's successors, though, chose to ignore his warnings and instead sought a solution not in strategy but in overwhelming professional competence, the meticulous planning and organization of industrial war, and the elimination of any elements of surprise. Through this technocratic approach they hoped to square the circle of avoiding a long people's war by waging a short war based on decisive battles. This, of course, in their own mind seemed to mark a return to Prussian tradition, but it also divorced military operations and tactics from any larger political or grand strategic considerations. War was to be a professionally autonomous action controlled by decision-oriented specialists. A high-quality army, stress on the offensive, and willpower: these were the nonmaterial factors that would decide any future war in Germany's favor. The outlook of the new breed of German officers thus combined professionalism and technical competence with a dangerously limited perspective that saw all matters through a narrow military viewpoint.

If war was to be run by a professional elite, General Alfred von Schlieffen then provided the solution to the related problem of how actually to fight and win this war. Given Germany's geographic position and its economic and military inferiority to its likely opponents, Schlieffen rejected as unwinnable the idea of a long war of attrition. For him, the offensive remained the only alternative. Instead of seeking a quick decision through one or two decisive battles, though, Schlieffen proposed a breathtakingly elegant alternative. Tactical attacks, emphasizing fire and movement, would create a fluid situation from which would develop a dynamic operational advance that would sweep all before it and allow the complete annihilation of the enemy forces. Seizing the initiative, creating a central point of attack (*Schwerpunkt*), continuous movement, joint operations, flexible leadership, and mission-oriented tactics (*Auftragstaktik*) would cut the Gordian knot of a two-front war and permit the German army to triumph over superior enemy forces. Clausewitz's argument that defense was the stronger form of war was rejected in favor of the notion that to make war meant to attack. In the concept of "total battle," Schlieffen believed he had found the answer to the related problems of the expanding size of the theater of operations and the increasing mobility of troops. Individual battles would be merged into one continuous operation that generated a self-sustaining momentum, the culmination of which would be the absolute destruction of enemy forces in a gigantic encirclement battle. If the model was Cannae in 216 BC during the Second Punic War, the key to achieving it was war as uninterrupted movement. Victory, Schlieffen thought, would emerge out of operational decisions. In this schema, operations reigned supreme; politics had little place.[16]

Schlieffen's ideas also had the great advantage, in the eyes of German generals, of corresponding to their understanding of the Prusso-German military tradition and, above all, of the campaigns of Frederick the Great, who was upheld as the great practitioner of the art of the quick battle of annihilation. But as Hans Delbrück, the prominent military historian and fierce contemporary critic of Schlieffen and his successors, pointed out at the time, this obsession with the decisive battle was an egregious misreading on the part of German generals of both classical and Frederician reality. Cannae, for example, which so excited Schlieffen's imagination, had not resulted in a decisive strategic victory over the Romans; indeed, it proved largely inconsequential in the course of the Second Punic War. By the same token, Delbrück insisted, Frederick's primary strategy, as often as not, and certainly during the Seven Years War, had been attrition rather than annihilation; the goal was to outlast his enemies, with the means being the strategic defensive. Hitler understood this, praising Frederick in a speech on 12 April 1922 for his unmatched brilliance in successfully prosecuting a war of attrition (the Seven Years War), in contrast to his recent successors, that not only ended in victory, but also left no crushing debt for the Prussian state and people. Above all, Frederick understood that political goals reigned supreme, with military strategy simply the tool to establish the preconditions for an advantageous peace. Ironically, the dogma of a quick, decisive battle owed as much to Moltke's successes as to the example of Frederick or the writings of Clausewitz. His near perfect victories at Königgrätz (1866) and Sedan (1870) seemed to prove the efficacy of the battle of annihilation, even as Otto von Bismarck, after the former, asserted political control to end the war immediately rather than pursue total Austrian defeat, and the French, in the latter case, simply continued fighting by irregular means. In remembering the battles, but forgetting the outcome of the wars, Moltke's successors neglected to register his profound insight: decisive battles were not likely to decide a war's outcome. Thus, an irony developed in German military thinking: while Moltke's successors stressed the need to be tactically flexible, they made the destruction of the enemy's force the absolute goal.[17]

Clausewitz, like Frederick the Great, insisted that politics must determine the ultimate goal of a war, and that the means to achieve these ends must be included in the strategic calculations. A government could not expect its soldiers to do the impossible. But in abdicating their responsibility to inform political leaders of the insufficient strength of the army to accomplish its strategic goal, in favor of a functional, narrowly military approach that stressed professional competence, Bismarck's successors did just that. Schlieffen's grand notions died quickly in 1914, with disastrous consequences for Germany. The war of continuous movement he envisioned ended abruptly at the Marne in early September; early triumphs had not resulted in the annihilation of enemy forces nor had they been a prelude to a negotiated peace. Helmuth von Moltke (the Younger) had pursued Schlieffen's vision despite his awareness that non-military factors could negatively influence operations and his unease at the inadequate forces at his disposal, and he had failed. If victory depends on a definition of aims, then Germany now had no clear goals and insufficient resources for a protracted war of attrition. This made the ideas of Moltke's successor, Erich von Falkenhayn, especially suspect. Falkenhayn correctly assessed the new relationship between attack and defense as favoring the latter, but in ordering that the front lines be held at all costs, and immediately retaken after an enemy break-in, his tactic of unyielding linear defense squandered lives needlessly (and also influenced a young soldier who participated in many of these grinding defensive battles in 1915–16). Falkenhayn's notion of attrition – based as it was on the idea of destroying enemy forces, threatening him with collapse, and thus forcing him to seek a way out through negotiations – seemed almost criminal both in its execution at Verdun in 1916, and in his disregard for the fact that Germany might suffer the same fate. Ironically, the one success during Falkenhayn's tenure as chief of staff, the 1915 operation in Russia that shattered much of the Tsarist army, had little impact – like France in 1870, the Russians simply continued to fight.[18]

The situation inherited by the Third Supreme Command under Paul von Hindenburg and Erich Ludendorff – that Germany was neither winning nor clearly losing the war – thus offered at least a slim possibility that politics could reassert itself at the strategic level and forge a solution to Germany's dilemma through diplomatic negotiations. Hindenburg and Ludendorff, though, had other aims: to win the war through innovative tactics. Not only had strategy been abandoned at the grand political level, but even operations now became the slave of tactical activity. The ultimate technocrat, Ludendorff confronted the failure of Falkenhayn's tactics head-on and made a virtue of necessity. Confronting a war of increasing scarcity, Ludendorff's answer was efficiency and the optimization of all available means. A static linear defense would now be replaced with the concept of an elastic defense in depth. When attacked, German troops would conduct a mobile defense, giving ground and withdrawing to a system of prepared defensive strongpoints, drawing the attacker away from his artillery support and into that of their own, reducing enemy strength and wearing him down in grinding combat; and, using another Clausewitzian concept, as the enemy passed the culmination point of his attack, launching a counterattack to retake the lost positions. Like a rubber band being stretched taut and released, German troops would absorb the enemy blow and then snap back to, or beyond, the starting point. No longer would German troops be ground up in senseless linear defense; it would be enemy forces that were squandered against a seemingly endless series of strongpoints and that would fall victim to the well-timed counterattack.[19]

If the efficacy of these new defensive methods was proven in 1917 (an example that would be of significance in the next war), German military leaders still could not envision these means as leading to any victorious ends. American entry into the war seemingly forestalled any hope that these defensive triumphs could be translated into a negotiated peace, or that they might enable a favorable outcome in the war of attrition. As so often in German history, offensive action was seen as the only way out of their dilemma. While the Allies saw the solution to the superiority of the defensive in new technology and weapons, the Germans introduced new tactics, again based on fire and movement. Well-equipped, specially trained small combat units (*Stoßtruppen*) supported by effective artillery fire and utilizing light machine guns, mortars, hand grenades, and flamethrowers, would use the element of surprise to penetrate enemy lines and flow to the rear, thus unsettling the enemy position. With emphasis on surprise, movement, flexibility, individual initiative, and independence at the lower echelons, these stormtroop methods marked the definitive triumph of tactics over strategy. These highly skilled, self-willed soldiers, given a task and expected to carry it out on their own initiative, shouldered an immense burden. In a very real sense, they had been made responsible for the outcome of the war, a realization that placed enormous physical and mental strain on them – but also led them to fight with extraordinary tenacity. In order to survive, soldiers had to kill; further, only through annihilation of the enemy could the combatant be liberated from the deadly threat facing him. Movement and aggression thus formed the basis for survival. Ludendorff's famous comment explaining his plan for the Spring Offensive of 1918 – "We will punch a hole. For the rest, we shall see. This is also how we did it in Russia" – illustrated perfectly the new functional mind-set. Strategy had lost its defining character as war increasingly became an end in itself.[20]

Two corollary factors also contributed to this development. This type of war, as Hitler realized in the next one, was best conducted by troops fortified by propaganda and ideological indoctrination. Since the new method of fighting (Auftragstaktik) placed extraordinary emphasis on personal initiative, motivation, rapid decision-making, and freedom of action – all largely outside the direct control of general officers – the men needed to be sustained by a powerful idea. Indeed, the importance of propaganda and psychological warfare might have been Ludendorff's most important contribution to ideas of war. From this, and the related notion of the significance of the cohesion of the domestic population, flowed the concept of the total mobilization of a nation, including industry and society, for the purposes of war. In such a situation, the connection between means and end was broken, as strategy became primarily an effort at total social mobilization. As Ludendorff realized, this turned Clausewitzian theory on its head. If war and politics existed only to ensure the survival of a nation, then any and all means were acceptable. Politics thus lost its role as a restraining force and became instead a radicalizing one. Total mobilization, Ludendorff stressed, required total goals. Total war thus aimed not only at the enemy army, but also directly against its people. And the logical consequence of total war, as Hitler understood, could only be the complete destruction of the enemy nation. In a very real sense, then, Hitler embraced the ideas of both Clausewitz and Ludendorff, but combined them in his own logic. He agreed with the former that war was essentially political, but accepted the latter's arguments that it was for the very survival of the nation. Since the best guarantee of that was the total annihilation of enemy nations, war would inevitably escalate to its absolute state.[21]

For Hitler, then, political aims of necessity shaped strategy. Most German generals, not having read Clausewitz, or at best only superficially, failed to comprehend this fundamental point. They saw war as an operational exercise, largely in the perceived manner of Moltke (the Elder): win enough battles and the rest (victory) will follow. This dichotomy framed a basic conflict between the concepts of Hitler and his generals. In good Clausewitzian fashion, Hitler as political leader shaped the larger policy goals, so he believed the military should defer to his political judgments. Then, in accordance with the astonishingly efficient methods of Auftragstaktik pioneered in the last year of the First World War, after he had set the goal Hitler expected his generals to be fanatical in the attainment of it, regardless of whether they fully understood or agreed with it. The military leaders, steeped in the tradition of Moltke, Schlieffen, and Ludendorff, stressed operational competence, technical proficiency, and combat effectiveness, but gave little attention to larger matters of diplomacy or strategy. Nor did they initially believe that a mere corporal from the First World War could possess acute insights into the European power-political sphere, and thus be able to manipulate it to advantage. The difference between traditional Prussian/German strategic thinking and Hitler's, then, was that the former was oriented toward military-strength relationships, the latter toward political-ideological matters. Ever since Moltke, the generals had demanded autonomy in decision-making once war began; when the fighting commenced, the political leadership should turn direction of the war over to the military experts and allow them to deliver victory, after which the political leadership could resume authority. This resulted in an inevitable clash with Hitler, believing as he did, with Clausewitz, that policy shaped strategy and that even in war the political leadership should reign supreme. So, to understand Hitler's decision-making, it is necessary to delve deeply into his ideological and racial beliefs, to see the situation as he would have viewed it.[22]

For Clausewitz, the political objective framed the goal, and war was the means of attaining it, so that means had to be considered in relation to their purpose. Hitler, though, took Clausewitz one step further, even if his goals appear to us irrational or unacceptable, since he applied strategy to attain his goals, sought to keep the political in the ascendant, yet understood the key role of force. For him, war was not merely a continuation of politics by other means, but the highest expression of the life force of a people itself. Struggle was natural, legitimate, inevitable, and permanent; just as importantly, it was racial, and it would continue until the "racially more worthy" German people had achieved world hegemony. He thus saw no distinction between the political, the goal of Lebensraum, and the military, the instrument by which to wage war to attain it. In November 1939, in perhaps the purest expression of his views, Hitler proclaimed to his generals, "I see war as the essence of all things. No one can evade war if he does not want to succumb . . . A people that cannot summon the strength to fight must yield . . . Today, we can speak of a racial war . . . I will annihilate the enemy."[23]

Hitler would endlessly quote Clausewitz to his generals on the superiority of the political over the military, and the obligation of the military commander to obey the political leader. After all, soldiers, Clausewitz admitted, were "bound by the duty to conquer according to the political concept of the head of state." The Führer would almost certainly have agreed, as well, with Clausewitz's emphasis on the importance of willpower, determination, boldness, intuition, and personal experience for successful leadership. Clausewitz also emphasized, though, that strategy had to be in harmony with the political goal. In the event, Hitler was undone, in no small measure, because he had unlimited goals that Germany had neither the means nor resources to accomplish. In his role of statesman he claimed that "politics is and can be nothing other than the safeguarding of a people's vital interests with every means." Hitler then defined the securing of Lebensraum and destruction of Jewish-Bolshevism as the crucial interests of the German people, and thus the principal goals of a war that he thought absolutely necessary for German survival. For Germany to live, others had to die. This was a brutal and ultimately self-destructive policy, but one that guided and influenced Hitler's decisions. In miscalculating means and ends, in being unable to distinguish between a battle of annihilation and a war of extermination, though, he ultimately took too great a gamble. Germany lacked the means to attain his goals, which Hitler implicitly understood, but he risked war anyway, largely because of political imperatives that, according to Clausewitz's formula, should have restrained his actions. The distinction between politics and war had dissolved and then coalesced in Hitler's mind, with the notion of total war the logical result. In a fight for survival, any and all means for victory were acceptable. After all, in total war, the counterpart of victory was absolute destruction. It was a brutal logic: either win or die. In failing to win, Hitler ultimately assured Germany's death.[24]

2

Emergence of the Idea

Temporarily blinded during a British gas attack, the young corporal lay fretfully in a military hospital in Pasewalk, with rumors of impending revolution swirling around him, as the war in which he had so fervently participated came to its conclusion. Having failed in his earlier attempts at an artistic career yet convinced that his talent had been unfairly denied, he had embraced all the more the cause of German nationalism. Rushing to volunteer in the heady days of August 1914, he had served four long years on the Western Front. Informed by an elderly pastor on 10 November 1918 of Germany's defeat:

> sightless and helpless . . . his own personal failure seemed merged in the disaster of the whole German people. The shock of defeat . . . caused this convalescent regimental orderly an agony which consumed his being, and generated . . . portentous and measureless forces of the spirit . . . The downfall of Germany seemed to him inexplicable by ordinary processes. Somewhere there had been a gigantic and monstrous betrayal.

Once released from the hospital, adrift and without purpose, the corporal encountered shocking scenes:

> Fearful are the convulsions of defeat. Around him in the atmosphere of despair and frenzy glared the lineaments of Red Revolution . . . As in a dream everything suddenly became clear. Germany had been stabbed in the back and clawed down by the Jews, by the profiteers and intriguers behind the front, by the accursed Bolsheviks in their international

conspiracy of Jewish intellectuals. Shining before him he saw his duty, to save Germany . . . avenge her wrongs, and lead the master race to their long-decreed destiny.

In these remarkable passages from the first volume of his memoirs of the Second World War, Winston Churchill offered a penetrating insight into the searing experience of 1918–19 – the collapse of a society – a national nightmare that decisively shaped the mind of Adolf Hitler.[1]

Despite his later claims in *Mein Kampf* that his political ideology had already crystallized as he left Vienna in 1913, Hitler's own account of his experience at Pasewalk, although certainly dramatized after the fact, nonetheless conveyed an authentic sense of the deep despair and primal bitterness aroused in him by Germany's capitulation. On hearing that Germany was now at the mercy of the victors, he wrote:

> I could stand it no longer . . . Again everything went black before my eyes; I tottered and groped my way back to the dormitory, threw myself on my bunk, and dug my burning head into my blanket and pillow . . .
>
> And so it had all been in vain. In vain all the sacrifices and privations; in vain the hunger and thirst . . . in vain the hours in which, with mortal fear clutching at our hearts, we nevertheless did our duty; and in vain the deaths of two million . . . Had they died for this, the soldiers of August and September 1914? . . . Was this the meaning of the sacrifice which the German mother made to the fatherland? . . . Did all this happen only so that a gang of wretched criminals could lay hands on the fatherland? . . .
>
> The more I tried to achieve clarity on this monstrous event in this hour, the more the shame of indignation and disgrace burned my brow . . .
>
> There followed terrible days and even worse nights . . . In these nights hatred grew in me, hatred for those responsible for this deed.
>
> In the days that followed my fate became known to me . . . There is no making pacts with Jews; there can only be the hard: either – or.
>
> I, for my part, decided to go into politics.

Although easy to dismiss, then as now, as comically pretentious, Hitler's self-imposed mission to "save" Germany would have the deadliest of consequences, transforming not only his life, but the lives of millions. Here, in retrospect, we can see the essential elements of Hitler's later appeal: the shock and confusion of defeat; the search for those responsible; the obsession with exacting revenge against those, especially the Jews, who had allegedly caused the ruination of Germany; and the determination to redeem the suffering of the war.[2]

For Hitler, war truly was the father of all things; as Thomas Mann put it at the time in an essay, "How could the artist, the soldier in the artist, not have thanked God for the breakdown of a peaceful world which was so very sick?" It was, he concluded, a "cleansing liberation." Yet in a twist on that popular theme, it was not merely the experience of war but even more the defeat and the catastrophic peace that shaped the "artist" Hitler, defined his career, and determined his worldview. For Hitler, the defeat fused the personal with the political. The soldiers of August 1914 had died for the great spirit of unity and camaraderie so lacking both in pre-war Germany and in his own life. The creation of a united community, a Volksgemeinschaft, bound in common purpose to the fate of the nation, had been the cardinal achievement of the war. This alone made the crushing fear, the unceasing hardships, and the otherwise inexplicable sacrifices bearable. All this had now been squandered – worse, snatched away from Germany, and himself, in the chaos of defeat and revolution. Defeat had not been merely a disinterested verdict of history, but both a personal and national cataclysm. There had been no justice; if not victorious, then Germany should have perished, with flags flying, in glorious battle. Instead, there had been the tawdry, ignominious surrender in a railway carriage. This demanded explanation, as well as a national renewal that would ensure such a humiliation never recurred.[3]

By most accounts, Hitler had been not merely a dutiful soldier but absolutely committed to German victory. Many others undoubtedly felt a passionate attachment to the German cause, but Hitler seemed different, as if married to the war exclusively. In the 1920s he often referred to his six years in uniform, suggesting that he regarded the initial post-war years as a continuation of the military struggle. Like many, he greeted the war with enthusiasm, but his first encounter with combat – the frightful slaughter in Flanders that pitted the hurriedly trained German volunteers against experienced British professionals – made a powerful impression on him. His unit, the 16th Bavarian Reserve Infantry Regiment – or List Regiment, named after its first commander – suffered horrific casualties, losing almost 3,000 of the original 3,500 men in less than a week. These experiences at the First Battle of Ypres in 1914 – with its profligate sacrifice of idealistic young Germans for the sake of the nation later the stuff of myth – affected him greatly. Indeed, the ubiquitous Nazi slogan of the Second World War, "the individual must die so the nation can live," seemed perfectly to reflect

Hitler's mental image. In thinking back on those days in late September 1941, in fact, he emphasized that, on the battlefield, "when you see thousands get injured and killed, you become aware that life is a constant, terrible struggle, which serves to preserve the species – someone has to die so that others may survive." Three weeks later, returning to the same subject, he asserted, "I am ice-cold on these matters. I feel myself to be the executioner of a historic will."[4]

After this initial intense spell of combat, his duties as a dispatch runner – present at regimental and battalion headquarters, exposed to danger and artillery shelling (and twice wounded) but not precisely at the front, with its attendant hardships and drudgeries – allowed him the time and opportunity to ponder the larger meaning of the war. He valued the power and emotional pull of camaraderie. Its ability to dissolve the bonds of previous group loyalties and draw men of all backgrounds together made a lasting impression on him as a superior organizational idea for a new, unified society. He showed remarkably little interest in the mundane affairs that occupied his comrades – mail from home, talk of family and friends, smoking and drinking, women and sex. Utterly lacking a sense of humor, he was unable to join in the easy jocularity and bantering of his mates, and his one diversion, his incessant drawing and sketching, also set him apart. When not sketching, he spent his free time reading and, while it is a stretch to credit his claim that he "carried five volumes of Schopenhauer around . . . throughout the war," he certainly understood the concept of will as the insatiable expression of life. To his comrades, the gaunt, unsmiling, serious young man, always on the edge of the few group photographs of him from that period, seemed odd and quirky, but no less liked or respected for it. He possessed physical courage, was reliable, and rarely tried to shirk his obligations.[5]

Given his later career, one other thing seemed strange: he evidently spoke very little about politics or the Jews to his comrades. Except for a February 1915 letter to a Munich acquaintance in which he bemoaned Germany's struggle against an "international world of enemies," and – in perhaps a hint of his later attitude – expressed the wish that both its "external enemy" as well as its "inner internationalism" be crushed, he largely kept his ideas to himself. Significantly, his first serious injury, and thus an opportunity to spend time on home recuperation leave, occurred just four days after his regiment had arrived at the front in the later stages of the archetypal battle of attrition, the Somme. Although spared the worst of the horrifying carnage and psychological torment of this battle, he witnessed the scenes of unrest and discontent, hunger and starvation, grumbling and plummeting morale back in Germany, and they shocked and dismayed him. Although he claimed in *Mein Kampf* that in December 1916 he first saw "the truth" about alleged Jewish shirking and profiteering – that the Jews were "sucking the blood . . . of the people" and that "the offices were full of Jews. Almost every clerk was a Jew and almost every Jew a clerk" – this smacks of post-war bluster, especially since no evidence exists of him making anti-Semitic statements at the time. Still, it seems unlikely that he would remain completely unaffected by either the general coarsening of anti-Jewish attitudes or the growing defeatism on the home front. Indeed, like many other soldiers, he expressed his "wish . . . to return to [his] old regiment and comrades." Unlike most of them, though, for Hitler defeat did not mean the end of the war. Peace left him utterly disoriented and adrift. Deeply invested emotionally in the war, Hitler simply could not let it go. Instead, he now began a long process of thinking through his experiences and observations, trying to draw some meaning and conclusions from them, seeking, above all, to explain the precipitate outcome.[6]

Historians have long debated the relative importance of his time in pre-war Vienna and post-war Munich as the key formative period of Hitler's ideological evolution, but this largely misses the point by making artificial either/or distinctions. Despite his later claims, he did not develop any notable anti-Semitic views during his time in Vienna, although he certainly absorbed important lessons, perhaps none more than the belief that life is an unrelenting struggle between the strong and weak, as well as the power of populist resentments. But it was the trauma of defeat that set him searching for concrete answers. For Hitler, the defeat meant both national and personal betrayal, certainly, but more, it was utterly shameful because seemingly unnecessary. After all, Ferdinand Foch, former commander-in-chief of Allied forces, admitted that Germany, instead of capitulating, "could have held the line on the other side of the Rhine in November 1918." His British counterpart, Field Marshal Douglas Haig, concurred, expressing his belief that the German army was "capable of retiring to its own frontiers and holding the line," a reality that made it likely that "the war would continue for another year." David Lloyd George admitted after the war, "All our plans . . . were made on the assumption . . . that the war would not conclude before 1919." Winston Churchill, in his history of the Great War, estimated that it would have taken the Allies six months and heavy losses just to reach the Rhine. Having thus bought itself time, Germany might well have split the enemy coalition, or at least ensured better terms, by offering the Allies the option of continuing the bloody fight, at the cost of millions more casualties, or accepting a peace based on German withdrawal from the occupied territories and the payment of reparations for war damages. Indeed, the official post-war German investigating commission concluded that only the outbreak of the revolution prevented this continued resistance, and thus, by implication, better terms for Germany.[7]

This, for Hitler, was the key point. Was this not historically unique, not only in the suddenness of the surrender but also for the fact that no nation had ever laid down its arms while its forces were still so deep in enemy territory? In mid-May 1918 London endured the last and largest aerial attacks and as late as that summer German artillery shelled Paris while Berlin lay untouched. In the east, Russia had been defeated, while the territory controlled by Germany seemed vast enough to absorb military setbacks and provide sufficient resources to carry on. If so many Allied leaders evidently thought the German situation in November 1918 was anything but hopeless, what had happened? Hitler himself, in a speech in September 1923, just two months before his ill-fated Munich putsch, favorably contrasted the actions of the French in 1870, in refusing to give up the struggle and so preserving national honor even in defeat, with the servile German submission of 1918. So, again, what had happened?[8]

"No enemy has defeated you. Only when the enemy's superiority in numbers and resources became suffocating did you relinquish the fight," exclaimed Friedrich Ebert, the Socialist leader, as he greeted troops returning from the front in December 1918. It was, many believed, the home front that had collapsed; indeed, German soldiers, *im Felde unbesiegt* (undefeated on the field of battle), were greeted as the "victors of yesterday, today, and tomorrow." For a brief moment at the end of the war, it seemed that this formula might serve to unite a nation facing the shattering collapse of its expectations of victory and struggling to come to terms with the bitter reality of defeat. The rhetorical equivalent of the popular uprising, the *levée en masse*, that never materialized, this formula aimed at restoring the nation's lost honor. To nationalists it seemed reprehensible enough that one of the few prominent leaders to call for such a people's war, Walther Rathenau, a Jewish industrialist and intellectual, had done so against the objections of General Erich Ludendorff, the dominant figure in the Supreme Command, who had lost faith in victory and so could no longer justify the struggle. Worse, to many, this slogan rang hollow. In losing the war without suffering defeat in a decisive campaign, the rallying cry, "undefeated in battle," could just as easily mean "quit without putting up a fight." Further, if the army had been unconquered in the field, who was responsible for the shameful capitulation? Here were sown the seeds of the destructive "stab-in-the-back" legend. Facing an enemy coalition vastly superior in numbers and resources, so the myth ran, German soldiers had struggled valiantly in the field, only to succumb to pernicious domestic forces that had exploited the impact of the "hunger blockade" in order to destroy Germany from within. This, of course, got the chronology backward, for it was the decision of the Supreme Command not to fight on that had led to the dissolution of the home front. Not surprisingly, though, the very military leaders who bore the greatest share of blame for the national collapse most ardently promoted this notion.[9]

Feelings of national honor, which many in both Germany and the enemy camp had expected would fuel a tenacious resistance, proved nonexistent. Frederick Maurice, the English general who allegedly coined the term "stab in the back" to describe the unexpected German collapse, asserted in 1919, "There was no precedent for a great and powerful nation, which was fighting for its existence, surrendering while it still had the means to resist." More than defeat, this was national humiliation, the absolute repudiation of the spirit of August 1914. Instead of a heroic saga it was, in the words of Heinrich Mann, "a pathology report." Was this, as Hitler cried in despair in *Mein Kampf*, the meaning of all the sacrifices of the war years? Carl von Clausewitz had written in *On War* that a nation must fight on, if necessary by means of a popular uprising, even in the face of a certain defeat, for:

> Even after a defeat, there is always the possibility that a turn of fortune can be brought about by developing new sources of internal strength or through the natural decimation all offensives suffer in the long run or by means of help from abroad . . . [I]t is the natural law of the moral world that a nation that finds itself on the brink of an abyss will try to save itself by any means.
>
> No matter how small and weak a state may be in comparison with its enemy, it must not forgo these last efforts, or one would conclude that its soul is dead . . . A government that after having lost a major battle is only interested in letting its people go back to sleep in peace as soon as possible and . . . lacks the courage and desire to put forth a final effort . . . shows that it did not deserve to win, and, possibly for that very reason was unable to.

Whether Hitler ever read this passage is unclear, but he knew well Clausewitz's famous exhortation, written a century earlier in response to Prussia's defeat and humiliation at the hands of Napoleon, in what must have seemed eerily similar circumstances, namely that:

a people must never value anything higher than the dignity and freedom of its existence; that it must defend these with the last drop of its blood . . .; that the shame of a cowardly submission can never be wiped out . . .; that a bloody and honorable fight assures the rebirth of the people even if freedom were lost.[10]

By first internalizing and then externalizing Germany's shame, and drawing on his own observations and experiences, Hitler began a quest to understand what had brought this disgrace on Germany, slowly assembling a worldview that, although violent – indeed, almost apocalyptic – nonetheless possessed for his adherents a compelling logic and considerable explanatory power. The key themes – a war forced on Germany by envious rivals, social collapse caused by internal agitation, the crushing burden of an enemy coalition superior in numbers and raw materials – that form much of the leitmotif of Hitler's early political speeches exemplified an attempt to explain, perhaps to himself as much as his audience, what had happened and why. For Hitler, the First World War never really ended; he drew from it the essential features of his ideology and future policy, including the determination to fight on in hopeless circumstances, which ensured that Germany's defeat in 1945 approximated what had been lacking in 1918.

Although Hitler developed his worldview in a tumultuous post-war atmosphere, the fundamental elements of his ideology comprised an amalgamation of various nineteenth-century ideas. From Darwin came the notion of life as struggle; from Marx, the idea of history as a product of conflict. The alleged existence of a Jewish threat that had to be countered had many fathers, not least Houston Stewart Chamberlain, the racialist philosopher and Richard Wagner's son-in-law, who, late in his life, met Hitler and in 1923 anointed him the "chosen one." Populist (*völkisch*) ideas of nationalism flourished in the era prior to the First World War, as did obsessive fears of racial and social degeneration caused by miscegenation. None of these ideas, individually, were unique to Germany, nor did German society contain within it some hidden pathology. What gave Hitler's worldview its power and insistent dynamism were the elements added as a by-product of Germany's war experience: the elevation of violence to a universal law of nature; the expression of despair, shame, and hatred at the defeat of Germany; the combination of nationalism and socialism resulting in the redemptive idea of a Volksgemeinschaft that would provide a new meaning to life; the potency of wartime popular mobilization that bestowed social recognition on the masses; the obsession with an existential threat to Germany's very being; the rejection of pre-war society and the determination to build a wholly new one;

and a radical, uncompromising spirit and willingness to use force to attain this new existence.[11]

That, out of this jumble of ideas, Hitler assembled an internally coherent, explanatory system that connected the points of the puzzle for many Germans, had much to do with the larger social context. The early 1920s in Germany were years marked by social collapse, an evident decline of morals and values, hyper-inflation, and periodic revolutionary outbursts that created a sense of a world on the brink – all of which gave a certain credibility to Hitler's warnings. He embodied all the anxiety, pessimism, fears, hatreds, hopes, and desires of the era. More than that, though, he expressed the yearning of a younger generation – those of the war, perhaps, but also the "not quite old" enough who had just missed combat but longed for the comradeship, belonging, and meaning of fighting at the front – to burst free of the constraints placed on Germany by history and geography. This was, as Michael Wildt has put it, an "unconditional generation" that refused to accept what had come before, that wanted to break out into the wider world, not only to reverse the stigma of November 1918, but also to create a society worthy of an ultimate fight to the finish. For them, Germany's collapse was not an act of treachery so much as the inevitable end of a tawdry drama. The "November criminals" had simply exploited the masses' justifiable desertion of a decadent and incompetent regime that had not merited a defense to the last drop of blood. "The military defeat of the German people," Hitler wrote in *Mein Kampf*, in an echo of Clausewitz, was in no way "an undeserved catastrophe . . . We have more than earned this defeat." And why? Largely, he claimed, for reasons of "an ethical and moral poisoning" from within that had to be eradicated. "The core of the state," he asserted in May 1927, "was rotten." This explanation for German defeat evoked images of contagion, of contamination, of being undermined from within by a disease, a virus. In contrast to the stab in the back, which seemed by comparison an explicable, almost classical treachery, this bacteriological metaphor posited a weak and vulnerable German "body" helpless in the face of a mysterious disease – a "body" that needed "cleansing" to be strong and healthy again.[12]

Hitler, then, was opposed not to revolution as such, just this particular revolution which had been engineered by the wrong forces and had led to capitulation, not fanatic resistance. The "front fighter" had of necessity to save Germany – to rescue suffering virtue, furnish redemption for all sacrifices, and provide salvation for the future. Early on, Hitler adopted this image of the redemptive *Frontkämpfer* as the revenge of the trenches against the November criminals. In his myriad speeches, he rarely mentioned his own personal experiences, preferring instead to emphasize the sacrifices of all the nameless frontline fighters. Invariably, this led him, and other National Socialists, to stress that the true inheritance of the war had been the idea of August 1914. "The march of German soldiers into the Third Reich," proclaimed the *Völkischer Beobachter*, the Nazi Party newspaper, in early August 1933, "began on 2 August 1914 . . . Out of the socialism of the front . . . arose National Socialism as a new life form for the entire nation." The idea of 1914, Joseph Goebbels boasted, had not only finally eradicated the notion of individualism, the poisonous content of the French Revolution of 1789, but this "German Revolution" also marked a watershed moment in history. The example of the "front community," with the mythical "front fighter" at its core, formed the model for the now-to-be constructed Nazi Volksgemeinschaft that would be both redemptive and offer a new purpose to national life. But, of course, the picture would not be complete without reference to November 1918, the humiliating counterpoint to the glory of 1914. Although the Nazis managed to transform defeat in 1918 into a moral victory of sorts, the threat of disintegration, from forces both internal and external, still hung over the vulnerable German nation.[13]

This sense of fragility and vulnerability, of a continuing threat to Germany's existence, represented the starting point for Hitler. As his local popularity in Munich grew, he began in his speeches to work through what he regarded as the specifics of Germany's defeat. As his few remaining wartime letters illustrated, Hitler already had a sense of England as the principal enemy, of Germany being worn down by the might of the British Empire and of succumbing to a world of enemies. This was a theme to which he returned in 1919. In some of his earliest public speeches, Hitler launched bitter attacks on the Anglo-Saxon powers (Great Britain and the United States) for their alleged determination to prevent Germany's rise to world-power status in order to preserve their own "world monopoly." The Anglo-Saxons, in combination with the Jews, he pointedly asserted, had provoked war and prolonged it in order to make money that was "soaked in blood." In June 1920 in Rosenheim, he emphatically blamed English greed, envy, and fear of German economic competition for the outbreak of the war, tying their actions with those of Jewish financiers, profiteers, and black marketeers. He gave further vent to these intimations of the key role of racial factors for German defeat, arguing in September 1920 that, while Imperial Germany had failed spectacularly in solving Germany's demographic problem, with the result that millions had emigrated from – and thus been lost to – the Reich, the British had created a great empire whose sheer numbers had crushed German forces. Worse, America, the foremost beneficiary of those German émigrés – the best, most dynamic elements of the population – had in 1918 sent these Germanic sons back to fight against the Fatherland. In March 1921, Hitler again returned to the theme of English culpability, this time raising the issue of the unfair distribution of land and sharply criticizing British hypocrisy in blaming alleged German imperialism for the outbreak of war. This seemed to Hitler especially vulgar coming from a nation that had "subjected the Chinese through opium, the Indians by means of hunger, and had sought the destruction of the Boers." Again in the autumn of 1922 Hitler returned to the theme of territory and space, but his incessant politicking before the failed putsch attempt of November 1923 simply did not allow the time for sustained conceptual thinking.[14]

Two things were evident, though. The first was his changing self-perception. Hitler increasingly saw himself less as the "drummer" rallying support for the leader who would save Germany; instead, he, the unknown front fighter, one of the tough "new men" produced by the war, would be that savior. Secondly, he had already begun, however haltingly, to articulate a set of ideas that connected German defeat with the old regime's lack of an effective demographic and territorial policy. Ironically, it was the enforced solitude of Landsberg prison, to which he was sent after the failed Beer Hall Putsch of November 1923, that allowed Hitler the time to think through his jumbled ideas. "Landsberg," he later confided to his lawyer Hans Frank, "was my university education at state expense." Particularly important in this education was his introduction to ideas of geopolitics popularized by the Munich professor Karl Haushofer. An ardent nationalist, Haushofer believed that German defeat in the war stemmed partially from the failure to prepare the home front for the hardships of a long struggle, but more importantly because no grand concept had guided the decision to go to war. Disgusted by the inept wartime German leadership, he wrote to his wife at the end of 1917, "You see how ready for a Caesar I am, and what kind of a good instrument I would be for a Caesar, if we had one and if he knew how to make use of it."[15]

Haushofer cobbled together geopolitics out of an amalgam of borrowed concepts. From the German geographer Friedrich Ratzel he took the notion of space or territory (*Raum*), a concept that quickly evolved into *Lebensraum*, or living space. In explaining the vital importance of *Raum*, Ratzel interpreted Darwin's struggle for survival as a struggle for territory, which alone would guarantee a people's existence. From the English geographer Sir Halford Mackinder, Haushofer appropriated the concept of the "heartland," which stressed the key position of the Eurasian landmass in the eternal struggle for supremacy with the maritime powers of the world. Indeed, Mackinder argued in 1919, with Germany in mind, "Whoever controls eastern Europe commands the heartland. Who rules the heartland . . . commands the world." Rudolf Kjellén, the Swedish political scientist who coined the term geopolitics, contributed the notion of autarky, or economic self-sufficiency. To Kjellén, as to Ratzel, the state was a biological being, a living organism driven by the imperative of territorial expansion via conquest, colonization, or amalgamation. The pre-war pan-German movement lent the concept of pan-regions, large areas controlled by a dominant state. To all this Haushofer added the explosive notion of the impermanence of borders, not only rejecting concepts of natural physical or ethnic borders, but also dismissing legal boundaries as well. Instead, borders were fluid and dynamic, mere temporary pauses for virile states in the process of expansion. Boundaries were thus the eternal object of struggle and frontier regions were nothing but dynamic, ever-changing battle zones. Far from demarcating permanent limits, borders were inherently changeable, unstable, and impermanent.[16]

Although there is some controversy over just how much Haushofer's ideas influenced Hitler, there can be little doubt that they played some appreciable role. The concept of Lebensraum, for example, had not been part of Nazi terminology before 1923, yet after 1924 it emerged in both parts of *Mein Kampf* and, especially, in the *Second Book*. Already in 1919 Haushofer had been introduced to Rudolf Hess, a bright and attentive student with whom he formed close ties that would last until Hess's flight to England in May 1941. Now, in 1924, on every Wednesday between 24 June and 12 December, Haushofer made the seventy-five-mile round trip to Landsberg to tutor both Hess and his "master," Adolf Hitler. In both morning and afternoon sessions, he offered intense personal mentoring to his "young lions" in history, philosophy, and, of course, geopolitics. Although later falling out with the professor and publicly dismissing his influence, Hitler privately admitted in February 1942, "Without my imprisonment, *Mein Kampf* would never have been written; . . . after constant rethinking, many things that had earlier been stated simply from intuition for the first time attained full clarity." Among these must be included the concepts of Lebensraum, autarky, the fluidity and impermanence of borders, forcible acquisition of resources, a people's struggle for survival, and war as the test of a nation's will to live – all key components of Haushofer's notion of geopolitics. In a deposition after the war, in fact, in circumstances that certainly would not have favored association with Hitler, Haushofer still asserted his influence, claiming, "These ideas came to Hitler from Hess."[17]

After his imprisonment in Landsberg a new intensity of thought emerged in Hitler. Now, in his mind, it all seemed to make sense. The war had indeed been forced on Germany out of greed and envy. Nor, according to him, was this the first time Germany had been victimized by predatory neighbors. A persistent theme in his speech-making in the 1920s and early 1930s had been the devastating nature of the Thirty Years War, which not only cost Germany a third of its population but also, after 1648, assured its fragmentation and international impotence. This "loss of world supremacy" that "should have been ours by right" especially grated on him since "no other race had as much a right . . . to take part in ruling the world." Once again, in the World War, threatened by the upstart nation's achievements after two centuries of quiescence, Britain and France, countries that disproportionately possessed the great land areas of the world, had forced Germany into an unwinnable struggle against all other great powers. Unprepared, without a clear goal or powerful motivating idea, Germany had been ground down by a material war of attrition. The home front, reduced to starvation by the pitiless British "hunger blockade" and lacking any reason to fight on, had collapsed, delivering Germany to its enemies.[18]

The lesson of the First World War seemed clear: the world of the future belonged to the self-sufficient imperial states that could secure reliable sources of food and vital raw materials. The enemy, Hitler insisted throughout the 1920s, had simply been too strong. From the outset, Germany had been forced to fight three major empires, with the continent-state of America eventually joining as well. In the future, then, Germany had to emulate them and pursue policies that guaranteed "the existence of the race for all eternity." Its dilemma was simple: a country lacking land and raw materials, it had to adjust its population to its available land. This could be done through birth control or overseas colonization, both of which Hitler rejected. He also dismissed a return to an export-based commercial policy, such as had been pursued in the pre-war period, for the obvious reason that any reliance on exports to earn the money to buy imported food and raw materials left Germany vulnerable to an Anglo-American blockade. Nor, given the reality of post-war economic protectionism, was Germany likely to have unfettered access to foreign markets. Only through a territorial policy focused on expansion in Europe could Germany acquire the vital raw materials necessary in the national struggle for existence. "The size of a people's living area," he stressed, "constitutes an essential factor in determining its external security." National Socialism, then, "would be worth nothing if it were limited only to Germany."[19]

By 1926, with the completion of the second volume of *Mein Kampf*, Hitler had clearly conceptualized the inescapable consequences of his new geopolitical reasoning. "The foreign policy of the *völkisch* state must safeguard the existence ... of the race embodied in the state ... by creating a healthy, viable, natural relation between the nation's population and growth ... and the quantity and quality of its soil and territory ... Only an adequately large space on this earth assures a nation [its] freedom of existence." Territory, for Hitler, possessed a racial, economic, and military-political significance. Not merely the acquisition but also the cleansing of the living space would provide the increased resources and internal unity that translated into greater power. Indeed, he noted, Germany had not really been a world power before 1914 since it completely lacked the key requirement of *Raum*, nor, without adequate space, could it ever be a world power. Obsessed with living space, Hitler early on in his speeches had taken to throwing around numbers relating to total area and population density to prove just how "cheated" Germany had been in terms of territory and world power. Behind this was more than just a propagandistic justification for aggression; for Hitler, this was a matter of justice and national survival. The "great mission" of the National Socialist movement, he stressed, had to be to secure living space for the German people. Hitler thus contemptuously rejected conservative nationalist demands for a return to the borders of 1914 as an "absurdity," since they were inadequate from both a racial and a geo-military standpoint. The only true goal must be "to secure for the German people the land and soil to which they are entitled on this earth."[20]

The only way to accomplish this, of course, was by force, since no nation could be expected voluntarily to surrender its territory. Nature, he stressed, knew no political boundaries nor did any higher law confer territory on a given people. Instead, the stronger race drove out the weaker; the "hard, inexorable struggle for existence" favored the strongest in courage and will, for "only children could have thought they could get their bananas ... by friendly and moral conduct." In pure Haushoferian fashion, he proclaimed that "state boundaries are made by man and changed by man." Since Germany was doomed to destruction if it failed to attain adequate living space, it thus followed that "Germany will either be a world power or there will be no Germany." More concretely, Hitler had a precise vision of where this land and resources would be acquired. "And so we National Socialists consciously draw a line beneath the foreign policy tendency of our pre-war period," he wrote. "We take up where we broke off six hundred years ago. We stop the endless German movement to the south and west, and turn our gaze to the land in the east ... If we speak of soil in Europe today we can primarily have in mind only Russia and her vassal border states." Russia, for

Hitler, had the twin virtues of being nearby and vulnerable, since "Jewish-Bolshevism" had fatally weakened the Russian state from within:

> Here Fate itself seems desirous of giving us a sign. By handing Russia to Bolshevism, it robbed Russia of that intelligentsia which previously brought about and guaranteed its existence as a state. For the organization of a Russian state ... [was] a wonderful example of the state-forming efficacy of the German element in an inferior race ... For centuries Russia drew nourishment from this Germanic nucleus ... Today it can be regarded as almost exterminated and extinguished. It has been replaced by the Jew ... He himself is no element of organization but a ferment of decomposition. The giant empire to the east is ripe for collapse. And the end of Jewish rule in Russia will also be the end of Russia as a state.

In breathtakingly radical fashion, then, Hitler not only laid out the enormous task before Germany, but also explicitly linked the acquisition of living space in Russia with the destruction of the Jews living there. In his view, "Jewish-Bolshevism" had already destroyed the Germanic element in Russia; now, they too would be eliminated.[21]

Hitler's social Darwinism and racial thinking, combined with his analysis of the reasons for Germany's defeat, thus led to a logical conclusion: a superior race could not remain forever confined to such a small and unsuitable living space. The process of European decolonization had already begun during the late nineteenth century in the Balkans with the erosion of the Ottoman Empire. The collapse of empires following the First World War, accompanied by changing borders, territorial alterations, and population migrations, simply reinforced his contention that borders were shifting and man-made, not fixed and permanent. These fluid borders not only offered the prospect of German settlement and colonization, though, but also served as a threat, for others could exploit them as well. These lands – these spaces – thus had to be filled and secured, and the threat from a numerically superior but racially inferior people eliminated. Historically, its neighbors had always placed limits on what Prussia and then Germany could hope to accomplish. But Hitler glimpsed a rare opportunity. Everything was in flux, up for grabs, and in this power vacuum the stronger had the right (and duty) to seize available territory and shape it for its own survival; Germany could take advantage of this to establish its empire. After all, if the British had built their great empire on the ruins of earlier ones, why should Germany not do the same, especially since the First World War had left no less defunct empires in central Europe? In so doing, Germany could also strike a death blow at the alleged Jewish-Bolshevik menace. History operates in both space and time; for Hitler, the opportunity was there. The traditional Prussian goal had typically been the attainable rather than the ideal. Hitler now altered the formula: it was the ideal to which he aspired. Lebensraum, then, neatly tied together a number of key themes in Hitler's thinking and justified Germany's need for a continental empire as an existential necessity. His vision of Germany was clear: a *Herrenvolk* (master race) without sufficient territory, a victim of envious neighbors throughout its history, plagued by its own hesitations and indecisiveness – now was the time to fight back. It was a simple matter of national justice.

Hitler expressed all these ideas with startling clarity in his *Second Book*, written in the summer of 1928 but never published largely because of his fear that it revealed too much. In it, he again argued that people were driven by laws of nature to reproduce and acquire food. The job of politics was merely to carry out the people's struggle for survival. Foreign policy, then, aimed at securing for a nation the Lebensraum necessary for existence, while the task of domestic policy revolved around ensuring that a people's racial quality and numbers were sufficient to achieve this. The German Reich had to be enlarged, while its enemies, the Jews and Bolsheviks, had to be annihilated. This whole process, of course, required the use of force. Nothing new here; the novel aspect of the *Second Book* related to Hitler's conception of the decisive new factor in world affairs. The United States, an emerging colossus that threatened to nullify all previous power relationships, loomed above Europe and lent urgency to the imperative to acquire space. Lebensraum now had to form the basis of a world empire that would allow a German-dominated Europe to meet the challenge of competing empires. Without the right policies and a sense of urgency, he feared, Germany might lose its second and final chance at world power, "even though we possess the highest entitlement not only to take part in this dividing of the globe that is once again taking place, but actually to play the most important part."[22]

The impact of defeat had led Hitler to develop a worldview of considerable consistency. The traumas of war and defeat also served to reinforce the notion that the nation was in a struggle for its very being, and that any future war would be in the fullest sense a "total war." To a greater extent, perhaps, than normally acknowledged, these same experiences and conclusions were generally shared by the men who would form the senior officer corps in the Third Reich. Although in the next war Hitler frequently tried to throw his frontline experience in the face of his generals, whose knowledge of the earlier war had primarily been formed at the staff level, the differences between them were often more of degree than kind. When, for example, exasperated by Hitler's reproaches after the battle of Stalingrad that his generals, not having served in the trenches, had too little experience of real war, Colonel-General Rudolf Schmidt remarked acidly to the dictator, "Your war experience could be carried on the tail of a sparrow," his observation illustrated differing perspectives rather than incompatible goals. For Hitler, the experience of war had been personal and emotional, one of immediate confrontation with life or death. His generals, on the other hand, with less intimate knowledge of the rigors of combat, viewed things from an analytical perspective, attempting in a professional manner to make sense of what had happened and why. Hitler viewed the army as an instrument of ideological war, ready to sacrifice itself to the last man, if necessary, while his generals saw it as a professional organization that must always strive to maintain its striking power. Although these differences in conception were real and would have significant consequences during the war, they also tended to obscure the extent to which a coincidence of interests existed between Hitler and his military elite – and the general lack of military opposition to his ideas.[23]

The traumas of war, collapse, defeat, and revolution served for his officers, as for Hitler, to reinforce the notion that the nation, the *Volk*, was in a struggle for its very being, and that any future war would be in the fullest sense a "total war." No less than for Hitler, the immediate aftermath of war had been a visceral emotional experience for the young officers. For both, the events of November 1918 contrasted sharply with the euphoria of August 1914. Since the German collapse, most believed, had resulted from a breakdown of the social compact between leadership and people – initiated, claimed Gotthard Heinrici (a future army and army group commander), in October 1918 in an anticipation of the stab-in-the-back myth, by "a clique of Jews and Socialists" – a prerequisite for success in any future war would be a unified society under the direction of a strong leader. Not surprisingly, those officers with more direct and lengthy experience of the hardships of the front became Hitler's most trusted subordinates and staunchest supporters, but even the more staff-oriented officers of the First World War shared a conception of a *Frontgemeinschaft* experience that bound them to Hitler. For both, the one tangible accomplishment of the war, the creation of a bond of unity across social or class lines, had been shattered by the events of November 1918. The revolutionary chaos, societal breakdown, and red flags waving in the streets of German cities all confirmed their worst fears – Germany was descending into the same sort of disintegration perpetrated by the Bolsheviks in Russia. Not just the government but the national community itself seemed to have dissolved in the last months of 1918, with most identifying socialists, communists, and Jews as the culprits.[24]

Moreover, those young officers with experience of war in the east gained the lasting impression of fighting a different enemy, one who was wild, primitive, brutal, and less civilized – and thus one for whom less restraint could be exercised. Heinrici expressed the feelings of others when he wrote of witnessing in the east "scenes of blind and senseless destruction that we had never thought possible." Even the environment appeared backward, alien, and sinister to these future generals, as they encountered "caftan Jews" living a meager existence in dirty, impoverished dwellings. The officers' experience of defeat, revolution, and chaos in Germany, their encounters with the so-called *Ostjuden* (eastern European Jews) and Bolshevism, and, especially, their post-war *Freikorps* experience fighting communist insurgencies both internally and in the chaotic areas of east-central Europe still under German control – all these strengthened and sharpened anti-Semitic views and confirmed in the minds of many of these future generals the reality of a "Jewish-Bolshevik" threat to Germany. One of them, Werner von Fritsch, in a letter written in December 1938 just after his ouster as army chief, warned that if "Germany wanted to be powerful again," it would have to battle three mighty enemies: the working class, the Catholic Church, and the Jews. "And the battle against the Jews," he stressed, "is the most difficult. Hopefully people are clear as to the difficulty of this struggle." The experience of war and revolution had radicalized these officers, stamping upon them a mentality characterized in equal measure by contempt, hatred, and fear of the "barbaric eastern peoples" and of "Jewish-Bolshevism." Significantly, as well, it also marked a key step in the process of the "totalization" of their conception of war.[25]

Deeply affected by war, defeat, and revolution, these future generals also worked assiduously to draw professional lessons from their own personal experiences and observations. Like Hitler's, their analyses led to military as well as political and social conclusions that would have lasting consequences in the next war, especially in the east. In abandoning strategy for tactics in 1918, Ludendorff's notion of fighting and winning battles – "punch a hole and the rest will follow" – proved disastrous. Many of these young officers likely agreed with the devastating assessment of the future field marshal and commander of Army Group North, Wilhelm Ritter von Leeb, that, in unleashing an offensive without a clear goal, Ludendorff had exposed the German army to "unnecessary losses" and therefore he "had the complete ruin of the German people on his conscience." Ironically, though, in conceptualizing the war of the future, the thought process of these young professionals seemed logically to culminate in a notion popularized by Ludendorff in his famous 1935 work, *Der Totale Krieg* (*Total War*).[26]

As the First World War came to be understood as a new type of conflict, one that seemed to combine Clausewitz's notion of "absolute war" with Moltke's conception of an industrialized "people's war," certain important points emerged. Since this war had required the unprecedented mobilization of large numbers of men, and was one in which the achievements of industrial workers seemed as significant as frontline fighters, the home front assumed a new importance. The entire population, in all its forms, conducted modern war. From this followed the realization that a nation, if its home front was unprepared, might well collapse without suffering a decisive defeat in battle. The political goal, survival of the nation, thus gave war a deeper meaning, but it also elevated national unity to an absolute necessity. The total state and total mobilization thus formed the prerequisites for fighting a successful war. "Total war," Ludendorff had come to understand, "is not only aimed against the armed forces, but also directly against the people." Moreover, since any future war would be one for national existence, it required the ruthless exploitation of any conquered resources. This raised a new dimension, as the legitimate objective of the war, survival of the nation, in essence meant the annihilation of other nations. Total war thus required total mobilization by the total state in pursuit of total aims, but also the abandonment of traditional values and moral restraints. For Ludendorff, in rejecting Clausewitz, war had become supreme; politics had to yield completely to the imperatives of the military. Hitler, though, merged war and politics, since the former was the means of realizing the essential requirements for national survival, the ultimate political goal. As an *Existenzkampf*, both realized the potential for unlimited violence that lurked in the concept of total war.[27]

In practical terms, for both Hitler and German military leaders the First World War had shown that the superiority of any likely enemy coalition in manpower and resources meant that Germany needed in the future to avoid a two-front war – although Hitler was always willing to gamble all or nothing, relying on his political instincts and calculations of the likely reactions of potential opponents to triumph. This material superiority of any potential enemy coalition also had to be overcome through the operational and tactical superiority of the German army. Technical modernization, mobility, speed of operations, avoidance of attrition battles through forcing quick decisions – all of these now were crucially important. In addition, though, improvements in the fighting power of the troops could be obtained through better training, discipline, and instruction – and especially through further application of the principle of Auftragstaktik, the mission-oriented tactics that placed a premium on individual initiative and motivation. Along with this, issues of propaganda and *wehrgeistigen Erziehung* (military-spiritual education) formed an integral part of the interwar military discourse. A materially superior enemy thus must be confronted both with a technically superior army and with a fanatic, decisive will – of the leadership as well as of the people. For Hitler's future generals, success in war could only be achieved through a united Volk; to them, in turn, this meant a rejection of parliamentary democracy and a willingness to embrace a strong (even dictatorial) leader.[28]

In addition, German economic inferiority, as shown in the recent war, had to be overcome in any future war through a massive expansion of the economic basis supporting the military. This meant not only an enlargement of the German Lebensraum, a notion shared with Hitler, but also a recognition that the resources of occupied countries needed to be better exploited for the German war economy. Of necessity, though, there would be a "danger period" in the next war, as Germany would be forced to use conflict to expand even as the economic basis for such a war was insufficient. The solution was to conquer the essential resources as rapidly as possible, then exploit the conquered areas quickly and thoroughly. The experience of blockade, food shortages, and hunger all showed the mistake of relying on imports and the necessity of creating a blockade-proof continental empire. A corollary of this was the absolute necessity of delivering foodstuffs from occupied areas to the German home front in order to ensure that a collapse like that of November 1918 did not reoccur. The primacy of feeding the German population at a high level, and Hitler's later explicit promise that in a future war no German would go hungry, of course, meant that occupied populations would have to starve.[29]

The logic of all this was clear – the First World War had shown that the structurally weaker nation could not allow itself to be strictly bound by any rules of war, and thus had to act in a ruthless fashion. This was especially imperative in quickly eliminating any partisan resistance that might pose a threat to the supply of food and vital raw materials. It applied as well, though, to the use of human resources. Here, too, better use had to be made of the occupied populations, with the further implication that Germany could not afford the luxury of winning over conquered peoples through a lenient occupation policy. The twin pressures of economic necessity and racial ideology thus led in the direction of brutal exploitation, which would have both political and military consequences. A future war against the western colonial empires could only be fought by means of a German colonial empire in the east. For the young officers who had served in the east in the First World War, moreover, encounters with Ostjuden and Bolshevism had not merely sharpened their anti-Semitism and anti-communism. For most, the Ukrainian "railroad campaign" of 1918 had also provided an apparent example of just how quickly and easily vast swathes of territory could be conquered – the very same resource-rich Lebensraum that would make Germany impregnable in the next war.[30]

For Hitler and his future generals, the violence of war and the shock of defeat and revolution had imposed new conditions and opened novel possibilities. War was no longer merely an instrument to regain lost prestige or territory. Instead, total war offered a radical new way to solve the eternal German dilemma imposed by its geographic position and lack of resources. Paradoxically, as well, the earlier war seemed to have created more favorable preconditions for success in the next one: the pre-1914 encirclement of Germany had been broken; a deep ideological conflict divided Great Britain and the Soviet Union; the Anglo-French relationship had cooled considerably; the United States had withdrawn into isolationism; Italy and Japan might be possible allies; and east-central Europe was in flux. To Hitler, then, both National Socialist goals and objective circumstances were aligning propitiously for one further German attempt at world-power status. In his writings and speeches Hitler had suggested that his own war experience had provided him both the ideological and the practical insight necessary to wage successful war. Ultimately, he believed, this required not only the acquisition of the essential territory and raw materials that formed the sinews of world power, but also the elimination of the "Jewish-Bolshevik" threat to German existence. What the would-be Führer and his future military leaders required now were new means and methods by which to execute this grasp at world power, while at the same time avoiding the attrition and trench stalemate of the First World War – but also, given Hitler's racial thinking, the massive loss of valuable German blood.

3

War in Peace

In March 1933, shortly after the National Socialists assumed power in Germany, perhaps as a warning, perhaps in an attempt through a calculated policy of pressure to force the new regime in Berlin into negotiations, the Polish leader Józef Piłsudski ordered a temporary occupation of the Westerplatte peninsula that controlled access to the city of Danzig. In response, General Werner von Blomberg, Hitler's minister of war, ordered the head of the Truppenamt, General Wilhelm Adam, to undertake a study of Germany's military situation. Adam's report proved sobering. Despite all the efforts of the Reichswehr leadership in the Weimar period to strengthen German defenses, Adam described the military state of affairs in the spring of 1933 as hopeless. The armed forces, he concluded, might be able to block a Polish advance on Berlin, but they lacked trained reserves, officers, and sufficient equipment and modern weapons. More crucially, a crippling shortage of ammunition meant that German troops could only fight for about two weeks. In the event of a Czech or, worse, French intervention, the Reichswehr would only be able to "administer pinpricks here and there." Adam thus stressed that everything had to be done to avoid military confrontation, "even at the price of diplomatic defeat."[1]

Despite Hitler's February assurance to the generals that he intended to free Germany from its international restraints and rebuild its power, the Polish show of force served as a rude reminder of the stark reality. The restrictions placed on it by the Treaty of Versailles had left the Reichswehr barely a second-rate force, unable to guarantee that a Polish or Czech invasion could be repulsed, to say nothing of a French incursion. Aware that it was little more than a domestic security force, but determined to reestablish

Germany's position as a European great power, German military leaders spent much of the 1920s thinking of and planning for a future war. Crucially, most either began with, or quickly arrived at, the assumption that conflict was inescapable: for Germany to regain its status as a great power, the Versailles system had to be broken. Having embraced the basic premise, officers also accepted the extreme consequences; professionalism and radicalism thus fit together quite well, setting the officer corps on a path of intersection with their future Führer, Adolf Hitler.[2]

The immediate problem, though, was resolving the conundrum posed by the outcome of the First World War. If the reestablishment of great power status, which required the use of military force, constituted the goal, the Great War had shown that Germany lacked the material and personnel resources to win a war of attrition; that tactical innovations could not in themselves alter the balance in Germany's favor; and that defensive action could result only in an unwinnable war of attrition. How, then, could the German military again become a serious instrument of national policy? Interestingly, in light of what was to come, one writer in the early 1920s sought the key to success in any ensuing war in the redemptive figure of the "Führer," the Feldherr who could fuse military and psychological insight into a powerful whole. Germans, Lieutenant Kurt Hesse claimed, "waited full of yearning . . .":

> From where he will come no one can say. Perhaps out of a princely palace or a day laborer's hut. But everyone knows: He is the Führer . . . And why? Because he exerts a strange power: He is a master of the soul . . .
>
> A brutal man yet gracious . . . Everyone who encounters him . . . has confidence in him, for his eyes are clear and deep . . . But his speech is the best about him; for it rings so full and so pure like a bell and presses on each heart.
>
> But what he thinks to himself lies as in the depths of the ocean. Only his actions tell us what it is: the life, the fate, the happiness of a people.

This Führer, perhaps a "martially inclined statesman" or a "politically minded soldier," suggested another writer, would not only prepare "war in peace" but would also be a Feldherr, the unquestioned leader in time of war.[3]

As a sign of the extent of national trauma and yearning for redemption, such writings yield a valuable glimpse into the collective psyche of the German people. Still, most thinkers sought a solution to the problem of the war of the future by returning to the foundation of the past. They, although not Hitler, largely ignored the real strategic reason for defeat, Germany's inferior resource base. No, the failure in the Great War, they believed, lay not in any fault in the operational doctrine of a war of movement, but in how it had been implemented. Initially, then, there was little break in the continuity of German military thinking, since the political and geographic reality confronting Germany remained constant: a string of enemies with superior resources on multiple fronts still dictated swift attacks before its opponents could coordinate a response.

The first effort to rebuild the army, undertaken in the early 1920s by Hans von Seeckt, the *Chef der Heeresleitung* (commander-in-chief of the army), imprinted the gospel of mobility on the new Reichswehr. While working to reestablish a formal military structure, and in the process favoring former staff officers over frontline fighters, a bias fraught with future implications, Seeckt also emphasized skill-oriented training as well as a modernized and mechanized army. Above all, he stressed the efficacy of a small, elite motorized force proficient in fighting a combined arms battle. With a nod to Germany's current situation, and a firm belief that its very immobility had played a major part in the development of positional warfare, he downplayed the importance of a mass army. Instead, he emphasized the vital role this elite force would assume in a future war. By exploiting the advantage of Auftragstaktik in orchestrating a mobile defense, it would set the stage for a quick, wide-ranging, and decisive counterblow against any invader. Seeckt's operational notions, though, not only assumed an army that did not exist but raised problems of their own. His focus on a small number of elite units, with the rest left as unmotorized infantry, as well as his operational fixation on quick victories close to Germany's borders, provided little assurance of any ultimate victory. An army designed to fight battles within a 200-kilometer range faced obvious logistical problems when extended beyond that distance. Moreover, notions of Auftragstaktik focused more on the tactical or operational than strategic level. A basic deficiency lay at the heart of operational thinking: Seeckt hoped through skill and cleverness to attain hegemony without having an adequate economic, military, or political power base.[4]

The Reichswehr's inability to hinder the French occupation of the Ruhr in January 1923, and the reality of budgetary limitations that would not permit a comprehensive motorization program, quickly caused Seeckt's vision of the future to lose much of its shine. The stark fact of German weakness, enshrined in the suffocating restrictions of Versailles, forced military planners to think in unconventional, often radical, fashion. Among the first to tackle this problem and, by rethinking all aspects of war, to attempt to reconcile the gulf between hope and actuality, were a group of young officers led by Joachim von Stülpnagel, head of the army operations department, and Werner von Blomberg, the future minister of defense under Hitler. In his "Thoughts on the War of the Future," issued in February 1924, Stülpnagel began from the commonly accepted premise that the German goal had to be restoration of its great power status, which would require a conflict with France. Rejecting Seeckt's rather quixotic views, Stülpnagel realistically assessed the current limited abilities of the Reichswehr. Its seven divisions had, he noted caustically, only enough ammunition to fight for about an hour. The operational experience of the Great War thus provided no guide.[5]

Instead, combining elements of both Germany's War of National Liberation in 1813 and the larger lesson of the First World War, Stülpnagel developed the concept of a *Volkskrieg* (people's war) to be fought in the border areas of the Reich. As in the World War, all powers of society, including, crucially, the will of the people, had to be mobilized to carry out a guerrilla war against an invader. The initial aim would be to harass and disrupt an advancing army, especially its supply lines, so thoroughly that the military leadership would have time to mobilize all available human and material resources in defense of the nation. In theory, this would enable the Reichswehr to strike the enemy an annihilating counterblow with a strong armored force. Volkskrieg would, Stülpnagel thought, in an echo of Moltke the Elder, lead to a radicalization of war, rising national hatreds, and brutalities of all kinds. It would be a war of no rules, of terrorist actions and general destruction – a self-inflicted scorched-earth operation that would leave the country in ruins. It might also, he conceded, amount to no more than a "heroic gesture," since in the mid-1920s Germany had neither the will nor the resources to fight such a war.[6]

Still, in embracing Volkskrieg, Stülpnagel had outlined a radical new vision of war. Domestic unity, an absolute national will to fight (and sacrifice), and the integration of technology in the form of mobile, mechanized units formed the essential prerequisites for successfully fighting such a war. Given this potent mix, the Clausewitzian battle of annihilation could easily change into a war of annihilation. Stülpnagel's vision lacked only the economic component of total war, a deficiency that would be made good at the end of the decade by Wilhelm Groener, the minister of defense from 1928 to 1932. Groener grasped the essential point that a Volkskrieg and the modern, mechanized force with which to fight it depended on solid economic growth that forged domestic unity and provided the necessary funds for the creation of a new type of army. Groener also recognized that, at present, Germany possessed neither the social unity, economic strength, nor logistical ability to fight a long war. Since a two-front war, he thought, would be a disaster, and the Great War had shown how enormously expensive modern war could be, Germany's only alternative in case of war was to act quickly and decisively to win it. For Groener, though, military means and political goals had to harmonize: since the creation of a powerful force poised to strike a rapid blow was beyond Germany's means, it had to avoid war altogether. If Germany could not win a war, it was best not to fight one. For Groener, a regenerated army should be employed within the Versailles system as the military instrument of a policy of peaceful revision. Although this conclusion deeply disappointed younger staff officers, Groener had highlighted the importance of economic mobilization as a precondition for victory and had clearly defined the role of the military as an instrument of the political leadership. Both of these accomplishments would, ironically, provide Hitler with leverage in his future relationship with army leaders.[7]

Younger officers associated with Stülpnagel and Blomberg grudgingly came to accept, or at least acquiesce in, Groener's assessment because their own ideas had hit a dead end. Not only did the notion of Volkskrieg assume a level of national unity and fiscal strength that simply did not exist, but the results of two war games in the late 1920s also proved devastating. German forces, not surprisingly, had been destroyed in a simulated two-front war, but they had been unable to check even a Polish invasion. The Reichswehr possessed neither the means nor the capabilities to carry out tactical attacks, let alone launch a decisive counterstrike. Despite these depressing results, though, younger staff officers, foremost among them Blomberg, simply ignored the relationship between means and ends that Clausewitz had considered of crucial significance, and defined future war only in terms of the means to be used. In thus separating political and economic concerns from military planning, they turned inward, focusing almost exclusively on technocratic, operational matters, with little interest in larger questions of strategy. Instead, they would be the functional instruments of a larger policy, the military experts who correctly implemented operations on behalf of a strategy determined by others.[8]

Throughout the 1920s, German planners continued to think in terms of mobile warfare, while studying developments in other countries. As mechanization increasingly came to be seen as the key to any future war, the proper use of the tank assumed critical importance. French experience initially shaped German notions that the tank could best be used in support of infantry attacks, but evaluation of English maneuvers began to convince them otherwise. As early as January 1927 the later commander-in-chief of the army Werner von Fritsch asserted that the tank would be the decisive offensive weapon of the future and would be most effective if concentrated in independent units. The later apostle of mobile warfare, Heinz Guderian, also promoted the tank as the means to overcome static, positional war and regain movement on the battlefield. Others envisioned a synthesis of Volkskrieg and a mobile, armored force as the key to successful offensive action. Movement and firepower, in this vision, would combine to create independent, free-flowing forces able to exploit opportunities as they arose in a continuous offensive operation.[9]

Although in hindsight this seems a clear anticipation of Blitzkrieg strategy, at the time there was little development of any such specific doctrine. It is, in fact, difficult to find more than a handful of German references to Blitzkrieg in the pre-war period. Hitler himself, although often credited with promoting the Blitzkrieg idea, seems to have known little of it in formal terms. He would occasionally talk of falling on his enemies in *blitzartig* (lightning-like) fashion, and, given the all-or-nothing aspect of his character, clearly preferred aggressive, offensive warfare. In *Mein Kampf* he had deplored the alleged half-heartedness of pre-war Germany as a symptom of decay and rejoiced at Ludendorff's March 1918 offensive as a resumption of the offensive spirit of August 1914. His deep admiration for Frederick the Great also fortified his embrace of the offensive. "World history," he declared in August 1941, "knows only three battles of annihilation: Cannae, Sedan, and Tannenberg. We can be proud that two of them were fought by German armies. Today we can add to them our battles in Poland and the West." Even after Hitler had lost the strategic initiative in the Second World War, he remained wedded to the notion of offense as the only way to win a war. "Defensive operations alone," he stated in August 1943, "are not enough. We must resume the offensive." As late as autumn 1944, just before the Ardennes Offensive, he again stressed the need for offensive operations in order to achieve decisive results and avoid a stalemate as in the First World War.[10]

Shaped by his own experience, Hitler regarded the trench stalemate of 1914–18 as a "degenerate form of war" and the shedding of precious German blood as a biological crime. Trench war, he despaired in *Mein Kampf,* had "drained the . . . best humanity almost entirely of its blood . . . irreplaceable German heroes' blood." In his unpublished *Second Book* he again decried the disproportionate destruction in war of the best German racial elements as a sin against the nation's future, and vowed in 1932 that it "will not return. I guarantee that." His preoccupation with the loss of German blood, in fact, seemed almost an obsession. "Whoever has experienced war at the front," he allegedly told Hermann Rauschning, "will want to refrain from all avoidable bloodshed. Anything that helps preserve precious German blood is good." Even at the height of his evident triumph in Russia, he returned often to this theme. "The offensive at Verdun . . ." he remarked acerbically on the night of 13 October 1941, "was an act of lunacy . . . [and] the commanders responsible for that operation should have been put in straitjackets." By contrast, he claimed, as a former frontline soldier he could imagine situations the troops had to face and so could take appropriate steps to avoid a repetition of such slaughter.[11]

Nor, despite the obvious gap between his rhetoric and reality, can Hitler's statements be easily dismissed as mere hypocrisy. After all, in *Mein Kampf* he had admitted his own personal battle with fear, when "the time came when every man had to struggle between his instinct for self-preservation and the admonitions of duty." For a man who claimed to have known "only the dark side of war," for whom it held no fascination as an adventure, such an attitude is consistent. For Hitler, the attraction of war had been the camaraderie and sense of belonging, of participating in something deeply meaningful, not the thrill of fighting. Indeed, he disliked unnecessary heroics on the battlefield and, despite his own undoubted personal courage as a dispatch runner, often recalled bitterly how he had been forced to risk his life in the Great War to deliver a postcard. In his memoirs, Erich von Manstein reported the views of a former OKW (*Oberkommando des Wehrmacht*) officer, not a Hitler admirer, who thought him too soft-hearted and emotional to be a good commander, which might explain his reluctance to visit hospitals or bombed cities. Hitler was, thought this officer, who had virtual daily contact with him, afraid of his own softness and fear at war's horrors, which hampered him in making difficult decisions. War, for Hitler, posed a conundrum: it was a vital necessity in order to achieve the Lebensraum on which Germany's existence depended – and it was essential for the preservation of the German nation in its struggle for existence – but, by shedding precious German blood, it also threatened that very existence. Precisely because war was a serious, grim affair, then, it had to be waged with utmost brutality, with humanitarian considerations swept aside. It had to be total, in the fullest sense of the term, fought with absolute determination and with the mobilization of all resources of the nation.[12]

Hitler's approach to war was a radical, all-out one, with little tolerance for half measures. Victory had to be achieved quickly at the least cost to German blood, so he hoped to avoid a head-on, attritional confrontation. But, like Clausewitz, he was also determined to force a decision. Personally attracted to bold, imaginative, daring solutions, Hitler increasingly saw mobility and maneuver as the key. "That's what I need," he exclaimed in

February 1935 after witnessing a demonstration of motorized units. "That is what I want to have." Hitler clearly appreciated the importance of new technology and the skillful interaction of all branches of the military, while Blitzkrieg suited his fascination with speed and his fear that time was always on the enemy's side. In the context of Blitzkrieg, war could be turned into a series of quick strikes in which the enemy would be dealt an indirect blow, thus avoiding the problems of attrition and an indecisive static war. Additionally, the centrality of surprise, deception, and psychological disruption appealed to Hitler as being the military analog to his successful political campaigns of the *Kampfzeit* (struggle for power). Finally, as a kind of military opportunism, an avalanche of action that would be sorted out by success, Blitzkrieg fit well with Hitler's unsystematic and impulsive nature. Still, beyond his attraction to its promise to avoid a repetition of trench war – of defeating an enemy through paralysis rather than the loss of substantial German blood – it is debatable how far Hitler conceptualized a Blitzkrieg doctrine. He noted disdainfully in November 1941, "I have never used the word Blitzkrieg, because it is a very stupid word," while in early January 1942 he remarked contemptuously to his entourage that evidently "the expression 'Blitzkrieg' is an Italian invention . . . I've just learnt that I owe all my success to an attentive study of Italian military theories."[13]

If the core of Blitzkrieg consisted of operational opportunism, the fullest possible exploitation of an initial breakthrough with all available means, and a torrent of action designed to unhinge the enemy's ability to respond, then little had changed in German thinking. Given their geographic position, Prussian and then German military leaders had traditionally sought, to use Clausewitz's term, a *Blitzeschnelle* (lightning-quick) decision. Blitzkrieg, to German thinkers, was less a doctrine than a practical solution to the ever-present dilemma confronting them. In the Great War, operational strategy had lagged behind technology; now, some Germans saw the chance to rectify that imbalance. The emergence at the end of the World War of new technologies and methods of combined arms combat raised the possibility of once again restoring a war of movement. As with Schlieffen's original intent in invading France, the goal was not so much a single, decisive battle of encirclement as unleashing a cascade of action. After the initial breakthrough had been achieved, exploitation of myriad local successes would then produce an irresistible dynamic that would overthrow an opponent as much by disorientation, dislocation of command and control, and breakdown in will as through force of arms. Speed, initiative, flexibility, and momentum were the keys. Younger German officers, receptive to new ideas and dismissive of their senior colleagues as hopelessly out of date, thus saw in emerging technologies such as the truck, tank, and airplane the means by which to restore the war of movement. To them, Blitzkrieg represented merely a new means to an old end; it was less a revolutionary doctrine than a return to an older attitude.[14]

For all the talk of the integration of tanks and airplanes in a modern war of movement, though, the value of tanks was still very much in question in the interwar period. Given the meager resources available, tanks were a risky investment, costly to build and consumers of scarce steel and gasoline; and, while their tactical utility was largely accepted, any operational value had yet to be demonstrated. Not until 1933 did guidelines for the first time stress the significance of combined weapons in a war of movement, although even then the infantry continued to be regarded as the principal instrument of war, with the implication that a primary task of tank units was to assist it. Nor, despite all the earlier discussions of a mobile defense, did these guidelines outline any such strategy. Instead, reverting to the early years of the First World War, they prescribed the holding of a main battle line to the last man. Not until the 1936 *Truppenführung* (German field service regulations) did the purely supporting role of armor finally change, with the recognition that tanks would lose their vital advantage of speed if tied too closely to the infantry. The concept of defense also evolved to reflect the experience of the last years of the Great War. Wilhelm Ritter von Leeb outlined an active, aggressive defense in which small numbers of well-armed men would hold the front line while mobile reserves with stopping power would seal any breaches and launch immediate counterattacks. Still, the 1936 manual left tanks in an ambiguous position, emphasizing their independent use while also binding armor to the support of infantry in defensive battles. The 1936 manual, as well, contained the basis of the future conflict between Hitler and his generals over the proper conduct of a defense. Even as armor doctrine evolved, then, many leading German thinkers still conceived the tank as primarily an infantry support weapon.[15]

These conservative tendencies persisted well into the late 1930s. In January 1936, Major-General Friedrich Fromm, then head of the general army office and later head of the replacement army, outlined in a memo his opinion that "the over-refinement of weapons and the fear of blood" resulted in "tactical degeneration." A determined opponent of the creation of independent tank formations, although in general he understood the efficacy of motorized forces, Fromm believed the main function of tanks should be to support infantry attacks. Before the Polish campaign, one unnamed major-general expressed skepticism about the value of tanks based on supply difficulties. It would be no problem, he argued, to find oats for horses in Poland, but where, he wondered, would they get hold of the necessary petroleum for tanks. Even Guderian encountered more scorn than encouragement. One senior general dismissed his ideas as utopian and ridiculed the whole notion of large armored units. Gerd von Rundstedt, pithier, if not more generous, characterized his ideas as "all nonsense." Erwin Rommel, later so closely associated with tank warfare, was in the 1930s a leading opponent of armor. Even in 1940 a German army manual asserted that the infantry remained the chief branch and that other weapons merely supported it. Despite this persistent skepticism, though, German army leaders in the 1930s proved willing to allow tank advocates to continue to experiment with the new weapon. Most did not doubt that the tank could be useful; the question was how to employ it most profitably.[16]

During the Weimar period, military leaders sought various expedients to nullify basic German weakness, but time and again, to their dismay, they discovered that clever ideas could not overcome their fundamental inferiority. The surest way to regain the ability to fight the wars necessary to restore Germany's position was military strength – and the requirements for that were more weapons and troops. This, then, set the stage for the "marriage of convenience" between the Reichswehr and Hitler, a marriage that proved easy to consummate, since there already existed a partial identity of interest between leading officers and Hitler. Most agreed with his foreign policy goals and the need for a buildup of the armed forces; from their experience of the First World War they also accepted the importance of a strong, unified domestic society, something Hitler had promised at his fateful meeting in early February 1933 with the generals.

Moreover, most officers were not unreceptive to the notion of collaboration with the National Socialist regime. While older generals, men such as Rundstedt, Leeb, Fedor von Bock, Ewald von Kleist, and Günther von Kluge, with roots in the monarchy and suspicious of the revolutionary energy (and brutality) of the Nazis, largely adopted a wait-and-see attitude, this should not be construed as anti-Nazi. Even Ludwig Beck and Werner von Fritsch, along with other later active anti-Hitler conspirators such as Erich Hoepner and Carl-Heinrich von Stülpnagel, broadly supported National Socialism as a positive development for Germany. Two other groups proved more willing collaborators. The first, and by far the smallest, consisted of convinced Nazis, men such as Reichenau, who embraced the new regime, welcomed the creation of a National Socialist Wehrmacht, and demanded that officers and troops alike embrace the Nazi ideology. Younger officers with a modernizing vision for the army made up the largest and most influential group. Blomberg, although slightly older, was the prototype, an enthusiastic modernizer who had visited both the Soviet Union and the United States and been stunned by what he saw, so much so that on his return from the former he had remarked, perhaps only half-jokingly, that he had become a convinced Bolshevik. Energetic, impulsive, politically naive, easily influenced, with an expansive imagination, he proved the ideal intermediary for Hitler. Not a Nazi himself, although sympathetic to party goals and ideas, Blomberg understood the industrial logic of total war and saw the advantages offered by a totalitarian state for a rapid rearmament program. He established an atmosphere that allowed ambitious, energetic, technocratic young officers, men such as Guderian, Hermann Hoth, and Georg Hans Reinhardt – all enthusiastic advocates of motorization and armored forces – to flourish. Non-Nazi themselves, they nonetheless supported the new regime for its promise to reestablish the power of the army, for reasons of their own personal career advancement, and from a conviction that Hitler offered the best opportunity to restore Germany's status as a European power.[17]

Hitler's appearance on the scene, at the moment when they had concluded that Germany had to rearm and that such rearmament likely made a future conflict unavoidable, came at an opportune time for the generals. Just as significantly, the officer corps saw themselves in the ascendancy, as evidenced by Reichenau's remark in early February 1933 that the interests of the armed forces and the state had never been more identical. A premature observation, perhaps, but certainly the new Chancellor's actions in taming the left and quickly establishing domestic order resonated with the generals. Nor, given Blomberg's goal of preserving the military as the sole instrument of national defense, could Hitler's purge of the *Sturmabteilung* or SA (Stormtroopers) in June 1934 have been unwelcome. After all, the SA leader Ernst Röhm challenged the very self-conception of the professional military elite, both with his notion of the SA as the basis of a people's army and his claim, as a former frontline officer, to better represent the war experience. Even the swearing of the personal oath to Hitler, after the death of President Hindenburg in August 1934, might be open to reinterpretation. Although Beck and Fritsch later claimed to be deeply troubled by such an oath, most officers seemed little bothered. It was, in fact, not so dissimilar from the oath to the Kaiser in imperial times, and Hitler, in a public letter, expressed his thanks to Blomberg and promised that the army would remain the sole bearer of arms in the new state. Since this was precisely what Blomberg wanted, he and Reichenau must have thought that they had bound the Führer to them, and not the other way around. Nor did Hitler and his generals disagree over the purpose of rearmament, only over its speed and timing. Paradoxically, then, the most important outcome of the first year of Nazi rule seemed to be the establishment of the army as the key force within Germany.[18]

Blomberg apparently had seized control of the issue of rearmament as well. In early 1933 it had been the defense minister, not the rather more cautious Hitler, who emphasized the necessity of unilateral rearmament and withdrawal from the ongoing Disarmament Conference. Hitler initially hesitated to take this step, not from any reluctance to rearm, but because he better understood the foreign political dangers. German goals and the Versailles system were mutually exclusive, so any unilateral rearmament would challenge the existing order and provoke a reaction. As Germany began to rearm, therefore, it had to traverse a "danger zone." During this period of vulnerability any overly hasty action might alarm its neighbors and threaten potentially disastrous consequences, whether an outright military intervention or rearmament on their part, thus touching off an arms race that Germany could not win. The military's single-minded insistence on unilateral rearmament, and its failure to grasp the consequences, thus put Germany in a foreign policy quandary, one that Hitler resolved with great proficiency, providing him growing leverage over the military. In skillfully withdrawing Germany in October 1933 from the Disarmament Conference and League of Nations, Hitler acted while his officers dithered and blustered, nervously planning for a war they could not win. When faced with British enquiries about German intentions, the Chancellor demanded a 300,000-man army and one-year military service, while ostentatiously renouncing heavy artillery, tanks, and bombers. Although infuriating military leaders who saw it as a breach of their autonomy, Hitler's offer seemed reasonable to the British, who viewed it as an acceptable basis for future negotiations. Hitler thus defused a potentially tense international situation, while demonstrating to the officers, not for the last time, that they needed him to implement their ideas.[19]

Still, Hitler's sway over the military seemed more apparent than real during the initial stage of rearmament, as his actions appeared to confirm the relative dominance of the military. The self-described "technology nut" largely confined his role to promoting rapid economic recovery, creating the unified Volksgemeinschaft necessary to conduct successful war, providing budgetary support, and bolstering younger officers in the debate over emerging notions of mobile warfare. The one foreign policy stumble – the premature attempt by the Austrian Nazis to seize power in Vienna in July 1934, which temporarily threatened war and led to a confrontation with Benito Mussolini's Italy – also seemed to strength the position of the army.

As a result, between 1933 and 1935, the generals had little to complain about, as, guided by political and military objectives held in common with Hitler, they designed and ran the rearmament program. In hindsight, in fact, Hitler might well have intervened more. In the absence of clear goals or a specific time frame – other than creating a force as quickly as possible, given the external and financial restrictions, that could defend Germany – the three services each developed their own plans and fought each other for scarce resources. German rearmament was thus less a rational optimization of resources than, typical of Hitler's organizational style, a product of an institutional Darwinism in which each service strove to get as much as it could without much consideration for economic or resource limitations.[20]

Paradoxically, each step of rearmament produced a foreign policy crisis rather than more security. Hitler then successfully resolved each crisis in turn – and, in a decided contrast with his timid and vacillating generals, generally maintained a cool, resolute approach. Rather than stabilizing the situation, though, the outcome of each crisis resulted in a spiral of further escalation and intensification of armament production, followed by another crisis. By 1935, as well, the scale of rearmament could no longer be concealed. Germany simply had too many airplanes flying in the skies, while its shipyards were clearly assembling submarines from prefabricated sections and constructing conspicuously large surface vessels. Most pressing, the army needed general conscription in order to continue its expansion. The original plan of December 1933 envisioned a peacetime army of 300,000 men in twenty-one divisions, ready for use by March 1938 and able to fight a defensive war on several fronts with a possibility of success. In view of new armament measures taken by France and its eastern European allies, in March 1935 Chief of Staff Beck revised his goals upward. In order to provide "at least a minimum guarantee of the security of our living space," he now demanded a peacetime army of thirty-six divisions (520,000 men), capable of expansion to sixty-three divisions (1.5 million men) in the event of war. This, of course, clearly violated Versailles restrictions and raised the prospect of foreign retaliation.[21]

The introduction of general conscription was thus both vital to a continued army buildup and a delicate foreign policy matter. Hitler had already shown his diplomatic prowess in extricating Germany from the Disarmament Conference and League of Nations, and in signing a Non-Aggression Pact with Poland in February 1934. Now, in early 1935, he used the decisions made in Czechoslovakia and France to increase the size of their armies, as well as a British announcement of increases in arms spending, as a pretext for conscription. Acting with typical surprise and misdirection, he first had Hermann Göring casually reveal to a reporter from the *Daily Mail* on 10 March 1935 the existence of a Luftwaffe allegedly nearly equal the size of the Royal Air Force (a gross exaggeration). Having caught the British and French off guard, and while they discussed a response, on 16 March Hitler announced the reintroduction of general conscription and plans to expand the army. While Blomberg, Fritsch, and the army leadership fretted about a possible war, British, French, and Italian leaders met on 11 April at the resort town of Stresa to discuss a diplomatic response to German actions. The resulting agreement, the so-called Stresa Front, aimed at upholding the 1925 Locarno Treaty that guaranteed the Franco-German border and the demilitarized status of the Rhineland. A few weeks later, on 2 May, Paris and Moscow agreed to a mutual assistance pact. With the fears of the German generals seemingly confirmed, Hitler now played his trump card. He reiterated a tantalizing offer to London, originally made in late March, for an accord on naval armaments. This resulted in the signing on 18 June of the Anglo-German Naval Agreement, a deal which in allowing Germany a navy a third the size of the British both implicitly legitimized German rearmament and shattered Versailles restrictions. It also stunned Britain's Stresa Front allies. When, in October 1935, Mussolini invaded Ethiopia, the anti-German coalition was in tatters, while Hitler glimpsed the possibility of creating the dream outlined in his *Second Book*, a deal with Italy and Great Britain that would isolate France. "Rearm and get ready," Hitler told a gathering of military leaders on 18 October, "Europe is on the move again. If we are clever, we will be the winners."[22]

Hitler's next move, the reoccupation of the Rhineland on 7 March 1936, seemed to verify his assertion, as well as demonstrate his expert grasp of the international situation. It is perhaps impossible to overstate the importance of this move. Not only was control of the Rhineland essential to any defense of the crucial armaments industries in the Ruhr, but, given Hitler's Lebensraum goals in eastern Europe, it was vital for all future operational planning. As long as its western border with France remained undefended, Germany could not possibly pursue a policy of aggressive expansion in the east. Although Hitler later claimed that "the forty-eight hours after the march into the Rhineland were the most nerve-racking in my life," he had chosen the ideal time for action. In mid-February he had remarked that "the right moment psychologically" had come, since the USSR would not act, "England was in bad shape militarily and seriously burdened with other problems, and France was domestically divided." As a consequence, he thought, "no military action would be forthcoming" if he remilitarized the Rhineland. Blomberg and other top generals, in a reprise of their earlier worries about the announcement of conscription, anxiously anticipated a forceful French response that would leave Germany humiliated. Hitler, though, proved shrewder than them in understanding that the Stresa Front had crumbled and the great powers, deeply involved in the Ethiopian crisis, had no stomach for a fight.[23]

He thus scored a tremendous victory at little cost. Not only did his personal popularity soar, but he also gained a significant psychological triumph over his generals, who, by comparison with their Führer, seemed timid and inept in foreign policy matters. The change in the European situation had also been decisive: Germany's military position had improved immensely; both the Versailles Treaty and the Locarno Pact had been invalidated; French inability to act reduced its influence; Italy edged closer to Germany; and the British clearly wanted to come to some arrangement with Hitler. Domestically, Hitler's self-confidence, belief in his own infallibility, personal authority, and leverage over the military grew. "I go," he told a gathering in Munich on 14 March 1936, "with the certainty of a sleepwalker along the path laid out for me by Providence." Although the generals were pleased with his diplomatic successes, which permitted more rapid rearmament, they seemed less aware of the way Hitler had subsumed them, and Germany, fully under his control. That autumn, at the annual party rally in Nuremberg, he expressed his sense of the mystical bond he had created: "That you have found me . . . is the miracle of our time! And that I have found you, that is Germany's fortune!"[24]

Despite his growing hubris, the Führer grew increasingly frustrated as he came to realize that the current pace of rearmament would never allow for the military superiority his generals deemed necessary to wage a successful war. The Versailles restrictions had so weakened the German military that even the rapid rearmament of the past few years barely sufficed to bring it to the level of its likely enemies. The tempo of rearmament had to be accelerated if Germany was to be ready for war by the target date of 1939–40. March 1936 thus clearly marked the point at which Germany made the transition from defensive to offensive armaments. On 1 April the goals for a new armaments cycle were set out that envisioned an increase of the peacetime army from 36 to 41 divisions (now including 3 armored divisions of 500 tanks each, a mountain division, and a cavalry brigade). By June, this plan had been amended to include 4 fully motorized infantry divisions, 3 light divisions (each with 200 armored fighting vehicles), and 7 independent Panzer brigades. The size of the peacetime army would swell to 793,410 men, while the fully mobilized strength of the field army in the autumn of 1940 would be 3,612,673 men. This rapid buildup aimed at "the creation of a mobilized army with the highest possible mobility and offensive potential," to be ready for combat by 1 October 1939.[25]

Just as impressive as the ambitious armor component of this new force was its sheer size. Hitler clearly wanted a powerful army in the shortest possible time. This aggressive program had staggering implications for the German economy, as Fromm, head of the general army office, pointed out with stark clarity in a memorandum of 1 August. It would likely lead to "serious difficulties . . . in the area of tanks and munitions deliveries, fulfilling truck requirements, and . . . with regard to raw materials, machines, and skilled workers." Crucially, Fromm also raised the question of whether the problems of foreign exchange and raw materials could be solved within the present system. The military had embarked on building a gigantic army explicitly intended for mobile, offensive operations, but its creation would stretch the German economy to the limit and require its immediate use in war once the buildup was complete. Given the amount of resources required, it was debatable whether this force could even be assembled under existing economic constraints. Every warning of economic limits, though, only further convinced Hitler of the need for Lebensraum.[26]

In his earlier writings and speeches Hitler had already outlined a compelling logic for territorial expansion. Modern weapons required a plentiful amount of a great variety of crucial raw materials. Germany, as a "have-not" nation, needed resources if it was to compete in the struggle for existence with the powers that monopolized the world's raw materials: Great Britain, France, the Soviet Union, and the United States. Importation of these vital commodities, though, proved increasingly problematic. Free trade had declined sharply during the Great Depression because of the imposition of protectionist tariffs, Germany lacked foreign currency to pay for such imports, and, in any case, since its likely enemies controlled the vital resources (and the sea lanes), they could always cut off supplies, as they had done in 1914–18. German vulnerability thus dictated territorial expansion to acquire essential raw materials and foodstuffs, but these could only be secured through war, for which, paradoxically, Germany was not prepared because of a lack of resources. Hitler proposed to cut this Gordian knot through an effort at autarky based on the intensive exploitation of all available resources under German control. To this point, the regime had relied on a complex and intricate system of currency controls and trade agreements, devised by the financial wizard Hjalmar Schacht, to secure the raw materials necessary for rearmament. This system had largely reached its limits by 1936, as shown by persistent foreign currency crises, a huge balance-of-payments deficit, and crippling shortages in raw materials that led to bottlenecks in armaments production. Schacht urged a slowdown in the pace of military spending as the logical solution to the looming crisis. This, though, meant reining in German arms production precisely at the moment when Hitler was pushing an accelerated program. In order to pay for the necessary imports, Schacht pressed for a renewed export offensive, which meant an end to unilateralism and some cooperation with Britain and France, which Hitler and the military refused to accept. Blomberg, the apostle of unilateral rearmament, was already struggling to sort out the bureaucratic strife between his service chiefs over distribution of scarce resources. Now he faced a bitter dispute with Schacht over the pace of rearmament and extent of raw material imports. Given his enthusiasm for the efficiency of the authoritarian state in matters of rearmament, Blomberg naturally sought a solution in terms of an economic dictator.[27]

Typically, Hitler initially did not intervene himself but directed Göring to sort out the mess. This suited the latter's bullying personality and desire for all-out rearmament, but his lack of any fundamental economic understanding resulted, as Schacht had foreseen, in a major economic crisis in late summer 1936. Stocks of vital raw materials had been seriously depleted, the country faced a foreign currency crunch, factories worked at reduced capacity, and shortages in iron, steel, and non-ferrous metals affected all weapons production programs. With a sharp reduction in the pace of rearmament the only alternative, Hitler in late August put pen to paper and personally outlined a new Four-Year Plan for the German economy. In a long preamble on the political situation, he stressed the growing threat from "Jewish-Bolshevism," reiterated the necessity for Lebensraum, and posed a stark choice for Germany: either strengthen the military or face annihilation. In the second part, he made clear, the economic dilemma facing the nation could ultimately be resolved only through acquisition of new land. In the meantime, though, Germany would turn to autarky in order to create a military-industrial state. This meant a drastic increase in the exploitation of available domestic resources, a sharp decrease in non-essential imports, and an all-out effort to substitute synthetic alternatives for essential imports. Not even vital food imports could be allowed to impede the pace of rearmament: the needs of the war economy were paramount. If private industry failed in its tasks, Hitler threatened, the National Socialist state would fulfill them on its own. Autarky was to be pursued regardless of economic efficiency; all difficulties would eventually be resolved through the acquisition of Lebensraum.[28]

Hitler's memorandum not only emphatically rejected Schacht's vision of a slower pace for rearmament and a strategy of stockpiling raw materials and hard currency, but also directly threatened German industry. In an economic version of Auftragstaktik, private industry would be given goals to fulfill but would, in principle, be free to choose its own methods. State control would be imposed if the private sector failed to meet targets set for it. Additionally, the memorandum delineated Hitler's rejection of any further British attempt to accommodate Germany within the existing system. With the Four-Year Plan, Hitler clearly revealed his intention not just to accelerate rearmament, but to launch a war in the near future. "The extent and pace of the military development of our resources cannot be made too large or too rapid!" he stressed, underscoring this point for emphasis. His final directive could hardly have been clearer: "I thus set the following task: I. The German army must be operational within four years. II. The German economy must be fit for war within four years."[29]

The first four years of his regime, he confessed to his intimate associates, had been largely wasted in "determining what we could not do." Now, he said, it was time "to implement what we can." Underscoring this urgency, Hitler on 18 October named Göring general plenipotentiary for the Four-Year Plan and authorized him to take responsibility for virtually every aspect of economic policy. Since Fromm's memo of 1 August had already noted that the army had to be used shortly after the completion of rearmament, the Four-Year Plan sharply increased the likelihood that Germany would be at war by 1940. At that point, as Hitler realized, the country would have achieved the best relative superiority against its Western foes it could expect under the conditions of temporary autarky. At the latest, then, Germany needed by 1940 to have begun the permanent solution to its economic problems: acquisition of living space.[30]

To this point, Hitler had, to a great extent, allowed his generals to shape the rearmament process, but the Four-Year Plan marked a significant change in his outlook. Although he and his military leaders generally shared similar goals, they diverged on the issue of ways and means. To men like army chief of staff Beck, war could only be waged after a careful arms buildup that allowed the necessary superiority to win such a conflict. Although an ambitious project, the Four-Year Plan in itself could not produce a rapid enough rearmament to meet this criterion. As Hitler began to question whether, by their definition, the armed forces would ever be ready to fight a war, he also challenged the entire system of orderly military planning. Ironically, Beck's increasingly forceful assertions that fighting a major war would continue to be beyond the army's ability did less to restrain Hitler than convince him to abandon a measured, professionally controlled, and carefully planned preparation for war in favor of a politically and

militarily improvised course of taking advantage of opportunities as they
arose. For Hitler, who ridiculed military "bean counting" in favor of a will
to fight, this strategy had the twin advantages of playing to his improvisational strength in the diplomatic arena while promising to increase his
leverage over the military. Significantly, despite the fact that Beck's arguments pointed to a strategic dead end, neither he nor Hitler remotely
contemplated halting rearmament or renouncing the use of force to achieve
their goals. With no viable alternative to offer, the military now became
hostage to Hitler's impulses, a clear reversal of roles since 1933.[31]

By 1937, as well, Hitler had concluded that a goal outlined in his *Second
Book*, for an understanding with Great Britain, offered few concrete advantages for Germany. This was the context that framed yet another fundamental restating of Hitler's strategic priorities in a meeting with the senior
military and diplomatic leadership on 5 November 1937. Although the
impetus for the conference had initially come from Blomberg and Admiral
Erich Raeder, both of whom wanted Hitler finally to make a decision on
allocation of resources for rearmament, he typically avoided such a decision and instead chose to outline his ideas on the foreign policy situation.
According to notes taken by Colonel Hossbach, his adjutant, Hitler spoke
for several hours, prefacing his main points with a long background exposi-
tion on the need for Lebensraum. What was new, and for much of his audience unnerving, was an indication of his willingness to act immediately to
expand the territory of the Reich. Gaining space was the vital issue, he
stressed, and resolving this problem was the crucial task of his foreign
policy. "The necessary space . . .," moreover, would "have to be found in
Europe," since "areas containing lots of raw materials were better located in
direct proximity to the Reich." History had shown, Hitler asserted, leaving
no one in doubt as to his intentions, "that expansion could only be carried
out by breaking down resistance and taking risks; setbacks were inevitable.
There had never in former times been spaces without a master, and there
were none today; the attacker always comes up against a possessor." The
declining powers, Britain and France, he asserted, were hate-filled antagonists with whom no accommodation was possible. Still, he thought both
had written off Austria and Czechoslovakia. In the event of an internal
crisis in France or an Anglo-French war with Italy over Spain, Germany
would exploit the favorable moment to seize both. In any case, and here
Hitler showed an acute awareness, the key issue was one of timing. Germany,
he emphasized, had to resolve the matter of Lebensraum at the latest by
1943–5, by which time the country's relative armaments advantage would
have disappeared, but he was prepared to act as early as 1938.[32]

He also noted the threat posed by the rearmament of its adversaries, whose programs would in the near future overtake those of the Reich. "Germany's problem could only be solved by means of force," he stressed, "and this was never without attendant risk ... If one accepts ... the resort to force with its attendant risks, then there remain still to be answered the questions 'when' and 'how.'" The answers, of course, were soon, and with whatever force Germany had available at the moment in swift, decisive actions. Hitler understood military preparations were not complete, but he had now articulated a decision to go to war as soon as the opportunity arose. Nor did he evince much concern about Western reaction. The British Empire, he thought, was rotting away and could not be maintained, while he dismissed France as seriously weakened domestically. Just as the strategic dead end of the generals led to dependence on Hitler, the Führer's notions of a military policy dictated by circumstance resulted in a dynamic in which expansion became necessary for economic, financial, and technological reasons. Germany would fight not when it was ready, which might be never, but when the situation seemed propitious. Technocratic and ideological thinking had now replaced professional strategic planning.[33]

Hitler's remarks stunned Blomberg and Fritsch (and Beck, when he heard of them) – not because they opposed rearmament, annexation of Austria or the destruction of Czechoslovakia, or his general concept of Lebensraum, but from a fear that an aggressive, opportunistic foreign policy would plunge Germany into a premature war it could not win. For these men trained to think in terms of a rational application of force for attainable ends, the idea that Germany had to exploit a supposed lead in the arms race seemed reckless and dangerous. Although all three tried to persuade Hitler over the next few weeks that provoking Britain and France was unnecessary, since much of what he wanted could be achieved peacefully, their efforts availed little. Ernst von Weizsäcker, deputy head of the Foreign Ministry and a Hitler opponent, displayed a remarkable obtuseness in a memo urging negotiation with Britain, since "time is in England's favor and not ours in the matter of rearmament." If its intent was to restrain Hitler, it backfired spectacularly. Joachim von Ribbentrop, then ambassador to London, captured his Führer's mood better, whispering in his ear that Britain was using appeasement as a mere pretext to buy time, since its leaders believed they would win any rearmament race with Germany, given their greater resources and American support. Nor, after a meeting on 19 November 1937 with Lord Halifax, a close associate of Prime Minister Neville Chamberlain, did the Führer have any reason to doubt Ribbentrop's assessment. Britain's own rearmament and unwillingness to concede German hegemony on the continent, he believed, meant that any negotiations would only be a ruse to buy time. When Foreign Minister von Neurath warned him in mid-January 1938 that his policies meant war, but that most of his plans could be obtained by peaceful means, albeit more slowly, Hitler replied simply that he had no more time. In any case, he aimed to fundamentally transform Europe, not tinker with minor frontier revisions. Hitler saw the trend better than his generals: at some point the military advantage would pass from Germany to its enemies. "I bet you," he told Ribbentrop, "that in five years Churchill will be Prime Minister and then we will be in a fine mess! I can assure you that I won't wait until I have been cornered. I will strike before then and tear up the web that the English spider wants to weave around me."[34]

In November 1937, Hitler indicated to his generals that he meant to be more forceful in taking advantage of opportunities as they arose, only to encounter opposition, a fact that fueled in him a growing distrust of his military leaders. Their arrogance, isolation, and self-conscious elitism irritated him. Not only did they look down on him socially (and as an Austrian) with aristocratic disdain, but now they seemingly also dismissed his skills as a diplomatist and strategist – and this, after his undoubted triumphs of the past few years. Just as crucially, they seemed to be interfering in the political sphere. After all, he had restored domestic order, supported their rearmament plans, and adroitly distracted Western attention, but now his generals presumed to know better than him. A deeper divergence had also appeared: whereas they saw the economic and political difficulties resulting from rearmament as requiring a slower pace in foreign policy, Hitler perceived more danger in waiting. In early February 1938, then, he acted swiftly to assert control over foreign policy decision-making, reacting to a sense of personal betrayal and demonstrating his uncanny ability to profit from the imponderables of history. Blomberg and Fritsch both resigned on 4 February as a result of separate scandals; on the same day the conservative foreign minister, von Neurath, was sacked, to be replaced by Ribbentrop. Hitler exploited the crisis by naming himself minister of defense and establishing a separate organizational entity, the Oberkommando des Wehrmacht (OKW, or Armed Forces High Command) with Wilhelm Keitel, a pliant but effective administrator, as its head, to coordinate policy. At the same time, Walther von Brauchitsch, a capable if weak-willed officer, replaced Fritsch as the new commander-in-chief of the army. In breathtaking fashion, Hitler had concentrated all military and political power in his own hands. He had long held the ineffectual elite of Imperial Germany responsible for defeat in the First World War; now, the former frontline fighter who had risen on merit would decide all matters. No longer a potential "state within the state," the army became a mere instrument of the Führer's will.[35]

Hitler's assertion of control over the armed forces and tensions surrounding the dismissal of Fritsch tended to obscure the extent to which he and the army continued a mutually beneficial relationship. Although some generals expressed doubt over the timing of Hitler's moves, and resented the crude manner in which Fritsch had been ousted, few really objected to their ultimate purpose. Moreover, younger officers inclined to be more supportive of Hitler. Eager to put new operational ideas and weapons to the test, they evinced a more audacious and technocratic outlook. If rearmament had driven Germany into a dead end, they sought a way out not by developing any coherent strategy within the larger diplomatic context, but by focusing on novel ways to use the weapons available. Given a boost in their career path by Hitler's rearmament program, these were enthusiastic modernizers eager to innovate and receptive to Nazi ideas. In a powerful mixture of ideology and technocracy, Hitler, who insisted that the will to fight was more important than power relations, found willing partners among the officers of the *Frontkämpfer* generation, who perceived themselves as the capable instruments of the fulfillment of Hitler's restorative foreign policy.[36]

The inauguration in March 1938 of an expansionist foreign policy marked by a run of spectacular successes hardly imaginable a few years earlier also cemented Hitler's dominance. The first blow came with the annexation of Austria (the *Anschluß*) in March 1938, an action that again seemed to confirm the Führer's improvisational genius. By late 1937, economic, ideological, and strategic imperatives had intersected nicely with diplomatic realities to render Austrian independence increasingly tenuous. Still, Hitler seemed in no immediate rush to achieve Anschluß. Events, however, forced his hand. At a meeting at Berchtesgaden on 12 February 1938 he bullied the Austrian chancellor, Kurt von Schuschnigg, into making further economic concessions, as well as taking two Austrian Nazis into his cabinet. On returning to Vienna, though, Schuschnigg recovered his nerve and, aiming to stop any further erosion of Austrian sovereignty, on 9 March called for a referendum four days later on Austrian independence.[37]

The news stunned Berlin; not only would the referendum, if allowed to take place, reaffirm Austrian sovereignty, but it would also be a public humiliation of Hitler. Spurred on by Göring, he quickly ordered preparations for an invasion of Austria. While staff officers led by Manstein (and including many future commanders on the Eastern Front) hastily threw together an invasion plan, Hitler issued an ultimatum demanding Schuschnigg's resignation. Under enormous pressure, and wishing to avoid bloodshed, the latter complied and, on 12 March, to scenes of wild jubilation, German forces, not without some mechanical problems, entered Austria. This bloodless triumph sent Hitler's prestige soaring, not least among his younger officers. Maximilian Weichs had "never experienced such jubilation" as displayed by the Austrians, while their "tremendous enthusiasm" deeply impressed both Guderian and Manstein. As Hitler had predicted in November 1937, the great powers did nothing, while Germany, buoyed by the economic, manpower, and, above all, financial resources of Austria, enhanced its strength. At a stroke, the national exhilaration in March 1938 dispelled any lingering unrest in the officer corps over the Blomberg-Fritsch crisis and cemented their loyalty to Hitler. Just as importantly, he had demonstrated, to himself as much as them, his apparently unerring political instinct and improvisational genius. He could do anything he wanted, and was impatient to do more.[38]

Any annexation of the next obvious target of German expansion, the Czech Sudetenland, would clearly be riskier and more problematic than that of Austria. Hitler's foreign policy moves to date had been bold but not reckless, revealing a keen appreciation of the diplomatic situation, a shrewd awareness of his opponents' weaknesses, and a sure instinct for exploiting opportunities as they arose. Now, his impatience to achieve his historic mission, as well as a deep hatred of the Czechs that had its origins in his Austrian heritage, began to overwhelm sound political calculation. Already on 21 April, just five weeks after the Anschluß, Hitler directed Keitel to initiate planning for a confrontation with Czechoslovakia. The imperatives driving his foreign policy were clearly evident; while irritated by the slow tempo of German rearmament, he nonetheless judged the relative power balance to be favorable. Further, he explained, the operation would be modeled on the Anschluß. War against the Czechs could not "come out of the blue," he noted in a realistic assessment, because that would provoke the great powers into action. Events would have to escalate rapidly out of some incident, leading to a justification for intervention. He did not intend to start a war right away, he informed Keitel, but wanted to be able to act quickly once the opportunity presented itself. The army and air force would only have a few days to defeat the Czechs in a quick blow. "Faits accomplis," he stressed, "must convince foreign powers of the hopelessness of intervention."[39]

Whether from Hitler's instructions or fear of the likely reaction from his fellow officers, Keitel, with General Jodl's help, prepared a directive for the operation, but held it back from the army. Nor did he give any indication of Hitler's intentions. Beck, though, got wind of the preparations, and on

5 May he sent Brauchitsch a sharply worded memo arguing forcefully against any military confrontation with Czechoslovakia. Although admitting that the German position had improved considerably over previous years, he nonetheless invoked visions of 1914 and the creation of a powerful hostile coalition in response to any German action. The point was clear: a German–Czech war could not be limited, and the intervention of Britain, France, and (possibly) Russia would lead to a long war of attrition that Germany could not win. Brauchitsch, unwilling to face the Führer alone, immediately took the memo to Keitel. The two of them filtered out the sections dealing with political and strategic matters before presenting it to Hitler, who predictably rejected it in the harshest terms.[40]

The brewing dispute grew more intense on 21 May when, in reaction to purported German troop movements and erroneous reports of an impending attack, the Czechs mobilized along the border. British and French officials, in apparent confirmation of Beck's prediction, quickly warned Hitler that they would not sit idly by if Germany invaded Czechoslovakia. The crisis passed just as rapidly as it had erupted, with the Western press trumpeting Hitler's climb-down in the face of united pressure. There had, in fact, been no German troop movements or plan to invade, but this perceived loss of prestige enraged the Führer. His response came quickly. On 28 May he informed a gathering of diplomatic and military leaders of his intention to destroy the Czech state as soon as possible, despite the risk of war. Thoroughly alarmed, Beck drafted an even longer and harsher memo. While agreeing with Hitler's goals of eliminating the Czech state and attaining Lebensraum, and conceding his undeniable successes to date, Beck nonetheless reiterated in the strongest possible terms the army's unpreparedness for war. It was also illusory, he emphasized, to believe a quick, limited victory could be achieved without outside intervention. The Führer's response was equally swift and uncompromising. "It is my unalterable decision," he asserted in a directive of 30 May, "to smash Czechoslovakia by military action in the near future. It is a matter for the political leadership to await or bring about the suitable moment from a political and military point of view." He also instructed the Wehrmacht to make preparations for war and to accelerate progress on the construction of the West Wall defensive fortifications along Germany's border with France, Belgium, and the Netherlands. In no uncertain terms, Hitler, in Clausewitzian fashion, had asserted political superiority over the military, as well as his prerogative as head of state to initiate a war at a time of his choosing.[41]

The explosive acceleration of German arms production in the summer of 1938 also reflected Hitler's acceptance that a war with Britain and France might follow any swift victory over Czechoslovakia. Completion dates for surface ships already under construction were brought forward and the tempo of submarine construction accelerated. Production of small arms, mortars, artillery, tanks, and ammunition for use by the army also increased, as did work on the West Wall. Angered by the slow pace of its construction, Hitler ordered Fritz Todt, the builder of the Autobahn, to undertake a crash building program. Aircraft production accelerated, most notably twin-engine bombers such as the Ju-88, which seemed ideal for use against Germany's western neighbors. Contrary to myth, Luftwaffe leaders, as their counterparts elsewhere, had early on embraced strategic bombing; German aircraft makers had even designed a prototype four-engine bomber, the so-called Uralbomber. Just at the time when British and American planners adopted long-range bombers as a potential war-winning weapon, though, German military leaders, influenced by the experiences of the Spanish Civil War, rejected them as too inaccurate to be of decisive importance. In addition, long-range, four-engine strategic bombers were expensive to build and gobbled up precious raw materials. The Ju-88, on the other hand, could not only be used for close air support of army units, but its superior accuracy as a dive bomber also seemed ideal for destroying enemy shipping or attacks on industrial targets in France and England. The medium bomber thus seemed more useful given the German situation. It also fed Hitler's preference for quick strikes, as well as large numbers of them. Göring calculated that German factories could produce two and a half of the twin-engine bombers for every one of the heavier ones, something he knew appealed to Hitler. Only later did its limited range and inadequate bomb capacity prove unequal to the challenge of a long-distance war. Similarly, the navy focused on an expensive surface fleet that, again, consumed limited resources, rather than on the more useful submarines, which, in the German estimation, had failed during the First World War.[42]

Despite Hitler's unequivocal directive of 30 May, Beck, in a series of memos directed at Brauchitsch, fought a rearguard battle throughout June and July, repeating his warnings that a war with Czechoslovakia would spread. "What sort of generals are these, whom I, the head of state, have to force into making war?" Hitler fumed, then added pointedly, "I don't ask my generals to understand my orders, but to obey them." Intimidated, Brauchitsch cast himself as a mere instrument of the Führer, but in reality most other generals also thought the matter of war or peace lay in Hitler's hands. Even Manstein, a protégé of Beck's, advocated putting trust in the Führer, since he had, until now, been an astute judge of the political situation. Increasingly isolated, Beck issued a memorandum on 16 July in which he tried to pressure Brauchitsch and other top commanders into resigning if their warnings went unheeded. "Their soldierly obedience has a limit," he asserted, "where their knowledge, their conscience, and their responsibility prohibits the carrying out of an order." Hitler, he argued, was putting the future of Germany at risk; therefore, they had the obligation before the nation and history to resign. Beck's impassioned plea fell largely on deaf ears, though, and on 4 August one last effort to rally support failed. Top army commanders, summoned by Brauchitsch to discuss Beck's objections, agreed that Germany was unprepared for a war, but expressed reluctance, as one general put it, "to get involved in matters that are the concerns of the politicians."[43] With that Beck's isolation was complete. Hitler, well aware of opposition to his plans in the military, met with younger generals, who owed their careers to him, for three hours on 10 August, during which he dismissed Beck's concerns and shared his own conviction that, given their state of unreadiness and internal crises, England, France, or Russia would not intervene to save Czechoslovakia. That proved sufficient to sway most in attendance. Beck drew the logical conclusion and on 18 August resigned as chief of the general staff, which Hitler accepted three days later, although delaying the announcement for foreign policy reasons.[44]

Beck's successor, Franz Halder, also harbored doubts about Hitler's plans, but found his scope for action limited. With a rather pedantic, stiff personality, more a competent technocrat than a strategist, conservative, with a strong sense of duty, but at the same time sensitive and given to emotional outbursts, Halder had a complex relationship with Hitler. Unlike Beck, Halder tended to cast his dissent indirectly, expressing disapproval with acerbic, biting remarks, and working behind the scenes to obstruct or modify Hitler's plans. This irritated the Führer enormously, as did the fact that Halder had spent his entire career as a staff officer. Hitler, of course, boasted frequently of his frontline service and distrust of staff officers, jibes that Halder could hardly misinterpret. Still, he appeared more modern and dynamic than Beck, with considerable technical skills, which Hitler appreciated. Halder, like his predecessor, drifted into resistance more from his practical objections to war than from any principled opposition to its intent. Although he certainly disliked Hitler personally, Halder, like most officers, supported the goal of restoring Germany's great power status. The whole early resistance effort, in fact, had a whiff of ineffectuality about it not so much because the plotters were amateurs "playing at" conspiracy – the risks and dangers were real enough – but because they largely agreed with the substance of what Hitler was doing, objecting only to the timing.[45]

Any plan for a nascent coup against Hitler depended on the outcome of the developing crisis over Czechoslovakia. Although Halder, along with a few other staff officers, believed that Hitler's actions would lead to war, he also recognized that most of the officer corps, as well as the general public, had faith that the Führer would again win a bloodless triumph. Ironically, while Hitler initially followed the Austrian script and justified his demands for annexation of the Sudetenland on grounds of national self-determination, he appeared increasingly unhappy with a possible peaceful outcome of the crisis. More than merely desiring war for its own sake, Hitler believed that war and economic power went hand in hand, that violence was a necessary and thus legitimate way to obtain essential economic resources in areas contiguous to the Reich. Czechoslovakia was just such an area and, significantly, Hitler had given instructions that Czech industry should not be damaged, but integrated into the German war economy as quickly as possible. The timing seemed opportune as well. After all, his fascist counterparts in Italy and Japan were waging war largely unhindered by the Western democracies, while the ongoing crisis in Spain promised to keep France distracted. Then, too, after assuming control over the armed forces earlier in the year, and fresh from the triumph of the Anschluß, Hitler likely also aimed to demonstrate to his timid generals that he was now fully in control.[46]

The key to success in his pulling off a limited war lay in separating the British from the French, and encouraging the former to stand aside. Following demands raised in a meeting with Chamberlain in Berchtesgaden on 15 September, though, the British and French pressured the Czechs into conceding to Germany the disputed territory. This evidently caught Hitler by surprise; throughout September, in fact, he seemed disconcerted by Chamberlain's relentless diplomatic efforts at maintaining peace. He responded by raising the stakes; the Czechs would also have to make territorial concessions to the Poles, Hungarians, and Slovaks, a demand, presumably, Prague would reject. Hitler thus hoped to isolate Czechoslovakia and ensure a limited, local war, but could not be certain of Britain's reaction. Although earlier he had told Goebbels that England would not intervene, and assured his skeptical generals that the West was bluffing, he was aware of opposition within the military to his policy and, worse, vacillation among top Nazis. Göring, for one, took Western threats seriously and urged Hitler to avoid war. Having adopted a confrontational course, though, Hitler could not abandon it without risking a loss of prestige, and perhaps even a coup, since the shadowy conspiracy against him was predicated on a foreign policy disaster.[47]

Visibly strained, with some observers of the opinion that he was close to a nervous breakdown, Hitler now began to waver. Czech rejection of his

latest ultimatum was hardly surprising, but he was rattled by evident steadfast British and French support for Prague. On the evening of 26 September
he gave a wild, hate-filled speech – extreme even by Hitler's standards – at
the Berlin Sportpalast in which he threatened the destruction of
Czechoslovakia. But that same day, in comments to Goebbels, he also gave
the first indication that he had moved away from his intent to destroy
Czechoslovakia in one, high-risk blow, instead raising the possibility of a
two-stage process: first, the Sudetenland, then shortly after, the remainder
of the Czech state would be occupied. Moreover, his gamble on war being
dependent on a quick-blitz military victory, he had been deeply upset by
the timid and uninspired operational plan originally drawn up by
Brauchitsch and Halder. Nor, after he had explained what he wanted, had
they altered their plan. Infuriated, the Führer had ordered both to meet
with him on 9 September, where he demanded a change in the military
dispositions, then abruptly dismissed them, leaving Brauchitsch badly
shaken by the encounter. After the two had left, Hitler remarked caustically
on their fear and cowardice, on how much the army had disappointed him.
Worse, Hitler's plan was daring and bold, aiming to hit the Czechs where
they least expected it, promising a quick victory; in all, a seeming confirmation of his own superior operational abilities.[48]

With tensions at breaking point – on 28 September Halder, in a state of
collapse, sat at his desk crying that all was lost – with the conspirators on
the point of launching a coup, and with Germany seemingly on the verge of
a war it could not win, Hitler relented and accepted Mussolini's offer to
mediate the issue, with his changed perception of Britain's willingness to
fight the key to his decision. The hastily arranged conference in Munich on
29–30 September resulted in a quick agreement on German annexation of
the Sudetenland, as well as a joint Anglo-German declaration of their desire
for peaceful relations. An action that succeeds always appears to have been
well planned, and so it seemed after the Munich Conference. At a stroke,
Hitler pulled off his greatest diplomatic triumph, confirming Germany's
status as a great power. He achieved his immediate aims peacefully, plans
for the coup collapsed, opposition in the army dissolved, to be replaced by
renewed faith in the Führer's genius, and his personal popularity in
Germany soared. If war had come, Hitler might well have been overthrown;
as it turned out, if he had died at that moment, he likely would have been
remembered as one of the greatest statesmen in German history, having
accomplished the unity of German lands without war. Despite his triumph,
though, Hitler was deeply troubled by the obvious popular longing for
peace, manifested both by the hostile response to German mobilization

and the enthusiastic crowds that greeted Chamberlain in Munich. "There is no way," he remarked in disgust, "that I can wage war with this people." He complained further on 10 November that the years of peaceful rhetoric, designed to camouflage his true intentions from Western observers, had lulled his own population. It would be necessary, he concluded, "to recalibrate the German people psychologically and make it clear that there were things which . . . would have to be pushed through by force."[49]

Revealing of Hitler's attitude, as well, was the way in which anti-Jewish policy, always an accurate barometer of his mood, moved in tandem with foreign policy. All during the summer and fall of 1938, as the Czech crisis simmered and his frustration grew, anti-Jewish actions intensified domestically. The one, of course, culminated in the triumphant annexation of the Sudetenland, and the other in the violence of Kristallnacht, an apparent dichotomy that was less than it seemed, for the outcome of the crisis left Hitler dissatisfied; he did not see Munich as a victory. The German people had reacted sullenly when faced with war, he anticipated yet another confrontation with his generals, and he had failed to isolate and destroy Czechoslovakia. He was well aware that he had suffered a setback, for he genuinely desired war in 1938, only to lose his nerve. His political instincts had told him to hold out, but at the last moment he had backed down, a fact that troubled him to the last. As late as 21 February 1945 he complained to Martin Bormann that "we ought to have attacked in (September) 1938. It was the last chance we had of localizing the war." Britain and France, he thought, would have remained passive, a stance that would have destroyed their political position. Then, Hitler mused, "we would thus have gained the time required . . . to consolidate our position . . . and would have postponed world war for several years," to a time when Germany would have been better prepared. Conscious that the arms race and time were running against him, aware that Chamberlain had outmaneuvered him and hoped to contain him with future negotiations, Hitler vowed that never again would he be drawn into an international conference or fobbed off with partial solutions, a posture he maintained when faced with a similar crisis a year later.[50]

In a further irony that fueled Hitler's sense of urgency, German rearmament had spurred Great Britain, France, the Soviet Union, and the United States to increase their armaments production, with the result that even after a concerted military buildup Germany had gained no appreciable advantage. The impact of Versailles meant that, starting from so far behind, the ambitious rearmament program of the 1930s had barely gained them parity, let alone any decisive edge. Additionally, scarce resources had been squandered because of the lack of coordination among the various services. Despite its evident diplomatic triumphs, German preparations for war in the 1930s had largely failed. The country had effectively been on a war footing from at least 1938, if not from the inauguration of the Four-Year Plan in late 1936, but this feverish economic and military activity had produced meager yields. While the Four-Year Plan did cushion the blow of the allied blockade, Seeckt's elite mobile units, while effective tactically and operationally in defeating France, could neither knock Great Britain out of the war nor inflict a strategic defeat on the Soviet Union. Hitler had largely let his generals define the shape of the new army and then accelerated his foreign policy, resulting in inevitable war, before it was fully ready. The triumphs of 1939–40 failed to produce a decisive victory, with the result that most of the rearmament effort of the 1930s was largely undone in 1941.[51]

Hitler, in the 1930s, had proven to be shrewd, incisive, and insightful in foreign policy matters, but utterly lacking in patience and caution. Although Nevile Henderson, the British ambassador to Germany, thought that he had "now become quite mad," his actions resulted more from a calculated assessment of likely Western reactions. With great trust in his own intuition, Hitler was prepared to gamble all-or-nothing with Germany's future. And, in truth, he saw the country's survival linked inextricably with expansion, which required war. For Hitler, a conflict was inescapable, so to him the element of risk was largely irrelevant. Nor did German military leaders, who largely shared his vision, restrain him. The narrow focus on how to fight the war of the future had thrust to the forefront the generation of officers from the First World War who valued activism and innovation, firepower and speed, over politics and strategy. These officers also proved less inclined to oppose Hitler, whether from agreement with him or because of their more limited, technocratic perspective. The only real difference was one of timing, not methods or goals. Military leaders hoped to avoid a premature conflict, but Hitler was correct that he could not wait indefinitely. "Hitler," the French premier, Edouard Daladier, remarked presciently shortly after Munich, "will find a pretext for an armed conflict before he loses his military superiority." If Lebensraum to safeguard the very existence of the nation was the goal, then he had to get on with war since the Wehrmacht's lead in modern, mobile weapons was diminishing rapidly.[52]

4

Blitzkrieg Unleashed

Although seen at the time as a great personal triumph, the outcome of the Munich Conference had done little to resolve Hitler's dilemmas. Strategically, the problem of raw materials had not been solved, the economy was sputtering alarmingly, and Germany remained restrained by its potential enemies. Personally, despite his soaring popularity with the majority of Germans – a striking outburst of enthusiasm based largely on avoiding conflict, not propagating it – the Führer still faced an officer corps skeptical of his rush to war with an insufficiently strong military force. Despite all the speeches he made to his generals over the course of the Third Reich, arguably none were more decisive, both in terms of number and importance, than those given in 1939, in which he sought to secure active support for his policies from the ranks of the officer corps.

Hitler provided the three service chiefs a glimpse of his thinking on 25 January, when he returned to a theme from his early period as a populist crusader. The catastrophe of November 1918, he stressed, had resulted from the failure of the entire leadership elite of a corrupt system. This, he remarked pointedly, would not happen again, as he expected – demanded – absolute personal loyalty from those who served the regime. Precisely what that meant became clear in a speech to his troop commanders on 10 February, in which Hitler aimed to make the "responsible elite" of the Wehrmacht aware of the "inner motives" of his policy. Carefully, almost as a lawyer would, Hitler established the basis of his case. Although 1938 had ended with resounding success, he noted, many officers failed to understand his actions or their role. He then outlined their duty to defend a cause to the death, a task made easier if they understood the basic principles behind his actions. "In the end," Hitler emphasized, "one can only audaciously and energetically represent that which one understands." As if still agitating during the Kampfzeit, he reiterated the necessity of acquiring Lebensraum. Thus, 1938 did not represent any special action, but "only a consistent continuation of decisions which originated in 1933." The timing of these actions, in turn, depended on circumstances, which had allowed the unfolding of his program more quickly than envisioned.[1]

This program was far more than rearmament and the restoration of German power. Revealing a deep sense of urgency, Hitler returned to a theme from the 1920s: "We have to catch up on things that have been neglected for three hundred years . . . and led us away from world power." No one, he stressed, should suppose "that our path has ended here. On the contrary, gentlemen, this is where our path starts." Noting the uniqueness of his rise, in only twenty years, from a demobilized soldier without prospects to the leader of a rejuvenated Germany, he declared, "I have taken it upon myself to solve . . . the German space problem . . . As long as I live, this idea will rule my entire being . . . One way or another, this question must be resolved." No one, he emphasized, should be surprised "when I seize every opportunity to achieve this goal." Nor should anyone be in doubt as to the nature of the coming conflict, which would be "an ideological war . . . a deliberate people's and racial war." The task of the officer corps thus went beyond merely carrying out military decisions; they should be ideological fighters able to inspire and motivate the troops in this existential struggle. Only so, he insisted, could the coming war be won. His policies and actions, he observed pointedly, had made them the leaders of a powerful Wehrmacht, so they owed him a debt of obedience. Given the difficulty of the task ahead, they needed to put their "devout trust" in him and embrace their role as an ideological example for the troops. In February 1939 the theoretical had turned real; none of the assembled generals could doubt in the slightest that war – and an ideological, racial war of extermination – loomed in the near future.[2]

Hitler thus pointed to the way out of his dilemma not through economic measures, which would have meant a policy of restraint, but through fanatical ideological zeal, trust in his intuition, and war. In truth, the outcome of Munich left him with only two feasible choices: either expand on the deal offered by Chamberlain, or launch a war in the near future while the relative arms balance still favored Germany. Hitler never seriously considered the former option. Indeed, immediately following the signing of the Anglo-German declaration he issued orders to accelerate war production and to have plans drawn up for the absorption of the remainder of the Czech state. He clearly understood that his unalterable goal of Lebensraum could not be realized within the confines of a political agreement regulated by the other great powers. War was the only option, but the question of how, with its insufficient military means, Germany could hope to win such a conflict remained unsettled. In the months ahead he seemed to perceive, in the British and French attitude at Munich, the glimmer of a solution. Although he suspected that Britain would not concede German dominance of Europe without an eventual fight, the trend toward imminent war might be slowed with clever diplomacy that isolated Poland and split the great powers. This had been the goal outlined in the *Second Book*, where Hitler talked of reaching an accord with the British that would isolate France. The key, he thought, lay in avoiding antagonizing Britain through a pointless naval arms race and in making clear that he had no desire to see their empire destroyed. In the early years of the Depression, Britain had been an understanding creditor (more so than France or the United States), and in June 1935 it had reached a naval deal with Germany. The policy of appeasement also seemed to confirm Hitler's opinion that the British might be kept out of a war in the next few years.[3]

The problem, of course, lay in reconciling his words with his actions. Both Hitler and Chamberlain recognized that the post-Munich German armaments expansion, a program that, Göring boasted, would "make all previous ones pale into insignificance," had resulted in serious economic problems. With insufficient financial and raw material resources, with factories clogged with orders, with the success of Hitler's employment policies ironically increasing the problem of military mobilization (the limited manpower could not be used simultaneously in both army and industry), and facing a demographic dilemma of declining numbers born during and immediately after the First World War, it appeared Germany had finally run up against its limits. The Führer also understood that Chamberlain, while continuing his peace efforts, had launched Britain on a rapid rearmament program and that his conservative critics, foremost among them Churchill, were pushing for a stiffer anti-German policy. In reacting to the same developments, both leaders formed vastly different interpretations. Chamberlain thought Germany was too weak militarily and economically for a war, and that the pressures of the arms race had made the Nazi regime unstable. These factors, he assumed, would lead Hitler to avoid war.[4]

Instead, these difficulties simply reinforced the latter's belief that time was not on his side and encouraged him to go for broke and launch a war before it was too late. In a series of lectures in early 1939 to high officials in the armaments industry and Foreign Ministry, General Georg Thomas, Head of the Defense Economy and Armament Office in the OKW, provided a clear glimpse into the Führer's mind. "In the past," Thomas argued, "the Clausewitzian view that he who destroys the enemy army will win the war was true. Today the Anglo-Saxon view holds the same validity: destroy the economy, then you also destroy the armed forces and . . . the people in question." The key point, he emphasized, was that for the next twelve to eighteen months Germany still possessed an armaments edge. This would not last, though, since the "vast economic power of Britain, the U.S., and France is in the long run greater than that of the Axis." This formulation precisely mirrored Hitler's assessment of the state of affairs. Looking back on the situation in a March 1940 letter to Mussolini, he explained, "The time gained by postponing a general conflict with the western powers would have worked out definitely to Germany's advantage only if England had not meanwhile . . . embarked on large-scale rearmament." Despite the many obstacles facing Germany, therefore, Hitler pressed on. The moment seemed propitious to strike, since action against Poland enjoyed wide-spread support within the ranks of the officer corps, who, in any case, had long since become merely Hitler's military instrument. War, à la Clausewitz, was again a matter of political policy. In Hitler's mind, Chamberlain's continued peace offensive in early 1939 meant nothing more than an attempt to buy time to complete Britain's military preparations. If Hitler did not act soon, Germany would no longer be in a position to act.[5]

Economic as well as military-strategic considerations dictated his next move. The Czech state contained valuable raw materials and diverse industries, while geographically it was the key to any move into eastern Europe; German occupation of the Sudetenland had also left the remnant state defenseless. As a result, Hitler assumed, not illogically, that the West had conceded German hegemony over it. Nor had British diplomatic actions following Munich indicated much awareness that Hitler would seek immediately to absorb the remainder of the Czech state. Only belatedly, in late February and early March 1939, was notice taken of German intentions, but by then it was too late. Always a devotee of a sudden coup that took an opponent by surprise, Hitler took advantage of a domestic crisis between Prague and the Slovak government, exacerbated by German actions, which provided the pretext for the absorption of the Czech state. On 15 March 1939, following the brutal bullying of Emile Hacha, the Czech president, the night before in Berlin, German troops entered Prague, completing the dissolution of Czechoslovakia that had begun at Munich. Chamberlain's initial reaction was weak, telling the cabinet that same day that Czech frontiers had been guaranteed against external aggression, not internal pressure, so he saw no cause for action; that, although Hitler had dealt a blow to confidence, he would continue to prefer discussion to violence. This tepid response only reinforced Hitler's belief that Britain had washed its hands of eastern Europe. Thus, he failed to notice the stiffening resolve in Parliament, or the pressure now exerted on Chamberlain to take a firmer stance. The prime minister's subsequent guarantee of Polish independence on 31 March therefore angered Hitler and took him completely by surprise – but without having the intended effect of deflecting him from the path of war.[6]

Hitler had a vision of how things should be; when reality failed to accord with this image, he typically refused to adjust his views to circumstances, but sought instead to transform reality itself. So it was in the spring and summer of 1939. Thus, when Hjalmar Schacht warned that accelerated rearmament would lead to economic chaos, Hitler fired him. When shortages of fuel and raw materials restricted expansion of the Wehrmacht, Hitler took comfort in the massive haul of military equipment looted from the Czechs, material that, in the words of Quartermaster-General Eduard Wagner, meant "an enormous increase in [German] military power." Enormous, indeed: in April 1939 an average of twenty-three trains a day, laden with ammunition and weapons sufficient to equip thirty divisions, left Czechoslovakia bound for Germany. When Brauchitsch, commander-in-chief of the army, worried about stagnation in the manpower growth of the German army just at the moment when Britain introduced general conscription, Hitler responded by unleashing Ribbentrop in a diplomatic campaign to secure a formal military pact with Japan and Italy. When Poland refused to be drawn into an alliance with Germany as a junior partner, then Hitler reversed his original intention of waging war in the west to secure his rear before seizing Lebensraum in the east. Instead, he would now smash Poland first. That, in the event, Hitler largely failed in all of his initiatives did little to dent his confidence that he could transform reality and establish the preconditions for isolating his enemies and waging a limited war.[7]

Here, of course, the key point would be that his efforts to prepare the ground for a limited war appeared not altogether unsuccessful, encouraging his belief that he could pull off yet another triumph. Once Poland, for example, fortified with the guarantee from Britain, refused to make concessions on Danzig and the Corridor, Hitler's attempt at a "reasonable solution" of the Polish question was doomed to failure. In early April 1939, then, he issued orders to the OKW to prepare plans for an invasion of Poland that could be launched from 1 September. This, in turn, increased the importance for Germany of access to key raw materials, especially Romanian oil, in southeastern Europe. In a furious race to assert economic dominance over the area begun immediately after the Prague coup, Hitler nimbly outmaneuvered British efforts to deny vital resources to Germany, thus securing continuing supplies of crucial raw materials and foodstuffs. Lebensraum, for Hitler, always meant territorial conquest in European Russia, but this successful short-term move toward autarky meant that he had punched a hole in the British effort at economic blockade and encirclement. Moreover, the great powers had long since squandered a superior diplomatic and military position vis-à-vis Germany, going back to the reoccupation of the Rhineland, so Hitler might be forgiven for thinking that it was hardly likely that they would now intervene on behalf of an anti-Semitic, semi-fascist Poland that had eagerly participated in the territorial division of Czechoslovakia. Moreover, deterrence would work only if Hitler thought he faced an extended war against the West. It had less force as a disincentive in an isolated, short-term war with Poland, which Hitler thought possible.[8]

Typically, though, his mood fluctuated constantly, as continuing British support for Poland gnawed at his self-assurance and seemed to indicate the likelihood of war with the great powers. Less than a month after a brilliantly mocking performance before the Reichstag, in which, in response to a telegram from the American president, Franklin Roosevelt, seeking clarification of German intentions, he had savagely criticized Western hypocrisy on matters of imperialism and territorial expansion, on 23 May he gave a rather more revealing talk to his top military leaders in the Reich Chancellery. It was, in retrospect, a curious address, almost rambling, as if the Führer was trying to convince himself of the way forward. In presenting his view of the current situation, he boasted that Germany had a far superior military position to that of 1933, internal unity had been achieved, and the "idea" problem had been solved. All true enough, but still, he admitted, economic problems remained that could only be resolved through the acquisition of Lebensraum. As if trying to steel himself, he asserted that it would take courage to solve this problem and, typically, the key would be not to reconcile his demands with circumstances, but to shape circumstances to meet his aims. The problem of Lebensraum, he noted realistically, could not be solved without violence, so he had decided to attack Poland at the first feasible opportunity. The object of the war, he stressed, was not the recovery of Danzig or the Corridor, but expansion of Lebensraum in the east; Germany had no alternative in order to secure foodstuffs.[9]

Continuing his sober assessment, Hitler indicated that the Polish problem could not be separated from conflict with the West, so the danger existed of sliding into war with England. Suddenly pessimistic, he "doubted the possibility of a peaceful debate with England" since, in an acute insight, the British "saw in our development the foundation of a hegemony that would weaken

England. Therefore ... the confrontation with England will be one of life and death." Nor could he predict with any certainty the course of this conflict. The British, he stressed, were "proud, capable, tough," and knew that failure on their part meant an end to their empire. A short war was the goal, but Hitler doubted that either Britain or Germany could be knocked out in a single blow, so it was necessary to prepare for a long war. The army needed to create the conditions for success by defeating France and providing the navy and Luftwaffe with the positions from which they could cut off England's lifeline (a remarkably accurate vision of what would happen a year hence, but without the intended result). Reversing his earlier view, he now dismissed France and saw in Britain the motor that drove opposition to Germany. Less the bombastic "mad dog" than a leader beset by a sober realism bordering on fatalism, Hitler again revealed his twin obsessions with Lebensraum and time: Germany had to begin securing the former and now was as good a time as any, and better than most, given the Reich's relative military superiority. War with the West, he admitted, was likely, and he had no clear idea how to win it. Still, the prospect of a quick German triumph that they could do little to prevent might cause the Western powers to renege on their pledge to Poland, as they had earlier with Czechoslovakia. The gamble, though, was clear: if a major war resulted, Germany was not ready, for its latest armament program would not culminate until 1942–3.[10]

The remainder of the summer was a rather curious interlude between peace and war. Driven by his determination to resolve Germany's "space" problem, Hitler oversaw preparations for war even while Chamberlain seemed not to have realized the true extent of the German threat. Then, when he did, he found the only feasible way to deter Hitler, an agreement with Stalin, unpalatable. Although the French were eager for an alliance, Chamberlain hesitated. Anti-communist himself, deeply suspicious of Soviet motives, unsure whether he could trust Stalin, his military leaders dismissive of the Red Army, fearful of antagonizing Hitler, the prime minister vacillated between an agreement with Stalin and a further attempt at direct negotiations with Hitler. As the key position of the USSR became clear, Stalin, frozen out at Munich, now became the object of everyone's attention. If he sided with the West, it would be difficult for Hitler to proceed with the attack on Poland. Such a move might mean danger for Stalin, though; in the event that Hitler attacked Poland, the Soviets faced war with Germany (and ran the risk that the West would betray them). An alliance with Germany seemed the safer, more immediately beneficial, choice. This meant the destruction of Poland but also a German–British–French war in the west. Stalin could then anticipate a long conflict that would exhaust the capitalist powers and allow the USSR to choose the proper time to act to further its own interests.[11]

Hitler, earlier than Chamberlain, recognized the key position of Stalin, and pushed with increasing urgency for an agreement that would undermine Western efforts at deterrence. Trade talks led to an economic agreement that presaged deeper political ties. Stalin craved the prospect of security and territorial gains in the Baltic and eastern Europe; for Hitler, a deal with Stalin would not only deprive the Western powers of any leverage in the east, but also provide Germany access to the raw materials of the Soviet Union and make it blockade-proof. If in late May he had been unsure about waging an isolated war against Poland, Hitler's self-assurance returned as the prospect of a pact with Stalin seemed likely to destroy the underpinnings of Western policy and give the West an incentive to disavow its Polish commitment. In a meeting with the Italian foreign minister at the Obersalzberg on 12 August, Hitler revealed to the startled Galeazzo Ciano his decision to force a war with Poland at the earliest opportunity. When the latter expressed his fear that this would lead to a wider conflict, the Führer replied that he "was absolutely convinced that the Western democracies would, in the last resort, recoil from unleashing a general war." While impressed with the Führer's detailed knowledge of military matters, Ciano nonetheless returned to Italy determined to keep his nation out of what he was certain would be a war with the Western powers.[12]

Hitler remained outwardly confident that he could isolate a war against Poland. On 17 August, the chief of the general staff Halder recorded the Führer's assessment of the situation, an account notable for its evidence of Hitler's thinking. "There can be no success without risk," he began, emphasizing a common theme. Britain, he claimed, would not have intervened in 1914 if it had suspected the consequences. "No nation wants a long war . . . Britain stands only to lose . . . A wealthy nation has little to gain, but a great deal to lose . . . every nation must pay with blood . . . even with a victorious war . . . the victor emerges diminished in strength." Moreover, he asserted, "Britain [was] overburdened with commitments in all parts of the world . . . In view of their experience in World War I, there is little chance that [they] will deliberately run the risk of a major war." Militarily and politically, as well, things had turned against the Western powers. Their rearmament program would not bear fruit for another year or two, while Russia would certainly not help the West. Nor, in light of the German trade deal with the USSR, would a blockade avail much. No, he concluded, there would be no general war: "The men I met in Munich are not the kind that start a world war." Even to a skeptic like Halder, the Führer's assessment appeared rational and logical. The British had frittered away a superior position, faced serious global challenges, and were still in the development stage as far as their army was concerned. "All these factors," Halder agreed, "argue for the likelihood of Britain and France refraining from entering the war."[13]

The imminent prospect of a deal with Stalin had persuaded Hitler that the risk of a larger war was minimal, but there still remained his generals to convince. In an effort to bolster their confidence in his actions, on 22 August he gathered fifty top military leaders at the Obersalzberg for a pep talk. His generals harbored mixed emotions: apprehension at the prospect of a two-front war mingled with anger at the Western powers' effort to contain Germany and support for an isolated war with Poland to regain Danzig and the Corridor. Some also believed that Hitler's actions were all a bluff, and that, as in September 1938, at the last moment he would pull off a diplomatic triumph. The Führer quickly put an end to those illusions. He had, he stated bluntly, decided on war against Poland. The relatively favorable military and political situation, as well as his own limited life-span, compelled him to act quickly. If war was unavoidable, as Hitler knew it was, then there was little reason to wait. "We have nothing to lose," he asserted; "we have everything to gain . . . Our economic situation is such that we can only hold out for a few more years. Göring can confirm this. We have no other choice . . . Our enemies have leaders who are below the average . . . no men of action." They were, he assured his generals, in words dripping with utter contempt, "little worms"; he had seen them at Munich. Then, rehashing the arguments used a week earlier, he stressed that the Great War had seriously weakened England and France, so they would hesitate to risk another war; that their rearmament efforts would not culminate before 1941–2; and that unrest in other parts of the world would keep the British fully preoccupied. The staggering news of the impending pact with the USSR also calmed misgivings. "We need not be afraid of a blockade," he reassured the generals, in an effort to remove the trauma of the World War. "The East will supply us with grain, cattle, coal, lead and zinc." It was, he concluded, time to get on with ending English hegemony. His only concern was that "at the last moment some swine . . . will submit a plan for mediation." There would be, he stated emphatically, no second Munich.[14]

The true extent of his radical determination was revealed in a second address that afternoon before a smaller circle of officers. All wars, Hitler admitted, entailed risk, and this one might not be contained to Poland. If necessary, one must be prepared for a "life and death" struggle. No mere figure of speech, he meant this quite literally, demanding from his generals understanding for extraordinary measures that would be taken in the

upcoming Polish campaign. "The destruction of Poland is in the foreground," he stated bluntly. "The goal is the elimination of its life-force, not
reaching a specific line. Even if war in the west breaks out, the destruction
of Poland stays in the forefront." His officers, he urged, "should close their
hearts to pity. Brutal action. Eighty million people must get their rights.
Their existence must be secured. The stronger has the right. Great hard-
ness." The means to the end, Hitler emphasized, were irrelevant. "The victor
is never called upon to vindicate his actions."[15]

After his speech, revealingly, the Führer charged his army adjutant, Rudolf
Schmundt, with sounding out the reaction among the generals. Although the
latter reported that the officers in attendance had been "very impressed by the
speech . . . and would tackle what lay ahead with confidence," the overall mood
was more circumspect. Some, such as Rundstedt and Georg von Küchler,
maintained that Hitler was bluffing and it would not come to war. Bock, on the
other hand, thought it a "terrific speech" that had clearly explained the political situation. Halder, as we have seen, had already accepted Hitler's reasoning
and conclusions. Virtually all embraced the prospect of war with Poland. The
surprising news of the pact with Stalin allayed the worst fears of a possible
wider war, even if it could not dampen all concerns. Leeb, for example, simply
noted in his diary that the "Führer is determined to finish Poland off." The
British and French declaration of war on 3 September, though, caused him to
sharpen his tone considerably. "Hitler," he thundered, "is a deluded fool, a
criminal." Still, Leeb's attitude was an outlier; while dreading a conflict with the
West, most generals accepted it when it came with a professional, even fatal-
istic, attitude. Many would have agreed with Gotthard Heinrici, who saw it as
a "preventive war." If Germany had not acted now, he thought, in a few years,
when they had built their strength, its enemies certainly would have attacked
the Reich. It was, he concluded, an unavoidable war for the German "right to
live." Quartermaster-General Wagner agreed, writing that one needed simply
to "be strong and do the best . . . it was difficult to find another solution or go
a different way." All likely shared General Georg Hans Reinhardt's formulation
that they faced their task "without enthusiasm, in no war frenzy, but serious
and conscious of their duty."[16]

The striking thing in all this was not merely Hitler's radicalism and determination to press forward with his ideological agenda, but his arguably
rational assessment of the situation. The dynamic of the arms race was
against Germany. Hitler, Albert Speer recalled, argued that from 1940
Germany's arms advantage would constantly diminish, so immediate action
had to be taken. Britain, and especially France, had suffered grievously from
the First World War, with the French adversely affected both economically

and demographically. British economic experts warned Chamberlain that the country was not in the same strong financial position as in 1914 and would be unable to sustain a long war. Tensions in the Mediterranean, East Asia, and the Middle East burdened the British. Nor could the Western powers provide much aid to Poland in case of a war, as a blockade would be mitigated by German access to the raw materials of the Danube basin and Russia. A Western attack on Germany in support of Poland also seemed dubious, since in the short term Britain could furnish only a handful of divisions and the French, influenced by the wildly unrealistic image of the strength of the West Wall fortifications created by German propaganda, were unlikely to venture out from the Maginot Line. Hitler based his perception of Britain's unwillingness to go to war not merely on his conviction of Chamberlain's personal weakness, but also on his belief that the prime minister understood the logic of the situation as he did. To Hitler, the Nazi–Soviet Pact was the trump card that would allow him to break external constraints and solve the "German dilemma." Flush with the agreement with Stalin, he thought he had established the conditions necessary to fight an isolated war against Poland. What he failed to realize, though, was that Chamberlain had never put much faith in Soviet assistance, so the pact did not undermine his resolve to fight. By now, as well, Western leaders believed that their armament preparations ensured that they would win a long conflict, so they were prepared to accept war in 1939.[17]

Hitler wavered briefly on the evening of 25 August in the face of the news of the Anglo-Polish military alliance and Mussolini's decision to opt out of war for the time being, ordering a postponement of the attack scheduled for the next day. Although the Duce's action seemed to unnerve the Führer, most German officials understood that Italy was more valuable as a benevolent neutral that could serve as a conduit for vital imports than as an active ally that had to be supplied with scarce resources. While Halder raged that Hitler was "playing fast and loose with the army," Brauchitsch, hoping that the Western powers would again back down, reassured him that the Führer merely needed time to let the "political game" play out. In truth, though, Hitler had no intention of seeking another Munich. He aimed, as he told Göring, merely "to see if we can keep the British out." At a conference on 28 August, looking, to Halder, "worn, haggard, [with] creaking voice, preoccupied," the Führer vowed that if push came to shove, "I will wage a two-front war." With no freedom of maneuver, he seemed to have hoped that the British were bluffing and would bow to his reality. A letter from Chamberlain the next day, meant to reaffirm British commitment to Poland while offering Hitler a way out, merely reinforced the latter's impression that Britain remained "soft on the issue of a major war." At worst, perhaps, he accepted the risk of a conflict with the Western powers because he did not expect to be confronted immediately with a two-front war, while a quick victory in Poland might yet dissuade Western intervention. What appeared to outsiders as a reckless gamble, then, was for Hitler the result of a cost assessment that persuaded him that, based on their recent actions, the West would not respond.[18]

Indeed, even when war came, it came in stages, and, initially, it appeared Hitler had pulled off his gamble. Although the German public reacted frostily to the outbreak of war, most were also inclined to see it in defensive terms, as a result of British and French actions, so Hitler had little to fear from popular opinion. The rapid German advances on the first two days also nourished hopes that Poland could yet be defeated in isolation. While Brauchitsch on 2 September reassured Leeb that "bridges [to the west] must definitely not be broken," Halder recorded in his diary, "The Führer wants to receive the ambassadors of France and England . . . links must not be broken off." Given this delusory perception of reality, when the Western powers finally declared war on 3 September, it provoked a completely disproportionate reaction of anger mingled with shock and dismay. Hitler had long been aware that his daring gambles had succeeded more from his opponents' weakness than German strength. His early triumphs, though, when he could wait on events and use his keen political instincts to good advantage, then act quickly to exploit favorable opportunities, had only fueled his recklessness, ultimately provoking a reaction from his adversaries. Under pressure of time, he became even more impatient and thrashed about, trying to shape the external situation to his needs. Then, just when it appeared he had outmaneuvered his opponents with the Nazi–Soviet Pact, they confounded him by taking a step he had not really expected of them.[19]

Typically, though, Hitler perceived in Western inaction a way out. Having declared war, the British and French proceeded to do nothing to help the Poles. Nor did they really intend to do anything. Although Halder fretted over developments in the west, and Brauchitsch considered every day that brought no attack "a gift from God," Hitler grew increasingly confident that no French attack was imminent. In this, he had a keener appreciation of his opponents' strategy than did his advisors. To the British and French, winning meant playing for time and securing aid from the United States. With memories of the massive bloodletting in the opening months of the First World War still fresh, the Western powers embraced the idea of initial defensive measures, a slow buildup of strength, and an economic blockade. Acting from the assumption that Hitler wanted and needed a short war, they intended to turn it into a long one. They focused on a long-term plan to unhinge the German economy in the hope it would collapse under the pressures of war, a rational strategy but one that overlooked short-term possibilities. They failed to realize both the weakness of Germany's western border and that, although its position had been enhanced by access to essential raw materials in eastern and southeastern Europe, the country still remained vulnerable to economic pressure. Ironically, both the British blockade and their efforts at denying Romanian oil, which sharply reduced German supplies, did serious damage to the German economy in the fall of 1939, a period before the commencement of large-scale Soviet deliveries. But Allied military passivity, as well as synthetic fuel production, allowed the Germans to evade the worst consequences.[20]

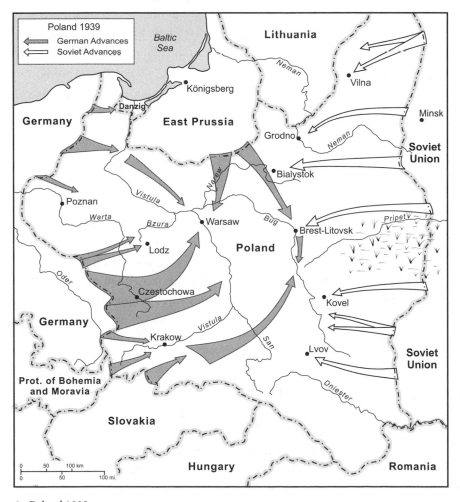

1. Poland 1939

In the absence of Western opposition, then, German action against Poland was shockingly decisive. Still, although it substantiated the notion of a motorized war of movement, it did not clarify the situation as far as the doctrine of Blitzkrieg (as a consciously new method of waging war) was concerned. German planners simply took advantage of circumstances, so that the initial position of both combatants largely determined the course of the operation. In fact, it is difficult to find any distinct conception of Blitzkrieg underlying German planning. Geographic reality meant that Polish forces already faced encirclement, so the campaign unfolded naturally from that fact. The nature of Polish troop dispositions, particularly their determination, for economic reasons, to defend the former German industrial areas in the western part of the country, also ensured that large numbers of Polish troops would be cut off and trapped once German forces effected a breakthrough. Nor, given the disparity of forces, was that much in doubt. The Poles suffered not so much from a numerical disadvantage, with both sides fielding roughly equal numbers of men, but from inadequate leadership, training, organization, and, above all, modern military equipment. Although their tanks compared favorably with German Panzer Is and IIs, the Poles had few of them and, most damaging, were completely deficient in terms of number and quality of aircraft. The Poles were also hurt by Allied pressure to delay their mobilization so as not to provoke a German attack, an action that seemed to corroborate Hitler's perception that the British, especially, still hoped to avoid war. And, in truth, the Poles themselves hesitated to mobilize because of their weak economic and financial situation, so that the German attack came before they were fully ready.[21]

From the German point of view, the only real difficulty lay in coordinating the operations in the north between the 3rd and 4th Armies of Army Group North (Bock), which were separated by the Corridor. As a result, OKH (*Oberkommando des Heeres*, or Army High Command) located the focal point (*Schwerpunkt*) of the attack in the south, where three powerful armies (8th, 10th, 14th) of Army Group South (Rundstedt) would break the Polish defenses and then advance to the northeast and east, in the direction of Warsaw. At the same time, after the 3rd and 4th Armies linked up, Army Group North would proceed in a southeasterly direction, along the line of the Vistula–Narew rivers, toward the capital. As the operation unfolded, OKH faced only two major surprises. The first was the Polish decision not to withdraw its forces in the west, which meant, both Brauchitsch and Bock agreed on 5 September, that "the enemy was as good as beaten," a fact confirmed by Halder's observation two days later that the Western powers showed "no real intention of waging a war." The Germans, in fact, were taken aback by the complete passivity of French troops along the border. Aided as well by absolute Luftwaffe domination of the air, the Germans had in effect defeated Poland within ten days of the opening of hostilities. As a result, despite sharp fighting along the Bzura River between 9 and 16 September – itself more an act of desperation than an organized battle, as Polish troops fought to escape to the east – the focus of German debate centered on Bock's proposal, endorsed by Hitler, for a deeper move to the east, thus preventing a Polish withdrawal. By 17 September the Germans had largely encircled Warsaw, and, despite their determination to fight on, the Polish fate had become clear, for on that same day the Soviets had invaded from the east.[22]

The other surprise for the general staff, no less pleasant, was Hitler's willingness to let Halder run the show, rarely interfering with military operations. When he did intervene, much to the consternation of OKH, his actions proved both sound and justified; any tensions between Hitler and OKH generally related to political-strategic matters, such as his concern for the rapid fall of Warsaw, rather than purely military affairs. Strains caused by the touchy issue of coordinating contact with the Red Army, and withdrawal from territory ceded to the Soviets, resulted primarily because Hitler had failed to inform OKH of the terms of his secret deal with Stalin, so that Soviet intervention had caught German military leaders unawares. Disputes over the demarcation line proved especially vexatious. Since some German units were 100 miles east of the proposed line, and had suffered casualties taking this territory, OKH acquiesced only reluctantly in their withdrawal, Halder writing bitterly in his diary of the "disgrace for the German political leadership!" Still, the army command had little to complain about, given the ease of the campaign and the fact that the Führer's political and military judgments had so far proven sound. For the most part, Hitler, unsure of his role, acted more like a "war tourist," flitting from place to place to get a look at the action, than a Feldherr. Significantly, though, in ideological as well as political and strategic matters, the Führer clearly ruled. In moving to implement his vision of Lebensraum, he had instructed the SS leader Heinrich Himmler to begin the process of intellectual and ethnic cleansing in Poland. The brutality of this deeply shook Halder and others in the officer corps, whose nerves, according to an observer in the Foreign Ministry, "suffered considerably." Hitler, typically, ridiculed the "infantile attitude" at OKH. "The war," he said, "could not be run with Salvation Army methods."[23]

The overwhelming triumph in Poland had both reinforced Hitler's ideas of Blitzkrieg and seemed to offer a way out of the dilemma created by the

Western declaration of war. A swift blow in the west would free him to turn back to the east, and, in any case, the critical economic situation also seemed to warrant immediate action. Still, despite the spectacular success, the Polish campaign had been more proving ground than revolution. While the Germans recognized the significance of new technologies such as the tank, airplanes, and radio in ensuring, unlike in the First World War, that a second-rate power would not be able to hinder a quick victory, the enemy's rapid encirclement and defeat had resulted as much from geographical factors as complicated maneuvers. Indeed, the campaign had not been all that dissimilar to the one in the east in the autumn of 1914, a point made by some older officers. Nor was the relentless drive to get at and destroy the enemy in any way outside the German tradition.[24]

Despite the boldness, daring, and initiative shown by its officers, though, the performance of German troops had disappointed OKH. Given their assumption that German forces had to be superior in performance and execution, since they were always likely to be materially inferior to their enemies, it was not surprising that OKH first wanted to correct the problems revealed by the Polish campaign before embarking on a new adventure. In an action that would have important consequences in the west, OKH swiftly took steps to rectify the army's deficiencies, not least improving the coordination of combined arms operations and inculcating a more offensive spirit into the troops. In the interim, many top generals discounted the notion that the Polish campaign offered any guidance in a future conflict with the Western powers. Memories of the earlier war, and respect for the French army, remained too strong. Already on 29 September, Halder stressed that Hitler had to be made aware that the "techniques of [the] Polish campaign [were] no recipe for the West. [They would be] no good against a well-knit army." Leeb voiced even stronger concerns. "Surprise [is] not possible," he noted in his diary, dismissing the idea that France could be defeated as quickly as Poland. "Our sacrifices in blood will be tremendous, and we will not be able to defeat the French." General Georg von Sodenstern, chief of staff of Army Group A, while recognizing the efficacy of the tank forces, nonetheless expressed well the pervasive pessimism of the top generals: "Paying due credit to our Panzer successes in Poland, we must nevertheless note that armor has little or no chance of success against such defenses [in the west]." While Hitler grew increasingly confident of German chances in the west, many of his generals – and, interestingly, Western military leaders as well – largely dismissed the Polish campaign as any sort of yardstick by which to measure a conflict with the Western powers.[25]

5

The Blitzkrieg Paradox

In his January 1939 address to his top commanders, Hitler had stressed, in contrast to the prevalent stab-in-the-back theory, that Germany's failure in 1918 had stemmed not from the people but from the political and military elite. This, he implied, would not reoccur, since he had combined both functions in his own person and had the fervent will necessary to see his war to a successful conclusion. Then, when doubts reemerged on the eve of the attack on Poland, Hitler had used the impending Nazi–Soviet Pact to reassure his generals again that all would be well: the British and French would not intervene, the German–Polish war would be localized, and the Soviet Union would make the Reich blockade-proof. For the first time, though, Hitler had misjudged the diplomatic situation and committed a serious blunder; the Western Allies had, after all, stood with Poland, and Germany now faced the prospect of an extended war. As a result of this blow to his prestige and confidence, Hitler had largely let the professional military men run the show in Poland, exerting his influence only indirectly. The swift conclusion of the Polish campaign, however, did little to clarify the larger strategic situation or alter the basic rearmament equation that favored the Allies. Germany still faced a prolonged war in the west and the prospect of serious economic dislocations. Nor was Hitler likely to remain content in the role of "battlefield tourist."[1]

While the triumph in the east raised hopes among some generals that a political solution might be possible, Hitler, impressed by the speed and power of the Wehrmacht, sought a way out of his dilemma through yet another application of force. With their declaration of war, the Western powers threatened a complete disruption of his strategic concept; now, though, he might finally be able to win freedom of action through a rapid offensive in the west. On 27 September 1939, then, even before the fighting in Poland had ended, Hitler gathered his top commanders at the Reich Chancellery to sketch out his ideas for the next offensive. As a strategic thinker, he was not a mere lucky amateur; indeed, he had demonstrated real insights. Trusting his instincts, over the past few years he had won one diplomatic victory after another; now, he had triumphed militarily in what, to date, had been a localized war. The problem was not that he was incompetent – the victory over Poland had raised his reputation with his generals – but that he could not put his many genuine insights into an appropriate context. He concentrated, for example, more on political, ideological, strategic, and economic considerations than on purely military factors, such as training, troop levels, combat readiness, and state of equipment, as if, once a decision was made, everything else would fall into place. In this political focus he acted in a Clausewitzian fashion, but he was then unwilling to consider or defer to the judgments of his military leaders as to the practical feasibility of his ideas.[2]

This was the pattern on display on 27 September as Hitler the political leader revealed to his startled generals his reasoning, itself quite lucid, for an immediate attack in the west. More clearly than them, most of whom favored a negotiated peace, Hitler recognized the firm disinclination of the British to negotiate. In addition, while his generals, influenced by the nightmarish trench experience of the Great War, still held a healthy respect for France, the Führer regarded it as militarily weak, with little fighting ability. In this, he implicitly understood the demoralization of the French; that, for them, war in 1939 meant the sacrifices of 1914–18 had been pointless. Acknowledging the Western strategy of a slow military buildup, Hitler stressed that German superiority would not last. "Lost time could not be recovered," so now was the moment to strike, while its enemies were not ready; this unique opportunity could not be squandered. Nor, given German economic constraints, did a long war on the cheap hold any attractions. After all, the Ruhr, Germany's economic Achilles heel, lay dangerously exposed to potential enemy bombing attacks. "The economic means of the other side are stronger," he noted, which only reinforced his resolve to get on with acquiring Lebensraum. Wilhelm Keitel, head of the OKW, later chided skeptics by noting curtly, "the Führer himself has recognized that we cannot last out a war of long duration. The war must be finished rapidly . . . since it was not clear how long the Russians would hold to us." In short, Germany needed to safeguard its own vital economic area and acquire the industrial infrastructure of the western European states if it was going to wage a successful war for living space in the east. Strategically, Hitler emphasized, swift action was necessary in view of growing American hostility and the inherent unreliability of Stalin. "Great victories have little staying power . . .," he observed, in an echo of Napoleon. "All historical successes come to nothing when they are not continued." Britain, the main opponent in the west, must thus be "forced to its knees."[3]

Ironically, Hitler's assessment of the situation differed little from that of Allied leaders, who planned a delaying game in the short term coupled with a steady long-term buildup precisely because they too assumed that time favored them. Hitler, impressed by the possibilities of mobile operations, thus sought to build on initial success and go for broke in an effort not to allow positional war to develop. If he had logically assessed the situation in political, strategic, and economic terms, though, which seemed to argue against a wait-and-see policy, he completely neglected the pressing military and logistical problems that troubled OKH planners. While the Führer identified Britain as the key obstacle thwarting his ambitions, it was precisely German inability to defeat the British, as well as a general unpreparedness for any further action, that distressed military leaders. In mid-October 1939, when Hitler wanted to launch his attack, not only could Germany marshal merely half as many divisions in the west as France, but many of the units awaiting transfer from Poland were in deplorable condition. In truth, the Polish campaign had largely exhausted the German army. Critical ammunition shortages loomed, while the Panzer forces urgently needed repair and replacement vehicles. The fighting in the east had also revealed acute deficiencies in training and logistics. The German army, in short, needed time to reequip its forces, implement better training methods, improve supply capabilities, build up stocks of ammunition, and learn the lessons of the campaign. Taking all of these factors into consideration, Halder's assistant chief of staff for operations, Carl-Heinrich von Stülpnagel, gloomily predicted that an operation against France could not be launched until 1942 – the same year the Western powers expected to be ready. As General von Kluge confided to his wife in mid-October, Germany could not "think in terms of a final knockout of England and France, for we simply lack the strength." Paradoxically, then, in the event, the breathing spell in autumn 1939 that Hitler feared would aid the West actually benefitted Germany.[4]

Nonetheless, sensing only defeatism among his generals and certain that he had correctly assessed the mood of the Allies, the Führer insisted on an autumn attack. Already on 29 August he had expressed his utter contempt at "those German soldiers who feared battle. Frederick the Great would turn in his grave if he saw today's generals." Little that transpired in the fall altered his opinion. Despite the great success in Poland, OKH still clearly lacked faith in Blitzkrieg as a war-winning doctrine. In trying to dissuade Hitler from proceeding with a fall offensive, in fact, on both 29 September and 7 October Halder and Brauchitsch argued that the methods used in Poland offered no guide to the west, since they would be useless against a well-organized army. Their effort availed nothing, and in a memo of 9 October that established the basic guidelines, Hitler ordered an operational plan be drawn up as quickly as possible. In it, he revealed his characteristic combination of acute insight with an almost complete lack of regard for the practical context within which his proposed actions would take place. "Time," he wrote quite clear-sightedly, "in this war . . . is not a factor that has inherent value in and of itself, but one which has to be evaluated. In the current situation . . . time can be seen more probably as an ally of the Western forces than of us." The danger of doing nothing, he asserted, betraying his strategic and economic concerns, as well as revealing lessons he had drawn from the World War:

> is that in a long war some states might be drawn to the opposite side . . . The second danger is that a long war could alarm states that in principle wish to join on Germany's side . . . The third danger in a long war is the difficulty, in view of the restricted food and raw material base, of securing nourishment for the people and creating the means to conduct war. Also, the mental attitude of the people would be burdened.

Above all, Hitler emphasized, "The precondition for any successful conduct of the war is the maintenance of the production of the Ruhr [industrial] area." Its exposure to aerial attack, as "the enemy well knew," represented Germany's greatest vulnerability.[5]

This, to Hitler, posed an intolerable danger, one that Germany had to eliminate. The goal, he stressed, consisted first of "the destruction of enemy forces," with the occupation of territory only of secondary importance. He also accentuated, in the actual conduct of the campaign, the importance of improvisation, massed tank forces, and – intriguing in light of later claims of its inspiration – the use of the 88 mm anti-aircraft guns, which accompanied Panzer units into battle, as anti-tank weapons to shatter enemy counterattacks. Still, at this point, Hitler envisioned largely a replay of the Schlieffen Plan, admittedly with a broadened axis of attack, the aim being the destruction of the French army – which he dismissed as inferior to the German – and the securing of Channel ports. This, in turn, would safeguard the Ruhr, allow the Luftwaffe to launch aerial strikes against British industrial targets, and enable the navy to conduct successful U-boat attacks on enemy shipping. Britain, not France, was clearly viewed as the primary adversary. Strikingly absent, perhaps because of the haunting memories of 1914, was any notion of a swift knockout blow. Although Hitler had outlined relatively limited goals, his top generals reacted in horror, aware as they were of the unprepared state of the Wehrmacht. Brauchitsch termed the idea "insanity," Leeb dismissed it as "madness," and Reichenau, a Nazi sympathizer, characterized it as "almost criminal." The latter evidently also went so far as to pass Hitler's plans along to the Dutch. Even Keitel, otherwise so compliant, offered his resignation, while Göring expressed skepticism about the prospects of an early attack.[6]

OKH could hardly disobey a direct order but its planning was desultory at best. The initial plan, finished by 15 October and issued four days later, proved unimaginative and uninspired; complying strictly with Hitler's directive, it aimed merely at pushing Germany's security zone outward. Although derided by some at the time as a repetition of the Schlieffen Plan, it was decidedly not that, for it lacked the boldness, the daring gamble on the rapid destruction of the French army, that had characterized the former. This was not a knockout blow, but merely a hard punch to force the opponent to his corner. What Hitler had asked for, and OKH delivered, was a plan directed more against Britain than France. The Schwerpunkt, or focal point, was to be in the north, with the limited aim of eliminating a major portion of enemy forces, gaining control of the Belgian-French coast, and then forcing Britain to its knees, although there was no clear idea of how that was to be accomplished. Doubtful that a Blitzkrieg operation would work in the west, OKH had produced an ill-considered, garbled plan that seemed designed more to deter Hitler from attacking than assuring any sort of victory.[7]

Not surprisingly, Hitler reacted disparagingly. A chronic "outsider" and autodidact, he had little respect for the closed circle of elite, educated experts. Indeed, he took pleasure in attacking and undermining the received wisdom of the professionals precisely because of their lack of imagination or creativity; his embrace of unconventional ideas and explanations thus was a way of asserting his own primacy, if not of credentials, then of merit. Although Brauchitsch, Halder, and Reichenau continued their efforts to dissuade him, he stood firm in his demand for a quick strike in the west. At daily briefings he increasingly vented his frustration with OKH, on 25 October subjecting its plan to particularly sharp criticism. He then "completely surprised" those present, especially Brauchitsch and Halder, by

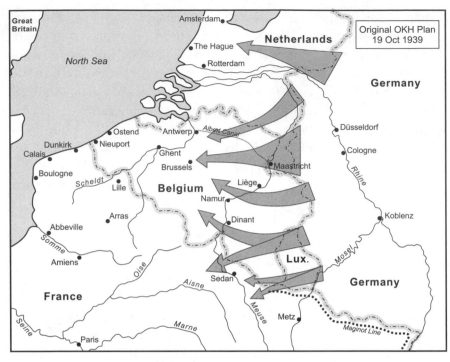

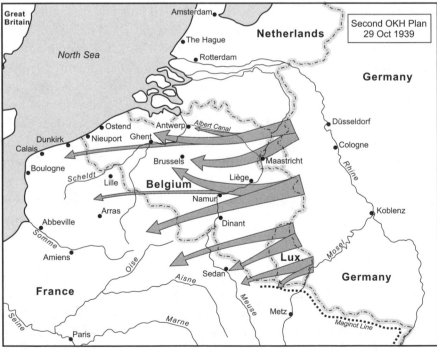

2. The Original OKH Plan, 19 October 1939, and Second OKH Plan, 29 October 1939

proposing a shift in the main focus of attack to south of the Meuse River "in order to advance west and then northwest and cut off and destroy the enemy forces in and moving into Belgium." This first indication of what would evolve into the Sickle Cut (*Sichelschnitt*) plan touched off a "lively exchange," with OKH instructed "to assess the new ideas." By 30 October it produced a second deployment plan that featured a double Schwerpunkt, in itself a problematic notion, but a clear indication that Hitler had forced a shift of focus south. Less than two weeks later, he ordered yet another main thrust even farther south, through Sedan, as the most likely avenue for success. This resulted in a simultaneous triple Schwerpunkt, "a risky game," Bock noted contemptuously, in which a main effort everywhere meant none anywhere. The idea seemed to be to attack and then create a Schwerpunkt based on initial success, a notion that in some respects mirrored Ludendorff's in 1918 (as well as Halder's later intent at the outset of Operation Barbarossa in June 1941). Despite the lack of clarity, Hitler's thinking had shifted in favor of a southern focus of attack, an alternative that provided the possibility for a quick victory. He had also, just as significantly, begun to assert his authority over OKH in matters of operational planning. As yet, though, this could not be termed a Blitzkrieg plan, for Hitler aimed only at achieving limited objectives as the basis for favorable future operations.[8]

One consequence of Hitler's insistence on moving ahead with the offensive had been to intensify Halder's growing unease and so resurrect his loose ties to the anti-Hitler opposition. As always, the key issue was more timing than goals, for Halder accepted the need for war against Britain, objecting only to an early attack. The strain, though, clearly affected him. On 31 October, with tears in his eyes, he confided to Lieutenant-Colonel Helmuth Groscurth, himself a member of the resistance, that "for weeks he had carried a pistol in his pocket" with the intention of killing Hitler. Although Groscurth tried to draw Halder into the ranks of the active conspirators who were plotting a coup, the chief of staff had little stomach for such an action. He well knew that he could not secure the support even of a majority of the top generals, let alone the army as a whole, for such a move. Not only did most, despite their misgivings, still regard Hitler as indispensable, but, to the extent that a coup rekindled the traumatic memories of November 1918 and the alleged stab in the back, it was an inconceivable act, as confirmed by the reaction of most generals to the attempted assassination of Hitler at the Bürgerbräukeller in Munich on 8 November.[9]

In the event, any nascent plans Halder might have entertained collapsed on 5 November. In the hope of convincing Hitler of the folly of a late autumn attack, Brauchitsch, at a conference with the Führer, suggested that inadequate training of the infantry had in the Polish campaign, as in 1918, resulted in an insufficient will to attack, poor morale, and acts of indiscipline among the troops. This, predictably, sent Hitler into a frenzy. In his fury, he demanded that the army chief provide any court-martial files as evidence, as well as a list of the affected units. The fact that Brauchitsch had no such evidence simply made matters worse. On the way back to army headquarters at Zossen, Brauchitsch, "pale as a ghost" and totally shattered, told Halder that Hitler had raged against the "spirit of Zossen," which he vowed to exterminate. In his "panicked confusion," Halder assumed, incorrectly, that the Führer knew about the conspiracy and would now act to crush it. On his arrival at headquarters he thus ordered all incriminating documents destroyed. Brauchitsch, who had utterly crumbled emotionally, offered his resignation on 23 November, but Hitler, finding no one to replace him, refused to accept it. Halder, for his part, retreated to the safety of "doing his duty," a withdrawal into a technocratic sphere where his primary concern was now to defeat the Allies. Having abandoned all notion of formal resistance, his attitude seemed to be that if he could not prevent the campaign in the west, at least it should be won, after which, in a typical example of self-deception, the army would be strong enough to rein in Hitler. Still, the events of 5 November at least clarified the situation in one respect: from early November 1939 the offensive in the west was no longer in doubt.[10]

The expected catastrophe, however, failed to materialize, since the miserable weather that grounded the Luftwaffe, whose role Hitler deemed crucial to the success of the operation, forced one postponement after another. Still, Hitler's determination to attack remained firm, as shown in a conference with 200 of his top officers, from the heads of the armies to the commanding generals and their chiefs of staff, on 23 November. Once again, the key theme was Lebensraum, along with an effort to stiffen the resolve and dispel the crisis of confidence afflicting the officer corps. He had, he asserted pointedly, always been underestimated only to be proven correct; and just as former German leaders, such as Frederick the Great, Bismarck, and Moltke, had prevailed against the skeptics, so would he. Clearly shaken by the recent attempt on his life, he felt a special urgency, as an "irreplaceable" figure, to settle the crucial issue facing Germany, that of space, which could only be solved "with the sword" in a "racial war" that would determine who ruled Europe. "Today we are fighting," he stressed, "for oil fields, rubber, the treasures of the earth." His preoccupation with Russia was clear. It had "far-reaching goals" in the Baltic and Balkans that conflicted with German interests, but "we can oppose Russia only when we are free in the west." The choice for the German future, he insisted in his typically Darwinist fashion, was stark, "victory or downfall." Offensive action was thus an absolute necessity, since the war would only end "through annihilation of the enemy. Anyone who believes otherwise," he said, in a barely concealed jibe at his generals, "is irresponsible." In any case, he remarked acidly, "I have not created the Wehrmacht not to use it. The resolve to strike was always in me." And now was the time to attack, when the Western Allies, sheltering behind their defenses until their rearmament programs took effect, would not act. This, though, would not last, for, in an oft-repeated worry, "time worked for the enemy. At present there is a balance of force that for us will not get better but can only worsen . . . I will therefore act. Today we still have a superiority such as we never had [in 1914]." Moreover, he stressed, in another pointed barb, "One can do anything with a German soldier when he is well led." Victory required fanatic will and blind allegiance from his generals, whose apparent belief that the task in front of them was overwhelming he found "deeply offensive." It was, he reiterated, mocking his officers, "childish" to hope for a compromise peace. He himself, in this struggle for "the existence of the nation," would "shrink at nothing" and, in a sinister threat his generals could not have missed, vowed to "destroy anyone who is against me . . . I will stand or fall in this struggle. I will not survive the defeat of my people." Then, with reference to 1918, he pledged, "Externally, no capitulation; internally, no revolution."[11]

Although the prevailing theme of this remarkably radical speech remained his obsession with settling the question of hegemony in Europe, it clearly also aimed at rooting out defeatism among the generals. Most were suitably chastened by his threats and, in any case, remained convinced, as Hermann Hoth later put it, that Hitler was the only person with the strength of will to see Germany through its time of peril. Only two younger generals, Manstein and Guderian, wanted to protest Hitler's lack of trust in the army. They, however, elicited little support, although the next day Reichenau did send Guderian to remonstrate with the Führer; not for the last time, though, his encounter with Hitler accomplished rather the opposite of what had been intended. When Guderian assured the Führer that only a few generals opposed him, and that they should be gotten rid of, the latter replied that his lack of confidence centered on Brauchitsch. To this, Guderian, revealing his contempt for the army chief, said simply that he should be fired. In reply, Hitler implicitly conceded that he had temporarily been bested in the power struggle with his generals, confessing that he could find no one better to take Brauchitsch's place, especially since he was loath to name any strong-willed personality to lead the army. Still, like Halder, most generals retreated into a narrow technocratic role of fulfilling their duty, serving, as in reality they had since 1938, as an instrument of Hitler's will. Despite this, Hitler grew more mistrustful of his generals. Ever the resentful populist, by December 1939 he was certain that his ideas were being deliberately sabotaged, though he, revealing a gnawing sense of inferiority, "would prevail even if he didn't happen to be a learned General Staff officer." Indeed, his November speech had betrayed a hint of doubt, a fear that he had stumbled into an unwinnable war and had no way out other than sheer force of will. Soon enough, though, dazzling military successes would confirm in his mind that he was right and his generals had been miserably wrong all along, as his personal triumphs bred contempt for his professional officers.[12]

Ironically, Hitler's great victory was made possible by the fact that weather concerns, his own uneasiness over the operational plan, and a plane crash that allowed detailed orders to fall into Belgian hands forced him to postpone the attack – all of which permitted the conceptual rethinking that resulted in the eventual Sickle Cut plan. The Führer had not been alone in his contempt for the unimaginative effort produced by OKH, as Manstein almost immediately emerged as the most vocal critic among the generals. On 21 October, Manstein, then chief of staff of Army Group A (Rundstedt), received the first deployment directive, which he quickly dismissed as a watered-down version of the Schlieffen Plan that would end in a stalemate. In a flash of inspiration, he began developing an alternative that addressed the weak points in the original plan: it would send the German army crashing head-on into the main enemy forces, and, by proposing a narrow advance along the Channel coast, it invited a counter-attack from the south. By contrast, he devised a bold and astonishingly simple plan: the Schwerpunkt would be shifted south to the Ardennes Forest, which the French regarded as impenetrable for armored forces. If fast, mobile Panzer units could effect a quick crossing of the Meuse River, the enemy would be caught by surprise, opening the possibility of a swift advance to the west into the rear of the main Allied armies that would trap them against the Channel. At the time, Manstein had the good fortune of being stationed in Koblenz along with Guderian, the foremost German tank expert, who knew the terrain of the Ardennes quite well. Guderian not only shared Manstein's enthusiasm for this daring operation, but assured the latter of the feasibility of his plan.[13]

In a series of memoranda from late October through January, Manstein peppered OKH with his ideas. Army High Command simply ignored

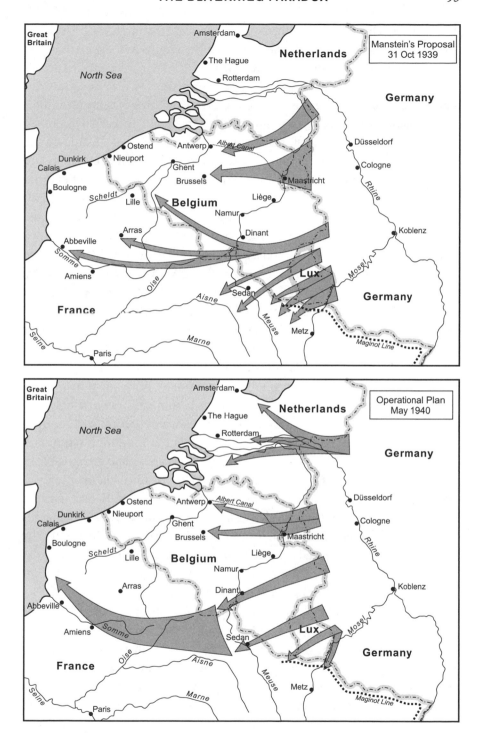

3. Manstein's Proposal, 31 October 1939, and Operational Plan, May 1940

him, not even bothering to inform Hitler, who had instinctively grasped the southern focus as the key to the attack, of the similarity between his and Manstein's views. In late November, in fact, the general confided to his diary, after Hitler's speech, "[His] explanation was, as always, extraordinarily gripping and logical . . . The only distressing thing was the clear indication that the army leadership did not want to attack." By early December, according to Gerhard Engel, his army adjutant, Hitler had "dismissed the 'old Schlieffen ham'" and broached various ideas "to split the British and French," only to have his ideas, he complained, "deliberately sabotaged." Both thus found themselves opposed by conventional, conservative generals who tried to marginalize their conceptions. Halder initially dismissed Manstein's plan as merely an attempt to inflate the importance of his own command, while Brauchitsch praised his innovative ideas, only to stress the lack of any available force to implement them. Pressed by Hitler, though, who on 20 January 1940 had again spoken out in favor of an offensive through Sedan, Halder began to take the idea more seriously. As he realized the possibilities of Manstein's plan, Halder wearied of the overly eager general, whom he termed an "annoying pest," and with whom he had a personal rivalry dating back to his appointment over the latter as chief of staff. Halder now made Manstein the first casualty of his own plan, gleefully dispatching him to "the desert," a corps command in Pomerania. The chief of staff also sought to usurp Manstein's plan and present it as his own, but his machinations had an unintended result. Hitler's adjutant, Schmundt, aware of the similarity of their ideas, arranged for a personal meeting on 17 February between the Führer and Manstein. Despite his usual proclivity to interrupt briefings, on this occasion Hitler listened silently as Manstein outlined his arguments. Indeed, his growing enthusiasm at seeing his "favorite idea" confirmed even overcame his personal aversion to the general, whom he regarded as clever but also a typical representative of the aristocratic officer caste. "The man," he admitted, "is not to my liking, but he knows something of how to get things done."[14]

The matter was now settled. As early as 13 February, even before his meeting with Manstein, Hitler had decided to shift the main effort to the south, a decision with which Halder concurred; Manstein's presentation merely provided reinforcement. On 24 February, OKH issued a fourth deployment directive for *Fall Gelb* (Case Yellow), itself the result of a convergence of Hitler's and Manstein's ideas, which clearly placed the Schwerpunkt in the south. Now fully converted, Halder set about developing the plan further, even going so far as to defy military orthodoxy and advocate an independent crossing of the Meuse by the Panzer forces, which should then ignore any threat to their long exposed southern flank in the dash to the Channel. The extreme risks this posed resulted in sharp criticism – prefiguring the later dispute between Hitler and Halder – from within the ranks of the generals, especially from General Georg von Sodenstern, Manstein's successor as chief of staff of Army Group A. In his rejoinder, Halder admitted that there would be crisis-filled hours, but argued that the very speed, violence, and momentum of the attack, combined with superior German leadership, would overcome every difficulty. In March 1940 the man who had sought so ardently in the autumn to delay a German attack, now, with all the enthusiasm of the convert, could barely contain his impatience to get going.[15]

The dispute over plans for the western campaign also demonstrated that Hitler's instincts were at least as good, if not better, than most of his generals'. In reality, no one had a clear idea of how to proceed, and all were influenced by the failure of the 1914 offensive. While the generals preferred a wait-and-see approach that played to the strength of the Allies, though, Hitler showed concern for protecting the Ruhr, the vital German economic area, from British air attacks. In operational terms, he evinced a flair for surprise and rapid action, an instinct for the weak point of the enemy, and some appreciation for the use of tanks and aircraft. Moreover, his stress on quickly smashing the French and forcing the British off the continent revealed far less respect for the fighting ability of the former than that held by OKH. Most generals not only had an exaggerated opinion of French prowess, but also thought that mobile warfare, so successful against Poland, would not work against a well-trained, highly organized force. By defeating France, Hitler betrayed his hope that the British, having lost their ally, would relent and accept German hegemony on the continent. Both his economic concerns and assessment of the French army were well founded, but he utterly failed to see that London would not concede German dominance, since that would reduce Great Britain to the status of a second-rate power.

Nor did he have a clear idea of how to proceed operationally. That was the genius of Manstein's plan, which, by its southern thrust, aimed to force a conclusive decision by land, a key facet that appealed to the Führer. As Manstein later admitted, Hitler "had a keen eye for the art of the tactically possible and spent much time brooding over maps. He may have spotted that a crossing over the Meuse was most easily achieved at Sedan . . . He may also have recognized that a crossing at Sedan would represent a promising spot [to force a breakthrough]." Indeed, perhaps because of his artistic background, Hitler possessed a great facility for map reading and visual deduction. In February 1940 he "pored over relief maps of the Ardennes all night long," gaining a valuable understanding of the relationship between space and time. Hitler's insights, though, could only come to fruition through the military expertise of a professional officer, something that Manstein also recognized. Although the general hoped that this would keep Hitler's excesses in check, it simply prefigured the later structural conflicts between the Führer and OKH.[16]

After the war many German generals would attempt to disparage Hitler's insight as merely tactical rather than strategic, but in the autumn of 1939 he had clearly perceived a breakout and encirclement plan not dissimilar from that of Manstein. This not only enhanced his military credibility, but allowed him to assert a claim to the tradition of the elder Moltke, whom he greatly admired. Organizational ability alone, he argued, with a view to the uninspired technocrat Ludendorff, could not guarantee victory. "How could a Feldherr draw up a battle plan," he asserted in accord with Moltke and Clausewitz, "without inspiration from the grace of imagination?" To Hitler, factual knowledge and will had to be balanced with creativity, so that military leadership was as much art as science. True enough, but as a key architect of the triumph over France, he soon entered the dangerous path of overvaluing his own ingenuity and disparaging the factual knowledge of his military professionals. They lacked, he thought, the requisite inspiration: "These generals are too ... rooted in outmoded concepts ... They should read more Karl May!" Military leadership certainly required creativity, but Hitler neglected Clausewitz's admonition that these creative forces be disciplined with professional knowledge.[17]

Meanwhile, amid the intense debates and preparations for Case Yellow, events elsewhere forced Hitler's attention toward Scandinavia. The Soviet invasion of Finland in late November 1939 had immediately raised fears that supplies of Finnish nickel could be imperiled, as well as concerns that any Allied move to aid the embattled Finns might serve as a pretext to occupy Norway, thus threatening Germany's supply of vital Swedish iron ore. As early as February 1937, Admiral Raeder had drawn Hitler's attention to the importance of acquiring naval bases in Norway and western France, while in the spring of 1939, in a study, "Conducting War in the Baltic," Admiral Conrad Albrecht emphasized the key importance of Swedish iron ore for the Reich war economy. In October, Raeder combined both strategic and economic issues in arguing again for the importance of Norway, a line of reasoning now fully embraced by the Führer. As early as 12 December he ordered Alfred Jodl, the head of OKW, to prepare a study on the feasibility of occupying Norway before the Allies could act, which resulted, on 24 January 1940, in the establishment of a Special Staff North within OKW. In response to the British seizure on 16 February of the German ship *Altmark* within Norwegian territorial waters, Hitler demanded accelerated preparations. On 21 February, General Nikolaus von Falkenhorst assumed command of the operation, now code-named Weserübung. Significantly, for the first time Hitler had given OKW, under Jodl's operational leadership, responsibility for the planning of a campaign. Since both the navy and Luftwaffe retained the political clout to keep OKW out of their respective areas, in practice this meant a loss of authority for the army. Additionally, it also signaled Hitler's intent to assert more personal control over the preparation and conduct of an operation.[18]

In the event, Hitler's fears were justified, since the British and French had begun planning a move against Norway. Although Allied strategy remained focused on a long war, the Nazi–Soviet Pact and the rapid German victory in Poland forced some rethinking. The long-war scenario made sense only if Germany could be pressured economically, but the prospect of Soviet deliveries punched a hole in any Allied blockade. In order to plug the gap, strong blows against Germany's most vulnerable areas, Swedish iron ore in the north and Romanian and Soviet oil fields in the south, appeared particularly promising. In both cases, a conflict with the USSR had to be anticipated, a prospect the Allies accepted with remarkable equanimity, since they had a low estimation of the Red Army. The French, eager to divert German attention from their own border and themselves increasingly concerned by the financial and economic strain of a long war, pressed for operations in Norway, as well as the bombing of Soviet oil facilities in the Caucasus, as the best way to strike a decisive blow against Germany. Since the British opposed any southern operation as ensuring continued German–Soviet cooperation, Allied attention centered on occupation of the key iron-ore port of Narvik. Curiously, then, by mid-March 1940 the focus of both antagonists had shifted north, with Chamberlain convinced that the Allies were set to steal a march on the Führer. Hitler, who he thought nearly "off his head altogether," had, the prime minister boasted in a public speech, "missed the bus." He had failed to attack France and had let the moment for success pass; the Allies would now seize the initiative. On 28 March they agreed to a mining operation off Narvik, to begin on 8 April, designed to impede the flow of Swedish iron ore to Germany.[19]

Hitler, long worried by the possibility of just such a crippling blow to the German war economy – but unaware of the Allied decision – by coincidence, a few days later, ordered Weserübung to begin on 9 April. Even as the British began their mining off Narvik on the 8th, then, the next day the

Germans seized the initiative in a daring and risky operation. With paratroop drops on key Norwegian airfields and bold seaborne assaults on the principal coastal towns, the Germans achieved virtually complete operational surprise. Still, all had not gone as smoothly as was hoped. While the Germans swiftly took key ports at Bergen, Trondheim, and Stavanger, they faced heavy fighting at Kristiansand and Oslo. Narvik, seized virtually unopposed on the first day by a force of 2,000 mountain troops under General Eduard Dietl, quickly developed into a contest between the Germans and the British, its key importance understood by all. The British dispatched an expeditionary force to retake the city, and on 13 April its naval forces entered the fjord and annihilated the German destroyers protecting the port. Some 2,500 crew members of the sunken ships now augmented Dietl's meager forces, but they found themselves in a dangerous position, surrounded and cut off from any aid.[20]

The events of 13 April also touched off a serious crisis of nerves in Berlin, revealing for the first time a pattern that would become chronic. Having authorized and unleashed a bold plan, one run under his own personal supervision through OKW, Hitler, faced with the vagaries of execution, reacted to the bad news from Narvik with a near nervous collapse. While Raeder despaired that the attack had come two days too late, the Führer, in his baptism of fire as operational leader, reacted with extreme agitation and a "panicky excitement" that, in the contemptuous words of one witness, revealed his "pathetic shortcomings" as a commander. As the situation at Narvik deteriorated over the next few weeks, with Dietl's troops forced out of the town into the hills above it, Hitler grew even more agitated, often issuing hasty and contradictory orders. On 18 April, in a fit of panic, he directed Keitel to draw up orders for Dietl's force to withdraw into neighboring Sweden, allowing itself to be interned there. Only the extraordinary refusal of a junior officer, Lieutenant-Colonel Bernhard von Lossberg, to transmit the order – on the grounds that it reflected the same loss of nerve that had cost the Germans victory at the Battle of the Marne in September 1914 – prevented a disaster. In view of the seriousness of the situation, Halder even overcame his antipathy to his rivals at OKW and implored Jodl to hold Narvik under all circumstances. Hitler, though, was not done. Following Allied landings in mid-April north of Trondheim at Namsos and Andalsnes, designed to interdict any German ore shipments, he cooked up a scheme to send reinforcements by sea, a plan that Raeder, after much remonstrance, managed to scuttle as unrealistic.[21]

In the end, largely because of events in France and Jodl's steadying presence, Dietl held on at Narvik and the Allies were forced to abandon Namsos, but at a relatively high price paid by the German navy. Although the key iron-ore port of Narvik had been secured, the other goal, establishing the operational basis for an effective naval war against Great Britain, had been less successful. In an ironic twist, during the Great War, Germany had had a large navy but no ports from which to confront the Royal Navy; now, in 1940, they had obtained the strategically important ports, but, because of losses sustained in the Norwegian campaign, lacked the requisite fleet. Perhaps the most significant result of the operation, though, had been Hitler's erratic behavior, which had sent shock waves through his high command. To Brauchitsch and Halder, the sight of the Führer losing his nerve over Narvik seemed an ill omen for the impending offensive in the west. Hitler's foresight had undeniably enabled the Germans to preempt the Allies and move expeditiously to safeguard the essential Swedish iron-ore shipments, while his flair for surprise enabled the Germans to seize the initiative. But the Norwegian campaign also revealed the duality in his temperament: boldness in conception and planning dissolved, in execution, into extreme anxiety, occasional panic and near hysteria, and erratic, impulsive decisions. It was as if, knowing the weakness of his own position militarily, aware he was always risking everything on one big gamble, he shrank at the moment of decision from the enormity of what he was doing. Narcissistic and self-absorbed, with no trusted friends or advisors to whom he listened, Hitler had a need to maintain a facade of absolute confidence and iron will. Still, at bottom, he remained the lonely outsider aware of his parvenu status, with an inkling of self-understanding that his whole enterprise hinged on a gigantic deception; that he had one chance and one chance only, with the odds greatly stacked against him. Typically, as well, once the operation succeeded, he forgot (or repressed) the moments of weakness and gloried in his personal triumph.

A similar pattern was soon to be repeated in France. Having finally gotten the high command on board – in his new-found enthusiasm Halder had made Manstein's original plan even bolder and more daring – all was set for the decisive blow to be struck in the west. Brimming with confidence, Halder expected a great victory, at whose "end will stand the United States of Europe." Few other senior army officers expected it to work; for them, a bold plan simply seemed better than no plan at all. From the very start of the campaign, though, things fell into place almost exactly as envisioned. As in Poland, even the response of the enemy aided German operational success. Certainly, the French army had crucial defects in communications, air cover, and reaction time, but as Army Group B under Bock launched its attack through the Low Countries, perhaps the worst fault was the overly ambitious defense plan of the French commander-in-chief, General Maurice Gamelin. In the late 1930s, B. H. Liddell Hart had confidently asserted that "the only serious chance of French resistance collapsing completely is as a sequel to a rash offensive on their part and the crippling of their forces in it." Gamelin clearly did not intend an offensive, but in seeking the most advantageous defensive line, he sent his best units hurtling into Belgium and southern Holland in an effort to engage and halt the advancing Germans as far from French soil as possible. When German Panzers unexpectedly penetrated the weak French defenses in the Ardennes, though, and turned west across northern France, the best French units found themselves cut off. "We have been defeated . . .," admitted Paul Reynaud, the new French premier, in a terse 15 May telephone conversation – just five days after the start of the German attack – that rendered Winston Churchill, himself only in office those same five days, momentarily speechless, "we have lost the battle." The crucial absence of a strategic reserve, which in many respects decided the outcome, thus resulted not from an overcautious French plan, but from a gamble every bit as risky as the German Sichelschnitt through the Ardennes. In May 1940 both Hitler and Gamelin had gambled all or nothing on a bold move – and Hitler won.[22]

The Führer, though, had been just as astonished by the success of the breakthrough as anyone else, proclaiming it to be "an absolute miracle." Paradoxically, in these heady days of mid-May a personality inversion seemed to occur between Hitler and Halder. The former, by nature a gambler willing to stake all on one throw of the dice, who had taken almost criminal risks in his foreign policy, now became timid; the latter, so opposed to all of Hitler's adventures that he had contemplated a coup, now exuded confidence. At the moment of triumph, when Halder glimpsed the possibility of turning the operational breakthrough into a strategic one, Hitler began to lose his nerve. "Frightened by his own success," "terribly nervous," insisting that the "main threat is from the south," Hitler, the man who had pushed the bold Sickle Cut plan forward, suddenly saw danger everywhere. As early as 17 May, as Halder pondered an armored thrust to the southwest that would alter the original plan in order to complete the campaign in one rolling operation rather than in two separate phases, Hitler intervened for the first time in operational matters. The day before, Rundstedt (Army Group A), in overall command of the key tank forces although a decided skeptic of their value, had ordered the Panzer formations to halt, even as the entire French front threatened to collapse, to enable the infantry divisions to "close up." This view was shared by other "old school" generals such as Ernst Busch, commanding the 16th Army, who feared a French counterattack and preferred the cautious approach of gathering the divisions before again setting off. The "progressives," by contrast, urged an immediate westward attack with armored spearheads in order to exploit enemy disarray.[23]

On 17 May, at Rundstedt's headquarters, the Führer not only reaffirmed the halt order but extended it, justifying his decision on political and psychological grounds. Any setback now, he asserted, would give "a fatal boost . . . to the political leadership of our enemy." Then, incredibly, he claimed that "the decision is not to be found so much in a rapid thrust to the Channel coast but rather . . . in as quickly as possible establishing absolutely reliable defense readiness along the Aisne . . . [and] the Somme," that is, along the southern flank of the advance. Given the tenuous state of the French leadership, Hitler could perhaps be credited for his psychological insight, but militarily he seemed not to have liberated himself from the demons of the First World War, particularly the specter of another "miracle on the Marne," any more than many of his generals. As he pored over the situation map and saw the narrow line of the German Panzers, exposed and with no flank protection, he suddenly refused to take any risk, assuring Mussolini on 18 May that the trauma of 1914 would not be repeated. The more successful Sickle Cut appeared, the less Hitler seemed able to grasp the implications, and no amount of logic could dislodge his fear. Guderian, leading the tank spearhead, railing against having "the brakes put on" him, expressed well the disappointment of the advocates of mobile war when he noted his astonishment that the man who had approved the bold idea had now ordered "our advance to be stopped at once." Less discreetly, a staff officer at Army Group A exploded, "But that is sheer madness. We have the whole thing rolling now. We have to get to the coast as quickly as possible. And we are supposed to stop?"[24]

Even on the morning of 18 May, as Halder urged action to prevent Allied forces from forming a front to block the German advance, Hitler still raged that the whole campaign was being ruined and refused to continue the westward thrust. Further infuriated by Halder's furtive efforts to circumvent his order, not until early that evening did the Führer relent and permit the Panzer forces the next day to resume their push to the Channel, but the damage had been done. Not only had the French been granted an unexpected breathing spell, but the episode had rekindled an atmosphere of mistrust and ill-feeling at the Führer's headquarters. At bottom, this was an issue of authority and power. Hitler, who had used OKW as his personal command staff in Norway, felt no hesitation in intervening in operational matters in France, even though it came under OKH's purview. Halder, influenced by his sole conduct of the Polish campaign, saw France as "his" operation, so chafed at the Führer's interference in day-to-day military matters. In response, the army chief of staff developed a form of "indirect leadership" that further incensed the Führer. Halder, in effect, systematically ignored or undermined Hitler's orders and attempted to run military operations independently. His hope seemed to be that if he placed all the pieces correctly on the chessboard, the resulting success would overcome Hitler's irritation at being undercut. Instead, Halder's style backfired, as the Führer, ever protective of his power, began to factor issues of authority into his decision-making calculations.[25]

Despite this temporary halt to their operations, by 20 May German tanks had advanced to the area around Amiens and Abbeville and appeared poised to seize the ports of Boulogne and Calais, trapping the Allied forces. Once again suspicious of his own success, Hitler now not only failed to appreciate the precariousness of the Allied situation, but also succumbed to a bout of overrating the French, itself surprising since earlier he had expressly ridiculed their capabilities. This might perhaps have been a response to unexpected counterattacks launched by General Charles de Gaulle's 4th Armored Division on both 17 and 19 May, the first of which caused the Germans some consternation. In any case, a stronger British counterattack at Arras on 21 May provoked even greater anxiety and seemed to confirm the worst fears of many German commanders. The rapid push to the coast had left the strung-out Panzer forces isolated and vulnerable. An enemy pincer attack just behind the tank spearhead might well have resulted in a Dunkirk in reverse, what Clausewitz termed "the encirclement of the encircler."[26]

Although Halder had accepted that risk when he warned of crisis moments to be overcome, when it happened it sent shock waves through the German command. Rommel's 7th Panzer Division, strung out and exposed, bore the brunt of the counterattack. Although initially a close-run thing, it ended in catastrophe for the British, who lost sixty out of eighty-eight tanks engaged, many of them victims of devastating fire from 88 mm anti-aircraft guns used in defense – as Hitler had earlier suggested. Despite this result, the British push at Arras had a decidedly outsized effect on the Germans. Rommel, perhaps feeling the belated impact of a mad dash through enemy lines a few days earlier that had exposed his division to destruction, first inflamed the atmosphere by dispatching exaggerated reports that claimed "hundreds of enemy tanks" had attacked. This exacerbated the worst fears of Hitler and some of his generals, who, like Churchill on the other side, regarded a strong Allied counterattack as inevitable. Their nerves already at breaking point, this troubling news from the battlefield only confirmed their expectations. The situation at Arras, they worried, was not a mere isolated incident but portended the major enemy assault they had anticipated. General von Kleist, commanding the Panzer forces, suddenly saw a "serious threat" to the operation, reporting on 23 May that he had lost more than 50 percent of his tanks and was "no longer strong enough to mount an attack to the east against strong enemy forces." Nor, he continued ominously, could he fend off an enemy counterattack in major strength. This message, in turn, persuaded Kluge, commanding the 4th Army, to halt his movements. Concerned by reports of mounting tank losses, and worried about holding bridgeheads across the Somme, the now panicked Führer, as well as some field commanders, believed it advisable to concentrate all motorized formations before proceeding. Although Allied attacks had undoubtedly grown stronger, their psychological impact was out of all proportion to their actual military effect, a classic case of leaders seeing what they want to see and then imputing design to what was, in fact, desperation. Fearful of another "miracle on the Marne," German actions now created the conditions for a "miracle at Dunkirk."[27]

Even as the crisis at Arras dissipated – the British declined to pursue any more attacks southward, instead withdrawing to Dunkirk – Rundstedt remained determined to clear up the situation before pushing on. He later admitted to Bock that he had feared that Army Group A would be overrun by British forces fleeing Bock's attacks. This was the background to the famous halt order. Like the initial one a week earlier, it originated not with Hitler but with Rundstedt, with Kleist's message of 23 May the decisive catalyst. Kluge, late that afternoon, first suggested that formations close up, which meant that the motorized units of the left wing of his army should be halted. Rundstedt agreed and issued orders for the Panzer forces to be halted on 24 May, with preparations to be made to resume the attack the next day. Despite this concession, tank commanders in the field exploded in anger at the delay, however temporary, in their attack on Dunkirk, the last remaining Channel port in enemy hands. As Reinhardt argued, any halt could only help the weak enemy construct defenses. Guderian's war diary warned that Rundstedt's order would "practically discard the attack concept" despite the "essential [need] . . . to push toward Dunkirk . . . whose fall would make the encirclement complete." Nor were Brauchitsch and Halder pleased with Rundstedt's action. Although the latter was skeptical, at best, of modern mobile operations, in the course of the campaign all tank forces had come to be concentrated under his command. Halder found this problematic, since he believed that Rundstedt was not using these forces energetically enough. So, when OKH learned of the temporary halt order during the night of 23–24 May, even Brauchitsch, who until now had left execution of the operation to Halder, exploded in anger. Around midnight Brauchitsch sent a brusque order to Rundstedt informing him that Kluge's 4th Army, which contained all Panzer divisions, would at 8:00 p.m. on the 24th be transferred to Bock. In doing this, he ignored Halder's misgivings; it would, thought the OKH chief, cause "serious trouble" in coordinating the final phase of the encircling operation, especially since Bock had no effective communications with the Panzer troops. This action not only stripped Rundstedt of most of his striking power, but also changed the basic tenor of the operation. Where, originally, Army Group A (Rundstedt) was to be the hammer that drove the enemy from the south onto Bock's anvil in the north, now Army Group B (Bock) was to assume the role of hammer and anvil, with Rundstedt's forces serving mainly as flank protection along the Somme.[28]

As fate would have it, Hitler visited Rundstedt's headquarters on the morning of 24 May, where he learned both of Rundstedt's halt order of the previous day and Brauchitsch's action. Not only did Hitler share Rundstedt's cautious assessment of the situation as "entirely identical" to his own, but he was outraged that the 4th Army was to be turned over to Bock. Irritable and petulant, his anger resulted less from the military logic of the order than the fact that this shift in the operation had been made without his knowledge or approval. Already suspicious of OKH undermining his authority, Hitler immediately invalidated the transfer of the 4th Army and reaffirmed Rundstedt's halt order. Despite the latter's post-war protestations, Hitler neither forced the halt order on him nor tied his hands in terms of the duration of the halt. Instead, he expressly gave Rundstedt freedom of action to determine the duration of the stop and in handling the 4th Army. Although Halder and others exploded in anger at this extended halt order, which resulted in the absurd situation of some Panzer units having to sit by and watch Allied troops march past them unhindered toward Dunkirk, the object of their rage more properly was Rundstedt rather than Hitler. None, though, had the nerve to point out Rundstedt's mistaken assessment of the situation. The unfortunate Brauchitsch bore the brunt of Hitler's wrath, as the Führer subjected him to vehement reproaches for his unauthorized actions and stripped him of his authority to direct the field armies; future decisions would be dependent on Hitler. As this drama raged, Halder on the evening of 24 May conceived a way around Hitler's obstruction. Without specifically lifting the halt order, he issued an instruction that gave Panzer units the go-ahead to act locally to prevent enemy troops from escaping, trusting that lower-level commanders would understand his intent and that the principle of Auftragstaktik would do the rest. While Bock clearly got the message, Rundstedt refused to pass the directive to his Panzer commanders, on the grounds that Hitler had left it to him to handle operations of the 4th Army – a clear example of Auftragstaktik backfiring on Halder – and he considered it more urgent to allow units to close up before resuming the attack.[29]

Not until the morning of 26 May did Rundstedt, himself apparently uneasy over the halt, drive to the front to consult Kleist and Hoth, both of whom urged a resumption of the attack. Rundstedt then dutifully contacted the Führer, who lifted the halt order at 1:30 that afternoon. Since the Panzer units were now in the midst of reorganization and repair work, it was not until the next day that they resumed the offensive. Without Manstein, the original motivating force behind Sichelschnitt to encourage him, Rundstedt had forgotten the key to its success, its very forward momentum. At the moment of triumph, faced with the risk of an enemy counterattack without flank protection, he undermined any chance of decisive victory by impeding his own Panzer forces. The Allies used this pause not only to withdraw their forces into the Dunkirk pocket but also to construct more effective defenses, so the German attack, when it resumed, bogged down immediately. Left temporarily on their own, the infantry divisions proved unable to make headway while the Luftwaffe, not expecting to bear the full burden of destroying the enemy pocket, was unprepared. Not only did they have to deploy aircraft from airfields in Germany, which meant they were at the end of their effective range by the time they reached Dunkirk, but they then encountered British Spitfire squadrons from England, with planes that were equal or superior to their own. The persistently rainy, cloudy weather also hindered aerial operations during the evacuation. Finally, the Luftwaffe was unable to concentrate all its force against the pocket because it still had important ground support tasks elsewhere, especially along the Somme and in preparing for the second phase of the campaign, the strike south into the French hinterland.[30]

Thus, the Luftwaffe proved unable, and tank forces were not allowed, to prevent large numbers of Allied troops from escaping at Dunkirk. As the importance of this gradually became apparent, Hitler justified his actions with various arguments, some of which were more compelling than others. Certainly, rain made the marshy area around Dunkirk difficult for tank forces, and he expressed legitimate concern that these tanks would be needed for the second phase of the operation. Both of these worries reflected an intensified "flank psychosis" that had developed in Hitler and some of his advisors. The Allies had launched increasingly spirited counterattacks in recent days that confirmed German expectations, but their calculation went awry on one key point. Hitler, and others, failed to grasp that although the Allies could launch local counterstrikes, they had neither the strength nor the coordination to pose any real threat to the overall outcome of the campaign. Their counterstrikes amounted to desperate local actions, not portents of a grand counteroffensive. Nor, despite later allegations, did Hitler "allow" the British to escape as part of some clever diplomatic ploy to encourage them to make peace – the fact that the Luftwaffe had been ordered to wipe out the pocket is evidence enough to disprove that claim. More plausibly, Hitler did not expect the British to be able to evacuate. Göring, the head of the Luftwaffe, provided the "logic" behind the decision. Halder later asserted that at the decisive moment Göring, a master intriguer who knew how to play on Hitler's instinctive dislike for the aristocratic officer corps, argued that the victory (and glory) at Dunkirk should go not to the conservative army but to the National Socialist Luftwaffe. This remark hit home doubly since Hitler had grown progressively suspicious of Halder's efforts to undercut his orders and thus his authority, and likely now saw a chance to reassert his dominance. His decision, then, rested less on military factors than on this ongoing power struggle, in the determination of the Führer to assert his authority over OKH and, in the words of his adjutant Engel, let his generals "know that he was in command and nobody else."[31]

Still, there was more to this than just a power struggle; it also entailed a real difference in vision, as shown in a subsequent disagreement over the goal of the second phase of the campaign, which itself prefigured later disputes during Operation Barbarossa. While Halder focused entirely on the military goal of destroying "the living fighting forces of the enemy," Hitler for the first but not the last time intervened in operational matters using economic arguments, in this case the priority of quickly seizing the Lorraine iron-ore mines in order to cripple French armaments production. Halder, with less understanding of economic imperatives, saw this as yet another example of Hitler wanting "to play it absolutely safe . . . We have the same old story again," he fumed in his diary, with no hint of any recognition of the irony in the situation. "On top, there just isn't a spark of the spirit that would dare put high stakes on a single throw. Instead, everything is done in cheap piecemeal fashion." Although Halder complained a week later of the impossibility of finding any "operational picture" amidst all the Führer's talk, and muttered that he would just have "to figure these things out for myself and see how I can get on," he was being overly dramatic. Indeed, in his earlier diary entry he had himself noted Hitler's argument that he intended "to deny the enemy possession of his iron-ore resources in Lorraine. With them gone, it's all over with his armament industry." After all, as both Halder and Hitler knew, destruction of French armies in 1870 had not, in contradiction of Clausewitz, led to an end to that particular war, since the French still retained the means to fight on. Halder's real objection, then, lay less in Hitler's lacking a vision than in its being primarily an economic and not operational one.[32]

It is also well to remember that Hitler was hardly isolated in his views. In fact, he had considerable support in the very highest ranks of the officer corps: Rundstedt, the commander of an Army Group, as well as his chief of staff, Sodenstern; Busch, the commander of an army; and, at least temporarily, Kluge and Kleist, both key army commanders – all assented to the halt order. In retrospect, Hitler's mistake lay not in initiating the halt order, which he did not, but in allowing it to stand. At the time, though, the swift implementation of the second phase of the operation seemed most urgent, and only later did the full import of Dunkirk become clear. We need to bear in mind too that from Hitler's perspective the French campaign had been his operation, one that he had forced on reluctant commanders, many of whom were certain it would fail. Then, when it resulted in a brilliant triumph, it seemed that people like Halder, initially an arch skeptic, were trying to claim credit for all successes and pin the blame for failure at Dunkirk on him. Hitler could argue, reasonably enough, that he was being criticized by one group of generals for a decision based on input from another group. Moreover, when, in accordance with German tradition, he allowed the ranking field commander to decide for himself, Rundstedt had reaffirmed and extended the halt order. Hitler thus believed himself unfairly criticized while concluding that his own judgments, given the divided nature of opinion in the officer corps, were at least as sound as theirs.

In any case, the breathtaking swiftness with which the Germans completed the second phase of the campaign quickly swept aside any initial unease over Dunkirk. Within two weeks of their renewed attack on 5 June the Germans had shattered remaining French defenses and forced their capitulation. As General Maxime Weygand, who had replaced Gamelin, woefully put it, "We have gone to war with a 1918 army against a German army of 1939. It is sheer madness." This was a remarkably accurate assessment, since Weygand's observation ignored the impact of the so-called "Maginot mentality" as the cause of defeat. Certainly, France had not fully recovered physically or mentally from the extreme exertions (and manpower losses) of the Great War, and an undercurrent of defeatism and pacifism existed. But as Churchill pointed out after the war, there was nothing intrinsically wrong with defensive fortifications designed to safeguard long stretches of border, and thus economize one's own use of troops while "canalizing" the enemy attack into a certain area. The problem lay more in the French response to that attack when it came. While the delay of the *Sitzkrieg* had reinforced their notions of linear defense, with the bulk of the fighting (and physical destruction) of what presumably would be another positional war to take place in Belgium, the Germans instead turned their attention to the rebirth of operational movement. The anachronistic command structure of the French army, the detailed and time-consuming planning of all combat operations down to the minutest detail, the almost unbelievable lack of direct communications between headquarters and the front – Gamelin had no radios at his command center, while, at one point, Weygand was out of touch by phone every afternoon between noon and two o'clock because the local switchboard operator insisted on her lunch break – meant that the French were incapable of seizing the initiative.[33]

To the Germans, this seemed a miracle. They had accomplished in five weeks in 1940 what they had been unable to do in fifty-two months in the earlier war. In many respects, this success marked a return to traditional German notions. As Napoleon had noted, a nation's military policy is dictated by its geography, which for Germany meant a preference for quick decisions through battles of annihilation. The German assumption had virtually always been that its forces would be inferior to those of the enemy, so personal qualities, such as skillful leadership, top-notch training, and adept operational maneuvering on the battlefield, had to trump material inferiority. The First World War, in which command skills had been subordinated to the mere accumulation of artillery shells, had seemingly changed this calculus of victory. Ironically, the post-war restrictions on the German military forced a revival in operational thinking and an emphasis on quality leadership as decisive factors. Nothing distinguished Allied and German commanders in 1940 more than their command methods. The cumbersome, methodical manner of the Allied high command, with its obsessive issuing of orders down to the smallest detail that left junior officers unable to react to the dictates of the rapidly changing battlefield, amazed German officers. By contrast, Auftragstaktik specified what the mission was, but not how it was to be accomplished. Of necessity officers on the spot would have to seize the initiative, make decisions rapidly and on their own, and exploit any opportunities even without specific orders from above. They would also have to lead from the front to maintain control of a constantly changing battlefield. German commanders would make up for what they lacked in mass with speed. Given this ingrained infrastructure of operational thinking, it was perhaps not surprising that even generals who thought such a mobile war of movement could not be waged successfully in France quickly embraced it once its efficacy had been shown.[34]

While much of this marked a return to traditional German methods, the all-out emphasis on the operational breakthrough, itself the result of a further refinement of tactics used at the end of the First World War, appeared more daring, especially since it seemed to flout the evident lesson of trench warfare, the innate superiority of the defense. To break the stalemate and restart the war of movement, the Germans developed a tactical approach that emphasized independent, flexible maneuvering. Enemy strongpoints should be avoided as much as possible; the attacking force should flow around obstacles, then advance quickly into rear areas without concern for the flanks or attempting the immediate destruction of enemy troop concentrations. These spearhead units were instead to threaten enemy supply lines and command centers, sow confusion, create panic, and, like water trickling through a small gap in a dam, create an "expanding torrent" that eventually collapsed frontline defenses. Instead of systematic, planned battles, the Germans sought to create and then exploit chaos, reinforcing local success in a continuous, uninterrupted battle. Although used with some success in March 1918, the overall impact of this approach had been blunted by the absence of the means by which to convert this tactical break-in into an operational breakthrough that would yield decisive victory.[35]

In 1940 the effective combined use of tanks and aircraft, coordinated and directed through new means of communication, especially the radio, made good this gap. The Germans created a "total system" that not only emphasized teamwork between tanks, aircraft, infantry, and artillery, but also stressed speed, movement, maneuver, and low-level individual initiative. Rather than a methodical battle constrained by reliance on the slow pace of infantry and artillery, they stressed swift movement by motorized and mechanized formations, supported and protected by "flying artillery," the Stuka dive-bomber. This approach allowed them to think again in terms of the decisive breakthrough, with speed and surprise used as psychological weapons to sow confusion and panic in the enemy. Ideally, it aimed to avoid destruction of the enemy in costly pocket battles, instead unhinging him and encouraging him to stop fighting. It worked to perfection in France, with its relatively short distances, good road network, and ability to pin the enemy against the sea. The Allies, trapped in thinking governed by the set-piece materiel battles of the Great War, could not cope with an opponent who seemed to disregard the basic rules and whose system evidently consisted of little more than a mad dash forward. The more chaotic the battle became, the less the Allies seemed able to respond. In relying on their tactical and operational skill to produce order out of chaos, the Germans seemingly had created a new, war-winning doctrine that could produce victory from material inferiority. In the blaze of glory of 1940, though, they failed to consider what might happen, as later in Russia, if an enemy refused to surrender, so that pockets of resistance would have to be reduced in costly fighting.[36]

Although this latter point crucially affected future events, the key to victory in France ultimately lay in the shift in the focal point of attack. If the Germans had gone with the original plan, and slammed into onrushing Allied forces in Belgium, the result might well have been stalemate and a debilitating war of attrition. Instead, Gamelin's gamble failed, as the very best Allied divisions and their operational reserve rushed north, only to be cut off and trapped. In both 1914 and 1918 the Germans had come close, but ultimately failed to separate the British and French armies; in 1940 they succeeded, with devastating consequences. The German triumph thus resulted as much from a demoralized opponent unwilling to offer resistance as from a new conceptual method of war. Moreover, everything had been gambled upfront on a knockout blow. Virtually all available frontline aircraft had been employed in the initial assault – the Allies, anticipating a longer struggle, had withheld large portions of their air forces – as well as all Panzer units; the Wehrmacht, like the French, had no armored reserves. After an earlier dazzling military triumph over France, Friedrich Nietzsche had warned his countrymen that a victory can be more dangerous than a defeat, especially one whose sources were misconstrued. And so it was in 1940; the sensational triumph in France transformed the generals' thinking. Blitzkrieg had earlier been viewed as an opportunistic "torrent of action" to unhinge the enemy on an operational level. Now it was elevated to a strategic principle: the encirclement battle as a war-winning method. While Blitzkrieg had proven successful in Poland and France, it was less likely to be effective in the USSR, given the size of the country, the absence of a clearly decisive Schwerpunkt, deficiencies in German forces, Stalin's systemic control, and the doggedness of the average Russian soldier. The generals, though, thought they now had a war-winning formula that could overturn the importance of numbers and economic power, while avoiding the egregious loss of life that had dissipated German strength in the First World War. Germany, it seemed, could finally break free of its geographic and strategic dilemma. In so thinking, the generals ignored the obvious: the most spectacular encirclement battle in history, Cannae, was only a passing triumph and, in the end, Rome had defeated Hannibal. Even Clausewitz, the supposed apostle of the quick strike, warned against making the outcome of a war totally dependent on one decisive battle of encirclement.[37]

For Hitler, the victory over France seemed both a personal triumph and a vindication, a perception aided by the immediate Nazi propaganda efforts to portray the victory as a result of the personal work of the Führer. He brushed aside his anxieties and hesitations, convinced that his inspired insights and good luck were signs of his martial genius. Brauchitsch, completely browbeaten, declared him "the first soldier of the German Reich," while the sycophantic Keitel transformed him from Führer to "the greatest field marshal of all time." Göring, not to be outdone, credited the Führer alone with the creation of Blitzkrieg strategy, gushing, "Adolf Hitler's genius as a warlord caused a revolution in warfare in that it breached strategic principles that had been held sacrosanct until now." He also fused the political and military in Hitler, claiming that he, like Frederick the Great, "combined in his person the wisdom of the statesman and the genius of the Feldherr." Certain that his talents matched those of his generals, and with his distrust of OKH growing as a result of Halder's efforts to undermine him, Hitler now proved even less willing to listen to their advice. His triumphs also overwhelmed his generals' hesitations. Even a traditionalist officer such as Quartermaster-General Wagner, who praised Halder's behind-the-scenes management of the battle, nonetheless credited Hitler alone for the triumph, "for without his will it never would have come to such an action." In all, he thought it a "masterful interplay between military and political leadership that no one but the Führer could do." Others were bought off with promotions, material rewards (such as estates or stipends), and even bribes. In praising the many, of course, Hitler assured that no single general would be identified with the great triumph in the west. In the summer of 1940, Hitler was at the height of his power and prestige, with most generals, whose mood since 1938 had vacillated wildly between despair and elation, now confident that the war could be won. Giddy with success, they buried their reservations and accepted Hitler's – admittedly unorthodox – military genius.[38]

Ironically, both Hitler and Halder believed the outcome of the French campaign had confirmed their judgments and actions although, in a further paradox, the situation in the summer of 1940 resulted from failed expectations by both. Hitler had gambled that the Western powers would not go to war over Poland, so had been forced to improvise. For his part, Halder sought to obstruct a premature Western offensive, toyed with a coup, doubted the prospects of success in the west, was uncertain and without any conception of how to proceed, and ultimately (but only after Hitler's decision) adopted the offensive plan of his bitter rival. As for Hitler, bold as he had been in planning, with his flair for surprise, instinct for the weak point of the enemy, and appreciation of the use of tanks and aircraft, in the implementation, as a military leader, he was anxious, uncertain, panicky, and afraid of his own success – all of which encouraged Halder to believe that, as in Poland, he should be left to manage the campaign.

But it was also true that Hitler had created the conditions necessary for victory, had pushed the campaign in the west against the doubts of his generals, and appeared confirmed in his overall strategic concept. Moreover, Hitler had also demonstrated a talent for reading situation maps. "Many times," he told his intimates in October 1941, "I would go over to the map room at three in the morning to study the relief map." This skill, though impressing his general staff officers, masked a latent conflict, for it enabled him to visualize the unfolding battles from his headquarters and thus interfere more readily in their conduct. The more Hitler interfered in operational matters, though, the more Halder resorted to an indirect form of exerting influence by quietly obstructing him. This proved a problematic and self-defeating form of leadership, not least because Hitler, with a good portion of the officer corps, had come to accept the infallibility of his own judgment. He neither could nor wanted to disavow this myth, for he saw in it a confirmation of his own superiority. It destroyed all sense of his own limits or capabilities; while Halder grudgingly accepted Hitler's strategic dominance in hope of retaining operational autonomy, the Führer increasingly believed he was best suited to conduct operations as well. It seemed to Hitler that he had been correct all along and that it had been so easy to be right. He had not had to have any special training or skills in order to conceive the key to success; his intuitive understanding and flash of insight had sufficed. He had, he said in October 1941, become a Feldherr "against my own will. If I deal with military matters, it's only because at the moment there is nobody who can do it better than I can." Germany, he complained, had no Moltke, no commander who was a "military genius." In the absence of that, he himself would fill the void as de facto Feldherr.[39]

Ultimately, neither Dunkirk nor the complete neglect of any plan for an invasion of Britain constituted the major fault of Blitzkrieg in France. After all, it would have been almost impossible to predict Churchill's defiance in the face of all odds (although Hitler had an inkling in 1938). Even if the British Expeditionary Force had been destroyed at Dunkirk, the Germans still had no certain prospect for success in any attempt to ship invasion troops across the Channel, given British control of the sea and at least

equality in the air. Thus, although Blitzkrieg had been a brilliant operational success, victory on the continent could not provide the leverage to
force Britain from the war, while it made a more activist American response
virtually certain. The ultimate flaw, and one that again emphasized the
operational-economic divide in the German leadership, was that success in
France failed to secure the resources necessary for Germany to make the
leap to great power status. That still required the conquest of Lebensraum
in the east. France had been a necessary preliminary, but that's all it was.

Hitler clearly understood that Germany possessed insufficient means to
assure a successful invasion; indeed, in June 1940, the Italian foreign
minister Ciano thought he resembled a successful gambler who "has made
a big scoop and would like to get up from the table, risking nothing more
. . . He speaks with a reserve and a perspicacity which, after such a victory,
are truly astonishing." Hitler, in fact, expected the British to agree to a negotiated peace. After all, he remarked in July, with unintended irony, "the
outcome of the war had already been decided", but London was still "not
aware of it." He was thus uncertain, indecisive, and had no answer, no bold
plans or ideas, when Churchill refused to play his assigned role and enter
into peace talks. For a time Hitler put his hopes in an alleged "peace camp"
in London, but German soundings went unanswered. Fearing the risks
involved, he shrank from an invasion, an attitude shared by the navy leadership. Unlike Halder, who regarded England as the principal enemy, he
saw an invasion as only a final expedient – one he was reluctant to undertake – and, again unlike Halder, he did not consider defeat of Britain a
necessary precondition for the later invasion of the Soviet Union. Nor, in
truth, did he want to destroy the British Empire, believing that this would
only benefit the United States and Japan. Hitler thus saw the Battle of
Britain as an alternative to an invasion as much as a prelude. Although air
superiority was the key precondition for an actual landing, Hitler seems to
have seen the aerial combat more in psychological than in operational
terms. As it became apparent that the Luftwaffe could neither compel
London to negotiate nor clear the way for an invasion, Hitler drew the
obvious lesson and lost interest in the project. Nothing would destroy his
invincible image as rapidly as a botched invasion, so he decided not to take
a chance. Although justifiably skeptical and realistic enough not to risk a
direct attack on Britain with meager prospects of success, its failure to
materialize nonetheless left Germany's dilemma unresolved.[40]

As Hitler had indicated on any number of occasions since late May, his
ultimate aim still lay in securing Lebensraum in the east, but the question
now was how to proceed in the interim. England would not concede, the

America factor gained in importance with Roosevelt's increasing commitment to the British, the Soviet Union was growing stronger, western Europe provided inadequate resources to prosecute a long war (and, in fact, was a drain on food, coal, and oil), and increasing dependence on Russian deliveries of essential foodstuffs and raw materials exposed Germany to economic blackmail. Increasingly fearful of a long war, he believed time, as always, to be against him, especially given the hugely ambitious rearmament program that Roosevelt had put before Congress in mid-May. Aware that the United States would not be ready for action on the European continent before mid-1942, and that Germany had a temporary window of opportunity, Hitler grew increasingly impatient. He could only achieve his objectives through conquest of Lebensraum in the east, not by the destruction of the British Empire. Already in the summer of 1940, then, Hitler, to whom Russia was "the great problem of Europe," had returned to his ideological fixation. The Soviet Union had to be destroyed as soon as possible. He ordered the army to begin planning for an invasion of the USSR, and he did so not primarily as a means of knocking Britain out of the war, but because his ideology made no sense otherwise. If London had suddenly made peace it would have made no difference. Hitler still would have launched an attack on the Soviet Union as a matter of principle and because he had to attack now, when the time was right. Ultimately, he believed, only securing Lebensraum in the east would liberate the Reich from its resource dilemma and afford Germany its chance at world power status.[41]

Unable to strike immediately against the USSR, though, in the meantime Hitler pursued a half-hearted attempt to rid Germany of its British enemy, in the vague hope that something would work. Although possessing long-term goals, Hitler was an opportunist in terms of achieving them; now he seemed out of opportunities. While the Führer, typically, vacillated and hesitated to make a decision, his subordinates outlined two strategies aimed at negating the Anglo-American threat. The first, associated primarily with Foreign Minister Ribbentrop and based on Hitler's belief, shared by others, that Britain's obstinate stance depended on continued aid from America, sought to neutralize both by erecting a "continental bloc" against them. The conclusion on 27 September of the Tripartite Pact between Germany, Italy, and Japan sought to achieve part of this aim by using rising Japanese power to distract and negate American influence in Europe. An isolated Britain would then be neutralized, or forced from the war, through the creation of a continental European alliance, under German direction, of Spain, France, Italy, and the USSR. Given Hitler's resolve to achieve Lebensraum at the expense of the Soviet Union, any alliance with the latter would only be tactical and temporary, but if Stalin could for a time be deflected to other historic areas of Russian expansion – India and Persia – this would pressure Britain and provide Germany a breathing space. The other, somewhat complementary scheme, since it also aimed at knocking Britain out of the war, sought indirectly to pressure the British through a peripheral Mediterranean strategy. By seizing Gibraltar and the Suez Canal, Axis control of the Mediterranean would be assured, oil from the Middle East would be made available to Germany, Turkey might be brought into the war on Germany's side, the raw materials of the Balkans would be secured, and control of the Iberian peninsula and Atlantic islands would push German power westward, threatening American supplies to England. Its advocates, primarily Admiral Raeder (and to an extent Göring and Halder), perceived the Mediterranean as the pivot of the British Empire – a defeat there might well deal Britain a mortal blow and force it from the war.[42]

Hitler saw things differently. Given the level of mistrust between the Axis partners, the paucity of available German forces, and the limited port facilities at Tripoli, any swift move into North Africa in the fall of 1940 was problematic. Nor, given their geographic location, and in view of their force limitations, could the Germans entertain any realistic idea of seizing the crucial oil fields of Iraq and Iran, let alone the Baku fields; and, if by chance they did take some or all of these fields, they faced the immense difficulty of repairing what would presumably be wrecked facilities and oil pipelines, and then of transporting the oil to European refineries against the opposition of the British Mediterranean fleet. Not even the loss of the Suez Canal would necessarily have proved a war-winning blow against the British. America, and its ties to the dominions, would enable Britain to carry on; defeat in the Mediterranean would have been embarrassing but not fatal. To Hitler, the Mediterranean would merely drain and scatter German forces without providing any decisive results in ending the war; operations there thus served a defensive purpose, to secure his rear. The same could be said for the idea of seizing strategic points in West Africa and the Atlantic, such as Dakar, Casablanca, the Canary Islands, and the Azores, a move that would serve the dual aims of enhancing German security by pushing its defense zone to the west and hindering any American action against the periphery of the Nazi empire, while providing bases for future action against the United States. Determined to achieve a continental empire and now under no illusion about Britain's willingness to make peace, Hitler pursued the Mediterranean strategy primarily to secure his southern flank when he turned east against the Soviet Union. The key weapon in his arsenal, the army, had to be used in Russia to force a decision before

Germany found itself squeezed between east and west. Although Hitler in late May 1941 betrayed some misgivings that he had overlooked a grand strategic opportunity, the true losers in the Mediterranean were the British, who in late 1940 and early 1941 had, to their later regret, squandered an opportunity to secure North Africa and forestall any German campaign there, with all of the later drain on limited British resources.[43]

Hitler's analysis was both logical and consistent with his thinking, but again undercut OKH intentions. Halder strongly supported action in the Mediterranean on the grounds that it represented a concentration of German forces designed "to force England to understand that the war is lost." The OKH chief envisioned a comprehensive series of campaigns in Gibraltar, Libya, Suez, Anatolia, and the Near East that would climax in a gigantic pincer operation directed against the British position in the Mediterranean. Brauchitsch, too, had been enthusiastic, as had Admiral Raeder, who in September 1940 urged Hitler to consider a Mediterranean alternative. Even before his key December decision to turn Germany against Russia, though, Hitler had made it clear that his goals in the Mediterranean were purely defensive: securing key strategic or economic areas and safeguarding Germany's flank. Hitler, then, turned against the Soviet Union not in order to end British resistance, but in spite of it, as the culmination of the ideas that had motivated him since the beginning of his political career.[44]

In the event, even these limited aims exceeded German abilities. Unwilling to commit extensive German resources to the area (and lacking the requisite naval and air forces in any case), Hitler made the realization of his strategy dependent on a coalition of nations with mutually antagonistic goals that could be achieved, he admitted to Mussolini, only by "a gigantic fraud," primarily at France's expense. Perhaps sensing the impossibility of his goal, or simply aware that the time to hammer together such an unlikely coalition had passed, Hitler's late October diplomatic offensive achieved nothing of consequence. In July 1940, Vichy France and Spain might have been pressured to assume their assigned roles; by October, neither Marshal Pétain nor General Franco was quite so certain of British defeat, so preferred to hedge their bets. Facing massive Anglo-American economic pressure and dependent on imports that Hitler could neither guarantee nor supply, the Caudillo remained noncommittal, a stance that effectively doomed any joint seizure of Gibraltar. Likewise, although Hitler professed admiration for Pétain, his talks with the aged president proved no more productive. Since both Spain and Italy coveted French colonies in Africa, the "deception" could be pulled off only if Hitler was prepared to make generous concessions to France in the matter of the occupation, as well as guarantee French acquisition of British colonies after a peace settlement. Since he was not prepared to grant the former, and could not ensure the latter, he had no leverage over Pétain, who also preferred to await developments. Nor could Hitler make any substantive concessions to Spain or France without offending Italy. Thus it was that after his talks with Franco – a meeting that left both leaders visibly irritated – and Pétain he went to meet Mussolini with the intention of assuaging the Duce's anger over a possible Franco-Spanish-German collaboration at Italy's expense, as well as to prevent any Italian attack on Greece. Hitler's arrival in Florence on 28 October, though, came too late. Fueled by resentment at his perceived slights, as well as a desire to play an independent role in the alliance, Italian troops had invaded Greece. Although annoyed by the Duce's actions, Hitler could do little under the circumstance of impending Axis disaster than refrain from criticism and offer Mussolini German help.[45]

Developments since the fall of France had clearly perplexed the German leadership. Its attempt to retain control of events had so far proven unsuccessful. The Luftwaffe had failed to achieve the aerial superiority necessary for an invasion of Britain, Hitler had been unable to produce the political conditions for a successful Mediterranean strategy, and time still worked against him. In a profusion of ironies, Hitler, the leader who had roiled European politics for nearly a decade, now pursued cautious and defensive aims in the Mediterranean, preferring stability to the more adventuresome ideas of some of his generals. Having unleashed the dynamic of war, though, he discovered he could not control it, as Mussolini and Churchill disrupted his plans. Both had offensive ambitions: the former to win his own glory and imperial expansion and the latter to distract Germany and defeat Italy, the weakest of the Axis nations. Hitler had been slow to realize both the depth of Mussolini's pique and London's determination to carry on in what it now viewed as an all-or-nothing struggle for existence. He thus showed none of the audacity, boldness, or keen psychological insight in the Mediterranean that had been on display in Poland, Norway, and France. As he returned to Germany, then, Hitler was more convinced than ever that he had been correct all along – the solution to Germany's dilemma lay in conquest in the east. He retained some fleeting hope that Franco might yet be persuaded to cooperate in seizing Gibraltar, but his attention focused chiefly on what he had preferred to do all along, wage war against Russia. If defeat in the Mediterranean would not force Britain from the war, he could see little point in devoting scarce time to creating the necessary political coalition or diverting valuable resources to that area. Decisive victory, he believed, could only be achieved through an attack on Russia. That would mark a return to his original strategic and ideological focus, while a defeat of the Soviet Union would have the beneficial side effect of knocking Britain – so he thought – out of the war.[46]

There still remained the other option outlined by Ribbentrop – a continental bloc that included the USSR – but Hitler, ever wary of Stalin, did not put much hope in it. Although normally attracted by grandiose geopolitical schemes, he seemed skeptical of Ribbentrop's vision of a Eurasian alliance with the Soviet Union, even if it offered at least temporary autarky. Troubled by Stalin's war against Finland and pressure on Romania, concerned by Germany's dependence on Russian supplies of food and raw materials, and fearful of Soviet economic blackmail, Hitler resented the leverage Stalin had over him. "Every weakness in the position of the Axis," he complained, "brings a push by the Russians." Even though he had mentioned to Mussolini his hope of bringing the USSR into the recently formed anti-British front, he remained convinced that Russia was the "great problem" of Europe and seemed to his aides depressed and uncertain, as if "he [did] not know how it would turn out." On 12 November, the very day Soviet Foreign Minister Molotov arrived in Berlin for a two-day discussion on bringing the USSR into the Tripartite Pact, Hitler issued Directive No. 18. Although it laid out various possibilities for action in the Mediterranean, and noted the inauguration of political discussions with Molotov designed to clarify the Soviet position, it nonetheless concluded with Hitler's order to continue preparations for an attack on the USSR, "regardless of the outcome of these discussions." In the event, the meeting with Molotov did not go well, a result that seemed to please the Führer. He had viewed the talks as a chance to gauge Moscow's intentions, to see whether Germany and the Soviet Union stood "back to back or chest to chest." He now had his answer, confirming his suspicions that German and Soviet positions were incompatible. Hitler clearly believed that the Mediterranean strategy, by delaying the confrontation with Russia, posed unacceptable risks. Order in Europe demanded the liquidation of the Soviet Union.[47]

By mid-November 1940, then, Hitler had reverted to the view he had expressed that summer: German interests would most optimally be served by a quick military solution in the east. In order to secure his western and southern flanks against any Anglo-American action, plans were drawn up for a seizure of Gibraltar and efforts intensified to persuade Spain to enter the war, although by mid-December Hitler realized that, given Franco's continued obstinacy, nothing was likely to come of such exertions. As a consequence, the Germans turned their attention to the more pressing concern of stabilizing the Italian position and safeguarding supplies of raw materials from the Balkans. Italian failures in Greece and North Africa had gone far beyond an embarrassment; by opening the possibility of a British presence in the Balkans, Mussolini's misadventures threatened the entire southern flank of any German invasion of Russia and forced Hitler to react. By early January 1941 he had resolved to introduce German forces into both North Africa and Greece to back-stop his Axis partner. Even as preparations intensified for Operation Marita, the invasion of Greece, and the insertion of troops into North Africa, the Germans kept imperatives in the east firmly in mind: all these operations had to be completed in time to allow for the invasion of the Soviet Union. British dispatch of troops to Greece, then, determined the timing of the German action, but was not its cause.[48]

In the event, the bold German operations in Yugoslavia, Greece, and Crete proved spectacularly successful (and reinforced both the Wehrmacht's and Hitler's reputation for swift, explosive actions), but these were largely defensive operations designed to protect the German flank, not the first step in an aggressive move against Britain in the eastern Mediterranean and Suez. Similarly, Field Marshal Rommel's successes in North Africa made for great theater and provided splendid newsreel footage, but were largely irrelevant since Hitler was unwilling to follow them up. His focus fixed firmly on the Soviet Union, his hope for the Mediterranean was merely that Rommel and the Italians could stabilize the situation on a shoe-string budget. Although large German forces were not committed to the Mediterranean, this still represented a dissipation of men and materiel that could better have been used in the USSR. Ironically, then, even as Hitler was skeptical of any Mediterranean involvement precisely because he feared a dispersal of force, events in this area, largely out of his control, caused it eventually to become an even greater drain; for Germany, the Mediterranean proved more of a dead end than a strategic opportunity.[49]

By late spring 1941, Hitler had secured his southern flank but had been forced to admit that German power was insufficient to fully resolve the Mediterranean question or force Great Britain from the war. Although he had largely left the planning and conduct of these campaigns to others, he still exerted a decisive strategic influence, and the operations bore his stamp of boldness, audacity, willingness to take risks, and skillful execution. Nothing that transpired had challenged the image of the triumphant Feldherr first achieved in France. Nor, despite later claims, had the Balkan campaign fatally disrupted the timing of the invasion of the Soviet Union. It had strained German logistics, and added wear and tear to German armored vehicles, but it was not the cause of any delay in launching Operation Barbarossa. That resulted from production difficulties, as well as the fact that, due to a late thaw, most of the western USSR was under water. When Germany turned decisively against the Soviet Union, then, Hitler (and his generals) fully expected to achieve the final victory that had eluded them to date.

In January 1941, Hitler confessed to Mussolini that he felt like a hunter with only one bullet left in his gun, so it had to hit the mark. Although it is often argued that, in view of economic and manpower disparities, Germany had no chance of winning the war, the fatal Allied coalition did not come into being until December 1941, so for a time it seemed that the bullet might yet strike true and German victory might be possible. In retrospect, Hitler devoted an amazing amount of time and effort from 1939 to mid-1940 to delivering speeches to his generals designed to convince them of exactly that point, to rouse them to support of his policies and actions. As perhaps befitting the almost messianic role he now assumed, his speeches revealed a compulsive need to evangelize. In this cycle of talks with his generals, the recurring themes are clear: his intention to inform and prepare his generals for a war – not merely for Lebensraum but a racial war for global supremacy – is apparent, as is the fact that this was not a sudden impulse or a fit of madness, but a long thought-out calculation. "The earth," he said any number of times between 1919 and 1944 with only slight variations, "is there for whoever will take it." Clearly evident, as well, was Hitler's intention to assert the primacy of politics, to use the military as his instrument, one whose generals had to assume the role of the ideological fighter, ready at all times to obey and follow the Führer. After all, as he had remarked years earlier, a battle plan could not be drawn up without the inspiration and imagination of a genius behind it. Finally, there was the theme of compulsion, fate – he had to solve the problem of Lebensraum now, through war, before Germany's enemies grew stronger. After the triumph in France, most German generals mistakenly believed that they had uncovered the means to achieve hegemonic status, and the actual realization of it would be relatively easy – and nothing that had transpired in North Africa or the Balkans had substantially shaken that conviction.[50]

6

The Lure of Lebensraum

In February 1933 a clearly nervous Adolf Hitler had appeared before a small group of prominent generals at the home of the head of the army to outline his vision of the German future. Barely eight years later, on 30 March 1941, roughly a hundred top officers, arriving on a late Sunday morning, were led through the Court of Honor of Albert Speer's monumental New Reich Chancellery, its very size a suggestion of both German rebirth and claim to a preeminent status in Europe. After entering a door flanked on either side by Arno Breker sculptures of two muscular men, one holding a sword and the other a torch – representing the armed forces and the Nazi Party – they crossed the splendid Mosaic Hall, then passed the main entrance to the Round Hall, again flanked by two Breker statues, the Fighter and the Genius. The group then traversed the 467-foot-long, 38-foot-wide, and 30-foot-high Marble Gallery – twice the length of the Hall of Mirrors at Versailles – with its walls covered in tapestries meant to evoke images of German fame and glory. On the way to the Reception Hall, they passed Hitler's office, with its 20-foot-high door topped by a cartouche of his initials done in the style of Albrecht Dürer. The symbolism of this journey could not have been lost on the generals: the political genius of Hitler, unyielding faith in the party, and the strength of the Wehrmacht had, in less than a decade, transformed Germany from a weak and broken nation into a dominant power. No less important was its staging: no longer the supplicant going to the generals to gain their trust, he was now the Führer, in complete control, letting it be known what he expected of them.[1]

Hitler had over the years frequently addressed his generals to cajole, convince, and convert them. In finally moving to realize his aims, this speech was different, and not merely for its sheer radicalism. Less the military impresario than the coolly calculating strategist, he had little need to persuade his listeners of the necessity of an attack on the Soviet Union, an action with which most agreed; instead, he sought to reassure them that the time was propitious, that they had little to fear from a two-front war. The war in the west, he assured the generals, was essentially finished, a statement replete with both insight and illusion. In the short term, Hitler's argument was cogent: the British could do little other than dispense pinpricks designed more to promote Italian collapse than confront Germany. For all his acuity, though, he could never quite grasp that his aims were so radical and far-reaching, and in their intent to destroy the existing order so menacing, that the British, as the foremost upholder of that system, would never allow him a free hand in eastern Europe. Britain fought on, the Führer argued, primarily because of American support, which was true, but as the other power most vested in retention of the existing order the United States was also bound to oppose Germany. American aid, though, would not be substantial for another year or so, which to Hitler meant that Germany still had time to defeat the USSR if it acted immediately, before a Western Front could become a meaningful reality. Herein lay the second illusion. German intelligence knew remarkably little about the Red Army but, based on its limited information, Stalin's purge of senior commanders, and the poor Soviet performance against Finland, it initially judged its future adversary a "colossus of clay" unequal to the mighty Wehrmacht. In particular, underestimation of both the size and equipment of the Red Army, as well as the economic strength of the USSR, caused German planners to misjudge Soviet ability to absorb a punishing blow and keep fighting.[2]

Ironically, Hitler seemed more attuned to this reality than many of his generals. In early January 1941 he had pointedly warned against underestimating Russia and Stalin. The Soviet leader, he claimed, had gambled on Germany being bled to death by the Western powers in 1939; if not for the triumph in the west, the Russians would now be in Germany. In hinting at the necessity of an attack against the USSR as a sort of preventive war against the threatening "shadow" of a "Russian-Asiatic danger," Hitler struck a responsive chord in the officers present, but he did not try to sugarcoat the difficulties of the upcoming campaign. He left no doubt that the Red Army possessed modern armament: he judged Russian tanks favorably and noted that the Red Army had the strongest tank force in the world, although Halder dismissed the bulk of them as obsolete. Hitler also regarded the Red Air Force as formidable. "Our air force," he noted soberly, "cannot eliminate [the] enemy air force" in a single blow, as in France; the huge space of the USSR simply would not allow it. The Luftwaffe would thus have to coordinate its activities closely with the ground operations. The goal of the attack would be to "crush the armed forces, break up [the] state," but the Führer acknowledged the "problem of Russia's vastness: [the] enormous expanse requires concentration on decisive points. Massed planes and tanks must be brought forward to bear on decisive points." The enemy would, he thought, not withdraw, allowing for their rapid destruction. With a nod to his own particular economic concerns, Hitler emphasized that Soviet "armaments factories had to be destroyed or occupied . . . and cut off from oil." In all, the Russians would prove a "tenacious adversary," but one "without leadership."[3]

In the second part of his speech Hitler made clear that the two facets of his war against the USSR, the military and the ideological, were different sides of the same coin; the ultimate end of the racial struggle that had broken out in 1939 also determined the means to be used. It would be, he told his generals, a "clash of two ideologies" that necessitated a "war of annihilation." Here, he harked back to his earliest notions of total war: since politics aimed ultimately at safeguarding a people's vital interests, and he had defined these as the securing of Lebensraum and destruction of Jewish-Bolshevism, a war for German survival had to be fought with any and all means. The traditional military notion of destruction of enemy forces would, as Ludendorff had advocated in the mid-1930s, be extended to encompass annihilation of the enemy nation. Bolshevism, the Führer thundered, was tantamount to "asocial criminality . . . an enormous danger for our future." He implored the officers to "forget the concept of comradeship between soldiers. A communist is no comrade . . . We do not wage war to preserve the criminal enemy." The generals, he stressed, had to overcome their scruples in this "fight for our survival"; no false humanity should hinder the execution of the necessary tasks. Bolshevik commissars and the communist intelligentsia had to be destroyed. It was, he suggested, to be a sort of colonial war, one fought against an alien culture, a war of conquest that demanded a "hard understanding." With the relatively favorable situation facing Germany, he could not, he concluded, leave this urgent task to future generations.[4]

Although he claimed that his decision was not easily made, this was mere posturing; shorn of its expansive and ideological elements, Hitler's program made no sense. Autarky had long preoccupied him as the only way by which Germany could be competitive in the world of global empires and continent-states. Through ruthless economic exploitation and harsh rule the vast expanse of European Russia, he thought, would be the key to a large, integrated economic area that would provide prosperity and economic security for the Greater German Reich. "The struggle for hegemony in the world will be decided in favor of Europe by the possession of the Russian space," he declared to his entourage. "It will make Europe into an impregnable fortress, the most blockade-proof place on Earth." The United States could then "get lost, as far as we are concerned." He remained obsessed with the American example, though, in October sketching his vision of the future: "Here in the east a similar process will repeat itself for a second time as in the conquest of America." The Volga, he insisted, indicating the German colonial empire would be in the east, and not in Africa, must be "our Mississippi . . . not the Niger," then "Europe – and not America – will be the land of unlimited possibilities." His consistent social Darwinism, in fact, provided Hitler with all the justification he needed for his actions. In order to secure the existence of the Volk, all measures were acceptable: a culturally superior people denied adequate living space had an obligation to take what it needed. For Germany to live, others had to die. His vision of making Germany "the most autarkic state in the world" could be realized only by defeating the Soviet Union. Shaped profoundly by his own experience of war, Hitler saw in it the essence of human activity; what her first sexual encounter with a man was for a woman, war meant to him. Living meant killing. "Life is a cruel struggle," he declared, whose only object was the preservation of the species. "Coming into being, existing, and passing away, there's always a killing. Everything that is born must later die." By making sacrifices today, he insisted, future Germans would be spared. Far from an act forced upon him, this was the culmination of his career as politician, and now, as military leader.[5]

Despite their later protestations of shock at the radical tasks demanded of them, Hitler was not leading his generals anywhere they were not willing to go, nor did any of those generals present express opposition. Although Hitler left the gathering immediately after his speech, the post-war claim of Brauchitsch and Halder that the leaders of the army groups – Bock, Leeb, and Rundstedt – rushed up to them in indignation and emphatically stated that "a war of this type would be intolerable" lack credulity. Bock, Leeb, and Halder mention nothing of the sort in their diaries, nor did Hoth or Walter Warlimont, in post-war statements, recall any discussion among the generals. At the lunch that followed, there was, in fact, remarkably little comment or grumbling. Bock's only criticism was that he was "not fully convinced that an Anglo-American landing is impossible." Indeed, the entire tenor of his diary entry suggests that he had been convinced, not repulsed, by Hitler's explanations, noting only that the "plans and goals" were "gigantic." An operational conference that afternoon that included, among others, Hitler, Halder, Bock, Leeb, Rundstedt, and

Guderian, also elicited no negative comments, Halder concluding laconically, "nothing new." Bock complained only of ambiguous instructions
from Halder, while noting mundanely that "the Führer appeared very . . .
concerned about my health." Far from any eruption of protest, the generals
fully accepted the validity of Hitler's assertions, both strategic and ideological. Heinrici, for example, had earlier noted, "It appears almost to be a
law that a war against Britain must lead to Russia. It was no different with
Napoleon." Nor was it merely on a functional level that Hitler's arguments
resonated. Like their Führer, the generals were convinced that an unbridgeable racial and ideological gulf separated National Socialist Germany and
communist Russia. Hitler's speech had shaken neither the conscience of
military leaders nor their trust in him. He had handled his generals with
great aplomb, ensuring their support for his life's goal, the showdown with
the Soviet Union.[6]

In the long, eleven-month planning and preparation phase of Barbarossa,
this remained the dominant theme. Not only was there little opposition to
the intended operation from his generals – at no time during this period
did fundamental disputes erupt between Hitler and his military leaders, as
in the months before the invasion of France – but there was, as well, remarkably little self-reflection on the German ability to defeat the USSR; the
generals just assumed they would. As the planning and decision-making
for this operation evolved over a period of months, they reflected complex
and competing motivations. The spectacular German victory in France had
obscured equally important geopolitical alterations in eastern Europe.
With attention riveted on the west, Stalin had acted quickly to secure his
territorial gains under the Nazi–Soviet Pact. Soviet action against Finland
and the Baltic states was to be expected, but the move to annex the Romanian
regions of Bessarabia and Northern Bukovina stoked German fears that
Stalin's ambitions extended to the vital Romanian oil fields. They also raised
uncomfortable memories of German dependence in an earlier war on
outside sources of raw materials. For now, Russia proved a reliable supplier,
but the longer-term prospects of continued cooperation seemed dim.
Stalin, after all, had originally gambled that the 1939 pact would entice
Germany into a war of attrition with the West from which he would profit,
while the massive buildup of the Red Army not only seemed aimed at
Germany but also threatened to consume the very raw materials they
needed. Hitler, aware of his own duplicity, was only too quick to see it in
others. The German war economy, he fretted, could not "become dependent
on forces or powers over which we have no influence." Nor did he leave any
doubt as to which power he was referring. "Every weakness in the position

of the Axis," he complained, "brings a push by the Russians . . . They utilize every opportunity to weaken the Axis position."[7]

In the event, though, it was not Hitler but Halder who initiated the movement of German forces to the east; indeed, at times it seemed that OKH was more eager for action than the Führer. Halder was a staunch anticommunist concerned by the threat raised by Soviet actions, as well as increasingly in accord with the Führer's notion that British obstinacy was based on its hopes in Russia. Seeing the need for "striking power in the east," on 26 June 1940 he ordered the transfer of the 18th Army to Poland. A week later, he instructed Army HQ to prepare a plan that envisaged the possibility of a limited preventive strike, perhaps as early as the autumn, if German intelligence identified a threatening Soviet buildup. Hitler's thoughts had not gotten that far, as at the end of June he still hoped for "an understanding with England." As for the east, that was a task he might tackle "in ten years' time." This attitude clearly persisted into mid-July. After a conference on 13 July, Halder noted:

> The Führer is greatly puzzled by Britain's persisting unwillingness to make peace. He sees the answer (as we do) in Britain's hope on Russia, and therefore counts on having to compel her . . . to agree to peace. Actually that is much against his grain . . . [for] a military defeat of Britain will bring about the disintegration of the British Empire. This would not be of any benefit to Germany. German blood would be shed to accomplish something that would benefit only Japan, the United States, and others.

Driven by his own logical assessment, Hitler seemed genuinely unable to accept that Britain refused to come to terms, finally bowing to the inevitable only on 20 July with Lord Halifax's definitive rejection of his peace proposal.[8]

Hitler's changing attitude was evident in a meeting the next day with Brauchitsch and Halder, although as yet he still had no firm view of the strategic situation. Like his military chiefs, Hitler intended to keep the initiative firmly in German hands, but was uncertain how to proceed. Clearly loath to launch a risky invasion of Britain at the height of his prestige, the Führer groped around for alternatives. Perceiving a threat to the German position, especially to Romanian oil, from possible Anglo-Russian agitation, his thoughts turned toward a settling of scores with the Soviets. Since Halder had already solicited plans for a limited offensive action that would force Russia "to recognize Germany's dominant position in Europe," he was able to present Hitler the outline of what was clearly more than a spoiling attack, since it aimed at the breakup of the Soviet state, but not yet the long-prophesied war for Lebensraum. Hitler, though, responded skeptically to both proposals for action. He explicitly criticized Halder's depiction of a cross-Channel invasion as a river crossing, noting that it was "not just a river crossing, but the crossing of a sea dominated by the enemy." Nor did he put much faith in the proposed action against the Russians, citing time, space, and weather factors.[9]

Still, once planted, the idea of an attack on the Soviet Union grew rapidly in his mind. To this point, Halder alone had promoted all such planning and preparation, with no formal guidelines or directives from Hitler. But the risk of a failed invasion of Britain, economic needs, growing awareness of dependence on Soviet supplies of raw materials, fear of blackmail by Stalin, time pressures, and the desire to retain the initiative all argued in favor of an attack on the USSR. So too did Hitler's ideological and strategic inclinations. Not only was a war for Lebensraum at the core of his racial-ideological program, but victory in the east might cut the Gordian knot and enable Germany to break its restraints. Yet again, he sought to resolve Germany's strategic dilemma through force. On 29 July, then, Hitler surprised everyone when he had Jodl inform OKW of his decision to invade the Soviet Union in May 1941 and ordered it to prepare plans. Two days later, he confirmed his decision at a major conference with his top military leaders at the Berghof, his mountain retreat. Destroying the Soviet Union, he now believed, would not only eliminate the threat of Judeo-Bolshevism and provide Germany with crucial economic resources, but would limit any American aid for Great Britain by vastly increasing Japanese power in the Pacific. To do so, Hitler proposed a two-pronged thrust toward Kiev in the south and the Baltic States and Leningrad in the north. Only then would a vast encircling movement be launched toward Moscow.[10]

Although in retrospect a watershed moment, at the time Hitler's decision resulted in anything but intensive and single-minded planning. He remained uncertain how to proceed, so reacted in typical fashion, exploring other options and procrastinating. In this interregnum, Hitler weighed a number of factors. At the forefront was the utmost importance of obtaining food and oil, with all the complex mix of memories of the First World War, the impact of the blockade, Germany's humiliating surrender, and the chaotic, revolutionary post-war years that this entailed. His ideological goals meant the destruction of the existing Anglo-American order and the construction of a New Order that was intended to reassert European world hegemony. This, though, entailed a war that put Germany at a disadvantage, since it had first to fight to secure the raw materials and food that were the precondition for success. Germany had to fight a short war because it could not win a long one. Hitler's strategic focus had always been how to break this conundrum.

Earlier annexations and conquests provided some additional resources, but they also imposed economic burdens that could be resolved only by gaining access to larger supplies. The triumph in France, then, had been more apparent than real, as Germany neither defeated Britain nor ensured necessary resources. Moreover, its significance would quickly fade if the war was not brought to a swift end, and Hitler saw no clear way to do that. The irony, he realized, was that both Germany and Britain were dependent on noncombatants, the Soviet Union and the United States. Hitler had no way to get at America and knock that prop from under the British, so explored other options – the Battle of Britain, the Mediterranean strategy, a continental bloc – all to no avail. At the same time, he recognized the significance of vastly increased American armaments output and feared that if he sat tight and did nothing, time would work against him and the war would become unwinnable. For all his victories, he had been unable to free himself, to break out of the cage of restrictions: Germany was never quite powerful enough to achieve his hegemonic goals.[11]

Nor was aid from the Soviet Union a long-term solution, since it still left Germany dependent; and, in any case, Hitler increasingly perceived Stalin's actions in the Baltic and southeastern Europe in 1940 as dangerous pressure on Germany. More crucially, his ideology always assumed the inevitability of war in the east. This was of vital importance since, in a sort of circular reasoning process, events reinforced his preconceived ideas. The logic of the situation seemed to be that the only way to end the war was to expand it in a campaign against the USSR, which he had always anticipated as necessary and which seemed less risky than an invasion of Britain. Thus, the political-military situation offered legitimacy and justification to his ideological vision. Hitler's analysis and logic was consistent: he had to take the initiative in order to secure crucial living space, which meant war with the Soviet Union. But this action, which formed the core component of his ideology, seemed to offer a way out of his dilemma; defeating the USSR would allow Germany resource independence and undercut American aid for Britain. What on the surface seemed opportunistic, improvisational, or grasping at straws thus fit easily within Hitler's larger strategic, ideological, and economic goals; he was not forced to do something he would not otherwise have done. For Hitler, the issue had always been what he desired most. There was no single factor pushing him to war with the USSR, but instead a complex mix of interwoven motives, ideological, political, economic, and strategic. All of them, though, reinforced his long-held idea: only through the conquest of territory in the east could Germany master the threats to its existence and emerge a world power. Hitler believed it absolutely essential for Germany's survival that it obtain Lebensraum; he thus willingly risked war against Russia rather than submit to what he saw as the alternative – Germany as a permanently second-rate power.

Having willed the end, he also had to will the means. Possessing insufficient means, though, Germany had to employ new methods; politics and military operations had to complement each other to enable an objectively inferior Germany to prevail. Since this would be a war for national existence, it had to be absolute, with no compromise. Hitler's decisions, therefore, were not those of a "mad dog," but were based on rational, if totally amoral, calculations of how to achieve his goals. He displayed a rather clear sense of German economic weaknesses and needs, as well as a keen appreciation of strategic realities and power relationships. Still, although clearsighted about many of the constraints on Germany, he was also a man mistrustful of his military advisors and too certain of his instincts. Nor was he resolutely critical enough about the deficiencies in the German armed forces, the problems of a war in the Soviet Union, and the limits of German strength. He and his generals believed the newly demonstrated power and efficacy of Blitzkrieg would sweep aside all difficulties. Ironically, in an early May 1941 speech, just six weeks before the German invasion, Stalin alluded to this pervasive over-confidence of German leaders, noting, in what might have been a revealing glimpse into his own mindset, "From the military point of view there is nothing special about the German army in terms of tanks, artillery, aviation ... [It] has become boastful, self-satisfied, and conceited ... [while] German leaders are already beginning to suffer from dizziness [of success]. They think they can do anything." In terms of equipment the German army had, he thought, fallen behind the Red Army, which itself was "amply supplied with equipment for modern battle."[12] Given the tremendous boost to his self-confidence by the victory over France, and now firmly convinced of his own genius, Hitler took little notice.

From the early planning stages neither the Führer nor his military leaders gave much thought to the possibility of defeat in the east. They began with the premise that they would prevail; after all, the new gospel of Blitzkrieg had proven the experts wrong in France. So it would be again; the only question was how best to proceed in terms of a Schwerpunkt. If the operational plan encompassed too large a theater of operations, the effort would disappear into thin air; too small, and the objective of the campaign would not be achieved. The key, then, was to define an operational area that was limited enough to enable a decision, but not so small that the decision was minor in its effects. The other looming problem was that, largely for geographical reasons, the operational possibilities open to the Germans did not match their strategic goals. The Wehrmacht, despite its impressive triumph in France, was designed to fight close to its frontiers. In invading the Soviet Union, though, it would be engaged in something that exceeded its geographical range – in terms of transport and supply, operations, and strategy. Encirclement battles made sense where, as in France, distances were short and the enemy could be pinned at fixed points, but on the Eastern Front space for maneuver also allowed space for the Russians to retreat. What looked good on paper would be invalidated in practice, as geography overcame operational competence. As the Germans were to discover, operational triumphs by themselves could not produce strategic results.

Hitler's directive of 31 July had specified that Russia should be crushed in a single blow, with powerful thrusts toward Kiev and the Baltic states, followed by a drive on Moscow, a strategy that placed the flanks above the center in terms of importance. Over the next few months OKH, OKW, and Hitler all developed operational plans to achieve this victory, which, while diverging in some areas, shared two basic premises: the inferiority of the Red Army in quality of leadership and equipment, and a time frame of three to four months for completion of the campaign. In the event, both of these assumptions, based on an astonishing lack of knowledge about their future enemy, proved wrong. In underestimating the Red Army's size, resilience, and quantity and quality of weapons, Wehrmacht planners committed an original sin of analysis from which the army never recovered. Interestingly as well, especially in light of the later controversy between Hitler and Halder over the focal point of the attack, most plans – including those submitted even before Hitler's 29 July announcement by Lieutenant-Colonel Eberhard Kinzel of Foreign Armies East and Colonel Hans von Greiffenberg, Chief of OKH Operations Division – proposed strong actions on the flanks rather than a direct advance on Moscow. Kinzel advocated a strong push in the north to secure the Baltic, followed by a turn to Moscow, with a subsequent drive toward Ukraine to force the Soviets to fight on a reversed front, whereas Greiffenberg suggested a main thrust into Ukraine to confront the bulk of the Red Army and capture key industrial areas.[13]

Neither of these proposals accorded with Halder's own rather uninspired preference for a direct assault on Moscow, followed, if necessary, by a turn south to Ukraine. He rejected Greiffenberg's plan both for its reliance on an attack out of what he regarded as an unreliable Romania and, more importantly, because of false information from Foreign Armies East that indicated the bulk of the Red Army's strength lay north of the Pripet Marshes. Given his own preference for a main thrust north of the Pripet, Halder delegated Major-General Erich Marcks, the chief of staff of the 18th Army and a man highly regarded for his "razor-sharp intellect," to draw up a plan for the eastern campaign with the main advance to the north of the marshes. Working rapidly, Marcks's initial proposal for how best to defeat the Soviet Union proved closer to Hitler's ideas than Halder's. Marcks placed the Schwerpunkt in the south aimed at Kiev, on the assumption that a powerful assault from Romania would safeguard the essential oil fields from Soviet attack, allow for the rapid seizure of critical foodstuffs and raw materials in Ukraine, and provide the optimal basis for taking Moscow. In his original conception, then, Marcks appeared to validate Hitler's economic as well as strategic judgment. Halder, in a preview of the persistent deception that fueled so much of the later conflict with Hitler over the Schwerpunkt of the operation, immediately rejected Marcks's proposal. His objections centered both on practical difficulties – the political uncertainty of staging an attack from Romania and the difficult rivers to be crossed – and on his dogmatic belief that the capture of Moscow, as with Paris, would result in final victory, and that such an assault had to proceed along the most direct line to the capital. Significantly, even though the political situation in Romania, which loomed large in Halder's rejection of Marcks's initial plan, changed definitively in Germany's favor in early September, the OKH chief refused any reconsideration of his operational focus, yet another indication of his rejection of any focal point of attack other than the central sector.[14]

For a time Halder, never an original thinker, seemed to have considered a reprise of the Schlieffen Plan of 1914, this time with German forces sweeping along the Baltic coast, wheeling toward Moscow, then, having seized the Soviet capital, turning to the southwest to pin the enemy against the Black Sea and Carpathians. This was a plan so outlandish, entailing an unbroken advance of 1,000 miles, that Hitler's notion, by comparison, seems the height of strategic logic. Although more sensible heads prevailed upon him to drop this idea, he merely shifted to another failed avenue of attack, that of Napoleon in 1812. Marcks, under Halder's influence, duly switched the Schwerpunkt to Moscow and on 5 August resubmitted his study for approval. In his now acceptable second draft, Marcks sketched a four-stage plan of operations – with the focal point a drive down the Minsk–Smolensk axis – that depended on surprise and speed for success. The presence of the natural barrier of the Pripet Marshes, a reality that bedeviled every German planner, forced him to divide the operational area into two distinct parts, which meant that from the start the attack eastward would lack cohesion and coordination between its two wings, with each essentially moving away from the other, as opposed to the converging trap created in Sichelschnitt. Marcks attempted to overcome this difficulty by reuniting the secondary southern thrust into Ukraine, after the capture of Kiev, with the northern wing advancing toward Moscow.[15]

In the key first phase of the attack, requiring roughly three weeks, German armored units would break through and trap the bulk of the Red Army, which would be destroyed by the trailing infantry west of the Dvina–Dnieper line (itself some 250 miles east of the starting point). If the advance proved rapid enough, Marcks thought the outcome of the campaign might be decided in this first stage. But if the bulk of enemy forces had not been destroyed, the second phase, lasting two to four weeks and covering a depth of 100 miles, aimed to force a decisive breakthrough and elimination of resistance. Success in this second phase would be the key to the nature of the third. Its objectives would be the capture of Moscow, Leningrad, and penetration of the eastern Ukraine, all another 250 miles to the east, but, significantly, its timing depended on the extent of enemy opposition, the supply situation, the condition of the army's motorized vehicles, and the need for rest and replenishment of tanks and equipment. This might necessitate a pause of up to three weeks, followed by another three weeks of fighting. Marcks envisioned the fourth stage, following the capture of Moscow, as a largely unimpeded pursuit, a "railway advance" to the Don, Volga, and northern Dvina. Marcks assumed that the crushing blows administered in the first three phases would eradicate any cohesive Soviet resistance, so full occupation of the Archangel–Gorky–Rostov line would not be necessary. The campaign, he reckoned, would take between nine and seventeen weeks, although Halder, who expected the war to be over with the seizure of Moscow, thought even this ambitious timetable too long, a belief based on illusion rather than evidence.[16]

In the meantime, Jodl, Halder's rival at OKW, instructed Lieutenant-Colonel Bernhard von Lossberg, the same man who had coolly prevented a calamity at Narvik in March by refusing to transmit Hitler's withdrawal orders, to prepare its own study, which was completed on 15 September. Like Marcks, Lossberg had to confront the difficulty of the Pripet Marshes, which he chose to solve by clearly focusing the main effort to the north of the swamp in the central sector, where the road and rail systems were better and where the bulk of enemy forces could be swiftly destroyed. In contrast with Marcks, though, and perhaps reflecting Jodl's awareness of Hitler's inclination, Lossberg stressed the importance of a thrust in the Baltic; where Marcks had proposed only two army groups, Lossberg advocated the formation of a third in the north. Intriguingly in light of later events, Lossberg urged that after reaching Smolensk the central army group be halted so that part of its armor could be turned north to destroy enemy formations there. He also

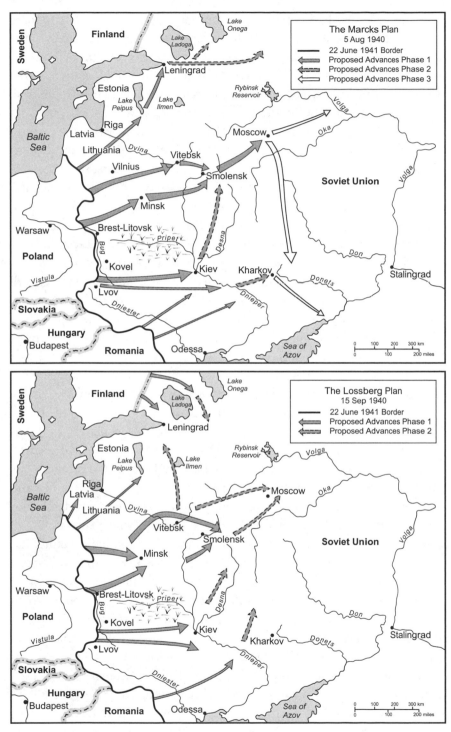

4. The Marcks Plan, 5 August 1940, and Lossberg Plan, 15 September 1940

assumed that after this operation had been completed, a pause of up to three weeks would be necessary in order to replenish the exhausted forces. In the south, he envisioned an encirclement movement by German forces operating from southeastern Poland and Romania that would destroy Soviet formations in Ukraine. Then, showing a strategic flexibility that would have made Moltke proud, the southern army group would, depending on Soviet actions and continued ability to resist, either move on Moscow in conjunction with the northern army groups, or pursue objectives in the eastern Ukraine up to the Volga. Lossberg clearly tried to address logistical requirements as well, stressing both the shortcomings of the Russian railways and the fact that a transport system based largely on roads would be insufficient. This observation also pointed to the importance of a northern thrust, since quick capture of Baltic Sea ports would ease German logistical restraints.[17]

Although Hitler evidently never saw the Lossberg Study (it was suppressed by Warlimont for two months), and it is unclear whether Jodl communicated the main ideas to him, in its strategic flexibility, stress on strong flank moves to secure economic resources, and indirect approach to Moscow, it anticipated many of the Führer's concerns, and again illustrated the logic of his arguments. After the war, in fact, Rundstedt stated that Lossberg's plan corresponded to his own preference for an attack toward Leningrad, followed by an operation against Moscow from the north. Hitler's intention to encircle and destroy Russian forces mirrored that of OKH, but he believed this would be more readily achieved by large, sweeping, indirect movements than by the frontal thrusts advocated by Halder, which risked merely pushing back rather than destroying the Russians. Further, Hitler showed a greater sensitivity to economic and logistic concerns than did his OKH chief. Significantly, neither Marcks nor Lossberg doubted the Wehrmacht's ability to defeat the Red Army, nor, despite the latter's better appreciation of the size of the undertaking, did either seriously consider the impact of Soviet resistance, countermeasures, or even capacity for absorbing blows and continuing to fight. Just as damning, the assumption in each of their plans that the army would have to pause for up to three weeks after an initial advance of 250 to 300 miles to allow for resupply and replenishment seemed to cause neither man to reflect on the implications for success in the upcoming campaign. That this swift triumph would automatically result in Soviet defeat, though, had already been put into doubt by a study completed on 10 August by OKH's Military Geography Department. It stressed that Ukraine, Leningrad, and Moscow were all important targets for occupation but that, contrary to Halder's assumption, Ukraine, with its industrial and agricultural resources, was the most valuable part of the Soviet Union. More troubling, it concluded that the oil fields of the Caucasus were probably beyond German striking power and that even if the Wehrmacht conquered all the above-named areas, the war would not necessarily be over since the USSR now had the means to fight on based on industrial infrastructure and resources beyond the Urals.[18]

Indeed, further reflections by Marcks himself indicated as much, since he fully expected a coalition between Great Britain and the Soviet Union, to be joined by the United States, as a certain result of a German invasion. This meant an intensified blockade of German-controlled Europe, with all the haunting memories and fears of hunger that conjured. At the same time, it also implied that the Soviets would only have to survive the initial German blow in order to take advantage of the economic and military power of their new allies. They would thus likely respond with delaying actions, counterattacks, and systematic construction of a series of defensive lines, all of which cast doubt on his initial timetable for the operation. In addition, Germany would be forced to defend on all sides, thus allowing Britain and the United States a better opportunity to launch counterattacks in coordination with the Soviets. Marcks expected these attacks to begin in 1942, a view reinforced in a report by Lieutenant-General Kurt von Tippelskirch, head of OKH Intelligence Staff. In response to a query from Marcks, Tippelskirch pointed to the likelihood of an Anglo-American offensive in North Africa, expulsion of the Italians, establishment of air bases for use against Italy, and the defeat of Italy, all consequences that would make the conduct of the war more difficult, although not necessarily pulling large German forces away from the Soviet Union. Even though he expected Japan to enter the war, none of his predictions alleviated Marcks's gnawing fear that the Russian campaign might take longer than envisioned – indeed, might result in an indefinite state of war – and expand into a global conflict. This suggested the only solution for Germany was the rapid conquest of Ukraine and control over the Baltic, both of which Marcks, again mirroring Hitler's assertions, now regarded as crucial for German conduct of the war. Despite the red flags he had raised, Marcks took comfort by clinging to his earlier belief that the loss of industry, raw materials, and foodstuffs in its western borderlands would cause Soviet resistance to crumble.[19]

Nor did his report do much to dampen the general mood of optimism since there is no evidence that it reached either Halder or Hitler. In any case, Halder was largely dismissive of the Red Army, an attitude shared by many top German military leaders, who, shaped by traditional assumptions of Russian cultural inferiority, personal impressions formed during the First World War, and the influence of Nazi ideology, tended to discount Soviet abilities. Foreign Armies East, in one such typical assessment, judged Soviet strengths to be – apart from the vast size and sheer primitiveness of the USSR – the great numbers of simple, tough, courageous soldiers, an asset more than offset by allegedly poor organization and the incompetence and lack of training of its leaders. Russian officers, most believed, were sluggish and slow-witted, unsuited to the demands of modern mobile warfare. Warnings from one of the most knowledgeable German observers of the Soviet Union, General Ernst Köstring, the military attaché in Moscow, had little impact on the OKH chief. In a September conversation Köstring advised Halder that the Red Army had made improvements, especially in defensive capabilities, and that terrain, weather conditions, and lack of roads would make rapid movement difficult, but then tempered his remarks with the estimate that it would be another four years before the Red Army regained its former effectiveness. Gebhardt von Walther, a councilor at the German Embassy in Moscow, provided a more sobering foretaste of the probable Soviet response, predicting fierce resistance, a surge of patriotic support from the Russian populace, and little likelihood of an internal collapse of the regime. His memo, which Halder almost certainly saw, also raised troubling questions as to whether Germany would even benefit economically from conquered Soviet territory. All this points to a professional failure by Halder, who had personally dissuaded Marcks from launching the main thrust of the operation in the south, in favor of his *idée fixe* of Moscow, but also to a larger failing of OKH and the army commanders. Blinded by the apparent success of their new method of war, they gave remarkably little attention to whether Germany had the physical means to defeat the Soviet Union.[20]

In order to coordinate all the preparatory planning done to date, Halder had secured the appointment of Major-General Friedrich Paulus as OKH Quartermaster-General – Ludendorff's old position. On 3 September Paulus gave Halder an analysis based on Marcks's plan that clearly, and alarmingly, showed the absolute necessity of a three-week pause for rest and resupply after completion of the second phase of the operation. Paulus, in studying the practical problems related to the campaign, quickly realized that logistic and supply difficulties would impede German action, a conclusion reinforced by a November study by Eduard Wagner, the army Quartermaster, who believed transportation problems would force a halt to German operations east of Minsk. This meant that Soviet forces would have to be brought to battle and destroyed considerably west of the Dnieper line or else German forces, spreading out in a fan shape as they advanced into the USSR, would be too dispersed to destroy the Russians. Given such uncertainty about operational premises, Halder instructed Paulus to oversee a series of war games, with the goal of putting preparations for the campaign on a surer footing, especially distribution of forces and selection of objectives.[21]

Conducted in late November and early December, the results proved sobering. Paulus quickly realized that not only could the Soviets generate a very rapid troop buildup, but their likely goal would be to blunt the force of the German attack by launching a series of counterattacks that would impede the mobility of the German armored units. The solution, he thought, was to attach strong infantry forces to the armored groups in order to fight the great battles of encirclement that were envisioned. Still, this was merely a bandage, not a cure, since it failed to resolve the inherent problem of the speed differential between man and machine, nor could it guarantee that Soviet forces would be prevented from withdrawing intact. The Germans, it seemed, would be able to strike deep into the enemy rear, or destroy large numbers of troops in cauldron battles, but would not be able to do both simultaneously. In addition, the rapid destruction of enemy forces in the central sector could only be accomplished if the attacks by both neighboring army groups were made secondary, meaning that they would necessarily lag behind, thus dangerously exposing the flanks of the central army group to counterattack. Also sobering was the fact that after reaching the first goal, the Dnieper River line, the overstretched German forces would have to pause for up to three weeks to allow for rest and resupply; only then, roughly forty days after the start of the invasion, could the decisive attack on Moscow be launched. Above all, Paulus warned against allowing the Red Army to withdraw into the depths of the country, noting that Russia had few natural barriers (unlike the English Channel) against which an enemy could be pinned following a breakthrough. The outcome was thus crucially dependent on the effectiveness of German mobile units in destroying the Red Army quickly and as close to the border as possible.[22]

The conclusion seemed inescapable that, as in 1914, Germany lacked sufficient forces to accomplish its goals. Not only was its initial strength barely adequate, but it could not hope to match a Soviet force buildup; indeed, Paulus warned that Germany's meager reserves would be exhausted within two months. Writing in 1946, he dismissed the whole idea of an advance to the Archangel–Volga line as "far beyond anything that the German forces available could hope to achieve." In retrospect, the focus on relatively short encirclements because of the Wehrmacht's limited striking range should have been a profound indication that it lacked the ability to deliver a knockout blow against such a numerous enemy. At the time, though, Paulus seems not to have taken any action to persuade Halder or anyone else in OKH of the implications of the war games, nor was there any comprehensive attempt within OKH to digest the lessons. Perhaps this reflected yet again the hubris afflicting the general staff at this time, or perhaps it resulted simply from the fact that the analysis of the war games was not complete when Hitler met on 5 December with Brauchitsch, Halder, and the OKW chiefs to discuss operational planning.[23]

Hitler began the conference typically, with a rather rambling survey of the general war situation, reinforcing the impression that he remained uncertain as to how to proceed. He quickly dispelled that idea, though, as just three weeks after his disastrous meeting with Molotov in Berlin, he reaffirmed that the question of hegemony in Europe would be decided in the struggle against the Soviet Union – and now was an "especially favorable" moment to embark on it. Since the United States would not be in a position to interfere in Europe until 1942, he stressed, all continental problems had to be solved in 1941. Hitler then sketched his plan that favored an indirect approach: an attack in the center would prevent the enemy from falling back, while powerful flank assaults in the Baltic and Ukraine would destroy enemy formations west of the Dnieper (an absolute necessity to secure a quick victory) and secure crucial supply bases and raw materials. Although still hazy in concept, Hitler's plan seemed to envision a dual envelopment of Soviet forces, much like the Polish campaign, with the larger, outer ring based on advances through the Baltic and Ukraine, while the shorter inner ring featured thrusts north and south of the Pripet Marshes, with the central army group prepared to send "considerable forces," if necessary, north to assist the drive in the Baltic. After encircling the enemy facing it, the southern army group would turn north and cooperate with the northern groups in a giant pincer movement circling behind Moscow; following this, depending on circumstances, German forces would either occupy Moscow, which Hitler dismissed as "of no great importance," or move further east. His intentions were confirmed at a conference held on 3 February 1941, when he stressed that the task of Army Group Center was primarily to pin Soviet troops in place so that both Army Groups North and South could "thrust in the rear of the Russians without a frontal attack. It is essential to wipe out large sections of the enemy and not to put them to flight." This, Hitler argued, could best be achieved by holding the Russians in the center while strong flanking forces enveloped them from both north and south.[24]

This savage blow, he believed, would cause the communist state to collapse, with German forces eventually advancing to the Volga. Even then, in recognition of the changes wrought by Stalin's industrialization campaign, Hitler thought it would be necessary for the Luftwaffe to carry out "destructive raids" into the Urals to destroy the widely dispersed armaments facilities in that area. In all, though, he had outlined an operational vision very similar to Lossberg's, one bold in conception that combined the military goal of the rapid destruction of enemy forces with the recognition of the importance of economic factors (opening a Baltic supply route and securing food, resources, and oil in the south). Just as importantly, he had noted the dangers in a frontal assault in the central sector of a Russian withdrawal, a direct confrontation with the Red Army, or attacks on the exposed flanks of Army Group Center. This was a comprehensive, imaginative plan that played to German effectiveness in mobile warfare while recognizing its economic deficiencies, with an eye as well for the enemy's strengths and weaknesses. Whether the Wehrmacht had the strength to accomplish this task, though, was unclear, an issue left open.[25]

By comparison, when Halder took the floor he outlined a rather uninspired plan – based on the twin false assumptions that the bulk of Soviet forces were north of the Pripet Marshes and that the Red Army could not withdraw without sacrificing the economic infrastructure vital to waging war – that threatened merely to push the enemy back rather than annihilate him. Unlike Hitler's conception, it also took no note of German economic requirements or likely Russian responses. All previous army studies had initially rejected the traditional, Napoleonic invasion route into Russia, only to be overruled by Halder, so it was not surprising that, once again, he sketched an unimaginative approach to a problem that demanded a more creative solution, choosing to follow in the French emperor's footsteps. For that reason, if no other, it was not likely to appeal to a man like Hitler, who valued creative insight and, based on the rather lackluster ideas provided him to date by OKH, harbored a growing disdain for the "learned gentlemen" of the general staff. For him, Halder was a capable technocrat, to be sure, but lacked an intuitive feel for modern strategic concepts, an "army cadet" rather than a Moltke. Nor was Halder's presentation entirely truthful. Although he accurately noted that the road and rail system in the center was better than in the south, he falsely claimed that the mass of the Red Army was being deployed north of the Pripet Marshes, an assertion at variance with the increasing flow of intelligence information and designed to bolster his claim for Moscow as the key target. The Soviets, Halder claimed, would be forced to protect their armaments industries, so would have to stand and fight west of the Dnieper–Dvina line, exposing themselves to destruction in encirclements in the Minsk–Smolensk area. This, not coincidentally, would also generate momentum for a thrust toward Moscow. With the way cleared to the Soviet capital, Halder assumed,

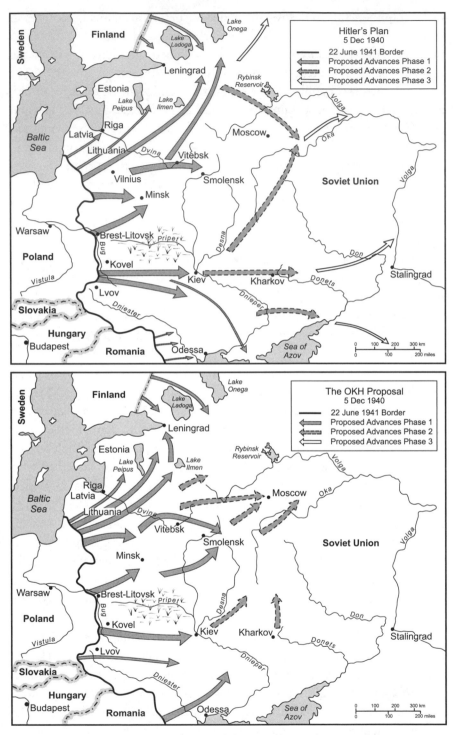

5. Hitler's Final Plan, 5 December 1940, and the OKH Proposal, 5 December 1940

without providing any evidence, that its fall would end the campaign, much as a year earlier in France. Nor did he indicate concern for any enemy responses, again ignoring the possibility of counterattacks or flank attacks from the Pripet Marshes.[26]

After Halder spoke, Hitler ended the conference by stressing what he understood to be the key points: a choice had been made to put the Baltic and Ukraine ahead of Moscow in terms of strategic importance; in order to facilitate this, forces from the central army group were to be used to aid in the north; the foremost operational goals had to be destroying enemy forces west of the Dnieper and preventing the Red Army from forming a cohesive defensive line. In contrast with Halder, the Führer clearly stressed the importance of destroying enemy forces, not taking Moscow. He also emphasized that the areas of the two flanking army groups had to be cleared, with help from the central army group, before the thrust on Moscow could commence. This challenged the fundamental principle of Halder's concept, a question of Schwerpunkt that would be left unresolved and, typical of the Hitler-Halder relationship, never openly discussed. Hitler's reply at the time to Halder's outline – that he was "in agreement with [Halder's] proposed operational considerations" – betrayed key aspects of Hitler's personality and Halder's leadership style. Contrary to the persistent image of Hitler browbeating his long-suffering generals, at this stage of the war he was not running roughshod over them. He had deferred during the Polish campaign, his intervention in operational planning for France had proved fully justified, and even his famous "decision" to halt the Panzers before Dunkirk, as we have seen, largely involved deferring to the commanding general on the spot.[27]

To paraphrase the historian Percy Ernst Schramm, from 1943 keeper of the OKW war diary and a shrewd observer of the Führer, it would be wrong to diminish Hitler as a strategist. Nicolaus von Below, his Luftwaffe adjutant, thought he exhibited a "sharp logic and extraordinarily fine feel for military situations," was "very good at placing himself in the enemy's shoes," and displayed a "balanced and accurate" military judgment. Manstein, certainly no friend of Hitler's, readily conceded that his arguments, military as well as political-economic, could not be "dismissed out of hand." The field marshal, in fact, believed Hitler had "a number of qualities indispensable to a supreme commander." Not only did he have a strong will and nerves, but he was also "highly intelligent" with an "undeniably keen brain," possessed "an astoundingly retentive memory and an imagination that made him quick to grasp all technical matters," and displayed "a certain instinct for operational problems." What he lacked, Manstein thought, was military experience and a sense of what could be achieved, for which his intuition could not compensate. Ironically, Manstein also believed that this led Hitler, as a military commander, to recoil from risk-taking and to substitute willpower and brute force for the art of war.[28]

Nor, for all his private muttering about the "mediocre quality" of the general staff officers, did Hitler typically seek confrontation, but rather sought to persuade through his arguments. This leadership style, though, often resulted in protracted discussions with no quick decisions taken, itself an indication that Hitler was not imposing his will. At this time, his customary method of dealing with OKH was to ask searching questions to understand the overall picture, defer a contentious decision for further study, support officers who shared his views to gain credibility, but then, as often as not – as Halder had realized and used to his advantage as early as the French campaign – acquiesce to OKH while seeming to stamp the decision as his own. He was not a man impervious to counter-argument, if convincing and presented properly, but he tended to regard direct challenges as an attempt to undermine his authority. As Manstein admitted, "the arguments with which Hitler defended his point of view . . . were not usually of a kind that could be dismissed out of hand . . . Hitler frequently showed himself to be a very good listener even when he did not like what was being asked of him . . . and quite capable of objective discussion." This pattern resulted in part, as his close associates knew, from his dislike of personal conflict, and in part from his assumption that once he had outlined an idea others would put it into practice. Indeed, after the conference on 5 December he largely left OKH to get on with the detailed planning. This worked well with someone like Himmler, who was adept, in Ian Kershaw's apt phrase, at "working toward the Führer," but less effectively with Halder, who typically attempted to subvert Hitler's intentions and pursue his own plans, on the assumption that he would be proven correct and the Führer would then acquiesce. Nor, despite his later criticisms of Hitler's interference, was Halder blameless in this regard. While he systematically sought to circumvent Hitler's authority, his subordinates were largely denied any particular independence of thought, with one complaining, "We are trained to be machines and must adapt our opinions." In fact, as we will see, it was Halder, not Hitler, who in the autumn of 1941 first began to rein in the traditional operational freedoms of German frontline commanders.[29]

In the planning run-up to Barbarossa, Halder, in fact, seems routinely not to have involved Hitler in details and also withheld important information on German weakness from him. This raises a basic question: How much were Hitler's decisions based on an inaccurate estimate of Soviet strength and an exaggerated belief in German striking power? After all, over-optimism and supposition of a quick victory were apparently the basis of OKH operational planning. Hitler can hardly be blamed for making decisions based on the often incorrect or misleading information being furnished him, something that he often complained about. Nor is it valid, as many historians have done after the war, to dismiss Hitler's operational views as faulty because he allegedly stressed economic over military priorities. Not only did he emphasize the key importance of destroying enemy forces over the capture of Moscow, but he also raised very valid concerns about flank security. Indeed, a mid-January 1941 report by Foreign Armies East corroborated Hitler's fears, predicting that the Red Army would try to stymie a German invasion by means of flank attacks. Hitler's idea, like Lossberg's and Marcks's original plans, also had the benefit that it brought the wings back together in coordinated action; Halder's did not, with each army group flailing out on its own. In its outline, Hitler's plan largely mirrored that of Lossberg, and was not dissimilar from Marcks's early conception, thus providing it some credibility. As with France, moreover, he showed an appreciation for the indirect approach. Further, given his awareness of Germany's serious economic weaknesses, as well as of the growing importance of the United States in any future conduct of the war, it is at least arguable that his conceptions were more nearly of a strategic nature than those of Halder, who routinely dismissed Red Army abilities and refused to allow economic or logistic issues to determine his decisions. When, for example, Wagner told him in mid-March 1941 that fuel supplies sufficed only for three months, Halder merely noted in his diary, "Fuel preparations adequate."[30]

Halder and Hitler thus held differing conceptions of Operation Barbarossa. While the OKH chief saw Moscow, in classic operational terms, as the focal point of attack, for the Führer it was a mere geographical object. The key for him was an awareness of time and resource limitations, a concern growing acute in spring 1941 given dwindling food and fuel stocks and forecasts of dire shortages in the near future, all of which evidently could be made good through territorial acquisition in the Soviet Union. He thus focused on larger economic and strategic goals: Lebensraum, food, oil, other resources, so as to fight the eventual war for world hegemony against the Anglo-Americans. His focus was firmly set on the north and south (the first to gain ports and relieve supply problems, the second to win vital resources); above all else loomed the absolute need for oil. Germany was dependent on supplies from Romania and Russia, but faced a dilemma: any invasion of the USSR to secure vital oil would, in the short term, disrupt the supply of that same scarce and critical commodity and confront German forces with shortages. The solution to the conundrum, for Hitler, had to be to give priority to the northern and southern thrusts; thus, his operational goals were logical within his larger strategic conceptions. Halder, though, saw the solution in classical terms: destroy Soviet armies in the center and seize Moscow. Whether this would compel Stalin to yield, as the French had, or whether he would fight on from beyond the Urals, remained an open question, one that troubled some top generals, among them Hoth, who openly wondered how the campaign would end.[31]

Hitler also had a clear awareness of problems raised by the size of the country, likely enemy resistance, and flank dangers, all of which he thought could be overcome by sweeping enveloping movements from the wings. That his concerns were not unfounded was shown by further war games overseen by Paulus on 13–14 December and 17–20 December. These focused on key practical problems that would be crucial to the success of the operation, and that challenged the fundamental premise of a swift Blitzkrieg triumph: how to coordinate the movements of armored units with marching infantry; and how to supply a large army deep within the vastness of the Soviet Union. This was uncharted territory, for the Wehrmacht had not yet attempted a Blitzkrieg campaign into a vast geographical space characterized by the absence of an extensive transportation system. Typically, despite Hitler's stated preference for a flank strategy, these war games were based on Moscow as the prime objective. They also betrayed the rather dubious assumption that the Germans had a decisive superiority in the quality and quantity of tanks, aircraft, artillery, and infantry. Even then, the results proved discouraging. After reaching the Dnieper River line, and agreeing to halt for three weeks for resupply and regrouping of forces, both Army Groups North and South had clearly lagged far behind and would need the loan of armored units from Army Group Center to aid in entrapping enemy forces facing them. In an amazingly accurate forecast of what actually transpired, this resulted in vigorous debate among the generals, with the ultimate result that Army Group Center was to continue on toward Moscow, with the other two army groups offering as much flank protection as possible.[32]

In reviewing the war games, Paulus again concluded that the army was "barely sufficient" for the tasks assigned it and would be shorn of reserves by the time of the final assault on Moscow. He also began to realize the difficulties associated with time and space in the vastness of the Soviet Union, which opened like a funnel to an invading force. The disparity of speed between armored and infantry units presented a particular problem, with Paulus now deciding that the best option was to allow the armor to forge ahead in free-wheeling pincer thrusts into the enemy rear. This, though, left two issues unresolved that, in the event, proved especially thorny: first, the threat of counterattacks into the exposed German flanks; and, second, the difficulty the slower-moving infantry would have in closing up and sealing off the encirclements to prevent large numbers of enemy troops escaping (swift destruction of enemy forces was, after all, regarded as the key to success). Logistics also challenged Blitzkrieg theory. German supply depots located close behind the starting line could sustain a drive only for about 300 miles, but Smolensk and Moscow were a distant 400 to 600 miles away. To maintain the drive eastward new supply areas would need to be established, but they would be dependent on the inadequate Soviet rail system – which had to be rebuilt to correct the different track gauge – and trucks operating over poor or nonexistent roads. The conclusion that shortages and interruptions of supply could not be avoided, and improvisation would be necessary, was realistic if not very comforting. Although an accurate predictor of what would happen, Halder ignored Paulus's conclusions either because they were unwelcome or because he simply failed to understand the full extent of the problems posed by the vast distances of the Soviet Union. Halder knew, for example, that the railroad system would have to be rebuilt, but simply assumed that supply by truck would be a suitable alternative, despite an insufficiency of motor vehicles, fuel, and good roads. He neither discarded nor significantly altered his preferred operational scheme, let alone presented Hitler the hard information with which an alternative plan might have been devised.[33]

At the same time, Halder acted behind the scenes both to undermine Hitler's conceptions and to weaken his arguments. At meetings on 13–14 December with the chiefs of staff of the armies and army groups, he failed to mention any dispute over the Schwerpunkt, implying that Moscow was the agreed target. The first draft of the war directive, prepared by Lossberg of the OKW staff, thus adhered closely to Halder's preferences. When he saw it on 17 December, Hitler ordered a "considerable alteration." The new text, issued next day as Directive No. 21 "Case Barbarossa," reflected more of Hitler's preferences, as expressed on 5 December. As in all previous plans, the bulk of the Red Army was to be prevented from withdrawing and destroyed in the western borderlands of the Soviet Union. Although the main weight of the attack lay with Army Group Center, which should rout enemy forces in Belorussia, its other principal task would be to turn north at the appropriate time to aid Army Group North in clearing the Baltic. Only then, with the Baltic made safe and Leningrad secured, could the attack be continued with the goal of occupying Moscow; only a surprisingly rapid collapse of enemy resistance would allow both objectives to be pursued simultaneously. Army Group South, operating below the Pripet Marshes, was to destroy enemy forces west of the Dnieper and seize Kiev, then advance and capture the economically important war industries of the Donets Basin. In a significant contrast with earlier conceptions, Army Group South was not now expected to turn forces north and aid in the capture of Moscow, but would move independently away from the other two army groups, thus dissipating German striking power.[34]

Although seeming to acquiesce with Hitler's ideas, Directive No. 21 was, in fact, an ill-chosen compromise between Hitler's and Halder's conceptions, with none of the strengths and all of the weaknesses of both. In place of the two-pronged offensive of earlier plans – whether a focus in the center and supporting drive from the south, or the sweeping envelopments preferred by Hitler – there now emerged a three-pronged attack with no main point of effort, and with each army group lacking the strength to accomplish its tasks without major shifts of forces between sectors. The army had two challenging, and not entirely compatible, objectives: to defeat Soviet forces west of the Dnieper; and to seize Leningrad and the natural resources of Ukraine and the Caucasus. Halder had also inserted language that allowed the OKH chief wiggle room based on semantics, subjective interpretations, and the misrepresentation that Hitler had fully endorsed his plan. Rather than resolve the sticky issue of differing conceptions of how the operation should unfold, Halder, in hoping to run the campaign according to his vision, again resorted to deception, of both himself and the Führer. At the decisive operational moment in the campaign, he simply assumed he would be proven correct, and Hitler would yield; in the event, this was a grievous mistake.[35]

Halder's deceptions continued into the New Year, with growing impact on planning for the campaign. On 9 January 1941, Hitler again outlined the main operational goals as "severance of the Baltic region," followed by "annihilation of the Russian army, seizure of the most important industrial regions, and destruction of the remaining industrial regions." Although these put clear emphasis on destruction of enemy forces and economic priorities – that is, on elimination of the enemy ability to wage war – with no mention of Moscow, Halder made no comment or objection. Hitler also pointedly noted that, while the Red Army was "a clay colossus without a head," the enemy should not be underestimated, for Stalin was tough and clever. Halder, though, continued to dismiss or understate potential difficulties. On both 20 and 28 January he received reports on projected supply difficulties, but

6. Operation Barbarossa Final Directive, 31 January 1941

offered completely contradictory responses. On the former date, he stressed
the key importance of railroads to maintain the pace of the advance, whereas
on the latter day he noted realistically that railroads initially would not be of
much use for supply purposes because of their destruction and the different
gauges, so logistic support depended on trucks. Halder made little attempt to
reconcile these disparate views, even though he knew Germany lacked sufficient motor vehicles for the task at hand. He understood both that the Red
Army had to be destroyed "without pause" in the initial phase of the campaign,
and that there were no ready means by which to supply such an advance. In
the German army, though, everything revolved around the operational
concept, so rather than adjust those goals he simply assumed that, logisti-
cally, what must be done would be done. Significantly, as well, he failed to
communicate this disturbing information to Hitler.[36]

Nor did OKH necessarily bow to the concerns of others. At a conference on 31 January, Brauchitsch and Halder showed themselves untroubled by possible enemy reactions to an attack, brushing aside Bock's worry of what would happen if the Russians failed to oblige and instead withdrew forces into the interior. This, despite the fact that in late November 1940, Halder had voiced similar doubts about German ability, after achieving their initial objectives, to operate effectively in the immense spaces of the Soviet Union. Bock raised his fear the next day in a meeting with Hitler, who glossed over the issue by stating that if the loss of Leningrad, Moscow, and Ukraine did not induce the Soviets to surrender, then the Germans would just have to continue operations eastward. In retrospect, this conveyed a sense of optimism and unreality bordering on self-delusion. While Jodl and Manstein complained after the war that Hitler did not fully appreciate the difficulties of mobile warfare, in fairness he was not being given the full picture. Nor, despite their belated reservations, did any of the top planners at the time, although fully aware of German deficiencies, harbor any serious doubts about German victory.[37]

This subterfuge was shown again in a planning conference on 3 February. Halder disclosed none of the troubling supply or logistic difficulties with which he was grappling, such as a severe oil shortage, although he inadvertently supported Hitler's operational argument by conceding the necessity of securing Baltic ports as soon as possible for supply purposes. He also acknowledged that the Soviets had numerical superiority in manpower, but dismissed any advantage because of an alleged German qualitative edge. Similarly, although disparaging their quality, he grudgingly admitted that the Red Army had more tanks, without mentioning estimates of their number, even though the day before he had noted in his diary that the Soviets possessed 10,000 tanks to only 3,500 for the Germans. In the event, even this estimate proved false, for the Soviets actually had between 20,000 and 25,000 tanks, including growing numbers of the T-34, a model the Germans could not match. This would seem to be something that Hitler should have been told. In an unsubstantiated claim, Guderian wrote after the war that the Führer told him in early August 1941 that had he known how many tanks the Soviets actually had, he would have hesitated to launch the attack. Nor was this empty hyperbole, for the Führer's adjutant Gerhard Engel had observed in late December 1940, after the Barbarossa directive had been issued, that Hitler appeared very unsure what to do: "Distrustful of his own military leaders, uncertainty about Russian strength . . . continue to preoccupy him." On 3 February, Hitler seemed more concerned than his generals about Soviet reactions, specifically noting the threat from the

Pripet Marshes and the importance of destroying enemy forces before they could withdraw, as well as stressing that the enemy could not be expected to easily give up the Baltic area and Ukraine.[38]

Hitler's uneasiness, in fact, led him to order new studies on the Pripet Marshes and Soviet industrial areas. Foreign Armies East completed an analysis on 12 February that came to the unsettling conclusion that by using the railways the Soviets could effectively move troops anywhere, warning, "a threat from the Pripet to the flank and rear of the armies advancing toward Moscow or Kiev is very much within the realm of possibilities." In yet another indication of his scheming and determination to bend everything to his operational concept, Halder had that reference deleted in the final draft presented to Hitler on 21 February. Hitler, even without the benefit of the study's full conclusions, remained unconvinced, telling Halder on 17 March, "It is a terrain in which armies could maneuver freely." Moreover, in a report from 20 May that likely never reached Hitler, Foreign Armies East once again supposed, based on its deployments, that the Soviets meant to counter German breakthroughs with counterattacks by their own rear-massed armored units. In the event, of course, Hitler proved correct about both the Pripet Marshes and the likelihood of Soviet flank attacks, despite being denied access to information that supported his view. In over three years of occupation the Germans never succeeded in subduing the Partisan forces, operating very effectively from the area, that posed serious problems for two army groups; and the ferocity of Russian counterattacks blunted German momentum and upset all their operational plans. Finally, Halder's "indirect" method of ensuring that his view prevailed furthered an atmosphere of distrust with Hitler, contributing to the ultimate breakdown in the German command structure.[39]

As for Hitler's other concern, economic assessments had been ongoing. In November 1940, Göring commissioned a report from General Thomas of the OKW Armament Office. The latter had already been warning of a severe shortage of oil if the war continued into 1941, and in late January repeated his concerns to Wilhelm Keitel, head of OKW, about the economic implications of the planned eastern campaign. On 8 February, therefore, just three days after Hitler's request, Thomas provided Keitel and Jodl with a memorandum revealing serious fuel and rubber deficiencies. Keitel, fearful of the Führer's reaction, peremptorily dismissed these warnings, so it is unlikely that Hitler ever saw this report. Instead, Thomas revised his study and, in a memo dated 13 February, sent it to Göring; it finally reached Hitler on 20 February. In it, Thomas again pointed to deficiencies in oil and fuel but now stressed the economic benefits to be gained from the rapid conquest of Ukraine and the Caucasus oil fields, while ignoring the actual German ability to achieve this. When he met Göring in late February, Thomas warned that the eastern campaign "would be completely supplied with fuel for only two months," to which Göring replied that this only emphasized that the "Baku oil-producing region, too, had to be seized at all costs." Göring's discussions with Hitler, then, would only have reinforced the Führer's sense of urgency, since he certainly understood that both the German war economy and his room for maneuver were shrinking. Indeed, after the war Speer claimed, "In the case of Russia, the need for oil certainly was a prime motive" for the attack.[40]

This willingness to risk war with only limited supplies of oil on hand was a key indicator of Hitler's state of mind strategically. Although he needed a secure source of oil for the final showdown with the Anglo-Americans, Hitler, fearing blackmail by Stalin, trusted neither the flow of continued supplies from the USSR nor Soviet forbearance in exploiting German vulnerability. In January 1941 he told his generals, "Now, in the era of air power, Russia can turn the Romanian oil fields into an expanse of smoking debris . . . and the very life of the Axis depends on those fields." Another comment to Fritz Todt, Reich minister for armaments and ammunition, and Keitel, put in a memo to Thomas on 20 June 1941, just two days before the attack, again reflected his anxieties over oil. "The course of the war," he claimed, "shows that we went too far in our autarchical endeavors. It is impossible to try and manufacture everything we lack by synthetic procedures . . . One must choose another way. What one does not have, but needs, one must conquer . . . The aim must be to secure all territories which are of special interest to us for the war economy by conquering them." Ironically, Hitler's argument was supported by one other interested character in the unfolding drama: Stalin. The Soviet leader, believing correctly that German military-economic abilities depended on the capture of Ukraine's grain, the Don Basin's coal, and oil from the Caucasus, had steadily shifted Russian forces to what he considered the most probable direction of a German attack: the southern USSR. Contrary to Halder's expectations, the bulk of Soviet forces would not be exposed to destruction by Army Group Center.[41]

Some field commanders had also begun to express uneasiness about the operational plan, although their criticism was directed more at Halder than Hitler. On 17 March the Führer himself questioned Halder's design, noting that "it would be fundamentally wrong to attack everywhere," while on 30 March he again stressed that after advancing to the Dnieper, Army Group Center was then to send forces northward. Halder, though, confident that the development of the campaign would prove him correct, remained riveted on Moscow. It was not surprising, then, that in undermining Hitler and seeking to assure priority for his own idea, his operational directives were vague and subject to misinterpretation. The army group and Panzer commanders, whose job it was to execute the plan, all to varying degrees complained of the ambiguity emanating from OKH. General Hoth, the leader of Panzer Group 3, for example, had made his initial deployment with an eye toward a rapid advance to the upper Dvina, thus putting the weight of his advance on his northern, left flank. This would allow either for a large encirclement, in cooperation with Guderian's Panzer Group 2 striking north along the Dnieper, or a favorable position from which to move his forces northward to aid Army Group North, which reflected Hitler's wishes. Halder, though, fearing that this might dilute the push toward Moscow, insisted that the bulk of Soviet strength lay between the border and Minsk. He wanted Hoth's armored forces redirected to the center, for a shorter encirclement, in tandem with Guderian, centered on Minsk. This raised a dilemma for Hoth and his commander, Bock, both of whom clearly saw the incompatibility of reaching the Dvina quickly with a southeasterly diversion to Minsk. When pressed on this, Halder purposely gave vague, noncommittal replies, for he could not risk being exposed for what he was doing. He hoped, rather, that the commanders would understand his ulterior goal and "do the right thing." Bock was highly frustrated both because he recognized merit in Hoth's solution, and because he realized that a diversion of forces to the Minsk-Smolensk axis brought into play the difficult area of the Pripet Marshes, "making it very detrimental to their further forward movement."[42]

Halder continued to evade Bock's attempts to clarify the issue, much to the latter's irritation. Not until mid-May did the commander of Army Group Center receive a "rather foggy order" that his two Panzer Groups were to close on Minsk, although this hardly satisfied either his or Hoth's concern that the first encirclement was too small and too early. At the same time, further OKH analysis of the problems of coordinating the differing speeds of the armor and infantry had led to the conclusion, voiced months earlier by Paulus, that the Panzer forces would have to include strong infantry contingents. Further, Brauchitsch insisted that reserve units be pressed close to the front and congregated on the right wing of Army Group Center. Hoth, Guderian, and Bock, to one degree or another, all voiced concern about these proposals, since they threatened to produce monumental traffic jams and slow the movement of the armored formations. Halder, meanwhile, was primarily interested in two things: that the right wing of Bock's army group be heavily weighted for a thrust in the direction of Moscow, and that Hitler not be made aware of the dispute so that OKH would be able to control the operation. The key point of disagreement, the Schwerpunkt, was thus left unresolved, with Halder remaining silent about his true intentions, preferring to work behind the scenes to ensure that his operational concept prevailed. Although Hitler consistently articulated his primary goals as being the destruction of enemy forces and the conquest of resources for the war economy, Halder simply ignored him. Additionally, while Hitler thought the operational achievement of strategic goals had to be left flexible, dependent on enemy reactions and the degree of resistance, Halder, in his fixation on Moscow, promoted a rather inflexible strategy that largely ignored the threat of any Soviet counterattacks on the flanks; enemy concentrations in the Baltic or Ukraine would simply be disregarded. This virtually guaranteed a future conflict, since from the outset Hitler had left little doubt that he intended to take a more active role in the conduct of this campaign.[43]

From the beginning, then, the absence of harmony between Hitler and OKH ensured that the implementation of a coordinated plan of action was impossible, and that key decisions would be made in a heated atmosphere of mistrust, rivalry, and intense competition for authority. And, of course, there existed a major problem in both conceptions: once again, as in France, the Germans were gambling on Blitzkrieg as an all-out, front-loaded, knockout blow. It was a plan for war without sufficient reserves or adequate material supplies – made especially acute by the demands of the Balkan campaign – a plan for a single campaign with little thought to the consequences if it failed. For all their other disagreements, there was remarkably little doubt among the top Nazi leadership, whether political or military, that they would prevail. Hitler's remark to Jodl on 22 June – that they had "only to kick in the front door and the whole rotten structure will come crashing down" – betrayed an expectation of victory based on the experience of the First World War, when Germany had defeated Russia because of the political collapse of the Tsarist system. That, though, had followed three years of war and had not been achieved through a single campaign. Rather than base their prospects on a poor historical analogy, German leaders should have asked whether they had the power to defeat the Soviet Union in one season.[44]

Hitler's decision to eliminate the threat from the USSR, though, found general acceptance among the officers, those few skeptics suppressing any qualms. All believed the *Gesetz des Handelns* (the law of war) required action to retain the initiative; in view of British stubbornness and growing

American animosity, the "gigantic task" in the east had to be disposed of to better the military-strategic situation, something with which most generals agreed. Nor was there much criticism as strategic and economic arguments yielded to ideological and racial justifications for war against the Soviet Union, both of which led in the direction of Ludendorff's "total war" against both the enemy army and nation. In spite of post-war claims, few top generals at the time expressed unease with this looming reality. Halder, for example, far from being morally repulsed by Hitler's speech on 30 March, merely observed, "commanders must make the sacrifice of overcoming their personal scruples." Frontline commanders such as Reinhardt, Hoth, Hoepner, Küchler, Kluge, Heinrici and others in the weeks and months before the attack on the USSR expressed support for the necessity of a showdown with Bolshevism and the conquest of Lebensraum. Far from being horrified by the task ahead, most saw it, whether enthusiastically or fatalistically, as something that had to be done. Few would have agreed with Edmund Glaise von Horstenau, a leading Austrian Nazi and general born in Braunau seven years before the future Führer, who in April 1941 asked prophetically, "Isn't a man . . . with an eerie yet at the same time untamed genius running amok here through the streets of world history, shooting down everything around him, reducing it to rubble?"[45]

On the morning of 14 June, just over a week before the invasion, Hitler once again, as before all previous campaigns, gathered his top commanders to hear a lengthy and comprehensive explanation of his decision. This time, though, it was hardly necessary. Whether it was understood strategically as an act against Great Britain or to gain European hegemony, economically to secure vital Lebensraum, or racially-ideologically as a blow against "Judeo-Bolshevism," the generals recognized and accepted the fusion of pragmatic with ideological motives. While his commanders, in their presentations, painted a picture of a large but inept Red Army, Hitler warned that the campaign would be a hard-fought affair, with the Russian soldier fighting stoutly and offering tough resistance. For that reason, he insisted, "every soldier must know what it is we are fighting for . . . Bolshevism [must be] destroyed." In contrast with earlier campaigns, there was virtually no protest against the meaning and goals in this one, nor were there any particular attempts at obstruction. The only unease, and that mostly muted, was directed at the "criminal orders," and as often as not this resulted from pragmatic reasons – the maintenance of discipline, fear of reprisals – and not from any pronounced moral qualms.[46]

More curiously, in retrospect, neither Halder nor Brauchitsch objected when, in the afternoon, Hitler emphasized, in accordance with what he thought were the operational goals of Barbarossa, that after reaching the Dnieper forces from Army Group Center would be sent both north and south. Halder's silence has to be seen not as a sign that he had given up his preference for Moscow, but merely as a further indication of his determination to control operations indirectly. His later, rather hollow, complaints of Hitler's interference notwithstanding, he knew from the outset the Führer's priorities and chose to subvert them when they conflicted with his own. As Hitler's adjutant Below noted rather ominously, Germany was embarking on its great offensive in the east not merely with a disjointed leadership, but one that seemed to be pulling in different directions. Hitler, he observed, grew increasingly nervous and apprehensive, remarking in the early hours of 22 June 1941, "It will be the most difficult battle which our soldiers will have to undergo in this war." Nor was this merely a sign of pre-attack jitters, for on the eve of his great crusade he seemed less optimistic than anyone around him. "The Führer estimates the action at around four months," Goebbels noted on 16 June. "I estimate much less. Bolshevism will collapse like a house of cards." Hitler was not so sure, a few days before the attack sharply rebuking Göring for his sanguinity. "It will be our toughest struggle yet – by far the toughest. Why? Because for the first time we shall be fighting an ideological enemy . . . of fanatical persistence." For his part, Hitler was perfectly clear about the risk his action entailed, remarking a few weeks before the beginning of Barbarossa, "Should we fail, it's all over anyway." In October, Hitler again gave his intimates a frank glimpse of his mental turmoil at the time. "At the moment of our attack, we were entering a totally unknown world . . . On June 22 a door opened before us and we did not know what was behind it . . . The heavy uncertainty took me by the throat." Time, though, worked against him; waiting would only strengthen his enemies. Barbarossa offered a geo-strategic way out of his dilemma, while Blitzkrieg provided the means; but more, conquest of Lebensraum and the final confrontation with the alleged Jewish-Bolshevik enemy represented the apotheosis of his ideology and life's work.[47]

7

Barbarossa
THE LAST BLITZKRIEG (JUNE–AUGUST 1941)

In the spring of 1941, with the imminent invasion of the Soviet Union, Hitler's thoughts turned to his place in history. To ensure that he, like Napoleon, would be remembered as one of the greatest military leaders of all time, he authorized the creation of a military history section in OKW to collect documents and relevant materials from the upcoming campaign – in which he clearly intended to take a leading role – that would be the raw stuff of a future history of the Russian war. In essence, it was to be a "*Mein Krieg*" sequel to *Mein Kampf*, a chronicle of his genius as a Feldherr that paralleled his foresight as a political leader. His proclamation to the German people on 22 June 1941, a remarkably dreary, tedious speech in which he gave vent to his resentments, sought to combine these two roles. In it, he defined the eastern campaign not as a war of conquest, but as an existential struggle for German and European civilization. As usual, he blamed those he held responsible for defeat in 1918 – above all, the Jewish-Bolshevik conspiracy – for thwarting his desire to end the current war, for engaging in economic blackmail of Germany, and for threatening German and European civilization. Only by destroying "this conspiracy of the Jewish–Anglo-Saxon warmongers and . . . the Jewish ruling powers in the Bolshevik control station in Moscow" could Germany fulfill its "mission" of "the securing of Europe and, hence, the salvation of all." Likewise, in his order of the day to the soldiers of the *Ostheer* (Eastern Army), Hitler stressed that "the fate of Europe, the future of the German Reich, the existence of our Volk now lie in your hands alone."[1]

Nor was this mere hyperbole. In a remarkable response on the evening of 22 June, Winston Churchill, after terming Hitler a "a monster of wickedness, insatiable in his lust for blood and plunder," and a "bloodthirsty guttersnipe" bent on "slaughter, pillage, and devastation," declared his "one single, irrevocable purpose" the destruction of "every vestige of Hitler and the Nazi regime." As an assertion of undying hatred for Hitler, Churchill's utterances could hardly be bested, to the extent that this lifelong opponent of Marxism, who even in this speech professed Nazism "indistinguishable from the worst features of communism," nonetheless proclaimed his willingness to ally with any nation fighting Hitler. Still, the anti-Hitler coalition was not fully forged until December 1941, so at least for a time it seemed Germany had a possibility of success. Indeed, the idea of Germany attaining an empire in the east seemed hardly less fanciful than the notion of a small island nation with few resources ruling a global empire. Hitler, after all, often used British control over India – without really understanding its ruling methods – as an example of how a small nation could dominate and exploit a large area in order to create the wealth that ultimately led to world-power status. Habsburg rule in his native, unloved, Austria also served as proof of his mission. "If the ten million Germans in Austria-Hungary were able to rule forty million non-Germans . . .," he told Luftwaffe General Alexander Löhr, also a native of the defunct monarchy, "then it will not be difficult for the eighty million in Greater Germany to rule the same number of non-Germans." With the political vacuum left by the collapse of empires following the First World War, Hitler believed he had both the opportunity and the examples for what he proposed to do. At other times, of course, he cited the bloody conquest of the American West as both historical precedent and justification. That he largely misinterpreted both examples is less important than his own belief that his was a "civilizing" vision, one that promised that Germans would finally have a material quality of life commensurate with their alleged racial value. Achieving it seemed possible, given German faith in Blitzkrieg – and their faulty view of the Soviet Union.[2]

This, though, would be the last time that Germany would be in such a position of potential victory, which meant that the decisions made during the next six months were crucial – and the source of much later controversy. In the post-war period, German generals, especially those influenced by Halder under the auspices of the U.S. Army's Historical Division, proved adept at creating an image – one that persisted for decades among both historians and the general public – of a fanatical, incompetent, amateurish, and irrational Hitler who at every turn frustrated or undermined the professional judgments of his generals with his erratic and flawed decisions. This reconstructed history, in demonizing Hitler and whitewashing the complicity of the military elite in this criminal war of aggression, obscured both the complex divisions in the German leadership and other factors that contributed to German failure in 1941. The articulate and ambitious Halder, in contrast to the compliant Brauchitsch, was a crafty and devious bureaucratic in-fighter who consistently sought to safeguard and enhance the power of both himself and OKH. In addition to the complex Hitler–Halder relationship, conflict also raged between various field commanders (Bock, Hoth, Guderian) and OKH, as well as between infantry and armor generals. Throughout much of the campaign, in fact, criticism by those in the field was more likely to be directed at Halder, a career staff officer with no front-line experience, than Hitler. Nor did these divisions reflect mere personal animosities. They stemmed, in pursuing the common goal of defeating the Soviet Union, from differing notions of how to accomplish that task, as well as from the effort to find solutions to fundamental problems that arose as the army advanced eastward. The interplay of forces often resulted in a confused, contradictory strategy, but one for which Hitler alone was hardly responsible, as Halder, Bock, and headstrong generals such as Guderian fully contributed to the blunders that plagued Barbarossa.[3]

The initial assault, though, fueled German expectations of a swift campaign. "Tactical surprise of the enemy has apparently been achieved along the entire line . . .," Halder noted drily in his diary. "As a result of this tactical surprise, enemy resistance directly on the border was weak and disorganized, and we succeeded everywhere." In launching the largest military operation (to that point) in history, the Germans had assembled a force of over 3 million men, 3,600 tanks, 600,000 motorized vehicles (as well as 625,000 horses), 7,000 artillery pieces, and 2,500 aircraft in a crusade to win Lebensraum and destroy the alleged "Jewish-Bolshevik" menace. This huge array, although not significantly stronger than that assembled a year earlier against France, was opposed by an even larger force: the Red Army fielded well over 5 million men, 24,000 tanks (of which almost 2,000 were new type T-34 and KV models superior in armament, speed, and fighting power to anything the Germans then possessed), over 91,000 artillery pieces of all types, and over 19,000 aircraft (with some 7,000 based in the western districts). Most Soviet tanks were, admittedly, obsolete, but the Germans still had to destroy them, a process that would bleed lives, time, and a staggering quantity of munitions. The Red Army could also exploit an enormous pool of manpower to make good its losses, something the Wehrmacht, despite – or perhaps because of – its conquests, could not match. As in 1940, the Germans gambled on throwing all their available resources into a quick knockout punch. If, however, the Red Army did not disintegrate at the first blow, the Wehrmacht was too small, too poorly equipped, and too badly supplied to defeat its foe before the onset of winter. In 1941, with its

Stalinist apparatus of control fully functioning, the USSR would prove far more resilient than the Germans anticipated. The Wehrmacht's qualitative edge in terms of training, leadership, and equipment provided it an advantage in a short struggle, but in the long term the Soviets had the capability of overwhelming Germany.[4]

Mesmerized by the stunning collapse of France, though, the expectation of a quick victory dominated all German assessments. European Russia, however, was a different animal than France: a vast area traversed by few paved roads; a region of rough terrain, harsh climate, and poor infrastructure in which the dense woods and swampy marshlands offered perfect conditions for partisan warfare; one, moreover, in which the railway system would have to be rebuilt to the narrow-gauge European standard, a process that would require manpower the Germans lacked. These problems had all been foreseen in early planning and in war games, but their implications seem not to have been fully realized. German planners expected difficulties with supply, logistics, and transportation, for example, but inexplicably failed to anticipate either Soviet destruction of railroads, rolling stock, and locomotives, or the withdrawal of those that could be saved. This, in turn, forced more reliance on road transport, itself dependent on an insufficient quantity and quality of trucks to move supplies over inadequate or nonexistent roads. Nor, despite their recognition that after the initial advance of some 300 miles the Wehrmacht would have to pause for up to three weeks for supply and replenishment, did German planners seriously reflect on whether a Soviet defeat in the western borderlands would put Moscow in the same immediate danger that the drive to the Channel had put Paris. The Soviet capital, after all, lay another 350–400 miles to the east of the Dvina–Dnieper line, so presumably there would be less likelihood of the same panic affecting Soviet leaders as that which had overwhelmed their French counterparts, seemingly a key consideration in a plan based on the assumption that the Stalinist system would collapse after an initial hard blow.[5]

Much of the later wrangling over operational strategy was thus conducted in a surrealistic atmosphere, since logistical difficulties rendered many of these disputes meaningless. German leaders, though, acted as if the campaign was a map exercise and they could simply impose their will on the battlefield. This blithe assumption quickly began to fade in the face, not merely of fiercer than expected resistance, but of a Red Army whose troops were better led and more tenacious than previously believed, and whose equipment often proved superior to German weapons in both quantity and quality. In a cascading chain of causation, then, this opposition not only upset German timetables, but also forced a conceptual change upon them. As they struggled to control the battlefield, and as the Red Army refused to play its assigned role, the result was not just a slowing of momentum and the emergence of something that resembled positional war (which favored the Soviets), but a rethinking by German leaders of the entire notion of Blitzkrieg. The doctrine they had confidently expected to be the vessel that produced victory rapidly sprang leaks, forcing them beyond debates over short versus large encirclements to consider whether, given its immense size, poor infrastructure, and seemingly unending resources, such a strategy could ever compel Stalin to surrender. Finally, these disputes were intensified and made more vitriolic and consequential by Halder's policy, itself a carry-over from France, of misleading and manipulating Hitler in the expectation that he could then ensure that OKH goals (i.e., Moscow) would ultimately prevail. In the course of this, it was Halder, not Hitler, who initially interfered in the command freedom of field generals and who tried to centralize decision-making in his own person.

The larger problem, of course, was the conundrum at the heart of the German war effort: they first had to conquer the resources they needed in order to prosecute the war successfully. Lebensraum, in terms of gaining economic resources, had long been Hitler's goal in the east, but the realities of war had given its attainment a much greater urgency. The British blockade had left Germany in a precarious position with regard to many key raw materials, and none more critically than oil, especially given its almost complete dependence on imports from Romania. Additionally, even though the western conquests in 1940 had temporarily augmented the stocks of oil available, the Third Reich now found itself responsible for supplying the needs of both the occupied countries and its oil-poor allies. Germany, as General Thomas warned in February 1941, would run out of oil by October; only the capture and exploitation of Soviet oil fields could alleviate this desperate shortage. Moreover, economic resources had to be seized quickly in order to prosecute both this campaign and the anticipated global war of attrition with Great Britain and the United States.[6]

The questions of the main focus of the attack and how to win a quick victory, though, had never been resolved. Hitler's ideas, at first glance, seemed to violate Clausewitz's principle that the defeat of the enemy's military forces in the field was the aim of any campaign. In stressing the quick destruction of the Red Army west of the Dnieper–Dvina, while simultaneously seizing key resources, he hoped to square the circle, to reconcile both military and economic priorities. In view of the later criticism of his meddling, it is worth mentioning that Hitler had a far keener appreciation of the economic weaknesses faced by Germany than did his military advisors, something Manstein admitted after the war. The fundamental problem was not the self-evident superiority of one strategy over the other, but the failure to make a clear decision for one or the other. Hitler and Halder never resolved the incompatibility in their views, so no single objective dominated planning: three primary goals were identified, with an army group detailed to each, but with little regard for an eventual concentration of force. In trying to do everything at once, German planners merely ensured that none of the three army groups had the means by which to achieve success. Their operational plan thus failed to achieve clarity in how to destroy the Soviet will and ability to fight on: by crushing the main Soviet forces and seizing the capital, by conquering the key military-industrial areas of the country, or by a combination of the two. Given the army's limited quantities of oil, along with serious deficiencies in logistical preparation and supply capabilities, Barbarossa was from the outset a hazardous undertaking. Success meant that Germany would have the resources to fight a war of attrition against the Anglo-Saxon powers; failure would convert the temporary risk of a two-front war into strategic disaster. Little wonder that Goebbels noted on the second day of the campaign, "There's a somewhat depressed mood among the people ... [E]ach newly opened theater of war causes concern and worry."[7]

Still, the impressive successes achieved in the opening phase of Barbarossa seemed to vindicate German assumptions of a quick destruction of the Red Army. Along the entire front, German infantry and armored forces caught Soviet defenders by surprise and advanced quickly against initially weak and patchy resistance. In places, Russian troops fought stubbornly to the last man and delayed the German advance for a few hours, but this failed to alter the larger picture: the invaders had completely shattered Soviet border defenses. In the skies above the onrushing German forces, the Luftwaffe destroyed over a thousand enemy planes, most on the ground, on the first day alone. The Germans had seized the initiative and now aimed to develop such momentum that the Soviets would be unable to organize an effective resistance. Leeb's Army Group North, for example, spearheaded by Hoepner's Fourth Panzer Group (consisting of Reinhardt's and Manstein's 41st and 56th Panzer Corps), advanced rapidly through the Baltic states with the objective of seizing the Dvina River crossings before sizable Soviet forces could escape. By 1 July the Germans had ripped apart Soviet defenses, crossed the Dvina, seized Riga, and advanced into Estonia and the Leningrad region. While enjoying shorter supply lines and better railroads, the invaders were also aided by the quick capture of Baltic seaports, something Hitler had stressed, as well as the seizure of large quantities of

7. Operation Barbarossa

Soviet supplies. Although Russian resistance increased steadily in early July, the initial defeats threatened Leningrad with disaster.[8]

While operations in the north proceeded smoothly, in the south the Germans experienced less initial success. Halder's original plan for a large envelopment operation from Romania and southern Poland had been abandoned for lack of reliable allied forces, so Rundstedt's Army Group South faced the difficult task of destroying Soviet forces in western Ukraine in a single thrust from Lublin to Kiev, followed by a drive down the Dnieper River to the southeast to prevent Red Army troops in the west from escaping. Two factors made Rundstedt's undertaking challenging: first, the vast expanse of the Pripet Marshes impeded his initial assault and precluded any assistance from Army Group Center; secondly, Stalin and his military advisors assumed the goal of any German attack would be to seize the economic riches of Ukraine, so Soviet forces in the area were numerous, well trained, equipped, and led, and prepared for the German onslaught. As a result, the invaders struggled against stiff enemy resistance along the borders. Strong Soviet counterattacks slowed the German advance, as did heavy rains that turned the primitive road system into muddy quagmires and impeded supply efforts. Fierce fighting at Lvov, as well as furious Soviet counterattacks to the northeast at Rovno and Dubno, along the main axis toward Kiev, slowed the German advance for a week, creating a persistent threat that helped fuel the German command crisis of late July. As Rundstedt's forces lagged behind, Hitler, fearing for the southern flank of Army Group Center, early on considered redirecting units from the center to the south to secure Ukraine. Significantly, this energetic and stubborn Soviet defense came in the area that held, to Hitler's mind, the most important objectives of Barbarossa, the raw materials and industrial centers of Ukraine, and the oil of the Caucasus. The border battles in Ukraine also clearly demonstrated that, given time and leadership, Red Army soldiers were capable of effective resistance.[9]

In the main area of operations, Army Group Center's sector, the magnitude of the initial German triumph seemed most evident. Here, Bock's armies aimed to penetrate Soviet defenses north and south of the Bialystok salient, advance eastwards along the Minsk–Smolensk axis, then encircle and destroy enemy forces west of the Dnieper River. To accomplish this, his two mechanized formations, Panzer Group 2 (Guderian) and Panzer Group 3 (Hoth), were to strike rapidly to the east on either side of the sector and then converge to envelop enemy forces, which would then be destroyed by the infantry of Kluge's 4th Army. Although several major rivers posed an obstacle to a swift advance, this area of rolling land was generally favorable to mobile warfare. On the army group's southern sector, Guderian's Panzer Group 2 caught the Soviet defenders by surprise, quickly crossed the Bug River, bypassed the fortress of Brest-Litovsk (which held out until 12 July), ignored enemy units on their flanks, and advanced rapidly to the east. On the northern wing, Panzer Group 3 captured three bridges over the Neman River intact and by 24 June had seized Vilnius, the capital of Lithuania. Two days later units of Guderian's force took Slutsk, sixty miles south of Minsk, while Hoth's troops were only eighteen miles to the north of the city. The rush to the east stalled, though, as Guderian had already received orders to turn the bulk of his forces northward and close the pocket by linking up with Hoth in a short encirclement. Halder, determined to maintain firm control of the operation and worried that his headstrong Panzer commanders might exert too much independence, had acted to rein in the dash eastward. Although both Panzer generals preferred to continue the advance to Smolensk some 200 miles to the east before closing the pincers, they reluctantly obeyed the order to close the outer ring.[10]

The emerging picture created by the Soviet response thus seemed to confirm both Hitler's and Bock's arguments. Fierce Soviet resistance in Ukraine reinforced the Führer's belief that Stalin had accorded its protection, for economic reasons, highest priority. By implication, then, and contrary to Halder's assumptions, the real strength of the Red Army lay not in front of Army Group Center but to the south; destruction of enemy forces in the center thus might not result in the shattering triumph Halder anticipated. Meanwhile, enemy withdrawals in the north had opened a favorable path to Vitebsk and the "land bridge" between the Dvina and Dnieper, the route preferred by Bock and Hoth as the optimal way to get at Moscow. This fact, and the inadequacy of German power, now sparked the first signs of disagreement. Bock and his Panzer commanders urged a deep envelopment, while Hitler leaned toward the certain destruction of enemy forces in smaller, tighter pockets, fearing that otherwise the encircled area would be so large that German forces would not suffice to destroy the trapped Russians. Halder, while ridiculing Hitler's fears, nonetheless wanted to ensure his own direction of the campaign, so he supported Hitler and on 24 June ordered the Panzer groups to close in on Minsk, not least because a turn in there accorded with his view that the Minsk–Smolensk route was the best path to Moscow. Although neither Guderian nor Hoth saw any point in wasting time and resources on mopping up an enemy they regarded as already defeated, they grudgingly turned in at Minsk. Hoth's troops seized the city on 28 June and, with Guderian, snapped the trap shut the next day. Since Kluge's infantry had closed an inner ring around Bialystok, instead of one larger encirclement, two pockets had been formed, one around Bialystok by infantry with no armor support, and the other around Minsk with Panzer units but virtually no infantry. As a result, the Panzer troops could not prevent large numbers of Red Army soldiers from escaping, where their presence as partisans and roaming bands caused continuing difficulties in German rear areas, tying down mobile units and delaying their advance eastward. They also fed Hitler's anxiety that deep penetrations and weak encirclements simply allowed Soviet forces to escape through the overextended lines, a fear not without justification.[11]

Neither Hitler's nor his generals' view was fully correct or inherently superior to the other, nor did the German command necessarily throw away a chance at victory by reining in the Panzers. Given the continuing furious Russian resistance that alternately amazed and impressed German observers – Goebbels conceded that they were "fighting bravely" and effectively, while those on the spot admitted that the exceptionally bitter fighting already strained German troops to the limit – any notion that the enemy was defeated was profoundly mistaken. Hence, the irreconcilable operational dilemma: the Panzer commanders were right in seeking a rapid solution through deep penetrations, but failed to appreciate the severity of the threat to their rear and flanks posed by the allegedly "beaten" enemy. At the same time, shorter encirclements did cost time and tie down the Panzer units, but were the only way to seal pockets tightly and ensure destruction of the enemy, which all agreed was the main goal. The bold action that had proven successful in the past now only increased the danger, while safe, conventional decisions threatened to mire the Germans in a positional war that they were ill-prepared to fight. The uncomfortable reality, of course, was not merely that the Germans were attempting too much with too few resources, but in seeking a way out of the dilemma OKH failed to fully support either option, instead choosing to split already inadequate forces in pursuit of both alternatives.[12]

Although Halder seemed to believe that German forces could both close on Minsk and continue the advance eastward, Hoth dismissed it contemptuously as a "safe, but time-wasting tactic." Bock, too, doubted that anything decisive could be achieved at Minsk, suspecting that little was left inside the pocket. "We are," he fumed, "unnecessarily throwing away a major success!" He also fretted that the diversion of Hoth would allow the Russians, with their considerable tank forces, to build a defense line behind the Dvina and Dnieper, while accurately noting the problem with encirclements. "If we turn in at Minsk," Bock complained, "there will inevitably be a stop there until the entire Bialystok-Minsk pocket has largely been cleared. I wanted to take possession of the Dnieper or at least the Beresina bridges quickly, so as not to have to fight for them later – which unfortunately will now be the case." That, in fact, seemed precisely what the Soviets intended. Despite the persistent image of Red Army formations floundering about wildly, already on 23 June Halder admitted that the Soviets "might be attempting to concentrate armor far in the rear," while acknowledging a 4th Army report that indicated "the enemy in the Bialystok pocket is not fighting for his life, but to gain time." Still, he dismissed the notion that the "enemy High Command really has unified and organized control of the situation." By early July, though, the Soviets had clearly switched from reckless counterattacks to actions aimed at allowing their troops to evade German pincer movements and withdraw across the Dvina and Dnieper rivers.[13]

Paradoxically, it was Halder who seemed to be grasping at control. Bock and his Panzer commanders, for example, attempted to ignore OKH instructions in pursuit of their own preferences – a tactic that infuriated Halder but which he used extensively against Hitler. Indeed, when Hitler on 25 June expressed concern about the Panzer groups operating in too much depth, Halder, who had pushed through the shorter encirclement at Minsk against Bock's and Hoth's objections, ridiculed the Führer's fear as "[t]he old refrain" – adding significantly, "[b]ut that is not going to change anything in our plans." At the same time, Halder took a decision that elicited furious protest from his Panzer generals, and in retrospect seems to have been his first effort at centralizing control over operations in his own person. On the 25th he issued orders that both Panzer Groups 2 and 3 be placed under the command of Kluge, a conservative infantry general in agreement with Hitler on the necessity of tighter pockets, in a newly created 4th Panzer Army. Although the actual shift in command, which also included the transfer of most infantry units from the 4th to General Weichs's 2nd Army, would not take place until 3 July, Guderian and Hoth reacted sharply to this perceived brake on their drive east, Guderian even threatening to resign rather than submit to Kluge's authority. Halder, though, seems to have been playing a duplicitous game. Allowing the Panzer groups freedom to roam eastward would surely have aroused the Führer's suspicion, so instead he placed them under the command of a cautious general whom Hitler respected, then expressed the hope on 29 June that Guderian and Hoth would on their own initiative "do the right thing [i.e., advance toward Smolensk] even without express orders." OKH, Guderian realized, expected the Panzer commanders, "whether without or even against orders ... to carry out the previously accepted plan" and advance rapidly to Smolensk, but he must have felt considerable unease about being left out on a limb, buffeted by contradictory orders that, he admitted, generated "a considerable amount of ill-feeling." Less noticed at the time, though, was that OKH, and not Hitler, had acted to significantly reduce the traditional freedom of action of field commanders. Brauchitsch, in fact, claimed that both tough Russian resistance and the enormous expanse of the combat area – which threatened to swallow up German forces – compelled OKH to interfere in operations. In the event, of course, it would be Hitler, not Halder, who profited from the centralizing tendencies begun by OKH less than a week into the campaign.[14]

Initial German difficulties, then, stemmed not so much from Hitler's meddling as from fundamental problems with the operation itself, such as the tangled supply system and the unexpectedly stout Russian resistance – which, it might be noted, Hitler had predicted in his 14 June address to the generals. The Führer, though, had clearly lost faith in large encirclements. This was not merely the repetition of his familiar pattern of bold concepts followed by timidity in execution, but rather the impact of accumulating evidence that indicated the difficulty in sealing off pockets. The scale of maneuver in Russia, much greater than anything the Germans had previously encountered, combined with the almost complete absence of all-weather surfaces – less than 5 percent of roads in European Russia were paved in 1941 – meant that from the outset their truck-dependent supply system would be hard pressed. Within the first days it was obvious that the rutted paths that passed for roads placed great demands on the trucks, causing maintenance problems and soaring consumption of fuel and oil. In addition, the Landsers, marching on foot through the choking dust and oppressive heat, found the going exceedingly difficult. Moreover, Red Army counterattacks, although largely ineffectual and carried out with appalling casualties, nonetheless inflicted not insignificant losses in men and materiel on the Germans. Perhaps more importantly, the constant small group attacks and ambushes by the Russians on German troops and strung-out supply columns produced a wariness and exhaustion out of all proportion to the larger significance of the Russian endeavors. By early July these factors had forced a noticeably slower tempo on the German infantry, as it struggled to reduce pockets and deal with large numbers of bypassed Soviet troops, at the cost of falling behind Panzer units.[15]

Confirming Bock's fear, the battles at Bialystok-Minsk tied down roughly half the strength of Army Group Center in an effort to destroy enemy forces that refused to surrender. Previous experience with Blitzkrieg in France, when an enemy maneuvered into a trap lost the will to fight, was turned upside down, as the encircled Soviet units fought with a disconcerting fury that unnerved even veterans of previous campaigns. His unit, remembered one officer, "suffered considerable losses inflicted by . . . [cut-off] enemy troops . . . [who] hid beside the march routes, opened fire by surprise, and could only be defeated in intense hand-to-hand combat. German troops had not previously experienced this type of war." Another officer, a veteran of the First World War, claimed that the bloody forest fighting was "worse than at Verdun." Bock, who had earlier noted, "The Russians are defending themselves desperately," on 28 June conceded, "Our losses are not inconsiderable. Thousands of Russian soldiers are sitting in the forests . . . [and] refuse to give up. Each fellow has to be killed one at a time." Even Guderian, who regarded the Red Army as beaten, conceded in a letter to his wife on 27 June, "The enemy resists bravely and bitterly. The fighting, therefore, is very hard. One just has to put up with it." By themselves, the Panzer units lacked sufficient forces with which to seal off an encirclement totally, and since poor roads, lack of vehicles, and tough fighting delayed the Landsers, the gap between the slogging infantry and the driving Panzers steadily widened, with the result that large numbers of Soviet troops slipped through German lines.[16]

After the chaotic first days of the invasion, the Soviets regained a good deal of control over their units – Goebbels admitted on 29 June, "Their command is functioning better than during the first few days" – brought up reinforcements, and, in some areas, launched vigorous counterattacks using reserve divisions equipped with armor. This Russian resistance, despite the sledgehammer blows of the first days, clearly disrupted German plans, since the armored formations, confronted with continuing Soviet opposition, were unable to race eastward, thus maintaining the momentum of the attack, until the slower advancing infantry units arrived. In one of the first indications of the later fierce, and complex, controversies over problems raised by encirclements, Halder on 2 July indicated to Bock that OKH might halt the Panzer groups entirely in order to better seal off the pockets and destroy enemy troops. When Bock protested, the OKH chief cut him off by relating Hitler's skepticism at professions of a great triumph at Minsk: "Where are the prisoners then?" the Führer had asked pointedly. When Bock pressed not to have the armored forces halted, Halder's reply must have shaken him: "Thrust an entire corps into the swamps . . . in order to eliminate a threat to the inner flanks of Army Groups South and Center." Precisely this threat from the swamps, of course, had led Bock to favor the more northerly route to Moscow via Vitebsk and had occasioned Hitler's early, prescient warnings about both the swamps and exposed flanks. Neither could have been impressed by Halder's initial direction of the campaign; Hitler, in fact, urged on by his adjutant Schmundt, evidently early on considered replacing Halder with a frontline commander.[17]

In his sharp query on 2 July, Hitler, though perhaps without fully realizing it, had identified the central difficulty of Blitzkrieg in the vast spaces of the Soviet Union, one that meant the spectacular early victories were more apparent than real. German forces were destroying large quantities of mostly obsolete equipment and some Red Army formations – losses the USSR could make good – but at an unacceptable cost to themselves, since they could not easily replace either lost equipment or lost manpower. Clausewitz had warned against any campaign in Russia precisely because the endless spaces allowed the Russians to absorb numerous defeats while drawing the enemy into the middle of the country where, exhausted and past its peak offensive strength, it was most vulnerable to counterattack. The vastness of Russia now exposed a fatal flaw: Blitzkrieg would founder if the enemy was not induced to surrender quickly. Far from a steady unbroken advance that devoured the Red Army, as misleadingly suggested by operational maps, German forces had simply bypassed vast swathes of territory (and enemy resistance). To work, though, Blitzkrieg depended not merely on deep penetrations but on the chaos, confusion, and disruption occasioned by the initial blow – the basic loss of command and control – inducing the enemy to surrender even though it was capable of fighting on. It worked well in France, but less so in the Soviet Union. After initial paralysis, Stalin quickly regained his will and reasserted control. When faced with continued resistance and refusal to surrender – as with Great Britain in 1940 – the Germans were left adrift, with no clear idea how to proceed. In the USSR, the elusive decisive operational victory became the German goal, which merely raised the very real danger of winning themselves to death. Soviet resistance also forced a resurfacing of the unresolved conflict between Hitler and Halder over the principal goals of the campaign and how to attain them, disputes that spread throughout the command structure and took on a new urgency and rancor.[18]

In the first weeks of the campaign, the Führer was rarely able simply to push his ideas through. He yielded, for example, on 30 June to pressure from Brauchitsch and Halder – perhaps influenced by extremely optimistic situation reports – not to divert forces from Army Group Center to the north, trusting Halder's judgment that Leeb's forces were sufficient to achieve their tasks on their own. OKH, not Hitler, dominated operational decision-making and sought to restrict freedom of command in an effort to keep field commanders from bypassing its instructions. In creating the 4th Panzer Army, for example, Halder meant to assert more control, but his action failed to resolve important questions. Should pockets be reduced by Panzer or infantry forces? How could the differing speeds of the two be reconciled? Should armor be used to seal encirclements or drive eastward? Within the first few weeks, this had clearly become an odd sort of war: Panzer units raced ahead on the few good roads to enlarge the front, but without actually extending their control to areas off the roads or destroying enemy forces, thus leaving large numbers of them "behind the lines" to wreak havoc. "The whole war takes place, more or less, on the roads," Wilhelm Prüller noted on 3 July. "Without securing the land lying to the right and left of the road, we move along . . . How many Russians must be cruising around the country still! How many enemy tanks are off the road . . . Funny the way this war is being waged."[19]

The gap between the infantry and armor had distinctly serious ramifications, though, since supply lines for the Panzers had to be pushed out in advance of the infantry and through long unsecured stretches of territory, leaving the columns dangerously vulnerable to destruction. Moreover, the trailing German forces had enormous difficulty in pacifying the rear areas. This, in turn, slowed the momentum of the armored forces, thus reducing the prospect of decisive success for the increasingly unsupported Panzer thrusts, which began to resemble isolated raids more than powerful, coordinated enveloping movements. Many Panzer generals, in fact, felt they had been left vulnerable and exposed, with little support, to do the bulk of the fighting on their own. Letters by Guderian and Kluge to their wives on 12 July captured perfectly this sense of two different wars being fought. While the former expressed the feeling that this campaign, even more than the French, was "almost completely an affair of the Panzer troops," who, despite being restrained by the plodding infantry, nevertheless stood before a "campaign-deciding success," the latter noted soberly, "The Russians are fighting excellently with newly brought up forces, among them new armored divisions that have been created on a scale we did not suspect."[20]

Above all, supply and transport difficulties fueled the insoluble problem of the difference in speed between infantry and armored forces. The limitations imposed by the Versailles Treaty and the subsequent rush to build the armed forces in the 1930s had strained German capabilities to the limit. They had thus entered the war with inadequate railroad capacity and an incompletely mechanized Wehrmacht. In order to standardize the bewildering variety and quality of vehicles possessed by the army, Halder had actually proposed in February 1940 a "demotorization" program. In Russia failures of both the railways and trucks forced the Germans to rely on horse-drawn transport for much of their supply needs, a reality that greatly influenced operational decisions, even if Halder was reluctant to accept it. Even as he pressed frontline commanders to take the initiative and surge ahead, then, facts on the ground forced different conclusions. Given the reality of Soviet resistance and their own supply difficulties, the real issue facing the Germans was not that OKH decisions were better than Hitler's (they were not) or that Hitler was an interfering dilettante (not so much at this point), but that this was an intractable problem, one Heinrici pointed out in a letter of 11 July to his wife. For the infantrymen, he complained, the task of clearing the pockets, securing the rear areas, and engaging in forced marches to catch up with the rapidly moving Panzer forces meant "walking until their tongues hang out, always marching, marching, marching. I believe that after the war the infantry will be disbanded. The difference between motor and human power is too great." Insufficient motorization, in fact, meant that the Germans lacked the basic requirement for successful deep encirclements. Instead, they were left with impressive, but not mortally decisive, Panzer thrusts. Despite Halder's irritation at Hitler for pointing this out, large numbers of enemy troops were escaping the porous pockets, which undermined the stated goal – that all agreed held the key to victory – of destroying the enemy west of the Dnieper. After all, what was the point of having the Panzers race ahead if they were not disrupting enemy organization or the ability to resist, nor demoralizing the enemy, nor bagging large numbers of prisoners? The German command, then, could not avoid making contentious decisions on the thorny issues of how to proceed – large versus small pockets; destroy the enemy versus gain territory – as well as over the primary goal: economic resources versus taking Moscow.[21]

At the time, though, these problems seemed to many merely inconvenient irritations, since the seemingly shattering opening triumphs convinced even German commanders, who might have been expected to know better, of the imminence of victory. In his memoirs, Weichs admitted that most thought that the hammer blows delivered to the Soviets would cause the entire Bolshevik system to collapse within six weeks. Halder was even more optimistic, recording in his diary on 3 July: "On the whole, then, it may be said even now that the objective to shatter the bulk of the Russian army this side of the Dvina and Dnieper has been accomplished . . . [E]ast of the Dnieper . . . nothing more than partial forces [remain], not strong enough to hinder realization of German operational plans. *It is thus probably no overstatement to say that the Russian Campaign has been won in the space of two weeks* [emphasis added]." He did allow that "this does not mean that [the campaign] is closed. *The sheer geographical size of the country and the stubbornness of the resistance, which is carried on with all means*, will claim our efforts for many more weeks to come [emphasis added]." Hitler, privy to the same intelligence information, also shared Halder's optimism, remarking the next day that, in his opinion, Stalin "has practically lost the war already." Although false, this assumption would have significant consequences beyond battlefield decisions. On 14 July he ordered a reorientation of armaments production to favor the navy and Luftwaffe, a clear indication that he expected success in the east and, in contrast to the previous year, intended to be prepared for the next showdown, that with the Anglo-American powers. It also meant that while the Soviets ramped up their production – making good their staggering tank losses, for example, and with better models – German tank production declined throughout the remainder of 1941. This lack of equipment would prove especially irksome later in the year.[22]

Although long regarded as an example of a lethal combination of hubris and braggadocio, Halder's diary entry, curiously enough, mentions all the factors that contributed to German defeat, from the larger dangers of space, time, and fierce Soviet resistance, to specific references to threats from the Pripet Marshes and operations being slowed by bad weather. His, therefore, was a hubris based on obliviousness more than smugness; it was a failure of imagination, a refusal to consider the implications of enemy resistance or poor road conditions, let alone credit the Soviets with the ability to affect German operations. Reports from the field, though, already hinted at the problems ahead. The war diary for Panzer Group 3, for example, noted, "[T]he enemy . . . fights tenaciously and courageously to the death . . . The struggle, as a result, will be harder than those in Poland and the Western campaign." Heinrici similarly noted in a letter to his wife on the third day of the attack that the Soviet soldier fought "very hard" and was "a much better soldier than the Frenchman. Extremely tough."[23]

In retrospect, 3 July was to mark a key point in the campaign, but not in the way Halder believed. Attacks by both Hoth's and Guderian's Panzer groups met markedly stiff resistance, while in Guderian's front, enemy counterattacks caused not inconsiderable difficulties. Halder also seemed not to understand the real strength of the Russians or his own knotty logistical situation. It had, in fact, become increasingly clear that the results of the December war games had been dishearteningly accurate, that the German army lacked the ability to accomplish all of the objectives set for it. The planners' assumption had been that the Red Army would collapse at the initial blow; if it survived, the Wehrmacht had insufficient strength to finish the task. The Lossberg plan, Major-General Paulus's analyses of the war games, and Hitler's operational directive of December 1940 had all pointed to the intractable problem of inadequate German strength, so they had stressed the importance, after the initial victories on the central front, of shifting forces to both the northern and southern sectors. Halder, though, remained stubbornly focused on a direct thrust on Moscow, admittedly an important industrial and communications center, as the best way to trap and destroy the Red Army. From the beginning, then, he intended to launch an attack in the center that would develop such impetus that Hitler would be forced to bow to OKH wishes. But by early July, although Hoth's and Guderian's Panzer forces had made impressive progress, increasing Russian resistance, spiraling supply difficulties, and the growing threat to Army Group Center's flanks – which even Halder was beginning to acknowledge – had noticeably stalled its momentum. The assumption that Stalin, like French leaders, would just give up was now tenuous, at best. Winning battles was not enough; a way had to be found to translate operational success into strategic victory, a problem reflected in the growing tension between Hitler and OKH.[24]

Since the army lacked the necessary resources to execute both conflicting operational conceptions, a decision had to be made soon on whether to sustain the drive of Army Group Center toward Moscow or adhere to the original plan and turn forces to the flanks. "Turn to the north or south?" Hitler pondered on 4 July, recognizing that the time had come to decide the future direction of the operation. "It will perhaps be the most difficult decision of this war." The next day, he again stressed, presciently, that this would be the "critical decision in this war, perhaps . . . the only decisive decision in this war," but, typically, he hesitated to pull the trigger. Not until 8 July did he defer to OKH and outline his "perfect solution," one that owed much to Halder's influence and to the erroneous information the OKH chief was supplying him: Army Group North would continue toward Leningrad with its own forces while Army Group Center would destroy the enemy north of the Pripet Marshes and open the way to Moscow. In a nod to the original plan, Hoth was to assist Leeb in the north, if necessary, while Guderian would strike to the south. In a stunning failure to comprehend the true strength of the enemy, Halder anticipated that Bock's infantry forces alone, or aided only by Hoth's Panzers, would suffice to eliminate the last elements of the Red Army in the central sector – an assumption that in the event proved wildly overoptimistic.[25]

Although he knew that the enemy had not been fully destroyed west of the Dnieper line, Halder nonetheless assumed that the serious losses suffered by the Red Army had nearly exhausted its ability to continue fighting. On that same 8 July he received estimates that 89 of the 164 known enemy infantry divisions, and 20 of the 29 armored units, could be considered destroyed or largely eliminated, with only 46 Russian combat divisions left to contest the Germans. By his reckoning, the Soviets could no longer organize a continuous front, nor would activation of new units offer much help since they would lack officers, equipment, and training. To Halder, the Soviet goal seemed simply to drain German strength through ceaseless counterattacks. These, although admittedly worrisome, paradoxically encouraged – because of the sizable enemy losses – his belief that the resistance must soon slacken. The erroneous estimates of enemy strength supplied by Foreign Armies East misled Hitler as well. He justified his decision to keep new tank production at home rather than ship the tanks to the front both because of their unsuitability in urban warfare – in retrospect, more than a bit ironic – and with reference to "missions still ahead" that would "extend over thousands of kilometers," by which he meant future operations against the British position in the Middle East. On 8 July, then, both the Führer and his OKH chief clearly thought the Russian campaign was well in hand. Despite the continual appearance of fresh enemy divisions, especially armored units equipped with new model tanks, as well as evidence that the Soviets were evacuating entire factories to the east, the Germans were slow to draw the proper conclusions.[26]

Between 8 and 13 July, though, persistent Soviet counterattacks forced Halder to a reappraisal of the situation and an implicit admission that his assessment of the threat the Red Army posed to the German flanks had been wrong – and that Hitler had been correct. Although Hoth had crossed the Dvina on 4 July and Guderian pressed over the Dnieper on 10 July, both, in classic Blitzkrieg fashion, had done so largely by avoiding the largest enemy concentrations. As a result, they faced growing pressure on their flanks, Hoth from the direction of Nevel and Velikie Luki to the northeast and Guderian on his southern flank from Mogilev and Rogachev. Guderian's situation was also exacerbated by the lagging advance of Army Group South, whose operations had been distinguished more by a laborious "pushing back" of a well-organized enemy than any bold operational breakthroughs. Because of these twin threats, within days Halder's optimistic assumptions had been shattered. On 12 July, in response to Hitler's concerns about the slow pace of Leeb's advance, Halder reluctantly conceded that Hoth might have to swing north. The next day, the growing Russian threat forced him to recommend to Hitler that the "dash toward Moscow" by Panzer Groups 2 and 3 be halted until "enemy strength on the present front" had been destroyed, an action that accorded both with the intent of the original Barbarossa plan and with Hitler's oft and continually expressed opinion that the destruction of enemy forces was more important than the capture of the enemy capital. Still, the OKH chief's concession was more apparent than real, for, with his sights firmly set on Smolensk and an eventual resumption of the push on Moscow, Halder ordered Hoth's forces to swing northeast and Guderian's Panzers southeast with the object of clearing their flanks before pivoting to converge east of Smolensk. As Halder tried to juggle Hitler's wishes against his own and those of his field commanders, though, he was caught in a predicament of his own making, which Bock neatly expressed on 13 July: "I consider diverting elements of Panzer Group Hoth to the north while elements continue to march east to be futile . . . [T]he Panzer groups are only an effective striking force if employed in unison . . . [E]mploying individual Panzer corps to operate alone [is] pointless [since] their fighting strength has become too low." After all, Bock warned the next day, "One must be careful not to take the overall situation too lightly . . . A victory has not yet been won." Hoth noted more bluntly in his diary on the 13th, "The expenditure of strength is greater than the success."[27]

In seeking an offensive solution to the problem on his flanks by splitting his already overstretched forces, Halder continued to overstate German and underestimate Soviet abilities. Despite his OKH chief's persistent optimism, Hitler, impatient for the decisive victory he had been led to believe was imminent, expressed increasing concern at the slow pace of operations. According to his adjutant, Schmundt, the Führer remarked on 13 July, "The Russian is a colossus and strong," while worrying that the Panzer groups were expending their strength – something Bock noted the same day – before "the coming wide-ranging operations." Even as Hitler deduced from the slowdown that Guderian's Panzer group would have to be turned south to Ukraine to seize the harvest – itself an implicit recognition that the campaign would likely extend into 1942 – while Hoth's Panzers conserved their strength for a later assault on Moscow, Halder delivered an upbeat assessment, claiming the enemy front was "weakly held or manned by troops of dubious quality." Not only was this an erroneous appraisal, but he also failed to realize that German strength limitations and logistic difficulties made Moscow an increasingly unattainable goal, at least in 1941. On 15 July, though, when he reiterated his belief that the Soviets lacked the ability to impede the German advance, Paulus, pointing to Russian troop concentrations to the east, raised the disconcerting possibility that the Soviets had succeeded in creating an operational reserve that would be used to attack the flanks of any German push on Moscow.[28]

Just getting to Smolensk, as was becoming uncomfortably apparent, strained German logistic capacity to its limit. Despite warnings on 14 July from Quartermaster-General Wagner – and by others over the next few days – that the supply situation did not allow a further advance to the east, OKH remained unmoved, or worse, uncomprehending. Brauchitsch admitted to Bock on 15 July that "a continued drive to the east by the Panzers after the capture of the area around Smolensk is out of the question . . . [and an] advance by the entire body of infantry is no longer possible for reasons of supply." Then, seemingly unaware of the implications of what he had just said, Brauchitsch continued, "We will have to make do with a sort of 'expeditionary corps,' which together with tanks will have to fulfill far-reaching missions." Amazingly, no one in the German command structure saw Brauchitsch's ludicrous proposal, which assumed a colonial campaign rather than the one at hand, for what it was: an admission that Blitzkrieg had run its course. The key to victory lay in retaining superior mobility, both to outmaneuver and to destroy enemy armies as well as to seize the crucial economic and industrial resources that would assure German survival and Soviet defeat. After just one month of the campaign, though, the Germans already suffered from overextension and exhaustion of their Panzer forces. In a disturbing omen, their drive eastward was stalling not because they had been defeated in a major battle but because of their own deficiencies.[29]

If not yet a recognition that the campaign could not be won, a troubling sense of unease was nonetheless palpable; from mid-July the question of how to achieve victory dominated discussions between Hitler and OKH. The enemy had been pushed back but not destroyed – precisely what Hitler had warned against – so uncertainty reigned as to how to proceed. The fall of Smolensk on 16 July provided little relief, since the encirclement was incomplete and the Germans lacked the ability to close the pocket. Also unsettling was the realization that the Soviets had now consciously begun to use encircled forces as a means to tie down German units, inhibit their freedom of action, and disrupt the pace of their advance. The debacle at the strategically important city of Velikie Luki proved sobering as well. Although Hoth's forces seized the city on 19 July, ferocious Soviet counterattacks compelled him to withdraw the next day, a blow to Halder's plan to clear the northern flank of Army Group Center before closing the Smolensk pocket.[30]

Substantial Soviet combat power still confronted Army Group Center, a realization that sparked a downturn in the mood at OKH, if not yet in that of its chief. Halder on 20 July recorded that "the costly battles involving . . . our armored forces," as well as the "loss of time . . . and the weariness of the troops marching and fighting without a break," had plunged Brauchitsch into utter despair, but Halder concluded, "There really is no call for this." That same day, Bock complained that the constant friction between Kluge, Guderian, and Hoth was "getting on his nerves," not least because "Guderian is in fact right in his push to drive east . . . until the last enemy reserves . . . have been crushed." This, of course, was the crux of the problem. A rapid push east was the textbook solution, but the stubborn reality of the battle-field meant the slower advance of the infantry delayed progress while steadily bleeding German strength made any further push eastward impos-sible. Bock, with an inkling of the problems ahead, chided OKH: "The assumption . . . that the enemy is not acting according to a plan does not coincide with the facts . . . I think it doubtful that the enemy will allow the fighting here to cease when it suits us . . . If full freedom of action is to be won, then . . . [enemy forces] must be destroyed."[31]

The logical place to destroy them was Smolensk, but the key decision in that regard had already been made on 19 July, but by Guderian, not Hitler or Halder. Having swept south of Smolensk, he chose not to turn north to link up with Hoth and close the pocket, but, hoping to seize an advantageous jumping-off point for the eventual push on Moscow, to move east in the direction of Yelnya. As a result, he squandered the chance to seal the pocket quickly and prevent large numbers of enemy escaping, Bock lamenting on 20 July, "At the moment there is only one pocket on the army group's front! And it has a hole!" Guderian's action, which the annoyed Bock blamed on Kluge's lack of control over the headstrong general, also ensured battles in the Yelnya salient whose ferocity led many officers to compare them to their Great War experience at Verdun. Moreover, the delay in reducing the pocket at Minsk, along with the yawning gap between German infantry and armored units had, just as Hitler predicted (and feared), invited Soviet counterattacks along the long, exposed flanks of Panzer Group 2. Fierce enemy attacks against Guderian's southern flank at Propoisk, southeast of Mogilev, forced Bock to send forces from the 2nd Army to his relief. Thus, although Bock had earlier pressed Guderian both to close the Smolensk pocket and to continue to advance eastward, on 21 July he admitted of the Soviet action, "A quite remarkable success for such a badly battered opponent!" The next day, Guderian conceded to Kluge – an action that must have pained him greatly, given the bad feeling between the two – that "securing of the flanks . . . has become very difficult and takes away the strength from our spearheads." Clearly, both Guderian's and Hoth's Panzer forces – dispersed, exhausted, fighting with no infantry support, and at the end of a barely functioning supply system – needed to refocus their power. The stubborn Soviet resistance had succeeded in derailing German plans and enabling large numbers of their own men to escape the pocket at Smolensk; but more, it also revealed the extent to which Stalin was now determined to force the Germans to react to Soviet moves.[32]

After a month of fighting, the Wehrmacht desperately needed a period of rest, as all plans for Barbarossa had anticipated, but the planners had assumed this would not be a problem since Soviet resistance would long since have been shattered. Instead, on 20 July, Stalin telephoned Marshal Semyon Timoshenko to inform him that the time had come for a Soviet strike to gain the initiative. The plan entailed three simultaneous blows directed at Smolensk, with the aim of cutting off both German pincers east of the city and transforming the would-be encirclers into the encircled. Although Stalin intended this attack to destroy Army Group Center and produce a decisive turnabout in the war, command and control problems meant that the assault that began on 21 July unfolded in a piecemeal fashion. The Soviets did manage to delay the closing of the pocket until 27 July, while their relentless assaults also put intense pressure on the seriously overextended Panzer units. This was, Bock marveled on 26 July, "astonishing for an opponent who is so beaten. They must have unbelievable masses of materiel, for . . . the field units still complain about the powerful effect of the enemy artillery." Although the Germans managed to repulse these attacks, the Russians persisted through August in intense fighting that resulted in frightful casualties to both sides. Repelling these vigorous enemy assaults, in fact, left Army Group Center so weakened that a direct thrust on Moscow was out of the question until the precarious supply situation had been remedied. Once again, as in the border battles, the Germans had landed a series of body blows but failed to inflict a knockout. This, in turn, encouraged a flare-up of the long-simmering dispute over the focal point of the operation, as German leaders struggled to prevent the campaign from deteriorating into a war of attrition.[33]

Ironically, this crisis of command erupted in large part from Halder's chronic over-optimism and ongoing deception of Hitler. On both 8 and 13 July he had agreed with Hitler that troops from Army Group Center should be shifted to aid the lagging efforts in both the north and the south. The result, on 19 July, was Führer Directive No. 33, which reflected Hitler's recognition that large-scale encirclement operations had not achieved decisive success. He now declared the immediate aim to be the final reduction of pockets and destruction of enemy units still within reach, a process that would entail shifting the bulk of the two Panzer groups from Army Group Center to support the drive on Leningrad and to clear Soviet troops from the Pripet Marshes. Although Hitler has since been criticized for this order, it was both true to the original Barbarossa directive and based on OKH recommendations. More to the point, it also relied on faulty German intelligence assessments; as noted, Hitler can hardly be rebuked for making decisions based on the information and advice given him by his professional military elite. Since the Panzers had largely outrun the supply system, the infantry struggled to keep pace with the armor, frontline units had received scant replacements, and the lagging effort in Ukraine threatened the entire southern flank of Army Group Center, Hitler's order was neither unrealistic nor unreasonable. Even Halder realized a period of retrenchment was needed before resuming the drive toward Moscow.[34]

By the time the order was issued, though, another fact dominated: the Russians, not the Germans, were dictating the terms of fighting at Smolensk. This reality forced Halder on 21 July to finally deal with the threat to the flanks – and to alter the plan he had proposed to Hitler. He now told Bock and Kluge that he meant to move Panzer Group 2 and the 2nd Army south into Ukraine, with the ultimate objective – stunning, in retrospect, in its deluded optimism – of seizing Stalingrad, although, Bock noted critically, "The big strategic idea is still unclear." Significantly, and despite this move to the south, Halder remained intent on pushing on to Moscow, so instead of shifting part of Panzer Group 3 to the north, after clearing its flank it would now advance on the capital in coordination with the infantry of 4th and 9th Armies. This, though, contradicted his earlier pledge to shift forces from Army Group Center to the north. The stagnation of Leeb's forces and loss of Velikie Luki seemed to confirm the need for troops there, while the inability of German infantry to even reach Smolensk in order to relieve the armor and seal the pocket had led to a daily erosion of Panzer strength. The developing impasse thus seemed to belie Halder's confident assumption that Moscow could be taken with only one Panzer group and two infantry armies.[35]

More importantly, Hitler had not approved any change in plans, and certainly not an assault on Moscow. His dawning realization that Halder was deceiving him, as well as his dissatisfaction with OKH's rather inept handling of German armies at Smolensk – especially the inability to concentrate forces and close the pocket – crystallized his growing lack of confidence in Halder's direction of operations. He had long regarded the OKH chief as a competent bureaucrat but inept strategist, and nothing that had transpired in recent weeks had changed his opinion. Given his seemingly valid suspicion of Halder, he was now inclined to rely more on his own instincts and judgment, which he believed had been vindicated by past successes. The conflict between Hitler and Halder thus erupted because of a failure of the campaign to produce decisive results. Halder had hoped to subtly manipulate Hitler and convince him of the superiority of OKH actions through the cumulative effect of success, but now the obvious failure to destroy Soviet resistance and the creeping exhaustion of the Wehrmacht forced choices to be made. In response, on 22 July, in Directive No. 33a, "Supplement to Directive No. 33," which was issued the next day, Hitler reaffirmed the earlier decision to shift forces from Army Group Center to the north and south.[36]

Halder immediately understood not only that this threatened his push on Moscow, but also that his chicanery had been found out. He met with Hitler throughout the day and evening of 23 July, trying to sway the Führer with his own economic arguments. Halder conceded that even if he scraped together all available reserve units the infantry of Army Group Center alone was insufficient to take Moscow, with any such attack resulting in a laborious, costly "biting through." Thus, Hoth's Panzer Group 3 would have to clear its flank, strike in the direction of the Valdai Hills, then turn in on Moscow from the northwest. Taking the capital was critical, Halder asserted, not merely because a majority of enemy forces would be concentrated there, or because it was the communications center of the Soviet Union, but – a new argument for him – because the Moscow region also contained significant armaments industries, the loss of which would make further organized enemy resistance "extraordinarily difficult." Moving with the zeal of a convert to buttress this economic argument, Halder admitted that it was impossible to defeat the USSR without eliminating its economic base, a point already made by Hitler. He also raised a new and disquieting concern: the Germans lacked sufficient time and strength to complete the Barbarossa plan before winter. If the fighting was reduced to "positional warfare," the enemy would be able to organize its defenses and mobilize its industries so that next spring the Wehrmacht would face newly raised and equipped Soviet formations. As a result, "the military goal of the war against Russia, the rapid elimination of one opponent in a two-front war in order to turn full strength against the other (England), could not be achieved." Halder claimed that the Soviets had been "decisively weakened" but not yet "completely defeated," so future operations had to aim at destruction of the enemy ability to resist. This meant that German forces should also strike southeast toward the Volga at Stalingrad and on into the Caucasus to seize key oil facilities.[37]

In his diary, the OKH chief seemed to reveal a different opinion. "Subsequently (and into the rainy fall season), he [Hitler] imagines one could drive to the Volga and into the Caucasus with armored divisions alone," Halder remarked disdainfully, adding, "Time spent in such a conference is a sad waste." This cynical tone – ridiculing Hitler for repeating the same ambitious goals that he himself had just outlined – reinforces the impression that Halder was merely manipulating Hitler's twin concerns with destroying enemy forces and securing economic resources. Such an interpretation might not be completely warranted, though, for at a meeting with army group commanders on 25 July, Brauchitsch, who closely followed his chief of staff's line of thinking, stressed, "Our main task remains to shatter Russia's capacity to resist . . . [and] to bring their . . . production centers under our control . . . We must seize their armament centers before the onset of winter . . . If we succeed . . . their superiority in manpower alone will not win the war for them." Nor, seemingly, did he foresee any imminent possibility of a swift victory, envisioning future Panzer operations – in a startling reversion to First World War thinking – less as far-ranging "raids" than as "a tactical break-in into the enemy front so that 'piece by piece' it would be broken." Halder was just as forthright, if equally clueless as to how to proceed. After praising the "ruthless use of troops," the "remarkable achievements," and the "tactical agility" of this toughest opponent of the Wehrmacht, he then declared that "for the time being an [enemy] collapse could hardly be hoped for," regarding the "system of piecemeal break-throughs and smashing [of the enemy front] . . . the only method of battle . . . New operations can no longer be conceived in such wide-ranging fashion . . . All actions against this enemy [must aim at] limited goals and be tightly reined." Although certainly a belated recognition that economic factors were important, these extraordinary statements can also be seen as a frank admission that both strategically and operationally the campaign had failed, and – notwithstanding Hitler's intervention – the only option for Germany in the interim was a method of war remarkably similar to attritional British tactics in 1916–18.[38]

In any case, Hitler feared that any frontal assault on Moscow, especially with the depleted Panzer forces, would simply allow the enemy once again to withdraw, a belief apparently confirmed by the bungled operations at Minsk and Smolensk. Worried by the gap between armor and infantry that resulted in porous encirclements – Göring, much to Bock's disgust, had informed Hitler that aerial reconnaissance showed large numbers of enemy troops streaming eastward out of Smolensk – as well as the high losses suffered by Panzer units in the pocket battles, the Führer advised using infantry and artillery to eliminate the pockets rather than risk high casual-ties and further reduce the striking power of the tanks. He had also concluded that the Russians did not care if their flanks were endangered or units encircled, so his advice, that the army should concentrate on "tactical battles of destruction over smaller areas in which the enemy could be pinned down and completely destroyed," came as a stinging rebuke to Halder and his conduct of operations. Over the next few days, the OKH chief fumed that the campaign was deteriorating into static warfare, even as he admitted the weakness of German units, the extreme supply difficulties, that large numbers of enemy were escaping the encirclements, and that the Soviets were assembling yet more forces for counterattacks. On 26 July he bluntly told Hitler that he was playing into Russian hands by resorting to "tactical envelopments." His claim, though, was undercut by the fact that each gamble on a large encirclement, however successful it appeared, merely exhausted German forces without achieving anything decisive, a vicious cycle that was eroding the strength of the army. Hitler expressed the dilemma well, complaining to Halder on the 26th, "You cannot beat the Russians with operational successes . . . because they simply do not know when they are defeated."[39]

Although Halder conceded that Hitler's observation had some merit, he nonetheless complained that following the Führer's prescription would let the enemy dictate German actions, reduce the campaign to a series of minor successes, and slow the tempo of operations – as if this was not already happening. Ironically, in a letter to his wife two days later Halder voiced exactly the same complaint as Hitler, while claiming it was the latter who did not understand the reality of war in Russia. "He is playing warlord again and proposing such absurd ideas . . . The Russian won't simply go away, like the French, when he has been operationally beaten. He has to be killed one at a time . . . This takes time and [Hitler's] nerves won't stand it." In reality, though, it was Halder's own clumsy direction of the campaign – especially at Smolensk, where Soviet attacks prevented both closure of the pocket and replenishment of the Panzer forces – not Hitler's intervention, which dispersed German forces and allowed the Russians to dictate terms. Hitler's prescription to rely more on infantry and artillery to seal and eliminate the pockets rather than reduce the striking power of the tanks by using them for this task was valid, but, of necessity, also meant adjusting the pace of the advance to that of the infantry – and thus, as Halder feared, slowing German progress.[40]

Halder was himself disconnected from reality, since the inadequate transportation and logistic network, and consequent lag in supplies, meant that the war of movement could not be sustained in any case, especially as the front both deepened and widened – a dispersal of strength that Brauchitsch warned about on 25 July. His complaint, then, although correct, was largely irrelevant; Russian counterattacks and their own logistic weakness, not Hitler's orders, caused the loss of momentum. Further, Halder had already established the precedent of short encirclements at Minsk, while at Yelnya it was Halder, Bock, and Guderian who insisted – ironically, in view of the later harsh criticism of Hitler for just such stubbornness – on holding this untenable salient at exorbitant cost, only then to have to give it up. On 27 July, Bock admitted that Army Group Center was in the interim incapable of anything more than local operations: "Whatever can be found in the rear army area is being scraped together for the coming missions, for the army group is much too thin . . . to undertake anything serious." The next day he noted, "Halder is in no doubt that under these circumstances a significant advance to the east by the weak forces left to the army group . . . will be impossible." Taken together, these statements hardly constituted a ringing endorsement of German ability to renew and sustain a war of movement.[41]

Despite his jab at Hitler, Halder's nerves were suffering as well, as the realization took hold that his operational ideas had failed and that the fighting might well last into the winter. The Red Army had not been destroyed west of the Dnieper and clearly had more strength and resilience than thought, while supply problems, threats to its flanks, Soviet resistance, and high casualties were all forcing a halt to the advance. Adolf Heusinger, head of the Operations Section in OKH, thought, in fact, that the strain of the campaign had put Halder "near his end, on the one hand he allocates everything to me and on the other hand he constantly comes to interfere," a charge the OKH chief often made against his Führer. There is a curious and persistent disconnect between the image of sweeping German successes, since perpetuated in many histories, and the reality of bitter, bloody combat at Smolensk. "The fighting around Smolensk in July and August," recalled one veteran who experienced war on five fronts, "was the heaviest and deadliest I saw during the war," a claim substantiated by the statistics. More Germans died on the Eastern Front in July 1941 than in any other month until December 1942, at Stalingrad, a sober corrective to the triumphalist myth. On the last day of July, both Guderian and Bock conceded German difficulties. While the former noted simply, "The battle is harder than anything before," the latter complained, "I have almost no reserves left to meet the . . . constant counterattacks . . . With the present state of the railroads I can't receive any help from home or through the shifting of forces."[42]

Indeed, one reason why the dispute between Hitler and Halder now flared with such intensity was the growing sense, as Goebbels put it, "that we have underestimated Bolshevism." Bock agreed, conceding on 28 July, "A collapse of the Russian system is for the time being not to be expected," an admission that demolished the basic assumption upon which victory was predicated. Astonishment at the unexpected fighting abilities of the Red Army was widespread. Kluge confessed that "the Russians fought much more skillfully than we had assumed," while Reinhardt, referring to the period of cooperation between the Reichswehr and Red Army in the 1920s, now feared that "the brothers with me in the classroom learned too much." The "good times," as Manstein termed them, when one could make swift advances, were gone, replaced by "slow strangulation." "All of us," agreed Heinrici, "misjudged the Russians." Hitler surely concurred, which, given the corollary that the war would continue into 1942, elevated economic concerns – and seizing industrial centers – to a top priority for him.[43]

Typically, though, when faced with a contentious decision, Hitler wavered, uncertain how to proceed. He was, according to his adjutant Engel, beset with doubt and indecision, torn between "political-strategic and economic" concerns, although, in truth, he rarely made decisions based exclusively on one or the other consideration. Although Moscow was a key industrial center, if the fighting was to continue into 1942 Hitler considered the south, "a land where milk and honey flowed," to be more important, since that was "where oil, wheat, more or less everything was located necessary to keep the country going." Additionally, he believed it vital to have "a proper concentration of forces. To use Panzers in fighting to demolish cities . . . was a sin . . . They had to operate in the open areas of the south." On 26 July, in fact, Paulus solicited information from Hoepner, Manstein, and Reinhardt, the Panzer commanders of Army Group North, as to the feasibility of using tanks in the area between Lakes Ilmen and Peipus. All agreed on their unsuitability, with Manstein – who from the start had doubted that he had sufficient strength for the tasks assigned – recommending an advance on Leningrad with infantry alone, while turning the army group's Panzer forces toward Moscow. The next day, Jodl, who had earlier favored a turn north but was now skeptical, intervened with Hitler to urge a drive on Moscow. Hitler tended to listen to Jodl, so even though the latter was unable to secure a renewed thrust on the capital, his influence was nonetheless apparent. On 28 July, Hitler told Brauchitsch that he had decided to suspend the Leningrad operation in favor of clearing up the situation on the flanks of Army Group Center. Although the advance on Moscow would still have to wait, two days later, in Directive No. 34, Hitler again acquiesced to OKH proposals. Noting the appearance of strong enemy forces, the dreadful supply situation, and the need to rehabilitate the Panzer groups (which was expected to take ten days), he ordered Army Group Center, "for the moment," to go on the defensive, while the other two army groups continued on with their own resources. Halder, sensing victory, exulted, "This decision frees every thinking soldier of the horrible vision obsessing us these last few days, since the Führer's obstinacy made the final bogging down of the campaign appear imminent." Halder, though, overstated both the impact of Hitler's orders on the slowing of operations and the reality of Directive No. 34, for Hitler, still uncertain how to proceed, had simply put off a firm decision about Moscow.[44]

The key dispute in July 1941 was not one of space versus time (i.e., seizing territory as opposed to a rapid advance), but one of space, logistics, and mechanization (i.e., how best to deploy armor and infantry in the vast expanse of Russia). A critical failing of Barbarossa was inherent in the very structure of the Wehrmacht: it was not motorized enough nor did it possess sufficient manpower or logistic capacity to master the vast space of the USSR. There was thus no "correct" option available that would have guaranteed victory, so, in retrospect, the July crisis in command seems a bit unreal. German deficiencies, combined with continuing Soviet resistance, meant that the momentum of the campaign necessarily stalled. This raised the issue of how to proceed, given the increasing disparity in economic power between Germany and its enemies (now effectively including the United States). To retain operational command, Halder, who controlled the flow of information, gave Hitler overly optimistic assessments. Then, when the OKH chief began to face reality, he dispersed forces between the army groups – so that none had the resources needed to accomplish their goals, but in such a way as to continue the advance on Moscow – rather than just halt and clear the flanks, as war games had shown would be necessary, the Barbarossa directive indicated, and Hitler desired. This, in turn, crystallized the unresolved clash between military and economic goals. OKH sought to resolve the dilemma in operational terms, but by late July there was no reason to believe that Stalin, who was firmly in control and prepared to fight on from the Urals, would have quit even if the Germans had been able to solve their supply crisis and capture Moscow. Hitler, on the other hand, realized that Germany, desperately in need of food, raw materials, and oil, had entered an economic danger zone. If these could be captured, not only would it be able to fight on, as well as prepare for the eventual showdown with the Anglo-Americans, but their denial to the USSR (through conquest or destruction) might well force Stalin to capitulate or severely reduce the scale of fighting – as Stalin himself suggested in July 1942 in his "Not One Step Back" speech, and as Hitler had argued in June 1940 during the French campaign.[45]

Although historians have often addressed the conflict between military and economic priorities, in many respects the vital issue was the discrepancy between field reports concerning the level of enemy resistance – as well as supply and transportation difficulties – and what was being reported to Hitler. Halder, fixated on an advance on Moscow, wanted to create the impression that German power sufficed for a continued attack in that direction. This, then, raises the question of the extent to which Hitler should be criticized for making decisions based on misleading information. In evaluating even the incomplete evidence given him, the Führer recognized early in the campaign that large envelopments were not producing the intended results, which Halder only conceded weeks later. Hitler's decision for tactical encirclements was militarily sound – if limiting

– and hardly irrational. The first goal of the campaign, all agreed, upon which all else depended, was to destroy enemy forces, but in the event too many were escaping. Deep drives into the rear thus seemed pointless if they were neither disrupting enemy ability to organize serious counterattacks nor bagging large numbers of troops. The crucial fact, which Hitler had expressed on 26 July, was that Stalin, unlike the French a year earlier, maintained control and the will to fight on; the "expanding torrent" was not working. By late summer 1941 it is doubtful whether any option would have been successful in knocking the USSR out of the war that year. German striking power was so reduced and the Panzer forces so exhausted that, although they were still capable of operational successes at the points on the front where they were concentrated, they could not produce a war-winning blow. Serious logistic problems not only made the seizure of Moscow extremely doubtful, but, despite Hitler's insistence on destroying Russian industrial production facilities, the Germans had also been unable to prevent the Soviets from dismantling and withdrawing factories to the east. In fact, the Russians produced more tanks (and newer models) in the second half of 1941 alone than the Germans did during the entire year, a discrepancy intensified by Hitler's withholding of newer German models to be used elsewhere – on the assumption, based on the information he was receiving, that the campaign was nearing success.[46]

Smolensk, then, was a victory of sorts for the Germans, but one that in many ways was indistinguishable from defeat. By the time Bock officially declared the pocket eliminated on 5 August, his troops had taken far fewer prisoners at a much higher price than anticipated. The battered Panzer divisions were badly in need of rest and replenishment, struggling even at the end of the battle to keep the pocket closed against frenzied Russian break-out attempts. At the same time, the continuing enemy attacks at Yelnya, especially the devastating artillery barrages, cost men, munitions, and (perhaps most significantly) spirit. Although the Red Army had suffered grievously as well, it had achieved its goal – survival – while the Wehrmacht had been unable to eliminate enemy resistance in front of Army Group Center and clear the way to Moscow. In addition, Smolensk had upset Hitler's grand strategic calculations. An overwhelming triumph there, he reckoned, would lead to a rippling effect of consequences that would benefit Germany. Great Britain, he believed, without the prospect of future Soviet assistance, could be coaxed into cooperation against the hegemonic ambitions of the United States, while Japan would join the war against the USSR. On 14 July, in fact, Hitler told the Japanese ambassador, General Hiroshi Oshima, that the "destruction of Russia" should be the "political life's work of Germany and Japan." Instead, Soviet counterattacks in the second half of July persuaded Japanese leaders not to intervene against the USSR. Significantly, Foreign Minister Yosuke Matsuoka, the leading advocate of intervention in the Japanese government, was forced to resign on 16 July, after which Tokyo moved swiftly to assert its dominance in Southeast Asia. Bock, in fact, noted with disappointment on 25 July, "The Japanese are taking the opportunity to establish themselves in Indochina, but ... are only lukewarm about the hoped-for attack on Russia!" By mid-August, Japanese reports from Moscow concluded that the Germans could not hope for a quick victory over Russia. The Germans had thus lost time, momentum, irreplaceable men and materiel, the possible intervention of Japan – and still seemed no closer to knocking Russia from the war, as evidenced by the vigorous and continuing Soviet counter-attacks. Meanwhile, German forces were exhausted and in need of rest, while even optimistic generals such as Guderian feared the congealing of the front.[47]

Still, despite mounting evidence, German military leaders struggled to admit that the Soviets, far from beaten, could not be knocked out at one blow, that Blitzkrieg had reached its limits, and that a new approach was needed. And if the military professionals could not (or would not) see this, it is hard to expect Hitler to have a clearer view. Destroying the enemy west of the Dnieper–Dvina line was assumed by all German plans to be the key to success, but had not been accomplished. After the rest period a decision – for or against Moscow – would have to be taken. Nor, in retrospect, is it clear that Halder's arguments were markedly better than Hitler's. In view of the logistical situation and exhaustion of forces, any further advance on the central axis was for the time being out of the question; even the replenish-ment of frontline units proved difficult enough. Moreover, as the war games had predicted (and Hitler feared), strong Soviet forces in the Pripet Marshes – which six German divisions could not squelch – constituted a significant threat to the flanks of both Army Groups Center and South, menacing supply lines and any further advance, especially toward Moscow. "A precondition for any further operation," Bock emphasized, "is the defeat of the enemy on the army group's flanks, both of which are lagging far behind." That, in fact, was precisely what Georgii Zhukov, the Soviet chief of staff, feared most; specifically, an attack by Bock in the south that would cut off and destroy the dangerously exposed Soviet forces near Kiev. For his efforts at warning Stalin of this danger, Zhukov was demoted to command the Reserve Front, while Stalin's gross misreading of the situation would lead to the Soviet catastrophe at Kiev. By early August the Barbarossa campaign had already exceeded in length that in the west the previous summer, with no clear way to end it in evidence. Victories had been won, yet a terrible price had been paid. "[W]e are at the end of our tether . . ." Bock conceded on 2 August, "the nerves of those burdened with great responsibility are starting to waver."[48]

Hitler, faced with the vital decision of where to focus diminishing German power, was one of those so burdened. Typically, when beset with doubt and confronted by disagreement among his advisors, he tended to procrastinate and then defer to his generals. The delay in operations while the Panzer units were rested and replenished thus provided Halder another opportunity to regain control of strategic decision-making. Hitler, though, wanting to hear first-hand from his field commanders, whom he trusted more than the clique at OKH – his class resentment for the "learned gentlemen" of the general staff was never far from the surface – flew to Army Group Center headquarters on 4 August to discuss options with Bock, Kluge, Hoth, Guderian, and Heusinger (from OKH, who was likely there as Halder's eyes and ears). The situation was especially tense since a number of officers on Bock's staff had hatched a plot to kidnap the Führer, a plan foiled by tight security measures. Buoyed a bit by the recent encirclement in the south at Uman, where Rundstedt, after weeks of grinding battles, had finally destroyed a significant Soviet force, as well as the expectation that Leningrad would soon be surrounded, Halder had impressed upon Bock, Hoth, and Guderian the need to make Hitler aware of the importance of taking Moscow. This united front held, despite Hitler's insistence on meeting with each general individually and in private. In his audience with the Führer, Guderian pressed for more tanks and tank engines to be released to the Panzer groups. He also gave a rather upbeat assessment of the situation, reminiscent of Halder's early February 1941 attempt to convince Hitler that the Red Army was no formidable foe, claiming that the last Soviet reserves had been depleted and with one further effort the path to Moscow would be cleared. Hitler had been skeptical then, and was dubious now, remarking, according to Guderian, "If I had known about the Russian tank strength in 1941 I would not have attacked." Still, Guderian was a frontline commander, a man of action respected by Hitler, so the latter patiently heard him out and took his claims seriously, agreeing to release 400 new tank engines and 35 new production tanks to the Eastern Front – which, Halder noted smugly, OKH had already done without Hitler's knowledge.[49]

Releasing tank engines, though, had not relieved Hitler of his uncertainty; he was open to the possibility of a future advance toward Moscow, but Leningrad and the Donets had higher priority. When informed of the outcome of the meeting, Halder voiced frustration at the lack of a clear decision and the low priority for Moscow, but, significantly, did not dismiss the idea of a move to Ukraine for economic reasons. He merely noted that if this was the goal, then forces needed to be concentrated "for an invasion of the oil region . . . all the way to Baku." In a meeting with Brauchitsch, Hitler now conceded – a result, Halder boasted, of having the idea put discreetly into his head – that developments were moving in the direction of static warfare, as in the First World War, so the front had to be cracked open. The Führer again related three options for action: in the north Leeb would take the Valdai Hills, with support from Hoth; Bock would resolve the threat on the southern flank of Army Group Center; and in the south Rundstedt would eliminate enemy forces west of the Bug River. Although not the clear directive Halder had desired, he was nonetheless hopeful, since the first two suggestions would effectively clear the way for a thrust on Moscow and keep the campaign, in his mind, on track. Halder, in fact, was generally upbeat, concluding on 8 August that the Soviets had "only limited forces left," a situation he compared to that of France a year earlier when, having broken the last enemy defense line, the Germans advanced largely unopposed. Now, he supposed, the Wehrmacht was on the verge of a similar operation. Both Army Groups North and South, he thought, again displaying a bewildering optimism, could accomplish their goals on their own – and might even receive help from Army Group Center.[50]

His immediate goal, though, was to restore OKH operational supremacy, but in moving to do so Halder was too clever by half. Although he bemoaned Hitler's obsessive tactical thinking – itself a consequence of diminishing German power and options – he now outlined operational objectives with little regard for the realities of a tattered logistics system or Panzer forces desperately in need of rest and refitting. In a meeting with Jodl on 7 August – perhaps in order to coordinate action against the Führer now that the former was on board with the Moscow alternative – Halder, after posing the query, Moscow or Ukraine, decided the answer was "Moscow and the Ukraine . . . with the emphasis on the 'and.' We must do it, or else we shall not be able to eliminate this source of the enemy's strength before fall." Halder had now seemingly come to agree with Hitler that in order to defeat the USSR the Wehrmacht would have to seize its resource base and destroy its industrial war-making capacity, which meant a move into Ukraine and the Caucasus. Halder, though, as always reluctant to give up Moscow, preferred not to choose one over the other, so advocated pursuing both goals at once. With Jodl, one of the few generals who could influence Hitler, in agreement, he set about convincing the Führer that the Wehrmacht could do both. Typically, he overstated German abilities and underestimated those of the Soviets, creating dangerous illusions that fed Hitler's allegedly amateurish and mistaken decision-making. Halder controlled the flow of information; not even Jodl was completely aware of the actual situation or the full extent of Russian resistance, so his advice to Hitler was colored by Halder's opinion. The problem was that the entire premise of OKH strategy was wrong.[51]

As always, Halder believed that once the Germans regained freedom of movement, sweeping operational victories would follow, leading to ultimate triumph. On 7 August, though, while he and Jodl conspired to renew the push on Moscow, Bock expressed a clearer view of the difficulties ahead. "The situation is extremely tense . . .," he worried, "I don't exactly know how a new operation is to take place . . . with the slowly sinking fighting strength of our . . . forces." Still, he consoled himself with the thought that "things are undoubtedly even worse for the Russians!" That may well have been, but on 10 August he forbade an attack by Guderian precisely because of limited strength and the continued vulnerability of his southern flank. A few days later he noted, "In spite of his terrific losses in men and materiel the enemy attacks at several places daily, so that any regrouping, any withdrawal of reserves . . . has so far been impossible." He then added, in a revealing concession, "If the Russians don't soon collapse somewhere, the objective of defeating them so badly that they are eliminated will be difficult to achieve before the winter." Halder, too, succumbed, if only temporarily, to reality, noting gloomily on 11 August:

> On the fronts . . . reigns the quiet of exhaustion. What we are now doing is the last desperate attempt to prevent our front line from becoming frozen in position warfare . . . The whole situation makes it increasingly plain that we have underestimated the Russian colossus, who consistently prepared for war with that utterly ruthless determination so characteristic of totalitarian states . . . At the outset of the war we reckoned with about 200 enemy divisions. Now we have already counted 360. These divisions indeed are not armed and equipped according to our standards, and their tactical leadership is often poor. But there they are, and if we smash a dozen of them, the Russians simply put up another dozen. The time factor favors them, as they are near their own resources, while we are moving farther and farther away from ours. And so our troops, sprawled over an immense front line . . . are subjected to the incessant attacks of the enemy.

Although certainly a belated realization that his assumption of Soviet weakness was incorrect – an insight Hitler had had a month earlier – Halder could do little but press on with his plans.[52]

The day before, in fact, Walter Warlimont at OKW had produced a study, based on Halder's discussion with Jodl, which advocated both a resumption of the Moscow offensive and a push into eastern Ukraine. Halder, though, remained fixated on the idea that only a decision at Moscow could compel the Soviets to capitulate. As a result, Army Groups North and South were, unrealistically but deliberately, depicted as capable of achieving their goals on their own. Not surprisingly, since it seemed to offer a way out of the strategic impasse, the Führer embraced the document, which became the basis of Directive No. 34a, issued on August 12. In it, Hitler specified that the primary tasks were to occupy the Donets area, rectify the situation on Army Group Center's flanks, seize Leningrad, and only then move on the capital in order "to deprive the enemy, before the coming of winter, of his government, armament, and communications center around Moscow, and thus prevent the rebuilding of his defeated forces and the orderly working of government control." Although initially disapproving, since the Moscow operation was held hostage to progress at Leningrad, a powerful Soviet offensive two days later in the direction of Staraya Russa that threatened to disrupt Leeb's front forced Halder to admit to Bock, "I don't know myself what I should do. I am utterly desperate." Although he complained on the 15th that the frantic shifting of forces to meet audacious but limited enemy attacks was "a grave mistake for which we will have to pay heavily," he also conceded that Bock "had been playing an all-out gamble with the numerically superior enemy," before confessing, in a profoundly disturbing admission of failure, "all it [Army Group Center] accomplished to date is wasted." Even so, Halder quickly regained his balance and discovered a positive in Hitler's new directive, in that it "follows our conceptions by ordering Army Group Center to strike on Moscow and by calling off departure of forces from this army group to Army Group South." Thus, although the timing of the assault on Moscow was still dependent on Leeb's success in taking Leningrad, Halder's cherished dream of seizing Moscow remained intact. Even though Army Group Center had nearly won itself to death in the quest for the decisive encirclement battle – and had signally failed to destroy either Soviet will or ability to resist – Halder could think of nothing else but to try again. If the Red Army was to be destroyed, it would have to be done in front of Moscow. Significantly, he ignored the implicit admission in Hitler's directive that the war would not be over in 1941.[53]

Soviet attacks, though, created another pressing problem for Halder, since he had earlier told Hitler that Ukraine and Moscow could both be taken. The OKH chief now realized German forces were too weak to do both, but he had already implicitly agreed with Hitler on the importance of Ukraine. Faced with the choice between Ukraine and Moscow, Halder still favored the latter, so he had to backtrack on Ukraine. To provide justification, OKH on 18 August produced a new proposal, presented by Halder to Hitler that same day, clearly favoring Moscow over, not in addition to, Ukraine. The problem lay in convincing Hitler. The Führer had needed little persuasion when, in late July, Halder had first stressed that Ukraine should be taken quickly for economic reasons and assigned it equal priority with Moscow. The latter now had to deconstruct his earlier argument and make the case for Moscow instead of Ukraine. In addition to the economic rationale in favor of Moscow – it was, after all, a major armaments center – Halder admitted the ability of the Panzer groups to carry out long-range operations was limited. Thus, he suggested, given their restricted mobility, they had to be used over shorter distances, which implicitly excluded their use in Ukraine, and in support of both strategically and economically decisive goals. Although he conceded that the northern and southern army groups had important objectives to pursue – the capture of vital industrial and economic areas – an attack on the flanks, he insisted, could never achieve a decisive result. Only Army Group Center could accomplish both objectives: seizing a key armaments center and shattering the enemy defense line by destroying his last remaining large concentration of forces. In a double irony, then, Halder, who had consistently overstated German strength and, in his direction of the campaign, dispersed it, now conceded it was deficient and demanded that it be concentrated in the central sector. Army Groups North and South would thus be left on their own, with no promise of aid from Army Group Center, which would seek the decisive triumph at Moscow. In retrospect, given his admission just a week earlier that he had grossly misjudged Soviet military and economic strength, along with his awareness of German weakness, Halder's optimism is difficult to fathom. Perhaps he simply thought he could once again mislead Hitler, and concentrate all available German resources to pursue his cherished goal of Moscow. Or perhaps he was merely deceiving himself and engaging once again in his typical disregard of logistical realities.[54]

In any case, he had picked the wrong time for a showdown. Hitler almost certainly believed that in the Supplement to Directive No. 34 he had already made a major compromise. He likely also suspected that Halder was again trying to manipulate him. In any case, Hitler had formed his own conclusions from the information given him over the past few weeks. Although Jodl thought that Hitler had "an instinctive aversion to treading the same path as Napoleon," fearing a "life and death struggle with Bolshevism" at Moscow, he also had reasons that Jodl considered "well thought out." In particular, Hitler believed that the best chance to destroy enemy forces lay in the south, since their main grouping was now east of Kiev. Engel largely substantiated this, noting that the Führer regarded seizing economic resources as opportune precisely because "he is being advised from the front and by OKH that the enemy has taken such a beating that the prospect of his being able to mount an offensive in the foreseeable future . . . need no longer be taken into consideration." Ironically, then, having drawn Hitler a false picture of enemy strength, Halder was undone by his own deceptions: if the Soviets were indeed so depleted, then there existed no need for a hurried offensive toward Moscow. Another factor was at work as well, one that suggested that Hitler had a clearer view of reality than his advisors. The strain of the past month had clearly taken a toll on him both physically and psychologically. In mid-August, Hitler suffered an attack of dysentery, accompanied by evidence of rapidly progressing coronary sclerosis. When Goebbels visited the Führer's headquarters on 18 August he was stunned by Hitler's physical and mental exhaustion. Signs of extreme nervous strain abounded: he was obsessed with the gross underestimation of Soviet strength given him before the war by German intelligence, implying that had he known the truth he might have hesitated to launch the attack. Hitler also shocked Goebbels by suggesting that he might accept a negotiated peace with Stalin, and by the wholly unwarranted belief – more a desperate hope – that Churchill's government might suddenly collapse and the war end. Hitler's nerves were clearly frayed, while Goebbels was sobered by the realization that the campaign would not be over in 1941, and the best that could be hoped for were good winter positions.[55]

This was the key point, for Hitler certainly knew better than his generals that Germany was unprepared economically for the continuation of the war that he now thought likely. His flash of strategic insight had immediate operational implications. The realization that the campaign could not be won in 1941, and its corollary that the eastern war would likely be decided more by economic factors than military maneuvers, meant that control of material resources – and their denial to the Soviets – assumed even greater importance. The Russians could fight on, and surely would, even if Moscow was lost, but they could not continue without the economic resources of Ukraine and the oil of the Caucasus (a point Stalin was to stress in July 1942 in his "Not One Step Back" order). Material factors were thus crucial for Germany's ability to wage the next phase of the war in the USSR, and absolutely vital if Germany now faced, as seemed likely following the conclusion of the Atlantic Conference between Churchill and Roosevelt, a global war. After all, point six of the Atlantic Charter pledged the Western democracies to a complete destruction of Nazi tyranny, which, his adjutant Below claimed, caused Hitler to fly into a rage when he heard it.[56]

His detailed reply to Halder, then, came as a slap in the face, for it was a terse rejection of the army chief's proposals. Seizing on objections submitted to him by Jodl, who was having second thoughts about the drive on Moscow, on 21 August Hitler issued an order through OKW reaffirming the principal objectives to be attained before the onset of winter: the seizure of the economic and industrial areas of Ukraine, the oil region of the Caucasus, and, showing his extreme sensitivity to economic matters, conquest of the Crimea to secure the Romanian oil supply. As a last jab at Halder, the encirclement of Leningrad still took precedence over the capture of Moscow. The next day, in a detailed "Study," Hitler justified his operational priorities not only with the usual economic arguments, but with military considerations as well. Army Group South, he argued, in contrast to Halder, was not strong enough on its own to accomplish its tasks, so Guderian's Panzers would have to be turned south. Far better, he stressed, as Bock had already conceded, to eliminate the enemy threat on the flanks before launching any attack on Moscow, so the operation into Ukraine to gain economic resources would also serve the aim of securing the southern flank of Army Group Center.[57]

In any case, Hitler noted caustically, the original operational plan called for movements to the north and south, so not he but OKH had altered the script. Moreover, in a stinging rebuke to Halder, Hitler chided him for not knowing, in the vast spaces of the USSR, how to use tank and air forces in coordinated, concentrated fashion to achieve maximum destruction of the enemy. Göring, Hitler stressed, in a gratuitous swipe at Halder and his clumsy handling of operations, understood this. Not only had Halder deviated from the plan, then, but he failed to achieve a decisive victory. After all, the aim of the campaign, he reminded his OKH chief, was to eliminate Russia as a major power, and the best way to realize that goal was through "the destruction of the life force of Russian resistance" by eliminating its economic basis. The differing outlooks between Halder and Hitler had thus been laid bare. While the former sketched plans according to formal military doctrine, the latter's views reflected his long-held conviction, stemming from the First World War, that it had been the collapse of the German social-economic base – and not any failure of will on the part of the army – that had led to the destruction of the imperial regime. This view now informed his decision, so, although he ended with conciliatory words affirming his acceptance of the thrust on Moscow, Hitler emphasized that this would only be undertaken after the other operations had concluded.[58]

Furious at Hitler's reply, which he took as a personal insult, and perhaps embarrassed that his obstructionism had been found out, Halder raged against the Führer, blaming him for the vacillation and indecision of the past weeks. He also insisted to Brauchitsch that they should tender their resignations, a proposal the latter rejected since it would accomplish nothing. Deeply upset, Halder flew to Army Group Center headquarters on 23 August to rally support for resuming the offensive on Moscow. Bock, though, insisted that he could not advance on Moscow without Panzer Group 2, since the battle around Yelnya clearly showed the enemy was far from beaten. Halder thus arranged for Guderian, one of Hitler's favorite generals and especially vocal in his opposition to a move south, to accompany him to Führer headquarters in an attempt to dissuade the dictator from his course of action. On the night of 23–24 August, Hitler listened patiently, in the absence of Halder, as Guderian made the case for an attack on Moscow. The Soviet capital, Guderian asserted, was not only the political, transportation, and communications center of Russia, but, in a telling analogy that illuminated the military mindset, "the nerve center of Russia . . . like Paris is to France." Hitler then argued the alternative. In order to continue the war, he stressed, Germany needed the crucial raw materials and agricultural resources of Ukraine, as well as a secure oil supply. "My generals," he remarked in a biting comment, "know nothing of the economic aspects of war." Guderian, who the day before had asserted that an attack to the south by his forces was impossible, now reversed his position and affirmed his ability to launch just such a drive, as long as his Panzer group remained intact – a refusal to divide his forces that would have a crucial impact on delaying the later attack on Moscow. When they heard the news of Guderian's volte-face – aided, perhaps, by rumors, of which he was aware, that he was in line to replace Brauchitsch – both Halder and Bock were furious, with Halder particularly bitter. In reality, though, Hitler's decision had already been made and Guderian, always far closer to Hitler than supposed, was not the man to change it; the battle for Ukraine took precedence over Moscow.[59]

Despite the later self-serving assertions of the generals, Hitler's observations were not without merit. Indeed, German miscalculation of Soviet military capabilities – a failure made by the professional elite but for which Halder stubbornly insisted on blaming Hitler – had resulted in a fundamentally flawed conception of the eastern campaign, for which military skill alone could not compensate. The bulk of the Red Army had not been destroyed and Soviet leaders had managed to organize an effective defense in spite of catastrophic losses, while the steadily declining German strength and vastness of the area to be conquered posed almost insuperable difficulties. The German logistical system had also neared the point of collapse: railroads had not been repaired quickly enough and the dire state of Soviet roads overwhelmed German motorized transport. The number of trains arriving at Army Group Center could barely sustain daily operations, let alone allow a buildup sufficient to permit an advance on Moscow. Amazingly, though, Bock, supported by Halder, believed the only way he could sustain his position was through continued offensive action – this at a time when holding the ground already taken proved difficult. Despite Bock's claims, he did not possess the capacity to destroy the strong enemy forces in front of him. An admission of this came in early September, when, having been "bled white" through their own stubbornness – more on the part of the generals than Hitler – Bock finally withdrew from the Yelnya salient, important both as a psychological victory for the Soviets and as the German loss of a springboard for later operations. For his part, Hitler saw the continued Soviet pressure at Yelnya as proof of the need to eliminate the southern threat to any advance on Moscow – and, in truth, without such an operation, an attack in the center would not likely have reached the capital in any case. Nor, given supply difficulties, did the turn south substantially delay the eventual attack on Moscow, since Army Group Center could not have immediately jumped off for the capital in any case. Finally, despite his dismissal of the military elite's understanding of economics, many of his front generals – now faced with the prospect of the campaign lasting into the winter – had in fact come to agree with Hitler on the importance of material resources.[60]

In the command crisis of August 1941, then, the key point was not that one decision was right and the other wrong – they both had merits, and logical arguments could be made for or against each – but that it took Hitler six weeks to prevail. This not only belied the notion that he directed the campaign with an iron fist, but also left the eastern war running on an improvised basis. Hitler was neither irrational nor illogical in his judgment; in fact, his strategic assessment at the time was probably better than Halder's, especially given German logistical problems and the threatening Soviet force to the south. Economically and operationally, a move south made sense; striking toward Moscow might have seemed the strategic thing to do, but after Smolensk the Wehrmacht lacked the ability to do so immediately. As always, Hitler could marshal support from many generals for his view. Despite the prevalent image of Hitler today, at the time he shied from dictating to his generals in the way Stalin did; indeed, it is hard to imagine Stalin arguing with his generals for six weeks before imposing his will. Ironically, it would have been better had Hitler dictated operations from the start. At least then a swift decision on a clear Schwerpunkt and concentration of forces would have been taken.

In the event, though, this decision, itself a good illustration of the typical process by which Hitler sought to persuade his generals rather than impose his will on them, took weeks to arrive at amid paralyzing and debilitating discussions between Hitler and OKH. The German army traditionally put a premium on rapid decisions, preferring even a poor decision executed quickly to an ideal solution that cost time – but in this instance time had been wasted precisely because Hitler proved unable or unwilling to impose his will on OKH. Revealingly, Hitler chose not to communicate his ideas orally, his preferred style, but through a written memorandum (his "Study" of 22 August) that mimicked traditional general staff methods – a demonstration, perhaps, of the value he placed on convincing his generals through rational military arguments as opposed to simply ordering them to take his preferred course of action. This hesitation, though, put a heavy mortgage on German chances for victory in 1941. Although Guderian, Manstein, Hoth, and others complained of delays and the lack of a clear Schwerpunkt, at the time they tended to blame Halder rather than Hitler for the bungled direction of operations. Nor was there any particular unity of opinion among the generals as to where that Schwerpunkt should be, as Kluge, Weichs, Heinrici, Rundstedt, Reichenau, and Kleist all agreed with Hitler on the move south, with Weichs endorsing it as a precondition for an attack on Moscow.[61]

The real problem, as Hitler himself had remarked earlier – and Clausewitz had noted of the Napoleonic failure – was that it was difficult, in a country of such size, to break the will to resist even after a series of devastating defeats in battle. The Soviets were proving, as had Tsarist Russia in 1812 and France in 1914, that it was hard to knock a major power out in one blow. Conversely, the Germans were learning, much to their distress, that despite their operational skill it was quite possible to win the battles and lose the war, that, as Michael Geyer put it, victory did not automatically result from "a mere accumulation of success." This, of course, should not have come as any surprise, since that had been the pattern of the First World War. German military leaders, though, thought the new operational technique of Blitzkrieg had eliminated this dilemma, so they largely ignored the logistical constraints that stymied their efforts at decisive victory. Of no one was this truer than Halder, who regarded Barbarossa as a short-term operation. When it threatened to go awry, he could think of nothing else but to redouble his efforts to launch a final offensive in the direction of Moscow that would salvage the entire campaign – itself, perhaps, an admission of intellectual bankruptcy. Having from the start made a serious miscalculation on Blitzkrieg as a war-winning strategy, German generals compounded this mistake by failing to realize, despite the ensuing triumph at Kiev, that Blitzkrieg had died at Smolensk.[62]

For his own part, as he began to perceive that the timetable was going amiss and that German victory in 1941 was problematic, Hitler reverted to the pattern of 1940; deeply hesitant and uncertain what to do, he fixated on the larger economic and strategic situation to justify his actions, while increasingly intervening in operational and tactical matters. Characteristically, having finally decided, given the likelihood of the campaign continuing into 1942, that securing economic resources had a higher priority than achieving another operational triumph, he justified his decision with the hope that destruction of enemy forces in the south, along with the loss of its vital sources of economic power, might at last break Soviet resistance. The deeper problem, of course, was that a war-winning strategy at this point likely did not exist. Hitler and Halder had never agreed on the fundamental aims of Barbarossa, so, from the start, it had been a muddled gamble on luck. But what many had expected as "a matter of course," as the commander of the 9th Army Corps lamented in early September, "has not occurred: victorious Blitzkrieg, destruction of the Russian army, collapse of the Soviet state." As Soviet resistance continued, all concerned had a haunting sense of time slipping away, aware as they were that Germany would never again possess a relative advantage that might bring victory.[63]

8

Barbarossa
CATASTROPHE (SEPTEMBER 1941–MARCH 1942)

"Soldiers of the Eastern Front!" began Hitler in yet another of his portentous declarations, this one proclaiming the "last gigantic blow which shall crush this enemy before the onset of winter!" To be read to the troops on 1 October 1941 just hours before Operation Typhoon commenced, on the surface it seemed a pompous hash of bluster ("When I called on you to ward off the danger threatening our homeland, you faced the greatest military power of all time"), boasts ("In barely three months, thanks to your bravery . . . it has been possible to destroy one tank brigade after another . . . to eliminate countless divisions, to take uncounted prisoners, to occupy endless space"), and bravado ("The world has never seen anything like this!"). Yet to a critical listener – or one who had experienced the fighting in the east – it was less what the Führer said than what he left unmentioned that was most revealing. Despite all the alleged success, why was this last "deadly blow" necessary? And why did he promise that "this time, everything was prepared . . . according to plan" so that the enemy would now be crushed? Did this mean that the earlier operations had been haphazard and slapdash? Just as crucially, given the weakened state of the army – apparent to all after three months of bitter, bruising combat – would this "last great decisive battle" really end the war before winter? Or, like the men of Napoleon's *Grande Armée*, would the Landsers of the Ostheer be forced to endure the bitter cold of Russia, a prospect that frightened even the toughest of soldiers?[1]

Despite Hitler's litany of success, German victories so far had been more apparent than real. The Wehrmacht had failed to attain the objectives set for it and the final triumph proved stubbornly elusive – a reality that Hitler's proclamation did little to conceal. Indeed, just a week earlier he had admitted, "We've forgotten the bitter tenacity with which the Russians fought us during the First World War . . . They are brutes." Having prevailed in the bruising six-week confrontation with OKH and secured the turn south into Ukraine, though, over the next two months Hitler stepped back and largely left direction of operations to Halder. Paradoxes abounded. While Hitler, Halder, and Bock, hoping for an imminent attack on Moscow, urged Guderian to move south quickly in a concentrated manner along the west bank of the Desna in order to smash enemy forces, the strong-willed Panzer commander, with an eye on the Soviet capital, overextended himself by crossing to the east bank, thus exposing his forces to continual Soviet attacks that slowed his advance. The command crisis that erupted this time, though, was between Halder/Bock and Guderian, as Hitler limited himself to support of his senior commanders, who thought that Guderian's strategy slowed his advance, led to unnecessary fighting, and endangered the entire operation to trap Soviet forces east of Kiev.[2]

In a further irony, a turn south was precisely the one German action that Zhukov most expected, and feared. He believed Army Group Center could not advance on Moscow without eliminating the danger to its flanks, while the lagging effort of Rundstedt's forces in the south presented the Germans with an obvious opportunity to destroy Soviet armies behind Kiev and then either advance on Moscow from the south or continue east to the Donets Basin. In the final paradox, Stalin, who at the start of the war had been most concerned with the defense of Ukraine, was now obsessed with safeguarding Moscow. He therefore ignored Zhukov's warnings, even demoting him when his constant admonitions became too annoying. By the time Stalin realized, in mid-September, the true nature of the impending disaster, he resorted to form. Instead of trying to extricate Soviet armies, he used the soon-to-be encircled forces much as he had at Bialystok-Minsk and Smolensk: as a way to grind the enemy advance to a halt, buy time, and exact a high price for German victory. The result was another in a long series of spectacular encirclements that netted impressive figures of Soviet prisoners but, in the inevitable fierce fighting to reduce the pocket, cost the Wehrmacht dearly, in both time and lives. Thus, although Bock exulted at the "dazzling success" at Kiev, a Landser noted more grimly, "Probably we will have to annihilate everything before this war is going to end." Still, the Wehrmacht seemed at last to have blown the front open, although the striking success at Kiev resulted as much (or more) from Stalin's blunders as German abilities. Despite evidence of insufficient strength, it seemed proof to most German commanders that the Wehrmacht still had the ability to seize Moscow.[3]

Kiev had also been Hitler's triumph, something he promoted against the expert advice of his military professionals. Although Zhukov had seen it as the most logical and dangerous German operation, it had been vigorously opposed by Halder, Bock, and even Jodl at OKW. Without a follow-up, though, Kiev would remain merely a tactical rather than a strategic victory. And the principal way – perhaps, at the time, the only way – to achieve a meaningful triumph was for the Germans again to do what Zhukov feared: continue their advance to the east against the exhausted enemy forces and seize the economic resources of the Donets Basin and the oil of the Caucasus. This, of course, would have meant giving up any chance of taking Moscow before the winter. After their victory at Kiev, the Germans had a chance, however slim, to accomplish Hitler's economic goals in the south, if all available strength was concentrated there. Given the pre-war dispersion of Soviet industry to the Ural region, as well as the growing importance of Lend-Lease aid to the USSR, this would not have ended the eastern war, as Stalin surely would have fought on, even in a reduced capacity. It would, however, have provided the Germans with the crucial economic means by which to conduct what was now effectively a global conflict; it would also have spared Army Group Center the disastrous losses incurred in the late autumn and winter of 1941–2. Even with this enhanced economic position, though, the Germans still would have struggled to defeat the Soviets in 1942 before the large-scale American presence was felt in Europe. In this devil's choice lay the grim reality facing the German leadership in the autumn of 1941: they could possibly have conquered Ukraine, or taken Moscow, but they could not do both. By this stage of the war, an outright German victory was already problematic, as the best they could realistically hope for was simply better odds in a grim global war of attrition.[4]

Even this chance, though, was denied the Germans, for Hitler, typically irresolute, yielded to the strong-willed Halder and approved a renewed offensive on Moscow. This meant, once again, a shifting of the Schwerpunkt, a failure to exploit gains, and further strain on the already overburdened army. The impetus for this gamble on a last effort to take Moscow stemmed primarily from Halder and Bock, with the former taking little regard of time or supply constraints. Both had succumbed to a "Marne psychosis," obsessed with not throwing victory away by failing to make a last, all-out effort to take the Soviet capital. Hitler, too, under intense pressure from his generals, had given in to the temptation of Moscow – believing that its capture was both crucial and possible. Reacting to OKH insistence, then, on 6 September, less than two weeks after Guderian had launched his push south, and well before any assessment could be made about possible future gains in Ukraine, Hitler directed that preparations begin for the attack on the Soviet capital. His order to concentrate all available forces for the Moscow operation unleashed new energy in both Halder and Bock, for the developing success in the south had renewed hope that the last reserves of the Red Army were being destroyed and the worst of the struggle was over. Kiev, Halder thought, had cost the Russians "an arm ... [Moscow] will break its back." Bock rejoiced that his "old wish, the attack on the main Russian forces, is yet to be fulfilled," while Halder admitted in a letter to his wife, "I have fought and struggled for this operation. I am attached to it as to a child for whom one has suffered greatly." Virtually all troop commanders saw it, at last, as the decisive battle, even as they understood that OKH was gambling everything on an exhausted army in the hope of final victory before winter. It was indeed a momentous decision, one taken with breathtaking nonchalance and recklessness, as the lure of the Clausewitzian battle of annihilation overwhelmed acknowledgment of the difficulties involved, which likely crippled any chance of German victory over the Soviet Union.[5]

The first indicator of looming problems should have been Halder's realization that the time required to reassemble and supply the necessary forces for the Moscow attack made it impossible to launch it until the end of the month. This raised the already high stakes even higher, since the *rasputitsa*, the rainy season when roads turned into impassable muddy quagmires, normally began in mid-October. Without substantial resupply and reinforcements, though, Army Group Center was simply incapable of attacking any earlier. The Germans had assumed all along that after the push to the Dnieper a pause for rest and resupply would be necessary, gambling that a logistical system dependent on truck columns would suffice. In the event, Russian resistance, the absence of paved roads, persistent rains that left muddy tracks, unexpected wear and tear on trucks, constant traffic jams, and high fuel expenditure produced a logistical nightmare. Preparations for the next phase of the operation thus proceeded much more slowly than anticipated. By the time the fighting at Smolensk had ended, German units were up to 450 miles from their original base, some barely within reach of motorized supply. The relentless Soviet counterattacks throughout July and August, moreover, not only prevented any rest for the troops, but also caused a serious ammunition crisis. German transport capacity was so limited, though, that a switch in priorities to munitions necessitated a drastic cut in the supply of fuel and food rations. Nor, despite his recognition that the fighting would continue into 1942 could Halder ensure that winter clothing would reach German units, since this limited the provision of other vital items. Expedients such as giving precedence in supply to motorized units also backfired, since this served only to increase the gap between armor and infantry. The supply situation was so tenuous that on 11 September the Quartermaster-General's office warned that the strength of the Ostheer might be "insufficient to bring the eastern campaign to a conclusion in the autumn. A great reduction in the fighting power and mobility of the army, perhaps at the crucial moment," might result unless drastic measures were taken.[6]

Just as worrisome, the combat power of the armored divisions meant to spearhead the attack on Moscow had declined precipitously as a result of the continuous fighting. Halder noted in early September that over half of the eastern army's tanks were out of action; in Army Group Center the situation was worse, with only a third of tanks operational, an astonishing situation since it was to fight the decisive battle of the campaign. Thus, although three of the four Panzer groups would for the first time be focused on the same target, each possessed only a fraction of its original strength, undermining the hope that sufficient force for a knockout blow could be assembled. Further, because of bad weather, muddy roads, and the inadequacy of the railways, redeployment of forces back to Bock crawled along. Guderian's Panzer Group 2, for example, had only a third of its armored vehicles in operation – with many of them hopelessly obsolescent older models – faced a precarious fuel situation, and struggled just to get to its starting point after the foray into Ukraine. To the north, Panzer Group 3 had left three motorized divisions in the Leningrad area, while combat and the strain of moving some 400 miles exacted a stiff price on both men and machines. Similarly, redeployment over hundreds of miles taxed Hoepner's Panzer Group 4, the strongest of the three with almost 800 tanks, double the number of the other two. German manpower reserves were also exhausted, as Halder well knew. By the end of August virtually all available forces in the Replacement Army had been brought to the front, so that casualties sustained after mid-September could not be replaced. Moreover, officer and NCO casualties – the experienced elite schooled in initiative and independent action that gave the Wehrmacht its qualitative edge – had been extremely high. Although Army Group Center had roughly 1.9 million men, it did not possess the fighting power these figures would suggest, since veteran soldiers were exhausted and the replacements lacked adequate training and experience. Halder thus knew from the outset that he was gambling everything on one card.[7]

Despite all the problems in preparing for Operation Typhoon, a generally positive outlook prevailed on the eve of the attack, even as the usual disputes over tactics and goals split the army command. Bock and his

Panzer generals demanded wide-ranging operations spearheaded by deep armored thrusts into the enemy's rear – even as these were impossible for supply reasons and, in any case, had not succeeded earlier – while Hitler and the infantry generals, mindful of previous experience, wanted to keep the gap between armor and infantry to a minimum. This, to Bock's great irritation, meant a shorter encirclement, although Halder, typically, indicated to him that he need not take his orders too seriously, even though the latter did not indicate, given German limitations, how the former was to accomplish a grand envelopment. Bock, also blind to reality, reacted angrily to his instructions: "The battle is to be 'even more limited' in scope! Narrow-mindedness is becoming an art! And after the battle we will again be facing the enemy's reserves!" Although Hoepner echoed Bock's complaint, and, like most generals, blamed OKH and Kluge specifically for the limitations placed on them, the real culprit was German inability to carry out such large encirclements. Tellingly, at the last planning conference on 24 September the decision was taken that Guderian's forces would launch their attack on 30 September, two days before the general offensive, in order to reach the surfaced road between Orel and Bryansk, vital for logistical purposes, as soon as possible. This meant that many of his formations would enter the attack after three months of nearly constant fighting with no rest or replenishment.[8]

Nonetheless, the Soviets, having expected the Wehrmacht to exploit its success in the south, were caught off guard. Despite the lateness of the season, the diminished fighting power of German units, and the time given the enemy to build defenses, by 7 October the Germans had closed pockets in the north at Vyazma and in the south at Bryansk that would eventually cost the Soviets 673,000 men and almost 1,300 tanks. Still, typically fierce enemy resistance prevented the Germans from taking full advantage of their success, as the "vast superiority" of the Soviet tanks caused "grievous casualties." In spite of this, optimism was widespread that the battles of Vyazma and Bryansk had at last broken any opposition. Guderian believed "the bulk of the Russian army to now have been destroyed," while Hoepner noted a "significant decline in the fighting morale of the Russians." Even skeptics such as Heinrici reckoned on 8 October "that the enemy is already beaten and the remaining core of his army that is supposed to defend Moscow is lost . . . By the end of the month he will be left standing there without a capital and without the famous Donets Basin industrial area . . . It will not be easy for the Russians to make good these losses." Nonetheless, he concluded, "Despite this, it is not to be expected that the struggle with him is over." Hitler thought that "if the weather stays moderately favorable the Soviet army will essentially be smashed within fourteen days," although, like Heinrici, he deemed it unlikely that Stalin would capitulate or the Soviet state collapse. Halder and Jodl both thought Vyazma to be decisive and with "moderately good weather" the encirclement of Moscow was certain to succeed. Bock also brimmed with optimism, believing this time he had sufficient force to clear the pockets quickly and push on to Moscow. Quartermaster-General Wagner was even more positive, anticipating "a collapse of the [Soviet] system" while exclaiming, "I am constantly astounded at the Führer's military judgment . . . [U]p until now he has always acted correctly. The great success in the south is his solution." The Stavka [Soviet Armed Forces High Command] too, was thunderstruck by the rapid encirclement and imminent destruction of its forward forces. Zhukov, hastily recalled from Leningrad, recognized the danger immediately: virtually all routes to Moscow lay open while available reserves had been sent south to deal with the consequences of the Kiev disaster.[9]

Even as the German leadership celebrated, and on 8 October began to discuss how to realize the encirclement of Moscow, events began to slip out of control. Impressed by the scale and magnitude of their victory, and expecting, as in 1918, little more than an unopposed march into empty space, Hitler and Halder expanded the offensive – in a characteristic effort to achieve several goals simultaneously – thus dispersing rather than concentrating forces for the final drive on Moscow. On 7 October, OKH, on the basis of a Führer directive, ordered Panzer Group 3 to advance north to Kalinin to assist Army Group North in seizing the Moscow–Leningrad railroad, thus further isolating Leningrad. At the same time, Panzer Group 2 (now renamed 2nd Panzer Army) was to send one wing northeast through Tula, then swing south around Moscow, while another arm was to take Kursk, nearly 100 miles to the southeast. Moreover, all these moves were to begin even as German troops struggled to reduce Soviet forces at Vyazma and Bryansk. Only part of the 2nd Panzer Army, the 4th Army, and Panzer Group 4 were now to envelop the capital. Bock, fearing the crippling of his striking power by this fragmentation of forces, protested vigorously, but to no avail. "Like after Smolensk," he complained bitterly, "once again the army group is to be scattered to the four winds and thus seriously weakened in its main direction of advance." While Halder believed that Bock had adequate forces to seize Moscow, Hitler thought the more important goal was to weaken the enemy decisively, achieve favorable winter positions, and prepare to resume the campaign in 1942, an admission that a defeat of the Soviet Union in 1941 was unlikely. As a result, Bock lacked sufficient forces at perhaps the (last) decisive moment in the campaign, when, for a fleeting moment, Moscow appeared undefended and vulnerable.[10]

The expectation of pursuing a defeated enemy against little resistance and encircling Moscow by the end of October soon proved illusory. Once again, the Russians recovered their equilibrium and put up stout resistance, throwing fresh reserves into battle against increasingly exhausted German troops, while the great qualifier in all optimistic assessments of the situation, the weather, took a sharp turn for the worse. The dry autumn changed to a typical mix of rain, snow, freezing, and thawing that turned the roads into a bottomless morass, halting the German advance. The Russian saying, "In the autumn a spoonful of water makes a bucketful of mud," proved devastatingly accurate. "The roads, so far as there were any in the western sense of the word, disappeared in mud," remarked one officer, "knee-deep mud . . . in which vehicles stuck fast." Another remembered, "Horses drowned on a road, although the Wehrmacht had proudly termed it a Panzer highway." Pursuit was impossible since supplies, equipment, and fuel simply could not be moved forward. "We can't go on," wrote one disgusted Landser. "There is no more gasoline and nothing is coming up behind us." Just two weeks after his joy at final victory, Wagner admitted, "we are hung up in muck." Thousands of trucks were stranded, while moving a few miles might take a day or two. "In some cases," Bock observed, "twenty-four horses are required to move a single artillery piece." The already inadequate motorized supply could no longer be maintained, nor, given the huge losses of horses, could the Ostheer move even by traditional means. The operational mobility of the troops had been so reduced that, amazingly, the foot soldiers were beginning to overtake the "fast" motorized divisions. Once again, the pursuit of the enemy failed to deliver the expected results and German triumphs, as Bock admitted, were only partial successes that "mean nothing. The splitting apart of the army group together with the frightful weather has caused us being bogged down. As a result, the Russians are gaining time to . . . bolster their defense." While at the beginning of October, German commanders had exulted at the imminent exhaustion of the enemy, by the end of the month it was their own troops who neared the limits of endurance; for many men the most important thing was no longer a strategic objective, but simply finding shelter.[11]

Bock's hope that this time the pockets could be reduced quickly proved false as well. The fighting at Vyazma and Bryansk proved, if anything, even more intense than in previous pockets, and some of the hardest fighting of the entire eastern campaign. Once again, maneuver alone failed to induce Soviet troops to surrender. The fighting in the pockets raged for nearly two weeks, tying down some 70 percent of the army group's divisions and, in the process, bringing the offensive to a standstill amid irrecoverable losses in men and materiel. As the infantry fought to the limit of their endurance, Kluge believed "the psychologically most critical moment of the campaign in the east" had arrived, while Bock conceded, "A success for the Russians, whose stubbornness paid off." By 1 November he admitted the obvious. With his units exhausted and out of fuel, doubtful that Hitler had been made aware of the bleak situation at the front, and reduced to the absurd proposal that detachments equipped with machine guns mounted on horse-drawn *panje* wagons be employed as mobile combat teams, he ordered that "further advances should be temporarily suspended" until supply problems could be overcome. "Our losses," Bock confessed, "have become quite considerable." The attempt to smash the remainder of the Red Army in a quick battle had failed. If the enemy was still to be beaten in 1941, a new, full-scale offensive would have to be launched, although it was problematic where Army Group Center would get the supplies or replacements needed for such a venture.[12]

The encirclements at Vyazma and Bryansk were for the Germans a typically equivocal triumph; savage fighting, poor mobility, abysmal weather, and inadequate supplies cost time and any chance at decisive victory. As well, constant operational improvisation prevented the necessary concentration of force, a shockingly flawed and negligent conduct of operations for which Hitler, Halder, and Brauchitsch shared equal blame. Once again, the high command seemed mesmerized by its apparent success in pulling off encirclements, so much so that they failed to realize that they were again merely winning themselves to death. Nor could frontline commanders act as a vital corrective to this flawed view, since Halder had long since taken away their customary freedom of action. It is revealing that Bock, Leeb, and Rundstedt, the army group commanders, played a surprisingly secondary role in planning and decision-making, while frontline generals remained too fixated on their own sectors – and Panzer and infantry commanders too competitive with each other – to form a united front against Hitler and Halder.[13]

Despite the fact that the German attack had passed the culmination point – the crucial stage at which an offensive degenerates into nothing more than a dangerous gamble vulnerable to enemy counterattack – Halder, and to a certain extent Hitler, still hoped to utilize the brief period between the onset of frost in mid-November and the commencement of heavy snowfall in early December for a last offensive. In truth, both men, tied together by Operation Typhoon, had little choice but to pursue the chimera of victory. At the beginning of the operation the Führer had publicly proclaimed the enemy broken, never to rise again, so his prestige, both domestically and internationally, rested on its success, while Halder, the individual most closely identified with it, who had pushed relentlessly for it, was now obliged to deliver results. What both envisioned now, admittedly, was not intended to produce a military decision – Hitler remarked to Brauchitsch on 7 November that Germany could not reach its farthest objectives in 1941, something he had suspected much earlier – but simply to further weaken the enemy and gain favorable jumping-off positions for the spring offensive. In order to accomplish this, Halder believed it necessary to capture key railway lines and armament centers, so that even the minimum goals – circling behind Moscow to reach the Volga at Rybinsk and Yaroslavl, almost 200 miles distant, while in the south advancing to the lower Don – were ambitious, if not completely unattainable given the parlous state of the Ostheer. The maximum goals set by Halder – advancing to Vologda, Gorky (Nizhny Novgorod), Stalingrad, and Maikop, in order to seize the oil fields of the Caucasus and the armaments centers of the interior, while cutting the transport routes for Lend-Lease supplies – were so utterly unrealistic as to be delusional.[14]

Halder's quixotic aims and failure to draw obvious consequences appalled Bock, who informed his superior, "the objectives ... surely cannot be reached before winter, because we no longer have the required forces and because it is impossible to supply those forces." Significantly, though, Bock did not oppose a resumption of the offensive – in fact, he advocated an immediate frontal attack on the capital – but instead insisted on the "realistic" goal of advancing to a line along the Moskva River and the Moscow–Volga canal (that is, the western outskirts of Moscow), since the reduced strength of the army group made any encirclement of the city unlikely. Even this was too much for most of his army commanders, as Guderian, Hoepner, Kluge, Weichs, and Adolf Strauss – only Reinhardt remained cautiously optimistic – opposed any further effort. The dismal supply situation, moreover, necessitated a staggered advance of individual armies rather than a unified strike against the capital, even though Bock knew a concentrated thrust offered the only chance for success. More worrisome, if anything went amiss, Bock thought the front as it then stood could not be defended. The determined Halder, though, brushed aside any consideration of the only sensible alternative – going over to the defense in order to conserve strength and prepare for the coming spring – and insisted on pressing ahead in an attempt to achieve the maximum disruptive effect in the time left for campaigning.[15]

Having failed to convince the skeptics, Halder chose to convene a meeting of his frontline commanders at Orsha, near Smolensk, on 13 November to discuss the situation. He – and Hitler, he emphasized – were still inclined to push for the maximum gains possible instead of halting to conserve strength. "It is possible," he stressed, in a remark that showed his preoccupation with the First World War battle at the Marne, "that the war is shifting from the level of military success to the level of moral . . . endurance." This very shift in September 1914, of course, had put a heavy burden on Imperial Germany, one that Halder hoped to avoid. The army, he stated, would thus have to take some risks to destroy enemy power, isolate Moscow from the hinterland, and seize economic resources in the south. The OKH chief, however, found himself opposed – even mocked – virtually across the board by his generals, who, concerned about the sheer survival of the Ostheer, argued that serious shortages in manpower and supplies, the looming physical and psychological collapse of the troops, and the lack of winter clothing and equipment ruled out any further large-scale offensives. Guderian complained vehemently that "nothing more could be achieved in winter," while Kluge described his 4th Army, the backbone of Army Group Center, as barely capable of attack. Weichs doubted that an operation against Moscow was still feasible and warned of the need to prepare winter positions. Even those generals, like Reinhardt and the normally cautious Heinrici, who did not completely rule out a renewed offensive, agreed with their brethren that Halder's plan was completely unrealistic. Guderian's chief of staff, Kurt von Liebenstein, in fact dismissed it with the sarcastic remark that it was "no longer May and we were no longer fighting in France."[16]

Despite this overwhelming opposition, Halder demanded that the attack on Moscow proceed and all the army groups push on until mid-December. Although well aware of the dire state of his troops, Bock – whose opposition to a further advance would have been difficult for even Halder to overcome – nonetheless decided to go ahead with a renewed but limited offensive toward Moscow, a direct thrust without any broad envelopment of the city whose success was highly unlikely. When confronted a few days later by a member of the Quartermaster-General's office, who pointed out that it would be impossible to supply Army Group Center even as far as the Moskva River, Halder replied disingenuously, "Your calculations are certainly correct, but we should not like to stand in Bock's way if he thinks he can succeed; you also need a little bit of luck in war." Having from the outset argued for the key importance of Moscow and done everything he could to force a decision there, Halder seemed compelled to push on, substituting the hope for a streak of gambler's good fortune for rational assessment of the situation. Perhaps, he thought, the capture of the enemy's capital would produce a Soviet collapse, just as little over a year earlier the fall of Paris had achieved such decisive results. The Russians, all were convinced, were making a last effort, so the stronger will would prevail. "We are not doing too well," Halder summed up the situation, "but the Russians are doing far worse!" Despite reports indicating the transfer of fresh Soviet units from the Far East to Moscow, OKH simply placed its faith in the alleged superiority of German soldiers. Moreover, as noted, Halder and others feared a repetition of the disaster at the Marne in September 1914, when the fight was prematurely abandoned and an imminent strategic victory thrown away by a failure of nerve. Having squandered possible triumph in an earlier war through a collapse of will, Halder would not make the same mistake. In view of presumed Soviet exhaustion he would not, he declared, allow the miracle at the Marne "to be repeated before Moscow; one could not break off the battle for it had obviously reached its decisive stage." After all, aid from the Anglo-Americans might enable Stalin to recoup his losses, just as France had recovered in 1914. A final effort thus seemed mandatory, even though most generals displayed little optimism.[17]

The recognition that no clear victory could be won, nor his military and economic goals attained, left Hitler, in contrast to Halder, in a resigned state, notably absent in the overall direction of operations. Engel on 12 November noted the Führer's "uncertain intentions" and failure to "express and explain clearly what it is that he wants," while over the next week he hit at the heart of the matter. Hitler, he observed, understood "that the objectives of the campaign have not been achieved," yet believed that "he had to . . . seize the initiative . . . [as] the precondition for final victory." The dilemma, though, lay precisely in the fact that Hitler remained unconvinced that Moscow was "decisive for the war," as he "entertains more and more doubts that new full-scale attacks . . . are right." In this vacuum, Halder – and to a certain extent Bock, "obsessed" as he was with the idea of getting to Moscow, just as he had been with Paris a year earlier – was the driving force. When Leeb at the end of October proposed a further offensive that would take the 16th Army beyond the Volkhov River and on to Tikhvin, for example, the Führer, unwilling to risk anything further in this now secondary front, expressed his doubts about the operation. Nonetheless, at Halder's urging, it proceeded and Leeb's forces took the important transport junction of Tikhvin on 8 November, although the "deplorable condition" of its units forced Army Group North shortly thereafter to go on the defensive.[18]

Similarly, in the south Rundstedt and his commanders, Reichenau, Hoth, and Kleist, with Manstein the exception, were notably hesitant about continuing the advance. Again, Halder and OKH pressed operations forward toward Stalingrad, the Don, and possibly beyond to the oil regions of Maikop and the Caucasus, even though Rundstedt preferred to halt after reaching the Donets Basin and lower Don. Brauchitsch confronted a skeptical Rundstedt and Reichenau with "OKH's demand that the areas of Maikop, Stalingrad, and Voronezh be taken as early as possible." Halder's insistence on pushing ahead resulted in the first significant prestige setback for the Germans. Although Kleist's 1st Panzer Army took the key city of Rostov, the gateway to the Caucasian oil fields less than 200 miles distant, on 20 November, a massive Soviet counterattack drove German forces from the city on the 28th. The loss of Rostov was yet another sobering reminder that the enemy was still resisting fiercely and the goals of the campaign would not be met. The setback at Rostov left Hitler noticeably nervous and irritable, as if his worst fear was being realized. It also, in a misunderstanding over obedience to orders during the ensuing retreat, cost Rundstedt his position, as Hitler, who in October and November had largely left direction of operations to Halder, now intervened, in a portent of what was to come, in a renewed effort to influence military decisions.[19]

To the north, with time short and facing the transfer on 18 November of part of Luftflotte 2 to the Mediterranean – a decision made by OKW, not Hitler – Army Group Center hastened preparations to resume the offensive. Having abandoned plans to envelop Moscow, Bock aimed for 9th Army and Panzer Group 3 in the north to advance to the Volga reservoir and Moscow–Volga canal, then turn south toward the capital. In the center, Panzer Group 4 and elements of the left wing of 4th Army would strike toward the northwest suburbs of Moscow. Meanwhile, 2nd Panzer Army was to swing north through Tula and Kolomna and approach the capital from the southeast, while 2nd Army was to protect the southern flank of the army group. Although pitifully weak, it was also ordered to thrust to the Don and capture Voronezh – yet another egregious dispersal of force – even though it could expect no help from 6th Army (Army Group South). Even this limited attack, which Bock dismissed as "no great strategic masterpiece," had little chance of success, since the mobile forces on the wings were too weak to meet at Moscow. To have any chance of success, moreover, the assaults would have to be launched simultaneously in every sector to prevent the Russians from shifting forces to imperiled areas, but 4th Army's inability to attack meant that it would be incapable of tying down enemy troops. Finally, the Germans faced crippling shortages of men and materiel, as Army Group Center had received no replacements since October and the flow of supplies had trickled to a virtual halt. In literally throwing his last units into the battle in hopes of tipping the balance, Bock had to remind his commanders at the outset that they were on their own, since the army group had only a single division in reserve. Worse, if unsuccessful, he had neither sufficient force to mount an effective defense, nor were his troops in any way equipped for a winter war.[20]

Still, when the offensive against Moscow resumed on 15 November, it made deceptive progress. In the north, Panzer Groups 3 and 4 succeeded, despite tough initial resistance, in breaking Soviet lines south of the Volga reservoir and moving on Klin. To the south, 2nd Panzer Army, reduced to only 150 tanks, on 18 November pushed around Tula, where it had been tied down for weeks, in the direction of Kolomna. The failure of 4th Army to attack, though, caused a salient to form based on Tula that immediately threatened the inner flank of 2nd Panzer Army's left wing. Nor could 2nd Army, on the army group's southern flank, offer any real support, since it was heading east toward Kursk and Voronezh. Army Group Center's attack thus resembled less a balled fist than a feeble thumb and forefinger unlikely ever to meet at Moscow. In a sorry refrain, the Germans had once again fragmented instead of concentrating their already insufficient forces, so, despite these early gains, the attack increasingly took on a surrealistic quality, as ever fewer freezing and exhausted men, with dwindling supplies and facing stout enemy resistance, lurched forward with no real hope of getting to Moscow.[21]

Even as frontline commanders realized that, at last, their strength was broken – that, as Hoepner put it, they had "achieved a great deal, but not the final goal" – Halder remained trapped in a delusion. He dismissed reports about the poor condition of the troops, writing on 21 November, "It is true, they did have to fight hard and a very long way; and still they have come through victoriously . . . So we may hope that they will be able to fight on . . . until a favorable closing line is reached." The next day, while admitting the enemy was not destroyed – though "decisively battered" – he breezily noted that "naturally from the beginning" he knew that "100% of the goal was probably not to be achieved." Still, the important thing – since "the army, as it existed in June 1941, will not be available to us again" – was to continue the attack until a favorable stopping point, wherever that might be, had been attained. This last task, however, was clearly beyond German abilities. By 20 November the offensive in the south had largely run its course. That day, Guderian informed the army group that his attack would have to be suspended because of the serious threat to his flank, heavy casualties, continuing fuel shortages, and the exhaustion of his troops. The next day Bock noted "the overexertion of units" and concluded dispiritedly, "It is doubtful if we can go any further." Nonetheless, he urged Guderian on but, his forces spent, on 23 November the Panzer general met with Bock to impress on him the reality of the situation. His troops could seize a few more objectives, Guderian stressed, but none would have any decisive impact while his army, bled to death, would be left "hanging in the air" with open flanks on both sides. Bock, sobered by this gloomy assessment from the usually optimistic Guderian, now realized the full gravity of the situation: "the eleventh hour" was approaching and his strength had been reduced to such a degree that his troops would be unlikely to mount any resistance in case of an enemy counterattack. Despite this, he complained, Brauchitsch and Halder insisted on a continuation of the attack.[22]

As signs of crisis and internal dissolution proliferated, the old divisions, especially between Panzer and infantry generals, reemerged, as each sought to blame the other for the looming catastrophe. While armored commanders faulted their infantry counterparts for slowing them down, a rather laughable charge given the weather and supply conditions, they in turn complained of being forced into risky ventures; almost all criticized Bock's lackluster leadership and the lack of support from neighboring army groups. Hitler, too, was noticeably uneasy, reckoning that the capture of the oil regions would have to wait until the following year. On 19 November he startled Halder with the sobering observation that it was likely that neither opponent could defeat the other, concluding, "the realization of the fact that the two groups of belligerents cannot annihilate each other will bring about a negotiated peace." On 24 November, General Fromm, head of the Replacement Army and Chief of Military Armaments, furthered the Führer's gloomy mood by warning that the "catastrophic worsening" of the situation in the armaments economy made an imminent peace a "necessity." The next day, according to Engel, Hitler expressed great concern about the Russian winter, fearing, "We began a month too late." Time, he mused, was "his greatest nightmare." Although Hitler appalled Engel by giving an exaggeratedly optimistic portrayal of the situation to the Italian foreign minister, Galeazzo Ciano, who had come to Berlin on 25 November, stressing that his goals extended to the Persian Gulf and Middle East, this was likely an attempt to persuade the reluctant Italians to go all out in North Africa. On 27 November, Quartermaster-General Wagner, who less than two months earlier had expected the imminent collapse of the USSR, warned Hitler of the looming crack-up of the Ostheer: "We are at the end of our personnel and material strength." Sobered by this, Hitler, true to his social Darwinist logic, remarked that same day to the Danish foreign minister, "If the German people are no longer strong enough and ready to sacrifice their own blood for their existence, they should perish." Two days later, on 29 November, one of his most trusted and able advisors, Fritz Todt, the minister for armaments and munitions, jolted him with yet more bad news. After describing serious supply problems and materiel deficiencies, and noting the superiority of Soviet tank production, Todt stated bluntly, "This war can no longer be won by military means." Hitler listened calmly, then asked, "How, then, should I end this war?" Todt replied that it could only be concluded politically – something Hitler had already considered in August – to which the Führer responded simply, "I can scarcely see a way of coming politically to an end." With his and his generals' calculations gone awry, Hitler had few options other than to grimly pursue some sort of military solution.[23]

Brauchitsch and Halder, too, insisted that the attack continue in order to inflict as much damage as possible on the enemy, despite the obvious fact that the Germans would also suffer heavy casualties for which they had no replacements. Halder conceded in a meeting on 23 November that the means for continuing the war were limited, that Germany would never again have an army like the one in June 1941, and that ultimate victory could not be certain, given "the vastness of this country and the inexhaustibleness of the people." Still, even as he urged commanders to maintain "frugality in the employment of our forces and … ammunition," he concluded the best response would not be to "signal, 'Halt into the barracks,' [but to] sustain the pressure on the enemy" by continuing to attack. Amazingly blind to reality, Halder still hoped to reach the Caucasus oil fields by the end of the year, while sustaining the attack everywhere else on the vast front line. His demand to accomplish this without proper winter quarters or supplies must have seemed a mockery to frontline officers, as did his assurance that Soviet forces were cracking under the German attack. "We are in a situation like the battle of the Marne," he claimed, once more invoking the historic memory that had such deep significance for German leaders. Halder sought a final decisive battle, "where the last battalion to be thrown in settles it." Bock, too, in spite of his deep reservations about his lack of strength and belief that it was "five minutes before midnight," accepted a continuation of the attack.[24]

The gap between rhetoric and reality, though, was now unbridgeable. Guderian halted his advance toward Kolomna on 25 November because of fierce enemy counterattacks, while the attempt to seize the key city of Tula failed. Immobilized by lack of fuel and bitter cold – temperatures plummeted to –30 degrees, which rendered vehicles and weapons virtually inoperable – on 5 December, with fewer than forty tanks in his entire army, Guderian suspended the offensive. Preservation of his fighting strength, he emphasized to the army group, now took highest priority. Northwest of the capital, Landsers struggled forward, sustained not by any belief that Soviet forces were near collapse, but by the hope that the capture of Moscow would bring some respite in a campaign that had now become a fight for self-preservation. As they inched nearer to the city, German troops found that Russian resistance grew even more determined. By 27 November, Panzer Group 3 had taken Klin while spearheads of Panzer Group 4 had pushed to within twenty miles of the Kremlin; but with the failure of 4th Army to attack in the center to prevent the Soviets transferring troops to the wings the two Panzer groups stood little chance of going any further. Capture of an intact bridge spanning the Moscow–Volga canal in the early morning hours of 28 November briefly raised hopes of a final push into the city, but a lack of troops to exploit the breach and a swift Soviet counterattack quickly dispelled any illusions. Similarly, twenty miles to the south, at Krassnaya Polyana, units from Panzer Group 4 came to a halt as they battered futilely against the minefields and earthworks of the Soviet defense line, with the spires of the Kremlin tantalizingly visible twelve miles in the distance.[25]

By now, Bock doubted that his forces could go any further. "If we do not succeed in bringing about a collapse of Moscow's northwestern front in a few days," he noted on 29 November, "the attack will have to be called off; it would only lead to a soulless head-on clash with an opponent who apparently commands very large reserves of men and material; but I don't want to provoke a second Verdun." Tellingly, in a matter of days the relevant Great War analogy had shifted from the Marne, where the Germans threw away a chance at ultimate victory through a failure of will, to Verdun, where the grinding battle of material attrition spotlighted fatal German weakness. Although Kluge now belatedly launched an attack with his depleted forces, an action urged by OKH despite Bock's reservations, the state of his troops ensured that it would sputter to a halt almost immediately. OKH's lack of realism seemed to Bock further proof that Brauchitsch and Halder failed to comprehend the weakness of his forces. On 1 December, then, he issued another stark warning. "I lack the strength for large-scale encirclement movements . . . ," he stressed, then outlined with precision the dire reality: "The attack will, after further bloody combat, result in modest gains . . . but it will scarcely have a strategic effect. The fighting of the past fourteen days has shown that the notion that the enemy in front of the army group had 'collapsed' was a fantasy . . . The attack thus appears to be without sense or purpose, especially since the time is approaching when the strength of the units will be exhausted."[26]

In fact, as events were to show, the Ostheer, both physically and psychologically, had passed the limit of its endurance; even before the Soviet counterattack, the Germans had ground to a halt. On 3 December, Bock, certain that Hitler was not receiving his reports on the appalling state of his troops, telephoned Jodl at OKW with a warning that his forces were so exhausted that even going over to the defensive would be very difficult. In fact, no preparations had been made for constructing a rear defense line; not until 1 December did Halder raise the issue with Paulus, even as Bock lamented that he was unaware of OKH intentions. This failure to plan and prepare a winter defense line was merely the last of a whole series of misjudgments and miscalculations. Driven by a sort of "Marne psychosis" to make one final effort – despite their realization that the war would continue into 1942 – OKH had pressed toward Moscow rather than begin the more mundane task of building winter positions by which the Ostheer could conserve its strength. Even in the absence of an enemy attack, German units would have been hard pressed to maintain their positions, since the lines reached by 5 December had long, unprotected flanks. Bock himself had succumbed to fatalism, refusing to challenge the soundness of OKH decisions, resigned to the fact that the offensive would continue to its bitter end. In this, he mirrored the attitude of most of the frontline commanders who, even at Orsha, challenged only Halder's unrealistic goals, not the wisdom of resuming the attack on Moscow. Hitler, too, remained detached amid growing doubts that he was fully aware of the true state of affairs. In fact, indications suggest that Halder neither informed him of what was actually transpiring nor passed on information from frontline commanders.[27]

When it came, then, the Soviet counterattack, beginning north of Moscow, caught the Germans by surprise, although earlier enemy attacks at both ends of the front, at Tikhvin and Rostov, should have given OKH pause. In addition, German intelligence at the end of November had noted a buildup of Russian forces behind the front, but in yet another sign of their continuing underestimation of the Red Army, believed it incapable of a serious counteroffensive. Despite their astounding losses, though, the Soviets managed to assemble slightly more than a million men, with more than 700 tanks and 1,300 aircraft for the operation; actual Soviet combat strength opposite Army Group Center was now greater than it had been when Operation Typhoon began in October. German troops, meanwhile – overextended, mentally and physically exhausted, without supplies or winter equipment, with dangerously vulnerable supply lines – had made no preparations for defense, nor could they now build any positions for, having thrown everything into the last effort at Moscow, they lacked both manpower and construction materials. The time was right, Zhukov stressed to Stalin on 29 November, for German strength was sapped.[28]

Zhukov's initial intent, though, was rather modest: simply to force the enemy some thirty to sixty miles away from Moscow in order to eliminate the immediate threat to the capital. Although possessing good intelligence indicating a lack of supplies and instances of panic among German troops, he was unwilling to risk anything more ambitious in view of the feeble state of his own men. He aimed at biting off Panzer Groups 3 and 4, as well as 2nd Panzer Army to the south, not at any large-scale encirclement and destruction of Army Group Center. The main effort was in the north, where German forces had penetrated closest to the city, with the central sector to contain German troops and prevent their deployment elsewhere. Meanwhile, a southern attack was to rupture the link between 2nd Panzer Army and 2nd Army and thrust deep into the rear of the former, threatening it with encirclement. Although the northern assault, led by Shock Armies heavy in armor, motorized vehicles, and automatic weapons, succeeded in breaking through German lines, both it and attacks over the next two days in the center and south failed to meet Soviet expectations. Enemy successes thus caused some concern, since efforts to shift troops to stem the tide were hampered by lack of fuel, vehicle breakdowns, icy roads, massive snowdrifts that blocked rail lines, and the general exhaustion of the troops, but no immediate fears at higher levels. Gradually, though, the many local penetrations and the serious damage done to some German divisions had a cumulative impact, as Soviet forces began to advance deep into the rear. Even as German frontline commanders sent increasingly panicked messages, Halder was slow to recognize the brewing disaster. On 8 December both OKW and OKH issued directives formally terminating offensive operations, but each still set out continuing operations that were ambitious and unrealistic. Brauchitsch blithely ordered Army Group Center to organize itself so as to turn away the Russian attacks, seemingly unaware that Bock no longer had the ability to do this. Halder was only slightly less deluded; he took note of Soviet actions but regarded them as merely of limited tactical importance.[29]

In fact, the stunning – and surprising – news of the Japanese attack on Pearl Harbor on 7 December appeared to be of more immediate significance. Although the Germans had pressed the Japanese to move south against British possessions, they had never pushed for a direct attack on American territory, believing the mere threat was sufficient to prevent the transfer of US naval forces to the Atlantic. Japanese action now brought America into the war, something that Hitler had long anticipated; a year earlier he had told Jodl, "We must solve all continental European problems in 1941, since from 1942 on the United States would be in the position to intervene." Thus, while others in the high command were shaken by the news, Hitler seemed relieved: a "millstone," he said, had been lifted off him. Nor was the reason for his almost euphoric mood hard to understand. His geo-strategic concept for the campaign in Russia had aimed at deterring American intervention in the European conflict by raising, after the defeat of the USSR, the specter of Japanese power in the Pacific. At the beginning of the month, with the failure of Barbarossa, he faced the prospect of fighting a prolonged war for which Germany was ill-prepared economically, with the United States aiding his enemies through Lend-Lease deliveries. The Japanese action, though, gave him a last chance to dispatch the unexpectedly resilient Soviets. In Japan – a nation "that has never been conquered in 3,000 years" – Hitler had an ally that, he thought, would tie down the Americans for the foreseeable future in the Pacific, forcing the United States to divide its naval resources and thus lessening its possible European impact. In addition, by removing the restraints on the U-boats in the North Atlantic, something for which the navy had pressed for months, Hitler anticipated reducing the flow of American aid to Great Britain. In a neat reversal, the United States, and not Germany, would face the immediate prospect of a two-front war. As a result, Hitler expected to have another year in which to defeat the Soviets before he had to face the full might of his Western foes, a calculation that proved highly accurate. Although conceding he had no clear idea how to defeat America, Hitler nevertheless hoped that some sort of victory over the Soviet Union in 1942, combined with a Japanese stalemating of the Americans in the Pacific, might yet retrieve the situation. In contrast to a year earlier, however, Germany had clearly lost its freedom of action. Hitler's worst fear was materializing: time and space were against him.[30]

While these developments played out at the level of grand strategy, the operational situation turned increasingly bleak. By 8 December enemy pressure on the left flank of Army Group Center had built to such an extent that Bock felt compelled to shake OKH out of its illusions. Not least, he was influenced by dire warnings from Panzer Group 3 that its forces were no longer operational, as well as a gloomy telephone call from the usually confident Guderian, who demanded reinforcements and warned of a growing "crisis of confidence." To this, Bock replied merely that he could give him none and that "either one held out or let himself be killed." Bock then called Halder and presented his plight in stark terms: "nowhere was the army group capable of withstanding a strong attack by the Russians." In order to hold the line, he stressed, in an assessment remarkably similar to Hitler's later observations, he needed immediate replacements and supplies, which were not likely to arrive in time. If, on the other hand, he attempted a withdrawal, the deep snow, shortage of fuel, and lack of tractors to pull the heavy weapons meant the unavoidable loss of a sizable amount of equipment and supplies. His troops would therefore arrive at unprepared defensive positions with no heavy weapons with which to halt the Russian advance. The Germans thus faced a devil's dilemma: they could fight where they were, and chance destruction, or carry out a large-scale withdrawal, with the threat that any retreat might turn into a rout. Halder, still obtuse, attempted to reassure Bock by dismissing the attacking Russian units as only rear elements and untrained recruits, adding, "I presume that [the Russian counterattacks] will continue until the middle or end of the month and then things will quieten down." To that Bock replied bitterly, "By then, the Army Group will be kaputt." Aghast, Halder tersely rejoined, "The German soldier does not go kaputt."[31]

Bock and other frontline commanders were not so sure, succumbing to a sense of impotence and impending disaster. While Reinhardt worried that all that had been gained would be lost, and Guderian described the situation as "unimaginable," Hoepner raised a frightening specter. At night, he admitted to his wife, he was "tormented by memories of 1918," confessing that he felt even more powerless than then. Heinrici, who declared tersely to a colleague, "The war is lost!", conjured a more terrifying analogy, that of the destruction of Napoleon's Grand Army in 1812. On 12 December, at last admitting the serious threat confronting the Ostheer, Halder confessed bleakly that Germany faced "the most serious crisis of the two (world) wars," although he still clung to the hope that if they could just hold out for two weeks the crisis would be over. Hackneyed depictions of an amateurish Hitler thwarting the cool decisions of his professional elite at OKH, then, simply miss the mark. Guderian, for example, put the blame for the "shocking bungling and aimlessness" on OKH, OKW, and Bock. "I would never have believed," he wrote on 8 December, "that a really brilliant military position could be so screwed up in two months. If a decision had been taken at the proper time to break off and settle down for the winter in a habitable line suitable for the defense, we would have been in no danger." In retrospect, he thought, "Our misfortunes began with Rostov; that was the writing on the wall." It was also an operation that had been pushed by Halder, not Hitler. Kluge similarly denounced Brauchitsch's lack of energy and unwillingness to acknowledge the true nature of the situation. Far from railing against Hitler, early on in the crisis frontline commanders desired a stronger personal engagement from him, to the extent that Bock, on 10 December, told Kluge that he was "about to send a personal telegram to the Führer that I face decisions that far exceed the purely military." Guderian, too, believed the time had come to report directly to Hitler, confessing that he himself did not know how to get out of this "very difficult situation." Rather than rejecting involvement by the dilettante Hitler, many frontline generals hoped that his reputation for luck and seeming unerring knack for transcending difficult situations would once more prevail.[32]

Something clearly needed to be done, as OKH remained drifting and irresolute. Bock complained on 11 December, again anticipating Hitler, "By constantly withdrawing we will never halt the Russians and a large-scale withdrawal under pressure from the enemy could have unforeseeable consequences." Yet the next day, when Halder persisted in doubting Soviet ability to sustain their initial success, he shocked the OKH chief by exclaiming, "Of course they can! We cannot stop our troops running away as soon as they see a Russian tank!" Both men appeared stunned and disoriented, seemingly unable to make a clear decision. On 13 December, Bock confessed to Brauchitsch, "I have no more suggestions to make . . . The Führer has to decide whether the army group has to fight where it stands, at the risk of being wrecked in the process, or whether it should withdraw, which entails the same risk. If he decides for withdrawal, he must realize that it is doubtful whether sufficient forces will reach the rear to hold a new, unprepared . . . position." This, in a nutshell, was precisely the point made by Hitler when he issued his "Halt Decree," for which he was, and has been ever since, roundly criticized.[33]

Still, Hitler appeared just as unsure as his advisors. Like Halder, he believed it necessary to hold firm against what surely must be the last Russian reserves, although on 8 December he allowed a withdrawal of forces threatened with encirclement around Tikhvin. This clearly put him in a sour mood. "He did not," Engel noted, "want to hear the expression 'pull back' again." In his own bow to the Marne trauma, Hitler remarked, "It would not be the first time that Germans had lost their nerve at the fateful hour," but Engel also observed "how unsettled and uncertain he is." By 10 December, back in Berlin, Hitler had begun to recover his confidence, telling Goebbels that although tactical withdrawals might be necessary, "Our position is so favorable, especially after the entry of Japan, that there certainly can be no doubt about the outcome of this enormous continental struggle." Relieved, Goebbels exclaimed, "Once again the Führer radiates a wave of optimism and confidence in victory." This new mood, compounded of hope in the Japanese and self-reverence at his own prophetic ability, would also seal a grim fate for the Jews of Europe. Two days later, in a gathering with old party comrades, Hitler referenced his January 1939 warning to the Jews not to foment another world war, then confirmed the plans, already in motion, for the annihilation of all Jews under German control. "The Führer," Goebbels related, "is determined to clear the table. He warned the Jews that if they were to cause another world war it would lead to their own destruction. These were not empty words. Now the world war has come, the destruction of the Jews must be its necessary consequence." A day earlier, in his speech declaring war on the United States, Hitler had admitted that German losses in the east, killed and wounded, were "somewhat more than double the losses of the Battle of the Somme in the First World War." Perhaps this reference was meant to offer context, however unsettling, to the German population; more likely, it served as Hitler's justification for "clearing the table" with the Jews. On 20 December, in his appeal to the German people to donate winter clothing for troops at the front, Hitler conceded that "after a year of the heaviest battles," German soldiers on "the greatest front of all time" faced "an enemy far superior in terms of manpower and materiel." For all concerned, a new war had dawned.[34]

Seemingly rejuvenated by his time with party leaders in Berlin, just a few days after Bock's injunction and shortly after his adjutant, Schmundt, returned from a fact-finding mission to the front, Hitler acted decisively to end the befuddlement and helplessness afflicting OKH. On 16 December he had dismissed the physically and mentally overwhelmed Brauchitsch, and on the 19th took the reins of army command himself. Although never explicitly stated, Hitler held Brauchitsch responsible for the nightmare that had developed; his (and OKH) fixation on Moscow and failure to take the supply situation into account had led to the crisis, which had then been made worse by his loss of nerve. Hitler, significantly, stressed that a centralization of control had been made necessary not only by immediate events in the east, but also by the great extent of the various fronts and the close interconnection of military, political, and economic matters. It was now a global war. Although Hitler's intervention was a step that would have profound consequences, at the time most generals, yearning, as did Reinhardt, for a strong hand, saw it as the last chance to save the situation. Guderian, as others, fully expected the Führer to act "quickly and energetically . . . with his customary vigor," while Fromm thought that this development would draw Hitler into tighter support for the army. Even Halder, believing that he might profit from the new situation, initially accepted the changed command with remarkable equanimity. Hitler, though, who had considered and rejected Manstein – on the grounds that he was too independent – as a replacement for Halder, soon let the OKH chief know that he was to be merely an instrument of policy, not its maker. Having allowed OKH to shape operations for the previous two months, Hitler now reasserted himself as Feldherr. In his first basic order as head of the army, revealingly, he demanded absolute honesty in the reports submitted to him, a clear indication of his belief that previously he had been left unaware of the true state of affairs. Brauchitsch, he told Goebbels in late January 1942, had built a wall between himself and OKH; that had now fallen away.[35]

The new head of the army faced three options: rigidly holding out; a flexible withdrawal; or a general retreat to prepared positions. Since the Germans had neither the means to carry out the second nor existing defensive positions vital to the third, he quickly settled on the first option as the only means by which to save Army Group Center until reinforcements could be dispatched to the front. Although Hitler had already issued a milder halt order on 15 December, on the night of 16–17 December he decided, based largely on Bock's earlier arguments, that any withdrawal that entailed abandonment of heavy weapons and artillery and retreat to unprepared positions risked turning into a panicked rout reminiscent of 1812. In a telephone call to Bock, Hitler concluded – "quoting my reasons almost word for word," Bock noted, not without some pride – that it made no sense to withdraw to an unprepared position, leaving behind artillery and equipment. "In several days, we would be facing the same situation again, but now without heavy weapons and artillery. There was only one decision and that was not to take a single step back, to plug holes and hold on." Bock, in reply, said little, since Hitler had merely complied with his own advice; and, in any case, the field marshal had little else to suggest, admitting to Schmundt, "In truth, counting one's buttons is the only way to determine which is the right thing to do." As the crisis peaked, Bock, the military professional, with no answer for how to proceed, voluntarily, almost with relief, conceded fundamental decision-making authority over the fate of his army group to the Great War corporal. Given the situation, though, not only was Hitler's a rational decision, but it was not all that dissimilar from those made earlier by Stalin that allowed Soviet troops to be encircled in order to slow and eventually halt the German advance. The Soviet dictator even mirrored Hitler's phrase, "not one step back," in his famous July 1942 order of the same name. Hitler knew that it would take weeks to assemble and transport divisions from France and the Balkans to the east, so it was imperative that the Ostheer hold out where it was and buy time until reinforcements could arrive.[36]

In contrast to the drift at OKH, moreover, Hitler had made a clear and definitive decision – probably the only correct one under the circumstances – and one that matched arguments made by many frontline generals. Although some commanders balked at this order and urged either a rapid resupply and reinforcement of the troops at the front, or a measured retreat to rearward positions, it is difficult, given the circumstances at the time, to see these proposals as anything other than illusory. Due to exhaustion, excessive strain, the extreme cold, and snow as high as six feet, the German logistics system had largely collapsed, while it is doubtful that the Soviets would have done the Germans the favor of easing pressure on the front or suspending attacks long enough to allow for construction of a new defensive line. At a time of confusion and creeping disintegration, Hitler's decision brought order and discipline back to the troops and almost certainly saved the army group from collapse. Halder, for one, acknowledged the soundness of the Führer's decision, not least because it freed him from the bugbear of a disorderly flight to the rear. "Given the conditions of the Russian winter," he admitted to General Hermann Balck, "any retreat meant a catastrophe of Napoleonic proportions." Hitler's first decision as the new head of the army – emphasizing the need to gain time to bring in reserves and supplies from the west, after which an orderly withdrawal could commence – was seen as a reasonable way to extricate the army from a difficult situation. His "stand and fight" order also finally stripped his generals of their accustomed flexibility and command initiative, a process, ironically, begun by Halder but whose realization would instead benefit Hitler. Bock, exhausted, resigned his post on 19 December, insisting, perhaps in an example of forced optimism, that "the end of the present 'dirty period' is in sight," to be replaced by Kluge, but his action had nothing to do with any protest against Hitler's orders. Bock, convinced that Hitler had never been properly informed of the seriousness of the situation, was anxious that the Führer understand that his stepping down was purely for health reasons.[37]

In contrast to the departed Bock, Guderian was not so ready to accept Hitler's halt order. Although he had welcomed Hitler's takeover of the army – and was always much closer to Hitler and National Socialism than generally acknowledged – Guderian still insisted on freedom of command in running his army group, which now included 2nd Army as well as 2nd Panzer Army. In reaction to an intensification of the Halt Order on 18 December, he insisted that he would act in the self-interest of his own forces. Given the implicit risk of such a stance for other sectors of the front, the headstrong general quickly found himself in conflict not only with

1. Hitler, seated on the far right with the moustache, with comrades from the 16th Bavarian Reserve Infantry Regiment. Although an Austrian citizen, Hitler's request to King Ludwig III of Bavaria to be accepted into the Bavarian army was approved. Hitler's beloved dog, Fuchsl, who was later stolen – an action that angered him to the end of his life – sits looking at the future Führer. Lying on the ground in front is Balthasar Brandmayer who published a book on Hitler as a dispatch runner in 1933.

2. Hitler speaking to an enthusiastic crowd, estimated at 200,000 people, gathered at the Heldenplatz in front of the Hofburg Palace in Vienna on 15 March 1938 to mark the occasion of the historic union of Germany and Austria. Just thirty years earlier he had lived in Vienna as a failed, would-be art student. Now he had accomplished a feat that had eluded even Bismarck.

3. After his return from Munich on 30 September 1938, Neville Chamberlain declared that the agreement signified "peace in our time." The document he waved in the air was actually a separate Anglo-German agreement bearing both Hitler's and Chamberlain's signatures, which declared the intent of the two nations never again to go to war with each other.

4. German troops crossing the Meuse River north of Sedan near Aiglemont, France, 14 May 1940. The swift crossing of the river was the key to success in Operation Sickle Cut, for it allowed German armored forces to proceed largely unhindered to the Channel coast.

5. British prisoners at Dunkirk, France, June 1940. Most of those captured by the Germans remained in captivity for the rest of the war. Despite the fact that nearly 60,000 British men were killed, wounded, or taken prisoner, the successful British evacuation at Dunkirk meant that Blitzkrieg had failed.

6. Hitler with Albert Speer (left) and the sculptor Arno Breker (right) at the Eiffel Tower, Paris. In the early morning hours of 28 June 1940 Hitler made a whirlwind tour of the city. He delighted in showing off his knowledge of the opera, and seemed awed by his visit to Napoleon's tomb, but was otherwise unimpressed with Paris.

7. Hitler at a situation conference with Keitel (far left), Brauchitsch (left), and Halder (right), c. 1940–1. Hitler was keenly interested in maps and would often pore over them for hours on end.

8. German troops from the Infantry Regiment "Großdeutschland" attack a village in Russia, summer 1941. The soldier in the foreground holds a flamethrower, while in the background a house is burning.

9. A German soldier saluting Colonel-General Heinz Guderian, Russia, *c*. July–August 1941. As the leading advocate of mobile warfare, Guderian urged deep encirclements as the best way to cripple the Red Army. By late July 1941, though, fierce Soviet resistance had already thrown this strategy into doubt.

10. German troops pulling a stuck vehicle out of the mud, November 1941. The Russian saying that in autumn a spoonful of water produces a bucketful of mud proved devastatingly accurate for the Germans, reliant as they were on unpaved roads to move supplies.

11. A German supply column struggles through the cold and snow during the advance toward Moscow, 21 November 1941. In the bitter cold that incapacitated trucks, German supply became dependent on horse-drawn transport.

12. Hitler at a situation conference at Army Group South headquarters, June 1942. From left to right: Lieutenant General Adolf Heusinger, an unidentified man, Adolf Hitler, General Georg von Sodenstern, Colonel-General Max Freiherr von Weichs, General Friedrich Paulus, Colonel-General Eberhard von Mackensen, and Field Marshal Feodor von Bock. In pointing to the map, Hitler was perhaps emphasizing the importance of the quick destruction of Soviet forces for success in the 1942 summer campaign.

13. German infantry battling in Stalingrad, late autumn 1942. As shown by their grim faces, by this point the struggle for the city named after Stalin had become a grueling house-to-house fight which taxed the nerves of even the toughest soldiers.

14. A Soviet soldier guards a wounded German prisoner of war in Stalingrad, c. January–February 1943. Following their capitulation some 90,000 German troops went into Soviet captivity, an outcome that few could have anticipated at the outset of the battle. Only about 5,000 survived to return to Germany in 1955.

15. Hitler greets Field Marshal Erich von Manstein upon the Führer's arrival at the field marshal's headquarters at Zaporozhye, Russia, 18 March 1943. On the right is General Wolfram Freiherr von Richthofen. This was the second time in a month that Hitler had flown to Manstein's headquarters, a revealing indication of the hopes he then had in the field marshal's ability to stem the Soviet tide.

16. Hitler portrayed as a Feldherr (military commander) for use in propaganda in Ukraine, May 1943. Although intended to influence sentiment in occupied Ukraine, the poster nonetheless accurately portrays Hitler's transformation from Führer to Feldherr.

17. Troops of the SS Panzer Division "Das Reich" take a rest from the fighting in the Belgorod area during Operation Citadel, July 1943. "Das Reich" fought under Manstein's command on the southern sector of the Kursk bulge. Its withdrawal following the Anglo-American invasion of Sicily effectively ended the battle, the first time the Germans had failed in a summer offensive.

18. Field Marshal Erwin Rommel on an inspection tour of the Atlantic Wall shortly before the invasion, June 1944. Rommel had brought a much-needed energy and sense of purpose to the construction of the Atlantic Wall, but his absence from Normandy on 6 June 1944 hindered a swift German response to the invasion.

19. American troops wade ashore at Omaha Beach, 6 June 1944. Although German defenses in this sector were the most formidable of any of the landing sites, the G.I.s managed to establish a beachhead by the end of the day, despite suffering some 2,000 casualties.

20. German troops move carefully along a house wall in Normandy in the summer of 1944. Although unsuccessful in throwing the invaders back into the sea, the Germans put up stiff resistance that stymied an Allied breakout for two months.

21. A German Panzer IV and a Panzer VI "Tiger I" sit destroyed in the ruins of Villers-Bocage,
Normandy, June 1944. The fierce battle for Villers-Bocage on 13 June 1944, and the British failure
to hold the town against a determined German counterattack, marked the beginning of the
attritional phase of the battle for Normandy.

22. Hitler at his "Wolf's Lair"
headquarters with Colonel Claus
Schenk Graf von Stauffenberg
(left) and Field Marshal Wilhelm
Keitel (right) on 15 July 1944, just
a few days before Stauffenberg
unsuccessfully attempted to
assassinate the Führer on 20 July.

23. Newly enlisted men of the Volkssturm march past Joseph Goebbels in Berlin in November 1944. Inspired by the example of the popular militias of the wars against Napoleon, the Volkssturm was a Nazi Party organized militia that consisted largely of young boys and older men. Although there is no clear figure for their casualties, the Volkssturm likely suffered losses of 35 percent killed or wounded.

24. Hitler planning the Ardennes Offensive with Hermann Göring (left) and Heinz Guderian (right), October 1944. Hitler began thinking of an autumn counteroffensive that would allow Germany to regain the initiative in the west as early as the Allied breakout from Normandy.

25. German troops crossing a Belgian road during the Ardennes Offensive, December 1944. Hitler counted on fog and poor weather, in addition to surprise, to give the German attack toward Antwerp a chance for success.

26. German troops advancing through dense woods during the Ardennes Offensive, 22 December 1944. Although achieving some initial success, the German attack quickly stalled as the troops struggled to overcome American resistance in the thickly wooded Ardennes region.

27. German SS Panzergrenadiers move through a burning village on the Western Front in early January 1945. Some of the heaviest fighting of the Ardennes Offensive occurred in January 1945 as German troops resisted American efforts to regain lost ground.

Wehr Dich oder stirb!

Die Plutokraten Churchill und Roosevelt lassen das deutsche Volk kaltblütig und gewissenlos durch

den Bolschewismus

ausplündern - schänden - morden!

Sie sind damit die wahren Mörder und Totengräber Europas.

- Das Blut unserer geschändeten und gemordeten Brüder und Schwestern im Osten aber schreit nach **Rache!** -

Was man dem Osten antat, wird der Westen nie vergessen!

- Die Rechnung werden **wir** den Anglo-Amerikanern präsentieren -

Wir kennen keine schwachen Herzen!

Nur das Volk ist verloren, das sich selbst aufgibt!

28. "Defend yourself or die!" Echoing Hitler's sentiments (and rationale) for fighting to the last, this placard warns Germans that the plutocrats Roosevelt and Churchill are cold-bloodedly and unscrupulously allowing Germany to be plundered by the Bolsheviks, then declares, "Only that people is lost that gives itself up!" Posters such as this were prominent in the west, where they aimed to stiffen resistance by dispelling the prevalent notion that the Allies would be lenient in their treatment of a defeated Germany.

29. German civilians in Berlin struggle to find a path through the debris after an Allied bombing raid, *c.* February–March 1945. In 1933 Hitler had boasted, "Give me ten years . . . and you will not recognize your cities." By late March 1945 perhaps half of all houses in Berlin had been damaged and a third were uninhabitable; some 20,000 Berliners died in the air attacks.

30. The destroyed Hohenzollern Bridge in Cologne (with the cathedral in the background) after an Allied bomb attack, early 1945. Cologne was one of the most heavily bombed German cities, and although the famous cathedral stood directly across from the main train station, it survived, damaged but intact.

31. U.S. infantrymen and armor advance amid the destroyed buildings of Cologne, March 1945. The third-largest city in Germany, Cologne fell after a brief fight on 6 March 1945, much to the anger and chagrin of Joseph Goebbels, himself a native of the area.

32. Hitler greets Hitler Youth conscripts guarding the Reich Chancellery, dated 20 April 1945 (but most likely 20 March 1945). Hitler had once boasted that with his magnificent youth he could do anything, but by the end of the war they were sacrificed in a meaningless fight to the last.

Hitler but with the hardly less adamant Halder and Kluge. Hitler, Engel recorded, was appalled at Guderian's psychological state, adding that it was quite clear to the Führer that he was no longer able to lead. Halder, for his part, agreed, noting that "Guderian seems to have lost his nerve completely." Embracing his new role as enforcer of the stand-fast doctrine, on 20 December he also insisted, with astounding optimism – and after Hitler, convinced of its necessity, had expressly agreed to a withdrawal by 43rd Army Corps to the Oka – "If we hold out everywhere, everything will be over in fourteen days. The enemy cannot pursue these frontal attacks forever." The view from the front looked much gloomier to Guderian, who insisted that his forces had to retreat or be destroyed, and was more than willing to act independently of orders. Kluge and Halder, shocked by both Guderian's pessimism and his open defiance, and more than a little moti-vated by personal distaste for the willful general, accused the Panzer leader of having "lost his nerve" and being "so pessimistic" that he was incapable of leading his men. Kluge, who like Hitler demanded clear obedience to authority, saw Guderian's willfulness not only as a personal affront, but also as a challenge to his larger strategy, which was simultaneously to enforce the stand-fast doctrine at the front while working to modify it with the higher authorities.[38]

Guderian's insistence on withdrawing his army, and using his personal connections with Hitler to influence decisions, brought matters to a head. Seemingly unaware of the intrigue against him, the assertive and self-confident general flew to Führer headquarters on 21 December in an effort to get Hitler to rescind or modify the rigid halt order. In a dramatic five-hour encounter, Hitler not only rebuffed Guderian, categorically forbidding any withdrawal, but also dismissed his concerns as exaggerated, pointing out that as a common soldier he had endured many enemy break-ins during the First World War. Guderian's troops, he advised, should dig in where they stood. When the Panzer commander replied that the earth was frozen to a depth of five feet, the Führer retorted that they would have to blast holes with howitzers as was done in the earlier war. When Guderian observed that the loss of life would be enormous, Hitler agreed that no one was anxious to die, but noted the hardships of Frederick the Great's soldiers; surely, the Führer asserted, he had the same right to demand sacrifices from his troops. Hitler then chided Guderian for being too close to the suffering of his men. "You are seeing events at too close a range . . .," he argued. "You should stand back more. Believe me, things appear clearer when examined at longer range." Disappointed but undeterred, and now aware of the intrigues against him, Guderian returned to the front determined to withdraw his army group, which made a final showdown inevitable. It came on 25 December, when he escalated the dispute by openly defying Kluge's orders, an action that led the latter to demand Guderian's ouster. Hitler complied, removing Guderian from his post the next day and replacing him with General Rudolf Schmidt.[39]

Although Guderian's removal resulted as much from personal intrigue and mutual dislike among top generals as any conscious assertion by Hitler of his dominant role in the army, it nonetheless sent an important signal, but one that is often misunderstood. The key point was not that Hitler would fire any general who disobeyed his halt order; many, in fact, did just that and were left in their positions. Rather, it revealed a more complex calculus of actions leading to a dismissal. If the army leadership was disunited and engaged in personal intrigues, if Hitler believed that a general had lost his nerve, and, especially, if a particular retreat or disobedience of orders threatened to collapse the entire front, then he would act decisively. In the absence of these factors he was inclined to overlook the infraction. Later, after the fact, he admitted as much, telling Goebbels on at least two, widely separated occasions, that he had fired Guderian because his disobedience in the crisis had threatened the entire front. In many respects, then, the command conflict revolved not, or not merely, around the issue of insubordination, but was one of focus as well. For Hitler, necessarily having to consider all aspects of the war, what seemed to be a temporary crisis on one narrow sector or other of the front could not be allowed to threaten the whole. As his adjutant Below wrote approvingly of him in a letter on 25 December, "There is no general or officer in the army who possesses such a comprehensive knowledge or skill in all questions of weapons, armament, production, supply and other necessities for the front army." For the Führer, the key point was not so much that a general defied him, but that the individual in question was a fighter and understood the larger issues at stake.[40]

His actions at the time, in fact, spoke volumes. Kluge, for example, chafing at Hitler's unwillingness to modify his stand-fast order and expectation that the troops could fight on with no food or ammunition, exploded to Halder in frustration on the day Guderian was fired, "Whether the Führer likes it or not he will have to order a retreat. If supplies cannot be delivered, things will soon collapse . . . The Führer will have to come down from cloud-cuckoo-land and . . . set his feet firmly on the ground." Kluge, though, had distinguished himself by his willingness both to hold the line and to enforce discipline himself, so Hitler's response was merely a refusal to accede to Kluge's demand for withdrawal, telling him that "one day the Russians will no longer have the strength to attack." Similarly, when

Schmidt, before assuming Guderian's position, was forced by events on 24 December to withdraw his 2nd Army without explicit approval, Hitler acquiesced, showing that some independent action was still possible. There were, however, limits to what he would accept. When, on 30 December, Kluge tried to make a case for retreat, Hitler chided him for wanting to "go right back to the Polish border." Unlike his frontline commanders, he stressed, confirming his decision-making paradigm, he had to see things with "cool reason," and logic told him that there was no alternative to holding out and buying time for the reinforcements that were now on their way to the front. Otherwise, he feared, any withdrawal would signal an unstoppable retreat of Napoleonic proportions. Hitler the Feldherr, after all, was also Hitler the Führer; unlike his generals, who busied themselves with immediate tactical concerns, he had to think in strategic and economic terms.[41]

In the event, continued Russian pressure forced German units back with or without Hitler's approval. By early January 1942, with one-quarter of the original Ostheer casualties, with shortages of all types of equipment, with deep snow and temperatures of –25 degrees Fahrenheit making movement nearly impossible, Hitler seemed at last to have realized that he was dangerously close to losing Army Group Center. The pull-back of 9th Army against his will occasioned a wild outburst at OKH headquarters that the army command had been "parliamentarized" and that commanders no longer had the courage "to make hard decisions." Still, the growing recognition that the Soviets, having modified their original plan, now intended to encircle Army Group Center, enforced clarity on German defensive measures. Efforts at holding out everywhere gave way to a priority for retaining key road and rail junctions and protecting critical supply lines. The precipitating event seemed to be a breakthrough in 4th Panzer Army's front that threatened 20th Army Corps with encirclement. Hoepner, in vain, requested permission on 6 January for these units to be withdrawn, since OKH still believed that the Russians were at the end of their strength and the situation would soon ease. By 8 January, with the supply route to the corps cut, Hoepner once again demanded that Kluge allow him to pull these units out of the looming trap. In response, Kluge indicated that because of Hitler's halt decree he could not issue such an order, although he implied that consent would be forthcoming. Hoepner, frustrated, tired of waiting, and under the assumption that approval was imminent, just after noon on 8 January ordered the army corps to break out. Kluge, as in Guderian's case, reacted violently to what he perceived as disobedience by another of his headstrong Panzer generals, so immediately reported Hoepner's action to

Hitler. That same night Hitler relieved Hoepner of his command and ordered that he be dishonorably discharged from the army. This, however, did nothing to improve the situation at the front, for as one commander succinctly put it, "I cannot put a policeman behind every soldier."[42]

Once again, the signal seemed clear: independent action in violation of the halt order would not be tolerated; but, as before, the message was more complicated. As with Guderian, Kluge's sensitivity to his own authority and the "disobedience" of his Panzer generals – with neither of whom he had good personal relations – was the immediate precipitating factor. Kluge, moreover, worried that Hoepner's action would undermine his own strategy of incrementally modifying Hitler's stand-fast edict. In addition, Halder continued to reinforce Hitler's halt order, noting on 11 January, "Fighting every day, every hour is a victory, even if the nervous strain is still so great." He, in fact, went so far as to express the belief in late January that "Hitler [was] the only man able to hold the Wehrmacht and the German nation together in the coming difficult times." Finally, the danger remained that a general withdrawal in one sector would threaten to put the entire front into an uncontrollable rearward movement. Faced with the inevitable, though, Hitler relented and on 15 January approved a general pull-back of the front, signing – for the first time in the war, he emphasized pointedly – an order authorizing a large-scale withdrawal. Even as he loosened the rigid halt order, itself as much because the situation had begun to stabilize and rein-forcements from the west to arrive, as from pressure from his generals, he began to replace many top commanders. It is difficult not to see in Hitler's sacking of Guderian and Hoepner a sense of disappointment, or perhaps betrayal, as these once dashing, confident Panzer generals had given way to deep pessimism and, from his perspective, loss of nerve at a time when strong will was needed above all else. Similarly, Leeb was sacked when his insistence on a wide-ranging withdrawal threatened the northern flank of Army Group Center. As Halder made clear on 16 January in denouncing the "operational mania" of the army group commanders – a charge, inter-estingly, to be repeated by Hitler later in the war – they only had one task: holding on. The high command would assume responsibility for the gamble.[43]

The ultimate fate of Guderian and Hoepner might also offer some further clues to Hitler's thinking: Guderian, generally a supporter of Hitler and Nazism, was rehabilitated and brought back into the center of power, whereas Hoepner, long skeptical of Hitler and then an opponent of the regime, was hanged on 8 August 1944, having been implicated in the plot to kill the Führer. Still, too much should not be made of this ideological dimension, since those now rising to take frontline commands were ambitious men who had proven themselves, in accordance with Hitler's *Führerprinzip* (leadership principle), in the cauldron of battle – men like Kluge, Dietl, Heinrici, Schmidt, Küchler, Richard Ruoff, Georg Lindemann, and Walther Model. Even a staunch Nazi supporter but much less adept commander such as Busch was limited in his independence. On 17 December, in a rant to Luftwaffe General Wolfram von Richthofen, Hitler had expressed dissatisfaction with the shortcomings of his generals, a harangue that continued the next day with Goebbels. His commanders, Hitler complained, were no longer physically up to their tasks, and this interfered with the necessary measures being taken. He wanted generals such as Kluge, "an energetic personality, a leader from head to toe . . . not a general staff general but a front general. We can now use such men . . . who have strong nerves and do not topple over at the first crisis. Our leading generals had gotten too old . . . [The new generals] are [men] of energy who, above all, possess a very strong connection to the front." Such leaders were necessary, he asserted, because of changed realities. "Nowadays," he remarked on the night of 17–18 January 1942, explaining the essential new tactics, "we allow the Russians to infiltrate while we remain where we are without budging. They get themselves wiped out behind our lines or gradually wither away . . . for lack of supplies. It takes solid nerves to practise such tactics . . . Generals must be tough, pitiless men . . . who impose their will on such a situation." Just such decisive personalities, not general staff officers but tough, front-experienced leaders who, like him, were part of the community of frontline fighters he so admired, were needed at the moment.[44]

Hitler saw this rejuvenation of the army by energetic new commanders as a positive aspect of the recent crisis. "This winter," he declared at a situation conference in late March, "has allowed us to find a group of truly tough generals. The longer the war lasts, the more valuable will be such personalities . . . Unknown men move to the foreground." Qualities such as mental toughness and frontline experience loomed larger in his mind than party loyalty, since Hitler made no deliberate attempt at this time to "Nazify" the army leadership. Already at the end of February, in fact, he had surprised some of his generals with an uncharacteristic openness. "They must have thought him perhaps obstinate," he confessed, "because up to now he had been so adamantly opposed to any withdrawal." This, he now explained – perhaps in an attempt after the fact to gain approval for his actions – "had been necessary . . . in order to stabilize the front. There were people who regarded our situation as hopeless. Only by insisting upon unconditionally holding out had it been possible to counteract a panic." One of those present, Heinrici, agreed with Hitler's overall judgment, although noting that at the tactical level his rigidity had caused many unnecessary casualties, an observation that betrayed his and others' belief that the situation in front of Moscow was not as desperate as higher commanders had painted it.[45]

This approach allowed Hitler an opening for a sort of reconciliation with his generals, one achieved partly by bestowing honors, medals, and money on key figures, but even more by restoring a bit of their old freedom of command against the centralizing tendencies of OKH. This did not sit well with Halder, who in his diary chastised the Führer for giving too much freedom of decision to his strong-willed army commanders. As the Soviet offensive ran its course, moreover, an increasing number of frontline generals conceded the wisdom of Hitler's halt order. More importantly, the sense that he had been proven right against his weak-willed generals came to characterize all his later dealings with the military elite. Hitler, the autodidact, had little respect for the educated, professional elite, the so-called experts, therefore he took pleasure that his solution had undermined the received wisdom. In future crises, as a result, Hitler was less willing to concede to their professional competence and expertise, believing they lacked his intuition, imagination, and creativity. He had been encouraged in January by the success of Rommel's audacious actions in Libya, while in mid-February, as if in confirmation of his self-opinion, he gloated over the escape of the *Gneisenau*, *Scharnhorst*, and *Prinz Eugen*, which raced from Brest through the English Channel in broad daylight to Norway, a daring operation that had been his idea. Finally, Japanese military successes in seizing the Philippines from the Americans and in humiliating the British with the capture of Singapore – the worst military defeat in its history – reaffirmed his belief that his ally would play its assigned strategic role of tying down American and British forces, although his pleasure was tinged with regret that the British had not thrown in their lot with a German-dominated Europe against the United States.[46]

Hitler, not without justice – as many of his critics among the frontline commanders conceded – believed that his iron will and energetic leadership had prevented a Napoleonic catastrophe, even if his strategy of standing fast had worked because of Soviet mistakes as much as German actions. Still, the crisis had exacted a physical and mental toll, and, in truth, Hitler had little idea how or even whether Germany could still win the war. Jodl, in fact, claimed in mid-May 1945 that from early 1942 Hitler knew victory could no longer be achieved: "Earlier than any other person in the world, Hitler . . . knew that the war was lost. But can one give up a Reich and a people before they are lost? A man like Hitler could not do it." Goebbels, too, was shocked by Hitler's appearance and outlook in late March – he talked openly of a "crisis in the regime" – and especially by the Führer's admission that at times he doubted whether the eastern army could be saved and the war won. Hitler railed at the incompetence and cowardice of his generals. He had wanted to seize the Caucasus and strike a mortal blow at the Soviet regime, but "they" – meaning the professional elite at OKH, especially Halder, whose animosity rankled him – knew better, had in fact consistently interfered with and undermined all his plans. Then, confronted with military reverses and a failing supply system, his generals lost their nerve. Only his iron will and determination had surmounted the crisis and avoided a "Napoleonic disaster." He had, he asserted, understood the necessity of turning the natural desire of the troops to cling to the shelter of the villages into a way to blunt the enemy attack; by turning the entire rear area into a defense zone, the Russians who penetrated would be denied food and shelter, then mopped up by hunting parties in the rear. In this way, the troops' morale had been restored and the enemy made aware of German superiority. Stalin, he thought, had done much the same in the summer battles; now the tables had been turned. The winter crisis had also intensified Hitler's belief that he had to struggle against not only external enemies, but those within his own ranks who were either inadequate or disloyal. "Stalin's brutal hand," he again remarked with approval, "had saved the Russian front [for them] . . . We shall have to apply similar methods."[47]

In retrospect, once Stalin – eager to deal the Germans the same fatal blow as suffered by Napoleon – had overplayed his hand and extended the Soviet offensive, the Germans were at no time threatened with a potentially decisive, war-changing operational defeat. The situation was certainly dangerous, but the Germans always possessed the ability to master it; that, of course, was precisely Hitler's point when he later complained that his generals had lost their nerve. Performance under fire, not professional credentials, now conferred status, and Hitler's success in preventing panic and stabilizing the front seemed, to him as well as many others, to justify his takeover of army command. By the beginning of the *rasputitsa*, when all movement stopped, Hitler could take justifiable pride in the fact that his army, despite all predictions and expectations, had avoided the fate of Napoleon's. As early as December, Goebbels had noted that enemy propaganda had dubbed Hitler a reborn Napoleon, whose troops would suffer a similar catastrophe. The fact that they did not, though, proved enormously important in propagating the "Feldherr" myth, especially among German generals, for whom the historical example of the French emperor and the specter of 1812 was never far from memory. Hoepner, for example, acknowledged, "Our situation has dispiriting similarities with that of Napoleon in 1812," while Heinrici confessed in a letter to his wife, "I don't know how it will end . . . but it is quite clear that . . . we do not know how it should be done."[48]

Although Heinrici's was as close to an admission of professional intellectual bankruptcy as one was likely to get, Hitler, contrary to expectations and seemingly through sheer will, prevailed and the Wehrmacht had not crumbled: 1941 was not a reprise of 1812. He himself was fully aware of what was at stake, that if history repeated itself then "I am a beaten man." Indeed, he confessed to his entourage in late February 1942, "Boys, you can't imagine . . . how much the last three months have worn out my strength, tested my nervous resistance." As if divulging secrets to a confessor, Hitler continued, "I can tell you now that during the first two weeks of December we lost a thousand tanks and had two thousand locomotives out of operation. As a result of the general lack of material, I seemed to be a liar . . . I told the front that trains were arriving, but the locomotives were always broken down. I told the front that tanks were arriving, but in what a state!" But, he concluded triumphantly, "Now that January and February are past, our enemies can give up the hope of our suffering the fate of Napoleon." Indeed, he boasted in April, "We have mastered a destiny which broke another man 130 years earlier." The lesson of the last few months seemed clear: he, with his unorthodox decision and will, and not his generals, had been proven right. "I've noticed, on the occasion of such events," Hitler bragged, "that when everybody loses his nerves, I'm the only one who keeps calm." Fanatic will, toughness, strong nerves, the ability to overcome great difficulties and solve the toughest problems – these, and not the professional training of the military academies, he asserted in a speech to his *Gauleiters* (regional party bosses) in May 1942, had averted disaster and prevented a repetition of 1812. The winter crisis had given Hitler final legitimation as a Feldherr, the culmination of a process that had begun in the spring of 1940. The survival of the Wehrmacht had been credited to his account, while their failure had tied the Wehrmacht leaders even tighter to him. His creative genius, as in 1940 exerted against the doubts and expert advice of his generals, had spared the Ostheer the fate of Napoleon's *Grande Armée*. He, like his hero, Frederick the Great, had proven his ability not only to win offensive victories but also to prevail in defensive battles. This, concluded his adjutant Below, was the proof of his genius as a Feldherr. As almost two years earlier, at the end of the French campaign, Hitler's reputation as a military leader had again risen.[49]

Despite the later fixation of historians on the winter crisis as the occasion of Hitler's centralization of military command authority and erosion of the principle of Auftragstaktik – a process begun, as has been noted, by Halder and greatly aided by the extensive use of radio – the really important question has often been left unasked: did OKH and army group commanders have any better ideas for how to prosecute the war in Russia? The answer is mixed, at best. It is well to remember that it was Halder who in August had assured Hitler that both Moscow and Ukraine could still be taken in 1941. In some respects, then, Hitler's great strategic mistake was that he took his OKH chief's advice seriously. Given Halder's predilection for dividing forces and his original intention of launching an assault on Moscow with only one Panzer group, it is improbable that the Soviet capital could have been taken even by an offensive launched in late August. More likely, Red Army resistance in the center and counterattacks against the weak and exposed German flanks would have caused the operation to fail, as Zhukov claimed after the war. Ironically, this probably would have been less disastrous than what, in fact, actually transpired. Hitler's intervention meant a focus on Kiev took precedence over Moscow, which in itself was a logical enough response to the serious threat to the German flanks. Having set the offensive in motion in the south, though, he did not act to see it through to its full conclusion, a failure he acknowledged with some bitterness to Goebbels in late March 1942. Germany, as he knew, suffered from serious economic deficiencies that, from the start, made victory a highly risky gamble. In the late summer of 1941, with at least a realistic possibility of seizing key economic resources in Ukraine and oil in the Caucasus, Hitler bowed to OKH pressure and approved the attack on Moscow. As Halder in the interim had come to realize, the Germans could do one or the other but not both, but he was done in by his own machinations; having promised the Führer both, in the event, he could deliver neither.[50]

Reality, as always, was far more complicated than myth. The Germans had seriously miscalculated the difficulty of applying a Blitzkrieg strategy, successful in France with its limited spaces and good transportation system, to the vast territory and abysmal infrastructure of the Soviet Union. They had then compounded this error by ignoring the problems raised by their own war games, so were unprepared for what eventuated. This, of course, was a failing of OKH as much as Hitler. To make matters worse, Hitler's mid-July decision – itself largely based on optimistic OKH assessments – to reorient armaments production away from the army in favor of the Luftwaffe and navy came at precisely the moment that stiffening Soviet resistance indicated an enemy far from beaten. Additionally, when it became clear by late July and early August that key decisions would have to be made, the interminable back and forth discussions between Hitler and Halder – which disproved the myth of Hitler's absolute dominance – cost valuable time and poisoned an already tense atmosphere. Halder's obstructionism and misrepresentations had not merely sown ill-will, but had eroded Hitler's inclination, evident in earlier disputes, to concede to OKH judgment, since he now thoroughly mistrusted Halder's motives or willingness to implement his orders.

Nor, despite the later assertions of some generals, was it likely that the already thin and overstretched German forces could have encircled and taken Moscow; indeed, their inability, in more favorable circumstances, to control earlier encirclements at Minsk and Smolensk was the best argument against this possibility. Hitler, in fact, had a realistic view of the problems raised by urban fighting, in late August explicitly assuring Mussolini that he would not be drawn into such warfare, at which the Russians were exceptionally adept. Moreover, given Stalin's firm control of the Soviet administrative apparatus, the corollary to this myth, that the seizure of Moscow would have caused a collapse of the USSR, is highly problematic. Stalin was fully prepared to fight on from the Urals, relying on new industrial areas and Lend-Lease to bolster his effort. Semyon Timoshenko, after all, reminded the Supreme Defense Council in December, "If Germany succeeds in taking Moscow that is obviously a grave disappointment for us . . . but that alone will not win the war. The only thing that matters is oil . . . So we have to do all we can (a) to make Germany increase her oil consumption, and (b) to keep the German armies out of the Caucasus." In retrospect, the only real possibility for German victory in 1941 was for the Red Army to have reacted as the French had a year earlier and, when encircled, simply surrender. When this failed to happen, all the skill and operational competence of the German military elite could not compensate for its economic and logistic deficiencies. The events of December 1941 meant Hitler's gamble on defeating the Soviet Union quickly in order to gain strategic freedom of movement to elevate Germany to world-power status had failed. The war had slipped out of his control; it had become a global war before Germany was ready. Hitler might well have saved the Wehrmacht from disaster in the winter crisis of 1941–2; a year later, however, his luck would run out.[51]

9

A World Power or Nothing at All (1942–3)

When the Führer mounted the stage at the Berlin Sportpalast on 30 January 1942 to deliver his customary "state of the Reich" address to a hand-picked audience of armament workers, nurses from local military hospitals, and convalescing soldiers, circumstances had changed dramatically, both for himself and for the German people. Just six weeks earlier, in addressing the Reichstag to announce his declaration of war on the United States, he had given a long, tedious, and disjointed speech – more a list of complaints of the evil done to him than an effort to rally the nation or seriously discuss the current situation – that sought historical vindication for the war that had just turned global. He now, pointedly, attempted to justify himself to the German people. "My German *Volksgenossen*. My comrades," he began. "In these times each [leader] speaks to the forum that appears to him most appropriate – the one [meaning Churchill] before a parliament whose existence, composition and origin we all know well enough – but I believe again that in these days I must return to where I came from, namely, the people. You are, you see" – and here he clearly was chiding the two democratic leaders, who allegedly spoke only to professional politicians, not to the average citizens who had conferred Hitler's legitimacy – "also representatives of the nation, only with the difference that you receive no allowances and have much more difficulty in coming to such a gathering than the so-called appointed representatives of these democracies."

This war, he continued, had become a second world war, a continuation of the first not only in the sense that it was a global war, but also because the same power had provoked it, and for the same aims. The British, he thundered, who for three centuries had promoted the growth of their worldwide empire through war and conflict, had fomented the First World War because of their jealousy of Germany and refusal to allow it an independent existence. Abetted now by the United States, they again sought the destruction of a National Socialist Germany that, in its achievements, exposed the lie of liberal democracy. Then, aiming to solidify his support, Hitler recited his domestic social, economic, and political accomplishments. He had, he exclaimed, taken over a Germany broken by a harsh peace, failed democratic policies, and economic depression. Despite this, he had inaugurated programs that created jobs, restored economic and social security, and promoted the unity of the German nation. What, he asked in a contemptuous tone, had his opponents really done? Roosevelt, "a wretched madman," bragged of his programs but, Hitler gloated, listing one after another social program, "We have long had that in Germany." Churchill fared no better. He was, Hitler bellowed, "a drunken babbler . . . who in reality had achieved nothing in his life . . . [a] lazy liar . . . if this war had not come, who would speak of [him]?" As for Bolshevism, German soldiers could see daily what it had wrought in Russia.

Having worked himself into a frenzy, Hitler now turned, in his mind, to the ultimate instigator of war, the Jews. Their agents, the British and Americans, had already spoken of breaking up the Reich. The Jews, he thundered:

> are in any case our old enemies; they have experienced a thwarting of their goals by us and they rightly hate us just as we hate them. Let's be clear about it, this war can only end with either the extermination of the German people, or that the Jews of Europe will disappear. I said as much before the German Reichstag on September 1, 1939 [*sic*] . . . that this war will not end as the Jews imagine, namely, in the extermination of the European-Aryan people; instead, the result of this war will be the annihilation of Jewry. For the first time, not merely others will bleed to death; rather, for the first time the old Jewish law "an eye for an eye, a tooth for a tooth" will be applied to them.

Similarly, Hitler cast the new global struggle as one of the "haves" versus the "have-nots." "Now we shall see," he declared, "who are the stronger in this struggle, those who have nothing to lose, but everything to gain, or those who have everything to lose and nothing to gain. For, what does England want to gain? What does America want to gain? What do they want to gain? They have so much that they do not know what to do with what they have . . . They have the whole world at their disposal. For decades they have plundered us, exploited us, squeezed us." In Japan, though, Hitler thought he had a suitable ally for the fight ahead. Germany, too, was different, reminiscent of a "Frederician Germany . . . that will not give up a foot of ground without a fight." The winter, he conceded, was difficult, but it was also the "great hope of our eastern enemy." The Ostheer had stood the test and now, just as Frederick the Great, a man of "iron will [who] through all setbacks . . . never despaired of victory," he would be the "first soldier of the Reich," standing with his people. "No other path remains but the path of battle and success. It may be difficult . . .," he allowed, "but never will it be more difficult than the struggles of our ancestors. It will also not," Hitler admitted grimly, "get easier." The war, he declared, had become an existential struggle "to maintain our freedom, our nation, our children and grandchildren."[1]

The electric atmosphere, the raw emotion of the speech, Hitler's resentful populist tone, Goebbels thought, had once more "charged the entire nation as though it were a storage battery" and prepared it for tough times ahead. The "turbulent enthusiasm," he claimed, was proof of the "tremendous impression" Hitler had made and demonstrated that the "psychological difficulties had been overcome." Despite his obvious relief that Hitler had once more rallied the German people, though, no amount of speechmaking could disguise the grim reality facing the country in early 1942. Hitler knew full well that victory could no longer be achieved, or at least not the way originally envisioned, nor did he have a clear idea how to end the war. He admitted as much in his Heroes Memorial Day speech in March, when, having generated an enthusiastic response with his vow that "the Bolshevik hordes, who were unable to vanquish the German soldiers . . . this winter, will be defeated by us this coming summer and annihilated," he then raised doubts as to what that actually meant by suggesting that Soviet borders would simply be pushed far from Europe. Still, he had reasons for guarded optimism. For one, he was on firm ground with the high command. Despite their testy relationship, Halder had conceded the Führer "to be the only man able to hold the Wehrmacht and the German nation together in the coming difficult times." Relief at the Ostheer's ability to blunt the Soviet counterattack, survive intact, and destroy many enemy units, combined with the spectacular early successes of their Japanese ally, also provided hope that the situation could still be turned to German advantage. If the Japanese could preoccupy the United States in the Pacific, and if the Soviet Union could be, if not defeated, then neutralized in 1942 before American power could be mobilized, it might just be possible for Germany to gain the resources necessary to fight a global war. Although the defeat in front of Moscow, as virtually all in the high command recognized, marked a turnabout in the war, it did not, they thought, necessarily have to be a watershed. German leaders agreed that 1942 would be the decisive year, indeed, for Germany, the last chance. One more successful campaign, they believed, would enable them to persist in what was now a war of attrition.[2]

Such, at least, were the expectations as outlined in a surprisingly optimistic study released by OKW on 14 December 1941. Japan's entry into the war and initial successes, it stressed, had deprived the Western allies of the strategic initiative, at least until late 1942. Operating on the assumption that Britain and the United States would then opt for a "Germany-first" strategy, which gave them only a limited window within which to wrap up the war in Russia, OKW analysts proposed operational goals for the summer campaign. The focus, they thought – betraying a belief that the Soviet Union could not be defeated militarily on the battlefield – should be on strangling the enemy's war economy by capturing the northern ports of Archangel and Murmansk, vital for Lend-Lease supplies, while in the south seizing the oil fields of the Caucasus. With the Soviets unable to receive Lend-Lease aid and denied oil, any further Russian resistance, it was assumed, would be at a low level. The high command having assured themselves of a steady supply of oil, the Caucasus would then serve as an excellent jumping-off point for an advance against the British in the Middle East; capture of the Persian oil fields and the prospect of an Arab rising might cause the entire British position to collapse. Furthermore, if the Mediterranean could be stabilized by the time Anglo-American forces were ready to act at year's end, the Axis would be in a formidable position from which to conduct a defensive war. This was, in retrospect, an astonishing misappraisal of Axis capabilities, given the woeful state of the Ostheer, the weakness of the Italians, and the inadequacy of German strength in the west. Moreover, even if everything unfolded as outlined, OKW staffers provided no explanation for how victory might be achieved; far from a strategy for success, this would merely put Germany in a better position to fight a long war. Whether they won or lost the summer battles, Germany still faced a loss of the strategic initiative and a protracted defensive war.[3]

Although in the event only OKW's assumption of the "Germany first" approach would prove correct, this study, reinforced by the fall of Singapore in February 1942, meshed to a great extent with both Hitler's and Halder's concepts. Hitler, in late October 1941, had already decided the eastern campaign could only be resolved through conquest of the Caucasian oil fields, an assessment with which Halder agreed. Even before his hope of reaching Moscow had evaporated, the latter pointed to the necessity of seizing the vital industrial and oil areas in the south; an attack toward Maikop and over the Caucasus to Baku, he believed, was the most urgent task in the coming year. Hitler agreed, thinking this blow, which would secure German oil supplies and cripple the Soviet war economy, would force Stalin to give up an active war policy. The Soviet Union, after all, obtained some 90 percent of its oil supplies from the Caucasus, so its loss, along with the other mineral, agricultural, and industrial resources of southern Russia, would, he reasoned, both boost the German war effort and throw the Soviet economy into an existential crisis. Hitler had also persuaded himself that it might well cause London, especially if accompanied by Axis successes in the Mediterranean, to finally see the senselessness of continuing the war and agree to a peace. In that event, his lack of any idea of how to deal with the immense power of the United States – he told his entourage on 15 January that he had an uneasy suspicion that only America would emerge a victor – might prove irrelevant. Shorn of a European ally from whose territory to build up an invasion force, American power would be nullified. This Hitler thought a plausible outcome, since he believed America's rise would come at England's expense. Britain, he asserted, would be the "only loser" in the war, and as that realization took hold in London, it would veer away from the United States and – in his wildest fantasy – even join with Germany in an anti-American coalition.[4]

In any case, he could see no alternative to an operation in the Caucasus. Hitler's thinking certainly violated Clausewitz's basic dictum, of which he was well aware, that the object of a campaign should be the defeat of enemy military forces in the field, from which the seizure of economic assets would follow. But, in view of the failure, in more favorable circumstances, to destroy the bulk of the Red Army the year before, along with his realistic assessment of the needs of the struggling German war economy, he saw a push south as the only option. Oil was essential to continue the war – as Hitler recognized, "Who loses oil, loses the war" – while time, he knew, was running against him. He only had resources for one major campaign, and just a few months to make "a clean sweep in the east" and create a defensible German-occupied Europe. In December 1941 he had ordered the construction of a "new West Wall" – the first appearance of his "Fortress Europe" concept – to ensure the protection of the North Sea and Atlantic coasts. Unlike the previous year, when the absence of an agreed goal for Barbarossa contributed to the campaign's failure, all was now clear: German power would have to be concentrated in the south for a sweeping operation that would take the Wehrmacht further into the depths of Russia, to the very gates of Asia.[5]

Without explicitly saying it, then, Hitler saw 1942 as a transitional year: after one last successful offensive campaign, Germany would pivot to a continental, defensive strategy. He had in fact already drawn lessons from the 1941 fighting, concluding that "the decisive factor for winning any war is that one constantly possesses the technically best weapons." Impressed both by the powerful Soviet tanks, as well as the development of the German hollow-charge anti-tank shell, he had decided that the tank in its present form – light, quick models used as an offensive breakthrough weapon – would not survive until the end of the war. The future, he thought, belonged to heavily armored tanks with powerful guns – "self-propelled fortresses" – that could be used in defense as well as offense. A British commando operation against St Nazaire on France's Atlantic coast on 28 March 1942 also exacerbated his anxieties about possible enemy action in the west, and the need for defensive preparations there. In July, at a crucial point in the eastern campaign, he would order the transfer of several combat-experienced SS formations from the east – putting a heavy burden on an already strapped Ostheer – in order to supplement the 22 infantry and 7 motorized divisions, some 500,000 men in all, stationed in the west. Still, despite some desultory offers, brusquely rejected, on the part of the Japanese and Swedes to mediate with the Soviets – and soundings put out by the Russians themselves – Hitler preferred to gamble that the Wehrmacht, which had mastered the winter crisis, could now achieve the goals set for it in 1942. He would, he indicated to Goebbels, be prepared to end the war once his ideological and economic objectives had been realized. He also thought that he had the advantage over his Soviet adversary, which he believed had been brought to the brink of collapse from the effort of the winter counteroffensive. The hope of wriggling out of the war with Russia and Britain with much of his gains intact – thus nullifying American power – proved much more tantalizing than a peace with the Soviet Union alone.[6]

At the end of March, Hitler revealed to Goebbels the outline of a plan that, if not exactly designed to end the Russian campaign – he talked of a "hundred years' war in the east" – would nonetheless by the end of October leave Germany in a very formidable position to wage a global conflict. This plan, submitted to Hitler for his review on 28 March under the code name *Fall Blau* (Case Blue), sketched the goals for the German summer offensive. After reworking by OKH, it received concrete expression in Directive No. 41, which Hitler signed on 5 April 1942. Declaring it vital to seize the strategic initiative and "force our will on the enemy," Hitler directed that "all available forces" would be concentrated in the southern sector in order "to wipe out the entire defense potential remaining to the Soviets, and to cut them off, as far as possible, from their most important centers of war industry." Interestingly, in view of its later importance, Stalingrad was hardly mentioned in the directive, nor was its capture a particularly critical goal. "Every effort will be made to reach Stalingrad itself," the order stated, "or at least to bring the city under fire from heavy artillery so that it may no longer be of any use as an industrial or communications center." Instead, seizing the Caucasus oil fields was the main prize. Hitler, in confirmation of his newfound wariness of a second front, also directed that "the security of occupied territories in western and northern Europe, *especially along the coast*, will be ensured in all circumstances." At the conclusion of this operation, which Hitler expected by the end of October, German troops would immediately go into winter quarters; haunted by the near-disaster of the previous winter, he was determined that strong defensive positions be prepared. All future plans, he told Mussolini at the time, depended on the outcome of the coming campaign. "When Russia's sources of oil are exhausted," he claimed, "she will be brought to her knees." Furthermore, he told the Duce, he expected Britain to make peace "once she no longer sees a chance of winning."[7]

As with the Blitzkrieg of the previous summer, it was an all-or-nothing gamble on a short campaign, but in the spring of 1942 there existed an even greater discrepancy than in the year before between Hitler's aims and military power. Clearly, too, the Germans had been sobered by their winter reverses. This did not resemble the bold, confident plan of a year earlier, which aimed at the swift annihilation of enemy forces as a prelude to a total defeat of the Soviet Union. Although ambitious, this plan accepted that a complete Soviet capitulation was not to be expected; instead, the goal now was merely to paralyze Stalin's ability to carry on active fighting. Despite the bitter debate of the previous year, there was now virtually no discussion of renewing the offensive in the direction of Moscow; Hitler (and Halder) meant to neutralize the Soviet Union not by destroying the Red Army and seizing the capital but by turning off the oil spigot.

The operational plan for 1942 outlined an exceedingly complex operation based on a series of successive actions. Problems raised by the great distances, the tenuous supply situation, and insufficient manpower meant that in order to achieve a maximum concentration of force at crucial points the campaign was planned as a series of mutually supplementary partial attacks, staggered from north to south. Rather than a sweeping envelopment movement, it aimed to compensate for German weakness through an intricate sequential operation in which each stage prepared the way for the next.

The aim, in short encirclements modeled on Vyazma and Bryansk, would be to seize Voronezh on the northern shoulder of Army Group South – thus providing flank support and threatening a further advance on Moscow – then sweep south to destroy enemy forces west of the Don to prepare the way for an advance to Stalingrad. This city, a major river port for Lend-Lease supplies and a key center of tank production, did not necessarily have to be entered. Indeed, Hitler himself had dismissed the idea, pointing out that Stalingrad could easily be destroyed from the air, while a German presence anywhere on the Volga would disrupt river traffic. Having neutralized this industrial and communications center and cut the Volga supply line, only then would the fourth, and most important, phase of the operation unfold: the rush into the Caucasus, presumably against now weak and scattered Red Army units, to seize the valuable oil fields. If all went well, Hitler expected the operation to be completed by early October. Although a complicated undertaking that depended for success on expert direction of forces, even as German commanders were to be denied much of their traditional freedom of action, neither war games nor simulations had been conducted. Success was also, to a large extent, predicated on the Soviets repeating their behavior of a year earlier and again cooperating in their own destruction.[8]

With Directive No. 41, Hitler affirmed his intention to make the Eastern Front the decisive theater of operations, a resolve surely strengthened by the steady flow of reports he received stressing the importance of oil for the war effort. In any case, with the failure of Barbarossa and the entry of the United States into the war, Hitler's options, none of which offered much certainty of victory, had been seriously constrained. He might have gone over to the strategic defensive and used the time to mobilize the German war economy and develop new weapons. Goebbels, in fact, referred in late March to a report indicating that German research "in the realm of atomic destruction has now proceeded to a point where its results may possibly be made use of in the conduct of this war." Hitler might also have ordered an increase in the production of weapons such as U-boats or anti-aircraft guns in order to more vigorously prosecute the war in the Atlantic and over the skies of Germany. He might have built on Japanese successes and revived the Mediterranean strategy rejected a year earlier, with the aim of striking east through Egypt to seize Suez and the oil fields of the Middle East and link up with Japanese forces in India. The naval leadership proposed just such a plan to redirect German efforts against the British Empire, but although Hitler found it intriguing, it was ultimately rejected because of time and force restraints. As Halder noted witheringly, "These people are dreaming in terms of continents" while the acute problems in the east were treated "with criminal unconcern."[9]

Halder, then, despite his post-war claims, neither opposed resumption of the offensive in the east nor challenged its conception and goals. He accepted Hitler's strategic assessment of the situation and agreed that it was vital to seize the oil fields of the Caucasus, both to secure the German war economy and serve as a jumping-off point for an assault on the British power-base in the Middle East. Despite his fear that losses in 1942 would be greater than the entire cohort of youth to be drafted into the army, the Caucasus operation, he concluded, was "an inescapable necessity." Although some senior military leaders complained privately of "Utopian plans for an offensive," none could offer a convincing alternative, especially since the Germans lacked the manpower, materiel, and economic resources to conduct a strategic defense. General Fromm dismissed the proposed operation as a "luxury" inappropriate to a "poor man," while General Thomas warned of "the disproportion between war requirements and the capacity to meet them." Albert Speer merely observed that if Germany had to fight another winter in Russia, then it would have lost the war. None, though, could offer a viable option, a fact that caused Hitler to note with asperity in late May, "Again and again so-called experts . . . declared: that is not possible, that can't be done . . . There are problems that absolutely have to be solved. Where real leaders are present, they have always been solved and will always be solved."[10]

Indeed, in an indication of his increased assertiveness and confidence in his own military abilities, Hitler had largely devised the operational scheme himself, thoroughly reviewed and "corrected" plans submitted to him by OKH, and added entirely new parts. His awareness of time limitations, German weakness, and the failure of the sweeping encirclement operations of the previous summer contributed decisively to his order that the armored forces should not go off on wild Panzer raids but focus instead on tight encirclement operations carried out in close cooperation with infantry. Given Army Group South's limited armor and the need to provide the Luftwaffe a smaller target on which to focus its own scarce resources, this methodical approach seemed reasonable. "Experience has sufficiently shown," Hitler's directive of April 5 stressed:

that the Russians are not very vulnerable to operational encircling movements. It is therefore of decisive importance that, as in the double battle of Vyazma-Bryansk, individual breaches of the front should take the form of close pincer movements.

We must avoid closing the pincers too late, thus giving the enemy the possibility of avoiding destruction.

> *It must not happen* that, by advancing too quickly and too far, armored and motorized formations lose connection with the infantry following them; or that they lose the opportunity of supporting the hard-pressed, forward-fighting infantry.

Moreover, his cognizance of the shortcomings of German tanks – another reason he was skeptical of the success of sweeping envelopments – in both quality and quantity vis-à-vis Soviet ones also helped determine the shape of the offensive. The Ostheer had almost 2,000 fewer tanks than the year before, while Hitler had gained a healthy respect for Soviet models. This meant that the armored forces alone were not likely to be a war-winning weapon in 1942. They would have to work more effectively in conjunction with infantry and air forces.[11]

The operational plan, though, concealed a larger dilemma. If the Red Army avoided being drawn into encirclement battles, destruction of its forces, given diminished German strength, would be beyond the capabilities of the invaders. At best, Hitler might hope to destroy sufficient numbers of Soviet units to hold the remnants of Stalin's regime at bay. Meanwhile, the Soviet Union's Western Allies were steadily assembling their massive economic and military resources, while the Germans were increasingly dependent on Italy, Romania, and Hungary, nations that drained already insufficient German economic strength rather than adding to it. As always, it seemed, the Germans struggled to do more with less. Having rejected any notion of ending the war politically or standing on the defensive, Hitler, like Napoleon in 1815, resolved to take offensive action in an effort to split his enemies and defeat one (and possibly even two) before the third was ready. Fall Blau was thus an operational attempt to pass through the "danger zone" before the Western Allies could intervene on the continent. As Hitler realized, American entry into the war put Germany under an extraordinary time pressure; a concrete threat of a "second front" had now materialized, so in order to avoid the strategic encirclement of Germany, as in the First World War, a victory in the east was vital. Above all, the absolute necessity of acquiring oil supplies seemed to validate Hitler's strategy. "The operations of 1942 must get us to the oil," Field Marshal Keitel admitted in late May, otherwise the army would be unable to sustain operations. A few days later Hitler made an even more startling confession to his assembled generals: "If I do not get the oil of Maikop and Grozny, then I must end the war." Control of the economic resources of southern Russia was the key. Without them, Germany had no hope of sustaining an attritional war; with them, Hitler asserted, "then the war is practically won for us," since the

Anglo-Saxon powers could not seriously challenge a German-dominated Europe. It was, though, a situation of "triumph or destruction": 1942 was to be the watershed year.[12]

Operation Barbarossa had been launched on the gamble of a quick knockout, which had failed because of unrelenting Soviet resistance; in 1942, Hitler now placed his hopes on a similar throw of the dice, but with even less chance of success. The Ostheer had suffered losses in excess of 1.1 million men, a shortage of troops that an influx of new recruits could not make good; in May it was still short by 625,000 men. Virtually all the units of Army Group South had been partially or completely rebuilt, stripping the infantry divisions of Army Groups North and Center – and thus leaving them dangerously weakened – to flesh them out. Nor, because of labor needs, could any more trained reservists be pulled out of the armaments factories. By 1942 the Germans had run out of manpower; only those recovering from wounds were left as a ready pool of trained personnel. Nothing reflected this stark reality more than the decision in the spring to increase the size of the Italian, Romanian, and Hungarian contingents fighting in the east: of the forty-one new divisions arriving in the south for Operation Blue, fully twenty-one were non-German. Although poorly trained and motivated, they were necessary to plug gaps in the overstretched front. Just as seriously, German factories struggled to make good the massive losses of tanks, vehicles, and artillery; even supplying adequate levels of ammunition proved difficult. As a result, the firepower of German units would be sharply reduced. In addition, cuts to its fuel rations dealt a serious blow to the Ostheer's mobility, despite the fact that the key to the entire operation lay in the swift encirclement and destruction of remaining Soviet forces in the south. The success of the campaign depended on seizing objectives more than 800 miles from the German start line, an operational and logistical challenge greater even than the previous summer. Although the rail system had recovered somewhat from its near-catastrophic collapse in January 1942, the lack of locomotives and rolling stock limited its ability to provide supplies for the offensive. The conclusion of all who looked objectively at the figures was inescapable: the Ostheer in the spring of 1942 lacked the means to achieve its ambitious objectives.[13]

Ironically, Hitler's confidence owed more to his assessment of Soviet weakness than his belief in German strength. His operational thinking, based on the assumption that the Red Army was at the end of its strength and had only limited powers of regeneration, stemmed from incorrect information. Foreign Armies East reported in April that Soviet manpower reserves were "by no means inexhaustible" and, if subjected to losses such as those suffered in 1941, would run out by the onset of the muddy season. This appraisal, though, was flawed in two respects: Soviet reserves were larger than assumed, while there was no guarantee that devastating losses could be inflicted on the Red Army. Moreover, German economic analysts had misjudged Soviet industrial capacities in the eastern part of European Russia, as well as the extent of the factory evacuation program and the speed with which production could be resumed in the Urals area. In the second half of 1941, despite the loss of its key economic areas, the Soviet Union had nearly equaled the entire German yearly production of tanks, aircraft, artillery, mortars, machine and submachine guns, and rifles. Since receipt of Lend-Lease aid would, as the Germans realized, result in a "substantial strengthening of the Soviet Union's power of resistance," a key goal of the summer offensive was to cut the Allied supply line via Murmansk and Archangel, as well as from Persia up the Volga River. Given limited German capabilities, the northern operation was highly doubtful from the start, so even if the Ostheer succeeded in reaching the Volga and seizing the oil fields of the Caucasus, a fatal weakening of the Soviet ability to continue fighting would not likely have resulted. Even the Führer seemed to recognize this, remarking to Goebbels in April that it would be necessary to build a stronger defensive line this coming winter.[14]

Germany thus faced the same ticking time bomb as in the First World War: inferiority in resources, manpower, and production would eventually prove decisive on the battlefield, despite their operational successes. Hitler fully understood this. If he had any hope of a successful outcome of the war, he had to cripple the Soviet Union by the end of autumn. The Red Army had suffered staggering casualties in 1941; perhaps, the Führer thought, they could not now resist another onslaught. Having concentrated his forces in the south, and phased even that operation into staggered assaults, he believed he had made sufficient allowance for the Ostheer's loss of strength. His keen strategic insight was clouded, though, by his compulsive wishful thinking; declaring belief in the success of an operation did not guarantee its realization. The gulf between reality and perception was thus bound to widen if the situation developed contrary to his hopes. Such, of course, would be the case in the second half of 1942, when his denial – or, perhaps better stated, his realization – of unpleasant facts led him, in a state of growing nervous anxiety, to make a number of operationally flawed decisions. Believing the war to be essential to the very existence of the German nation, he could not easily adjust reality to his perception of German needs. This would be one reason for his later decision to stubbornly hold on. Germany needed resources; if they were given up, then they could never be recovered. In the spring of 1942, his grand strategic vision reduced to little more than an operational advance on a distant target that might, in any case, not provide the necessary oil to continue fighting, Hitler risked everything on yet another calamitous miscalculation.[15]

The chaotic situation at the end of the winter fighting necessitated a series of preliminary operations to stabilize the front, provide flank protection, safeguard vital oil production, and free up additional forces for the main offensive. Foremost among them was control of the Crimea, important both as a springboard to the Caucasus and, if left in Soviet hands, a persistent threat to the Romanian oil fields. After bitter autumn and winter fighting that resulted in staggering casualties, Manstein's 11th Army in April 1942 controlled the bulk of the Crimea, excluding Sevastopol and the Kerch peninsula. Taking them, Manstein realized, would be a formidable endeavor. From Hitler's perspective, though, concern over the safety of his sole source of oil more than justified the operation. Moreover, the Führer had repeatedly expressed interest in the Crimea, which was to be "cleansed" of its native population and resettled by "pure Germans," as a key area of colonization that would secure Lebensraum as far as the Urals. Complete control of the peninsula, including the fortress of Sevastopol, would also limit the effectiveness of the Soviet Black Sea Fleet, as well as possibly influence the neutrality of Turkey. Finally, army planners saw strong Soviet formations in the Crimea as a persistent threat to communications and supply lines along their long, exposed southern flank.[16]

As a result, Hitler took a lively interest in the campaign, not least because of the "expertise" he had gained from personal experience during the First World War in fortress warfare. In mid-April 1942 he had detailed discussions with Manstein about the operation – an exchange of views that Manstein regarded as quite positive – advising him of the importance of firepower and sharing his experiences of the earlier war. While Manstein in May displayed his operational flair in seizing the heavily fortified Kerch peninsula in stunningly swift fashion, he also made extensive use of gigantic artillery pieces, the largest in the German arsenal, and large-scale aerial attacks (i.e., the firepower recommended by Hitler) to subdue the fortress of Sevastopol, finally taking it on 1 July. This brilliant operation spotlighted German strengths in planning, tactical skill, optimum coordination of air and ground forces, risk-taking commanders, and well-trained combat troops. But it also demonstrated the key weakness of the Wehrmacht: it had too few resources to enable it to transform tactical victories into strategic triumphs. Victory in the Crimea depended on concentration of Luftwaffe forces in the region, but this superiority could be achieved only by stripping other sectors of the front of vital air power. When deprived of much of its air power in mid-May because of emergencies elsewhere, Manstein's forces took longer to capture the fortress of Sevastopol than anticipated, thus contributing to a holdup in launching other preliminary operations, which in turn delayed the main summer campaign. Finally, the operation resulting in the seizure of Sevastopol, which for all of its brilliance may not have been necessary, cost the Germans considerable numbers of casualties they could ill afford.[17]

The conquest of Sevastopol – an attack, he thought, "that no other army but the German could have pulled off" – confirmed Hitler in his opinion, shaped by his First World War experience, that firepower created by dense concentration of artillery played the decisive role in reducing fortresses. Not surprisingly, then, later that summer he dispatched Manstein to Leningrad with instructions to reduce that fortress. In line with his reassessment of the use of tanks, he also advised using the new heavy Tiger tank, just rolling off production lines, in defensive operations on the Volkhov front, where enemy attacks to relieve Leningrad were expected, as a sort of self-propelled artillery. If concentrated behind the front, Hitler declared to General Küchler, the commander of Army Group North, on 23 August, then "nothing can happen; they are invulnerable and can smash any enemy tank attack." In the event, the Führer's high hopes went unfulfilled, not least because the Tiger tanks were too heavy for roads and bridges in the marshy area and were thus rendered immobile. The Soviet attack, when it came on 27 August, quickly breached German lines, with enemy forces eventually thrown back only by the diversion of significant German forces to the area. The costly lesson was not lost on Hitler, who remarked in early March 1943 that the new large tanks were probably more suited for use in the west, where the roads were better. They were, after all, in line with his increasingly defensive thinking, "designed primarily to drive back attacks by enemy tanks and not to carry out independent strategic movements." At worst, he thought, they could just be buried "like the Russians do and . . . use the long gun" for defense.[18]

In the south, the Schwerpunkt for the summer campaign, Hitler initially proved more successful. The confused and desperate winter fighting had left the front line a tangled web of protrusions and salients that planners on both sides regarded as both a threat and an opportunity. The Germans had to eliminate these bulges in order to secure favorable jumping-off positions for their planned summer offensive. Nowhere was this more apparent than in the Izyum bridgehead, a protrusion some sixty miles in depth and breadth into their line on the west bank of the Donets River. Not only did it tie down many units, but Soviet forces jammed into the salient also menaced the key industrial city of Kharkov, less than forty miles to the northwest, as well as posing a threat to roll up the entire Southern Front. The menacing Soviet position, though, also posed an opportunity. To planners envisioning a summer campaign based on the rapid encirclement and destruction of enemy forces, the Izyum bulge, where the Red Army had already stuck its head in the noose, cried out to be snapped shut. As with the Crimean operation, elimination of the Izyum bridgehead would create an advantageous starting point for Fall Blau, as well as provide a morale boost for German troops left shaky by the winter crisis.[19]

The Soviets, too, saw an opportunity at Izyum. Stalin, like Hitler, thought the winter fighting had left the enemy on his last legs, so he favored aggressive offensive operations aimed at delivering the fatal blow. By contrast, his senior military advisors believed the most sensible approach in 1942 was to remain on the strategic defensive, build strength, absorb the anticipated German attack – which they expected to be aimed at Moscow – and only then, with the enemy exhausted, go over to the offensive. Stalin, though, embraced a limited offensive out of the Izyum bulge since even a short breakthrough, if circumstances fell right, might have an outsized strategic impact. Although the stated intent of the operation was simply to encircle and destroy German forces at Kharkov, by implication success here might lead to the collapse of the entire Southern Front. As a few months earlier, the lure of a single decisive blow proved irresistible to Stalin. Although the operation was originally scheduled to start on 5 May, difficulties in assembling forces caused Marshal Timoshenko to postpone it until 12 May. Still, despite repeated warnings by Foreign Armies East of the likelihood of an enemy attack out of Izyum, and the fear expressed by Bock to Halder on 5 May that "the Russians might beat us to it and attack on both sides of Kharkov," the enemy offensive caught the Germans off guard. The Soviets, employing concentrated forces on the German model for the first time – with a smaller infantry component supported by massively expanded tank, artillery, and air formations – quickly punched holes in the German line. Although these new tank corps performed poorly, primarily for lack of motorized infantry and anti-tank units, they nonetheless presaged a new style of waging war that aimed to match the Germans in shock, mobility, and coordination of supporting arms.[20]

The early success of the Soviet attack caused near-panic on Bock's part, although other German generals swiftly perceived an opportunity in Soviet actions, since a quick counterstrike could bag the entire attacking force. Having recognized the same possibility, Hitler on 14 May argued that the situation could be turned to advantage by an armored attack from the south. Fortified by his success during the winter crisis, and targeting Bock's panic, he also asserted the need to maintain nerves at this delicate moment. He even explicitly compared the situation at Kharkov with the legendary First World War battle of Tannenberg, where the steely nerved Hindenburg had surprised and destroyed an entire Russian army, declaring, as then, "This severe test must be gotten through." Hitler, like Hindenburg, was rewarded with a grand operational success. For the last time a German attack trapped and destroyed large numbers of the enemy: when resistance collapsed on 28 May, the Red Army had suffered 267,000 casualties, with another 240,000 men taken prisoner, in addition to losses of 1,200 tanks and 2,600 guns. In a brilliant display of skill and aggressiveness, the Germans had not only fought off a Soviet offensive but had then encircled the would-be encirclers. Although elated at their success, which had again been aided by mistakes in the Soviet command, sober German observers remained troubled by the other constant in the enemy: his seemingly bottomless reserves and the continued ferocity of his resistance. The fighting, in fact, stunned many, for it seemed "more fanatical, more ruthless" than the year before. Victory required "an all-out effort," including deployment of virtually the entire Luftwaffe on a limited area of the front, while the supply system was as dismal as ever. The Panzer units upon which the success of the summer campaign depended suffered significant losses in men and materiel, while time was slipping away. Still, these opening victories did much to restore German confidence and morale, while the shaky Soviet performance rekindled inflated notions of easy triumphs leading to a quick seizure of the Caucasian oil fields. Perhaps most significant, it again encouraged Hitler's belief in his own instinctive genius for battle, as well as the mistaken notion that German skill and proficiency in mobile warfare would always trump Soviet advantages in tanks and manpower.[21]

Fall Blau finally opened on 28 June, six days later than the previous summer offensive. Remarkably, the attack achieved almost complete surprise; accompanied by overwhelming air support, German units broke through Soviet lines and began racing eastward. With the Soviet defenders stunned by the speed and ferocity of the assault, about the only thing that slowed the Germans in the first few days was heavy rain. Even then, by 4 July lead units of 4th Panzer Army had crossed the Don, over 100 miles from the starting line, and reached the outskirts of Voronezh. Stalin, alarmed at the rapid German advance and fearful that this important armaments and transportation center would fall to the enemy, ordered strong

Soviet forces into position for counterattacks from the north. Still, the Red Army seemed in disarray and, in places, to have dissolved. With Panzer forces already across the Don, and with most of the Soviet defenders still west of the river, the Germans seemed poised once again to pull off a spectacular encirclement operation reminiscent of 1941. Doubts persisted, however. "The actual picture of the enemy situation is not yet clear to me," Halder admitted on 6 July. "There are two possibilities: either we have overestimated the enemy's strength and the offensive has smashed him, or the enemy is conducting a planned disengagement . . . to forestall being irretrievably beaten in 1942." In the event, the second assessment proved more accurate, as strong Soviet counterattacks at Voronezh allowed enemy forces time to withdraw, inciting yet another crisis within the German high command.[22]

Reports that the enemy had disappeared stirred increasing uneasiness in Halder and Hitler, since the goal of the first phase of the operation was the destruction of Soviet forces west of the Don. For them, the key was speed; German mobile formations in the north had to be turned south as swiftly as possible to trap the Red Army before it could escape. Nor could Hitler or Halder understand what appeared to be Bock's obsession with taking Voronezh. Bock, though, faced an increasing danger: Soviet attacks on his left flank had grown steadily, while enemy troops had been detected massing across the Don to the north. Bock was surprised to learn on 2 July that Hitler and Halder now placed no importance on the capture of Voronezh, and instead urged him to wheel his mobile units south. Bock was reluctant to do this as long as his left flank was unsecured and, in any case, he believed that the bulk of the enemy facing 6th Army, on his right flank, had already escaped.[23]

Fearful that the vital mobile units would get bogged down in urban warfare, Hitler flew to Bock's headquarters at Poltava on 3 July intending to order him to bypass Voronezh. The result was only further misunderstanding. In the presence of the aloof and aristocratic field marshal, the Führer, not atypically, lost his nerve and left the decision to Bock, who himself was confused. "Am I right in understanding you as follows," Bock asked, "I am to capture Voronezh if it can be done easily . . . But I am not to get involved in heavy fighting for the city?" Hitler confirmed this with a nod. Since General Hoth's Panzers reached the outskirts of Voronezh the next day and took it largely unopposed on 6 July, Bock felt confirmed in his command decisions, even as Hitler the day before had exploded in rage at what he considered the field marshal's inept leadership. Fuming that he had made it "emphatically clear" on 3 July that Voronezh had no value, Hitler now ordered Bock to detach two mobile divisions and send them south. The next morning, though, the Soviets launched a series of fierce attacks on Bock's left flank, which could only be stabilized with some difficulty. These assaults, along with a shortage of fuel, meant that Bock's mobile divisions, to Hitler's fury, were now tied down in fighting around Voronezh, threatening both a crippling delay in German plans and worsening the already acute time pressure.[24]

The Führer's anger at Bock's allegedly poor handling of the situation merely obscured the deeper problems confronting the Germans. Hitler, in the intimidating presence of a representative of the old Prussian elite, had typically shied away from making his desires clear and issuing specific orders. This command confusion, in turn, exacerbated the fundamental dilemma that the Ostheer lacked the mobile forces necessary simultaneously to defend its flanks against determined assaults and to press an offensive. Successful encirclement operations depended on both German skill and Soviet willingness to cooperate in their own destruction. While the Wehrmacht's skill was not in doubt, in the summer of 1942 it lacked sufficient quantities of tanks and fuel to drive deep into the enemy's rear, which, in any case, it was forbidden to do because of Hitler's demand for shallow pockets to ensure that the trapped enemy did not escape. But large numbers of Russian troops were escaping, even as Stalin insisted on a stubborn defense, only reluctantly authorizing a few tactical withdrawals in order to conserve strength. Although these evasive maneuvers often turned into headlong flight, the Germans, because of their lack of fuel and limited mobility, could not exploit this. While Soviet troops increasingly used American trucks supplied under Lend-Lease, German infantrymen undertook long, grueling marches in a futile effort to overtake their adversary. As Bock noted bitterly on 7 July, "The Army High Command . . . would like to encircle an enemy who is no longer there." The result, he concluded grimly the next day, was that the second phase of the operation "was dead." As in the previous year, the Germans could defeat but not eliminate the Red Army, a reality that undid their entire operational plan.[25]

Strategically as well, and despite his boast in late July that he had achieved great success against the "teachings of the war academy," an increasingly agitated Hitler suspected things were going wrong. He had devised an operational plan to minimize German weaknesses, but the enemy seemed to be foiling it simply by altering its response in the wake of multiple encirclement disasters. Moreover, after a promising start with the fall of Tobruk in June 1942 – Hitler, in an impassioned appeal to Mussolini, urged the Duce to exploit this "historic turning point" to destroy "the whole eastern structure of the British Empire" – the Axis push into Egypt stalled at El Alamein. Field Marshal Rommel, himself starved of supplies, now faced the prospect of a rapid Allied buildup, while large-scale British air raids on Lübeck (in late March) and Cologne (in late May) marked the start of a sustained area-bombing campaign that threatened civilian morale and resiliency, an issue of great sensitivity for Hitler. Finally, with the battle of Midway in early June, the Japanese, whom he had counted on to distract the Americans, had already reached the limits of their conquests and had been thrown on the defensive.[26]

Clearly, Soviet withdrawals had confounded the Germans and rendered their plans obsolete. Worried that the evaporation of Soviet forces was jeopardizing the entire operation, Hitler and Halder, at a time when the situation called for a concentration of power, and over the vigorous protests of Bock, on 7 July split Army Group South in two, beginning the fatal dissipation of force that would characterize German summer operations. Bock also fell victim to Hitler's mounting frustration. On the morning of 13 July the field marshal, now commanding Army Group B, protested an order to turn his units south, warning Halder that "annihilation of substantial enemy forces can no longer be achieved" in that direction. Bock argued instead that his troops should be sent east toward Stalingrad. Given the chaotic nature of Russian withdrawals, deep thrusts to the east might well have succeeded in trapping large numbers of the enemy. Any chance for success, though, given the chronically inadequate German logistical system, depended on a concentration of effort; and, contrary to Hitler's belief, the movement of armored units to the south had been hindered more by a lack of fuel than by Bock's alleged intransigence.[27]

Nonetheless, the reaction to Bock's proposal was swift and final: OKH curtly informed him that his mission lay in the south, not the east, while Hitler, who had fumed for days that Bock's decisions at Voronezh had undermined the entire operation, on 13 July relieved the field marshal of his command. That same day the Führer ordered "a thrust be made as quickly as possible from the north" toward the south to seize the Don River crossings east of Rostov in order to prevent the enemy from withdrawing. The firing of Bock and further marginalization of Halder meant that Hitler assumed increasing control over the day-to-day conduct of military operations, an action, in view of his growing irritability and impetuousness, with immediate consequences. He notably failed to concentrate German strength, instead sending divisions off in response to actual or presumed threats (such as blocking a Soviet spoiling offensive in Army Group Center's sector or dispatching troops to France to protect against a second front). He also abandoned the overall concept of Fall Blau as a sequential operation in which each stage was vital for the success of the whole. In its place he left only confusion, with German columns apparently advancing aimlessly, often across each other's line of march and with their supplies sent in the wrong direction. His hectic issuing of orders might have been comical, except for the very real loss of precious time, which Germany did not have, to sort out the mess. Hitler's impatience and tendency to understate enemy possibilities, now almost an obsessive desire to believe the Soviets beaten, were not merely typical aspects of his personality but also betrayed deeper worries. Indeed, combined with other decisions at roughly the same time, a pattern emerged that shows the way in which time pressures had begun to affect his decisions.[28]

Although continued success in the U-boat war and the surprisingly rapid advance toward the Caucasus offered some grounds for optimism, Soviet Foreign Minister Molotov's visit to London and Washington in May and June, and the Western Allies' apparent solid commitment to a second front in 1942, profoundly disturbed Hitler. The Anglo-Americans, he realized, would not tolerate a collapse of the Soviet Union. Ironically, then, the likelihood of an early Allied landing in Norway or northwest Europe increased with every German success in the east. His "window of opportunity" apparently narrowing rapidly, Hitler decided to forestall any Allied intervention on the continent. "The rapid and great successes in the east," he explained in an order of 9 July, "would face Britain with the alternative of either executing a major landing at once to establish a second front or losing Soviet Russia." As a result, the Führer transferred the powerful 1st and 2nd SS Panzer Divisions, which should have spearheaded 1st Panzer Army's drive into the Caucasus, to the west. Two weeks later he ordered that the elite Grossdeutschland Motorized Division be prepared for transportation west. Finally, he also decreed, despite the drain on the Wehrmacht's meager resources, that the Channel and Atlantic coasts be developed into an "unassailable fortress" in order "to avoid the establishment of a second front." There could be, he stated to Speer and Keitel, "only one fighting front." The German dilemma was clear: by fortifying his defenses in the west, Hitler hoped to deter the Allies from launching a second front in 1942, but at the cost of what was most immediately important, seizing the Caucasian oil fields.[29]

His timetable unraveling, Hitler, typically, reacted by attempting to do everything at once, thus ensuring that none of his key objectives could be attained. First, after having on 11 July ordered Manstein to prepare for an early August crossing of the Kerch straits in order to facilitate a rapid seizure of the Maikop region and its vital oil fields – a target date that suggested he planned to launch the thrust into the Caucasus before the Stalingrad operation was finished – just six days later he reversed the decision and ordered the bulk of 11th Army transferred north to the Leningrad front. At the same time, in the area around Rostov, German forces plunged ahead in the futile search for an annihilating battle, even as they continued, as Bock noted contemptuously, to strike "a blow into thin air." To Hitler's irritation, the thrust south merely confirmed Bock's prediction, as it bagged disappointingly small numbers of prisoners. Finally, in committing the bulk of Wehrmacht forces to Wilhelm List's Army Group A, Hitler and OKH starved 6th Army of the resources it needed to advance quickly to the Volga. Bock in mid-July had correctly observed that Stalingrad was ripe for the taking; by the time the Germans turned their attention to it, valuable days had been lost, giving the Soviets time to strengthen the city. The German triumphs in July thus seemed empty; despite impressive territorial gains, the Soviets had evaporated into the vastness of southern Russia. Time and space, in addition to the Red Army, had become very real enemies.[30]

Halder, for his part, had grown increasingly alarmed at the rapid Soviet reinforcement of both the Stalingrad and Caucasus fronts, a clear indication that they meant to hold both the city on the Volga and the vital oil fields. Upset by the "meaningless" concentration of forces around Rostov, which merely "crammed" the area "with armor which has nothing to do," and worried about fighting a battle at Stalingrad simultaneously with the move toward the Caucasus, Halder attempted without success to convince Hitler of the need to return to the original concept and make a concentrated thrust to the Volga. Then, with rear and flanks secured, and adequate logistics, the Caucasus operation could be unleashed. Hitler, though, dismissed the OKH chief's concerns. "The Russian is finished," he told Halder on 20 July, the next day expressing his belief that the Germans, on the verge of seizing the Donets industrial region, severing the Volga supply line, and taking control of 90 percent of Soviet oil production, had dealt the enemy a fatal blow. This, along with an outburst three days later of "insane rage and ... gravest reproaches against the General Staff" for its alleged negativity, caused the OKH chief to explode. "The chronic tendency to underrate enemy capabilities is gradually assuming grotesque proportions," he complained angrily, and more than a little ironically, given his own past tendencies, on 23 July, "and develops into a positive danger ... This so-called leadership is characterized by a pathological reacting to the impressions of the moment." Halder's objections served only to rekindle the poisonous atmosphere of the previous winter. Convinced (or hoping) that the Soviets were fleeing for their lives and not, as Halder argued, conducting a planned withdrawal, Hitler saw the swift seizure of Rostov as proof that the enemy was incapable of preventing a German occupation of the Caucasus.[31]

Despite the appearance of a great operational triumph, less than a month after it had begun Fall Blau had come apart, undone by both its own and enemy actions. The Soviets had clearly learned the lesson of the previous summer and avoided encirclement; when they did fight, as at Voronezh, they upset the fragile German timetable. German execution of the plan, moreover, proved surprisingly inept. The short encircling thrusts struck only air, while Panzer units, in pursuit of a disappearing enemy, raced about wildly, became entangled with each other, bagged few prisoners, and ended each phase of the operation – such as they still existed – in a poor position for the next stage. Rather than the precise movements envisioned in the original directive, Fall Blau had come to resemble a mad dash forward, with some units headed east, others south, with nothing coordinated, and with little sense of a realizable goal. Much of this was due to Hitler's increasing interference in the day-to-day affairs of the campaign. No longer content to set the larger goals or even take key operational decisions, he now made detailed tactical decisions, a role for which he was particularly unsuited. He had in the past displayed flashes of insight, often very acute, but his temperament – impatient, impetuous, impervious to mundane military matters such as transport, supply, and concentration of force – not only caused serious operational problems but also raised tensions with Halder (who still sought to control day-to-day operations and was himself quick to blame others when things went awry) to explosive levels.[32]

On 23 July, the same day Rostov fell, Hitler, against the advice of Halder, made perhaps the last fateful decision of the war, issuing Directive No. 45, which irrevocably severed the campaign into two partial offensives, to be conducted at the same time but in diverging directions. With their shoe-string operation, all had depended on everything going according to plan; Hitler now changed the plan. "In a campaign which has lasted little more than three weeks," he began, in an assessment more wishful thinking than hard analysis, especially since he conceded the Russians would likely defend Stalingrad tenaciously, "the broad objectives outlined by me . . . have largely been achieved. Only weak enemy forces . . . have succeeded in avoiding encirclement." As a result, he decided, instead of first taking Stalingrad and then launching the attack into the Caucasus, to do both simultaneously. This marked a watershed, a point at which the accretion of actions and events began severely to limit German options. This decision altered the fundamental nature of the campaign and risked, indeed courted disaster. Nor was it like the December 1941 Halt Order, which had been taken in the absence of any good alternatives. Hitler, in seemingly cavalier fashion, risked everything on an apparent whim. Insufficient German combat forces were to be split, sent off in different directions, and rely for flank protection on undependable Axis troops, all the while being supplied by a logistical system incapable of meeting the demands of even one operation. As both army groups drove eastward, moreover, they would advance further away from the railheads, so that precious gasoline supplies would have to be brought over increasingly long distances by trucks, which themselves consumed much of the petroleum they were hauling. At the height of their success, German forces in the Caucasus would be receiving only a trickle of fuel. This latter fact, though, furnished Hitler's decision with a certain logic, fixated as he was on the speedy acquisition of oil in order to tilt the imbalance of resources a bit toward Germany. He was well aware of the twin problems of time and oil. Germany had only one chance, he believed, to gain the oil resources crucial to fight a prolonged war against the Western Allies, an opportunity that had already been seriously compromised by delays in starting and executing the campaign. In making this decision, then, he perhaps acted more like a man who had his back to the wall – and knew it – than one who, in a hubristic outburst, plunged ahead blithely into the unknown.[33]

The problem remained that even if Hitler's strategic calculation was comprehensible it still had to be measured against military reality – and by late July the Wehrmacht had almost surely passed the limits of acceptable risk and entered the danger zone. If clear priority had been given to the Caucasus operation, the powerful armored units not transferred to France, and the move toward Stalingrad merely a secondary defensive action to secure the northern flank, then splitting the forces might have been justified. Instead, Hitler failed to define the priority of either advance. Any purposeful concentration of force in order to attain achievable goals had given way to individual advances that dramatically worsened the force-space ratio and lessened any possibility for overall success. Hitler had introduced a dangerous dynamic into the operation, outside of OKH control, with potentially disastrous consequences. Halder's helplessness, in fact, seemed plain to frontline commanders, who pleaded with Hitler's adjutant Engel to inform the Führer of the lack of manpower and other necessary resources "since, in the opinion of the front, [Halder] does not do this."[34]

At the end of July, Halder did warn Hitler of potential dangers lurking at Stalingrad, not least the possibility of a Soviet counterattack, and also took notice of Stalin's equally consequential Order No. 227 of 28 July, the famous "Not One Step Back" decree that signaled the days of endless enemy retreat had passed. Moreover, after having urged Hitler for a week to reinforce 6th Army in its advance to the Volga, Halder had to sit by while General Jodl, on 30 July, pompously announced that the "fate of the Caucasus will be decided at Stalingrad and that . . . it would be necessary to divert forces from Army Group A to Army Group B." Less than a week after the push into the Caucasus, then, Hitler impulsively redistributed forces yet again, even though the key to conquering the oil fields was the swift destruction of strong Soviet forces on the Black Sea coast. In order to have any chance of reaching the oil fields of Baku, Field Marshal List needed a massive influx of supplies and reinforcements. Instead, he now had to give up much of his armor to 6th Army, but to little immediate effect since fuel shortages left it immobile for over a week in early August, even as the Soviets worked furiously to build defenses in the city. Not until 23 August did German forces cross the Don and move swiftly to the Volga, reaching the northern suburbs of Stalingrad that same day. As Soviet resistance stiffened in the foothills of the Caucasus, List's forces lacked sufficient strength to realize its objectives. Frustrated and bitter, Halder harbored doubts that the overstretched Wehrmacht had the ability to effect a stalemate, let alone achieve some sort of victory. Of one thing he seemed certain, though, that if (or when) the crisis came, Hitler would react with unrestrained violence.[35]

By mid-August, with the sclerotic German logistics system unable to cope with supplying even the most basic necessities to the troops of Army Group A as they struggled through difficult mountain terrain, the tempo of operations slowed considerably. Worries also mounted over the failure to capture the first oil fields intact. German forces reached Maikop on 9 August, but Soviet sabotage of the wells meant they would have to be re-drilled, and even then it was unclear how or even whether large quantities of oil could be transported out of the Caucasus, problems that General Thomas had warned of in February. Hitler was kept informed of progress toward the oil fields, and the extensive damage done to them, so he could have been under no illusions that the Maikop wells had been rendered useless for the foreseeable future. In early June he had stressed to his generals the importance of the oil of Maikop and Grozny for the continuation of the war; now he talked openly of defeat and, in fact, stunned an audience of economic leaders by remarking that if the oil wells of the Caucasus could not be taken by the end of 1942, it would mean the end of the war. In contrast to Goebbels's glowing propaganda reports, Hitler betrayed a gnawing sense that the gamble had failed, and, in his increasing nervousness and agitation, that his personal leadership had in no small part contributed to this failure. Churchill had weathered a no-confidence vote and military setbacks earlier in the year, while the British had halted Rommel's advance at El Alamein, thus stabilizing their position in Egypt. Ever more fearful of Western invasion, Hitler on 13 August ordered accelerated construction on the Atlantic Wall and the transfer of yet more units from the already strapped Ostheer to the west. Zhukov's violent counterattack at Rzhev, in Army Group Center's sector, begun on 30 July and raging over the next two months, resulted in heavy Soviet losses, but also strained German resources, with the army suffering serious deficiencies in manpower that could no longer be made good. Hitler recognized the obvious: he only had a few more months to cripple Russia and weaken the anti-German coalition.[36]

The atmosphere of crisis was palpable. In a disturbingly familiar refrain, the German thrust into the Caucasus, after initial success, bogged down in the mountains in the face of impenetrable terrain and fierce Soviet counterattacks. Engel, on a visit to List to assess the situation, recorded in his diary on 15 August:

> Troops more or less at the end of their tether . . . Caucasus south of Krasnodar and Maikop only negotiable . . . by mountain troops with mules. No possibility of . . . a decisive attack . . . Operations off roads and paths totally out of question because of primeval-type jungle . . . A Panzer division is totally out of place there. Tough Russian resistance in the mountains, heavy casualties.

The next day, in reporting his observations to Hitler, Engel was shocked and surprised by his reception, the Führer scoffing, "Our friend Engel has been taken in." Although it was decided that Jodl would go to the front to clarify the situation, the truth of Engel's observations must have hit home. For weeks Hitler had alternated between euphoria and frustration, as if trying to convince himself in the face of increasingly negative news that the campaign was still on track. On 19 August, for example, he boasted privately to Goebbels that operations in the Caucasus were going extremely well, so much so that he expected not only to seize the oil regions of Grozny and Baku but also burst through to the Middle East. Just three days later, though, he flew into a rage when informed that mountain troops had planted a German flag on Mt Elbrus, the highest peak in Europe. Speer claimed that he had seldom seen Hitler so enraged; for days afterwards the Führer fumed at the pointless stunt of "these mad mountaineers" who had wasted valuable time and resources. It was, Speer said, as if Hitler believed these few men had ruined his entire operational plan. That, of course, was the crux of the matter.[37]

On 23 August, the day after Hitler's explosion at the mountain troops, Halder noted in his diary both the gravity of the situation at Rzhev and the Führer's extreme vexation at the slowness of the advance in the south. The next day, he wrote of his conference with Hitler simply, "Sharp clash over interpretation of the situation at Rzhev, where I perceive a distinct danger of attrition for our forces." This seemingly mundane comment, though, concealed an outburst of vitriol unusual even for Hitler. Despite his expressions of confidence in victory, the Führer had grown noticeably more irritated and nervous over the preceding days. Halder had been a frequent target of his anger, as Hitler openly mocked and ridiculed the OKH chief for his recent warnings of approaching danger. At the situation conference on 24 August, Halder noted the sharply increased casualties suffered by 9th Army at Rzhev, then pleaded for a pull-back to shorten the front. To that Hitler responded, "You always come to me with the same suggestion to withdraw ... We must remain firm in the best interest of the troops. I demand the same firmness from the leadership as I do from the front." Halder then lost his temper and retorted angrily, "[O]ut there brave riflemen ... are falling in the thousands, simply because their leaders may not execute the only possible decision and their hands are tied!" Hitler then exploded in unbridled rage, screaming at Halder with withering derision, "What do you want to tell me about troops, Herr Halder, you who [have] only, also in the First World War, sat on the same swivel [general staff] chair, you, who not once has worn the black wound badge?" Those in attendance, including Manstein, stood stunned by the outburst, which had an extraordinarily hurtful impact on Halder not least because – at least so far as the earlier war was concerned – it contained more than a kernel of truth. Halder's days were now clearly numbered, although the final break did not come for another month.[38]

In the meantime it was List, the man Hitler believed responsible for the failure to attain the crucial oil, who felt the brunt of the Führer's wrath. Seemingly trying to push German forces forward by the sheer force of his will – and fixated on capturing the key port of Tuapse in order to allow oil to be delivered to Romanian refineries – Hitler pressed List to shove forces over particularly difficult mountain passes in hopes of rekindling the momentum of the offensive. In view of his dwindling manpower and fretful supply situation, List proved skeptical and resistant. With tensions rising and time short, Hitler on 31 August ordered the field marshal to come to his temporary headquarters at Vinnitsa, where the stifling heat and mosquito-infested surroundings had not improved the mood. Little but further misunderstanding resulted from the meeting, with Hitler accusing List of spreading his forces too thinly, while the latter pointed to his own lack of troops. Significantly, the Führer issued a direct order to List to attack across the western Caucasus range and seize the Black Sea coast as far as Sokhumi, an assault that could not possibly be successful. As a result of its failure, Hitler's anger, mistrust, and suspicion of his generals, who he believed were sabotaging his orders, only grew. On 7 September, List requested that Jodl, who remained Hitler's most trusted advisor, fly to the front to observe conditions. Upon his return that same evening, Jodl, who rarely confronted Hitler, insisted to him that List had not been insubordinate but had faithfully carried out orders. At that, Hitler exploded in an "indescribable outburst of fury," his long-simmering resentment directed not merely at Jodl but at nearly the entire army officer corps. As Engel recorded, "Führer got more worked up minute by minute, sensing the failure of the offensive, had harsh words for the supply service, deficiency of initiative on part of the higher field commanders, placed all blame on OKH and Jodl." The latter's sin, evidently, was that in siding with List, he had implicitly criticized Hitler's own conduct of operations and placed the blame for any failures squarely on him. The eruption also reflected a deeper reality, Engel observing insightfully on 8 September, "the roots of the Führer's rage and aggravation lie much deeper . . . [He] sees no end to it anymore in Russia, particularly since none of the goals for summer 1942 have been achieved. He said himself how fearful he is of the winter . . . On the other hand, he will never retreat."[39]

After past blow-ups Hitler had always made small conciliatory gestures to those around him, but this episode marked a psychological watershed. Believing himself betrayed all around, especially by Jodl, whom he accused of falsely citing his orders, he reduced contact with his closest entourage to an absolute minimum. Hitler now ate alone, withdrew to his windowless hut, where the two daily military briefings were held "in an icy atmosphere" and which he would only leave at dusk, petulantly refused to shake hands with his generals, demanded to see all directives he had given to Army Group A, and ordered a verbatim record kept of all situation conferences to eliminate alleged distortions of his words – and to justify his actions to posterity. Although Hitler quietly dropped any further plans for an offensive in the western Caucasus, he nonetheless dismissed List on 9 September. When Walter Warlimont encountered Hitler a few weeks later, he was stunned by the malevolence of his stare. It was, Warlimont thought, as if he knew that his last gamble had been lost and he could no longer bear to have around him the generals who had witnessed his errors and illusions. Still, even now a certain delusion – and irony – persisted. The original goal had been to capture the oil fields, thus securing this vital commodity for Germany and denying it to Russia. By early September it was clear that capture of the oil fields was unlikely or, if achieved that they would be so wrecked as to be unusable, so the logical response would have been to destroy them, and thus deprive the Soviets of the oil. Hitler, though, inexplicably failed to take the decision to have them demolished by air power, although he was fully aware of that possibility; indeed, he had long worried about enemy air attacks on the Romanian oil fields. Given his understanding of the crucial aspect of oil for the Soviet war economy, his failure to order their destruction was likely an indicator that he clung to the slim hope, however rapidly it was diminishing, that the oil fields might yet be seized relatively intact. By the time he conceded the obvious, it was too late. On 7 October he ordered the destruction of the Caucasus oil fields, but this was now largely beyond the Luftwaffe's ability to accomplish.[40]

At the beginning of August, Hitler had prophesied that the next six weeks "would be decisive for the outcome of the war." By early September the balance sheet was clearly unfavorable: the Red Army had not been destroyed; the oil of the Caucasus was out of reach; heavy fighting had erupted in Stalingrad; Soviet forces were assaulting German positions at the northern end of the front; and Rommel's offensive had petered out at El Alamein. The second culmination point of the war had been reached, and with it, Germany's time had run out – even before Stalingrad – as Hitler realized. His late July decision to split the offensive had been crucial; German tactical superiority could not offset the strategic implications of this blunder. Moreover, he alone was responsible for this highly risky gamble and its consequences. His talk of creating a Fortress Europe to safeguard German gains was thus less a reasoned policy than an admission of strategic helplessness. Unwilling to consider a political end to the war and with diminishing means and resources, Hitler had little choice but to grimly hold on to what had already been conquered.

On 8 September, then, even as fighting at Stalingrad had barely commenced, he issued a directive on "fundamental tasks of defense" that, in its stress on holding the line "under all circumstances," not only mirrored Stalin's "Not One Step Back" decree, but harked back to an earlier war. Indeed, Hitler emphasized that in making this decision he was consciously turning back to the methods of defense, especially a reliance on artillery and firepower, used in the defensive battles of the Great War. He was now in a position similar to that of Ludendorff in late 1916, seeking, in unfavorable circumstances, to orchestrate a stalemate in a war that had turned attritional. Less than a week later he ordered battle-weary divisions from Russia to be sent west for the purpose of their rehabilitation, another implicit signal that the war in the east would not soon be over. Finally, on 14 October, he directed all forces, except those battling inside Stalingrad and pushing toward Grozny, to prepare winter lines of defense, an explicit admission of failure. Once the Soviets decided to withdraw their forces rather than squander them in encirclement battles, German deficiencies in manpower, fuel, and logistics had been exposed. Once again, operational victories had been more apparent than real; they had not resulted in a strategic triumph, nor was there any reason to believe that such could still be achieved in the Caucasus or along the Volga.[41]

By late September 1942, Hitler's trust in victory – and his military advisors – had been completely shattered. Frustrated by the Ostheer's failure to achieve success, fixated on seemingly decisive points on the map (Tuapse, Stalingrad) but with little understanding of the difficulties involved in seizing them, worried about a second front in the west, he insisted on his right, as Feldherr, to intervene in operational and tactical matters – and be obeyed absolutely; he raged, full of hate, that his officers had put words in his mouth and "curs[ed] himself that he had risked fighting a war with such generals." In adopting the role of infallible Führer and Feldherr, Hitler had to regard all military setbacks and defeats as betrayal. Engel, though, also noticed, next to "the fury . . . his uncertainty: What now?" He was, Engel concluded, "at the end . . . of his nerves . . . Basically he hates everything in field-gray . . . today I heard again the oft-repeated expression that he longed 'for the day when he could cast off this loathsome jacket.'" In the end, even the final break with Halder, a man who just a week earlier he had derided as being unable to "decide whether an attack should be carried out with 200, with 100 men, with 6 battalions or 2 divisions," proved anticlimactic, as if, with his plans in tatters, he could no longer summon the energy for a showdown. At the close of the midday briefing on 24 September, Hitler merely observed that Halder's nerves were shot, and that he had suffered from their confrontations as well. The Führer, though, took one final shot at Halder's perceived "negativity," pointedly remarking that he needed a general staff with fanatical faith in the Nazi idea, and that he was determined to force his will on the army. At that, Halder simply said that he would tender his resignation.[42]

Halder's successor, General Kurt Zeitzler, was already present at Führer headquarters. A relative outsider, and in many ways Halder's antithesis, he embodied traits desired by Hitler in an OKH chief. Zeitzler had risen through the OKW and was close to Schmundt, one of the few generals Hitler trusted, so he was not suspected of being in league with OKH to thwart the Führer's orders. Although a staff officer, Zeitzler's most recent duties were in the west as chief of staff to Rundstedt, where he had played a key role in defeating the Dieppe raid in August 1942. This was of special importance, given Hitler's growing fear of a second front and determination to fortify the western European coastline. Finally, in contrast to the often aloof and acerbic Halder, the younger Zeitzler exuded confidence, energy, and – not least significant – absolute faith in Hitler. He already had a reputation as a "Nazi" general, a charge seemingly verified by his demand, upon taking office, that his subordinates both work hard for victory and maintain an absolute belief in the Führer. Although understood at the time and since as Hitler's final assertion of control over OKH, the change of leadership was also his tacit acknowledgment that the war was not going to be won in 1942 – or, perhaps, at all.[43]

Despite his efforts to energize and streamline OKH, which included a growing emphasis on National Socialist belief and frontline service, Zeitzler faced the reality that in the last quarter of 1942, just as in the previous year, Hitler's strategy was coming apart. By early October the fighting in Stalingrad resembled that of Verdun more than Blitzkrieg, while in Egypt British preparations for a counterattack at El Alamein had been completed. The moment Hitler had anticipated and dreaded – when Germany could no longer concentrate on one front – had come, and victory was no nearer. Although certainly a fervent believer in Hitler, Zeitzler was also a competent military man who thought he could convince the Führer to see reason in the conduct of the eastern war. As any prospect of either strategic or operational victories disappeared, however, Hitler slid into an obsession with Stalingrad. On 2 October he "brusquely waved aside" the danger of "high losses in house-to-house fighting" and, for the first time, Engel heard him emphasize the "urgent necessity" of taking the city "not only for operational reasons but also psychologically for world opinion and morale among Germany's allies." A clearer sign of Hitler's understanding of the changed nature of the war could hardly be given. But as he got bogged down in the details of the fighting in the city – to the extent of calling on his First World War experience to urge the use of *Stoßtrupp* (shock troop) tactics (which were already being employed) even though, as in the earlier war, the Germans possessed insufficient strength to exploit this tactic – this distracted him from the reality of the overall situation. Indeed, whatever tactical or political advantage Hitler might gain at Stalingrad was out of all proportion to the enormous loss of men and equipment being suffered, resources that could have been put to better use aiding Army Group A in the Caucasus or shoring up the Don River defenses north of the city.[44]

Reality hit home in early November. Even as the fighting raged in Stalingrad, Hitler had departed the Wolf's Lair for Munich in order to give his traditional address to the *Alte Kämpfer* (old fighters) on the anniversary of the 1923 Putsch attempt. En route, his special train was halted early on 8 November so he could receive the urgent news that Allied troops were landing in North Africa. Hit hard as he was by the reversal of Axis fortunes at El Alamein, and especially Rommel's disobedience of orders and precipitous retreat across Libya, this development seemed to catch him off guard. Overnight, with this first commitment of American ground troops in the Mediterranean, the problems raised by a second front – even one in North Africa – had gone from theoretical to frighteningly concrete. Although Hitler instantly recognized the danger to the Axis – and Mussolini's personal position – and ordered the defense of Tunisia, reinforcements could come only at the expense of the already overstretched German forces in Russia. Aware that this would strain German resources to breaking point, Foreign Minister Ribbentrop pleaded with Hitler to allow him to put out peace feelers to the Soviets in Stockholm. This the Führer brusquely rejected with the observation, accurate enough, that "a moment of weakness [was] not the right time for negotiations with the enemy."[45]

Facing a key decision, Hitler the Führer put a heavy mortgage on Hitler the Feldherr by essentially premising any political solution to the conflict on a decisive military victory. Such a triumph could only come on the Eastern Front, and at Stalingrad, as Hitler admitted in his speech later that day. The "old fighters" in attendance, Goebbels observed, already troubled by the unresolved situation in the east and now confronted by a new fighting front in North Africa, realized that "a turning point of the war" had arrived. Nothing Hitler said, though, offered much reassurance. He specifically rejected a negotiated peace and reiterated his resolve to fight on; indeed, in the fight for Germany's very existence, he emphasized, there could be no compromise. As if to underscore that his regime had long passed the point of no return, he again took up his obsession with the Jews, smirking that this "eternal enemy" who had wanted war and Germany's destruction "are no longer laughing today." Although he then sought to reassure the faithful by boasting of Stalingrad's imminent capture – it was taking a bit longer than anticipated, he admitted, because he did not want "a second Verdun," itself hardly a comforting statement – the gap between rhetoric and reality was too large to be bridged by a few platitudes. For a public increasingly weary of the incessant fighting and soaring death tolls in the east, Hitler's claim that he only wanted to reach the Volga to cut off oil and military shipments must have rung hollow; worse, it was an implicit acknowledgment of his own inept handling of the military operation. If the goal was merely cutting river transport, why get bogged down in murderous urban fighting – which he had explicitly warned against a year earlier – since, as he had intimated, the city itself was irrelevant? In any case, his determination to seize Stalingrad now seemed less the prelude to a decisive triumph than the end of a misconceived policy. This sense that all had gone awry permeated his 17 November order to the troops in Stalingrad, which reeked of futility. It urged them on even as he acknowledged difficulties and as he now transferred significant forces from east to west to deal with the crisis in the Mediterranean. The 6th Army had indeed taken most of the city, but had destroyed itself in the process, and now its time, too, was up.[46]

German operations in the south had always raised the risk of producing a giant bulge in the front that would invite a Soviet counterattack; the gamble had been that remaining enemy forces could be destroyed and the Soviet war economy crippled before such an operation could be carried out. To Hitler's, and perhaps even Stalin's, surprise, Soviet forces stubbornly resisted and denied the Germans the decisive victories that would have rendered a Russian counter-thrust all but impossible. Now, with the failure to seize Stalingrad quickly, virtually everyone at OKH, as well as the Führer himself, recognized the threat along the undermanned Don front. In mid-August, in a flash of insight, Hitler had predicted that Stalin would likely repeat the crucial "[Bolshevik] attack of 1920" at Tsaritsyn (later renamed Stalingrad). This operation, attributed to Stalin, the local chairman of the military committee, had destroyed the White forces besieging the city by attacking them in the rear with a thrust across the Don aimed at Rostov. The problem, therefore, was not that Hitler was unaware of the danger – intelligence reports had consistently warned of a Soviet buildup – or that he could not conceive of such a possibility, since he could read a map as well as anyone. At a meeting with Manstein on 26 October he reaffirmed his earlier prediction by pointing to the existence of an especially dangerous situation between Voronezh and Stalingrad.[47]

The dilemma, rather, lay in his inability to convert his prescience into any effective response (as would recur with his later insight into the Allied landing at Normandy). Hitler's fixation on seizing Stalingrad, coupled with his recognition of the lack of available German manpower, led him to believe the best – indeed, the only – course of action was to capture the city as quickly as possible in order to free up the bulk of 6th Army for defensive duties in threatened sectors of the front. He did, in fact, order the fortification of the Don defenses (which had little impact because of material and equipment shortages), the shifting of a few Luftwaffe field divisions of dubious quality into defensive positions alongside Romanian and Italian troops, and the bombing of Don River bridges. In the absence of a really bold move, though, such as suspending operations in Stalingrad and pulling 6th Army out to defensible positions, there was little else Hitler could do. He could hardly strip Army Group Center, itself under significant pressure, of troops or abandon the Caucasus, since its oil had been the principal reason for the campaign. Another option, putting the 22 divisions (some 170,000 men) of the newly created Luftwaffe field divisions under army control, was rejected because of Göring's vehement objection to placing "his" National Socialist soldiers under reactionary army leaders. Hitler's attitude and actions thus betrayed a deep fear – and helplessness – at the prospect of powerful Soviet attacks directed at the weakest part of the Axis line. As his adjutant Below observed, Hitler "seemed unduly pensive and far away – almost as if he no longer had confidence in the strategy." Perhaps he hoped for a bit more of the fabled "Führer luck." If so, he was to be rudely shocked, as, in succession, the key events of the year, and perhaps of the war, unfolded: first, Rommel's retreat from El Alamein, followed by the Allied invasion of North Africa, and then the Soviet counterattack at Stalingrad.[48]

Ironically, it was Zeitzler, the military professional, and not the amateur Hitler, who believed the Russians incapable of launching an offensive. Just before dawn on 19 November, though, the Soviets proved him wrong. Having skillfully massed tanks, troops, and artillery against sectors manned by poorly trained, equipped, and motivated Romanian divisions, Soviet forces burst out of bridgeheads across the Don northwest of Stalingrad with the aim of advancing southeast toward Kalach and seizing its key bridge. The next day, Russian forces south of Stalingrad joined the attack, moving northwest in an effort to link up with their comrades and encircle 6th Army, as well as Axis forces in the Don bend. As German Panzer units, robbed of their mobility by the weather, inadequate fuel, and mechanical breakdowns, struggled to stem the Red tide, command disagreements between Army Group B and Zeitzler at OKH (backed by Hitler) resulted in a fruitless dissipation of already insufficient strength. Although by the end of the day the Soviets had ripped a fifty-mile-wide hole in the Romanian front and were halfway to Kalach, both General Weichs at Army Group B and General Paulus in Stalingrad reacted rather hesitantly. Not unlike the enemy counterattack a year earlier in front of Moscow, the German command had difficulty gauging the seriousness of the situation, as if they struggled to conceive that the Soviets could still have the strength and ability to pull off such an action.[49]

Not even the Soviet attack from the south the next day could dispel a cautious optimism at 6th Army headquarters that the situation could be managed. Indeed, only on 21 November did Paulus realize that Army Group B, lacking any mobile reserve, would not be able to check the Soviet columns advancing on Kalach and that at least a temporary encirclement was likely. Although Hitler's decision on 22 November to forbid any breakout attempt by 6th Army has been criticized ever since, in reality Paulus's forces, given their tactical position embedded deep in the city and with insufficient fuel reserves, had little immediate chance of pulling off such an operation. Instead, although neither he nor his staff had much faith in the viability of air supply – given the lack of transport aircraft and the unpredictable weather conditions – Paulus ordered 6th Army to form a hedgehog position in order to prepare for a later breakout to the southwest. Even as German troops, in appalling conditions, amid utter chaos, and fighting on all sides, struggled toward Stalingrad from outlying areas, Paulus evidently envisioned a breakout for 25–26 November. Little did he know that the Führer was thinking along different lines. With the gravity of the situation apparent, Hitler decided on the evening of 22 November to leave the Obersalzberg, where he had been resting, and return to his military headquarters in East Prussia. A few hours before departing, he discussed the possibility of air supply with General Hans Jeschonnek, chief of the Luftwaffe General Staff. Although aware of the problems of aerial supply, Jeschonnek, pressed for a quick answer by Hitler and evidently under the impression that any encirclement would be only for a few days, indicated, in principle, the feasibility of such an operation. The previous winter, he noted, the Luftwaffe had supplied 100,000 troops in the Demyansk pocket for 5 months, a comparison he likely regretted immediately. Just to supply Demyansk had required 500 aircraft to deliver 300 tons of supplies daily – and with little interference from the Red Air Force. The situation at Stalingrad was hardly comparable, since the 250,000 men trapped there would need 750 tons of supplies daily, and because many of the planes necessary for an airlift had been shifted to the Mediterranean, so the Luftwaffe had nowhere near the requisite transport capacity. The Red Air Force was also far stronger at Stalingrad, and in a better position to interrupt the flow of supplies.[50]

Jeschonnek's spontaneous answer, though, provided the Führer with exactly the assurance he needed, especially since he could hardly abandon the city he had twice pledged never to give up. In addition, considerations of prestige – the crisis at Stalingrad, after all, followed quickly on the defeat at El Alamein and the Allied landing in North Africa – and the belief, seem-

ingly validated in the previous winter's crisis, that holding on was preferable to a hasty retreat, played a role in his decision. Also, Hitler could not
quite concede that the power relationship between German and Soviet
forces had fundamentally changed. The Wehrmacht had proved its superiority in the past, so would do so again. Initially, in fact, few in the German
command even considered the withdrawal of Army Group A from the
Caucasus as the likely consequence of the Soviet action. Additionally,
although perhaps only as a show of bravado, in a meeting with the Italian
foreign minister Ciano in mid-December, Hitler still maintained that the
Soviets had suffered grievous economic and manpower losses, and
expressed confidence that this crisis could be contained. In any case, both
the expectation of a successful relief operation and the seemingly proven
feasibility of aerial provisioning argued against premature and dangerous
action. The 6th Army had already been receiving some of its supplies by air
even before the encirclement, so this did not seem to mark a radical new
departure but rather an intensification of the existing state of affairs. Nor
could the trapped forces break out without fuel, which would have to be
flown to them in any case. As with many of his key decisions, Hitler could
also point to the advice of others, so his decision to resupply the city from
the air had a military rationale. Jodl, for example, argued that a breakout
should not be attempted, and the gains of the summer abandoned, without
first attempting a relief operation. More crucially, Manstein, who had been
appointed commander of a new Army Group Don and given the task of
stabilizing the situation, initially agreed with Hitler's assessment that a relief
operation, especially one under his direction, was entirely possible. No one,
of course, expected an aerial operation of anything like the duration of
Demyansk. They anticipated that a relief attack could be launched in short
order; in the meantime, the fighting power of 6th Army would be maintained through supplies from the air.[51]

Discussions over what to do at Stalingrad also revealed tensions and
misunderstandings between army and air force commanders, as well as the
problems raised when a man such as Paulus – tactically cautious and unimaginative, without any real decisiveness or strength of character –
commanded the pocket. While Luftwaffe commanders tried to impress on
their army counterparts the impossibility of supplying 6th Army from the
air, especially since the needed transports had been sent to North Africa,
members of Paulus's staff simply referred to Hitler's order that the air force
would keep the trapped army alive until the breakout attempt. In almost
stereotypical fashion, the chief of staff of 6th Army, General Arthur
Schmidt, parried all objections from Luftwaffe officers with the comment

that since the Führer had ordered Stalingrad to be held at all costs, the air force must supply what was needed; what had to be done must be done. Paulus, hesitant and vacillating, could not summon the courage on either 22 or 23 November to confront Hitler or to order a breakout on his own authority. The best he could manage was to allude to doubts among his commanders and the difficulties in aerial supply. By 24 November, even as some of the Führer's generals, led by Walther Kurt von Seydlitz-Kurzbach (who, ironically, had personal experience with the Demyansk pocket), plotted a breakout on their own – an action, given the circumstances, that would almost certainly have resulted in disaster – any freedom of action Paulus might have had vanished, as Hitler declared that "Fortress Stalingrad" would vigorously defend itself, if necessary for the entire winter. A clue to Hitler's thinking might be found in a statement he made back in June 1938. The purpose of a fortress, he argued at that time, was not "to guarantee the lives of a certain number of fighters under all circumstances, but rather to warrant the maintenance of overall fighting strength." To Hitler, holding out at Stalingrad meant more than clinging to the city, but served as a way to tie down enemy forces and aid in stabilizing the entire Southern Front. Impressed, perhaps too much so, by the way in which Soviet resistance in the pockets the previous summer had disrupted German plans, and conscious of his successful "halt order" in the winter crisis of 1941–2, he failed to appreciate just how costly this strategy had been to the Soviets – and would be to his own forces.[52]

Hitler had also been strengthened immeasurably in his decision to hold on by the near-unanimous support he got from those around him. While en route to the Wolf's Lair near Rastenburg, he received no information directly from any generals who entertained doubts, let alone someone such as Richthofen, who was both violently opposed to an air supply operation and respected by Hitler. Ironically, about the only officer in his immediate entourage who dared express doubts was Jeschonnek, but his concerns were overridden by assurances from Göring. The Reichsmarschall claimed later he had little choice, since the Führer had told him that 6th Army was lost unless it could be supplied from the air, but even then he reiterated his assurances although he knew that his Luftwaffe could not accomplish the task set for it. Confronted by Zeitzler, in Hitler's presence, and informed that the tonnage figures that could be flown in each day did not square with his claims – as he well knew, having been informed of this earlier by Jeschonnek – Göring stubbornly persisted in his assurance to Hitler that Stalingrad could be supplied from the air. Even as Zeitzler lost his temper and called Göring a liar, Hitler coolly calculated his advantage. "The

Reichsmarschall has made his report to me," he said, "which I have no choice but to believe. I therefore abide by my original decision [to supply the army by air]." Again, the key point was not so much that Hitler made an incorrect decision, but that he made it based on the information and assumptions furnished to him: first, that a sufficient daily supply could be flown into the cauldron, and secondly, that this would only be a temporary operation. In addition, economic and political considerations played a role as well. Not only would a pull-back mean the loss of areas of vital economic importance, but, given recent events in North Africa, any retreat would also have a negative impact on Germany's allies. Operational ideas of pulling back everything south of Stalingrad, building reserves, and then resuming flank attacks were interesting theoretically, Hitler admitted, but were out of the question given the actual strategic situation.[53]

This decision was not well received by commanders in the field. Manstein's initially optimistic appraisal of the situation, though, effectively silenced all those who opposed Hitler's determination to hold fast on the Volga. The field marshal's thought processes at the time revealed a rather complex interaction of factors, from deep grief over the recent death of his eldest son to an under-appreciation – since he had only just been named commander of Army Group Don – of the serious dangers facing the entire southern sector of the front. Like Jeschonnek, he assumed that any airlift would be limited and temporary, and he agreed with Jodl that the hard-won gains of the summer should not be rashly given up. Although Manstein understood that 6th Army was in danger of destruction if it remained in Stalingrad with no relief, he saw no need for an immediate breakout attempt, which he regarded as "a last resort." He thought a relief operation could be successful if launched by early December, if he was given suffi-cient forces, and if the pocket received adequate supplies by air; only if it failed would a breakout be attempted. Manstein's evident support of Hitler, though, vindicated the Führer's decision, giving him an enormous boost and reducing OKH, in Richthofen's withering words, to a bunch of "highly paid NCOs." Although Manstein's goal might well have been to win Hitler over to a breakout by going about it gradually, the roles of manipulator and manipulated were complex and ever-changing. Hitler was certainly aware of the danger to his power position posed by a successful general such as Manstein, but like Abraham Lincoln in an earlier war, he was willing to risk the political challenge in return for the needed military victory. In any case, Manstein – an operational genius, perhaps, but slow to recognize the weak-ness of Germany's overall strategic position – had agreed with his assess-ment, not the other way around, so Hitler had hope that his "fireman" could not only restore the situation, but in so doing bolster his image as, if not a triumphant, then a coolly calculating Feldherr.[54]

Complicating matters was the fact that, from the outset, 6th Army had little ability to achieve a successful breakout on its own. Not only was the balance of force unfavorable, but the troops would also be exposed and vulnerable to Soviet attack as they broke out. In addition, there was no easily defensible (or easily supplied) position to which to withdraw. To paraphrase Napoleon, who supposedly said, "Space I can recover; time never," Hitler understood clearly that he could not regain any lost territory precisely because he was out of time. Indeed, Richthofen grasped the essence of the matter when he noted in his diary on 25 November, "The Führer . . . decides against [withdrawal] because he believes the army can hold on and he does not think we could reach Stalingrad again." Nor did anything alter his view in the following weeks. On 12 December, Hitler emphasized:

> We must not give it up now under any circumstances. We won't win it back . . . Things would have been quicker if we hadn't hung about Voronezh so long . . . But to imagine that one can do it a second time . . . that's ridiculous . . . We can't possibly replace the stuff we have inside. If we give that up, we surrender the whole meaning of this campaign. To imagine that I shall come here another time is madness . . . We are not coming back here a second time. That is why we must not leave here. Besides, too much blood has been shed for that.

The original purpose of the campaign, of course, had been to seize the oil of the Caucasus, not Stalingrad, but in the circumstances, staying put seemed the best option. And now the general whose opinion was most valued by his peers in the officer corps had largely supported Hitler's views. Although it is hard to take exception with Hitler's observation that the Germans would not be able to recover lost territory, his decision nonetheless had the ring of desperation, of a man who knew the game was up but hoped for one last winner that might retrieve the situation.[55]

Given German supply and force deficiencies, failure of the relief attack was predictable, especially since the goal of the operation – to get 6th Army out of Stalingrad (Manstein) or enable them to stay (Hitler) – remained unsettled. Even before the encirclement, 6th Army had been starved of supplies, with barely a week's worth on hand, so the loss of a large part of its outlying stores plunged it into a serious crisis. Since the Luftwaffe could not supply all the requirements, in anticipation of an immediate breakout attempt munitions and fuel rather than food supplies had taken initial priority in the airlift. Further, constructing adequate shelters and defensive positions for the men out on the steppe proved difficult. As a result, the fighting strength of 6th Army declined rapidly, making a breakout on its part to link up with any relief attack highly problematic. If, on the other hand, Army Group A had been withdrawn from the Caucasus at the beginning of the crisis, then perhaps sufficient strength could have been assembled to give the relief attack a reasonable chance of success in breaking into the pocket on its own and opening a supply corridor. No clear evidence exists, however, that such an option was presented to the Führer at the time, although both Zeitzler and Manstein claimed after the fact that they supported such a move. In the event, when the relief offensive was finally launched on 12 December, Manstein had only two armored divisions at his disposal, a force hopelessly overmatched by its Soviet adversary, while 6th Army no longer had the strength, if it ever did, to attempt a breakout. It had avoided destruction on the open steppe, but would now perish in the Stalingrad cauldron.[56]

More importantly, the Germans were not operating in a vacuum. A further Soviet offensive on 16 December threatened a "second Stalingrad," the cut-off of Army Group A in the Caucasus. At the same time, problems in southern Russia were compounded by Rommel's defeat at El Alamein and the Anglo-American landing in North Africa. Hitler recognized the threat to the Axis position in the Mediterranean (and to Mussolini's government), but transfer of units to that front impaired the desperate effort to stabilize the position in Russia. And, in any case, the only real possibility of salvaging the Axis position in the Mediterranean was by seizing Gibraltar (and possibly Malta), both out of the question because of force limitations. This growing interaction of fronts was an ominous development for Germany. In a negative sense, then, the Stalingrad "fortress" perhaps played the consequential role intended by Hitler even as it was doomed to destruction. Much as Soviet resistance in pockets the year before had tied down large numbers of German units and slowed their forward progress, so now German defenders at Stalingrad immobilized Red Army units, enabling Army Group A to wriggle free of potential disaster. Although not the decisive turning point in the war, as often asserted, Stalingrad nonetheless fundamentally altered the military and political situation in a way clearly unfavorable to Germany. At Stalingrad, the failure of all of Hitler's assumptions over the previous year had become clear: the Soviets had not been smashed in a single blow; the British had not sued for peace; the United States had not been deterred from entering the war; the resources necessary to prevail in a global conflict had not been secured; the Wehrmacht would no longer be able to concentrate its resources on a single front. Stalingrad thus marked a point of no return rather than a turning point, as the Germans plunged over the abyss.[57]

Thus, despite efforts to weave the "heroic sacrifice" at Stalingrad into the line of such mythical legends as Thermopylae – an attempt that could only succeed if the sacrifice ultimately led to a successful conclusion of the war – the early months of 1943 threatened a complete disaster. Doubts in the German command about Hitler's ability to master both the military and the political situation could hardly be hidden. Some openly expressed the belief that because of his failed decisions, he needed to give military oversight to a top general. In most instances, the man regarded as most likely to fill such a role was Manstein, whose initial support of Hitler's decision to hold on at Stalingrad, and then failed relief effort, had not damaged his reputation. This, the reasoning went, would allow the Führer to turn his attention to the political arena, where his proven abilities might yet extricate the country from a worrisome situation. By late January, there had already been talk in high military circles that Manstein suggest to Hitler a reorganization of command, with the field marshal assuming the role of overall military command in the east. Despite Hitler's latent fear of a too powerful general usurping his authority, Manstein seemed to have no overt political ambitions, instead insisting that "the Führer is the only man who possesses the trust of the people and soldiers and in whom they believe." Rather, Manstein seemed to envision his role as freeing Hitler from the burden of daily military decision-making in order to have the time to concentrate his "genius" on larger strategic and political matters. Through operational successes Manstein aimed to provide the space for Hitler, his role as Feldherr now subordinate to that of Führer, to find a political way out of the military dead end confronting Germany.[58]

Nor was Hitler as unyielding as often portrayed after the fact. Goebbels, who was angling in a similar direction to Manstein, observed in late January, "The Führer is not unreasonable, but like all geniuses he first insists on his own position and one must therefore marshal convincing reasons to move him to a contrary position." In the wake of the disaster on the Volga, though, Hitler was not averse to such suggestions. In remarks to his Gauleiters on 7 February 1943 he confessed that despite efforts to construct a heroic myth around it, Stalingrad had been "a military catastrophe," and that one had to avoid the delusion that militarily everything was as before. The previous day, in fact, he had met with Manstein and others at the Wolf's Lair and surprised all in attendance with his opening remarks, "Gentlemen, first

I would like to say a word about Stalingrad. I alone bear the responsibility for Stalingrad." Hitler's gesture impressed Manstein, who believed the Führer deeply affected by the tragedy and the failure of his leadership. Perhaps that explained his unusual willingness to listen to, and at least partially accept, the field marshal's ideas for how to stabilize the southern sector of the front. Since Manstein outlined a plan for a flexible defense that involved voluntarily giving up territory, Hitler, despite some desultory objections, evinced a willingness to learn the lesson of recent events, a point reinforced by Goebbels's "Total War" speech of 18 February.[59]

Although he appointed Manstein head of the newly reconstituted Army Group South, Hitler could not bring himself to anoint him as a military strongman in charge of all operations on the Eastern Front. Still, these actions demonstrated that as yet Hitler was not unwavering in his notion of holding firm to all territory and would acquiesce in a mobile defense when necessary to save his position. For all his political risk-taking, though, militarily he was loath to weaken some sectors of the front in order to achieve decisive strength in others. Manstein's idea was too bold, went beyond his comfort zone, and, in any case, required him to relinquish too much territory of industrial value. Where Manstein thought in terms of 1940 – allowing the enemy to place his forces in a precarious position, then attacking to gain a decisive operational triumph – Hitler saw things from the perspective of 1916: holding on to economically vital regions won at high cost. Thus, he gave Manstein some freedom of action, but denied him the necessary strength to attain potentially significant results.[60]

Nonetheless, Manstein managed to stabilize the situation with a nimble backhand blow at Kharkov. By late February the Soviet position was not as favorable as it had seemed. In hopes of completely shattering the Southern Front, the Soviet command had ordered that pressure be increased on the Germans with no pause for rest. Their offensive had thus outrun its supply lines and was vulnerable to counterattack from the south, which was exactly what Manstein proposed to do. By "leap-frogging" his armored forces from east to west, maintaining defensive shoulders to the north and south, and allowing the enemy to advance in the center, he lured the Soviets into a trap. Given unusual freedom of action by Hitler and bolstered by the addition of SS armored divisions newly arrived from France, he launched a strike on 20 February that caught the enemy completely by surprise. Although the imminent start of the *rasputitsa* forced Manstein to abandon his most ambitious plans, his forces still dealt the Soviets a stunning defeat, retaking Kharkov on 14 March, an act that revived Hitler's flagging spirits and occasioned much fanfare in Germany.[61]

Since the success enabled Hitler to reclaim some of his aura of military genius, he consented to make a radio address to the German people, his first in many months. Although Goebbels had pushed for the speech because of his sense of a renewed confidence in Hitler, he must have been disappointed in the Führer's performance. Far from a cheering exhortation, Hitler on 21 March delivered a short, uninspiring, workmanlike address, the theme of which – the danger in the east had passed – could hardly have been convincing to the German public, given the magnitude of recent military reverses. Indeed, in outlining measures to be taken in the coming year he seemed to highlight German weaknesses more than strengths. Nor could raising the image of Asiatic hordes who "bestially murdered multitudes" or mention of the "burned cities" and the "satanic destructive frenzy" of the Western Allies have been of much comfort. The most intriguing aspect of the speech, in fact, came afterward, when in a tour of an exhibit of trophies from the Eastern Front at the Berlin Zeughaus, a member of the resistance movement allegedly intended to kill Hitler. Major Rudolf-Christian Freiherr von Gersdorff, a staff officer at Army Group Center, itself a center of resistance activities, claimed later that he activated two ten-minute time bombs hidden under his coat. Hitler, though, again enjoying his proverbial luck, raced through the exhibit in eight minutes, leaving the would-be assassin barely enough time to defuse the bombs (and historians ever since wondering why he didn't just use a pistol). Despite the Führer's timely escape, though, Germany increasingly faced a situation of no return.[62]

The stabilization of the front brought a measure of relief and guarded optimism, certainly, but had been achieved at a high cost in men and equipment lost. Although Manstein's success demonstrated that the Wehrmacht remained a formidable fighting force, it had, crucially, depended to a great extent on Soviet errors in command and judgment that the Germans could not rely on to continue. The victory at Kharkov offered a temporary relief, but merely that; as Manstein and others realized, any sort of significant triumph would have to come later, in yet another summer offensive. Although the front line in March 1943 roughly approximated that of a year earlier – "We're in Kharkov again!" ran an inadvertently ironic headline trumpeting Manstein's achievement – that could not disguise the damage done to Hitler's hopes of achieving victory. The last quarter of 1942 had been broadly similar in its consequences to the same period a year earlier. If German options had been sharply limited then, now they had dwindled to two: attempt to stalemate the war or seek a political solution. As Hitler had already pointed out, the Germans were not likely to regain the Caucasus and eastern Donbas industrial area, nor could they easily make good the loss of men and materiel. In addition, the disaster in the east was about to be compounded by a similarly ruinous loss of precious manpower in North Africa, as that campaign ground to its inevitable conclusion. With the final surrender in Tunisia on 13 May 1943, some 130,000 German soldiers, mostly combat veterans of the Eastern Front, were taken prisoner. This loss, along with that of 2,400 aircraft, further burdened an already overmatched Wehrmacht. Hitler's decision to reinforce North Africa had kept the Mediterranean closed to the Allies for six more months, but, with no way to ensure the necessary supplies to stalemate the campaign indefinitely, in the end had resulted merely in unsustainable losses and irreparable damage to his Axis partner, Mussolini. The southern flank of Fortress Europe now lay open to Allied invasion.[63]

Nor could the twin losses at Stalingrad and what some had come to call "Tunisgrad" be blamed on others. Hitler had assumed total authority during the winter crisis of 1941–2 and had been given credit, however grudging, for his "halt order" that had stemmed the panic and seen the Wehrmacht through the crisis. His persona as Feldherr, during a period of undisguised disaster, now led some officers and many in the general public to call into question his military genius. Still, even as Hitler admitted that he "muddled through from one month to the next," his determination to fight on increased rather than slackened. Although any reasonable calculation indicated that the war could not be won with the means and resources available to the Germans, this realization resulted in little overt opposition to Hitler's strategy of holding on. Perhaps this reflected the altered reality created by the Anglo-American declaration of "unconditional surrender" in January 1943 at the Casablanca Conference featuring Churchill and President Roosevelt; any hope of a negotiated peace from that direction now seemed eliminated. Also, the Germans had considerable experience of "holding out" – and loathing of defeat – born in an earlier war. In any case, the price for the decision to fight on would be Germany's complete destruction.[64]

10

No Victory, No Peace (Summer 1943–4)

Faced with the loss of Kharkov amid the growing crisis on the southern sector of the Eastern Front, Hitler decided on the evening of 16 February 1943 to fly to Manstein's headquarters in the industrial city of Zaporozhye on the Dnieper for a three-day visit. This, of course, immediately raised suppositions as to the meaning of the meeting, since it was virtually unprecedented for Hitler to fly off to an Army Group headquarters for such a lengthy period. Historians have since focused primarily on the discussions of the perilous military situation that took place between Hitler, Manstein, and other top commanders over the next three days, although key points have often been overlooked. In an immediate, operational sense, the talks revealed that Hitler had no clear idea how to proceed, which was why, when pressed by Manstein, he consistently refused to outline his future plans or strategic views. Although unlikely to share them with someone whom he saw as a potential rival, he also genuinely had no real idea of what to do. If the outcome of the winter crisis of 1941–2 had ultimately reinforced his faith in his own decision-making ability, the disaster at Stalingrad had shaken him to the core. Seeking to disguise his confusion, he largely retreated into haggling over minutiae and asking detailed questions about weapons, troop numbers, or, reflecting his obsession with maps, the position and movement of various units.[1]

Despite efforts to portray him as either obtuse or obstructionist, though, Hitler betrayed less an absolute determination to impose his will than an effort to find common ground with Manstein in order to retrieve the situation. After all, had he wanted to dictate, he would have had Manstein come to him; and, in any case, it was consistent with his tendency, dating to his rise to power, periodically to curry favor with his generals. With enemy forces pouring through gaps north of Kharkov and in the south on the lower Donets, and in a position to trap seventy-five German divisions in Ukraine, a crisis greater than Stalingrad was brewing. Seen in this light, the meeting acquires a different tone. Despite initial disagreement over the direction and sequence of any possible action against the Soviets – Manstein wanted first to eradicate the threat in the south, and then turn toward Kharkov, whereas Hitler stressed taking Kharkov first, fearing that otherwise the onset of the *rasputitsa* would bog down German mobile forces in the south, a point Manstein conceded had merit – no real struggle took place here, at least not like Hitler's lengthy battle of wills with Halder in July and August 1941. A deadlock on the afternoon of 17 February resulted in Manstein's suggestion that any final decision be postponed to the next day, a proposal that cost him nothing since German troops would not be ready for action until the 19th in any case.[2]

By the morning briefing on 18 February, the situation had altered dramatically, an opportunity quickly seized upon by Manstein. With the SS Totenkopf division mired in mud between Kiev and Poltava, and thus unable to assist any strike toward Kharkov, Manstein, who recognized Hitler's urgent desire after all the recent setbacks to retake the city for prestige reasons, proposed an alternative. "The only thing to do now," he argued, was to "strike southeastwards and destroy the enemy advancing through the gap." Then, if all went well, his forces would turn north before the muddy season and seize Kharkov. Faced with reality, and sensing a way out of his dilemma, Hitler quickly agreed, as if relieved finally to have a plan of action. In the aftermath of this meeting, in fact, over the next month the field marshal enjoyed a decision-making freedom that made him a virtually independent army commander. In addition, in another sign of Hitler's sudden flexibility, having been convinced by Manstein of the dire shortage of troops and equipment afflicting Army Group South, already on 18 February – and not, as Manstein claimed in his memoirs, on the 19th – he affirmed, "we have no other choice but to bring the troops from the Taman peninsula as quickly as possible to Army Group South." Henceforth, the 350,000 men, 110,000 horses, and 27,000 vehicles of Army Group A, which Hitler had hoped to use as a springboard for a future return to the Caucasus, would be used as reserve strength for Army Group South, although the process of withdrawing them would be painfully slow. Even Manstein conceded at the time that Hitler's visit, far from being obstructionist, "had been very useful."[3]

More intriguing perhaps is what has generally not been emphasized about this meeting. On 18 February, Hitler also elaborated on a new concept for how to conduct the war, and perhaps regain the initiative, one that relied on the same weapon whose importance he had dismissed just over a year earlier: the tank. He prefaced his remarks with the cautionary statement – itself significant in view of later claims of responsibility (or blame) for the Kursk offensive – "We can undertake no great operations in this year. I think we can only strike small blows." At the time, indeed, he was preoccupied with the sputtering effort, for which he blamed an ineffective General Fromm, to raise an additional 800,000 men for the army. Still, Hitler betrayed his excitement over new technical developments. Totally new tanks (Panthers and Tigers) and a giant assault gun (the Ferdinand), he enthused, would soon be rolling off production lines, weapons of such decisive qualitative superiority that they would provide the critical edge to overcome Soviet quantitative advantages. "Most of these new weapons," he boasted, which would become available in large quantities from May, "are invulnerable. Their effectiveness is unequaled ... With these ... most modern weapons of attack we must succeed in regaining the initiative. With a hitherto unprecedented concentration of heavy artillery with these super-heavy tanks we must succeed in at least opening a hole [in enemy lines]. Then a new push must begin." The precondition for all of this, he acknowledged, was "naturally the stabilization of the front." After this had been achieved, though, the goal had to be "a gigantic massing of tanks and artillery." After Manstein objected that this would result in the loss of many men, Hitler replied, reasonably enough, "We must strive to reach our goals by means of the superiority of our weapons. We can't do much with men because we have too few, but with a massing of [our] best and heaviest weapons! . . . That is the way to regain the initiative."[4]

Manstein, clearly caught off-guard by Hitler's speculations – "two different worlds of thought," he remarked in his diary – sought to turn attention to present military realities and his own aim, by suggesting that, in view of the serious deficiency in German strength, the most logical action was a large-scale withdrawal of forces farther west to a more defensible line. The Führer, though, countered with economic arguments. Giving up the Donets Basin, with its steel production and vital raw materials, he emphasized, would not only strengthen the Soviet war economy but also cripple production of precisely those new weapons that offered Germany its best hope. In a further meeting with Manstein on 10 March, with the reconquest of Kharkov in sight, Hitler again stressed economic considerations, this time noting the urgent necessity of retaining the raw materials crucial for production of the steel needed for the anti-aircraft guns vital for home defense. Still, although unwilling to countenance a major withdrawal or a completely mobile defense – after all, he remarked pointedly on 5 March, "Space is one of the most important military factors. You can only operate if you have space" – the Führer conceded the need for the shortest possible fronts. He also advocated continuous attacks "with the most modern weapons" to weaken the enemy, retain the initiative, and hold on to indispensable industrial resources. Significantly, he again stressed that "large operations are not possible in the near future." Those would have to wait for the new tanks.[5]

As if to punctuate his newfound faith in the tank, Hitler brought Guderian back on 21 February, not as a troop commander, but to fill the new position of Inspector-General of Panzer Forces. In this role, he would be responsible for overseeing the organization and training of the rejuvenated Panzer wing. In rehabilitating Guderian, the apostle of tank warfare who had earlier been dismissed for his advocacy of command freedom, Hitler was essentially admitting he had made a mistake – not in his actions in December 1941, but over the future role of tanks. Although he still thought the new heavy models would be useful in defense in the west, where they could be maneuvered more easily and, if necessary, simply "bur[ied] like the Russians do and just use the long gun [to stifle attacks]," he now saw beyond a solely defensive utility. Used properly, the tank might yet be the key to recovering territory in the east. From early 1943, then, Hitler displayed an almost obsessive focus on *Leistung* (achievement), turning the new tanks, and the leap in technology that enabled them, into a virtual cult. Instead of wider considerations of strategy, or reflections on how to fight a global war, or any sober examination of the German situation, Hitler turned to a short-term focus on performance. He engaged Speer in detailed discussions about the new tanks throughout April and May, barely containing his enthusiasm. Quality, it seemed to him, could overcome quantity. Although he had talked vaguely of new wonder weapons since the previous summer, now, after the debacle at Stalingrad, it appeared to him that such arms were at last at hand. In a speech on 30 January, Goebbels had assured his listeners that new weapons would soon allow the Führer to again give the order to attack. As if to reinforce this claim, on 19 February, as Manstein's forces braced to launch the counterattack at Kharkov, Hitler's proclamation to the troops of Army Group South promised, "Previously unknown, unique new weapons are on the way to your fronts." This was intended to boost the morale of the troops, but it also reflected Hitler's own belief in the saving power of technology. The irony, of course, was that Hitler hoped to salvage the situation through new technology even as the army, over the past year, had been steadily demotorized.[6]

Here, if not the solution to the larger strategic dilemma, was perhaps a means by which to buy time. To a large degree as well, this overlapped with Manstein's concept. In early March, even as Kharkov was being retaken, the field marshal had drafted a memo to Hitler that concluded, realistically enough, that absolute victory in the east could no longer be attained. Still, Manstein suggested, it would be possible to achieve a stabilization of the front through mobile operations. This military impasse would then create the conditions for the "political leadership" to negotiate an end to the war. Even in his memoirs, Manstein clung to the notion that "the Soviet Union could be worn down to such an extent that it would tire of its already excessive sacrifices and be ready to accept a stalemate." Nor was Hitler opposed to a notion of flexible defense. In a conversation with Goebbels on 7 May the Führer expressed his opinion that the war was:

> chiefly a problem of movement. We lost Stalingrad because of the impossibility of mastering this problem of movement. We are now passing through a serious crisis in North Africa because of the impossibility of mastering this problem of movement. Whoever ... [solves] the problem of movement will be the victor in this war. From his viewpoint we have the advantage over our adversaries, for they must attack on exterior lines whereas we can defend ourselves on interior lines.

Thus, although politically naive about the prospect of serious peace negotiations, Manstein was not entirely off-base, for Germany in early 1943 did possess valuable trump cards: the Western Allies had not yet landed on the continent, the submarine war seemed to be producing positive results, German industry was experiencing a sharp rise in war production, as yet the bomber war had not begun in full, and German control over its occupied territories was not seriously challenged.[7]

Two interrelated themes, then, competed in 1943: hopes in new technology to stalemate the war intersected with the second motif, the possibility of a *Sonderfrieden* (separate peace). To Hitler, the first would allow the winning of battlefield victories that he believed essential in order to pursue a negotiated peace from a position of strength. At the same time, there was another, related, factor in his thinking. In a revealing, wide-ranging discussion on 8 March with Goebbels, who had flown to his headquarters in Vinnitsa, Hitler vented his rage at his generals. Although especially scornful of Göring and the Luftwaffe leadership, virtually all of his military advisors came in for criticism, with the notable exceptions of Zeitzler and, perhaps surprisingly, Jeschonnek, who was praised expressly for being a "fanatic about the truth; he sees the situation clearly and makes no false representations." Hitler was, Goebbels noted, full of contempt for his officers: "The experiences which the Führer had with the army generals have embittered him utterly." According to Hitler, they fawned over him and then lied to him, fed him false statistics that insulted his intelligence, and lacked technical knowledge. Worse, sensitive as he was to class slights, they belittled him for his lack of education. Still, he was forced to conduct the war "with the present corps of generals." Nor were his allies any better. They were responsible for the debacle on the Eastern Front, he claimed, and had shown themselves unsuited for fighting against Bolshevism. His particular scorn was reserved for the Italians, who had proved incapable of fighting anywhere. Why, the Führer asked, were they waging war in the first place?[8]

Given such a devastating appraisal of his officers and allies, his instinct, and advice from others, told him to reactivate his political genius and seek a way out through a separate peace. The most likely and promising would be with the Soviet Union. In tandem with his idea of building an *Ostwall* (eastern wall) behind which the Wehrmacht could go on the permanent defensive, any deal with Stalin would enable the bulk of the Ostheer to be withdrawn and sent west to confront the British and Americans, who had not yet established a presence on the continent. A clue to his thinking might be seen in a talk to his Gauleiters on 7 May 1943, when, among his most trusted associates, he confided that he had underestimated the inner stability of the communist state. It had not collapsed like a house of cards but had put up tenacious resistance and mobilized Soviet society. He also evinced a growing respect for Stalin, who he thought capable of strokes of genius, not least his elimination of Jewish influences and promotion of the Russian national element. He therefore no longer expected to defeat the Soviet Union, but hoped merely to hold onto what had been conquered. Germany would not attain the oil that had been the goal of the 1942 campaign, but the dire predictions of his economic advisors about the collapse of the German war economy if new supplies were not obtained proved exaggerated. In the event, the German oil situation actually improved a bit in 1943, as synthetic fuel production reached a peak and Italy left the Axis. The German ability to fight on did not suddenly dissolve with the failure of the Caucasus campaign, as the Führer had been led to believe. Moreover, by mid-1943, Hitler had achieved success in his other war in the east: the great majority of Jews under German control had now been exterminated. As a result, there was some reason for Hitler – and Stalin – to believe that Germany might be able to turn the newly stabilized

Eastern Front into a deadlock that would require enormous effort and sacrifice on the part of the Soviets to break. Indeed, Hitler was thinking in terms of turning all of German-occupied Europe into an unassailable fortress. The sober reality of the difficulties ahead, as well as the fact that his Western Allies still had no presence on the European continent, must have made a deal with Hitler that much more attractive to Stalin.[9]

The key question, then, was whether Hitler could now abandon his role of Feldherr and return to that of the Führer, the political virtuoso who had won so many early foreign policy triumphs. Although Hitler occasionally mused with his closest associates about making a separate peace with Stalin, it is debatable whether he was serious or merely hoped to exploit tensions in the enemy alliance – or whether Stalin would have made replacement of Hitler a requirement for any such peace. The situation had clearly changed since the summer and fall of 1941, when Stalin had appeared almost desperate for a deal. Now Soviet prospects had brightened considerably, although any complete defeat of the Germans lay in the distant future, especially given the uncertainty of a second front. Moreover, the Red Army had already suffered appalling losses, while the sharp reverse at Kharkov confirmed that the road to victory would be bloody and that they would continue to bear the burden of the fighting. The Soviet dictator must have been tempted to trade recent military success for a favorable political compromise: let the Germans go on fighting his less than enthusiastic Western Allies and then we'll see.[10]

Stalin, after all, knew his Clausewitz: primacy in war always belongs to politics. Even though Hitler, in early May, told Goebbels there was "practically no possibility of a compromise with the Soviets. They must be knocked out," secret discussions nonetheless took place throughout the spring and early summer. In Hitler's thinking, whether a deal materialized depended on a series of military successes. In March, Goebbels pushed a proclamation to the Eastern peoples that would promise more lenient treatment and distribution of land, but Hitler refused to agree to it until a new offensive commenced on the Eastern Front. A similar fate befell suggestions for raising an army of non-Russian (and then Russian) peoples to fight against Stalin's regime, as well as a Japanese offer to intercede diplomatically. In early April talks with the Führer, the same Mussolini who had criticized Hitler for the Nazi–Soviet Pact now implored him to make peace with Stalin. Hitler again rejected the suggestion on the grounds that without some sort of military leverage, any peace would merely allow Stalin to rebuild the Red Army. Germany would thus be hostage to Stalin's good will; he could simply choose to renew the war under more favorable circumstances.[11]

Stalin, though, seemed willing to test the waters of a separate peace, or at least put pressure on his allies to make good the proof of their sincerity to the alliance by opening a second front. Both before and after Stalingrad, he had suggested in radio addresses that he was not out to destroy Germany, while hinting at a desire to make peace with responsible, presumably military, circles in Germany. Significantly, he also refused to endorse the "unconditional surrender" doctrine laid out by his allies Churchill and Roosevelt at Casablanca in January 1943. In February and March he openly referred to the war as solely a German–Soviet affair, while again intimating that the Western alliance was perhaps not the most suitable vehicle for Soviet interests. Then, in mid-April 1943, German revelations of the mass graves at Katyn, in which thousands of murdered Polish army officers were found, victims of Stalin's NKVD, sent Soviet–Allied relations to their nadir. If ever the time was ripe for a deal with Germany, this was it. Unofficial discussions between Soviet and German agents, in fact, do seem to have taken place in Stockholm. Again, whether Stalin meant these as a viable alternative to continuing the war, or merely wanted to pressure London and Washington, is hard to determine. On balance, though, he likely sought to explore how serious Berlin might be to make a separate peace, and on what basis. After all, Allied reluctance to launch a cross-Channel invasion exacerbated his suspicion that the Western leaders were playing a duplicitous game, allowing the Soviet Union to be decisively weakened before they played their hand on the continent. At the same time, the inexplicable delay in the anticipated (and dreaded) German summer offensive might be seen as a signal that Berlin was willing to negotiate. Hitler showed no willingness to come to terms with his eastern adversary, however, without first regaining the upper hand. He had not yet concluded that the Wehrmacht had been so depleted that it required sacrificing the gains of the first two years of the war in Russia. Germany still held large swathes of territory containing valuable raw materials, while the enemy, he thought, was running low on manpower to continue the fight. Just as importantly, he feared that such a step might embolden his officers to overthrow him, especially in light of Stalin's none-too-veiled hints. This concern made Hitler the Führer hostage to Hitler the Feldherr. He believed he needed a series of military victories before seeking peace, both to force Stalin to deal with him on German terms and to reassert the legitimacy of his rule.[12]

The stumbling block, of course, was the Ostheer's inability to achieve anything like a decisive triumph. Germany faced a clear dilemma in spring 1943: it could not sit and wait for its enemies to attack, for it would then be overwhelmed, but there was no clear way forward operationally. Nothing illustrated this quandary more than the planning surrounding the Kursk offensive. It was neither, as often asserted, the turning point of the war, nor, as an offensive, comparable to its predecessors. In both 1941 and 1942 the Germans had aimed at decisive strategic triumphs, first on the entire 2,000-mile-wide front, then along the whole southern sector. Operation Citadel, by contrast, was little more than a grandiose spoiling attack designed, on a limited portion of the front, to shorten the lines, economize German manpower, and destroy a few Soviet armies. Despite Hitler's claim that the offensive would send a signal to his allies, the neutral nations, and to public opinion at home – as he put it pompously in the operational order, "Victory at Kursk must act as a beacon to the world" – it was primarily designed with a negative goal in mind: to prevent the initiative from slipping completely from Germany's hands. Still, even this limited aim had much to offer. A successful pincer attack at the Kursk salient would shorten German lines appreciably, knock Soviet plans for an offensive off-balance, and destroy large enemy forces. At worst, it would provide some well-needed breathing space in the east. At best, victory at Kursk might allow the Germans to further conserve strength, ramp up production of the new tanks, and focus on crucial matters in the west, such as the Battle of the Atlantic and the bomber war over Germany. If the latter two could at least be stalemated – and German failure in both would not be apparent for some months – then the threat of a second front might be greatly reduced.[13]

Nor, contrary to the later self-serving claims by various generals, was the Kursk operation primarily Hitler's idea or at his urging. The original inspiration for the attack came from Manstein and was intended – even as Hitler insisted that there could be no new offensives in 1943 – as a follow-up to his successful Kharkov operation. With Soviet forces off-balance and in apparent disarray, Manstein believed that in cooperation with Army Group Center his troops could continue north and "take Kursk without any great difficulty." Hitler, though, saw danger in a possible enemy attack in the south toward Izyum and the Donets area. On 10 March he once again flew to Zaporozhye to discuss the situation with Manstein, who tried to impress upon the Führer the need for immediate action. Although Hitler did not commit himself, three days later, at his behest, OKH issued Operational Order No. 5, which formed the basis for the future Kursk attack. Even though the city was not named specifically, the outline was clear enough: Army Groups Center and South were to prepare forces for an assault from both north and south of the Kursk salient, with the operation to begin by mid-April. Despite his apparent triumph, Manstein remained frustrated with what he considered the lack of urgency in preparations, and, in particular, with the failure to give him priority on the divisions being redeployed from the west. With such units, he claimed to Zeitzler, he could carry out "operations with deep objectives." Fearing that a golden opportunity was being lost, on 20 March he again demanded an immediate start to the operation, but to no avail.[14]

Some historians have claimed this delay resulted from Hitler's fear that, having given Manstein command freedom that resulted in his great triumph at Kharkov, any further successes would elevate the field marshal into a threat to his own authority. Goebbels and Himmler were certainly working assiduously to undermine Manstein's influence, but the Kursk operation was postponed for the most basic of reasons: the Germans lacked the means to launch it in late March or early April. Contrary to Manstein's overly optimistic assessment, and despite his impressive success at Kharkov, Stalingrad and the winter fighting had exhausted the Ostheer. Hoth, the notably aggressive commander of 4th Panzer Army, which would spearhead the southern pincer, was under no illusions. "The troops," he warned on 21 March in a response to Manstein's inquiry as to when he could resume the offensive, "having been in battle day and night without rest for months, are used up . . . Some are apathetic and have reached their goal – the Donets – only under strongest pressure from their officers. The truck situation was bad even at the beginning of the counteroffensive, while the equipment levels have sunk noticeably." Nor was Army Group Center, which had surrendered most of its armored formations to Army Group South at the start of Operation Blue, in any better shape. Without a pause for rest, resupply, and assembly of the assault formations, any attack had little chance of success. Moreover, the notoriously unpredictable *rasputitsa*, the season of mud, was fast approaching; without a drying up of the roads, virtually all movement was impossible. The Soviet general staff, more attuned to local conditions, assumed that any German offensive would be impossible until the second half of May.[15]

Even Zeitzler, who had emerged as the strongest supporter of Manstein in the high command, in Operational Order No. 6 – which he wrote and sent out over Hitler's signature on 15 April – envisioned 3 May as the earliest possible date for an attack. Much of the tone of the order betrayed more than a hint of desperation. In addition to outlining goals and means, it noted, in a section surely influenced, if not written, by Hitler, that the assault "must give us the initiative . . .," that "the best formations, the best weapons, the best commanders must be present . . .," that "every commander, every man, must be indoctrinated with the decisive significance of this offensive." This, Hitler knew, was a gamble in which the odds were decidedly unfavorable; therefore, it "must" succeed whether it had a realistic chance or not. In any case, Zeitzler's deadline too proved impossible, given the dreadful transportation situation in the area of Army Group Center. To complete its assault preparations, General Model's 9th Army needed some 300,000 soldiers and roughly 1,000 tanks brought in quickly and under the greatest secrecy, conditions that overwhelmed the available railroads. Model had also been forced to dispatch a Panzer corps to help combat partisans, while concerned by an obvious enemy buildup in his area.[16]

Troubled by the situation, he went to see Hitler in late April. Model was a Hitler favorite who, although not necessarily a Nazi fanatic, nonetheless embodied his preferred qualities in a commander – loyalty, optimism, toughness, ruthlessness, and an ability to get things done – so his report must have been sobering. In the Führer's presence, Model conceded that the operation was still possible, but only if he received considerable reinforcements, especially of the new tank models just arriving at the front, to provide the necessary offensive punch. This assessment, which played to both Hitler's faith in the Panthers and Tigers and skepticism about the Kursk offensive, combined with intelligence indicating large Soviet troop movements, seemingly confirmed Hitler in his doubts. Clearly worried by the growing problems confronting Operation Citadel, on 18 April, even before his meeting with Model, he had proposed an alternative. Instead of a pincer attack, Hitler suggested a frontal assault into the Kursk salient with the aim of splitting the assembled Soviet forces. Manstein, concerned by the uninspired nature of the proposed pincer attack, had developed a similar plan, one that sought to achieve surprise by striking at Soviet positions in the center, where their fortifications were weakest, then, after a relatively easy breakthrough, wheeling to the left and right to drive Soviet troops onto their own minefields. Unlike 1940, though, when Hitler's and Manstein's shared conception had led to the adoption of a bold plan, Zeitzler rejected the idea by convincing Hitler that any redeployment of troops would cause further intolerable delays.[17]

With his top generals riven by uncertainty and personal animosities, the Führer on 3 May convened a conference in Munich with Zeitzler, Kluge, Manstein, Jeschonnek, Guderian, and Speer to discuss the operation. This was not, contrary to the stereotype, a one-sided meeting where Hitler dictated to his cowed generals, but a genuine exchange of opinions. Given the difficulty of the moment – with the imminent disaster in Tunisia, problems in the U-boat campaign, and the ramped-up Allied bombing war over Germany – no one, including Hitler, had a clear idea how to proceed. Kharkov had provided a respite, but few believed it presaged a revitalized

Ostheer. The issue, rather, was how best to utilize this breathing-space and in Munich the Führer preferred to hear the ideas of his subordinates. Guderian, in his memoirs, noted that Hitler opened the conference with a factual description of the situation on the Eastern Front, then outlined Zeitzler's proposed operation and the views of Model, who had sent Hitler a memorandum containing his objections. Model's arguments, Guderian thought, were powerful and obviously made a deep impression on Hitler. Given recent intelligence information that showed the enemy had prepared deep and very strong defense positions – with unusually large concentrations of artillery and anti-tank guns – and had withdrawn its mobile formations precisely in the proposed areas of attack, Model feared that his forces were insufficient to achieve a breakthrough. This, he concluded, meant that Citadel had to be either abandoned, reworked, or delayed until the arrival of substantial numbers of Panthers and Tigers. If Model, one of the few generals Hitler trusted, doubted the feasibility of the operation, perhaps it was best to await the arrival of the new tanks.[18]

Hitler then turned to Manstein and asked his opinion. Guderian, who had long regretted that Hitler and his talented field marshal had a frosty relationship, thought that, "as often when face to face" with the Führer, Manstein was "not at his best." More likely, Manstein's response was ambivalent because he realized that his proposal had been the inspiration for Citadel. In view of the wider military and political situation, he admitted, a success in the east was necessary, especially before the fall of Tunis. An attack would have worked, he claimed rather feebly, and unhelpfully, if launched in April, but now its success was doubtful, especially if he did not receive two additional infantry divisions. To this, Hitler replied that such divisions were unavailable and Manstein would have to make do with what he had. When again asked his opinion by Hitler, the field marshal gave him "no very clear answer." Manstein claimed later that he had spoken against any postponement of the attack – on the grounds that it was pointless to wait for new tanks since the Soviets were already outproducing the Germans and any delay would allow them to further strengthen their defenses – but this seems more a case of self-justification after the fact. He evidently closed his remarks by emphasizing that Citadel would be difficult, but he was ready; even here, though, he was essentially evading an opinion and leaving any decision to Hitler.[19]

In contrast to Manstein, others questioned by Hitler proved more decisive. Kluge, commanding Army Group Center, both supported the operation and opposed any delay, a position endorsed by Jeschonnek for the Luftwaffe. Guderian, on the other hand, declared the offensive "pointless."

It would result, in his opinion, only in a substantial loss of tanks, which could not be made good in 1943, for little gain. Instead, he argued, the Ostheer should stand on the defensive and the new tanks should be sent to the west to form a mobile reserve in preparation for the anticipated Allied invasion of France in 1944. This was not, in light of Hitler's later hope of reversing the odds against Germany by defeating an invasion, an idea without merit, although Guderian assumed that the Ostheer could main-tain a stable defense line through the rest of the year. He also tried to lower Hitler's unrealistic expectations about the impact of the Panthers and Tigers. All new models, he stressed, had "teething problems" and it was unlikely that these could be made good before the attack. Speer, too, pointed to production difficulties in arguing against the offensive. In the end, then, the Munich talks resolved nothing: Zeitzler, Kluge, and Jeschonnek favored going ahead with Citadel, Model opposed it in its present form, Guderian and Speer rejected any attack, and Manstein evidently both favored and opposed it. Given the divided nature of his high command, Hitler, himself uncertain, not unreasonably chose to postpone the attack until 12 June. This would allow more time for production of the new tanks and perhaps bring Model on board as well.[20]

Although the Führer's "technology mania," along with division among his advisors, played a role in his decision to put off the operation, other factors were at work as well. Above all, strategic concerns, especially over developments in the Mediterranean area – the impending defeat of Axis forces in North Africa, the fear that Italy might leave the war, and anxiety over a possible Allied landing in the Balkans – influenced Hitler and convinced him of the need to keep sizable reserves available for any contin-gency. In early May he had speculated to Goebbels that it might be better "under the circumstances to wait to see whether the Bolsheviks want to beat us to it [an attack]. That might give us an even more favorable opportunity than if we seized the initiative." Guderian attempted to exploit just such doubts to get Hitler to cancel Citadel. At a meeting on 10 May to discuss tank production, Guderian asked him, "Why do you want to attack in the east at all this year?" At this, Field Marshal Keitel interrupted and declared, "We must attack for political reasons." Guderian, sharing the near-universal contempt for Keitel, replied derisively, "How many people do you think even know where Kursk is? It's a matter of profound indifference to the world whether we hold Kursk or not." At this, he turned to Hitler and repeated his question, to which the Führer confessed, "You're quite right. Whenever I think of this attack my stomach turns over." Guderian then responded, "In that case your reaction is the correct one. Leave it alone!"[21]

Hitler, of course, did not leave it alone, could not leave it alone. Throughout May and early June he closely monitored the situation in the Mediterranean. The defeat in North Africa had been a disaster for Mussolini, whose regime now appeared to be on the verge of collapse. In that eventuality, the entire Southern Front would be open to Allied invasion, so he had to consider the possibility of dispatching large German forces from Russia. Jodl, like Guderian, tried to use such a scenario to encourage Hitler to abandon Citadel. At the same time, Hitler returned to the notion of a frontal assault from the west on the Kursk salient, but Model and Hoth pointed to the unfeasibility of such a large redeployment at this late date. Manstein also confronted the Führer with the idea of abandoning the Kursk offensive and returning to his scheme of allowing the enemy to move first, then attacking from the "backhand." Although this was an elegant idea, and appealing to post-war historians, there remained the twin problems of predicting precisely where the Soviets would attack, or even whether they would do the Germans such a favor. Although Stalin favored a continuation of the winter operations, his advisors, most prominently Zhukov, supported the view that the Germans, known to be preparing an attack at Kursk, should be allowed to proceed. The Red Army would then absorb the blow and, turning the tables on Manstein, counterattack, thus executing its own backhand stroke. The final decision of course was Hitler's and by this time he was tired of Manstein's constant injunctions to operate. Now convinced that Italy would continue in the war and that sufficient defensive forces were available in the Mediterranean, he was prepared, largely, as Keitel had stated, for political reasons, to proceed with the Kursk operation. Significantly, though, he had also decided to transfer strong forces from the Eastern Front in the event of any danger in Italy, an action that would bring an immediate stop to Citadel. Strategic concerns and not an obsession with tank numbers played the key role in delaying the Kursk operation; more time to deliver Panther tanks to the front likely only influenced the last postponement, from the end of June to early July.[22]

Although Kursk was intended to send a political signal, its military purpose was far from clear. Conceived initially as neither a decisive battle of annihilation nor the prelude to a return to the Caucasus, it seemed primarily to be a spoiling attack that would knock the anticipated Soviet summer offensive off balance and allow the transfer of troops to the west. From the outset, though, the unfavorable ratio of forces made the attack highly risky, with much to lose and little to gain. Despite the qualitative advantage of the new tanks, the Germans confronted a staggering numerical inferiority in combat troops, armored vehicles, artillery, and aircraft.

Even given the undeniable superiority of the Panthers and Tigers, by 5 July, when the attack commenced, only 328 of them had been supplied to the units at Kursk: 128 Tigers and 200 Panthers. Since the Soviets had 8,200 armored vehicles, each new tank would have had to destroy 25 of the enemy before itself being immobilized. As Guderian predicted, however, the new tanks had serious teething problems. The Tiger suffered from track failures and breakdowns, while the Panther had a defective engine prone to catching fire. Both were formidable in their firepower – and the Panther would eventually become the premier tank of the war – but at Kursk their technical problems would limit their effectiveness. Nor could the Germans count any longer on a mobility advantage against an opponent whose forces had been substantially mechanized and motorized through Lend-Lease deliveries. Moreover, the interminable delays in launching the attack gave the Soviets time to construct a formidable system of fortifications, an elaborate labyrinth of eight separate defensive lines consisting of anti-tank ditches, tank traps, minefields, barbed-wire obstacles, anti-tank guns, flame-throwers, and machine gun nests that stretched 180 miles to the rear. Instead of the fast, free-wheeling, mobile operations in which the Wehrmacht specialized, the Germans now faced a static "biting-through" attrition battle reminiscent of the First World War that, at best, could achieve only a local success that would almost certainly be more costly than it was worth.[23]

Kursk, though, proved a failure. Lacking any element of surprise or materiel superiority, the German attack rapidly stalled. In retrospect, given the imbalance of forces, especially in armor, it is hard to see how any of the German generals pushing for the offensive believed it could succeed. General Model in the north, fearing a Soviet attack near Orel, opted to hold his armor back and use his infantry to clear the path for the tanks, but they made virtually no progress against the formidable Soviet defenses. Manstein, on the other hand, led with his armor and made some progress, but in deciding on two Panzer thrusts to the north he dispersed his tanks rather than concentrate them, so he struggled to force a decisive engagement. Even the climactic battle on 12 July – the so-called greatest tank battle in history at Prokhorovka – was not as it seemed, based largely on a myth constructed by Soviet General P.A. Rotmistrov to disguise his inept handling of the attack and explain to Stalin his astounding loss of over 400 tanks against a confirmed German total of three. Although certainly a mêlée of the first order, the German tank arm was not destroyed at Prokhorovka – in fact, the next day the German units involved reported more available tanks than the day before – nor did it cause Hitler to order a halt to the offensive. But neither was Manstein correct in claiming that he was on the verge of a great operational triumph – one of his supposed "lost victories" – when Hitler prematurely reined him in. The sad reality was, even if allowed to continue, Manstein had nowhere to go. Lacking sufficient force or logistical support, his troops could not possibly have hoped to break through each successive line of Soviet defense. And, even if they had, where was there to go? Moscow? The Caucasus?[24]

Prokhorovka, after all, took place not in isolation but against a backdrop of a rapidly deteriorating situation elsewhere. A Soviet breakthrough at Orel, just north of the Kursk salient, threatened not only the encirclement of 9th Army, but if left unchecked the destruction of Army Group Center. More importantly, Hitler's worst fear had transpired: on 10 July, Anglo-American forces had invaded Sicily, and with it the two-front war on the European continent had become a reality. Both Hitler and OKW had worried from the start about using the crucial German tank reserves for limited gains at Kursk, with the Führer determined to take immediate action in case of a threat in the Mediterranean. By 12 July it had become apparent that neither Sicily nor Italy could be held without significant German aid, triggering Hitler's decision to transfer strong Panzer forces to southern Europe. For the first time since the invasion of the Soviet Union, strategic concerns in the west superseded the war in the east. On 13 July, Hitler called Manstein, Kluge, and Rommel to his headquarters; after listening to their respective arguments for and against continuing the offensive, he confirmed his decision to break off Citadel and transfer the 2nd SS Panzer Corps to Sicily. Kluge, having already halted his portion of the attack and fearful of a collapse of his army group, received the news with relief. Manstein, believing his forces on the edge of victory – but characteristically taking little notice of the larger picture – protested vigorously, but to no avail, that to give up the battle at the decisive moment was like "throwing victory away." That night, in a revealing exchange over copious amounts of French wine, both Kluge and Rommel predicted a disastrous end and evidently indicated their willingness to serve under Manstein, as the only individual who could retrieve the situation. Manstein, again betraying his political naivety, thought the state of affairs not so bleak, anticipating that Hitler would surrender his overall military authority – presumably to him – before it got desperate. To that, Rommel could only reply, "He will never give up the Supreme Command. I obviously know him better than you do."[25]

In the event, only one SS Panzer division, the Leibstandarte Adolf Hitler, actually departed for Italy: too late, ironically, to help in Sicily, but too early for any successful end to the Kursk operation. For the first time, a German summer offensive had failed in its tracks and the attacking units were almost immediately forced onto the defensive, a situation, Goebbels noted laconically, to which "we . . . were not accustomed." Deficiencies in materiel · and manpower, the delay in launching the attack, the absence of the element of surprise, the decision to assault the enemy's strongest positions, along with an ill-conceived and badly executed plan – not to neglect Soviet skill, tenacity, and sheer numerical and material superiority – had led to the utter failure of the last major German offensive in the east. The growing interaction of fronts also played a major role. In mid-July 1943, Hitler faced a daunting reality: the surrender of Axis forces in Tunisia had cost almost as many men as had Stalingrad; the Battle of the Atlantic had turned decisively against Germany in May, when the loss of forty-one U-boats forced Admiral Dönitz to temporarily suspend operations; and the "Battle of the Ruhr," the five-month Anglo-American bomber offensive between March and July, had seriously disrupted war production.[26]

Paradoxically, although still regarded by some historians as the turning point in the war, or at least as the graveyard of the German tank corps, Operation Citadel resulted in relatively light German losses. For the entire operation, the Wehrmacht lost 252 armored vehicles, as opposed to 1,956 for the Soviets, an astonishing 8:1 kill ratio; of those 252, only 10 were Tigers. Similarly, German aircraft losses totaled 159 as against 1,961 for the Red Air Force, a 12:1 ratio. For the Luftwaffe, the invasion of Sicily was more ruinous, for it meant the opening of a third front which, combined with the costly defensive battles over Germany, proved insuperable. In July and August, for example, it lost 702 aircraft on the Eastern Front but 3,504 in the west and on the home front. Nor were manpower losses particularly severe, the Germans losing 11,000 dead, a rather low figure for an inferior force attacking into the heart of well-prepared and formidable defenses. Still, Citadel had only three modest goals – to shorten the front to conserve forces, to weaken the Red Army sufficiently to forestall its summer offensive, and to retain some initiative in the east – yet, despite an all-out effort, it had failed utterly at all of them. In the end, the only signal Kursk sent was that, given the strategic situation and balance of forces, Germany was not likely to achieve victory (or even stalemate) by means of technological superiority alone.[27]

After Kursk, Manstein redoubled his push for mobile defensive operations, still believing they could be a game-changer for Germany. But was this a realistic option, given the limitations of Wehrmacht resources? After all, war was not a game that could be won on points scored through skillful movement. If the goal was to wear down the Soviets by endlessly enticing them to advance too far, cutting them off, and destroying them in "backhand" counterattacks, as Manstein suggested in his memoirs, would not the enemy soon catch on to the German tactics and refrain from such actions in the future? Was it to be expected that the Soviets would never learn from their mistakes? Such an operational method also depended on the enemy attacking where the Germans expected and wanted them to attack. To concentrate the force necessary to deliver a sharp counter-blow, the Germans would have to assemble forces in the south, the sector Manstein believed most likely to be the focus of enemy attention, thus imperiling other areas and gambling the stability of the Eastern Front on the chance that the Red Army would attack precisely where the Germans wished. Since the Soviets had an advantage all along the front, they could (and did) choose the point of attack that favored them. In August 1943, for example, they caught the Germans by surprise with their focal point of attack. It was not, as expected, in the south across the Mius River or directly out of the Kursk salient, but at and a bit north of the Orel salient and in the Kharkov–Belgorod area. Ironically, the Germans actually lost more men in the July–August fighting in and around Orel – where Hitler, in line with his generals' pleadings, had allowed them to "maneuver" and withdraw to shorten the line – than they did at Kursk. Although the Germans inflicted massive casualties on the Soviets, Orel should have given even the staunchest advocate of operational mobility pause. They had skillfully executed a defense and withdrawal, had bloodied the enemy considerably, and the result had been, at best, a temporary stabilization of a small area of the front at a cost in manpower that the Germans could not afford. Whether in frontal defense or in mobile operations, the reality was that after Kursk the Germans had ceased to be the hammer so would now be the anvil.[28]

Manstein's conception, furthermore, rested on the assumption, growing ever more doubtful, that the Germans still possessed superiority in mobile warfare. German officers might be more skilled in operational techniques, and the average Landser might be better trained than his Soviet counterpart, but this strategy depended on an edge in physical mobility and air supremacy that the Germans no longer enjoyed. Lacking both, they could not outmaneuver the Soviets and were constantly left with choosing between two evils: either stand and fight – and face destruction – or withdraw prematurely in order to save heavy equipment and artillery. Army Groups North and Center, forced to transfer units to Army Group South, were in an especially acute situation in this regard, dangerously undermanned, with many of their divisions reduced to regimental strength, and with virtually no tanks or air support. Nor, in truth, did Army Group South possess the necessary men – outnumbered, as they were, five to one – or equipment to conduct an adequate flexible defense. Since the Luftwaffe had long since lost control of the skies, it could neither impede Soviet advances nor effectively cover German withdrawals. Ultimately, the problem with flexible defense, operating, or maneuvering – whatever it might be termed – was that sooner or later the Ostheer had to stand and fight, not least to prevent the defection of its allies. Manstein's notion of conducting operations independently of the larger strategic or political context of the war thus seemed disconnected from reality. The German dilemma was perhaps best summarized in a statement made in 1941 by Joe Louis, the famous heavyweight boxer, about one of his opponents, Billy Conn, who also intended to maneuver to avoid defeat: "He can run but he can't hide." Although the latter danced effectively for twelve rounds, he was knocked out in the thirteenth.[29]

Hitler, as well, grew weary of operations not only because his First World War experience had told him to hold on to territory once it was conquered, but also because there was no point to winning Lebensraum – which, after all, was the key reason for war against the Soviet Union in the first place – if it could not be controlled and exploited for German benefit. As his observation on 5 May suggested, there also came a point at which trading space for time, if unable to secure an end to the fighting, ultimately meant that both ran out. In this respect, the size factor, which Hitler had repeatedly emphasized in the past, also played a role. Despite all the undeniable German skill – and now, perhaps, technological superiority – the sheer mass of the Red Army had become a critical factor. While the Germans had stripped Army Groups North and Center of their armored forces in order to launch Operation Citadel, the Soviets repelled the onslaught even as they prepared attacks at other places along the front. This, then, raises again the issue of the ultimate purpose of a "backhand" strategy. What was it to achieve? To allow the possibility of winning the war, which was not likely? To parry the Soviets and stalemate the east, thus raising the possibility of a negotiated peace? To Manstein, that was evidently the aim, but was that ever a real alternative – and not only because Hitler insisted on negotiating from strength, but also because of the advantageous material position of Stalin and the Western Allies? If any political solution to the war required Hitler's ouster and change of regime – which Hitler suspected it did – then it was a non-starter. Especially after the Casablanca declaration of "unconditional surrender" in January 1943, there remained no particular incentive for Hitler to seek a political way out.

Still, in autumn 1943 he returned to thoughts of a Sonderfrieden. The only realistic chance at a negotiated peace, in truth, was probably the way

Hitler envisioned: win some operational victories, hold on as much as possible to economically valuable territory, stalemate the war, and hope for cracks in the enemy coalition. This latter was not such an outlandish hope, especially given Stalin's suspicion that his Anglo-American partners aimed to allow the Soviet Union and Germany to wear each other out before intervening decisively on the continent. Although, on 9 September, Hitler had voiced the opinion to Goebbels that he might be able to negotiate with the English – after all, he thought, they "will listen to reason at a certain point" – in another conversation with Goebbels on 22 September the Führer showed himself notably conciliatory and open to talks with Stalin, who himself in mid-August had again authorized peace feelers through contacts in Stockholm. Goebbels, surprisingly direct, confronted Hitler with the observation that Germany could not win a two-front war, so "must find some other way out" by coming "to an arrangement with one side or the other." When asked if he would eventually be ready to talk with Churchill, Hitler noted simply that he did not think such negotiations would be successful. He preferred, he indicated, to deal with Stalin, whom he regarded as a fellow revolutionary, though he also thought any talks would fail because what he would demand in the east would be unacceptable to the Soviet leader. Still, Hitler believed that the late autumn, when a *rasputitsa*-induced "quiet on the fronts" would again return, might offer "a certain chance for political arrangements."[30]

Similarly, on 18 October, he remarked to a Bulgarian delegation, "No one wants to conquer the world anymore, rather just reorganize it and, if possible, hold on to what the war has brought him. In the fifth year of war the behavior of war leaders is like the hamster." By late October, Hitler had warmed further to the idea of a separate peace with Stalin, telling Goebbels that "one could strike an arrangement with the Soviets, perhaps on the basis of 1939 after the Polish campaign." Following a deal with the Russians, he would then turn his attention to the west. Still, the tenor of his comments hardly indicated any real interest in an end to the fighting, since he could never reconcile himself to giving up the territorial gains of Barbarossa. "A later question would then be," the Führer pondered, "how we could create in the east the space that we need to live," a remark that revealed both his continued fixation on Lebensraum and suspicion that any deal with the Soviets would only be temporary. In any case, betraying his belief that the struggle was unending, Hitler thought himself "probably too old to also fight this battle." In the autumn of 1943 he thus showed some willingness to consider a separate peace – or at least try to exploit tensions in the enemy coalition – but not to the extent that he proved willing to pull the trigger.[31]

In large part, the reason for his hesitation has to be seen in his observation on 26 October: any separate peace had to come from a position of relative strength and had to be coupled with a stable military situation. "The precondition of such a still so tentative possibility," he emphasized to Goebbels, "is that we again achieve a (military) success." Since his personal rule now rested on military success rather than any residual charisma, the Feldherr needed a victory to boost the legitimacy of the Führer. There were also indications that he was worried about a threat to his rule from an external source, but one with potential domestic implications. In September 1943 the League of German Officers, formed from generals captured at Stalingrad and led by General Seydlitz, had proclaimed, "Hitler as statesman has welded together the most powerful states of the world into a crushing coalition against Germany. Hitler as Feldherr has led the German Wehrmacht into the most serious defeats."[32]

At roughly the same time, Stalin shifted his emphasis from talking with the Hitler regime to a willingness to respond to the initiatives of others. Both the National Committee for a Free Germany and the League of German Officers represented, for Stalin, the possible core of a new German government, but they were based in Moscow. More intriguing was the possibility of regime change from within. An article written on 3 October 1943 by the Moscow-based German communist, Walter Ulbricht – arguing that pressure in 1918 from the high command had forced regime change – must have further alarmed Hitler. "Today," he thundered, "Field Marshals von Bock, von Manstein, von Kluge, among others, know very well that the Hitler government has lost the war. Hindenburg had the necessary courage and acted." German generals, Ulbricht suggested, should show the same fortitude and move against "the bankrupt Corporal Hitler!" This barb at the incompetence of the military dilettante Hitler, the formation of the Seydlitz group of officers, and Stalin's new emphasis were all a not so subtle encouragement to the German officer corps to take matters in hand and form a new regime by overthrowing Hitler.[33]

Hitler certainly worried that any show of weakness might cause his officers to move against him. Revealingly, on 7 January 1944 he remarked to a small circle, "The most dangerous things currently happening on the front – various people have told me this . . . are the appeals coming from General Seydlitz." Just three weeks later, in fact, as if to inoculate against the "Seydlitz virus," he called many of his frontline commanders to a meeting at the Wolf's Lair, where, for almost two hours, he lectured them on National Socialist ideology and the need for fanatic belief. Putting out peace feelers, he must have feared, would be seen as a sign of weakness – as an admission of his failure – and would embolden his officers to overthrow him. Hitler found himself in a conundrum: he no longer thought military victory possible, but a Sonderfrieden raised dangerous uncertainties. In any case, he believed, a series of military victories that would allow a stalemating of the war and provide time for the enemy coalition to disintegrate formed the prerequisite for both a political solution and the reassertion of the legitimacy of his rule.[34]

That, though, was never a particularly convincing stratagem given enemy superiority in all phases and, in any case, it required Germany actually to win a victory or achieve a deadlock. In the event, the Germans proved unable to accomplish the first, nor could they stabilize the Eastern Front. After a pause to replenish following Kursk, the Soviets resumed a series of offensives in the late summer and early autumn that steadily pushed the Germans back to the Dnieper. While Army Group South desperately needed a quiet period in which to rest and build defenses, it instead faced a near constant series of enemy attacks that forced Manstein to react rather than dictate. Further, Soviet commanders had become more skillful, adopting German techniques of establishing overwhelming tactical superiority at the chosen points of attack, supported by massed air and artillery concentrations. With only meager reserves of armor, reliant on assault guns and tank-destroyers, and with their infantry largely immobile and dependent on horse-drawn transport, the Germans found it increasingly difficult to pinch off and destroy Soviet breakthroughs. Despite the punishment inflicted upon it, the Red Army also showed an ability to regenerate itself in a way the Wehrmacht could not match. It was, Manstein complained bitterly, like "confront[ing] a hydra: for every head cut off, two new ones appeared to grow." Thus, while he parried Soviet thrusts and oversaw a skillful scorched-earth retreat – which itself must have rekindled in Hitler and his generals memories of the German retreat to the Hindenburg Line in March 1917 – he could neither regain the initiative nor prevent German forces from being ground down by the incessant fighting. In spite of all his confidence in a mobile defense and all his considerable operational skills, the fall of 1943, then, proved yet another disaster for Manstein and the Ostheer.[35]

Significantly, German failure resulted primarily from the newfound Soviet ability to conduct continuous operations rather than any German withdrawal into a rigid defense or refusal to accept Manstein's advice on Hitler's part. Indeed, Hitler showed a willingness to embrace a flexible defensive strategy and, while often frustrated with Manstein, to allow the field marshal some autonomy in the hope that he could stabilize the front, and with it, his personal position. Hitler had not yet settled on a rigid "halt doctrine" on the Eastern Front despite his actions elsewhere. He ordered a defensive strategy in Italy because geographic factors made it sensible (and easy), as well as to protect Romanian oil. In the east, however, he showed a readiness to accept Manstein's advice, even when, as on 3 September, it was given very bluntly. Confronted with the loss of the Donets, the field marshal told him that he had only the choice of losing it with or without an army group. Facing ever more limited options, Hitler flew on 8 September to the field marshal's headquarters at Zaporozhye – again, perhaps, an indication of his desire for an accommodation with Manstein – to discuss the worsening situation. This, in retrospect, marked a symbolic day, for it was both the last time he would set foot on occupied Soviet territory and the same day as his Axis partner, Italy, surrendered to the Allies. In the preceding weeks tension had steadily built between the Führer and Manstein, not merely because of the problems caused by the aggressive Soviet actions, but also because Manstein had persistently raised the issue of unifying the command structure on the Eastern Front in his own person. This, of course, would deprive Hitler both of his day-to-day control over military activities in Russia and his ability to play OKH and OKW off against each other. More significantly, he perceived it as a challenge by a popular general to his overall authority, something he would not abide. On 3 September he had chided Manstein to his face, charging that "on the whole, [he] only wanted to conduct clever operations in order to be justified in the war diary." The point was clear: there could only be one military genius, and that was the Führer.[36]

Nonetheless, when Manstein, this time carefully avoiding any hint of a challenge to Hitler's command authority, again requested permission to retreat, the Führer stunned him by granting exactly what he had long demanded: the right to conduct mobile operations. Nor, despite his embrace of the Ostwall, construction of which had been authorized on 12 August, was he intent on a return to the stubborn defensive tactics of the winter crisis of 1941–2. In a meeting with his Gauleiters on 7 October, perhaps making a virtue of necessity, Hitler explicitly declared the foundations of his military policy to be a mobile defense. Precisely because of the great expanses east of the Dnieper, he explained, he could now trade space for time and give up territory without suffering any harm. As proof, he indicated his readiness – in actuality more forced upon him than voluntary – to give up the Donets, which he had long held to be indispensable, and the Kuban bridgehead, thereby signaling his realization that German forces would never resume the offensive toward the goal of securing Caucasus oil. The problem, then, was not so much Hitler's obstinacy as the fact that the Germans lost the race to the Dnieper, so the Ostwall quickly fizzled out as a potentially stabilizing factor. Just as significantly, despite his repeated exhortations to Hitler that his mobile, delaying operations held the key to Germany's ability to wage war, Manstein, like most generals, had at best a blinkered view of the overall strategic situation. He, like them, failed to appreciate Germany's strategic dilemma: stalemating the Eastern Front was in itself no guarantee if Germany proved unable to stabilize the other fronts.[37]

Forced to confront just such an unpleasant strategic reality, Hitler's attention increasingly turned to the west. From his perspective, the situation at the end of 1943, although serious, also seemed to hold some promise that, if the pieces fell into place and if he retained a fanatic will, it might just be possible to wriggle free. The Red Army, while pushing ahead, had been unable to rip a hole in German defenses, advance rapidly, or threaten destruction of an entire Army Group. The Ostheer, in falling back on its supply bases, was helped by both shortened supply lines and the narrowing of the front as it retreated west. Also, Soviet manpower reserves were not inexhaustible. In the west, the Allied advance in Italy had been stalled while, after the shock of the firebombing of Hamburg, the British had been unable to repeat the feat over Berlin (or any other city), while losing large numbers of planes in the effort. Unacceptable losses had forced the Americans to suspend daylight bombing raids, so there seemed to be grounds for guarded optimism that the Luftwaffe could regain control of the skies over Germany, the "house without a roof." As a result, the mood within Germany had improved. Although output had not fully recovered from the shock of the Battle of the Ruhr, by the end of the year Speer had weapons production again on an upward track. Enough tanks and arms were being produced to equip new divisions for the west and replace some of the losses in the east. Synthetic oil production had peaked, with stocks of aviation fuel at their highest since 1941, while the output of fighter planes rose spectacularly. Moreover, despite increased resistance activity, the continent was stable and there was no fear of a large-scale uprising. Furthermore, construction on the Atlantic Wall had increased in scale and pace. Under Rommel's energetic efforts, defensive preparations along the Normandy coast had accelerated. Finally, Hitler had high hopes for the technologically advanced "V"-weapons that might crack British morale, which seemed increasingly brittle, as well as for a new type of submarine that would enable the American supply line to Great Britain to be cut. By the end of 1943, the Germans seemingly had taken effective measures to stymie further enemy progress.[38]

Hitler thus considered the Allied invasion a great opportunity, perhaps the last such for achieving any sort of turning point. He knew Germany had to do more than just stand on the defense; to gain a way out, it had to win some tangible, significant victories. Germany, he believed, with the example of the First World War ever present, had to break out of this "unfruitful defensive" posture in order to bust the "unnatural alliance" of its enemies, itself an uneasy association of capitalists and communists. Germany, Hitler asserted, needed to achieve a great victory in order to demonstrate to its enemies that they could not win the war, or could do so only at unacceptable cost to themselves. Everything was premised on the expectation of defeating the impending Allied invasion of occupied France. This, after all, would be a risky endeavor, and Allied performance to date in amphibious landings, especially those at Salerno in September 1943 and Anzio in January 1944, hardly inspired any excess confidence on their part, or persuaded the Germans that it could not be crushed. Indeed, the potential effectiveness of Panther and Tiger tanks in western Europe merely increased Hitler's confidence. With the defeat of the invasion, then, the momentum of the war would be altered. Goebbels talked confidently of a "second Dunkirk," while the German public saw in the impending invasion the possibility for a "quick decision of the war."[39]

In such an eventuality, Hitler's expectation that the Allies would not try again – or at least not for a year – would likely have been correct. The invasion of France was a complicated operation that required months of preparation. If defeated, it could not simply be repeated any time soon. A failure, Hitler anticipated, would result in a severe political crisis in Great Britain and provide Germany with another opportunity to seize the initiative. After all, during the First World War an unsuccessful amphibious operation at Gallipoli had cost Churchill his position, a circumstance that might well repeat itself. Moreover, an abortive landing could have significant repercussions in the United States, especially in an election year, Hitler even asserting that it would cost President Roosevelt re-election. Failure of the invasion, plus a massive onslaught of V-weapons, might push Britain to abandon the war or at least suspend active operations. The impact of this might pressure the United States to shift its primary attention to the Pacific. In turn, this would put enormous strain on the enemy alliance, since Stalin would have no idea when, or even if, his Western Allies would again be in position to provide any significant help on the ground. An unsuccessful invasion would thus allow Germany to shift its focus to the east and concentrate its remaining resources against the Red Army. This would likely cause Stalin to think hard about whether to continue fighting. He had recovered most of pre-war Soviet territory, but at a staggering cost in lives and material destruction. Any further operations, in the absence of an active western fighting front, could be expected to be at least as debilitating, if not more so. Might it not be better to settle for a political solution that gave him most of what he wanted than continue the bloodbath?[40]

Above all, Hitler insisted, this point in time required fanatic belief. Just as the iron will of Stalin had saved Russia from collapse in the autumn of 1941, he argued, so now his own will would transform the bleak situation facing Germany. It was, he thought, reminiscent of the period of struggle in the 1920s, when a few determined individuals with a powerful belief in an idea created a movement with its own revolutionary dynamic that accomplished the seemingly impossible. Just as the street agitator had swept to power and achieved undreamt-of triumphs, so now in 1944 a few key victories would tip the balance and unleash an unstoppable momentum. The Germans had lost the First World War, Hitler believed, both from internal weakness and because the imperial leadership had given up too soon, mistakes that would not be repeated. He would supply the will, while in late May, in front of an audience of generals and other senior officers, he assured his listeners that there would be no inner collapse. "In removing the Jews I eliminated the possibility of creating some sort of revolutionary core or nucleus," he asserted, then reminded them, "Gentlemen, we are in a life and death struggle." He also conjured visions of a new "miracle of 1940," of a decisive triumph in the west that would free Germany from the nightmare of a two-front war. So confident did Hitler appear that Goebbels speculated that after the war was won, Hitler, having solved the "Jewish problem," would be able to eliminate two other obstacles: the Catholic Church leadership and the officer corps. After all, he noted, Stalin had already shown the way: he had made Orthodox leaders the servants of the state and simply shot officers who crossed him. Indeed, the mood at the Berghof in the weeks leading to the invasion was calm, almost peaceful. To dismiss all of this as irrational or unrealistic would miss the mark. Typically, Hitler mixed clear-sighted realism and gross self-delusion, a cogent understanding of Germany's predicament with little sense of its limitations. In truth, at least briefly, the prospects for victory in the west appeared not unfavorable.[41]

The precondition for all this, of course, was success in defeating the Allied invasion, an insight reflected in Führer Directive No. 51, issued on 3 November 1943, which, for the first time since the invasion of the Soviet Union, gave precedence to the war in the west. Despite the continued significance of the struggle against Bolshevism in the east, Hitler now declared that a greater immediate danger had arisen in the west: the threat of an Anglo-American invasion. "In the most extreme instance," he said, Germany could still sacrifice territory in the east, but in the west any breakthrough would have ruinous consequences "in a short time." Directive No. 51 in one sense clearly marked a turn toward the strategic defensive, but it also betrayed the way in which Hitler thought he could regain the initiative: hold on in the east and strike in the west. The Ostwall would shield against further Soviet advances, while the role of the Atlantic Wall was not so much to prevent an attack as allow German forces to defeat the invasion once it came. It also indicated the hopes being placed in the defeat of any second front in France. The Allied attack in the west, Hitler remarked in December, "will decide the war." The problem, though, was that any significant shift of forces to the west, in the absence of a strategic withdrawal to a line running from Riga to Odessa in order to free up troops, would stretch the overburdened Ostheer to breaking point. The Allied invasions of Sicily and Italy had already had a negative impact on the Eastern Front, one that no amount of maneuvering and operating could make good, so a correspondingly larger enemy effort in France would make the Eastern Front all that more brittle.[42]

Drawing on their experience of Allied amphibious landings in Sicily and Italy, German planners had concluded that the approach phase and initial landing offered the best chance of defeating an invasion and inflicting heavy losses on the enemy. This meant that strong forces had to be stationed in coastal fortifications and kept in a constant state of readiness. It also suggested that any quick Allied advance after the landing had to be blocked to allow time for deploying troops and mobile forces. If the Anglo-Americans could be "nailed to the beach for six to eight hours," Hitler thought, then German Panzer units could be sent hurtling into the landing zones and drive the invaders back into the sea. Anticipating that by the time of any landing the Luftwaffe would be equipped with new jet fighters, he also considered it important that the enemy "gets bombs on his head the moment he lands. Then we force [him to] take cover and that will cost him hour after hour." As if seeing the vision of future victory, he continued, "Imagine what this would mean for us . . . [if he is] nailed until our first reserves [arrive]." Successfully pinning the Allied landing force to the beach also demanded some sense of where that landing would take place. And again, despite his lament in late January – "Where will he land? Where are the clairvoyants?" – Hitler himself on several occasions from February on pinpointed the Cotentin peninsula, with the key port of Cherbourg, and the Normandy coastline as the most probable sector for an invasion. Indeed, in early April he demanded that this area be reinforced with the utmost speed, and when, in early May, Rundstedt rejected Rommel's recommenda-tion to strengthen the Cotentin defenses, Jodl, channeling his Führer, replied that the Cotentin peninsula "would be the first objective of the enemy." Others, too, most prominently General Marcks, commander of 84th Army Corps, supported this view.[43]

This provided the rationale for Hitler's often derided Atlantic Wall. Its construction had begun in September 1942, but then accelerated noticeably in November 1943 after the appointment of Rommel as commander of Army Group B, with responsibility for overseeing the coastal defenses. Despite Hitler's boast to Guderian that he was "the greatest builder of fortresses in history," the reality of the Atlantic Wall was quite different, as it consisted largely of thinly manned bunkers and fortifications. Neither was it, as often asserted, merely a gigantic trench fortification reminiscent of Hitler's earlier war, nor did it symbolize a withdrawal into an unthinking emphasis on linear defense. Instead, it was a rational effort to solve the problem of how to defeat an invasion, given the reality of insufficient manpower and military force. German planners had initially thought of using the Luftwaffe and navy to disrupt and destroy the bulk of any inva-sion fleet in the English Channel before it could even arrive at the French coast, with the Atlantic Wall acting as a further shield. By the end of 1943, given the weakness of both of these services, that idea was dead and the realization took hold that the army would have to bear the brunt of the fighting on its own. It also meant that the decisive battle would come after a landing. German planners, though, were clear that the Atlantic Wall by itself could not defeat an invasion. Its purpose, rather, was to allow the stationary defenders, made up primarily of second- and third-rate troops, to significantly weaken the invasion force, delay its progress inland, channel any advance to prepared strongpoints, and, in general, hold on to the forward beach positions long enough to provide the mobile reserve, espe-cially the Panthers, Tigers, and assault guns in which Hitler put so much faith, the time necessary to launch counterattacks. All of this was reminis-cent of Soviet defenses at Kursk. This delaying action, in fact, was consid-ered the crucial factor in defeating an invasion force. Rundstedt, *Oberbefehlshaber* (OB) West, emphasized that all coastal positions had to be held "to the last man," for "every half hour . . . [gained] can be decisive."[44]

Hitler and his generals largely agreed on all this; the explosive debate centered on how the crucial Panzer divisions, ten in total, were to be used. Rommel, shaped by his experience of Allied air superiority in North Africa – where it proved impossible for Axis forces to move anywhere unencumbered – advocated placing individual tank formations as close to the invasion beaches as possible so that they could go into action in the first hours after the landings. The advocates of this position, who included Hitler, OKW operations staff, and the commanders of the coastal armies, argued that the Italian experience had shown that German mobile units had been stationed too far away. They had then, given Allied air superiority, suffered heavy losses on the way to the landing site, so that they reached the invasion zone too late and too weakened to effect a decisive attack. The best thing, then, was to hold at the coast.[45]

Dispersing Panzer forces, though, ran counter to established Wehrmacht doctrine and practice. The commander of Panzer Group West, General Leo Geyr von Schweppenburg, supported by Rundstedt, favored gathering the armored units into a central reserve, allowing the now weakened Allied invasion forces to move inland, and only then, as at Kharkov, launching a devastating counterattack that would destroy the bulk of enemy forces ashore. Even though Geyr was a veteran Eastern Front commander, he had no experience conducting a battle against an enemy with anything approaching the absolute Allied air superiority; nor, for his part, did Rundstedt, who had commanded in the west in 1940 and then led Army Group South into Ukraine in 1941. Although they advocated a classic mobile defense, such as Manstein was futilely pursuing in the east, they also pointed to another aspect of the Italian experience. Allied naval artillery, they claimed, would decimate any Panzer forces stationed within their range – up to eighteen miles – so it was best to have a central armor reserve out of range of these guns. The Panzers could then be moved to key areas under cover of night or bad weather. Since a rapid response directly at the invasion beaches was not so vital in this formulation, a little delay, Geyr and Rundstedt thought, need not be fatal.[46]

While a logical case could be made for or against each of these positions, the so-called "Panzer controversy" was made more intense by the harshness with which Rommel and Geyr conducted the debate, and more consequential because of the ultimate compromise, which satisfied neither side and only exposed the convoluted German command structure. In late January 1944, Hitler intervened to settle the matter: part of the mobile forces would be sent to the presumed landing areas, while the rest would be stationed near Paris as a central reserve. Although it seemed the best solution at the time – theoretically, the armored divisions at the coast could intervene immediately, whereas those in the reserve would be available for any eventuality – it was undermined by the fact that there continued to be no clear lines of command authority between Rommel and Rundstedt. Only in April was the chain of command sorted out, to an extent, but Hitler then insisted on retaining control over the actual deployment of four armored units (the OKW operational reserve), with the rest split between Army Groups B and G. Thus, many people were made responsible for many things, but no one was in overall control, clearly an unsatisfactory situation. If the Germans were counting on the qualitative superiority of Tigers and Panthers to be decisive against overwhelming enemy numbers, then surely it would have been better either to have dispersed all the Panzer divisions to the coast in order to have a crucial advantage in firepower at the moment of greatest Allied vulnerability, or to have concentrated them for a massive counter-blow to destroy large numbers of enemy forces. In the event of course, neither of these approaches could overcome the reality of crippling German weaknesses in quantity and quality of manpower or the impact of complete Allied aerial dominance. Despite the frenetic efforts of Rommel, the Atlantic Wall fortifications remained incomplete by the time of the invasion, while both the number and quality of the defending forces raised concerns. The coastal divisions, often overseen by officers deemed inept on the Eastern Front and transferred west, largely consisted of overage, convalescing, or ethnically non-German troops poorly equipped with a variety of captured equipment. The critical Panzer divisions, while top-notch, were only just arriving in France, or, in the case of the 2nd SS Panzer Corps, being transferred back to Ukraine. Although the 2nd SS Panzer Corps finally brought a halt to the Soviet offensive, its absence from Normandy in June was to play a key role in the success of the Allied landings, a circumstance that Hitler complained of bitterly after the fact. Crucially, as well, Allied air and naval superiority would virtually paralyze German movement to or within the landing area, a circumstance that made the "Panzer controversy" even more of a map-table debate.[47]

Although in the spring Hitler had high hopes of turning the war around, in the event these proved illusory. Three interlocking factors undermined his strategy: first, the Allied introduction of long-range fighter escorts in early 1944 completely upset German calculations about the bomber war. They not only allowed the resumption of daylight bombing raids by the Americans, with devastating consequences, but the P-51 Mustang also proved a superior fighter that led to the crushing defeat of the Luftwaffe over Germany. As American bombers targeted oil production and synthetic fuel facilities, aircraft engine plants, and key rail yards, they also crushed any hope the Nazis had of winning the aerial war over Germany. By mid-May, Speer later conceded, "a new era in the air war" had begun, one that meant "the end of German armaments production." Hitler's hopes that a qualitative technological edge would prove decisive were being blown to bits by overwhelming Allied aerial superiority. The Germans could neither defend their home skies nor challenge Allied air supremacy over Normandy – nor could they hope to produce the quantity of weapons necessary to stymie their enemies.[48]

Secondly, unusually mild winter weather allowed the Red Army to press its advantage without let-up straight through to May 1944. By the time fighting in the east stopped, they had not only driven the Germans out of Ukraine in the south and Leningrad in the north, but had prevented the Wehrmacht from transferring large forces to the west in order to defeat the invasion. Hitler's deteriorating relations with Manstein reflected his realization of the ongoing failure of the latter's strategy in the east, which was the key to potential success in the west. In November, Hitler grumbled, "For weeks and weeks from the southern sector of the eastern front there have come one telex after another from Manstein: I must retreat . . . I cannot hold . . . I must evacuate . . . And between the lines of each telex we can read: I don't want to hold on, I want to retreat, I want to evacuate. For this is not my war but your war. See how far you get with the much praised command genius?" The key issue, again, was the urgent need to stabilize the Eastern Front in order to send troops west. "No other sector has received as much as . . . Manstein," Hitler bristled in December, with Zeitzler adding, "He devours everything." The problem, Hitler complained, was Manstein's negative attitude rather than deficient strength. If the field marshal was receiving more reinforcements than anyone else, the Führer suggested bluntly, then he should be producing results. Instead he issued only constant entreaties to retreat, which Hitler further mocked: "He should not speak of a 'counter-operation,' but call it by the right name: running away." Cutting to the quick, Hitler also ridiculed the key weakness of a mobile defense. In a recent telegram Manstein had expressed the hope that the Soviets would attack in a certain area and their forces would be exhausted. To this, Hitler replied scornfully, "we hope that the enemy . . . You know, when I hear such things: 'We hope it!' Because it suits us, right? And the enemy will do what we hope for! Is this a military term at all?" Instead, he insisted, the enemy would do "what will damage us the most." Nor did the atmosphere improve in the New Year. On 4 January, Manstein flew to meet with Hitler, itself a revealing change from September, to try to convince him, in view of the critical situation, to allow a withdrawal to close a dangerous gap in the north with Army Group Center. To Manstein, Hitler's now familiar economic and strategic arguments against withdrawal smacked of a return to the "halt doctrine," but to Hitler – with no new forces available for the east, facing the loss of critical resources that could not be replaced, and worried about a possible defection of his remaining allies – the only realistic course of action was "to play for time until things clarified in the west and our new formations were ready to go into action."[49]

Not satisfied with this response, Manstein requested a private audience with the Führer, where he stressed that the critical situation resulted not only from the enemy's superiority but also from the way in which Germany was led. This latter remark was a slap in the face to Hitler, who responded, according to Manstein, with a gaze that "wished to crush my will." Still, the field marshal proceeded once again to suggest an overall military commander in the east with full independence to act. To this Hitler replied sarcastically, made more biting by Manstein's recent complaints that other commanders were not carrying out Hitler's orders, "Even I cannot get the field marshals to obey me. Do you imagine that they would obey you more readily?" At this, Manstein countered caustically, and intemperately, that *his* orders were always carried out, a remark that certainly earned him no favor. Manstein had not only challenged Hitler's authority, both military and political, but also his strategic understanding that at some point the Germans had to hold the line and end their steady retreat in the east in order to build up sufficient forces in the west to repel the invasion.[50]

This seemingly endless withdrawal also made moot any further notions of a mobile defense, of trading space for time, or of attaining a separate peace from a position of strength, something that Manstein seemingly could not (or would not) admit. Although tactically clever and temporarily effective on a local level, a flexible defense was never likely to halt the Soviets for an extended period, given their immense superiority in manpower, materiel, and mobility. Manstein thus became a casualty both of his own popularity and the inability of the Ostheer to stalemate the Eastern Front. He had lasted as long as he had only because Hitler needed him to stabilize the critical situation, but the failure of his flexible defense to halt the enemy at a defensible position now made him superfluous. As the promised stabilization never materialized, Manstein's demands came to be seen by Hitler as a challenge to his authority, one that has to be seen within the context of the fears raised by Seydlitz's League of German Officers. Nor did Manstein, who believed he was operationally correct, help himself by continuing to fire off increasingly contemptuous and pedantic letters to Hitler instructing him on the art of command. The Führer, for his part, distrusted the field marshal precisely because he remained wedded to operational matters, seemingly unwilling or unable to comprehend the larger point of Hitler's defensive stubbornness: to have any chance of altering the outcome of the war, Germany now needed to hold at all costs in the east in order to effect a turnabout in its fortunes via success in the west. Manstein, evidently, could not accept the new reality: the west took precedence over the east.[51]

Hitler's suspicions boiled over on 27 January 1944 at a meeting of army group and army commanders called by him to ascertain their political loyalty and steadfastness. Just at the point in his speech where Hitler demanded of his top commanders that "in the critical hour" they should stay loyal, Manstein, impatient, frustrated, and with the "blood rush[ing] to his head," interjected, "And so they will, mein Führer!" Hitler, thrown off track, shot an icy glare in the direction of the field marshal, perhaps not least because, just over three weeks earlier in their private meeting on 4 January, Manstein had baited Hitler that *he* had no trouble having his orders obeyed by his subordinates. Whether intentional or not, Manstein was implicitly raising a further challenge to the Führer: the top commanders would remain loyal to Hitler not because of his authority, but because Manstein had guaranteed it. Although nothing further came of the incident immediately, as in the earlier break with Halder, Manstein's fate had been sealed. On 25 March, at a critical moment for his army group, he flew from his headquarters in Lvov to meet Hitler at the Berghof. There, the two engaged in a sharp exchange, the Führer complaining again of Manstein's endless "maneuvering" while the latter held Hitler responsible for the dire situation of his army group. Much to the field marshal's surprise, though, that evening Hitler conceded to Manstein's ideas for how to manage the situation. He then flew back to his headquarters the next day, only to be summoned back on 30 March to the Obersalzberg, where he was relieved of his command. "The time for grand-style operations in the east," Hitler pointedly told Manstein, "for which [you] had been particularly qualified, was now past. All that counted now . . . was to cling stubbornly to what we had." This was probably an accurate assessment, since the Germans had traded space for time but were now running short of both. Although Hitler had long disliked Manstein personally, he had respected his military ability and tolerated him as long as that had proved useful. But with his operational utility exhausted, and suspicious of his political loyalty and potential unreliability, Hitler had no further use for the field marshal. And, in any case, on 8 March, in Führer Order No. 11, he had already proclaimed a new strategy, that of the *festen Plätze* (fortified places).[52]

Festen Plätze, along with the Atlantic Wall, were intended finally to provide the defensive bulwark against which enemy attacks would shatter. According to Hitler's directive, "fortified places" were to be established in key towns or cities controlling railroad and highway supply and communications. By retaining them, allowing themselves to be surrounded, and then "holding down the largest possible number of enemy forces," the Germans could theoretically disrupt and eventually stall the momentum of the enemy advance. Taking or containing these fortresses, Hitler assumed, would cost the enemy more forces than were necessary for their defense, a crucial consideration in the face of critical German manpower shortages. In conception, these "fortified places" were to be a sort of "wave-breaker," doing to the enemy what Hitler thought Stalin had done to the Wehrmacht in 1941 and 1942. Jodl, in a lecture to the Gauleiters on 7 November 1943, appropriated Clausewitz to provide the conceptual justification for this defensive strategy: "Every attack that does not lead to an armistice or peace, must of necessity end in defense." As if anticipating skepticism, Jodl also used Clausewitz to quell any doubts about the Führer's strategy: "The most perfect General Staff with the most correct views and principles does not in itself represent perfect leadership of an Army, if the soul of a great General is missing." Although Goebbels understood the problem with such a defensive concept – "[It] contains only negative elements. A fortress can be besieged, and it is only a question of time when it falls" – it resulted largely from the recognition that Germany had been forced onto the defensive and had insufficient resources to defend all threatened areas.[53]

To the Führer, a "hold" strategy seemed to make some sense, at least on paper – not the last time he would pursue an idea that seemed promising in theory but was devoid of contextual understanding – especially as the Germans had lost their advantage in mobility and in the air. Simply put, in view of their limited manpower and resources, the idea was to meet the enemy in prepared defenses, force him to squander his forces, and thus blunt his advance. As early as 1938, Hitler had stated that the purpose of a fortress was to sustain overall fighting strength, and not necessarily preserve that of the fortress garrison. The problem was that the Germans could offer no key strategic point of such importance that it would draw the Soviets in and force a bloody showdown, such as at Stalingrad. Since most of the designated "fortified places" were never particularly formidable or threatening, the Soviets always had the option of simply bypassing them and reducing the pockets at a later time. The German forces trapped there, though, were lost for any future defensive operations, thus further aggravating the force imbalance. In the new era of mechanization, especially in the wide open spaces of the east, holding key transportation junctions had lost some of its earlier value, as most could simply be bypassed without seriously jeopardizing the flow of supplies. The assumption that these festen Plätze would tie down large numbers of Soviet troops seldom proved true; even when they did force the enemy to attack them, they usually employed second-rate follow-up troops while the frontline units continued on. Any benefit to holding the fortresses thus tended to be outweighed by the loss of the units defending them.[54]

Still, probably too much has been made of these "fortified places" as the key reason why Germany failed to hold the Red Army at bay. In early 1944 the strategy was primarily applied in four instances in Ukraine – Vitebsk, Cherkassy, Kovel, and Kamenets-Podolsky – where some enemy forces had been tied down and no great disaster resulted. In the end, these proved to be merely tactical defeats, for, ironically, Hitler did allow strategic withdrawals. In view of the criticism of this concept, it is well to remember that it was applied to great effect at Monte Cassino, where the Italian topography and the nature of Italian villages, with their thick stone walls and labyrinthine streets, greatly aided the defender in stalling the Allied advance. A similar policy of festen Plätze would also be successful when used in Brittany and the Channel ports after the Normandy breakout. By denying the Allies the ports they desperately needed for logistic reasons, it aggravated supply difficulties and contributed to the slowing momentum of their autumn advance.[55]

Any strategy, of course, requires both a coherent concept and the resources by which to carry it out. Hitler's "wave-breaker" idea had a logic to it but faltered for lack of the means by which to make it successful. The only alternative, a tactical mobile defense, suffered from a similar problem. Since the Wehrmacht no longer had the strength for major operations or counterattacks, so the idea went, combined arms battle groups could be formed that maximized remaining mobility in order to blunt Soviet attacks, then withdraw at the last moment to defensive positions. By taking advantage of the firepower afforded by new arms such as the MG 42 machine gun, the Panzerfaust anti-tank weapon, and the StG-44 Sturmgewehr assault rife, as well as the Panthers and Tigers – now overcoming their initial problems – in combination with the formidable assault guns and tank destroyers, the enemy could be harassed and worn down. While successful enough to dissuade the Soviets from attempting ambitious offensives, at least until the summer of 1944, this scheme was really not much more feasible than its alternative, namely, Hitler's halt policy. Given enemy aerial, mobility, and firepower superiority, it simply left exposed German forces vulnerable to relentless pressure. Germany's real dilemma was its fundamental weakness: any defensive strategy in the east was problematical, since the Soviets could choose to launch attacks anywhere they desired. Although Hitler's "halt doctrine" could offer little more than to delay the inevitable, it was probably no worse than Manstein's notion of maneuver, which had been unable to deliver the time necessary to allow Germany to marshal its resources for a decisive effort in the west or the victories from which to negotiate a separate peace. In any case, the key decision about the future of the war would come in the west; if the Allied invasion succeeded, then Germany had no further cards to play.[56]

Any realistic possibility of a military or political solution, then, finally dissolved as a result of the third factor: the Germans proved unable to defeat the Allied landings in Normandy. Even though an invasion had been expected in the spring, the long stretch of good weather in May without any Allied action, combined with bad weather in early June, induced a bit of complacency. Although German intelligence had picked up indications of the possibility of an imminent landing, they were largely discounted as false alarms, interpreted incorrectly or, according to Adjutant Below, not even reported to OKW or General Friedrich Dollmann, commander of 7th Army guarding the Normandy area. On the eve of the invasion, Rommel had returned home to Swabia to celebrate his wife's birthday – in retrospect an extraordinary lapse of command responsibility – while other senior generals had taken leave or organized war-games exercises. Reports of naval movements and paratroop landings in Normandy in the early morning hours of 6 June produced a flurry of activity – at 4:45 a.m. Rundstedt took the precaution of putting two divisions of the OKW reserve, the 12th SS Panzer and the Panzer Lehr, on standby – but in the absence of any confirmed invasion, the general attitude at OB West was that, although the Allies might be attempting a large-scale operation of some sort, the forces on the scene could manage without any outside assistance. When, shortly thereafter, full-scale landings began, the Allies had largely managed to achieve tactical surprise. Despite successful landings at Gold, Juno, Sword, and Utah beaches, though, the fierce German resistance at Omaha – and the apparent failure of the American landing there – initially persuaded both OB West and 7th Army staff that there were good prospects for driving other enemy forces back into the sea.[57]

This confusion continued until early afternoon; only then did Allied success become apparent. The delay in determining what was actually happening has led to the exaggerated claim that the fear of waking a sleeping Führer caused the invasion to succeed. While Hitler early on had correctly predicted a landing at Normandy, he and others in the high command tended to believe that this would be a diversion, with the real invasion – designed to trap the German forces that had rushed west into Normandy – coming further east in the Calais area. In effect, they mistakenly credited Allied

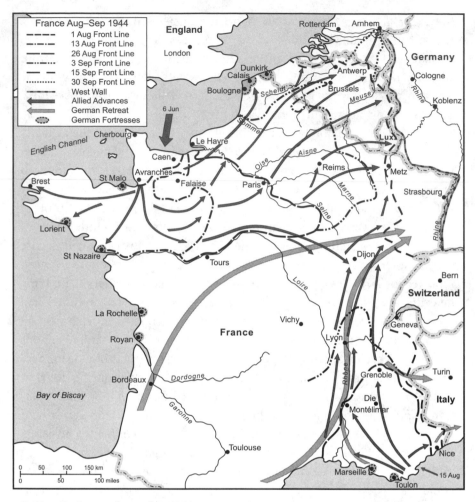

8. France, August–September 1944

planners with the same boldness as they themselves had possessed in 1940.
Given Allied deception measures, the uncertain information from Normandy,
and the reports of scattered enemy paratroop drops, though, Hitler was not
alone in believing that this was, indeed, a decoy. Rundstedt was decidedly
uncertain in earlier telegrams about whether this was merely a diversionary
attack, while Jodl opposed moving armored units toward Normandy. Both
Rundstedt and Rommel, who had returned by mid-afternoon, had doubts
that this was the main landing, seemingly more concerned with defense
preparations at Calais than Normandy. Rommel even declined to bring in
reinforcements from northern Brittany, a relatively short march away.[58]

Only at the midday briefing – where, according to Speer, Hitler still
expressed skepticism that this was the main attack – did he agree to

Rundstedt's belated request to release two Panzer divisions from OKW reserve to the beachhead. Since they were between fifty and a hundred miles away, however, their deployment would have to wait until that evening, for Allied air dominance made any movement by daylight virtually impossible. Thus, they could not play any role until the next day, a delay that would prove crucial. The uncertainty about Allied intentions, the failure of Rundstedt to send a timely situation report, and the reality of enemy air power, then, rather than Hitler's unusual sleep patterns – although, in truth, his aides were reluctant to wake him with possibly mistaken information – played the decisive role in the initially hesitant German response. As a consequence, the only serious counterattack on the first day was the mid-afternoon thrust by the 21st Panzer Division, which managed to split British and Canadian forces and reach the sea. Before it could exploit its success, though, reports of further airborne landings to its rear forced the division's retreat. Any further damage the 21st Panzer Division might have done remains debatable, since it had already lost two-thirds of its tanks and would now be fully exposed to Allied naval fire.[59]

Still, despite their successful landings, the Allies had not managed to achieve their day's objectives, let alone force a breakout. Hitler, in fact, seemed greatly relieved. "The Führer is in extraordinarily high spirits," Goebbels recorded. "The invasion took place exactly at the spot that we had expected." Although the propaganda minister conceded his concern that the Allies had succeeded in getting armored forces ashore, he nonetheless took heart from the fact that "two first-class Panzer units, 100 miles distant, were on the march." Hitler, too, remained "convinced that the enemy units that had landed would be evicted and above all the paratroops destroyed ... The Führer is absolutely certain and shows not the slightest signs of weakness." His adjutant Below, observing the scene at the Berghof and aware of the absolute enemy air superiority, could not comprehend this supreme confidence in the ability of the Panzer forces to get to Normandy intact and smash Allied troops. As if he was seeing his vision materialize, though, Hitler told Goebbels, "If we repel the invasion, then the ... war will be completely transformed. The Führer reckons for certain with this. He has few worries this couldn't succeed."[60]

The fact that it could succeed, however, did not mean it would. The initial delay in reacting meant that Rommel's idea of destroying the invaders on the beaches was already as good as dead. In the first days after the landing, not only did the Allies breach the Atlantic Wall fortifications but the Germans proved unable – in the absence of any aerial cover, insufficient fuel supplies, and the difficulty of moving forces – to assemble the armor concentrations necessary to defeat the enemy. As Roosevelt had pointed out in September 1943, Hitler's "Fortress Europe" had a decisive flaw: it had no roof. For weeks before the invasion Allied heavy bombers had systematically destroyed bridges and railway lines leading to Normandy, while the ubiquitous P-47 and P-51 fighter-bombers hindered any movement at a tactical level. German reinforcements thus dribbled in only in piecemeal fashion. Although these were enough to block British attempts at a breakout around Caen, they were insufficient to provide any decisive edge. The same proved true of Hitler's hopes in German technological superiority. Michael Wittmann's famed exploit with his Tiger tanks at Villers-Bocage on 13 June, where, in fifteen minutes – in "one of the most devastating ambushes in British military history" – his unit destroyed some fourteen tanks, fifteen armored personnel carriers, and two anti-tank guns of the British 7th Armored Division, seemed to validate Hitler's faith in the Tiger's capabilities. This action, greatly exploited by Goebbels's propaganda machine, stymied the British attempt at a breakout, while to the west, in the bocage country, Panthers, Tigers, and assault guns combined to slow the American advance to a bloody crawl. Just as Hitler had predicted, these deadly weapons proved especially effective in defensive warfare. Any hope that they could also lead an immediate, successful counterattack, though, was doused by the overwhelming firepower of Allied artillery, aircraft, and naval vessels. Significantly, Wittmann achieved his feat during a rare period of absent Allied fighter planes; the next day, the 3rd Company of his unit was torn to bits by a fighter-bomber attack.[61]

As a result of the inconsequential nature of the first week's fighting, both sides were forced to adapt. The Allies now largely discounted any notion of a quick British breakout to the east and instead settled on a slow, grinding battle of attrition, something that played to their material strength. Abandoning the original plan, British and Canadian forces would tie down the largest number of Panzer divisions, while the Americans to the west first cut off the Cotentin peninsula, took the key port of Cherbourg, then turned south into the bocage country to force a breakout in the western sector of the beachhead. For their part, the Germans combined bits of both of their contested strategies: fight on the beach but also organize a large counterattack. Neither worked because of Allied air and naval supremacy. The attempt to shift large numbers of troops and equipment into the Normandy area foundered because of Allied air dominance. Able to move safely only at night, the Germans found their ability to speedily build up their forces was limited. In addition, the earlier destruction of the French railway network and bridges meant that armored units, in particular, often had to take a long, circuitous route to their destination. Even then, many had to de-train sixty to hundred miles from the front and finish the march by road, which cost precious time and fuel, two commodities that were running in short supply for the Germans. Moreover, as the Panzer divisions trickled to the front, most arrived in disarray, with many of their constituent formations scattered or absent, missing equipment and spare parts, and lacking fuel. Any hope of using armor to crush the Allied bridgehead thus evaporated, as they were forced simply to plug the many holes in the defense line. Although the Germans eventually assembled some 1,200 to 1,300 tanks, these could never be concentrated for one great blow. Indeed, despite later complaints of German commanders, the most significant impact of Anglo-American aerial superiority was probably not its direct impact on the battlefield – the Wehrmacht quickly learned to disperse its troops into smaller battle groups and take advantage of the natural terrain and thick Norman stone farm houses for shelter against aircraft and naval bombardment – but the way in which it disrupted reinforcements, supplies, and communications.[62]

By 13 June, then, just a week after the landings, Rommel had abandoned the effort to drive the Allies back into the sea, focusing now on containing them until the second option, a powerful counterattack, could be organized. This, and the imminent launch of the long-awaited V-1 attacks on London, prompted Hitler, accompanied by Keitel and Jodl, on 16 June to fly for the last time to France – to the old Führer headquarters at Margival, north of Soisson – to discuss the situation with Rundstedt and Rommel and to bolster their flagging morale. Hitler was confident that the V-1, an early jet-powered cruise missile, if launched in mass quantities against the British capital, would have a devastating effect, inducing mass panic and disrupting the Allied war effort. Indeed, the reaction to the first small-scale launch on 12 June seemed to confirm his expectations. Although the Atlantic Wall had been breached, Hitler also had hopes that the other part of his fortress strategy, clinging to key ports needed by the Allies for supply purposes, would provide the time necessary for a counterattack.

On 17 June, though, in a frosty atmosphere, a pale and tired Hitler listened as Rundstedt reported on developments and concluded that the Allies could no longer be expelled from France. Rommel, too, emphasized the hopelessness of the struggle, given the massive material superiority of the Allies. He even broached the idea of a withdrawal to central France in order to shorten supply lines. Failing that, he insisted on a pull-back out of range of Allied naval artillery, where German armor could then pounce on the flanks of the advancing enemy, a notion, given Allied air supremacy,

Rommel must have known was faintly ridiculous. Hitler's reaction was predictable: seeing his whole strategy, not just for Normandy but for the larger war, threatened, he angrily retorted that he had not come to France to discuss retreats. When he mentioned the expected impact of the V-1, a weapon he thought would turn the tide of the war, both field marshals perked up, asking that it be employed against the Allied beachhead, only to be told that the weapon was not accurate enough for that. Hitler then promised that they would soon have jet fighters to regain control of the skies, even though he knew these had just gone into production. Rommel, again lapsing into despair, painted a gloomy picture of German prospects, concluding that a political solution to the war needed to be found. At that, Hitler retorted sharply, "Pay attention to your invasion front, not to the continuation of the war." Before flying back to the Berghof, he again ordered Rundstedt and Rommel to hold the line in preparation for a major counterattack, for which he promised to transfer the 2nd SS Panzer Corps (9th and 10th SS Panzer) to Normandy.[63]

That night, back at the Berghof, Hitler in disgust told his entourage that Rommel had lost his nerve. "Only optimists," he asserted, "can pull off anything today." The next day, American troops reached the west coast of the Cotentin peninsula, effectively isolating Cherbourg. Even though it had been designated a fortified place, the German commander, Lieutenant-General Karl Wilhelm von Schlieben – placed there personally by Hitler on 21 June with orders to hold out at all cost – surrendered the city on 27 June after putting up little opposition, an action that enraged the Führer. To him, Schlieben and other aristocratic officers like him were all "bastards." Although it took over a month to repair the damage, the Allies could now supply their troops for the breakout. Any prospect of the Allies being pushed back into the sea had now vanished, and with it, Hitler's hopes of regaining the initiative by defeating the invasion. About the only thing left was the effort at a counterattack that might at least delay or stalemate the Allied advance, but even here problems mounted. As Goebbels noted on 18 June, "the total superiority of the enemy in the air" had blocked all efforts at organizing the forces necessary for a major offensive. At a meeting at the Berghof on 21 June, the propaganda minister grew even more troubled by gloomy reports from Speer and Schmundt on the economic situation. Only the continued high hopes in the V-1 and soon to be deployed V-2 (early ballistic missile) offered any glimmer of a way out – that, and the Führer's hint that he might be willing to discuss the prospect of a separate peace with Stalin.[64]

The same day that Goebbels wrote this, though, the strategic situation altered conclusively in favor of Germany's enemies. Three years to the day after the launch of Barbarossa – a date Hitler had predicted Stalin could not resist, although, in truth, this was more coincidence than planned – the Soviets launched their largest offensive of the war, Operation Bagration. As Hitler also understood, any German hope of continuing to stymie the Allied advance in the west depended on Soviet actions in the east. The Soviet attack, the location of which caught the Germans by surprise, laid bare the last illusions of being able to manage the situation. When fighting had halted in May, Soviet forces had retaken most of Ukraine and, south of the Pripet Marshes, advanced far to the west, to within 150 miles of Warsaw. To the north, however, Army Group Center still occupied most of Belarus, including a bridgehead east of the Dnieper. Hitler was determined to hold this "Belorussian balcony" for defensive purposes, as well as for what it

9. The Eastern Front, April 1944–February 1945

represented: a threat in the rear of any Soviet thrust from the south and possible springboard for a future German counteroffensive. He also placed great faith in a string of "fortified places", including cities such as Vitebsk, Orsha, Mogilev, and Bobruisk, which, he thought, would deny the enemy key transportation and communication junctions, tie down considerable forces, and slow the momentum of any attack. Hitler, once again, was applying what he thought were Stalin's successful policies of the summers of 1941 and 1942. With regard to the former, he was perhaps overly impressed with Soviet actions in July–August 1941. While grasping how seriously the pocket battles had disrupted German plans, he failed to appreciate how destructive they had been of Soviet manpower and equipment. Similarly, in the summer of 1942, Stalin had stubbornly held on to bridgeheads across the Don that enabled his counterstrike at Stalingrad. Hitler thought it possible to pull off a similar feat that would restore the initiative to Germany, even though he lacked the manpower reserves necessary to assemble a counterattack. Convinced that the prolonged, costly Soviet winter offensive in Ukraine had finally bled the Red Army white, something that many of his Eastern Front generals believed as well, Hitler hoped to blunt the expected enemy offensive, wear down Soviet forces at the festen Plätze, then launch the game-changing German response.[65]

Despite the loss of some fortress troops at Kovel, Tarnopol, and Kamenets-Podolsky in March and April, the slowing of enemy momentum seemed to confirm Hitler's formula, reinforcing his determination not to yield. He simply ignored the fact that the Soviet offensive had ground to a halt because it ran out of steam, and not because of the "fortified places" doctrine. Given the extreme shortages of manpower and building materials, there existed no hope of ever actually making the numerous cities he designated as strongpoints into real obstacles, nor could they be relieved if besieged by the enemy. All his order did was to ensure that large numbers of men would be trapped in these indefensible "self-selected" encirclements. In a clear lose-lose situation, not only would the "fortified places" prove too weak to hinder Soviet momentum, but the overstretched German defense would be denied use of those forces trapped in static positions to plug the holes in the front created by the Soviet attack. In effect, the commanders and troops in a fortified place were like the crew of a warship: they were to fight to the last and all hands would go down with the ship. Hitler simply failed to realize, or refused to admit, that the German situation in the summer of 1944 was different from earlier examples. The Soviets had crushing superiority in men, armor, artillery, and aircraft, as well as the mobility to use this massive firepower to its utmost. In the event, the Red

Army's high level of mechanization – made possible to a great extent by American Lend-Lease supply of trucks and other vehicles – rendered these "fortified places" irrelevant, for the Soviets simply bypassed them on their sweep westward. The only forces they tied down were second-rate follow-up units; the crack Soviet combat divisions simply continued on their way. Only in the west, in holding on to the Channel ports, did the concept work to an extent, since it did impede the flow of supplies and thus helped slow Allied momentum.[66]

In any case, even if Hitler had allowed a more flexible defense, this would not likely have altered the overall result, although more German troops might have escaped the disaster. Even though Army Group Center still seemed formidable in terms of manpower, much of its strength consisted of sub-par Luftwaffe field units, security divisions, and Hungarian units, many of whom were behind the lines engaged in anti-partisan warfare. Only about 166,000 of their roughly 486,000-man strength (on paper) could be considered frontline combat troops, and they faced some 1.25 million Red Army soldiers. Adding to the imbalance, Army Group Center had lost virtually all of its tanks and aircraft to other fronts. When the offensive began, it had only one tank division (20th Panzer) for its entire sector, and a mere 118 battle tanks and 377 assault guns, against Soviet totals of 2,715 and 1,355 respectively, an astonishing 12:1 disadvantage. And this was only for the first phase of the offensive; for the second phase the Red Army had a further combined 1,748 armored fighting vehicles. Overall, it has been estimated that German forces in the "Belorussian balcony" were outnumbered four to one in men, nine to one in artillery, ten to one in aircraft, and twenty three to one in tanks.[67]

Moreover, the Germans lacked the mobility necessary to conduct a flexible defense. With only one Panzer division in reserve, and largely reliant on horse-drawn transport, Army Group Center more nearly resembled the German army of the First World War than a modern, mechanized force. To compensate for its lack of troops, for example, it had developed a defensive doctrine that stressed trenches, strongpoints, anti-tank traps and obstacles, artillery, and effective use of anti-tank weapons and tank destroyers in order to fight a delaying action and wear down enemy forces, much as the Soviets had done at Kursk. This strategy also relied on immediate local counterattacks at the base of the enemy breakthrough to blunt any momentum, but because of its lack of mobility the Ostheer could neither quickly pinch off an enemy penetration nor withdraw intact from defensive positions at the last minute. The Soviets had also caught on to a key German defensive tactic, itself perfected in the earlier war, which had enabled Army

Group Center to effectively defend itself in the winter. It had prepared defenses so that German forces, when faced with an attack, could withdraw to rear positions, shelter in bunkers during an artillery barrage – thus causing the enemy shells to hit largely empty trenches – then, when the firing stopped, rush back to the front lines to halt the attack. Now, Soviet artillery would shell intensively for a bit, then stop; when the Germans rushed forward, the bombardment would begin again, catching the defenders in the open. Lacking air power or reserves, Army Group Center had been so reduced in mobility that, once the Soviet offensive began, its troops either had to disengage early in order to salvage artillery and equipment or fight in place and be destroyed.[68]

Given the serious German weaknesses and lack of mobility, the key to defending successfully against any enemy attack was to identify the Soviet Schwerpunkt correctly. Since Army Group Center lacked the mobility and operational reserve to pinch off a Soviet breakthrough and prevent it from turning into a catastrophe – and could not count on reinforcements from the west – all depended on blunting the Soviet attack at the outset. In turn, any chance for a successful static defense hinged on identifying correctly the focal point of the enemy offensive and preparing adequate positions to counter it. This, though, relied on effective intelligence work, never a German strength. Although it had improved somewhat, too often the information gathered by the Germans was inaccurate, irrelevant, or purposely misleading. They expected the attack farther south, for example, where an enemy breakthrough at Kovel, at the southwestern edge of the Pripet, would allow them two great opportunities. Red Army forces could be turned southwest, with the goal of striking deep into Hungary and Romania, knocking these German allies out of the war, and encircling and destroying Army Groups North and South Ukraine. Or they could strike to the northwest through Warsaw and on to Danzig, thus bagging both Army Groups Center and North in a giant pocket. At one stroke, the heart of the German position in the east would be ripped apart, and the way to Berlin left completely open. In a single action, OKH feared, the Soviets would strike the death blow to the German war effort.[69]

Although unsure where the enemy would strike, Kovel seemed the key, so the bulk of German Panzer forces were concentrated there, under the command of Field Marshal Model (Army Group North Ukraine), a fact that seriously weakened Army Group Center. Ironically, though, just as OKH assumed that the Soviets would, once again, go for broke, Stalin turned cautious. Instead of a gamble that might invite a devastating German counterattack, he now settled for a sure thing: the Red Army would launch a series of sequential operations from north to south designed to swamp the strapped Ostheer. The main force would be concentrated against Army Group Center with the intention of encircling and destroying it in a giant pocket east of Minsk. If successful, the last bits of occupied Soviet territory would be regained and the Red Army would be well into Poland on the most direct route to Berlin. Since the first phase of the operation involved cutting off and destroying the German anchors at Vitebsk and Bobruisk – on either side of the great salient – and only then driving to the west, the offensive begun on 22 June developed relatively slowly. Initially, then, the Germans thought the situation under control, but on 24 June Konstantin Rokossovky's forces burst out of the Pripet Marshes, which the Germans thought impenetrable, north of Kovel, a flanking movement that quickly took them far into the German rear and threatened the destruction of the entire army group. Over the next few days enemy forces also drove through breaches in German defenses around Vitebsk, Orsha, Mogilev, and Bobruisk. Since these had all been declared festen Plätze, Hitler refused to authorize a full withdrawal, although, in a transparent effort at sparing himself total humiliation at the failure of his "fortified places" strategy, he issued vague and contradictory instructions that commanders on the spot eventually interpreted as permission to retreat, but not before much of their forces had been destroyed. Nor did Ernst Busch, the hapless commander of Army Group Center, respond with any initiative, repeatedly asking his chief of staff, "What shall I do?" By the time Busch, not merely obsequious but a Nazi loyalist, gathered the nerve to confront Hitler and request a withdrawal – flying to Berchtesgaden on 26 June – the Führer merely told him to hold Orsha and Mogilev, an order that had long been outrun by events.[70]

By 28 June, even Hitler seemed to realize the enormity of the catastrophe – that this was not like December 1941 and another halt order could not stem the Red tide – sacking Busch and replacing him with his favorite fireman, Model. This action, though, came too late, for the great majority of units the Germans would lose in Operation Bagration had already been destroyed. Model could do little immediately to stop the headlong Soviet rush westward. Minsk fell on 3 July, even as enemy forces raced on to Vilnius, seizing the Lithuanian capital on 8 July. The entire front seemed in flux, on the verge of collapse. As General Johannes Friessner, briefly the commander of Army Group North, told Hitler bluntly at the Wolfsschanze on 14 July, "One can hardly speak of a coherent battle line, such as I see here on your map." By the time the Germans slowed Soviet momentum in mid-July, the Red Army had destroyed Army Group Center – some 30 divisions and 300,000 men, a disaster worse than Stalingrad – and had driven

200 miles to the west. As they neared Warsaw in late July, the momentum of their great offensive now mostly spent, Model managed to pull off yet another minor miracle, launching a local counterattack that threw the Soviets back and finally halted their offensive. This, however, could not disguise the reality of the greatest German defeat of the war, with only the Somme in 1916 exacting a greater toll in German military history. The Germans had lost almost 400,000 men in roughly six weeks, and now possessed no reserves with which to contest a renewed Soviet offensive; only the fact that the enemy was exhausted allowed the Ostheer to stabilize the front yet again. The debacle of Army Group Center raised once more the threat of Seydlitz's League of German Officers, which had begun to bombard Landsers with flyers and loudspeaker propaganda. Goebbels conceded in early August that German soldiers "did not react to Bolshevik appeals, but when German generals addressed them . . . and told them the situation had become hopeless, that doesn't fail to make an impression." Even Hitler was forced to admit, "one could not have imagined a greater crisis."[71]

By the end of July, Hitler had also survived his most serious personal challenge, one that seemed to prove the danger emanating from the officer corps and raised the specter of a November 1918 in reverse. On 20 July military conspirators around Henning von Tresckow and Claus von Stauffenberg made a determined attempt to assassinate the Führer. Since the conspirators realized that they represented only a small percentage of the officer corps, and that the overwhelming majority of senior generals were either opposed or unwilling to commit to killing Hitler, they sought to trick the army into playing an unwitting role in overthrowing the Nazi regime. There already existed a plan, Operation Valkyrie, in which the Replacement Army would act in the event of a large-scale internal uprising or attempted coup. After assassinating Hitler, the conspirators hoped to make it look like an internal action of elements within the regime – most likely, the SS – then activate Valkyrie with the purported goal of restoring order. Top SS and Gestapo officials would be arrested, while the conspirators would install General Beck as the new head of an interim regime. The goal then was to initiate peace talks with the Anglo-Americans in order to end the war in the west, although the Germans expected to continue fighting the Soviets.[72]

This all failed, of course, with the unsuccessful attempt on Hitler's life, but even in the event of his death it was unlikely to have succeeded since it was doubtful that the army, either officers or men, would have supported this putsch. Nor would the Allies – who had already made it clear that they demanded an unconditional surrender and, in any case, were conscious of the extent to which the army had supported Hitler – have been inclined to negotiate. The most likely scenario in the event that the coup had succeeded would have been a (short-lived) civil war. Paradoxically, perhaps the most important consequence of the assassination attempt on Hitler, other than his survival, was that it, at least temporarily, restored some of his tarnished image as Führer and Feldherr and eroded much of what remaining influence the army had on him. Even Goebbels had begun to have doubts about Hitler as Feldherr, but the very act of survival seemed to verify his other-worldliness, while the genuine outrage at what was seen as a cowardly act – and the resulting outpouring of sympathy – distracted attention from his military failures. Moreover, the obvious betrayal by parts of the officer elite allowed him an easily understood excuse for these military setbacks: he had been sabotaged in all of his plans by his generals. After all, the people "that stood behind the Putsch," he told the Romanian leader Antonescu on 5 August, were the very same that "always wanted to withdraw the troops, allegedly to win more operational possibilities." That same day he addressed his Gauleiters at the Wolfsschanze – his most faithful followers now had to be checked for weapons – and demanded "loyalty, there is no loyal, more loyal, most loyal – there is only loyalty." Still, his physical appearance – he appeared, thought one, "old and shaky" and spoke in subdued tones – must have given even his most devoted followers pause. The stab in the back of November 1918, this time by traitorous generals, would not be repeated, he vowed; they would be rooted out and made to pay. Then, with the treacherous elements eliminated, ran the promise, things would be different.[73]

This, in the event, proved mere wishful thinking, as Soviet actions had fundamentally altered German calculations in the west as well. The anticipated counteroffensive at the junction of the British and American sectors had constantly been postponed by a chain of spiraling problems. The Panzer divisions took longer to arrive than expected, then they suffered from shortages of fuel, munitions, and supplies. Finally, the launch of Operation Bagration meant that German forces in the west could no longer count on receiving any reinforcements from the Eastern Front. They were now on their own and forced to rely on what they had available elsewhere in occupied France. The original intention of using the Panzer formations not merely in defense, but as a concentrated mobile force that would crush the beachhead, was also undone by Allied actions on the ground. When British forces on 29 June threatened a breakthrough west of Caen, 2nd SS Panzer Corps was forced to plug the hole, at high cost and for little gain. Instead of using it in a major attack to destroy the assembled enemy forces, as originally advocated by Geyr and Rundstedt, the tactical defensive counter-thrust at Caen was the only German attack at corps level during June and July. As with Rommel's concept, Allied air and firepower supremacy rendered Geyr's idea of striking a devastating "backhand" blow inoperable. Whether closer to the beach or in the hinterland, Allied might was simply too overwhelming to allow concentrated offensive action. Without any air cover, and thus effectively stripped of their mobility, the Germans discovered, to their great distress, that all their operational skills counted for little against the mass weight of Allied firepower. In the end, then, the "Panzer controversy" amounted to no more than an academic debate. Ironically, it had been Rundstedt, the advocate of maneuver and the "backhand" blow, who had first insisted on the priority of defending the eastern sector of the beachhead against British attacks, persuading Hitler on 24 June not to order an assault against the Americans on the Cotentin peninsula. By the end of the month, Rundstedt, Rommel, and Geyr were urging a withdrawal and a flexible defense, but as Jodl told his OKW staff on 3 July, the only course left was to "nail down the front where it now stands." Hitler opted for what he perhaps thought the lesser of two evils: continued exposure to Allied naval shelling, especially around Caen, rather than risk operating in the open in view of total enemy air superiority.[74]

By the end of June, then, it was clear to all that a second front had been established and that, despite the hopes of the spring, the German situation had dramatically worsened. The new wonder weapons were as yet having little impact, while in the east Army Group Center had disintegrated. Even a staunch Nazi and Hitler supporter such as Sepp Dietrich, commander of the 1st SS Panzer Corps, wondered whether the Führer had not given German forces an impossible task and should therefore seek a political solution out of the dead end. Hitler, though, reacted to the crisis in a now typical fashion: he blamed others and fired top generals. Rundstedt went, not entirely incorrectly, as too old and inflexible, while Geyr was deemed insufficiently rigorous, although his real sin was his willingness, as a representative of the old elite Hitler despised, to speak openly of painful realities. While the naming on 3 July of Field Marshal Kluge as new OB West or General Heinrich Eberbach as head of Panzer Army West could not have been surprising – both were competent, loyal, had Eastern Front experience, and were deemed steadfast – the new commander of 7th Army, SS General Paul Hausser, selected as a result of Hitler's personal intervention, was a clear signal of his dissatisfaction with the army. Rommel, despite his overt pessimism, was left in place, but only because his sacking would have been seen by the German public as an admission of defeat.[75]

For all their desire to clean things up and stiffen the resolve of German troops, all three newcomers quickly discovered that the crisis in the west had little to do with the alleged lethargy and defeatism of their predecessors. On 15 July, Rommel sent Hitler a stark warning, to which none of the new commanders could take exception. "The troops have fought heroically everywhere," he affirmed, "but the unequal battle is nearing its end." He then invited the Führer to draw the appropriate conclusions. But what did that mean in reality? Hitler almost surely realized that the attempt to defeat the invasion had failed, and with it his last potential strategic option. But he also knew that the Western Allies were not willing to negotiate a separate peace. Without stepping down himself, what other alternative to fighting on was there? After all, as he indicated, reasonably enough, to Field Marshal von Richthofen shortly after the assassination attempt, he "saw no prospect of obtaining an acceptable peace for Germany." Prodding Hitler to come to the appropriate conclusion, therefore, likely had unintended consequences. While Rommel clearly hoped the Führer would do the right thing for Germany and seek a political solution, Hitler likely understood his message as yet another reason to hold on, since his regime would collapse in either scenario.[76]

By this time, the Germans had given up any thought of launching a grand offensive and hoped merely to contain the Allied bridgehead. Endless pounding by enemy artillery and air bombardments, as well as high losses suffered by officers and NCOs had, by the end of July, sapped morale. Even the numerous SS units had begun to feel the strain. Despite their skill and stubborn defense, German forces were being ground down by relentless attrition. At the end of July, in perhaps the most telling statistic, Army Group B reported 116,863 men killed, wounded, or missing since the beginning of the invasion, but only 10,000 replacements. Hitler's musings on 31 July thus had a rather surreal quality to them. In a long, rambling discourse just eleven days after the attempt on his life, which was much on his mind, the Führer interspersed moments of clarity and lucidity with bitter denunciations of the plotters. In reviewing the strategic situation in the east, Hitler's assessment seemed realistic enough. "If the area that we are occupying now (in the east) can be held," he noted of the newly stabilized front, "then that is an area that we can still live in, and we don't have these huge communication zones," an observation with which his generals certainly would have agreed.[77]

"In the west," Hitler continued, "there is actually one very decisive question. If we lose France . . . ," he stressed, clearly with the technologically advanced Type 21 submarines in mind:

we will lose our point of departure for the submarine war . . . But it's also clear that an operation in France – and I believe we must be fully aware of this at all times – is totally impossible in a so-called open field of battle under today's circumstances . . . We can move . . . only in a limited manner . . . [not only] because we don't possess air superiority, but because we can't move the troops themselves: the units are not suited for mobile battle . . . [Our] total strength in France can't be measured by the number of divisions . . . but really by the limited number of units that are actually able to move. That's only a very small fraction. If the territory weren't that important . . . [we would] clear the coast without hesitation and lead the mobile forces immediately back into a line which . . . we would defend unyieldingly. But one thing is already evident now . . . [Our] forces are hardly enough to defend the narrow front . . . [so] we can see the complete hopelessness of holding such [a longer rear] line with the forces that are available to us . . . A change in France could only happen if we managed – even for a certain time – to establish superiority in the air.

This latter, he understood, depended on the large-scale introduction of the new jet-fighter aircraft, something he also admitted would take "many weeks." Hitler emphasized as well the importance of maintaining and safeguarding Hungary as the last remaining source of food and key raw materials, including oil, available to Germany; for good measure, he even dipped into the larger strategic realm by stressing Turkey's discomfort with Soviet advances toward the Balkans. In sum, Hitler's recitation of the situation confronting Germany was on the mark. Although not averse to a pull-back to a more defensible line, he clearly thought neither the Seine nor other unprepared lines could be held with the forces available, nor were they mobile enough to permit such a movement in the first place. What is breathtaking in all of this is not the often astonishing lucidity of his observations, but the fact that, with respect to the west, they were now completely outdated, for the American breakout that sealed the fate of German defense efforts in Normandy had already been launched six days earlier.[78]

Until now, and despite the heavy losses of officers, which resulted in a certain "de-professionalization" of the Wehrmacht, the Germans had mounted a stubborn and amazingly effective defense in the face of Allied superiority. Not only had so they contained enemy forces in a narrow area of Normandy, but in doing so they had also suffered fewer casualties than their adversary. Nonetheless, Rommel had accurately assessed the situation. Without significant reinforcements of men and equipment, the unequal struggle would soon be at an end. The manpower situation – the Germans fielded about 400,000 troops against 1.5 million for the Allies – verged on the catastrophic, while the Anglo-Americans had an overwhelming superiority in aircraft and tanks. By the end of July the Germans could muster barely 1,000 aircraft to their enemy's 11,000, and could manage only 300 to 350 sorties a day against roughly 4,000. Further, the Allies had assembled almost 3,800 tanks against a German total of 1,200 to 1,300. The sheer impact of this weight of materiel was finally brought to bear on 25 July, when, after earlier failed attempts by General Montgomery to force a breakout around Caen, General Bradley launched Operation Cobra in the vicinity of Saint-Lô, where the Germans could muster only two Panzer divisions and 190 tanks in opposition. British and Canadian efforts had paid off, in that the bulk of German armor faced them in the east. Preceded by a gigantic aerial bombardment – some 1,500 heavy bombers carpet-bombed the Panzer Lehr division, which lay astride the intended route of attack – the Americans at last bulldozed their way out of the bocage. As General Fritz Bayerlein, commander of Panzer Lehr, later recalled, "After an hour I had no communication with anybody . . . By noon, nothing was visible but smoke and dust. My frontlines looked like the face of the moon and at least seventy percent of my troops were knocked out – dead, wounded, crazed, or numbed." Although the cratering produced by the bombing initially slowed the Americans, the net effect was to destroy German defenses – the Landsers had, after all, been relatively safe when entrenched – while Allied air power also denied them the ability to assemble, maneuver, or counterattack. The morale of the German defenders now largely cracked; after all the failed promises and supply problems, the feeling of helplessness against the aerial onslaught was more than most could stand.[79]

General Patton's newly activated American 3rd Army moved quickly through the breach created, racing through Coutance and seizing Avranches, at the base of the Gulf of St Malo, by 31 July, the same day Hitler held forth on the larger strategic situation. The next day, American troops burst west into Brittany, with hopes of seizing key ports, while other units advanced south towards the Loire and east towards the Seine. Even as General Eisenhower began to conceive a broad envelopment of German troops against the Seine, Patton's rapid advance revealed risks that might be exploited. In advancing through a narrow bottleneck at Avranches, he had left himself vulnerable to a counterattack that, if successful, would cut off supplies to his forces to the south and east, thus leaving them exposed to destruction. As early as 2 August, in fact, Hitler had spied just this possibility and insisted on a counterattack at Mortain, with the intention of breaking through to the coast and cutting the vital American supply arteries. By now, Hitler's strategy of "hold in the east, strike in the west" had clearly failed, and with it his last realistic chance of significantly altering the direction of the war. The counterattack at Mortain thus has to be seen as a desperate effort to salvage something at least in the west, if only to deal the Americans a blow and blunt the momentum of the Allied advance across France. It again show-cased Hitler's eye for enemy weakness, but it also illustrated the extent to which he was now operating in a strategic and operational vacuum, with little regard for the overall context. The proposed counterattack lay more in the realm of a theoretical map study than any realistic assessment of the true balance of forces. There existed little chance that this counter-stroke could succeed; even if it did manage to reach the coast, any success would only be temporary, given the realities of insufficient German force by which to inflict any further damage and overwhelming Allied aerial, manpower, and fire-power dominance. The only practical impact would be like that of the Soviets at Izyum in May 1942: to simply put your head in the noose and invite your opponent to snap it tight.[80]

Despite this, Walter Warlimont at OKW on 3 August not only urged German commanders to hold out, since there were no prepared positions to which to retreat, but insisted that the attack proceed despite the low odds of success – a demand, curiously enough, not mentioned in his memoirs. He apparently hoped that a smashing defeat of the Americans, combined with an unleashing of the "wonder weapons" against London, would finally cause the increasingly war-weary British to opt out. In this, Warlimont outdid even his Führer, who, himself evidently not convinced that it would succeed, on 4 August ordered the rapid consolidation of a defense line on the rivers Somme, Marne, and Saône, all to the east of Paris. Nevertheless, preparations for the counterattack continued, even as difficulties mounted. Because of problems in transporting and assembling troops – and the impossibility of disengaging some armored units because of the fierce fighting around Caen – instead of the eight Panzer divisions originally envisioned by Hitler for the attack, by 6 August only parts of five motorized units had been concentrated at Mortain. In addition, the German task had become more difficult because the Americans had steadily widened the narrow bottleneck; instead of six miles, the Germans would now have to advance almost twenty miles in order to cut the corridor. Nor did they possess the requisite force to accomplish Hitler's ultimate goal: to drive the Allies back to the sea and out of Normandy.[81]

For his part, Kluge understood what was at stake. "I am aware," he wrote on the night of 6–7 August, "that a failure of this attack will lead to a collapse of the entire Normandy front, but the order is so unequivocal that it must be carried out unconditionally." Hitler, too, was clear about the possible consequences, although he just as obviously inhabited a dream world, declaring on 7 August, "the decision in the Battle of France depends on the success of the [Mortain] attack . . . [We have] a unique opportunity, which will never return, to drive into an extremely exposed enemy area and thereby change the situation completely." Despite his reservations, and even though preparations were not complete, Kluge nonetheless launched the attack on the night of 6–7 August, although, ominously, because of fuel shortages only 120 tanks participated in the initial assault. Still, the Germans had a local superiority at the point of attack, so despite Allied knowledge of their intentions – furnished by Ultra intelligence intercepts – the attack achieved some initial success. German forces seized Mortain, surrounding units of the American 30th Division, and moved some six miles toward Avranches. As the weather cleared on the afternoon of 7 August, though, Allied fighter planes pounced on German troops, despite Luftwaffe assurances of protection, inflicting great damage on the infantry and forcing German armor to disperse. At the same time, American artillery and anti-tank guns destroyed large numbers of Panzers, blunting any further German advance. Frustrated, Hitler, who had lost faith in the ability of SS General Hausser, ordered Eberbach to lead a further attack, but it too came to nothing, except to further position German forces for their own destruction. Kluge, on 10 August, complained bitterly of the "incredibility of a large military force . . . blissfully planning an attack while far behind it an enemy is busily forming a noose with which to strangle it."[82]

That, of course, was precisely what the Allies now planned. Instead of the larger encirclement at the Seine, which would probably still have been the best solution, they now sought a tighter envelopment focused on Falaise-Argentan. Although the pocket was more or less closed by 19 August, and savage fighting occurred throughout, the Allies achieved only a partial success. Instead of destroying the bulk of German forces in Normandy, when the fighting ended some 10,000 Germans lay dead, with the Allies capturing 50,000 more, a satisfying achievement, but far short of what had been desired. The Germans also lost 470 tanks and assault guns, most undamaged – abandoned for lack of fuel – but, in yet another irony, these losses could be made good, for August 1944 marked the high point of German armaments production. Any hope that those troops who escaped could mount a defense east of Paris had also collapsed, for on 15 August American and French forces had landed in southern France. Here, in contrast to Normandy, Hitler quickly realized the potential disaster awaiting all German forces in southern and southwestern France, well over 300,000 troops, and allowed a timely withdrawal. Although harassed by resistance fighters during their retreat, the great bulk of these troops nonetheless managed to escape the trap, marking the second failure of the Allies to destroy the German army in France and thus considerably shorten the war. One of the casualties in all of this was Kluge who, implicated in the plot on Hitler's life, had on 17 August been replaced by Field Marshal Model. Fearing that he would soon be arrested, Kluge committed suicide on 19 August, but not before declaring in a farewell note – an odd mixture of obsequiousness and pathos – "My Führer, I have constantly admired your greatness, your bearing in this gigantic contest, and your iron will . . . You have led a true, epic struggle. History will credit you with that. Show now the greatness that is necessary to end a pointless struggle . . . and above all to ensure that the Reich is not ruined by Bolshevism. I part from you, my Führer, to whom I was inwardly closer than you perhaps realized."[83]

Although Hitler and Jodl demanded a scorched-earth retreat in northern France, the headlong flight to the German border prevented much of this from being implemented. What slowed the Allied advance, in addition to the general destruction of bridges and railroads, were supply problems aggravated, ironically, by Hitler's "fortified places" policy. Although ineffective in the east, it now proved more successful in the west, where German refusal to surrender key ports in Brittany and the Channel coast impeded Allied supplies and drastically slowed the momentum of their advance across France. Indeed, by mid-September the "fortresses" of Calais, Dunkirk, and Boulogne had tied down a not insubstantial portion of the units of Montgomery's 21st Army Group. This, in turn, allowed the Germans a breathing space to collect troops and reform shattered units. As a consequence, the policy of holding on to the ports proved a sensible measure from Hitler's point of view, since they managed to prolong the war by a few months. As in the east, the loss of some 200,000 men in the "fortresses" has to be weighed against an overall weakening of the army, but in truth hardly any battle-worthy troops remained in them – most were naval or Luftwaffe personnel – and they had virtually no tanks or vehicles. In an open battle, these units could have offered little resistance to an Allied advance; in the fortresses, however, they sustained a not inconsiderable fighting power.[84]

As the Germans fell back on the Reich borders, they also benefitted from shorter supply lines and the advantage of interior lines of movement. Moreover, they made good use of the fortifications of the Maginot Line and West Wall, in effect turning areas such as Metz, the Saar, and the Hürtgen

Forest into impromptu festen Plätze. With the mid-September failure of Operation Market Garden, an uncharacteristically bold attempt by Montgomery to end-run German defenses in the north and seize the Ruhr industrial area, the Allies failed for a third time to deal a death blow to the German army in the west. Having used the last of the available Allied supplies to no effect, and facing a German force that had been recast remarkably quickly, any hope of an end to the war in 1944 had evaporated. So, too, had any prospect of Germany stalemating the war. Hitler had hoped 1944 would mark a turning point; instead, disasters in Normandy and Belorussia had accelerated the disintegration of the German position. Although enemy mistakes and weaknesses had prevented them from delivering the final blow – and despite the fact that the Germans continued to fight effectively in defense – the ultimate outcome of the war could no longer be in doubt, even if Hitler flailed away at imaginary options.

11

Never Again a November 1918

"War is of course a test of endurance . . . ," the Führer told the assembled audience of division commanders on 12 December 1944. "The longer the war goes on the more severe this test of endurance." Few in attendance would have disagreed with him on this point, although the next likely elicited doubt. "This test of endurance must under all circumstances continue," Hitler stressed, "as long as there is the slightest hope of victory. The moment all hope of victory disappears a people's determination becomes insufficient to withstand the test of endurance . . . It is therefore vital from time to time to destroy the enemy's confidence in victory by making clear to him by means of offensive action that his plans cannot succeed." Before virtually all major German campaigns, Hitler had gathered his generals in order to explain his military and political reasoning – and justify his actions in detailed historical explications. His speeches on both 11 and 12 December – he had addressed half the generals on the 11th – proved to be no different, for in launching a risky offensive he needed to deliver genuinely convincing arguments. "A successful defensive," Hitler went on, "can never achieve this as effectively as a successful offensive. In the long run, the principle that the defensive is stronger than the offensive does not hold . . . We must be clear," he explained further, "that, although a prolonged, stubbornly conducted defensive may wear down the enemy, it must in all cases be followed by a successful offensive. From the outset of the war, therefore, I have striven to act offensively whenever possible, to conduct a war of movement and not allow myself to be maneuvered into a position comparable to that of the World War . . ." This was a contention that many, accustomed to his demands to hold out, might have disputed – although, in truth, often enough his halt orders masked an intent to resume aggressive offensive action. "Wars are, however, finally decided," he asserted, "when one side or the other realizes that the war as such can no longer be won. Our most important task therefore is to force the enemy to realize this . . . The enemy must be made to realize that under no circumstances can he succeed."

This could only be done, Hitler thought, by destroying the enemy's strength and throwing his morale into crisis. History had never known, the Führer emphasized, such an unnatural coalition consisting of "heterogeneous partners with such totally divergent objectives as that of our enemies. The states which are our enemies are the greatest opposites which exist on earth: ultra-capitalist states on one side and ultra-Marxist states on the other; on one side a dying empire – Britain; on the other side a colony, the United States, waiting to claim its inheritance . . . If we can deal it a couple of heavy blows," he maintained, "this artificially constructed common front may collapse . . . at any moment." True enough, in the event, but Hitler overlooked the reality that the coalition would last just as long as his regime; Machiavelli's insight proved more correct: "the enemy of my enemy is my friend." And where would this offensive be launched? In the same area, he explained, that his critics – primarily his top generals, he added – had told him in 1939 and 1940 was impossible for a successful offensive: the Ardennes. "The official view," he noted, "was that we should conduct a defensive war . . . [T]o act against France and against England, that people thought was lunacy, a crime, a Utopia, a hopeless undertaking. The course of events proved the opposite." Now, he insisted, something similar could be achieved. Today, he claimed, except for the Luftwaffe, "there is little difference" from 1940. Enemy forces in the area were hardly first-class divisions and would be outnumbered at the point of attack; American morale was poor; and Germany not only had better but, in this sector, more tanks. His conclusion – that it just might be possible to pull off one last miracle – seemed indisputable, and certainly influenced many of those in attendance. General Manteuffel, for example, commanding 5th Army, thought that Hitler had provided a needed "assurance of favorable conditions."[1]

Two key themes emerge from this speech: his logic for how to alter the direction of the war; and, as we will see, his reasons for fighting on, which were closely related to the writings of Clausewitz a century earlier. Ironically, historians have criticized Hitler for his rigid "hold doctrine" at the end of the war, but when he clearly abandoned it to launch a counteroffensive, these same critics have assailed him for squandering forces that allegedly could have been better employed in the defense. Germany could, of course, have used the laboriously created last reserves of the army to remain on the strategic defensive and bolster the most threatened sectors of the front, especially in the east, where a major enemy offensive was anticipated. Although this offered the advantage of shifting forces along inner lines to counter enemy penetrations, a tactic that might prolong the fighting for some time, it could not substantially alter the situation or offer the prospect of a decisive change in the war.

Hitler clearly understood that the course of the war could not be affected by remaining on the defensive. The only way to loosen the growing economic and military noose, he thought, was to take bold offensive action. It offered the only chance, however slight, of altering Germany's position, and only in the west did offensive action make strategic sense. In the east, because of the sheer size of the theater, the Germans could achieve little more than local, tactical triumphs. In the west, though, there remained the possibility that successful action could create, at least temporarily, a political-military crisis that could offer a breathing space. Also, having made much of the east *Judenfrei* in the course of the war, Hitler glimpsed one final chance to deal a blow to the alleged conspiracy of international finance Jewry, which was based in London and New York. Clearly it would be an all or nothing gamble, something not foreign to Hitler, that, if it failed, would squander the last operational and fuel reserves and ensure that Germany would be left only with the option of total defeat. It did, though, offer enticing possibilities: if it succeeded, strong enemy forces would be destroyed, the Anglo-Americans might be plunged into crisis, troops could be assembled for counter-action in the east, and looming defeat would be avoided, at least for the foreseeable future. In effect, Hitler meant to replicate in autumn 1944 the miracle of spring 1940; this time, Britain would play the role of France, with the Americans mimicking the English response. This, along with a renewal of V-2 attacks, might be enough to get the Allies to mitigate their demand for unconditional surrender and negotiate an end to the fighting. It was a giant risk, but as Jodl explained after the war, "In a desperate situation the only possible hope lies in a desperate decision."[2]

Hitler had, in fact, as early as mid-August 1944 – in the days of crisis immediately after the American breakout from Normandy and the failure of the Mortain counteroffensive – begun thinking of a major counter-strike in the west. In a meeting on 19 August he startled his staff by announcing that twenty-five divisions were to be readied for a November offensive "when the enemy cannot fly." As he candidly admitted to General Balck two months later, the Wehrmacht was so reduced that this attack would have to rely on "muddy ground and foggy weather so that the enemy air forces and armored forces are neutralized ... We must do it like the Russians (in

1941)." His intent, though, seemed clear from a statement he made to two of his generals on 31 August:

> The time is not yet ripe for a political decision . . . [A]t a time of heavy military defeats it is quite childish and naive to hope for a politically favorable moment to make a move . . . The time will come when the tensions between the Allies become so strong that . . . the rupture occurs. History teaches us that all coalitions break up, but you must await the moment . . . [I shall] continue to fight until there is a possibility for a decent peace . . . Whatever happens we shall carry on in this struggle until, as Frederick the Great said, "one of our damned enemies gives up in despair."

Although remaining mum about his operational intentions, in early September he recalled Rundstedt as commander-in-chief in the west, teaming him up with the talented Siegfried Westphal as his chief of staff, and accorded the Western Front priority in receiving new artillery, tank, and assault-gun production. Not until 16 September did he reveal to a few trusted officers his aim to attack through the Ardennes in the direction of Antwerp, with the object of capturing the Allies' most important supply base. This would deliver them a sharp blow and confront the British with a "new Dunkirk." With much of the British 21st Army Group caught in a pocket and threatened with destruction, he also hoped to drive a political as well as a military wedge between the two allies. Discussions with Jodl at the end of September made it clear that Hitler now assumed a new Soviet offensive was some months off, so he meant to take advantage of the situation to radically alter the balance of forces in the west. An attack with thirty divisions, he thought, would inflict such heavy losses on the Allies that the Western Front could be stabilized. The offensive, though, would have to take place by late November and achieve a rapid success to enable large numbers of troops to be transferred to the east before the Red Army launched its winter offensive.[3]

Even as the Wehrmacht struggled with American attacks around Aachen – the city, the first to be captured by the Allies, fell on 21 October after three weeks of hard fighting – planning for the Ardennes Offensive (*Operation Wacht am Rhein*) continued apace. Early versions centered on the area just south of Aachen, where the difficult terrain and thinly manned American line seemed to offer good prospects for a breakthrough and advance on the key supply port of Antwerp. Both Rundstedt and Model, now commanding Army Group B, feared that Hitler's plans were too ambitious. Accepting the need for offensive action, though, on 3 November they proposed a "small solution": Model's troops would attack from Aachen with the aim of encircling and destroying Allied forces east of the Meuse, with the hint that, if successful, the offensive would continue toward Antwerp. Although such an attack offered the best chance of immediate tactical success, Hitler rejected it as too limited to offer any chance of fundamentally altering the strategic situation for the better or inducing the Allies to negotiate. Instead, he opted for a concentrated thrust by two Panzer armies (6th SS and 5th) toward Antwerp, supported by 7th Army on their left flank, in the hope that the 21st Army Group could be separated from the American armies to its south and destroyed.[4]

Although Rundstedt, Model, Manteuffel, and Dietrich, the key commanders entrusted with its implementation, harbored deep reservations about the operation – Model, for example, thought it had "no chance" for success – all suppressed their doubts. Hitler was thus prepared to accept the greatest risks – as Jodl put it, "in our current situation we cannot shrink from staking everything on one card" – in order to win the greatest possible rewards. However, continuing American pressure in the Hürtgen Forest and, farther south, at Metz, as well as difficulties in assembling the attack force, caused the offensive (as at Kursk) to be postponed from late November to 10 December, and then to 16 December. Enemy pressure in the east caused concern as well, with the Soviet threat to Hungary, the last important German source of oil and food, resulting in bitter attritional fighting around Budapest. This delay, along with continuing transportation and logistics problems, meant that, even if the attack were successful, the planned follow-up transfer of troops from west to east probably could not have been accomplished in time to contribute to any sort of defensive victory against the Soviets.[5]

Even though at first glance Wacht am Rhein (later renamed "Autumn Mist") seemed to have some rational arguments in its favor, once again, as with the Mortain counterattack, Hitler's instinct for the weak spot of the enemy and his eye for the main chance remained divorced from reality. Aerial supremacy – the essential guarantor of success in 1940 – was completely absent in 1944, which Hitler had acknowledged in both August and December. The very decision to time the attack during a period of bad weather so as to ground Allied aircraft clearly signaled this crucial weakness, and was also evidence of complete operational bankruptcy. In addition, though they had scraped together impressive-looking numbers of troops – Model had a total of nineteen infantry divisions and seven Panzer divisions available for the operation – many of them were Volksgrenadier

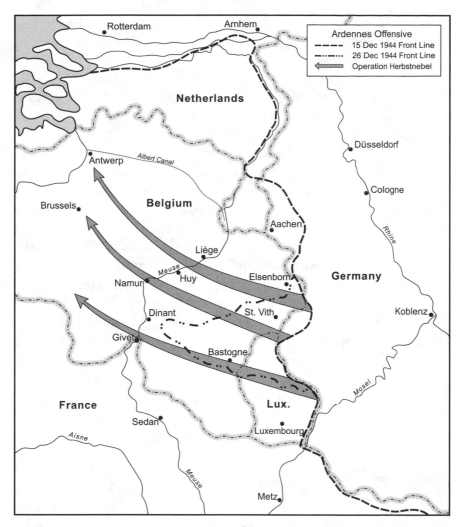

10. The Ardennes Offensive

units of varying quality and training; and, in any case, the Germans still needed at least ten more divisions to inflict any sort of knock-down blow on the Allies. Finally, the German logistical system could no longer cope with the demands of a large-scale offensive while simultaneously keeping other sectors supplied. Above all, they suffered from a serious shortage of fuel. Launching an attack in which the tanks had fuel for only about forty miles, which would barely get them to the Meuse River, with the rest of the eighty miles to Antwerp to be covered by captured Allied supplies, went beyond foolhardy; this was sheer fantasy, not a plan. Even though they managed to assemble over 1,500 armored fighting vehicles for the attack, including large numbers of Panthers, Tigers, and the excellent new Jagdpanther tank destroyers, the offensive capabilities of the Panzer units did not correlate to their strength on paper. Many of the existing tank crews were not of the same quality as in the past, or were battle-weary, while hastily prepared replacements, most with only a few weeks' training, could not hope to cope with the demands of battle.[6]

Still, the attack in dense fog on the morning of 16 December caught the Americans by surprise: they had only five divisions (one armored) in the assault sector. Hitler had insisted that the time was ripe to act against the battle-weary Americans, whose units had been worn down in bitter autumn fighting, and now he seemed vindicated. The initial success of Autumn Mist rekindled hopes that the once-fabled but now long-tattered "Führer luck" had returned. Announcement of the offensive lifted the mood, at least temporarily, among both soldiers and civilians; even Hitler seemed rejuvenated. Since success in the operation required rapid exploitation of a breakthrough along with continuing poor weather, the absence of Allied fighters, grounded due to the miserable conditions, seemed a particularly positive omen. Indeed, one German lieutenant exulted, after his unit had destroyed a fleeing American column, at "the glorious bloodbath, vengeance for our destroyed homeland . . . Victory was never as close as it is now. The decision will soon be reached." Even as some Panzer units rolled westward, though, it quickly became apparent just how misplaced German hopes were. Due to stronger than expected American resistance, the difficult terrain, poor roads, and ineffective commanders, 6th SS Panzer Army's advance quickly slowed to a crawl. As at Mortain, the performance of the SS failed to match the faith Hitler had placed in these elite units. Manteuffel's 5th Panzer Army made better progress in the center, although here too barely passable roads, destroyed bridges, and stubborn American opposition, especially at the key crossroads town of Bastogne, hampered German progress. More importantly, the Germans failed to shift forces quickly enough away from the stalled 6th SS Panzer Army to the advancing 5th Panzer Army, so that, although troops from the latter came within a few miles of the Meuse, they lacked the strength to cross the river and continue the offensive. Within a week it was apparent that the gamble had failed, and that the offensive had turned once more to grinding attritional fighting.[7]

Although they had stunned the Americans with the ferocity of the fighting, inflicting over 89,000 casualties, with 19,000 killed – the worst American losses in the European theater – the Germans had suffered as well, with over 10,000 dead, 34,000 wounded, and 22,000 captured, losses that could not be made good. They also lost 600 to 700 armored vehicles, many simply abandoned for lack of fuel. Stout American resistance, rapid Allied response, superior logistics, clearing skies that allowed enemy aircraft to dominate the battlefield, and effective use of towns and restrictive terrain to stymie the advance of qualitatively superior German tanks – once more undermining Hitler's hopes in the redemptive value of technology – along with crippling German shortages of fuel, poor command decisions, and the weakness of its infantry, combined to smash Hitler's hopes of a miracle that would reverse the situation in the west. The whole idea had been fanciful, as it was unrealistic to have expected the operation, dependent as it was on superior performance by poorly trained troops, continuing bad weather, and the avoidance of any tactical errors, to have reached Antwerp. "Brilliance," the Führer insisted on 29 December, "is just a phantom if it isn't supported by persistence and fanatical toughness." By now, though, his hope of emulating his hero, Frederick the Great, and of doggedly continuing the fight until the enemy gave up in frustration, had all but evaporated. As a soldier put it more realistically in his diary, "The superiority of our enemy is so great that it is useless to fight against it."[8]

In the end, Autumn Mist, militarily, proved little more than a flash in the pan, as did its analog in Alsace, Operation North Wind, launched on 1 January 1945, with the same results: initial success only to be checked by massive American material superiority. Politically, though, it had more important consequences, shaking Allied confidence and markedly slowing their advance to the Rhine. This, in turn, greatly enhanced Stalin's position, whose military task in the east had been made easier by the concentration of strong German forces in the west. By now, there existed little strategic rationale for continuing the war, other than vague hopes in some "miracle" weapon or another. Hitler, though, had long vowed there would never be another November 1918 in German history. That conviction, along with the realization – by himself, top members of his government, and senior military leaders – that the massive crimes committed in his name and because of his orders meant that neither he nor his regime would survive the end of war, also contributed to continued German defiance. In addition, as so often in the last year of the war, Hitler could draw on Stalin's example from 1941, when stubborn, determined resistance saved the Soviet Union from what seemed certain defeat. The Allies, Hitler vowed, would now suffer what had been inflicted on the Wehrmacht at Stalingrad, as the enemy would be bled to death in the streets of numerous German towns and villages. Eventually, the fanaticism of the German people would break the will of Allied soldiers to keep on fighting. As always, though, the problem in applying the "lesson" of one historical experience to another was contextual. In 1941 and again in 1942, Stalin could count on aid from allies; in 1945 Hitler had none. That, though, was irrelevant to his thinking. If the enemy could not be turned away, then the heroic fight to the last would inspire future generations of Germans to again take up the struggle.[9]

Clausewitz's exhortations on the value of fighting on, which Hitler knew and embraced, likely played the largest role in his intransigence. The great theorist of war had insisted that a nation must continue the struggle, even if by means of a popular insurrection, in order to preserve its national soul. "A people must never value anything higher than the dignity and freedom of its existence," he declared, insisting it must defend these with the last drop of its blood," for "the shame of a cowardly submission can never be wiped out." On the other hand, "a bloody and honorable fight assures the rebirth of the people even if freedom were lost." Hitler's stubborn continuance of the war was thus not based merely on some delusional, irrational, fanatical belief in ultimate victory, although in truth in the last months of the war he did descend occasionally into unreality. Rather, it stemmed in an odd sort of way from a realistic assessment of the situation. With the extermination of the Jews, he had burned all his bridges. The point now was to create a transcendent myth of heroic struggle to the end, of defiance in the face of certain defeat, of a valorization of National Socialism. He had failed to produce this at Stalingrad, he thought, because of the failure of Paulus to play his assigned role and commit suicide, but now he could stage German downfall according to his own design. He revealed this intent to Below at the end of 1944, after again complaining of betrayal by his generals: "We will not capitulate, ever. We may go down. But we will take the world down with us."[10]

That Hitler intended to continue the war for just such reasons was made further apparent in his proclamation to the German people on 1 January 1945. On the day he launched the war, 1 September 1939, he had vowed to the Reichstag, "There shall never ever be another November 1918 in German history!" Nor would he, in contrast to the cowardly Wilhelm II, survive a defeat, a theme that had become a fixation. In November 1942, at the height of the battle for Stalingrad, he again contrasted his determination with that of the Kaiser's government. "Germany back then," he emphasized in Munich to the Old Fighters in attendance at the annual celebration of the 1923 Putsch, "laid down its arms at a quarter to twelve – as a matter of principle, I never quit until five minutes after twelve." The enemy, he now claimed on the first day of the last year of his war, had "placed particular hopes on the year 1944. Never before did victory seem so close to them." Defeat had been avoided, he asserted, not only by the sacrifices and hard work of the German people, but because of his own commitment "that a day like November 9 [1918] would never repeat itself in the German Reich . . . The Jewish-international conspiracy has lived on hopes from the first day [of the war] . . . that an internal revolution and . . . collapse of the German Reich . . . was imminent." Germany's enemies believed, he continued, that the Nazi regime would crumble in August 1944, and had even planned, as in the First World War, once again to starve the German people after its surrender.[11]

The collapse, though, never happened, and precisely, Hitler asserted, because its enemies failed to understand that this was not the Germany of the past. This National Socialist Germany, he thundered, "will never capitulate . . . The entire German Volk knows what its fate would be if it lost this war . . . What we are fighting for is clear to all of us. It is the preservation of . . . our homeland, it is our two-thousand-year-old culture, it is . . . our Volk. It is, in short, everything that makes life worth living for us." After all, Hitler claimed, in an ironic projection of Nazi aims onto its enemies, "they intend to exterminate our Volk . . . By wrecking our cities, they hope not only to kill German women and children, but also and above all to eliminate . . . our thousand-year [sic] old culture . . . The existence . . . of a German future," he asserted ominously, depended on "uncompromising" resistance and great "sacrifices" by the German people. "A Volk that . . . suffers and endures . . . ," he declared, in echoes of Clausewitz, "can therefore never perish. On the contrary, it will emerge . . . stronger and firmer than ever before in its history." To accomplish this rebirth, though, the German people could not let up, but had "to fight this most difficult struggle for the future of our Volk with the greatest fanaticism."[12]

Although Hitler intended an epic struggle of Wagnerian proportions, a modern-day Götterdämmerung or "Twilight of the Gods," his charismatic authority had evaporated; he no longer had the ability to transform or mobilize his followers. Despite the collapse of his carefully constructed image as the infallible Führer and Feldherr, though, his control remained intact within his inner circle. What transpired, then, more nearly resembled murder than myth-making, the unparalleled destruction of an advanced industrial society, as Germany became a Totenland, a land of the dead. From January through May 1945 over 1.4 million German soldiers lost their lives, more than in 1942 and 1943 combined, and almost as many as were killed in all of 1944. The Wehrmacht lost over 450,000 men in January 1945 alone, more than the total of all American deaths during the Second World War; in each of the next three months almost 300,000 more perished. As a consequence of Hitler's refusal to capitulate, the Germans lost more killed in *each* of the first four months of 1945 than the *total* number lost at Stalingrad. Neither Operation Barbarossa nor the fighting in front of Moscow, neither Stalingrad nor Kursk, Normandy nor Operation Bagration, brought the Wehrmacht its greatest losses. These were suffered in the last bitter battles of the war, fought largely inside Germany. In addition, relentless Allied bombing not only killed over 1,000 people daily – roughly 130,000 in total in 1945 – but reduced the medieval splendor of many German cities to little more than heaps of rubble; not Germany's enemies, but Hitler himself, seemed bent on the destruction of the thousand-year-old German culture. Huddled in their ruined cellars beneath mounds of stone, much of the German population at the end of the war resembled nothing more than the cave dwellers of old. Hitler insisted that November 1918 would not be repeated. As a result, he ensured one last spasm of violence and destruction within Germany itself.[13]

Nor did Hitler have long to wait for these further sacrifices and hardships to be inflicted upon the German people. On the early morning of 12 January, with many German forces still tied down in the west, the Soviets, following a massive artillery bombardment, launched their long-anticipated offensive out of bridgeheads over the Vistula south of Warsaw. The Germans, taking their cue from both the First World War and the extensive Soviet defensive fortifications at Kursk, had aimed to create successive fortified lines to a depth of 120 miles that would slow the Russian advance by forcing them to fight through endless defensive emplacements while being subjected to mobile counter-thrusts. The backbone of this tactic was to be a series of fortified positions that, as in the Great War, would allow the defenders to withdraw from the exposed forward line during an enemy artillery bombardment, absorb the attack and slow its momentum, then launch tactical counterattacks that would snap the defenders back to their original positions. Evidently, though, no one at OKH had pondered the obvious lesson of July 1943: despite the formidable obstacles at Kursk, a far smaller German force had penetrated a much more elaborate Soviet defensive system. How a much smaller defending force in far less prepared positions would halt an attack by an overwhelmingly superior enemy remained unclear. So, too, did the question of precisely how, with limited fuel and no air cover, German armored units were to conduct a mobile defense.[14]

The key problem, then – that this type of defense required ample manpower, mobile reserves, and an active air force, none of which the Germans possessed – remained unresolved. Over Guderian's strenuous objections, for example, Sepp Dietrich's 6th SS Panzer Army, when brought back from the Ardennes, was dispatched to Hungary to protect the last oil fields, crucial for the German war effort, rather than being sent to reinforce the undermanned forces of Army Group A, then bearing the brunt of the enemy assault. On 9 January, just days before the attack, Guderian argued with Hitler for forces to be made available for the seriously overstretched Eastern Front. The Führer, though, still clinging to the hope of something decisive materializing in the west, insisted that the east "has never before possessed such a strong reserve as now," to which the OKH chief of staff could only reply, "The Eastern Front is like a house of cards. If the front is broken through at one point all the rest will collapse." Indeed, Army Group A had conducted its own study, with the sobering conclusion that the Russians could not only break through and reach the Silesian border in six days, but that even stopping them on the Oder was problematic. The Führer, though, refused to believe that the figures produced by Foreign Armies East on Red Army strength were anything more than an "enormous bluff" by the Soviets. Indeed, at his Evening Situation Report, he claimed the numbers were "a farce . . . We have approximately 3,000 tanks and assault guns in the East today. If I plan on the normal destruction ratio of three to one, the enemy needs 9,000 tanks . . . He doesn't have 9,000 tanks." He then added "not yet, anyway." Hitler's parting remark to Guderian, "The Eastern Front must help itself and make do with what it's got," could hardly have offered much comfort to the harried OKH chief. He knew full well that the available forces were insufficient, nor could reserves be quickly shifted from the west because of Allied air superiority.[15]

In any case, despite his complaints, Guderian must have known that, given the deplorable manpower situation, even if troops had been sent from west to east they could only have delayed, but not prevented, a Soviet break-through – and at the cost of deeply undermining defenses in the west. Of more immediate concern, on the tactical level the Führer's obsession with holding ground undermined the planned German defense in depth. At his insistence – itself perhaps a concession to German immobility – both the second and main defensive positions had been built within a few thousand yards of the forward lines, which made them vulnerable to Soviet artillery and thus negated the whole German strategy. Further, German unit commanders could only abandon their positions if given explicit orders from their divisions, which in practice meant approval from Hitler, again undermining the idea of a flexible defense. Finally, in view of enemy air superiority, many German mobile divisions had been deployed far forward in order to permit more rapid reaction. Not only did they have less room to maneuver, but they would also quickly get caught up in the main attack, thus limiting their assigned role of pinching off enemy breakthroughs.[16]

In the event, Army Group A's study proved uncannily accurate. Enemy forces quickly penetrated German lines and by the end of the first day's attack Soviet armored units had raced some twenty miles to the west. By the end of the second day, the enemy had blasted a hole in German defenses thirty-six miles wide and had penetrated twenty-four miles deep, while on 16 January advance units seized the city of Czestochowa, some 150 miles from their starting point. Having achieved an operational breakthrough, Marshal Konev's troops raced westward, sweeping aside or surrounding the remnants of the German defenders. Krakow fell on 19 January, with Red Army troops liberating Katowice – and the nearby camp complex at Auschwitz, now with only a few thousand ill and emaciated survivors – over the next ten days. By the end of the month the Soviets controlled nearly all of Upper Silesia, the last major German industrial center outside the Ruhr, with the exception of the capital, Breslau. It had been deemed a "fortress city," which, under fanatical Nazi leadership, managed to hold out until 6 May. Although to Hitler an impressive display of unbending determination, it proved a pointless act of defiance which, at the cost of enormous destruction and loss of life, did little to impede the enemy advance. By late January, as well, Soviet troops had reached the Oder – making the roughly 200-mile leap from the Vistula in three weeks – and vindicating the analysts in Army Group A.[17]

Even as German defenses in southern Poland collapsed, in the north the enemy on 13 January launched the second stage of a staggered operation designed to pin German forces in place before commencing the main attack in the center. Striking against 3rd Panzer Army of Army Group Center, troops of Ivan Cherniakhovsky's 3rd Belorussian Front sought to drive from the eastern border of East Prussia in the direction of Königsberg. Although ferocious German resistance and bad weather initially turned the attack into a prolonged penetration rather than a breakthrough, Soviet pressure nonetheless forced the German defenders back. Despite this momentary success, Army Group Center's situation deteriorated quickly, for the next day General Rokossovsky's 2nd Belorussian Front attacked 2nd Army out of bridgeheads across the Narew just north of Warsaw. Penetrating German defenses rapidly, Rokossovsky then unleashed his mobile forces into the enemy rear. Soviet tank units swiftly overwhelmed the 7th Panzer Division, the only formidable German mobile reserve in the area, forcing it to fight its way back to the west. Although Guderian that same day warned of an "extraordinarily serious situation," Hitler, as well as the army group commanders, seemed to have only belatedly realized the approaching catastrophe. On 13 January the Führer ordered two infantry divisions transferred from the west, but refused to move 4th SS Panzer Corps out of Hungary. The next day, with the situation of Army Group A nearing the critical point and the danger to Upper Silesia acute, Hitler ordered Army Group Center to transfer Panzer Corps Grossdeutschland and its two powerful divisions, "Brandenburg" and "Hermann Göring," to its neighbor to the south, a decision that hurt Army Group Center more than it helped Army Group A. The result was immediately apparent; by 16 January, 3rd Panzer Army neared breaking point and 4th Army faced encirclement.[18]

That same day, Hitler finally accepted defeat in the west and directed that 6th SS Panzer Army be transferred from the Ardennes to the east, but to Hungary, not Poland. Although Guderian, who planned to use these troops to attack the flanks of the advancing Russians, thus slowing their momentum, exploded in rage at Jodl, and strenuously argued his case to Hitler, he could not convince the latter to change his mind. The Führer merely reaffirmed his intention to attack in Hungary, throw the Russians back across the Danube, and relieve Budapest. As always, Hitler called up economic arguments to support his case. Retention of the Hungarian oil fields and refineries, he lectured Guderian, were essential to continuing the war effort. When the latter pointed to the immediate dangers in Poland, Hitler retorted, not incorrectly, "If you don't get any more fuel your tanks won't be able to move and the airplanes won't be able to fly." Then, with words dripping with contempt, he concluded, not for the first time, "But my generals know nothing about the economic aspects of war." On 18 January, 2nd Army's front snapped and by the 23rd the enemy had cleared the last defenses at Allenstein. The way to the sea was now clear and three days later Russian forces succeeded in cutting off East Prussia, and with it 4th Army and 3rd Panzer Army, from the rest of the Reich.[19]

Against the will and direct orders of a furious Hitler, the trapped 4th Army now attempted to break out to the west, in the process abandoning the heavily fortified fortress of Lötzen, the key to the defense of East Prussia. The 4th Army commander, General Friedrich Hossbach – who, as Hitler's military adjutant in November 1937, had secretly recorded the Führer's plans for expansion, notes soon to be used at the post-war Nuremberg Trials as evidence of premeditated Nazi aggression – on 26 January ordered an attack to the west, earning him a different sort of notoriety. Catching the Russians by surprise, units of 4th Army managed to push almost twenty miles to the west before furious enemy counterattacks halted their progress and forced them back on Heiligenbeil. Confronted with this clear violation of his orders, Hitler fell into a rage, accusing both Hossbach and General Hans Reinhardt, commander of Army Group Center, who had knowledge of his subordinate's intentions, of being "in the same racket with Seydlitz! This is treason!" Both were relieved of their commands, although neither, amazingly, was relieved of his life, a fact that owed much to the personal intervention of Guderian.[20]

To the east, the remnants of 3rd Panzer Army found themselves pushed into an enclave around the city of Königsberg and, critically, the port of Pillau. Around half a million soldiers were now cut off. These were troops, like the roughly 200,000 Germans in the Courland pocket, who might have been more useful elsewhere. Instead, they remained in place, albeit for different reasons. While both formed part of Hitler's "fortified places" policy, Königsberg, as the ancient coronation city of Prussian kings, loomed large in Hitler's mind for political reasons. If the Soviets took the city, he feared they would move quickly to install a puppet regime under the leadership of Seydlitz, one that might finally shake military support for his rule. As late as 23 April, amazingly enough, Hitler remained fearful of the influence of Seydlitz. In the case of Courland, and over the vigorous protests of Guderian, strategic reasons took precedence. Although the failure of the Ardennes Offensive meant the final collapse of his strategy of "strike in the west, hold in the east," the Führer clung to one last hope. If Courland could be held, it might yet be possible to unleash the new Type-21 submarines, currently undergoing sea trials in the Baltic, in an offensive in the Atlantic. Admiral Dönitz expected these new U-boats to turn the tide in the Atlantic, so it was largely at his urging that Hitler held on to the southern Baltic coast and not from any special aversion, at least in this instance, to withdrawals. At the same time, and in exploring any possibility of a chance at some sort of victory, Hitler envisioned an attack from Courland deep into the Soviet rear that might alter the situation in the east. Although he relented somewhat in mid-January and allowed seven divisions to be transferred from Courland back to the Reich, he could not completely abandon the illusion that Germany might somehow regain the initiative, thus leaving some 130,000 men trapped and besieged.[21]

With German defenses at both ends of the line shattered, on the morning of 14 January Marshal Zhukov unleashed his 1st Belorussian Front from bridgeheads across the Vistula south of Warsaw. As in Konev's successful effort farther south, after a twenty-five-minute artillery barrage Zhukov's forces launched a series of powerful probing attacks on the forward German positions, followed by the main assault. The effect was devastating; the power of the Soviet onslaught so unhinged 9th Army's defenses that by the end of the first day the Russians had advanced over seven miles to the west. The next day the Soviets shattered a determined counterattack by the 19th and 25th Panzer Divisions and achieved an operational breakthrough. While Russian armored units began their drive toward Lodz, eighty miles to the northwest, units of the 1st Polish Army moved north to encircle Warsaw, in combination with forces of the Soviet 47th Army that had pushed across the Vistula at Modlin, north of the capital. On 16 January, Hitler reacted in now typical fashion to the brewing disaster, sacking the commander of Army Group A, General Joseph Harpe, and replacing him with his new favorite, Ferdinand Schörner. At the same time, he issued a completely delusory directive, which Guderian termed "idiotic," that Army Group A should not only hold a line from east of Krakow to Warsaw and Modlin, but should also attack and destroy – or at least throw back the enemy – all along the line, even though it could expect no reinforcements for two weeks. Despite the Führer's will, the next day Polish and Soviet forces seized Warsaw against virtually no opposition. What they found, when they entered the city, was a picture of total devastation. So thorough had been German destruction – carried out on Hitler's orders following the August 1944 uprising – that scarcely a single building remained intact. The unopposed fall of the Polish capital, not surprisingly, touched off an explosion in Berlin. Hitler immediately suspected that OKH had sabotaged his orders, on 18 January ordering the arrest of the three senior officers at Operations Branch, and the next day signing an order that effectively directed all commanders down to the division level to obtain his permission for any operational movement, whether attack or withdrawal.[22]

Although the energetic and ruthless Schörner exuded will and confidence, and quickly emulated his Führer by sacking various commanders, he proved unable to slow the Soviet onrush. By the end of 18 January, Soviet forces, having destroyed forward German defenses and routed their counterattacks, were in a headlong dash westward, with some units advancing twenty-five to thirty miles a day. Behind the front, masses of civilian refugees, and not a few stragglers from combat units, fled westward in treks that would become all too familiar. Although the Grossdeutschland Panzer Corps, sent by train from East Prussia with orders to "restore the situation," and the remnants of the 19th and 25th Panzer Divisions, tried to halt the Soviet advance near Lodz, they did little to slow Soviet momentum. Russian troops seized the large textile city on 19 January and reached the outskirts of Posen, the administrative center of the Wartheland, on the 21st. Although Posen, yet another of Hitler's "fortified places," held out until mid-February, by now the Soviets had steamrollered any opposition in their way. Enjoying complete aerial domination, some units raced northwest toward the Baltic coast of western Pomerania, while others swarmed toward the

Oder. On 30 January, Zhukov's troops reached Küstrin on the Oder, the last major barrier before Berlin – fifty miles distant – some 260 miles from their starting point two weeks earlier. In the first few days of February they proceeded to establish bridgeheads across the river in preparation for what seemed an imminent strike at the Reich capital. Hitler reacted to this disaster by renaming his army groups: Army Group Center became North, North became Courland, and A became Center. At the same time, a new Army Group, misleadingly named Vistula, was created under the most improbable of commanders, Heinrich Himmler, with the task of defending western Pomerania and the port city of Stettin.[23]

Even though both Zhukov and Konev hoped for a rapid thrust toward Berlin, each envisioning a triumphal entry into the Reich capital, the Soviet offensive had now stalled. As they fell back on their own borders, German resistance had stiffened considerably, while the Red Army had suffered not inconsiderable losses in men, tanks, and assault guns. In the dash to the Oder, the Soviets had also bypassed numerous pockets of resistance – the "fortified places" so beloved by Hitler – that now had to be eliminated, especially those astride rail and supply lines. None of these in themselves posed a major threat, but they did demand troops and time. More to the point, German resistance on the flanks seemed to be stiffening appreciably. The heavy fighting in East Prussia not only tied down large Soviet forces, but in causing Rokossovsky to veer away from Zhukov's right flank, it had left the latter dangerously vulnerable to counterattack, which through hard experience the Russians had learned was a favorite German tactic. Nor was Zhukov's left flank fully secure. Although Konev's troops had pushed beyond the Oder and secured bridgeheads south of Breslau, he was also feeling increasing German pressure on his left flank. Any drive on Berlin, though, would require Konev to redeploy forces to his right flank in order to support Zhukov. Before such an operation could commence, then, he would have to clean up the situation on his left, as well as deal with the problem of Fortress Breslau. In February, therefore, the Soviets turned their attention to clearing up the flanks, especially the so-called "Baltic balcony" overhanging Russian forces in the north.[24]

By now it was also clear that any realistic possibility of prolonging the war had vanished. At the end of January, Hitler had expressed to Goebbels the hope that "our improvisations will stop the Soviets," but improvisations, no matter how skillful or creative, could no longer balance the impact of sharply limited resources. Speer detailed the inescapable reality in a memorandum to Hitler on 30 January: with the loss of the coal and industrial capacity in Upper Silesia, he emphasized, it would be possible to sustain armaments production for only a few more months. Weapons losses could no longer be made good, nor, he stressed emphatically, seeking to shake Hitler free of any remaining illusions about the transcendence of will over firepower, can "the material superiority of the enemy ... [any] longer be countered by the bravery of our soldiers." Still, it is difficult to determine what impact such a stark appraisal of the situation actually had on Hitler. Although Goebbels recognized the truth in Speer's assessment, noting in his diary that it showed "things as they really are," and concluded that the only way out was through a political solution, he had little success in persuading the Führer. When, in mid-February, Goebbels broached the idea of an opening to the British, Hitler, as always, brushed the suggestion aside with the comment that the time was not yet right. When the time might be right, of course, had become a moot point.[25]

Although Goebbels remained remarkably radical and fanatic – to the extent of advocating Stalinist methods to sustain military discipline and the mass execution of Allied prisoners in response to the fire-bombing of Dresden he also retained the capacity, seemingly absent in the Führer, to recognize reality. Hitler, though, might not have been as deluded as often portrayed. When shown the final communiqué from the Yalta Conference held between Churchill, Roosevelt, and Stalin in February 1945, at which his enemies had agreed on the destruction of the Nazi regime – which meant any hope of a negotiated peace had finally evaporated – Hitler reacted "as if it had nothing to do with him any more" and merely repeated what he had already stated at the start of the year. "I've always said," he declared, "surrender is absolutely out of the question. History is not going to be repeated!" Ironically, Speer noted in his memoirs, at the time the most popularly quoted statement by Hitler, from *Mein Kampf*, read, "The task of diplomacy is to ensure that a nation does not heroically go to its destruction but is practically preserved. Every way that leads to this end is expedient, and a failure to follow it must be called criminal neglect of duty." By now, though, the Führer had decided that a Clausewitzian struggle to the last, not capitulation, was the best way to ensure the rebirth of the German nation.[26]

Even as the enemy drive stalled in the east, from late January the Western Allies, having regained the ground lost as a result of the Ardennes Offensive, resumed their push to the Rhine. German combat forces in the west now comprised fewer than 500,000 men, about a third the number in the east, and faced a foe with over 3.5 million troops, as well as crushing superiority in tanks, artillery, and in the air. Given the virtual collapse of defenses in the east, commanders in the west understood that they could expect reinforcements of neither men nor equipment. Still, the Germans continued to fight stubbornly. Although American and French forces reached the Rhine at Colmar in Alsace, in early February the main Allied attacks came north, in the Rhineland. Despite bad weather and fierce resistance, British and Canadian troops pushed steadily toward the Rhine, seizing Krefeld on 2 March and capturing over 50,000 Germans near Wesel on the 10th. To the south, American forces made more rapid progress, gaining the Rhine south of Düsseldorf on 2 March and reaching the outskirts of Cologne on the 5th. The great Rhenish metropolis fell two days later, but not before the Hohenzollern bridge across the Rhine had been blown.[27]

American troops enjoyed more dramatic success farther south at Remagen, between Bonn and Koblenz, when on 7 March they seized the Ludendorff bridge intact. Although an explosive charge had been detonated and had shaken the structure, it remained standing, allowing the Americans to rush troops across and establish a bridgehead on the east bank of the river. During the month of March, American forces also cleared the Saar–Mosel area and on the 28th pushed across the Rhine at Worms. The next day Mannheim, Ludwigshafen, and Frankfurt fell to the onrushing Americans, and the basis was established for simultaneous drives to the north to encircle the Ruhr, Germany's last remaining industrial area, and to the south to forestall any enemy resistance in the Alps. Still, German opposition had not been broken, although they had suffered crippling losses in the effort to defend the Rhineland; more than 60,000 men had been killed or wounded, with almost 300,000 taken prisoner, along with significant losses of tanks and artillery.[28]

By now, Hitler had few options left. A mid-February attack against the Russians from Pomerania designed to strike a decisive blow into the enemy's flanks (finalized only after a tumultuous two-hour meeting during which Guderian claimed that Hitler, "with fists raised, his cheeks flushed with rage, his whole body trembling", hurled vile accusations at him) ended almost as soon as it began, a miserable fiasco. Enemy forces had also breached both the Rhine and Oder, the last major rivers along which a defensive line could be constructed. Hitler returned to the notion of fortress cities, although it was far too late in the war for these to be effective in tying down large numbers of enemy troops, let alone provide the circumstances for a decisive counterattack. The same was true of holding onto the Courland pocket, which resulted only in a senseless waste of German troops who could have been much more profitably employed elsewhere. Living in a simulated world of maps, one in which he still had the illusion of decision-making freedom, Hitler sought to exercise the last bit of his authority as Feldherr in order to prolong the war to the last. Whereas his generals had betrayed him, and Himmler, ostensibly in charge of the failed Pomeranian counterattack, had shown himself to be merely a pedantic bureaucrat, Hitler clung to the delusion that the armies he moved around on the map still had the ability to alter his fate.[29]

At Budapest, Königsberg, and Breslau, to be sure, German resistance did have an impact on Red Army progress. Hitler hoped that Budapest in particular would prove to be a "Stalingrad on the Danube." Fierce fighting for the city, including savage street fighting reminiscent of the battle on the Volga, continued until mid-February, making it one of the longest and bloodiest urban battles of the war. Both sides suffered appalling losses. While the Germans and Hungarians suffered 50,000 men killed and 138,000 taken prisoner, the Soviets lost, in the fighting for Budapest, some 100,000 men killed and almost 1,800 tanks destroyed. Even then, Hitler proved unwilling to concede the loss of Hungary and the last remaining oil fields under German control. He thought in terms of a strike around Lake Balaton that would safeguard the oil wells, guard the approaches to Vienna, and, if successful, allow troops to be transferred to the Oder. Against Guderian's protests, he – and it was his operation, for Hitler issued commands to units at the lowest level – launched the last German counterattack of the war on 6 March. Sepp Dietrich's replenished 6th SS Panzer Army crashed into Soviet forces, hoping to push them back across the Danube and retake Budapest. The Soviets resisted stoutly, though, and after ten days of heavy fighting in which they managed to advance only twelve to twenty miles, exhausted, mired in mud, and out of fuel, Dietrich broke off the effort. For the third time elite SS units, with their qualitatively superior Panther and Tiger tanks, had let the Führer down, and now he reacted with a fury savage by even his own standards at this late stage in the war. As it became obvious that these elite troops had violated orders to fight to the last, preferring retreat to death and abandoning much irreplaceable heavy weaponry, Hitler ordered that Dietrich's units, including his own Leibstandarte Adolf Hitler Division, be stripped of their distinctive armbands in disgrace. This humiliation notwithstanding – an act that appalled even the faithful Goebbels – by the end of March the last oil fields had been lost and the way to Vienna lay open.[30]

With the failure of the Hungarian counterattack, and having used up his last reserves, there remained little for Hitler to do other than ponder the destruction of Germany but, with a twist, this time at his own hand. By now his destructive rage encompassed his own people, disappointed as he was at their failure to prove the strongest in the Darwinian struggle for existence.

He was, it seemed, determined both to prevent a repetition of November 1918 and to stage a Götterdämmerung that would create a heroic myth of struggle to the end that would serve as the basis of a future national regeneration. As such, no price, even self-destruction – his own and Germany's – was too high to pay. Perhaps also drawing on Stalin's example, Hitler envisioned a scorched-earth policy that would deny the enemy any benefit from German industrial riches. How this might turn the tables in the late stages of the war remained far from clear, since the Allies could easily supply themselves from their own resources. Still, Hitler persisted in spinning fantasies, even assuring Albert Kesselring, who had replaced Rundstedt as OB West on 10 March, that he had plans to spring a historic reverse on his adversaries. His actions, though, only threatened the existence of the German people; in a dreadful paradox it was Hitler, who had long warned that the "Jewish conspiracy" was out to destroy Germany, who now resolved to do just that.[31]

If Hitler had, indeed, entered his own world of unreality, one in which his actions made sense in terms not of what was but what should be – a sort of "National Socialist realism" – the actions of those around him are more inexplicable and harder to justify. Speer, for example, had worked since late 1944 to water down Hitler's destructive orders, arguing that it was better to paralyze production by immobilizing industry than to destroy it entirely, since the former allowed the possibility of restoring production once the territory had been regained, an argument that played to Hitler's fantasy that the situation could still be reversed. Speer, of course, later claimed that he aimed to preserve Germany's material substance for the future, but his intentions at the time seemed less than clear. He had, along with Goebbels, long been an advocate of total war, a ruthless exponent of mobilizing the economy whose efforts had resulted in the steady expansion of armaments production through 1944. Until the end of January 1945, in fact, he projected a rather optimistic assessment to Hitler and other top Nazis, insisting that he could maintain armaments output as long as the Wehrmacht could hold the existing economic area and no more skilled workers were drafted into the army. His confidence had certainly influenced Hitler's January decision to launch attacks in Hungary rather than reinforce the Vistula, since Speer convinced the Führer of the importance of Hungarian oil and bauxite deposits.[32]

Speer's epiphany that the war could no longer be won seems to have come rather belatedly, only at the end of January with the failure of the Ardennes Offensive and the loss of the vital Silesian industrial area. Even then, his actions hardly resembled those of a man intent on ensuring a speedy end to the war, making it clear that he placed military needs above the interests of the east German population. He not only instructed Gauleiters in the east that the armaments industries should continue working to the last possible moment, but also demanded that the Wehrmacht be given absolute priority in all transport matters, dooming large numbers of civilian refugees. Speer remained determined to "force out of the arms production . . . anything which could still be forced out of it," especially fuel and munitions, so that the Wehrmacht could continue the hopeless fight. Speer's economic strategy of holding out to the last certainly contributed to the belated evacuation orders in the east that resulted in such human misery, but this was, he declared in the unmistakable language of a Nazi racial ideologue, "a tough selection . . . [which] would contain a good kernel of this unique people for the distant future." Although aware that the war could not be won economically, Speer nonetheless seemed intent on defending as much Reich territory as possible.[33]

This duality was clearly revealed in two memoranda he wrote to Hitler in mid-March. The first, written on 15 March but not delivered by adjutant Below to the Führer until the 18th, presented a blunt picture of reality, predicting that the war economy would collapse in four to eight weeks. Speer therefore urged the Führer not to destroy the industrial and economic infrastructure of the Reich but "to help the people wherever possible" and refrain from "undertak[ing] demolitions which may strike at the very life of the nation." Above all, he stressed, the material substance of Germany had to be preserved: the destruction of infrastructure "means eliminating all further possibility for the German people to survive." The German people, Speer concluded, had to be allowed "to maintain a basic standard of life . . . We have the duty to leave the people all possibilities that could secure them reconstruction in the more distant future."[34]

At the same time, though, he wrote Hitler another memorandum that substantially differed in tone from the first. If economic collapse was unavoidable, Speer stressed, drastic measures were necessary to defend the Reich at the Rhine and Oder. Since it would be impossible to defend Germany beyond those obstacles, he urged that ruthless measures be taken to mobilize all possible resources, including human, to defend these river lines. Troops should be transferred back from Norway and Italy to partici-pate in this last-ditch defense which, he thought, "can gain respect from the enemy and perhaps thus favorably determine the end of the war." What Speer meant by this remains unclear. Perhaps he hoped to ease the impact of his first memorandum by appearing to endorse a version of Hitler's downfall scenario. Or perhaps he really believed that a heroic defense that promised even more death and misery to its fighting forces might yet wring concessions from Germany's enemies. In any case, Hitler's response quickly dispelled any illusions that Speer had. On that same day, 18 March, he remarked acidly, "We can no longer take regard of the population," while the next day the Führer emphasized that if the war was lost, then the only thing left to do was to deny the enemy anything of value in Germany. Even if a miracle occurred and lost territory was recaptured, he insisted – displaying a touch of realism – it was foolish to believe the enemy would not himself engage in a scorched-earth policy and destroy everything. His "Nero Order" of 19 March 1945 ("Destructive Measures on Reich Territory") that ordered the destruction of all military, transport, industrial, and communications installations, as well as all material resources, also betrayed the iron logic of his own social Darwinism. "If the war is lost so too is the Volk," he declared, so no special measures need be taken to ensure its survival in the near future, as "the Volk [would have] shown itself to be the weaker." Large numbers of those Germans left alive would be the dregs of the racial stock, since the best would have been killed in the war. There was, therefore, no use in providing for their immediate existence, even on the most primitive of levels.[35]

Although, in the event, Speer stymied the "Nero Order" through his efforts to persuade political and military authorities not to carry out destruction, the reality of imminent German collapse was evident to all. Even as they managed to stabilize the Eastern Front, the Western Allies had resumed their advance. As long as German forces could hold the Rhine, there seemed to be some feasible strategy for defending the Reich, but once the enemy crossed that river any reason for fighting on largely evaporated. By late March, American troops were across the Rhine in numerous places and by 4 April they had completed the encirclement of the Ruhr, an action that finally sealed Germany's fate. Field Marshal Model's Army Group B, numerically strong but lacking heavy weapons, was surrounded and its destruction became only a matter of time. Although in places capable of stout resistance, the overall picture was now one of recognition of the inevitable, as numerous towns surrendered without a fight and troops began deserting wholesale. Model, too, who had long counted as one of Hitler's most trusted generals, drew the inescapable conclusion. Although not overt in his support of Nazism, his own hatred of communism and desire to stave off defeat served the regime well, as did his insistence to the troops in recent weeks that the struggle had to be continued even to the point of self-sacrifice. Even though Model cooperated with Speer in refusing to destroy vital economic infrastructure, his sense of soldierly duty could not bring him to surrender his encircled forces. Instead, on 17 April he dissolved his army group, thus sparing himself the humiliation of capitulation, and committed suicide. In the meantime, the Americans had also advanced into southern Germany, although even now German forces were still capable of inflicting sharp losses on the enemy despite the fact that their society was collapsing around them.[36]

The last enemy blow came on 16 April when the Soviets – with an enormous force of 2.5 million men, over 6,000 tanks, and an astonishing 42,000 artillery pieces and mortars – unleashed an attack across the Oder with the aim of seizing Berlin. Although they correctly anticipated the Soviet plan of attack, because they lacked sufficient manpower, fuel, and ammunition, there was little the Germans could do to contain it. To the south, Konev's army struck across the Lusatian Neisse toward Cottbus, then turned north toward the capital. Due east of the city, Zhukov's forces struggled for a few days against determined German opposition along the Seelow Heights – the last German tactical success of the war, pulled off by the defensive specialist, Heinrici – but that achievement proved fleeting. German defenses on the Oder collapsed on 19 April, while to the southeast of Berlin, Konev's troops surrounded the German 9th Army near the small town of Halbe. Although it eventually managed to fight its way to the west, some 40,000 Germans died in the Halbe Pocket. By 22 April, Soviet forces had seized OKH headquarters at Zossen, just south of the capital, and had reached the northern and eastern outskirts of Berlin. The next day, Soviet troops cut off the city to the north, east, and south, leaving only a thin corridor to the west open. Two days later, on 25 April, American and Soviet forces met on the Elbe at Torgau, effectively dividing Germany in half, while the next day Red Army soldiers began fighting their way into Berlin itself, which could now only be reached by air. Although Hitler had planned to turn the sprawling city, with its distinctive housing blocks, extensive subway system, and intricate network of canals, into a scene of prolonged urban warfare, this failed to materialize: the Soviets had cut the capital off from the outside world, preventing any remaining German troops from reinforcing it. Despite the Führer's wish, the decisive battle for Berlin had been conducted outside the city; it had gone down not, as the Führer had hoped, in a Wagnerian burst of glory that would serve as an inspiration for future generations, but in a ragged wave of destruction. Instead of being the rallying point, it served as the death knell of the Third Reich. By this time, too, any further coherent defense of the capital, or within what was left of Nazi-controlled Germany, had collapsed. While Hitler issued increasingly nonsensical orders, individual officers simply tried to save what could still be saved.[37]

Despite everything, Hitler remained determined to fight on, not necessarily from any residual belief in victory but in order to create the myth
essential for the rebirth, some time in the future, of a defeated Germany.
Although certainly a physical wreck – according to one general who was
summoned to the bunker, "he presented a terrible picture. He dragged
himself along slowly and laboriously . . . He lacked a sense of balance . . . He
had lost control of his right arm, the right hand trembled constantly . . .
Saliva often trickled from the corners of the mouth" – he nonetheless
remained mentally sharp. Heinrici observed in late March that Hitler "gave
me the impression of a man who was seriously physically ill. This changed
completely as soon as discussion with him got underway. Immediately he
became lively, answered with clear, considered arguments, and proved
himself to be most extremely strong-willed . . . He . . . held the reins himself
firmly in his grasp." Indeed he did, for Heinrici had been subjected to a
tirade of titanic proportions, as Hitler insulted him, the general staff, and
the entire officer corps. They all, he screamed, had never understood, or
refused to understand, his halt orders because of their "cowardice and lack
of steadfastness." Again, in early April, Heinrici witnessed the firm hold
Hitler retained on his entourage and the apparent conviction he conveyed
that the impending Soviet offensive would be "the bloodiest defeat of the
war for the enemy and the greatest defensive success." By this time though,
the general staff, whom Hitler dismissed contemptuously as those "learned
gentlemen with their book knowledge," had been reduced to irrelevance.
Goebbels, ever the radical, dreamed of a harsher fate for the institution
"within whose womb the assassination attempt against the Führer had been
born"; he thought they should be dealt with similarly to the SA in June
1934. In the end, Hitler, after yet another stormy scene on 28 March, settled
merely for ordering Guderian to take convalescent leave. Afterwards he
confided to Goebbels that it was Guderian who had been the first senior
officer to act against his halt order in front of Moscow, so "the blame for the
great crisis in the east in the winter of 1941–1942 should be ascribed to his
account." To the last, the image of the infallible Feldherr had to remain
intact.[38]

Even as this illusory world crashed down about him, however, it is not
quite accurate to see Hitler as someone who had descended completely into
irrationality or madness. He accurately predicted to Goebbels on 22 March,
"The enemy coalition will break up in any circumstance; the only question
is whether it breaks up before we are beaten down, or only after that."
Despite lingering hopes that a "political crisis in the enemy camp is a justification for our greatest hopes," that the British and Americans "would not

leave him in the lurch as the champion of western culture and civilization against the barbarity of the east," he was clear-sighted enough about what was actually happening and understood the hopelessness of the German situation. The death of Roosevelt on 12 April seemed temporarily to revive the Führer and give him hope that, as with his hero Frederick the Great, the sudden death of an enemy leader would shatter the unnatural coalition and provide an avenue of escape. In late December 1944 he had appealed to his generals to hold out using just such an historic example. "It is not a question," he declared, "whether Germany will be granted any kind of merciful existence by our opponents if they are victorious. Instead," he stressed, with obvious reference to the Morgenthau Plan for the destruction of German industry, "it is a question of whether Germany will continue to exist at all." Frederick, he emphasized, not entirely correctly, had held out against far larger numbers and in worse circumstances, and had in the end proved victorious. In such situations, he insisted, and in this he had long been convinced of the providential nature of chance, "the cast of mind is a decisive factor, making it possible to find new ways out and mobilizing new possibilities." Similarly, in early February 1945 he speculated to his inner circle that a change at the top in one of the Western democracies might create an entirely new constellation of power for, after all, "coalitions are also the work of men."[39]

Now, evidently, just such a miracle opportunity, the reason why he had stubbornly demanded the mobilization of the last German resources, had presented itself. For the man who always prided himself on playing for all-or-nothing stakes, the winnings seemed at hand. Roosevelt was, after all, not just any opponent, but, to Hitler, exemplified the "Jewish lackey," the figure whom the "Jewish conspiracy" in America had manipulated to their advantage. With his death, the United States would be released from the Jewish spell. Speer later claimed that Hitler, in a state of high excitement, declared that this was the "great miracle" he had anticipated, allegedly as a result of a horoscope Goebbels had commissioned two weeks earlier. Whether this was genuine conviction remains unclear, however. His adjutant Below, who was a close observer of Hitler in these last days, thought the Führer more sober about the news than Goebbels, who always had an eye turned toward possible propaganda advantages. To the end, most around Hitler found it difficult to discern his true belief about whether the war was lost, but this was largely irrelevant. He remained determined to stage his end according to his own scenario, a stance that forced him to maintain an unwavering posture of resistance; only occasionally did the facade crack, and even then, so briefly that drawing any conclusions proved problematic.[40]

Since defeat could not be avoided, and with it the destruction of both his regime and himself, the vital thing was to create a lasting myth of heroic defiance. Indeed, when on the night of 20–21 April, Walther Hewel, the Foreign Ministry representative on his staff, suggested that it was time for a political initiative, Hitler retorted in disgust, "I don't do politics any more. Politics makes me sick. When I am dead you will have to do plenty of politics." Hitler had now drawn the only remaining conclusion: he would stay in Berlin and die in the ruins of the capital. This decision had been confirmed on 22 April when he was informed, in the company of Jodl, Keitel, Hans Krebs (the new OKH chief of staff), and Wilhelm Burgdorf (chief adjutant to Hitler), that the attack by the combat group under SS General Felix Steiner – an assault on Berlin that was supposed to turn the tide – had not, indeed never could have, taken place, Hitler unleashed his last furious tirade. All had been the result of betrayal and "long-term treachery" on the part of the army, he screamed, in an outburst that lasted half an hour. At the end, though, he finally admitted the obvious: the war was lost. He would, he announced, stay in Berlin and "go down . . . with my soldiers and fall in battle for the symbol of the Reich." Nor was this the result of some sudden impulse, for in late autumn 1944 he had already pondered the idea of declaring his Wolf's Lair headquarters a "festen Platz" and dying there as a fortress commander.[41]

How much better, though, to die in Berlin, for, as he declared at his last situation conference on 27 April, it was "not a bad end to a life if one falls during the battle for the capital of one's Reich." For him, this was not a senseless act of despair; indeed, the later efforts by many historians to determine his psychological state, to locate his reasons for taking his life in his depressive attitude, seem irrelevant, almost surreal. Hitler, who had talked of suicide on numerous occasions throughout his life, asserted in his last testament that he chose death "of his own free will" and would die "with a happy heart." To him, taking his life offered the best alternative under the circumstances: a heroic struggle to the end that would symbolize eternal victory and a valorization of National Socialism. Heroic death, after all, had a redemptive quality to it; the courage to fight to the end, to death, with no hope of victory or even surviving, would lay the basis for the regeneration of Germany. As he had asserted on 25 April, his words dripping with contempt for those who urged surrender, "It was those smart-asses Clausewitz warned of – people who always see the easier way as more intelligent." If he fled, he insisted, he would "vanish from the stage of world history as an inglorious refugee . . . Only a heroic attitude can enable us to stand this difficult time." Hitler's physical condition prevented him from his preferred choice of staging his death in combat, since he feared either being taken alive and displayed by Stalin as an animal in a cage during a victory parade through Red Square – or having his corpse, if taken intact, displayed as a trophy of battle or left hanging, like Mussolini's, and exposed to public ridicule. Still, he could, at least, do what Paulus had been unable or unwilling to do in Stalingrad: commit suicide in the ruins of his fortress. This, to him, was the final service he could render, the last expression of his charismatic authority: in a terrible echo of the Nazi wartime slogan, "The individual must die so the nation can live," he would now die so that a destroyed Germany could be reborn. His example, he thought, would create a myth of resistance that would inspire a new generation of Germans. His authority and will, then, remained undiluted to the end.[42]

Indeed, the initial news of Hitler's death, broadcast over the radio on the night of 30 April, stressed that, "fighting to the last breath against Bolshevism," the Führer had "fallen for Germany." Not to be outdone, the Wehrmacht report of 2 May claimed that Hitler's example, "faithful unto death," was now "binding on all soldiers." The fact that he had committed suicide and so, in one sense, had abandoned his followers, was suppressed in favor of the fiction of a "heroic death." Still, Jodl's claim that in dying in the ruins of Berlin he died not an easier, but the surer death, was in some ways valid. It could not be otherwise; having willed the outcome, an appropriate myth had to be created to justify the destruction. The last communiqué issued on 9 May by Hitler's successor as head of state, Admiral Dönitz, confirmed this. Although defeated only by a "huge superior force," it read in part, "the German soldier, true to his oath and with the greatest dedication, has performed deeds which will never be forgotten. The home front" – in obvious contrast to the First World War, a point of emphasis that could not have been missed by its audience – "supported him to the last with all its powers [while] suffering the greatest sacrifices. The unique achievement of the front and the home front will find its ultimate appreciation in a future just verdict of history . . ." As a result, and already pointing to the future, "Every soldier can therefore hand over his weapons with honor and pride and begin work courageously and confidently for the eternal life of our people in the darkest hour of its history . . . The dead obligate us to unconditional loyalty, to obedience and discipline with regard to a Fatherland bleeding from countless wounds." In an almost perfectly phrased statement, in which neither the responsibility nor the crimes of Hitler were mentioned, the very fact of unbroken resistance to the last had provided the basis for rebirth in the future. In echoes of the cult of the fallen soldier from the earlier war, individuals had died so the nation might live again, thus providing redemptive meaning for the bitter hardships and sacrifices just endured.[43]

In the end, of course, there was no repetition of the much-feared collapse of military authority and humiliating capitulation of November 1918. Indeed, in many respects the amazing thing was not so much that Hitler persisted to the end, but that the great majority of Germans, especially workers, also endured to the last in a rather astonishing display, given the destruction of Germany, of national unity. In part, this resulted from the very determination of Hitler to prevent it; as Martin Bormann declared in a directive of 1 April demanding from party leaders utter ruthlessness in fighting to the last, "After the collapse of 1918 we devoted ourselves . . . to the struggle for the right of existence of our people. Now the high point of our test has come: the danger of renewed enslavement facing our people demands our last and supreme effort." These orders were accompanied by pitiless terror against Germans, especially in the west, inclined to surrender. In the east, fears of Bolshevik retribution, fanned by Goebbels and seemingly confirmed by the reality of Soviet revenge in territories they had overrun, encouraged continued resistance. Hitler had long imparted a potent sense of threatened national identity, which, when whipped up by Goebbels's propaganda, played an important role in stiffening and prolonging German resistance. The massive terror and destruction of the aerial bombing raids and the demands for unconditional surrender also convinced many Germans that Hitler's apocalyptic vision – that its enemies intended to destroy the nation – was correct. If its foes meant to annihilate Germany, then it was imperative to fight on. But people struggled on, as well, from a lingering affinity with Nazism, from a certain sense of satisfaction in defiance and self-assertion – almost a perverse pride in their ability to sustain punishment and stay standing – and from a refusal to accept the humiliation of defeat. Germans wanted, perhaps, to see the end of Nazism, but not the end of the German nation.[44]

At the same time, the total defeat and utter devastation of their homeland ensured that there would be no repetition of the stab-in-the-back legend following the First World War. The failure to fight on in 1918 had, in the post-war years, crystallized a sense of moral malaise, of corruption in the national body. A vibrant nation, it was argued, would have continued the fight beyond defeat and, in so doing, have gained redemption. Instead, the only thing epochal following the First World War was the outrage among nationalists that German honor had been besmirched. As Hitler had argued in the 1920s, salvation had to be found in the creation of a new society that would restore moral vigor and health to the nation, as well as deal out retribution to its enemies, both internal and external. In 1945, Hitler, according to Jodl, chose deliberately to continue the war precisely to ensure that the Third Reich would end in ruins. The only thing missing was the Führer's death in battle, fighting the Asiatic-Bolshevik hordes, which Hitler himself recognized. "I should already have made this decision," he told Jodl on 22 April 1945, "in November 1944 and should have never left the headquarters in East Prussia." To die in war, Hitler thought, meant being remembered, for both a leader and a nation. He preferred death, he asserted, to capitulation in order to sow "a seed . . . in German history that will one day grow to usher in the glorious rebirth of the National Socialist movement in a truly united nation." In addition, only such absolute destruction would compel future generations to seek to avenge the dead. "The more we suffer," Hitler proclaimed on 2 April, "the more glorious will be the resurrection of eternal Germany."[45]

As Hitler – "faithful," he claimed "to the ideals of the great Clausewitz" – asserted in his testament, "Centuries will pass but out of the ruins of our towns and of our art the hatred will be renewed against the people who . . . are responsible and whom we can thank for all of this: International Jewry and its auxiliaries." Ironically, though, Hitler's determination to fight to the finish in order to create the basis of a new myth only affirmed the reality of terror and hardship inflicted on the German people. Few, at the end of this war, could – or desired to – claim that Germany had not been defeated on the battlefield. In yet another paradox, Hitler's obsession with erasing the memory of 1918 had been accomplished, but not in the way he had intended. The horrors of the last months of the war had purged images of suffering following the earlier war. This time, Germans seemed merely to want an end to it all, quickly relegating Hitler and Nazism to the past. In one sense, though, Hitler had been successful. He wanted to create the conditions for a rebirth of Germany and this he had accomplished. With his own charismatic authority and the legitimacy of the Nazi regime completely shattered by this unparalleled catastrophe, the way was now clear for the emergence of a new and different Germany.[46]

12

Hitler as Feldherr
AN ASSESSMENT

"It is one of those queer twists of history," Hitler observed on 24 February 1945:

> that just as I was assuming power in Germany, Roosevelt, the elect of the Jews, was taking command in the United States. Without the Jews and without this lackey of theirs, things could have been quite different . . . The United States as a matter of fact could survive and prosper in a state of economic isolation; for us, that is a dream which we would love to see come true. They have at their disposal a vast territory, ample to absorb the energies of all their people. As far as Germany is concerned, my hope is one day to ensure for her complete economic independence inside a territory of a size compatible with her population. A great people has need of broad acres.

His ambitious plans for Germany, though, had been ruined "by the fact that world Jewry has chosen just that country [the United States] in which to set up its most powerful bastion. That, and that alone, has . . . poisoned everything." Earlier in the month, on 7 February, he had rued the fact that Germany's policy of colonization had failed, and had largely blamed the United States – that "monster" led by the "Jew-ridden Roosevelt" – for this result. He found some comfort, however, in the fact that:

> With the defeat of the Reich and pending the emergence of the Asiatic, the African and, perhaps, the South American nationalisms, there will remain in the world only two Great Powers capable of confronting each

other: the United States and Soviet Russia. The laws of both history and geography will compel these two Powers to a trial of strength, either militarily or in the fields of economics and ideology. These same laws make it inevitable that both Powers . . . will sooner or later find it desirable to seek the support of the sole surviving great nation in Europe, the German people.

Ironically, at the end of a lost war fought against the hated "Jewish-Bolshevik" enemy in order to secure Lebensraum, Hitler thought that Russia would shed its Marxism and return to an aggressive pan-Slavism, while America would be the vehicle for the Jewish "world conspiracy."[1]

Beyond these musings – part perceptive insight, part raving lunacy – Hitler provided a revealing glimpse into his mental world. He had been, we now know, concerned by the economic power and strategic potential of the United States since the late 1920s. He had also long been obsessed by the existential threat to Germany posed by the alleged Jewish world conspiracy. It was this power, he believed, that had been behind the German collapse in 1918. Jews had not only fomented chaos, but had then profited from it. The only possible response for Germany, he stressed continually, was to create a strong, unified society capable of waging war to secure the Lebensraum necessary to confront this threat and secure the existence of the German Volk. Against all logic, Hitler had risen to power and gone a long way toward realizing the first precondition for successful expansion. Nonetheless, despite his impressive rearmament efforts, in the summer of 1939, at the latest, the realization had sunk in that he might never be in a position to accomplish this historic goal. With Britain, France, and now the United States rearming as well, the opportunity might never arise to wage a successful war for living space. The leap into war, then, was based on a gamble that Germany could use whatever temporary advantage it had in order to secure, at least partially, the resources needed to win the larger war he envisioned. The spectacular Blitzkrieg triumphs in Poland, Norway, and France, though, obscured the deeper reality: Germany had possessed no clear economic, military, or technical superiority over its Western opponents, nor would it have any such advantages over the Soviet Union.

Any assessment of Hitler the strategist and military leader must take account of both his undeniable abilities and the closeness with which he came, in 1940 and 1941, to winning the war – or at least achieving the conditions for a favorable outcome. The widespread assumption that thereafter Hitler succumbed to hubris is only partly true: hubris is more a fault of character than vision, and in large part it was Hitler's vision, his expansionist and, ultimately, exterminationist aims, that proved his undoing. On the eve of the invasion of the Soviet Union, after all, Hitler hardly resembled the typical picture of an arrogant and self-assured leader, beset as he was by doubt and anxiety. In early January 1941 he had warned, "The Russians should not be underestimated," while on the eve of the attack Himmler had confided to Heydrich, "The Führer is not so optimistic as his military advisers." Indeed, that same night of 21 June 1941, Hitler, seemingly lost in thought, observed that Russia was like a ship in "the Flying Dutchman," then added somberly, "The beginning of every war is like opening the door into a dark room. One never knows what is hidden in the darkness." It was the striking tenacity with which he pursued his vision of Lebensraum – which could only be obtained by means of a war of conquest in Russia – rather than hubris that led him to launch such a risky enterprise. "No decision I had to make during the course of this war," he remarked to what remained of his entourage near the end of a conflict that had turned global:

> was graver than to attack Russia . . . For Time – and it's always Time, you notice – would have been increasingly against us . . . We had no choice, we had at all costs to strike . . . [because of] the mortal threat that Russia . . . constituted to our existence. For it was absolutely certain that one day or another she would attack us . . . Why 1941? Because, in view of the steadily increasing power of our western enemies, if we were to act at all, we had to do so with the least possible delay.

After all, he concluded, "raw materials . . . were essential to us."[2]

Hitler had internalized certain ideas from his First World War experience that became fixed points of his ideology, especially those of racial struggle (to revenge and expunge the alleged causes of defeat) and the absolute necessity of Lebensraum (to provide Germany the material basis for elevation to world power status). He was driven by his remorseless pursuit of Lebensraum, of restoring German pride, of return to great power status, and perhaps also of making good the shame of defeat in the earlier war. Implicit in all this were violence and war, which Hitler both understood and embraced. Indeed, an increasing aggressiveness and willingness to risk war were characteristic of his leadership. Crucially, to a great extent his ideas also overlapped with those of his generals. His rise to Feldherr would not have been possible based just on his ideas alone; he needed the framework provided by the military establishment as the context within which to achieve his first successes. They fully accepted his premise both of the necessity of securing Lebensraum and, by implication, of the murderous consequences such an effort would entail. Still, through the 1930s, and even in the Polish campaign, his generals, admittedly to a declining extent, constrained Hitler. German victory in the west, though, altered Hitler's relationship with his generals. In a very real sense it had been his triumph, one that brought German control over much of Europe, something unprecedented in German history that conferred on him enormous prestige.

This marked not the end for him, however, but only the beginning, for conquest of Lebensraum remained the one thing that made sense of the Nazi program, his program. Hitler prided himself on being a *Raumpolitiker*, a geopolitician who thought in grand terms of space, rather than a *Grenzpolitiker* who was concerned merely with border revisions. He thus combined his twin fixations, race and space, into one vision. He wanted, he proclaimed after the defeat of Poland, nothing less than "a resettlement of nationalities" in eastern Europe, an untangling of ethnic groups predicated on the establishment of a racially cleansed and powerful German core at the center of a larger European empire. This breathtakingly radical and overweening project could only be accomplished by a war of extermination, which he intended from the beginning. Moreover, not only did Hitler's total goals signify a total war, but such was also inherent in the means chosen to accomplish this. Blitzkrieg, itself, entailed a concept of total war; the surest way to defeat your enemy, after all, was to annihilate him. Since the dilemma of a two-front war and crippling blockade could only be resolved through territorial expansion and exploitation of conquered resources and manpower, it followed that decisions on how to fight a war should be influenced by these considerations. It had, therefore, to be swift, ruthless, merciless, brutal, and result in the destruction of all opposition.[3]

In the event, of course, the demands and pressures of a speedy advance and victory in Russia led to brutal actions, but their necessity had already been anticipated in the criminal orders issued before the offensive. In addition, memories of the First World War and the hunger that then seemed to sap the German civilian will to endure played a role in the conduct of the campaign in Russia. Not only was the Ostheer expected to live off the land, but scarce food resources had to be made available for delivery to the German home front. Harsh measures used to secure food supplies, though, provoked growing resistance, which caused Hitler and OKH to respond with even more brutality. This resulted in the thing they most feared, a prolonged and costly partisan war that spiraled out of control. Their response, absolute destruction in parts of the western borderlands of the Soviet Union, turned Clausewitz on his head: war was still the continuation of politics by other means, but both the means and end now involved total devastation.

Clausewitz also insisted that a Feldherr must control events instead of being overwhelmed by them. By that reckoning, Hitler had begun to lose command over the course of events in late July and early August 1941 at Smolensk. Already in mid-August, Goebbels had glimpsed a bit of Hitler's doubts, recording in his diary the Führer's musings, "Separate peace with Stalin? Will Churchill fall?" As early as mid-November 1941, that is, even before the setback before Moscow, Hitler realized that the war – at least his war, the way he had envisioned victory – could no longer be won, remarking to Halder, "The recognition, by both of the opposing coalitions, that they cannot annihilate each other, leads to a negotiated peace." Subsequent offensives, whether the triumph at Kiev or Operation Typhoon, always seemed a matter of "catching up" and trying to regain control, while the final assault on Moscow carried a whiff of desperation, of trying to avoid another Marne. Paradoxically, it was the failure of Blitzkrieg and the Soviet counterattack in December 1941 that cemented the Führer's transformation into Feldherr. The German officer corps already shared many goals with him, but the winter crisis of 1941–2 bound them tighter to the Führer, as he now seemed to be indispensable to mastering the situation. As Admiral Raeder insisted in August 1945, "the manner in which he [Hitler] took command of and handled military matters" appeared to verify that Hitler was "really a genius, a man called to leadership."[4]

Much the same sense of playing from behind, of frantically trying to gain some sort of victory in the Soviet Union before American power could be brought to bear, was apparent in 1942, with the offensive in the south designed less to achieve absolute victory than to gain the prerequisite to stalemate the war against the Anglo-American powers. Hitler might not be able to win the victory he originally envisioned, but he might be able to win a different type of victory – or at least not lose absolutely. However, he proved unable to make a separate peace because he could never relinquish his Lebensraum goals; they were simply too crucial to his understanding of continued German existence. Also, Hitler could never quite abandon his belief that he could yet make the unfavorable circumstances he faced conform to his ideas. As early as 1936, after all, he had told Speer he would either succeed entirely or fail – if he succeeded, he would be one of the great men in history; if he failed, he would be condemned and damned.[5]

Ultimately, as well, Hitler refused to consider the possibility of negotiating a way out of the war because that conjured up an image of the "shame of 1918" – and under no circumstances would he allow a premature end to the war to erode the possibility of avoiding absolute defeat, as he thought had happened in 1918. He persisted in the belief that, as with Frederick the

Great, one decisive German victory might convince one or another of his enemies that, in view of the cost of subduing such a stubborn opponent, it might be better simply to deal with him. As he remarked to two of his generals in August 1944, he would fight on "until, like Frederick the Great said, one of our damned enemies gets tired of fighting, and until we (get) a peace that will secure life for the German nation . . . and that doesn't damage our honor a second time the way it (happened) in 1918." He could also fall back on Clausewitz for justification of his decision to hold out, for the great theorist had insisted that a regime that did not pursue a final showdown, that failed to rally all its forces, including those on the home front, had, in the end, acted inconsequentially and showed "that it was not worthy of a victory and perhaps for that very reason was also not capable" of achieving one.[6]

Despite later post-war criticisms from his generals, Hitler had some undeniable strengths. He tried to anticipate or project how foreign policy matters would unfold – sometimes rightly, sometimes wrongly – and he stubbornly pursued his basic ideological objectives, especially Lebensraum. Germany, he thought, had to have sufficient space, which could only be achieved by war at the expense of the Soviet Union. His mistake, then, was not that he could have achieved his goal through continued clever diplomacy and bluff – he could not – but his failure to realize that Great Britain was not likely to grant him the free hand in the east that he thought he had after Munich. To return to Clausewitz, political aims and military strategy are indivisible. In planning and running a war, first one then the other is paramount. The dilemma for Hitler was that his political aims were so radical that he was faced with the problem of how to achieve so much with so little. He always intended to wage war sooner or later, but his understanding of the growing threat from America, especially Roosevelt's increasing support for the Western democracies, caused him to gamble on war in 1939, before Germany was fully ready. This decision was based on the not so irrational presumption that if he waited, the power of his enemies would become so overwhelming that he would never be able to win a war he deemed essential for Germany's survival as a people and nation. The fundamental problem, then, was one of grand strategy: Hitler's goal was not merely a revision of the Versailles system, but a complete reordering of Europe – and perhaps the world – for which the conquest of Lebensraum in the east was the essential first step. Thus, war against the Soviet Union was always the "right" war for Hitler; only then could he establish a German hegemony over Europe in order to confront the rising threat from the United States from a position of strength. To achieve his vision, he needed total war and total victory, but this absolute dominance would inevitably provoke absolute resistance.

Given his goals, his strategic decisions were neither as illogical nor as irrational as his generals claimed after the war; indeed, he almost always had the support of at least some key officers for his actions. He certainly had a clear view of his aims and possessed a keen strategic understanding, especially of the political and economic weaknesses facing Germany, but had less understanding of operations or logistics. His generals, on the other hand, often proved adept at operations and tactics, but not strategy or logistics. Hitler, though, proved unable or unwilling to combine the separate strengths into an effective command structure. Moreover, once the war turned defensive – that is, precisely when it moved out of the realm of "common sense" observations – Hitler needed to rely more on the advice of his generals. This, however, was precisely the moment when his distrust of them – at the scheming behind his back, the alteration of agreed plans, and his growing belief that they were neither particularly competent nor combative – caused him to interfere not only in operational decisions but also in tactical matters. Again, his early leadership style, the cult of *Leistung* (achievement), of the promotion of a meritocracy and individual initiative, fit well with the army's emphasis on Auftragstaktik. But eventually Hitler, with his lack of professional military training, could overcome neither his antipathy toward the elite with insider knowledge nor his burning resentment at social privilege. This led him to despise the whole notion of the general staff, as a socially exclusive and elite caste largely closed to outsiders like him, and to distance himself from their professional advice.

Still, at least until late 1942, he preferred, in a sense, to mimic the general staff, to persuade through the strength of his ideas and argument. Nor was his high command the apex of military wisdom so often portrayed after the war, being guilty of poor strategic thinking, inadequate concern for logistics, disregard for intelligence, and riven by political intrigue and infighting. Hitler was certainly an adept manipulator who took advantage of the tensions and divisions in his high command structure to promote his views, but it was also true that he did not take the officers anywhere they did not want to go; despite their differences, the high command remained loyal. Hitler was perhaps first among equals in military decision-making, but his generals were willing partners. Nothing demonstrated this more than their failure to object to the flood of criminal orders emanating from the Führer and OKW that meant, from the outset, that Operation Barbarossa would be a war of extermination. None of the top generals could have been in any doubt about this, since Hitler himself told them personally in March 1941 what he expected of them. Although Hitler was often guilty of self-deception, especially in believing in the innate superiority of the German soldier and the decisive importance of will, much the same could be said of his generals. Additionally, despite Halder's bitter complaints of Hitler's interference in the conduct of operations, the OKH chief also exercised minute control and was himself guilty of violating the principle of Auftragstaktik. Hitler at least understood the strategic dilemma facing Germany and the gambling nature of his endeavor, although his successes between 1936 and 1940 gave him a false sense that he could succeed in this high-risk venture.

Hitler undoubtedly also had certain strong points as a military leader: strength of will; a sense of the opponent's weak point and when to strike; an effective grasp of the larger strategic situation and economic considerations; and a gift for surprise and the psychological side of strategy. He also possessed good intuition and a creative mind, was quick to spot the value of new ideas and weapons, favored generals who had risen on merit, had an instinct for the unexpected, and often saw the fallacy of orthodoxy. He preferred bold strokes (at least initially), but early successes camouflaged German weakness. Although an amateur at operations, he did have some successes to his credit, most notably in the spring of 1940 and the winter of 1941–2; and even some failures were based on a certain logic, such as Operation Bagration. Bold, offensive action appealed to Hitler and played to his strengths, but he proved less adept at defense, where he relied on his First World War experiences. Like Napoleon, he believed that the offensive offered the solution to all problems, but had few answers when this failed. As everyone around him noted, he had an extraordinary memory and amazing grasp of military detail. Ultimately, Hitler defined his strategic goals in a manner consistent with his ideology, but failed to realize that they were not realistic in the sense of the "means–end" continuum – although that was not immediately apparent and his generals usually did not object or offer plausible alternatives.

Perhaps the principal difficulty in arriving at an objective assessment of Hitler as Feldherr – other than the obvious hesitation to credit such a detestable figure – lies in the fact that it was his generals who wrote the histories of the war afterwards. Unlike the post-First World War period, they could not blame defeat on a collapse of the home front, so they found the culprit in the leader who was no longer there. Thus, their advice was invariably correct, and if Hitler had only listened to them and not halted the Panzers at Dunkirk, or struck out for Moscow, or authorized timely withdrawals, or engaged in mobile defensive operations, the difficult situation facing the

Wehrmacht could have been avoided or turned around. The reality, of course, was far different; it was not true that the reasonable ideas of the professional elite were always overturned by the ignorant amateur, nor were their spectacular plans thwarted at every turn by the nonsensical notions of the mad corporal. His insight and operational changes – pushed through against Halder's opposition – in the French campaign, for example, long went largely unacknowledged, as did the fact that it was Rundstedt who ordered the halt before Dunkirk, not Hitler. In fact, Hitler's mistake, such as it was, lay not in halting the Panzers, which he did not, but in deferring to his commanding general. Similarly, after staking everything on a knockout blow in France, Hitler then refused a similar throw of the dice, largely as a result of pressure from the navy, in an attempt to knock Britain out of the war through an invasion. Along the same lines, while the Mediterranean seemed to offer some prospects for an indirect assault on the British position, which he certainly appreciated, Hitler's keen political sense told him that he could never reconcile the competing demands of the Italians, French, and Spanish. Early on, then, his primary leadership trait seemed not so much his overriding will or overestimation of his own military abilities, but his irresolution and inability to decide on a clear focal point on which to concentrate German resources. Manstein, for one, despite his difficult relationship with Hitler, nonetheless conceded the Führer's military talents at the strategic and operational levels. Where he fell down, the field marshal believed, was precisely in his indecision, lack of judgment, and tendency to pursue several objectives simultaneously, thus squandering limited German resources. Still, if Hitler is to be criticized for his later blunders, he must be credited with the successes in the early years of the war; the critics cannot have it both ways.

Similarly, in planning for Barbarossa, Hitler's conception was at least as sound as that of the planners at OKH; it was, after all, Halder who split the German invasion force into three separate armies, advancing in divergent directions, and with little concentration of resources. Once the campaign began it was Halder who schemed to alter the operational plan, often against the wishes of his commanders. Moreover, it was he, not Hitler, who initiated the process of denying commanders freedom of action over the battlefield, thus eroding the policy of Auftragstaktik that had guided earlier successful campaigns. Hitler certainly intervened more readily in this campaign than in previous ones, but he also voiced legitimate concerns about flank security in any attack against Moscow. Furthermore, he could rely on advice from top commanders to bolster his arguments. Ironically, even the one dispute with his generals – in August 1941 as Army Group

Center stood stalled at Smolensk for three weeks – that seemed to prove the validity of post-war claims that his obstruction prevented a victorious assault on Moscow, did nothing of the sort. Army Group Center could not have continued the advance in any case, for both logistical and supply reasons, and because of enemy resistance. Nor did the three weeks of wrangling reveal a Führer running amok over the determined opposition of OKH; after all, if he had wanted simply to impose his will, presumably he could have done so at the outset by executive fiat. Rather, he sought to convince Halder as much by the strength of his military, economic, and strategic arguments as by the force of his will. How else to explain the detailed memorandum he wrote, or the support he received from other military professionals?

It is also well to remember that Halder did, in fact – whether from conviction or the result of being caught in one of his schemes – urge a turn to the south, an action supported by many field commanders who shared the Führer's concern about vulnerable flanks and supply lines. Then, at the end of the wildly successful Kiev operation, Hitler, rather than continue the advance toward the Caucasus and the urgently needed oil, conceded to Halder's wishes and shifted the focus back to Moscow. Again, it was Halder and Bock, driven by memories of September 1914 and the Marne, who persisted in the attack on the Soviet capital, even after they realized the offensive had run its course. Finally, and most famously, it was Hitler's resolution – shown in his halt order – that prevented the disintegration of the Ostheer in the winter of 1941–2, a circumstance that virtually all top commanders came to acknowledge, whether grudgingly or openly.

Further examples could be found as well. Although criticized then and since for his stubborn refusal to retreat, Hitler allowed the withdrawal of Army Group A when it was threatened with being cut off in the Caucasus. Even though he then insisted on holding the Kuban bridgehead across the Kerch strait against the wishes of his military advisors, this did have a certain rationale: as a point from which to renew the offensive toward the oil fields. When it became clear that this was never going to happen, he then released the troops to fortify other sectors. Further, the flawed plan for the Kursk offensive owed more to his generals than to any conception by Hitler, who both proposed alternative schemes and was notably anxious before the attack. Similarly, he seemed to have a better understanding than many of his generals that, given the extreme limitations of the Ostheer by late 1943, a mobile defense of the sort urged by Manstein was not entirely feasible. It might, perhaps, in certain circumstances have delayed the Soviet advance, but, lacking the ability any longer to execute a successful Blitzkrieg-type action, it amounted to little more than moving pieces aimlessly on a chess-board.

Nor did his generals, especially on the Eastern Front, fully comprehend, after 1942, the growing demands of the other fronts. Again, Hitler's belief, expressed in late 1943, that the defeat of the imminent Allied invasion in the west offered Germany its best chance for retrieving the situation, seemed both logical and reasonable. The means by which to defeat that invasion, of course, became the focus of a furious debate between Rommel and Rundstedt, which Hitler never really resolved. He might have been better served to have imposed one solution or another – here again, he demonstrated a fatal indecision – but, in the event, given Allied material and air power superiority, neither really was feasible. The counterattack at Mortain certainly provided evidence that Hitler was losing his grip on reality – his instinct for the enemy's vulnerable spot was not matched by any realistic appraisal of German power – but he then allowed the with-drawal of German forces from southern France without protest. Moreover, the destruction of Army Group Center in the summer of 1944 owed at least as much, or more, to overwhelming Soviet strength and meticulous plan-ning as to Hitler's mistakes. Even his insistence on holding the French Atlantic ports, as well as Courland, had a coherent rationale to it and, in the case of the former, noticeably hampered enemy operations. The Ardennes Offensive was based on a miscalculation of the balance of forces, but resulted from a rational attempt to determine where the limited German forces might have the greatest impact – and, as well, on Hitler's calculation that the "unnatural" enemy coalition arrayed against Germany would disin-tegrate. Until late in the war, then, most of Hitler's military decisions had a reason and logic to them – and were largely based on considerations that seemed plausible at the time – certainly more so than his critics among the generals would lead one to believe. Even at the very end, when Hitler appeared to have descended into madness, moving nonexistent armies on a map, his words betrayed a certain cataclysmic logic: following Clausewitz's precepts, the fight to the last would provide the basis for eventual national renewal.

For Hitler, war was a liberation from restrictions; 1940 marked a caesura because it freed him from restrictions and he could now unleash his ideo-logical goals. From then on, his tendency to increasing radicalism was largely unchecked. As he turned to ideological goals, not surprisingly, he increasingly lost any willingness to be flexible in methods or resort to polit-ical solutions. His radical aims and actions also mobilized a powerful coali-tion against him. His political decisions, then, in a very real sense proved more decisive than his military ones. Having begun a war for economic and ideological reasons – with both rooted in his convictions as to why Germany had lost the First World War – he had to, and did not, win militarily in 1941. After 1941, given the enemy alliance arrayed against him, a military victory was increasingly unlikely, making a political solution the only way out. But here Hitler the Führer refused to allow Hitler the Feldherr any freedom of action: his decision to fight to the last reflected political more than military considerations. Hitler did what he promised to do: remake the German and European body politic. In attempting to redeem Germany from the trauma of 1918 – which, to him, as well as many other Germans, represented not just defeat but a complete end of collective national life – he implemented his vision of national regeneration and convinced ordinary Germans to take part in it. Then, in order to secure the existence of the new national community, he organized and fought a war for Lebensraum. Ultimately, he bet his life – and that of millions of Germans and Europeans – on undoing the trauma of defeat in the First World War, and he lost.[7]

Acknowledgments

It seems to be a truism that in the writing of acknowledgments two forms prevail: either the extended version that notes the contributions of very many people, or the brief variety. This will be of the latter sort. First, and foremost, this book would never have materialized without the efforts of Heather McCallum at Yale University Press. She proposed the original idea to me, persisted despite my rather considerable initial skepticism, and then finally persuaded me to undertake the project. Although now the managing director of Yale University Press London, it was her effort as editor that led to this book. Also at Yale I have been aided by, among others, Rachael Lonsdale, Marika Lysandrou, and Clarissa Sutherland, all of whom have been the epitome of professionalism in their encouragement, advice, help, and support. My copy-editor, Richard Mason, has been a paragon of efficiency. Through his outstanding efforts and astute suggestions he has made invaluable contributions to this book. I would also like to thank the anonymous readers of the manuscript for their helpful advice and comments. Closer to home, the College of Arts and Sciences and the Department of History at East Tennessee State University provided me with a Non-Instructional Assignment for the Fall 2015 semester, which greatly facilitated the writing of the book.

Like my other books, this one could not have been completed without the loving support and steadfast encouragement of my wife, Julia. Once again, she has devoted enormous amounts of time and effort to the creation of the excellent maps that add so much to this book. Her insistence on exactitude and prodding me to provide precise information on troop movements, front lines, and topographical factors also forced me to rethink many assumptions, which is always a good thing. To paraphrase Winston Churchill, my greatest achievement was to persuade her to marry me. In my last book I noted my joy at watching my daughter, Kelsey, grow from a small child to a young adult with an avid interest in European history. She is now in the process, as a PhD student at Emory University, of becoming an academic historian herself. It is both gratifying and humbling to see your child grow and develop into an articulate person able to more than hold her own with her father in a variety of historical discussions. More importantly, her enthusiasm for learning new things and exploring new areas helps keep me intellectually young and alert. If it is true, as the sixteenth-century Italian poet Torquato Tasso put it, that "Love gives you a piece of your soul that you never knew was missing," or as Zora Neale Hurston stated more bluntly, "Love makes your soul crawl out from its hiding place," then I have been illuminated and made whole by their love for me, and mine for them. Both Julia and Kelsey continue to enrich my life in ways I never thought possible, so to them this book is dedicated with love and gratitude.

Notes

Abbreviations

ADAP	*Akten zur Deutschen Auswärtigen Politik 1918–1945*
DGFP	*Documents on German Foreign Policy, 1918–1945*
DRZW	*Das deutsche Reich und der Zweite Weltkrieg*
GSWW	*Germany and the Second World War*
IMT	International Military Tribunal. *Trial of the Major War Criminals before the International Military Tribunal, Nuremberg, 14 November 1945–1 October 1946.* 42 vols. Blue Series
KTB/OKW	*Kriegstagebuch des Oberkommandos der Wehrmacht 1940–1945*
NT	*Nazi Conspiracy and Aggression.* 8 vols. 12 books. Red Series
TBJG	*Die Tagebücher von Joseph Goebbels*

Chapter 1

1. Domarus, *Hitler: Speeches and Proclamations*, 232–5; Kershaw, *Hitler: Hubris*, 440–1.
2. Wirsching, "'Man kann nur Boden germanisieren,'" 517–19, 542, 545–8; Vogelsang, "Neue Dokumente," 434–5; Eberle, *Hitlers Weltkriege*, 125–7; Megargee, *Inside Hitler's High Command*, 18, 20; Mitcham, "Generalfeldmarschall Werner von Blomberg," in Ueberschär, *Hitlers militärische Elite*, 28–36; Boll, "Generalfeldmarschall Walter von Reichenau," in Ueberschär, *Hitlers militärische Elite*, 195–202.
3. Wirsching, "Man kann nur Boden germanisieren," 545–8; Eberle, *Hitlers Weltkriege*, 127–8.
4. Wirsching, "Man kann nur Boden germanisieren," 545–8; Kershaw, *Hitler: Hubris*, 441–2; Vogelsang, "Neue Dokumente," 435; Geyer, "German Strategy," 564; Deist, "Road to Ideological War," 380.
5. Wirsching, "Man kann nur Boden germanisieren," 543–4; Kershaw, *Hitler: Hubris*, 442–4; Geyer, "German Strategy," 565; Vogelsang, "Neue Dokumente," 435–6; Vogelsang, "Hitlers Brief an Reichenau," 433–7.
6. Showalter, "German Grand Strategy," 66–70, Groß, "Dogma der Beweglichkeit," 144.
7. Clausewitz, *On War*, 13–31; Bassford, "Character of War in the Real World," in *Clausewitz and His Works*, http://www.clausewitz.com/readings/Bassford/Cworks/Works.htm#Categories (accessed 1 March 2014); Bahnemann, "Begriff der Strategie," 36–9; Aron, "Reason, Passion and Power in the Thought of Clausewitz," 601, 608–13; Showalter, "German Grand Strategy," 72–3.

8. Clausewitz, *On War*, 28, 44–60, 62–3, 65–8; Bahnemann, "Begriff der Strategie," 39–40; Kitchen, "Political History of Clausewitz," 29, 31–3; Bassford, "Character of War in the Real World"; Strachan, "Clausewitz and the First World War," 387–9.

9. Clausewitz, *On War*, 24–5, 160–3, 175, 209–18; Bassford, "Character of War in the Real World"; Strachan, "Clausewitz and First World War," 372, 376–80.

10. Clausewitz, *On War*, 31–44, 75, 77, 230–1, 260; Kitchen, "Political History of Clausewitz," 28–30, 36; idem, "Traditions of German Strategic Thought," 165–6; Honig, "Idea of Total War," 31–3; Aron, "Reason, Passion and Power in the Thought of Clausewitz," 606; Baldwin, "Clausewitz in Nazi Germany," 8–9; Groß, "Development of Operational Thinking," 3.

11. Clausewitz, *On War* (2007), 75, 77, 184–90, 223–5, 229–40, 252–7; Kitchen, "Political History of Clausewitz," 28–30, 36; idem, "Traditions of German Strategic Thought," 165–6; Aron, "Reason, Passion and Power in the Thought of Clausewitz," 606; Baldwin, "Clausewitz in Nazi Germany," 8–9; Honig, "Idea of Total War," 31–3.

12. Hitler, *Mein Kampf*, 533; Baldwin, "Clausewitz in Nazi Germany," 11–12; Kitchen, "Political History of Clausewitz," 35; Hitler, "Die 'Hetzer' der Wahrheit," speech of 12 April 1922, in Jäckel and Kuhn, *Adolf Hitler: Sämtliche Aufzeichnungen*, 620.

13. Kitchen, "Political History of Clausewitz," 34; idem, "Traditions of German Strategic Thought," 169; Bahnemann, "Begriff der Strategie," 41–2; Showalter, "German Grand Strategy," 73–4; idem, "From Deterrence to Doomsday Machine," 683.

14. Showalter, "German Grand Strategy," 73–4; idem, "From Deterrence to Doomsday Machine," 683; Förster, "Facing 'People's War,'" 214–15, 223–4; Echevarria, "Moltke," 91–9; Moltke, "First Debate," 137–8.

15. Förster, "Facing 'People's War,'" 216–24; Showalter, "German Grand Strategy," 73–4; idem, "From Deterrence to Doomsday Machine," 683; Moltke, "First Debate," 137–8.

16. Groß, "Dogma der Beweglichkeit," 144–6; Geyer, "German Strategy," 531–3.

17. Delbrück, *Warfare in Antiquity*, 336–9; idem, *Dawn of Modern Warfare*, 345–6, 352–3; Jäckel and Kuhn, *Adolf Hitler: Sämtliche Aufzeichnungen*, 608; Echevarria, "Moltke," 96.

18. Groß, "Dogma der Beweglichkeit," 144–6; Showalter, "German Grand Strategy," 80–2; Geyer, "German Strategy," 534–5.

19. Showalter, "German Grand Strategy," 83–4; Groß, "Dogma der Beweglichkeit," 148–51; Geyer, "German Strategy," 537–42.

20. Groß, "Dogma der Beweglichkeit," 151–2; Geyer, "German Strategy," 542–4; idem, "How the Germans Learned to Wage War," 32–3, 36–3, 44–5; idem, "Tötungshandeln," 122–37; Murray, Knox, and Bernstein, "Introduction," *Making of Strategy*, 3.

21. Geyer, "German Strategy," 546–9; Honig, "Idea of Total War," 34–8.

22. Geyer, "German Strategy," 582; Geyer, "How the Germans Learned to Wage War," 33; Jodl, "Jodl's Official Diary," diary entry of 13 September 1938, International Military Tribunal (hereafter IMT), XXVIII, Doc 1780-PS; Pyta, *Hitler*, 263–8.

23. Jürgen Förster, "Barbarossa Revisited," 21; idem, "Dynamics of Volksgemeinschaft," 181; Hitler, "Hitler's Speech to his Generals," 23 November 1939, IMT, XXVI, Doc 789-PS.

24. Baldwin, "Clausewitz in Nazi Germany," 11–14; Kitchen, "Political History of Clausewitz," 40.

Chapter 2

1. Churchill, *Gathering Storm*, 52–3; Lukacs, *Hitler of History*, 61.

2. Hitler, *Mein Kampf*, 204–6.

3. Mann quoted in Ullrich, *Hitler: Ascent*, 52; Schivelbusch, *Culture of Defeat*, 1–35. For Hitler's notion of conflict as the basic motivating force in both the natural and human worlds, see, among many others: Hitler, *Mein Kampf*, 96, 151, 177–8, 283, 288–9, 331–3, 388–9, 642–3, 652–3, 674, 680; Dusik, *Hitler. Reden, Schriften, Anordnungen. Februar 1925 bis Januar 1933*, II: *Vom Weimarer Parteitag bis zur Reichstagswahl: Juli 1926–Mai 1928*, 17–19, 136, 142, 191–2, 378–80, 406, 439, 625–6, 723–9, 764, 834; Trevor-Roper, *Hitler's Table-Talk*, 25–26 September 1941, 43–4; Jochmann, *Monologe*, 17 October, 28–29 December 1941, 3–4 January 1942, 71, 131, 144.

4. "Ich habe nahezu 6 Jahre lang den grauen Rock getragen," speech of 14 April 1926, in Vollnhals, *Hitler. Reden, Schriften, Anordnungen. Februar 1925 bis Januar 1933*, I, 383; Solleder, *Vier Jahre Westfront*, 60; Weber, *Hitler's First War*, 48–9; Trevor-Roper, *Hitler's Table-Talk*, 25–26 September 1941, 43–4; Jochmann, *Monologe*, 17 October 1941, 71; Simms, "Against a 'world of enemies,'" 321, 328.

5. Kershaw, *Hitler: Hubris*, 92–7; Eberle, *Hitlers Weltkriege*, 24–33; Ullrich, *Hitler: Ascent*, 50–72, quote on 63; Jochmann, *Monologe*, 19 May 1944, 353–4. For his few letters and postcards: Jäckel and Kuhn, *Sämtliche Auszeichnungen* (e.g. to Josef Popp, 22, 26 January 1915, 62–4). See also: Weber, *Hitler's First War*; Williams, *Corporal Hitler and the Great War*. For more contemporary accounts, see: Solleder, *Vier Jahre Westfront*; Brandmayer and Bayer, *Meldegänger Hitler*. For a good discussion of comradeship, see Kühne, *Rise and Fall of Comradeship*.

6. Kershaw, *Hitler: Hubris*, 92–7; Hitler to Ernst Hepp, 5 February 1915, Hitler to Joseph Popp, 12 February 1915, in Jäckel and Kuhn, *Sämtliche Auszeichnungen*, 69–70; Hitler, *Mein Kampf*, 193–4; Eberle, *Hitlers Weltkriege*, 33–47; Weber, *Hitler's First War*, 149–59, and passim; Ullrich, *Hitler: Ascent*, 64–72; Simms, "Against a 'world of enemies,'" 322. One lasting consequence of Hitler's, and other Nazi leaders', observations of domestic suffering due to hunger was the determination during the Second World War to ensure that Germans received a food ration that supplied their basic nutritional requirements, which meant that other Europeans starved.

7. Foch, interview in *Neue Freie Presse* (Vienna), 3 August 1928, quoted in Schivelbusch, *Culture of Defeat*, 189; Haig and Lloyd George quoted in Ferguson, *Pity of War*, 313–14; Stevenson, *Cataclysm*, pp. 386–8; Churchill, *World Crisis*, 800; Germany: Nationalversammlung (1919–20). Untersuchungsausschuss über die Weltkriegsverantwortlichkeit, *The Causes of the German Collapse in 1918*, Document 26: "Could We Have Kept on Fighting in the Autumn?," 86–8. More recently, Niall Ferguson, among others, has asserted the efficiency and lethality of German soldiers during the First World War. Right up until the end they regularly inflicted more casualties on their enemies than they themselves suffered. See: Ferguson, *Pity of War*, 282–317; McRandle and Quirk, "The Blood Test Revisited," 667–701; Geyer, "How the Germans Learned to Wage War," 26–7.

8. Jäckel and Kuhn, *Sämtliche Aufzeichnungen*, 12 September 1923, 1,007. The last Zeppelin raid on Britain came in early August 1918.

9. Schivelbusch, *Culture of Defeat*, 203–5; Geyer, "Insurrectionary Warfare," 459–63.

10. Maurice and Mann quoted in Schivelbusch, *Culture of Defeat*, 193, see also 190–203; Geyer, "Insurrectionary Warfare," 492–3; Clausewitz, *On War* 189; idem, *War, Politics, and Power*, 301–2; Hitler, *Mein Kampf*, 668–70; Lunde, *Hitler's Wave-Breaker Concept*, 22; Krüger, "Adolf Hitlers Clausewitzkenntnis," 467–71.

11. Plöckinger, *Unter Soldaten und Agitatoren*, 113–32, 283–316, 326–41; Töppel, "'Volk und Rasse,'" 1–35; Kroll, "Geschichte und Politik im Weltbild Hitlers," 327–53; Kershaw, *Hitler: Hubris*, 109–28; Eberle, *Hitlers Weltkriege*, 51–69; Weber, *Hitler's First War*, 227–54; Ferguson, *War of the World*, 19–31; Koenen, "Hitlers Russland," 2–4; Herbert, "Was haben die Nationalsozialisten aus dem Ersten Weltkrieg gelernt?," 21–4; Raphael, "Pluralities of National Socialist Ideology," 75–9.

12. Schivelbusch, *Culture of Defeat*, 209–14; Hirschfeld, "Der Führer spricht vom Krieg," 42; Wildt, *Generation des Unbedingten*; Hitler, *Mein Kampf*, 229–31; Simms, "Against a 'world of enemies,'" 332; "Aufgaben und Aufbau der S.A.-Förderung der Münchener S.A., Rede auf einer S.A.-Versammlung in München," 18 May 1927, in Dusik, *Hitler. Reden, Schriften, Anordnungen*, II, 310.

13. *Völkischer Beobachter*, 2 August 1933; Goebbels, *Wesen und Gestalt des Nationalsozialismus*, 7; Hirschfeld, "Der Führer spricht vom Krieg," 38, 44.

14. Simms, "Against a 'world of enemies,'" 321–5, 331–3; Jäckel and Kuhn, *Sämtliche Aufzeichnungen*, 96–9, 147–8, 335–6, 773.

15. Herwig, "'Daemon of Geopolitics,'" 5, 9.

16. Herwig, "'Daemon of Geopolitics,'" 7–9; idem, "'Geopolitik,'" 220–1, 226–9; Mackinder, *Democratic Ideals and Reality*, 194. See also: Haushofer, *Grenzen in ihrer*

geographischen und politischen Bedeutung; Dorpalen, *The World of General Haushofer*; Diner, "'Grundbuch des Planeten.'"

17. Trevor-Roper, *Hitler's Table Talk*, 3–4 February 1942, 287; Herwig, "Daemon of Geopolitics," 9–11; idem, "Geopolitik," 225–6. For a contrary opinion, see Diner, "Knowledge of Expansion," 46–8.

18. Herwig, "Daemon of Geopolitics," 10–11; Thies, *Hitler's Plans for Global Domination*, 45, 48–52; *Völkischer Beobachter*, 8 April 1927, 23, 25 May, 4 September 1928, 3, 6 August 1929.

19. Simms, "Against a 'world of enemies,'" 332; Hitler, *Mein Kampf*, 131–44; Horn, "Ein unbekannter Aufsatz Hitlers aus dem Frühjahr 1924," 280–94; Lange, "Der Terminus 'Lebensraum' in Hitlers 'Mein Kampf,'" 427–37; Thies, *Hitler's Plans*, 52; Zitelmann, "Zur Begründung des 'Lebensraum' Motivs in Hitlers Weltanschauung," 551–67; "Rede Hitlers am 10. Februar 1939 vor Truppenkommandeuren in Berlin," in Müller and Hansen, *Armee und Drittes Reich*, 365–75.

20. Hitler, *Mein Kampf*, 642–6, 649–52; idem, *Second Book*, 94–9; Jäckel and Kuhn, *Sämtliche Aufzeichnungen* (e.g. 123, 335–8, 420–5, 451–6, 613, 1,023–6); Zitelmann, *Selbstverständnis eines Revolutionärs*, 307–8, 316–23, 337–42.

21. Hitler, *Mein Kampf*, 132–42, 653–5.

22. Hitler, *Second Book*, 15–27, 90, 105–18, 128; Thies, *Hitler's Plans*, 51.

23. Schmidt quoted in Stahl, "Generaloberst Rudolf Schmidt," in Ueberschär, ed., *Hitlers militärische Elite*, 493; Hürter, "Hitlers Generäle," 261–4; idem, "The Military Elite and Volksgemeinschaft," 257–69.

24. Hürter, "Hitlers Generäle," 266–7; idem, "Kriegserfahrung als Schlüsselerlebnis? Der erste Weltkrieg in der Biographie von Wehrmachtsgeneralen," 764–5; idem, *Hitlers Heerführer*, 86–9, 139.

25. Hürter, *Hitlers Heerführer*, 73–4, 81–96; Crim, "'Our Most Serious Enemy',", 631–4; Liulevicius, *War Land*, 151–76; Herbert, "Was haben die Nationalsozialisten aus dem Ersten Weltkrieg gelernt?," 31.

26. Hürter, *Hitlers Heerführer*, 79, 86.

27. Hürter, *Hitlers Heerführer*, 79, 86, 112–13; Ludendorff, *Der totale Krieg*, 6; Honig, "Idea of Total War," 34–6.

28. Hürter, *Hitlers Heerführer*, 113–17; Herbert, "Was haben die Nationalsozialisten aus dem Ersten Weltkrieg gelernt?," 24–7; Pöhlmann, "Großer Krieg und nächster Krieg," 292, 295.

29. Herbert, "Was haben die Nationalsozialisten aus dem Ersten Weltkrieg gelernt?," 27–8; Hirschfeld, "Der Führer spricht vom Krieg," 48–50; Pöhlmann, "Großer Krieg und nächster Krieg," 294.

30. Herbert, "'Was haben die Nationalsozialisten aus dem Ersten Weltkrieg gelernt?,'" 29–30.

Chapter 3

1. Deist, "Rearmament," *Germany and the Second World War* (hereafter GSWW), I, 405–8; idem, "Road to Ideological War," 373.

2. Geyer, "Dynamics of Military Revisionism," 109–10.

3. Hesse, *Der Feldherr Psychologos*, 26–7; Schwarte, *Der Krieg der Zukunft*, 56; Deist, "Reichswehr und der Krieg der Zukunft," 82–3.

4. Groß, "Dogma der Beweglichkeit," 153–5; idem, "Development of Operational Thinking," 4, 7–8; Deist, "Reichswehr und der Krieg der Zukunft," 84; Geyer, "German Strategy," 554–6; Jablonsky, "The Paradox of Duality," 88; Pöhlmann, "Großer Krieg und nächster Krieg," 288; Citino, *German Way of War*, 240–4. For a deeper look at Seeckt's ideas and influence, see Corum, *The Roots of Blitzkrieg*.

5. Deist, "Reichswehr und der Krieg der Zukunft," 85–6; idem, "The Reichswehr and National Defense," GSWW, I, 377–8; Geyer, "German Strategy," 555–8; Megargee, *Inside Hitler's High Command*, 14–15. For a more recent assessment of Stülpnagel, see Vardi,

"The Enigma of German Operational Theory"; idem, "Joachim von Stülpnagel's Military Thought and Planning," 193–216.

6. Deist, "Reichswehr und der Krieg der Zukunft," 85–6; idem, "The Reichswehr and National Defense," GSWW, I, 377–8; Geyer, "German Strategy," 555–8; Megargee, *Inside Hitler's High Command*, 14–15.

7. Geyer, "German Strategy," 561–4; Deist, "Reichswehr and National Defense," 379–91; Megargee, *Inside Hitler's High Command*, 15–16.

8. Geyer, "German Strategy," 56–561; Deist, "Reichswehr and National Defense," 380; Groß, "Dogma der Beweglichkeit," 155; Murray, *Change in the European Balance of Power*, 29.

9. Geyer, "German Strategy," 558–60; Groß, "Dogma der Beweglichkeit"; Guderian, *Panzer Leader*, 18–46.

10. Harris, "The Myth of Blitzkrieg," 335–52; Frieser, *Blitzkrieg Legend*, 4–11; Raudzens, "Blitzkrieg Ambiguities," 77–94; Fanning, "The Origin of the Term 'Blitzkrieg'," 283–302; Wallach, "Misperceptions of Clausewitz," 213–23; Baldwin, "Clausewitz in Nazi Germany," 11–15; Jablonsky, "Paradox of Duality," 55–8; Trevor-Roper, *Hitler's Table Talk*, 8–9, 10–11 August 1941, 25; Warlimont, *Inside Hitler's Headquarters*, 486; "The Führer's Speech to Division Commanders, 12 December 1944, at Adlerhorst," Heiber and Glantz, *Hitler and his Generals*, 533–41. See also DiNardo, "German Armour Doctrine," 384–97; Murray, "German Army Doctrine," 71–94.

11. Hitler, *Mein Kampf*, 191, 197–9, 205, 240, 520–1; Hitler, *Second Book*, 11–12, 84; Trevor-Roper, *Hitler's Table Talk*, 13 October 1941, 56; Creveld, "War Lord Hitler," 67–8; Jablonsky, "Paradox of Duality," 57–60, 88–90.

12. Hitler, *Mein Kampf*, 165; Trevor-Roper, *Hitler's Table Talk*, 13 October 1941, 56; Manstein, *Lost Victories*, 281 (he did not share this view of Hitler); Creveld, "War Lord Hitler," 60–5; Jablonsky, "Paradox of Duality," 58–61; Hitler, *Second Book*, 11–12; Below, *At Hitler's Side*, 28.

13. Guderian, *Panzer Leader*, 29–30 (he mistakenly listed the date as 1933); Creveld, "War Lord Hitler," 65–8; Jablonsky, "Paradox of Duality," 57–60, 88–90; Domarus, *Hitler: Speeches and Proclamations, 1932-1945*, 8 November 1941, 2509; Trevor-Roper, *Hitler's Table Talk*, 172, 645–6. The notion of an Italian connection probably springs from the ideas of General Giulio Douhet, who conceived of a *guerra fulminante*, or "blitzkrieg." Douhet is more famous for his role and influence in developing revolutionary ideas on air power. Fanning, "The Origin of the Term 'Blitzkrieg'," 292.

14. Geyer, "German Strategy," 583–6; Murray, "German Army Doctrine," 71–94; idem, "Force Strategy, Blitzkrieg Strategy," 39–42; Jablonsky, "Paradox of Duality," 86–7; Citino, *German Way of War*, 238–67.

15. Groß, "Dogma der Beweglichkeit," 156–7; Murray, "German Army Doctrine," 80, 87–8; Jablonsky, "Paradox of Duality," 86. See also DiNardo, "German Armour Doctrine," 384–97.

16. Groß, "Dogma der Beweglichkeit," 156; Deist, "Rearmament of Individual Services," in Deist, GSWW, I, 436; Eberle, *Hitlers Weltkriege*, 155–6; Murray, "German Army Doctrine," 84–6. For a sense of the difficulties in developing a tank force, see Guderian, *Panzer Leader*, 24–39.

17. Hürter, *Hitlers Heerführer*, 123–31; Mitcham, "Generalfeldmarschall Werner von Blomberg," in Uberschär, *Hitlers militärische Elite*, 29–31; Megargee, *Inside Hitler's High Command*, 18–20, 26–7; Muller, "Werner von Blomberg," in Smelser and Syring, *Militärelite*, 50–65; Geyer, *Aufrüstung oder Sicherheit*, 161–3; Maiolo, *Cry Havoc*, 41–2.

18. Deist, "Rearmament," GSWW, I, 409–12; Hürter, *Hitlers Heerführer*, 134–5; Müller, *Das Heer und Hitler*, 53; Kershaw, *Hitler: Hubris*, 443, 729, fn 58; Megargee, *Inside Hitler's High Command*, 27–9; Geyer, "German Strategy," 567.

19. Geyer, "Military Revisionism," 109, 113, 118, 121–7; Deist, "Rearmament," GSWW, I, 412–13; Kershaw, *Hitler: Hubris*, 490–4; *Tagebucher Joseph Goebbels* (hereafter TBJG), 12, 16, 17 October 1933.

20. Eberle, *Hitlers Weltkriege*, 162; Jochmann, *Monologe*, 275; Deist, "Rearmament," GSWW, I, 417–23; Megargee, *Inside Hitler's High Command*, 30; Ullrich, *Hitler: Ascent*, 490–4.

21. Geyer, "Military Revisionism," 128-31, 134-5; Deist, "Rearmament of Individual Services," in Deist, GSWW, I, 421-3; Maiolo, *Cry Havoc*, 53; Ullrich, *Hitler: Ascent*, 497-8.

22. Maiolo, *Cry Havoc*, 53-5; Geyer, "Military Revisionism," 131; Hossbach, *Zwischen Wehrmacht und Hitler*, 81-3; Hitler, *Second Book*, chs. 14-15; TBJG, 18, 19 October 1935; Ullrich, *Hitler: Ascent*, 498-505; TBJG, 19 October 1935.

23. Geyer, "Military Revisionism," 128-30; Messerschmidt, "Road to War," GSWW, I, 615-19; Kershaw, *Hitler: Hubris*, 584-91; Shore, "Hitler, Intelligence, and the Decision to Remilitarize the Rhine," 5-18; Ullrich, *Hitler: Ascent*, 507-12; TBJG, 15 December 1935, 21 February, 2, 4, 6, 8, 31 March 1936.

24. Geyer, "Military Revisionism," 128-30; Messerschmidt, "Road to War," GSWW, I, 615-19; Kershaw, *Hitler: Hubris*, 590-1; Domarus, *Speeches*, 606, 643.

25. Deist, "Rearmament," GSWW, I, 437-40; Geyer, "Military Revisionism," 137-8; Tooze, *Wages of Destruction*, 203-13.

26. Deist, "Rearmament," GSWW, I, 437-45; Geyer, "Military Revisionism," 137-8; Tooze, *Wages of Destruction*, 203-13; Maiolo, *Cry Havoc*, 145.

27. For a thorough discussion of the economic problems facing Germany, see Tooze, *Wages of Destruction*, 203-43; Maiolo, *Cry Havoc*, 143; Kershaw, *Hitler: Nemesis*, 9-12.

28. Germany, Auswärtiges Amt, *Documents on German Foreign Policy* (hereafter DGFP), Series C, No. 490, 853-62; *Akten zur Deutschen Auswärtigen Politik 1918-1945* (hereafter ADAP), Serie C, No. 490, 793-801; Treue, "Hitlers Denkschrift," 184-203; Maiolo, *Cry Havoc*, 144-7; Ferguson, *War of the World*, 279-81; Tooze, *Wages of Destruction*, 219-24; Messerschmidt, "Road to War," GSWW, I, 623-4; Deist, "Rearmament," 447-8; Kershaw, *Hitler: Nemesis*, 18-23.

29. Germany, Auswärtiges Amt, *Documents on German Foreign Policy* (hereafter DGFP), Series C, No. 490, 853-62; *Akten zur Deutschen Auswärtigen Politik 1918-1945* (hereafter ADAP), Serie C, No. 490, 793-801; Treue, "Hitlers Denkschrift," 184-203; Maiolo, *Cry Havoc*, 144-7; Ferguson, *War of the World*, 279-81; Tooze, *Wages of Destruction*, 219-24; Messerschmidt, "Road to War," GSWW, I, 623-4; Deist, "Rearmament," GSWW, I, 447-8; Kershaw, *Hitler: Nemesis*, 18-23.

30. Eberle, *Hitlers Weltkriege*, 171.

31. Geyer, "Military Revisionism," 142-4; idem, "German Strategy," 570-1; idem, "Restorative Elites, German Society, and the Nazi Pursuit of War," 141-4.

32. "Niederschrift über die Besprechung in der Reichskanzlei am 5. 11. 37 von 16,15 - 20,30 Uhr," Doc. 386-PS, IMT, XXV, 403-13; "1. Nachtrag zur Weisung für die einheitliche Kriegsvorbereitung der Wehrmacht vom 24.6.37," 7 December 1937, Doc. 175-C, IMT, XXXIV, 745-6; Tooze, *Wages of Destruction*, 240-1; Maiolo, *Cry Havoc*, 224-5; Kershaw, *Hitler: Nemesis*, 45-51; Messerschmidt, "Road to War," GSWW, I, 635-6.

33. Doc. 386-PS, IMT, XXV, 403-13; Doc. 175-C, IMT, XXXIV, 745-6; Tooze, *Wages of Destruction*, 240-1; Maiolo, *Cry Havoc*, 224-5; Messerschmidt, "Road to War," GSWW, I, 635-6; Geyer, "German Strategy," 572.

34. Hossbach, *Zwischen Wehrmacht und Hitler*, 188-94, 217-20; DGFP, Series D, Vol. I, no. 21, 86, 93; "Bemerkungen General Becks zur Niederschrift des Oberst d. G. Hoßbach über die Besprechung in der Reichskanzlei am 5. November 1937, vom 12. November 1937," in Müller and Hansen, *Armee und Drittes Reich*, 323-4; DGFP, D, Vol. I, no. 31; TBJG, 21 November 1937; Neurath testimony at Nuremberg, 24 June 1946, IMT, XVI, 640-1; Kershaw, *Hitler: Nemesis*, 50-1; Maiolo, *Cry Havoc*, 223, 226-7, 243-4, 265; Wright and Stafford, "Hitler, Britain, and the Hossbach Memorandum," 95-106.

35. Megargee, *Inside Hitler's High Command*, 39-48; Kershaw, *Hitler: Nemesis*, 51-60; TBJG, 29 January and 1, 3, 5 February 1938; Pyta, *Hitler*, 272; Engel, *At the Heart of the Reich*, 22-23 April 1938, 40; Hossbach, *Zwischen Wehrmacht und Hitler*, 107-10, 115-18; TBJG, 27, 28, 29, 31 January, 1, 6 February 1938; Ullrich, *Hitler: Ascent*, 699-707; Mitcham and Mueller, "Generalfeldmarschall Walther von Brauchitsch," in Ueberschär, ed., *Hitlers militärische Elite*, 45-52.

36. Hürter, *Hitlers Heerführer*, 144-9; Geyer, "Nazi Pursuit of War," 144; idem, "Military Revisionism," 146-7.

37. Maiolo, *Cry Havoc*, 242–3; Hürter, *Hitlers Heerführer*, 149; Jodl, "Jodl's Official Diary, Covering Period from 4 January 1937 to 25 August 1939," IMT, XXVIII, Doc. 1780-PS, 31 January 1938, 362; IMT, XVI, 168–71; TBJG, 13, 16, 17, 21 February 1938; Kershaw, *Hitler: Nemesis*, 63–74; Ullrich, *Hitler: Ascent*, 710–13.
38. TBJG, 10, 11, 12, 13, 14, 15, 16 March 1938; IMT, XXXIV, Doc. 102-C, 103-C, 335–8; Göring Testimony at Nuremberg, 16 March 1946, IMT, IX, 393; "Philipp von Hessen verlangt den Fuhrer. 11.3.38," IMT, XXXI, Doc. 2949-PS, 368–9; Domarus, *Speeches*, 1,038–60; Maiolo, *Cry Havoc*, 242–3; Kershaw, *Hitler: Nemesis*, 74–83; Ullrich, *Hitler: Ascent*, 713–21; Messerschmidt, "Road to War," GSWW, I, 648–51; Hürter, *Hitlers Heerführer*,149; Guderian, *Panzer Leader*, 49–57; Manstein, *Aus einem Soldatenleben*, 320–32.
39. Kershaw, *Hitler: Nemesis*, 87–92; "Aufzeichnung Major Schmundts vom 22. April 1938 über eine Besprechung zwischen Hitler und dem Chef OKW, General Keitel, am 21. April 1938," in Müller and Hansen, *Armee und Drittes Reich*, 325–6; DGFP, series D, II, nos. 131–3; Jodl, "Jodl's Official Diary," IMT, XXVIII, Doc. 1780-PS, 372–3; Hürter, *Hitlers Heerführer*, 150; Megargee, *Inside Hitler's High Command*, 49; Maiolo, *Cry Havoc*, 244–5; Müller, *Heer und Hitler*, 300–1.
40. "Betrachtungen General Becks zur militärpolitischen Lage im Mai 1938 vom 5. Mai 1938," in Müller and Hansen, *Armee und Drittes Reich*, 326–9; Müller, *Heer und Hitler*, 301–5; Megargee, *Inside Hitler's High Command*, 49; Kershaw, *Hitler: Nemesis*, 97–8.
41. "Aufzeichnung General Becks über die Rede Hitlers vor den führenden Persönlichkeiten des Auswärtigen Amts und der Wehrmacht am 28. Mai hinsichtlich einer Aktion gegen die Tschechslowakei, vom 28. Mai 1938," in Müller and Hansen, *Armee und Drittes Reich*, 333–5; "Stellungnahme General Becks zu den Ausführungen Hitlers am 28. Mai 38 über die politischen und militärischen Voraussetzungen einer Aktion gegen die Tschechslowakei, vom 29. Mai 1938," in Müller and Hansen, *Armee und Drittes Reich*, 335–8; IMT, XXV, Doc. 388-PS; TBJG, 29 May 1938; Megargee, *Inside Hitler's High Command*, 49–50; Murray, *Change in European Balance of Power*, 172–3; Weinberg, "The May Crisis, 1938," 213–25; Messerschmidt, "Road to War," GSWW, I, 656; Maiolo, *Cry Havoc*, 261–3; Kershaw, *Hitler: Nemesis*, 99–101.
42. Maiolo, *Cry Havoc*, 263–4; Overy, "From 'Uralbomber' to 'Amerikabomber'," 154–78; idem, "Hitler and Air Strategy," 405–10; Corum, "Development of Strategic Air War Concepts," 18–35; idem, "From Biplanes to Blitzkrieg," 85–101; Maier, "Total War and German Air Doctrine," 210–19; Below, *At Hitler's Side*, 20–3.
43. "Denkschrift General Becks für den Oberbefehlshaber des Heeres über die Voraussetzungen und Erfolgsaussichten einer kriegerischen Aktion gegen die Tschechoslowakei aus Anlaß einer Weisung des Oberbefehlshabers der Wehrmacht, vom 3. Juni 1938,"; "Denkschrift General Becks für den Oberbefehlshaber des Heeres über die militärische Aussichtslosigkeit eines Krieges gegen die Tschechoslowakei, vom 16. Juli 1938"; "Vortragsnotiz General Becks über mögliche innen- und außenpolitische Entwicklungnen, inbesondere über das Verhalten der obersten militärischen Führung angesichts der Gefahr eines Krieges, vom 16. Juli 1938"; "Vortragsnotiz General Becks vom 19. Juli1938 mit ergänzenden Vorschlägen zur Vortragsnotiz, vom 16. Juli 1938," all in Müller and Hansen, *Armee und Drittes Reich*, 339–42, 345–9, 349–50, 350–1; idem, *Armee und Drittes Reich*, 108–14; Messerschmidt, "Road to War," GSWW, I, 659–60; Murray, *Change in Balance of Power*, 180–4; Hürter, *Hitlers Heerführer*, 150; Megargee, *Inside Hitler's High Command*, 49–52; Deist, "Rearmament," GSWW, I, 526–7; Kershaw, *Hitler: Nemesis*, 101–4; Jodl, "Jodl's Official Diary," 22, 23, 30 May 1938, IMT, XXVIII, Doc. 1780-PS, 373.
44. Ullrich, *Hitler: Ascent*, 728–30; Manstein, *Aus einen Soldatenleben*, 337–8; Jodl, "Jodl's Official Diary," 10 August 1938, IMT, XXVIII, Doc. 1780-PS, 374; Murray, *Change in Balance of Power*, 183–4; Megargee, *Inside Hitler's High Command*, 51–2; Messerschmidt, "Road to War," GSWW, I, 659–60.
45. Hartmann, *Halder*, 62–77, 99–116; Megargee, *Inside Hitler's High Command*, 51–4; Ueberschär, "Generaloberst Franz Halder," in idem, ed., *Hitlers militärische Elite*, 79–88.

46. Megargee, *Inside Hitler's High Command*, 54; Overy, "Germany and the Munich Crisis," 193–203; TBJG, 1, 2, 3 September 1938; "Besprechung am 3.9.38 auf dem Berghof," IMT, XXV, Doc. 388–PS, 462–4; Ullrich, *Hitler: Ascent*, 732–4.

47. Murray, *Change in Balance of Power*, 204–6; Megargee, *Inside Hitler's High Command*, 54; Messerschmidt, "Road to War," GSWW, I, 663–70; Maiolo, *Cry Havoc*, 269–71; TBJG, 1 September 1938; Kershaw, *Hitler: Nemesis*, 108–15; Ullrich, *Hitler: Ascent*, 735–6.

48. TBJG, 26 September 1938; "Besprechung Nurnberg 9./10. 9. 38, 22,00 – 3,30 Uhr," IMT, XXV, Doc. 388–PS, 464–9; TBJG, 23, 24, 26, 27 September 1938; Shirer, *Berlin Diary*, 22, 26, 27 September 1938, 137, 141–3; Murray, *Change in Balance of Power*, 225–9; Megargee, *Inside Hitler's High Command*, 54; Messerschmidt, "Road to War," GSWW, I, 663–70; Maiolo, *Cry Havoc*, 269–71; Hartmann, *Halder*, 105–6; Engel, *At the Heart of the Reich*, 53–4; Kershaw, *Hitler: Nemesis*, 113–19. For a good sense of the growing tension, anxiety, and evidence of his own and Hitler's thoughts, as well as for sharp observations on popular sentiment in Germany, see TBJG, 3 June–2 October 1938.

49. Engel, *At the Heart of the Reich*, 54; TBJG, 27, 28, 29 September, 1, 2 October 1938; Shirer, *Berlin Diary*, 30 September 1938, 144–8; Hartmann, *Halder*, 110–16; Messerschmidt, "Road to War," GSWW, I, 667–71; Hürter, *Hitlers Heerführer*, 152; Kershaw, *Hitler: Nemesis*, 119–25; Overy, "Germany and the Munich Crisis," 203–11; Ullrich, *Hitler: Ascent*, 737–46; Treue, "Rede Hitlers 10 November 1938," 182.

50. Murray, *Change in the Balance of Power*, 264, 266–9; Maiolo, *Cry Havoc*, 271–2; Overy, "Germany and the Munich Crisis," 191; Hitler, *Testament of Adolf Hitler*, 21 February 1945, 60–1.

51. Geyer, "Nazi Pursuit of War," 145–8; Tooze, *Wages of Destruction*, 287–93.

52. Kershaw, *Hitler: Nemesis*, 92, 123–5; Messerschmidt, "Road to War," GSWW, I, 638–9; Geyer, "Nazi Pursuit of War," 143–4; Maiolo, *Cry Havoc*, 280–1.

Chapter 4

1. "Rede Hitler vor den höheren Befehlshabern der drei Wehrmachtsteile am 25. Januar 1939 in der Reichskanzlei," in Müller and Hansen, *Armee und Drittes Reich*, Doc. 166, 360–5; "Rede Hitlers am 10. Februar 1939 vor Truppenkommandeueren in Berlin," in Müller and Hansen, *Armee und Drittes Reich*, Doc. 167, 365–75; Hürter, *Hitlers Heerführer*, 153–5.

2. "Rede Hitlers am 10. Februar 1939 vor Truppenkommandeueren in Berlin," in Müller and Hansen, *Armee und Drittes Reich*, Doc. 167, 365–75; Hürter, *Hitlers Heerführer*, 153–5; Thies, *Hitler's Plans*, 114–17.

3. Tooze, *Wages of Destruction*, 285–7; Maiolo, *Cry Havoc*, 272; "Directive by the Führer for the Wehrmacht," 21 October 1938, and "Notes for Wehrmacht Discussions with Italy," 26 November 1938, DGFP, D, IV, nos. 81, 411, 99–100, 530–2; TBJG, 24 October 1938.

4. "Besprechung bei Generalfeldmarschall Göring am 14.10.38, 10:00 im Reichsluftfahrtministerium," IMT, XXVII, Doc. 1301-PS, 160–4; IMT, XXXII, Doc. 3575-PS; Maiolo, *Cry Havoc*, 272–3, 279–80, 290–2; Murray, *Change in the European Balance of Power*, 287; Kroener, "Squaring the Circle," 285–7; Tooze, *Wages of Destruction*, 285–325; Kershaw, *Hitler: Nemesis*, 157–63; Overy, *War and Economy*, 93–6, 108–9, 196–7; Megargee, *Inside Hitler's High Command*, 62.

5. Maiolo, *Cry Havoc*, 289–91; IMT, XXVII, Doc. 1301-PS; IMT, XXXVI, Doc. 028-EC; Office of United States Chief of Counsel for Prosecution of Axis Criminality. *Nazi Conspiracy and Aggression* [hereafter NT, Red Series], VII, Doc. 028-EC; Hitler to Mussolini, 8, 18 March 1940, DGFP, D, VIII, no. 663 and IX, no. 1.

6. Messerschmidt, "Road to War," GSWW, I, 673–9; Murray, *Change in the European Balance of Power*, 265, 278–83; Kershaw, *Hitler: Nemesis*, 168–78.

7. Maiolo, *Cry Havoc*, 291–2, 443 fn 50; "Auszüge aus den Briefen des Oberst i.G. Wagner an seine Frau vom März 1939," in Müller and Hansen, *Armee und Drittes Reich*, Doc. 169, 376–7; Messerschmidt, "Road to War," GSWW, I, 675; Murray, *Change in the European Balance of Power*, 292–3. Watt, *How War Came*, 195, mentions the figure of twenty divisions, but without citing a source for this number; Müller, *Der Feind steht im Osten*, 105–22.

8. Hartmann, "Franz Halder und die Kriegsvorbereitungen im Frühjahr 1939," 467–95; Letter of Eduard Wagner, 24 March 1939, in Müller and Hansen, *Armee und Drittes Reich*, Doc. 169, 377; Messerschmidt, "Road to War," GSWW, I, 690–5: DGFP, D, VI, no. 78; Tooze, *Wages of Destruction*, 308–9.

9. Hitler Speech before the Reichstag, 28 April 1939, in Domarus, *Speeches*, 1,561–96; "Bericht über Besprechung am 23.5.1939," IMT, XXXVII, Doc. 79-L.

10. "Bericht über Besprechung am 23.5.1939," IMT, XXXVII, Doc. 79-L.

11. Messerschmidt, "Road to War," GSWW, I, 696–702, 706.

12. Messerschmidt, "Road to War," GSWW, I, 703–9; DGFP, D, VII, nos. 43, 47; Ciano, *Ciano Diaries*, 12–13 August 1939, 119–20.

13. Halder, *Halder War Diary*, 14 August 1939, 18–24; "Ausführungen Hitlers vor dem Oberbefehlshaber des Heeres und dem Chef des Generalstabes am 14. 8. 1939," in Müller and Hansen, *Armee und Drittes Reich*, Doc. 175, 385–7; Hartmann, "Halder und Kriegsvorbereitung," 467–95.

14. DGFP, D, VII, no. 192; IMT, XXVI, Doc. 798-PS; "Aufzeichnung Admiral Canaris' über die Ansprache Hitlers vor den Oberbefehlshabern am Vormittag des 22. 8. 1939," in Müller and Hansen, *Armee und Drittes Reich*, Doc. 174, 387–90; Halder, *Halder War Diary*, 22 August 1939, 28–32; Schramm, *Kriegstagebuch des Oberkommandos der Wehrmacht* (hereafter KTB/OKW), I/2, 947–9; Baumgart, "Ansprache Hitlers," 120–49; Pyta, *Hitler*, 273–4. In another version of the speech, Hitler allegedly pronounced the Four-Year Plan a failure, thus necessitating an immediate war. See Tooze, *Wages of Destruction*, 316.

15. "Zweite Ansprache des Fuhrers am 22. Aug. 1939," IMT, XXVI, Doc. 1014-PS; "Aufzeichnung Admiral Canaris' über die zweite Ansprache Hitlers an die Oberbefehlshaber am 22. 8. 1939," in Müller and Hansen, *Armee und Drittes Reich*, Doc. 175, 390–1; Halder, *Halder War Diary*, 22 August 1939, 31.

16. Engel, *At the Heart of the Reich*, 24 August 1939, 72; Bock, *Generalfeldmarschall Fedor Von Bock*, 22 August 1939, 34; Letter of Eduard Wagner, 1 September1939, in Müller and Hansen, *Armee und Drittes Reich*, Doc. 176, 393; Hürter, *Hitlers Heerführer*, 158–60.

17. Speer, *Inside the Third Reich*, 236; Murray, *Change in the European Balance of Power*, 295–7; Maiolo, *Cry Havoc*, 299–300; Tooze, *Wages of Destruction*, 316–17, 321–5.

18. Engel, *At the Heart of the Reich*, 25 August 1939, 73; DGFP, D, VII, Doc. 271, 285–6; Hartmann, *Halder*, 137; IMT, XXXIX, Doc. 090-TC, 107; Halder, *Halder War Diary*, 28, 29 August 1939, 37–9, 42; Messerschmidt, "Road to War," GSWW, I, 711–14; Megargee, *Inside Hitler's High Command*, 68.

19. Hartmann, *Halder*, 144; Halder, *Halder War Diary*, 2 September 1939, 47; Testimony of Jodl, 5 June 1946, IMT, XV, 372; Fritz, *Ostkrieg*, 8–9.

20. Hartmann, *Halder*, 144–5; Testimony of Jodl, 5 June 1946, IMT, XV, 373; Murray, *Change in the European Balance of Power*, 311–14, 326–34; Maiolo, *Cry Havoc*, 318–19, 323; Tooze, *Wages of Destruction*, 326–67.

21. Rohde, "Hitler's First Blitzkrieg," GSWW, II, 88–100; Hartmann, *Halder*, 141–3.

22. Rohde, "Hitler's First Blitzkrieg," GSWW, II, 101–26; Hartmann, *Halder*, 142–7; Murray, *Change in the European Balance of Power*, 326–34, 347–51.

23. Hartmann, *Halder*, 146–55; Hürter, *Hitlers Heerführer*, 177–95; Rohde, "Hitler's First Blitzkrieg," GSWW, II, 132–40; Megargee, *Inside Hitler's High Command*, 72–5; Halder, *Halder War Diary*, 20 September 1939, 58; Engel, *At the Heart of the Reich*, 19, 26, 28 September, 1, 8, 15 October, 18 November 1939, 75–80.

24. Citino, *German Way of War*, 264–7.

25. Murray, *Change in the European Balance of Power*; idem, "German Response to Victory in Poland," 285–98; Halder, *Halder War Diary*, 29 September 1939, 67; Frieser, *Blitzkrieg Legend*, 18–19.

Chapter 5

1. Pyta, *Hitler*, 274–5; Megargee, *Inside Hitler's High Command*, 76.

2. Hartmann, *Halder*, 157–58; Hürter, *Hitlers Heerführer*, 163–4.

3. Halder, *Halder War Diary*, 27 September 1939, 62–6; Frieser, *Blitzkrieg Legend*, 55–7; Hürter, *Hitlers Heerführer*, 164–5; Hartmann, *Halder*, 158–62; Tooze, *Wages of Destruction*, 336–7; Umbreit, "Battle for Hegemony in Western Europe," GSWW, II, 232–6; Megargee, *Inside Hitler's High Command*, 76; Murray, *Change in the European Balance of Power*, 326–33.

4. Hartmann, *Halder*, 159–60; Umbreit, "Battle for Hegemony in Western Europe," GSWW, II, 233; Megargee, *Inside Hitler's High Command*, 76; Frieser, *Blitzkrieg Legend*, 20–5; Murray, *Change in the European Balance of Power*, 326–33; idem, "German Response to Victory in Poland," 285–98; Hürter, *Hitlers Heerführer*, 165.

5. Engel, *At the Heart of the Reich*, 29 August 1939, 74; Halder, *Halder War Diary*, 29 September, 10 October 1939, 67, 69–72; "Unsigned Memorandum from Hitler to Brauchitsch, Raeder, Göring, Keitel, 9 October 1939: Directives for the Conduct of the War in the West," IMT, XXXVII, Doc. 052-L.

6. "Unsigned Memorandum from Hitler to Brauchitsch, Raeder, Göring, Keitel, 9 October 1939: Directives for the Conduct of the War in the West," IMT, XXXVII, Doc. 052-L; Jacobsen, "Winter 1939–1940," 436–7; Hürter, *Hitlers Heerführer*, 164–5; Umbreit, "Battle for Hegemony in Western Europe," GSWW, II, 236–7.

7. Halder, *Halder War Diary*, 14, 16 October 1939, 72; Jacobsen, "Hitlers gedanken," 437–9; Umbreit, "Battle for Hegemony in Western Europe," GSWW, II, 237–41; Frieser, *Blitzkrieg Legend*, 61–2; Hürter, *Hitlers Heerführer*, 166; Hartmann, *Halder*, 172–3, 179; Bock, *Diary*, 17 October 1939, 72.

8. Halder, *Halder War Diary*, 3 November 1939, 75–6; Jacobsen, "Hitlers gedanken," 437–9; Umbreit, "Battle for Hegemony in Western Europe," GSWW, II, 237–41; Frieser, *Blitzkrieg Legend*, 61–2; Hürter, *Hitlers Heerführer*, 166; Hartmann, *Halder*, 172–3, 179; Pyta, *Hitler*, 280–1; Bock, *Diary*, 25, 26 October, 1, 11, 18 November, 31 December 1939, 74–6, 79, 83, 86, 96; "Weisung Nr. 8 für die Kriegsführung, 20.11.1939," IMT, XXVI, Doc. 440-PS.

9. Groscurth, *Tagebücher eines Abwehroffiziers*, 31 October 1939, 222–3; Hartmann, *Halder*, 167–8; Hürter, *Hitlers Heerführer*, 167–8.

10. Hartmann, *Halder*, 169–71, 177–8; Frieser, *Blitzkrieg Legend*, 57–9; Hürter, *Hitlers Heerführer*, 167; KTB/OKW, I/2, 951–2; Engel, *At the Heart of the Reich*, 7 November 1939, 79–80; Groscurth, *Tagebücher eines Abwehroffiziers*, 5 November 1939, 224–5.

11. "Besprechung beim Führer zu der alle Oberbefehlshaber befohlen sind, 23.11.39," IMT, XXVI, Doc. 789-PS; Hürter, *Hitlers Heerführer*, 168; Hartmann, *Halder*, 175; Thies, *Hitler's Plans*, 120; Bock, *Diary*, 23 November 1939, 88; Halder, *Halder War Diary*, 23 November 1939, 80; Engel, *At the Heart of the Reich*, 23 November 1939, 80; Groscurth, *Tagebücher eines Abwehroffiziers*, 414–17.

12. Hürter, *Hitlers Heerführer*, 167–9; Hartmann, *Halder*, 175–7; Guderian, *Panzer Leader*, 86–8; Manstein, *Lost Victories*, 85; Halder, *Halder War Diary*, 23 November 1939, 80; Bock, *Diary*, 23 November 1939, 88; Engel, *At the Heart of the Reich*, 6, 10 December 1939, 81–2.

13. Manstein, *Lost Victories*, 84–5, 94–107; Guderian, *Panzer Leader*, 84–5; Frieser, *Blitzkrieg Legend*, 63–74.

14. Manstein, *Lost Victories*, 84–5, 94–107; Guderian, *Panzer Leader*, 84–5; Frieser, *Blitzkrieg Legend*, 63–74; Melvin, *Manstein*, 132–51; Pyta, *Hitler*, 278; Hürter, *Hitlers Heerführer*, 169; Jacobsen, "Hitlers gedanken," 441–6; Umbreit, "Battle for Hegemony in Western Europe," GSWW, II, 246–7; Hartmann, *Halder*, 179–84; Engel, *At the Heart of the Reich*, 6 December 1939, 19 February 1940, 81, 87; Halder, *Halder War Diary*, 18 February 1940, 100–2; Bock, *Diary*, 24 February 1940, 113–14.

15. Hartmann, *Halder*, 183–4.

16. Manstein, *Lost Victories*, 109; Jochmann, *Monologe*, 17–18 October 1941, 92; Pyta, *Hitler*, 285.

17. Frieser, *Blitzkrieg Legend*, 80; Pyta, *Hitler*, 266–7, 282–8. Karl May was an enormously popular German writer of adventure tales set in the American West. Hitler was a notable enthusiast of his books, which featured characters such as Winnetou and Old

Shatterhand. Hitler later recommended May's books to his generals, stressing Winnetou as a fine example of tactical agility.

18. Maier, "Securing Northern Flank," GSWW, II, 183, 188-91; Megargee, *Inside Hitler's High Command*, 77-8.
19. Maier, "Securing Northern Flank," GSWW, II, 197-205; Maiolo, *Cry Havoc*, 316-26.
20. Maier, "Securing Northern Flank," GSWW, II, 195, 206-19.
21. Maier, "Securing Northern Flank," GSWW, II, 195, 206-19; Warlimont, *Inside Hitler's Headquarters*, 76-9; Halder, *Halder War Diary*, 14, 15, 17, 18 April 1940, 120-3; KTB/OKW, II, Doc. 16, 15 April 1940, 963-4; Lossberg, *Im Wehrmachtführungsstab*, 66-9; Hartmann, *Halder*, 185-6; Megargee, *Inside Hitler's High Command*, 79.
22. Hartmann, *Halder*, 191-3; Harris, *Men, Ideas, and Tanks*, 291-2 (Liddell Hart); Maiolo, *Cry Havoc*, 335-6 (Reynaud), 340.
23. For the definitive account of the French campaign from the German perspective, see Frieser, *Blitzkrieg Legend*, 100-320; also Umbreit, "Battle for Hegemony in Western Europe," GSWW, II, 278-326; Halder, *Halder War Diary*, 16, 17, 18 May 1940, 145-9; Hartmann, *Halder*, 194-5.
24. Frieser, *Blitzkrieg Legend*, 256-9; Halder, *Halder War Diary*, 17, 18 May 1940, 147-51; Hartmann, *Halder*, 194-5; Guderian, *Panzer Leader*, 109-10.
25. Hartmann, *Halder*, 195-6; Halder, *Halder War Diary*, 18, 19 May 1940, 150-2.
26. Umbreit, "Battle for Hegemony in Western Europe," GSWW, II, 289; Frieser, *Blitzkrieg Legend*, 278.
27. Hartmann, *Halder*, 193-6; Umbreit, "Battle for Hegemony in Western Europe," GSWW, II, 288-90; Frieser, *Blitzkrieg Legend*, 264-5, 273-92; Halder, *Halder War Diary*, 21, 23 May 1940, 157, 161-4; Bock, *Diary*, 24 May 1940, 151-2.
28. Frieser, *Blitzkrieg Legend*, 287, 292-94; Bock, *Diary*, 29 May 1940, 157; Halder, *Halder War Diary*, 23 May 1940, 161-4.
29. Frieser, *Blitzkrieg Legend*, 294-9; IMT, XXVIII, Doc. 1809-PS (Jodl, "Jodl's Official Diary", 24, 25 May 1940); Halder, *Halder War Diary*, 24, 25, 26 May 1940, 164-8; Bock, *Diary*, 26 May 1940, 153-4.
30. Frieser, *Blitzkrieg Legend*, 298-302; Halder, *Halder War Diary*, 27, 29, 30, 31 May, 1 June 1940, 168-74; Bock, *Diary*, 30 May, 2 June 1940, 158, 162.
31. Frieser, *Blitzkrieg Legend*, 305-14; Engel, *At the Heart of the Reich*, 25 May 1940, 92.
32. Hartmann, *Halder*, 198; Halder, *Halder War Diary*, 5, 6, 13 June 1940, 179-82, 202.
33. Frieser, *Blitzkrieg Legend*, 320-6, 352; Churchill, *The Gathering Storm*, 474-5.
34. Frieser, *Blitzkrieg Legend*, 326-31, 334, 336-8.
35. Frieser, *Blitzkrieg Legend*, 334-6.
36. Frieser, *Blitzkrieg Legend*, 334-5, 339-46; Maiolo, *Cry Havoc*, 339.
37. Tooze, *Wages of Destruction*, 377-9; Nietzsche, *Thoughts Out of Season*, Project Gutenberg, May 2004, E-Book #5652, http://www.gutenberg.org/ebooks/5652, (accessed 7 March 2015) 14; Gibbons, "Opposition gegen 'Barbarossa' im Herbst 1940," 337-8; Frieser, *Blitzkrieg Legend*, 349-53; Hürter, *Hitlers Heerführer*, 175-6.
38. "Mein Führer, Sie sind des größte Feldherr aller Zeiten." This gave rise to the later derisory term, "Gröfaz"; Frieser, *Blitzkrieg Legend*, 326-7; Maiolo, *Cry Havoc*, 343; Pyta, *Hitler*, 289, 297, 301; Wagner, diary entry of 9 July 1940, in Elisabeth Wagner, ed., *Der Generalquartiermeister*, 195; Hartmann, *Halder*, 201; Hürter, *Hitlers Heerführer*, 174-6; Goda, "Hitler's Bribery of his Senior Military Officers," 413-52.
39. Hartmann, *Halder*, 201-6; Pyta, *Hitler*, 284-5; Trevor-Roper, *Hitler's Table Talk*, 17-18, 21-22 October 1941, 71, 82; Jochmann, *Adolf Hitler*, 21-22 October 1941, 101.
40. Ciano, *Diary*, 19 June 1940, 266; Umbreit, "Plans and Preparations for a Landing in England," in GSWW, II, 366-73; Halder, *Diary*, 13, 22, 29, 30, 31 July, 6, 26 August, 14 September 1940, 226-7, 230, 235-47, 251, 256-8; Hartmann, *Halder*, 211-18.
41. Fritz, *Ostkrieg*, 39-44, 75; Ciano, *Diary*, 28 September, 4 October 1940, 296, 298-9; Hillgruber, "Noch Einmal," 214-23; Tooze, *Wages of Destruction*, 402-3; Schreiber, "Mediterranean in Hitler's Strategy in 1940," 240-8, 257; Förster, "Hitler Turns East," 115-23; Halder, *Halder War Diary*, 4 November 1940, 279.

42. Fritz, *Ostkrieg*, 44–6; Megargee, *Inside Hitler's High Command*, 88; Umbreit, "Return to Indirect Strategy," GSWW, II, 408–11; Schreiber, "Mediterranean in Hitler's Strategy in 1940," 252–4; idem, "Political and Military Developments," GSWW, III, 209–46; Halder, *Halder War Diary*, 30 September, 15, 16, 24, 26, 27 October, 2, 4 November 1940, 260, 262–71, 274–9; Hartmann, *Halder*, 219–21.

43. Schreiber, "Mediterranean in Hitler's Strategy in 1940," 250–8, 272; Schmider, "Mediterranean in 1940–1941," 19–41; Eichholtz, *War for Oil*, 47–57; Engel, *At the Heart of the Reich*, 24 April 1941, 109 (although this is surely an incorrect date, since events in Iraq did not fully play out until the end of May; Hitler's aide, Walther Hewel, quoted in Thies, *Hitler's Plans*, 175, puts Hitler's musings on 31 May); Thies, *Hitler's Plans*, 165.

44. Halder, *Halder War Diary*, 2, 4 November 1940, 275–9; Hartmann, *Halder*, 220–3; Schmider, "Mediterranean in 1940–1941," 39.

45. Fritz, *Ostkrieg*, 46–8; Schreiber, "Mediterranean in Hitler's Strategy in 1940," 258–60; Umbreit, "Indirect Strategy," 411–15; Kershaw, *Hitler: Nemesis*, 327–31; Ciano, *Ciano Diaries*, 12 October 1940, 300; Engel, *At the Heart of the Reich*, 28 October 1940, 98–9; Creveld, "25 October 1940," 87–96; Halder, *Halder War Diary*, 28 October, 1 November 1940, 271–4.

46. Umbreit, "Indirect Strategy," 418–19; Schreiber, "Mediterranean in Hitler's Strategy in 1940," 271–72.

47. Fritz, *Ostkrieg*, 48–50; Halder, *Halder War Diary*, 1 November, 5 December 1940, 273, 294; Below, *Als Hitlers Adjutant*, 249–50; Engel, *At the Heart of the Reich*, 4, 15 November 1940, 99–100; Maiolo, *Cry Havoc*, 356–7; Schreiber, "Mediterranean in Hitler's Strategy," 262–6.

48. Directive No. 18, 12 November 1940, in Trevor-Roper, *Blitzkrieg to Defeat*, 39–43; Hartmann, *Halder*, 222–3; Halder, *Halder War Diary*, 16 January 1941, 310–11.

49. Halder, *Halder War Diary*, 11, 13, 14, 15, 23, 30 April, 3 May, 4 June 1941, 359, 362–5, 374, 380–2, 399; Schreiber, "Mediterranean in Hitler's Strategy," 262–70; Detlef Vogel, "The German Attack on Yugoslavia and Greece," GSWW, III, 499–556; Fritz, *Ostkrieg*, 71–2; Hartmann, *Halder*, 222–3; Schmider, "Mediterranean in 1940–1941," 37–40.

50. Ciano, *Diary*, 19 January 1941, 338; IMT, XXXIV, Doc. 134-C, 468; Maiolo, *Cry Havoc*, 349; Thies, *Hitler's Plans*, 118–21; Pyta, *Hitler*, 286.

Chapter 6

1. Hürter, *Hitlers Heerführer*, 1–3.

2. Förster and Mawdsley, "Hitler and Stalin," 61–9; Hürter, *Hitlers Heerführer*, 5–6.

3. "Besprechung des Führers mit dem Ob.d.H. . . . ", 9 January 1941, KTB/OKW, I/1, 257–8; Stahel, *Operation Barbarossa*, 71; Förster and Mawdsley, "Hitler and Stalin," 68–75; Hürter, *Hitlers Heerführer*, 7–8.

4. Förster, "Hitler Turns East," 130; Stahel, *Operation Barbarossa*, 96–7; Förster and Mawdsley, "Hitler and Stalin," 74–7; Hürter, *Hitlers Heerführer*, 7–9.

5. Fritz, *Ostkrieg*, 91; TBJG, 9 July 1941; Jochmann, *Monologe*, 5–6, 11–12, 27 July, 1–2, 8–11, 19–20 August, 17–19, 22–26 September 1941, 27–54; Kershaw, *Hitler: Nemesis*, 400–4, 434–5; Trevor-Roper, *Hitler's Table Talk*, 25 (evening), 25–26 (night) September 1941, 41–4. There is a lively debate over the extent to which nineteenth-century European colonialism in general, and the American example of Manifest Destiny in particular, influenced Hitler: see, for example, Westermann, *Hitler's Ostkrieg and the Indian Wars*; Guettel, "The US Frontier as Rationale for the Nazi East?"; Gerwarth and Malinowski, "Der Holocaust als 'kolonialer Genozid'?"; Zimmerer, "Holocaust und Kolonialismus"; idem, "The Birth of the 'Ostland' out of the Spirit of Colonialism."

6. Hürter, *Hitlers Heerführer*, 9–11, 215; idem, "Es herrschen Sitten und Gebräuche," 366; Halder, *Halder War Diary*, 30 March 1941, 345–6; Bock, *Diary*, 30 March 1941, 206–8; Warlimont, *Inside Hitler's Headquarters*, 162; Pyta, *Hitler*, 330; Förster, "Hitler Turns East," 131; on support of generals: Jodl, 15 May 1945, KTB/OKW, IV/8, 1503.

7. Fritz, *Ostkrieg*, 31–6; Hürter, *Hitlers Heerführer*, 213; Stahel, *Operation Barbarossa*, 33; Halder, *Halder War Diary*, 5 December 1940, 294.

8. Fritz, *Ostkrieg*, 36–7; Stahel, *Operation Barbarossa*, 34–5; Halder, *Halder War Diary*, 13 July 1940, 227.
9. Fritz, *Ostkrieg*, 37–9; Hürter, *Hitlers Heerführer*, 206; Halder, *Halder War Diary*, 3, 22 July 1940, 220–1, 229–32; Stahel, *Operation Barbarossa*, 34–5.
10. Fritz, *Ostkrieg*, 40–4; Warlimont, *Inside Hitler's Headquarters*, 111–12; Halder, *Halder War Diary*, 31 July 1940, 241–5; Leach, *German Strategy*, 100; Stahel, *Operation Barbarossa*, 37–9. Curiously, Halder's earlier enthusiasm for a confrontation, even a limited one, with Russia seemed to have abated. In strategic terms, he now thought it better to stay on friendly terms with Stalin until Britain had been forced from the war: *Halder War Diary*, 30 July 1940, 240–1.
11. Halder, *Halder War Diary*, 27 August 1940, 251–2; Hürter, *Hitlers Heerführer*, 207; Thies, *Hitler's Plans*, 176.
12. Förster and Mawdsley, "Hitler and Stalin," 80–1, 94–8.
13. Halder, *Halder War Diary*, 26 July 1940, 233; Below, *At Hitler's Side*, 81; Fugate, *Operation Barbarossa*, 63; Leach, *German Strategy*, 97; Klink, "Military Concept," GSWW, IV, 245; Stahel, *Operation Barbarossa*, 36.
14. Klink, "Military Concept," GSWW, IV, 258–60; Leach, *German Strategy*, 101–3; Fugate, *Operation Barbarossa*, 66–7; Hartmann, *Halder*, 227–8; Halder, *Halder War Diary*, 1 August 1940, 246.
15. Ritchie, "Russo-German War Plans 1941," 44; "Aus dem Operationsentwurf des Generalmajors Marcks für die Aggression gegen die Sowjetunion, 5. August 1940," Doc. 31, in Moritz, *Fall Barbarossa*, 121–6.
16. "Aus dem Operationsentwurf des Generalmajors Marcks," in Moritz, *Fall Barbarossa*, 121–6; Klink, "Military Concept," GSWW, IV, 259–65; Stahel, *Operation Barbarossa*, 40–2; Fritz, *Ostkrieg*, 52–5; Hartmann, *Halder*, 229.
17. "Operationsstudie des Gruppenleiter Heer in der Abteilung Landesverteidigung OKW für die Aggression gegen die Sowjetunion (Lossberg Studie), 15. September 1940," Doc. 32, in Moritz, *Fall Barbarossa*, 126–34; Klink, "Military Concept," GSWW, IV, 270–3; Leach, *German Strategy*, 108–10; Stahel, *Operation Barbarossa*, 47–50; Ritchie, "Russo-German War Plans 1941," 46.
18. Liddell Hart, *German Generals Talk*, 184; Klink, "Military Concept," GSWW, IV, 259–60.
19. Klink, "Military Concept," GSWW, IV, 262, 266–9; Stahel, *Operation Barbarossa*, 43–4.
20. "Aus der Einschätzung der politisch-moralischen Stabilität der Sowjetunion und der Kampfkraft der Roten Armee durch die Abteilung Fremde Heere Ost des Generalstabes des Heeres, 1. Januar 1941," Doc. 14, in Moritz, *Fall Barbarossa*, 79–80; Megargee, *Inside Hitler's High Command*, 111–12; Groehler, "Goals and Reason," 54–8; Stahel, *Operation Barbarossa*, 44–7; Hartmann, *Halder*, 230–1; Hürter, *Hitlers Heerführer*, 213–15; Halder, *Halder War Diary*, 3 September 1940, 255; Gibbons, "Opposition gegen 'Barbarossa' im Herbst 1940," 332–40.
21. Ritchie, "Russo-German War Plans 1941," 45–6; Klink, "Military Concept," GSWW, IV, 275; Fugate, *Operation Barbarossa*, 72–3; Vego, "German War Gaming," 135–6.
22. Klink, "Military Concept," GSWW, IV, 275–7; Stahel, *Operation Barbarossa*, 55–9; Fugate, *Operation Barbarossa*, 72–3; Vego, "German War Gaming," 136.
23. Stahel, *Operation Barbarossa*, 59; KTB/OKW, I, 5 December 1940, 203–9; Halder, *Halder War Diary*, 5 December 1940, 292–8; Klink, "Military Concept," GSWW, IV, 277–8.
24. KTB/OKW, I/1, 5 December 1940, 203–9; Halder, *Halder War Diary*, 5 December 1940, 292–8; "Conference of 'Fall Barbarossa' and 'Sonnenblume,' 3 Feb 1941," NT Doc. 872-PS, Red Series, III, 628; "Aus dem Protokoll der Besprechung Hitlers mit führenden Offizieren des OKW, des OKH und des OKL über die Operationen gegen die Sowjetunion und die Heranziehung der Satellitenstaaten, 3. Februar 1941," Doc. 40, in Moritz, *Fall Barbarossa*, 162–6; Below, *At Hitler's Side*, 83; Klink, "Military Concept," GSWW, IV, 277–8, 284; Hartmann, *Halder*, 233–4; Stahel, *Operation Barbarossa*, 64. On 7 December 1940, just two days after Hitler had outlined his ideas, General Sodenstern, chief of staff of Army Group A (later renamed Army Group South), completed a study

that similarly advocated a powerful inner thrust from either side of the Pripet Marshes, although in his plan Moscow loomed as the ultimate objective.

25. KTB/OKW, I/1, 5 December 1940, 209; Halder, *Halder War Diary*, 5 December 1940, 297.
26. KTB/OKW, I/1, 5, 18 December 1940, 208, 235; Stahel, *Operation Barbarossa*, 61, 90; Engel, *At the Heart of the Reich*, 19 February 1940, 31 May 1941, 87, 114; Fugate, *Operation Barbarossa*, 77; Klink, "Military Concept," GSWW, IV, 278; Hartmann, *Halder*, 233-4.
27. KTB/OKW, I/1, 5 December 1940, 209; Klink, "Military Concept," GSWW, IV, 278-9.
28. Below, *At Hitler's Side*, 38-40, 81-2; Manstein, *Lost Victories*, 74-5, 125, 274-8, 280, 282, 286.
29. Engel, *At the Heart of the Reich*, 28 July, 6, 8, 21, 23 August, 4 October 1941, 114-19; Fugate, *Operation Barbarossa*, 78-9; Manstein, *Lost Victories*, 286; Pyta, *Hitler*, 275, 327, 331-2; Stahel, *Operation Barbarossa*, 82.
30. Engel, *At the Heart of the Reich*, 31 May 1941, 114; Schramm, *Hitler*, 189; Messerschmidt, "June 1941 Seen through German Memoirs and Diaries," 216; Halder, *War Journal*, VI, 14 March 1941, 24-5.
31. Hürter, *Hitlers Heerführer*, 214-15, 226-7.
32. Fugate, *Operation Barbarossa*, 80-4; Vego, "German War Gaming," 138-9.
33. Fugate, *Operation Barbarossa*, 80-4; Vego, "German War Gaming," 138-9; Fritz, *Ostkrieg*, 53-5.
34. Halder, *Halder War Diary*, 13 December 1940, 302-6; Warlimont, *Inside Hitler's Headquarters*, 138-9; "Directive No. 21 'Case Barbarossa,'" in Trevor-Roper, ed., *Blitzkrieg to Defeat*, 49-53; "Hitlers Weisung Nr. 21 ('Fall Barbarossa') für den Überfall auf die Sowjetunion, 18. Dezember 1940," Doc. 36, in Moritz, *Fall Barbarossa*, 140-4; Klink, "Military Concept," GSWW, IV, 281-3; Stahel, *Operation Barbarossa*, 65-9; Hartmann, *Halder*, 234.
35. Klink, "Military Concept," GSWW, IV, 281-3; Stahel, *Operation Barbarossa*, 65-9; Leach, *German Strategy*, 101-3; Fritz, *Ostkrieg*, 55; Lunde, *Hitler's Wave-Breaker Concept*, 58-60. Halder used ambiguous terms such as "securing" the Baltic and misleading phrases such as "in accordance with plans submitted to me [Hitler]" in order to provide him with suitable leeway for action.
36. KTB/OKW, I/1, 9 January 1941, 258; Klink, "Military Concept," GSWW, IV, 283-4; Halder, *Halder War Diary*, 28 January 1941, 313-15; Stahel, *Operation Barbarossa*, 70-5; Megargee, *Inside Hitler's High Command*, 124.
37. Halder, *Halder War Diary*, 27 November 1940, 288; Bock, *Diary*, 1, 24 February 1941, 197-8, 200; Stahel, *Operation Barbarossa*, 77; Manstein, *Lost Victories*, 275.
38. Hartmann, *Halder*, 236-8; Hürter, *Hitlers Heerführer*, 213-14, 226; Megargee, *Inside Hitler's High Command*, 114; Stahel, *Operation Barbarossa*, 76-84; Guderian, *Panzer Leader*, 190; Engel, *At the Heart of the Reich*, 18 December 1940, 100-1; KTB/OKW, I/1, 3 February 1941, 297-302; "Conference of 'Fall Barbarossa' and 'Sonnenblume,' 3 Feb 1941," NT Doc. 872-PS, Red Series, III, 627-33; "Aus dem Protokoll der Besprechung Hitlers mit führenden Offizieren," in Moritz, *Fall Barbarossa*, 162-6.
39. Klink, "Military Concept," GSWW, IV, 287-8; Stahel, *Operation Barbarossa*, 85; Megargee, *Inside Hitler's High Command*, 115-16; Halder, *Halder War Diary*, 17 March 1941, 337; "Feindbeurteilung Stand 20.5.41," in Messerschmidt, "June 1941," 217-19.
40. Eichholtz, *War for Oil*, 36; Klink, "Military Concept," GSWW, IV 283, 287-8; Stahel, *Operation Barbarossa*, 85-6; Fritz, *Ostkrieg*, 58-61; Thomas, "Studie des Wehrwirtschafts-und Rüstungsamtes über das sowjetische Wirtschaftspotential und die voraussichtlichen kriegswirtschaftlichen Gewinne durch die geplante Aggression gegen die Sowjetunion, 13. Februar 1941," Doc. 108, in Moritz, *Fall Barbarossa*, 338-56; Speer quoted in United States Strategic Bombing Survey, *Oil Division Final Report*, 36-9.
41. Hayward, "Hitler's Quest for Oil," 99; "Memorandum, Chief of Agency for Armament Economy," 20 June 1941, NT, Doc. 1456-PS, Red Series, IV, 21; Larionov, "Why the Wehrmacht Didn't Win," 209.

42. Guderian, *Panzer Leader*, 146–7, 149; Manstein, *Lost Victories*, 177; Stahel, *Operation Barbarossa*, 88–95; Hürter, *Hitlers Heerführer*, 213–15, 226–35; Halder, *Halder War Diary*, 17, 30 March 1941, 338, 345–7; Bock, *Diary*, 18, 27, 30 March, 14–16 May 1941, 203, 205, 208, 213–14.

43. Halder, *Halder War Diary*, 17, 27, 30 March 1941, 338, 341, 345–7; idem, *War Journal*, VI, 21 March 1941, 32–3; Bock, *Diary*, 27 February, 18, 27, 30 March, 14–16 May, 4 June 1941, 201, 203, 205, 208, 213–14, 218; Stahel, *Operation Barbarossa*, 142–3.

44. Klink, "Military Concept," GSWW, IV, 284, 288; Fugate, *Operation Barbarossa*, 90–3; Fritz, *Ostkrieg*, 76; Bullock, *Hitler*, 652.

45. Halder, *Halder War Diary*, 30 March 1941, 346; Hürter, *Hitlers Heerführer*, 214–22; Pyta, *Hitler*, 329.

46. Below, *At Hitler's Side*, 101–4; Halder, *Halder War Diary*, 14 June 1941, 406; Bock, *Diary*, 14 June 1941, 220–2; "Richtlinien für die Behandlung politischer Kommissare vom 6.6.1941," Doc. 8, 259–60 (Commissar Order); "Erlaß über die Ausübung der Kriegsgerichtsbarkeit im Gebiet 'Barbarossa' und über besondere Maßnahmen der Truppe vom 13.5.1941," Doc. 6, 251–3 (Barbarossa Order: Kriegsgerichtsbarkeitserlass); "Richtlinien für das Verhalten der Truppe in Rußland, 19.5.1941," Doc. 7, 254–6, in Ueberschär and Wette, *Unternehmen Barbarossa*; Hürter, *Hitlers Heerführer*, 247–65; Weinberg, "22 June," 228–9; Stahel, *Operation Barbarossa*, 97–104.

47. Halder, *Halder War Diary*, 14 June 1941, 406; Bock, *Diary*, 14 June 1941, 220–2; Below, *At Hitler's Side*, 103; Stahel, *Operation Barbarossa*, 97–104; Fritz, *Ostkrieg*, 72–4; TBJG, 16 June 1941; Thies, *Hitler's Plans*, 166; Trevor-Roper, *Hitler's Table Talk*, 17–18 October 1941, 71.

Chapter 7

1. Domarus, *Speeches*, 2,444–51, 2,457–9; Pyta, *Hitler*, 313.

2. Domarus, *Speeches*, 2,457–9; Trevor-Roper, *Hitler's Table Talk*, 5–6, 27 July, 8–11, 19–20 August, 17–18, 25 September, 13, 17 October 1941, 5–6, 15–16, 23–4, 28–9, 31–5, 41–2, 52–3, 68; Kershaw, *Hitler: Nemesis*, 434; Pyta, *Hitler*, 373; Fritz, *Ostkrieg*, 91–3; Westermann, *Hitler's Ostkrieg and the Indian Wars*, 259–60.

3. Wette, *Wehrmacht*, 229–34; Fritz, *Ostkrieg*, 84–5; Hürter, *Hitlers Heerführer*, 281–2. See also Hartmann, *Halder*, 67–77, 343–53; Manstein, *Lost Victories*, 79–81; Engel, *At the Heart of the Reich*, 15, 36–7, 51.

4. Halder, *Halder War Diary*, 22 June 1941, 410–12; Fritz, *Ostkrieg*, 77–8; Leach, *German Strategy*, 172, 192; DiNardo, *Mechanized Juggernaut*, 40–50; Hoffmann, "Die Sowjetunion bis zum Vorabend des deutschen Angriffs," *Das Deutsche Reich und der Zweite Weltkrieg* (hereafter DRZW), IV, 88–99; Mawdsley, *Thunder in the East*, 26–31, 42–3, 46–51.

5. Fritz, *Ostkrieg*, 81–2. For a good assessment of German intelligence failures, see Thomas, "Foreign Armies East and German Military Intelligence in Russia, 1941–1945."

6. Fritz, *Ostkrieg*, 82–5; Hayward, "Hitler's Quest for Oil," 99–103; Cooke and Nesbit, *Target: Hitler's Oil*, 16.

7. Clausewitz, *On War*, 31–44; Manstein, *Lost Victories*, 286; Fritz, *Ostkrieg*, 82–5; TBJG, 23 June 1941.

8. Fritz, *Ostkrieg*, 85–8; Glantz, *Barbarossa*, 35, 42–6; Leach, *German Strategy*, 192–3; Kershaw, *War Without Garlands*, 37, 51–2, 55; Klink, "The Conduct of Operations," in GSWW, IV, 537–41; Megargee, *War of Annihilation*, 45–6.

9. Fritz, *Ostkrieg*, 85–8; Klink, "The Conduct of Operations," GSWW, IV, 546–69; Megargee, *War of Annihilation*, 47–9; Glantz, *Barbarossa*, 46–53.

10. Fritz, *Ostkrieg*, 85–8; Klink, "The Conduct of Operations," GSWW, IV, 525–32; Megargee, *War of Annihilation*, 46–7; Glantz, *Barbarossa*, 37; Stahel, *Operation Barbarossa*, 161–3; Guderian, *Panzer Leader*, 58–166; Bock, *Diary*, 23, 25, 26 June 1941, 225–8.

11. Fritz, *Ostkrieg*, 86–7; Fugate, *Operation Barbarossa*, 101–4; Leach, *German Strategy*, 194–5; Bock, *Diary*, 23, 25, 26, 29 June, 2 July 1941, 225–8, 232, 235; Halder,

Halder War Diary, 23, 25, 29 June 1941, 416, 424, 432; Stahel, *Operation Barbarossa*, 161–3, 177.

12. TBJG, 24, 29 June 1941; Stahel, *Operation Barbarossa*, 159–82.

13. Fugate, *Operation Barbarossa*, 104–6; Hoth, *Panzer-Operationen*, 60–3; Bock, *Diary*, 23, 25, 26, 29 June, 2 July 1941, 225–8, 232, 235; Halder, *Halder War Diary*, 23, 25 June 1941, 416, 424; Stahel, *Operation Barbarossa*, 204.

14. Fugate, *Operation Barbarossa*, 109–11; Stahel, *Operation Barbarossa*, 163, 177–9; Bock, *Diary*, 23, 25, 26, 29 June, 2 July 1941, 225–8, 232, 235; Halder, *Halder War Diary*, 23, 25, 29 June 1941, 416, 424, 432; Guderian, *Panzer Leader*, 166–7; Hürter, *Hitlers Heerführer*, 284–5.

15. Fritz, *Ostkrieg*, 87–8; Ziemke and Bauer, *Moscow to Stalingrad*, 14; Stahel, *Operation Barbarossa*, 137, 159–60.

16. Fritz, *Ostkrieg*, 87–8; Fugate, *Operation Barbarossa*, 106–9; Halder, *Halder War Diary*, 25, 26, 28, 30 June 1941, 421–2, 424–6, 430, 436; Ziemke and Bauer, *Moscow to Stalingrad*, 14; Stahel, *Operation Barbarossa*, 158–62, 169, 171–3, 181–2, 185; Bock, *Diary*, 24, 28 June 1941, 226, 231; Klink, "The Conduct of Operations," GSWW, IV, 531–2, 536.

17. TBJG, 29 June 1941; Fritz, *Ostkrieg*, 87–8; Fugate, *Operation Barbarossa*, 99, 106–9; Bock, *Diary*, 2 July 1941, 235–6; Stahel, *Operation Barbarossa*, 158–62.

18. Clausewitz, *On War*, 264; Groehler, "Goals and Reason," 51; Stahel, *Operation Barbarossa*, 169, 182, 200.

19. Halder, *Halder War Diary*, 30 June 1941, 437–8; Hürter, *Hitlers Heerführer*, 285–6; Stahel, *Operation Barbarossa*, 161–2, 189, 193–4; Prüller, *Diary of a German Soldier*, 3 July 1941, 73.

20. Stahel, *Operation Barbarossa*, 161–2, 170–1, 189, 193–4; Hürter, *Hitlers Heerführer*, 285–6.

21. Stahel, *Operation Barbarossa*, 127–38, Halder, *War Journal*, III, 4 February 1940, 55–8; Hürter, *Hitlers Heerführer*, 285; Fritz, *Ostkrieg*, 26, 52–7, 114–20; Hürter, *German General*, 68.

22. Fritz, *Ostkrieg*, 85–91; Hürter, *Hitlers Heerführer*, 282, fn 11, 283; Halder, *Halder War Diary*, 3 July 1941, 444–7; KTB/OKW, I/2, 4, 14 July, 16 August 1941, 1,020, 1,022–5, 1,047–54; Directive No. 32a, 14 July 1941, in Trevor-Roper, *Blitzkrieg to Defeat*, 82–5; Megargee, *Inside Hitler's High Command*, 171.

23. Stahel, *Operation Barbarossa*, 155; Heinrici letter of 24 June 1941 in Hürter, *Ein deutscher General*, 63.

24. Hürter, *Hitlers Heerführer*, 285, fn 24; Megargee, *Inside Hitler's High Command*, 132; Fritz, *Ostkrieg*, 112–13; Halder, *Halder War Diary*, 25, 26, 29, 30 June, 2 July 1941, 421, 424–6, 431–2, 434–6, 441–2.

25. Fritz, *Ostkrieg*, 113–14; KTB/OKW, I/2, 4, 5, 8 July 1941, 1,020–1; Halder, *Halder War Diary*, 8 July 1941, 457.

26. Fritz, *Ostkrieg*, 113–17; Halder, *Halder War Diary*, 8 July 1941, 457.

27. Halder, *Halder War Diary*, 12, 13 July 1941, 467, 470; Hürter, *Hitlers Heerführer*, 288; Fugate, *Operation Barbarossa*, 121–4, 155, 206–7; Stahel, *Operation Barbarossa*, 241–2, 245; Bock, *Diary*, 13, 14 July 1941, 247, 250; Hoth, *Panzer-Operationen*, 92–3.

28. Stahel, *Operation Barbarossa*, 237–41; Fugate, *Operation Barbarossa*, 124–5.

29. Stahel, *Operation Barbarossa*, 249–53, 259; Halder, *Halder War Diary*, 13, 15 July 1941, 469, 474; Bock, *Diary*, 15 July, 1941, 249–51.

30. Stahel, *Operation Barbarossa*, 252–3, 260–1; Fugate, *Operation Barbarossa*, 120–4, 128–9, 156.

31. Stahel, *Operation Barbarossa*, 252–3, 260–1; Fugate, *Operation Barbarossa*, 120–4, 128–9, 156; Kipp, "Barbarossa and the Crisis of Successive Operations," 114–17; Fritz, *Ostkrieg*, 123–4; Halder, *Halder War Diary*, 20 July 1941, 480–2; Bock, *Diary*, 20 July 1941, 255.

32. Stahel, *Operation Barbarossa*, 268–70, 280; Fugate, *Operation Barbarossa*, 128–35, 156; Bock, *Diary*, 20, 21 July 1941, 255–6, 258.

33. Fritz, *Ostkrieg*, 124; Kipp, "Barbarossa and the Crisis of Successive Operations," 124–30; Glantz, *Barbarossa*, 82–95; Mawdsley, *Thunder in the East*, 66–9; Bock, *War Diary*, 20, 21, 22, 23, 24, 25, 26, 31, July 1941, 255–69; Stahel, *Operation Barbarossa*, 271–3.

34. Directive No. 33, 19 July 1941, in Trevor-Roper, *Blitzkrieg to Defeat*, 85–8; Halder, *Halder War Diary*, 3, 9, 11, 12, 13, 15, 18, 19, 20, 26 July 1941, 448, 461, 465, 467, 470, 474, 477–82, 485; Fritz, *Ostkrieg*, 126–7.

35. Bock, *Diary*, 21 July 1941, 258; Halder, *Halder War Diary*, 21, 22 July 1941, 483–4; Fugate, *Operation Barbarossa*, 207–8; Stahel, *Operation Barbarossa*, 276, 283–5; Fritz, *Ostkrieg*, 126–7.

36. Fugate, *Operation Barbarossa*, 207–8; Stahel, *Operation Barbarossa*, 276; Fritz, *Ostkrieg*, 126–7; Directive No. 33a, 23 July 1941, in Trevor-Roper, *Blitzkrieg to Defeat*, 89–90.

37. Fritz, *Ostkrieg*, 127; Fugate, *Operation Barbarossa*, 208–9; Stahel, *Operation Barbarossa*, 276–8; Halder, *War Journal*, VI, 23 July 1941, 266–7; KTB/OKW, I/2, 23 July 1941, 1,031–4.

38. Halder, *War Journal*, VI, 23, 25 July 1941, 266–7, 269–270; Bock, *Diary*, 25, 27, 28 July 1941, 262–5; Fugate, *Operation Barbarossa*, 209–10; Hürter, *Hitlers Heerführer*, 289–90.

39. KTB/OKW, I/2, 25 July 1941, 1,035; Halder, *War Journal*, VI, 24, 25, 26 July 1941, 267–73; Bock, *Diary*, 24, 25 July 1941, 261–2; Fritz, *Ostkrieg*, 127–8; Fugate, *Operation Barbarossa*, 211–12.

40. Stahel, *Operation Barbarossa*, 298; Bock, *Diary*, 24 July 1941, 261; Halder, *War Journal*, VI, 26, 28 July 1941, 270–3, 276–8.

41. Fugate, *Operation Barbarossa*, 157–8; Bock, *Diary*, 27, 28 July 1941, 264–5; Halder, *Halder War Diary*, 26 July 1941, 484–7; Fritz, *Ostkrieg*, 121, 127–9; Stahel, *Operation Barbarossa*, 306–13; Fugate, *Operation Barbarossa*, 211–12.

42. Stahel, *Operation Barbarossa*, 280–3, 290–8, 312–15, 322–3; Hartmann, *Halder*, 279–81; Fritz, *Ostkrieg*, 121, 127–9; Frisch, *Condemned to Live*, 74; Overmans, *Deutsche militärische Verluste*, 277–8; Bock, *Diary*, 31 July 1941, 269.

43. TBJG, 31 July 1941; Bock, *Diary*, 27, 28, 29 July 1941, 264–6; Fritz, *Ostkrieg*, 121, 127–9; Stahel, *Operation Barbarossa*, 331–2, 349; Hürter, *Hitlers Heerführer*, 290–1.

44. Engel, *At the Heart of the Reich*, 28 July 1941, 114–15; Hartmann, *Halder*, 282; Hürter, *Hitlers Heerführer*, 288; KTB/OKW, I/2, 27, 28 July 1941, 1,036–7, 1,040–1; Halder, *War Journal*, VI, 26, 30 July 1941, 270–3, 281–4; Manstein, *Lost Victories*, 197–8; Hoth, *Panzer-Operationen*, 112; Bock, *Diary*, 28 July 1941, 265–6; Fugate, *Operation Barbarossa*, 215–17; Fritz, *Ostkrieg*, 128; Stahel, *Operation Barbarossa*, 323–4.

45. Pyta, *Hitler*, 353–66; Stahel, *Operation Barbarossa*, 23; Hürter, *Hitlers Heerführer*, 213–14, 291–2; Hartmann, *Halder*, 280–1; Hayward, "Hitler's Quest," 101–10.

46. Hartmann, *Halder*, 278–80; "The Strategic Situation in Late Summer 1941 as Basis for Further Political and Military Plans," OKW Memorandum to Hitler, 27 August 1941, DGFP, XIII, Doc. 265, 422–33; Warlimont, *Inside Hitler's Headquarters*, 192–3; Stahel, *Operation Barbarossa*, 24, 249; Fritz, *Ostkrieg*, 115–17, 230, 494.

47. Stahel, *Operation Barbarossa*, 324–34, 344–8, 353–6; Bock, *Diary*, 25 July 1941, 263; Hillgruber, "Der Zenit des Zweiten Welkrieges Juli 1941," 273–95; idem, "Die Bedeutung der Schlacht von Smolensk in der Zweiten Julihälfte 1941 für den Ausgang des Ostkrieges," 296–312; Pyta, "Bedeutung Japans," 21–44; Hürter, *Hitlers Heerführer*, 286–7.

48. Fritz, *Ostkrieg*, 128–9; Stahel, *Operation Barbarossa*, 362–3; Fugate, *Operation Barbarossa*, 245–8; Bock, *Diary*, 2, 5 August 1941, 271, 273.

49. Fugate, *Operation Barbarossa*, 217–18; Stahel, *Operation Barbarossa*, 338–42; Bock, *Diary*, 4 August 1941, 272; Fritz, *Ostkrieg*, 141; Guderian, *Panzer Leader*, 190; "Besprechung gelegentlich Anwesenheit des Führers und Obersten Befehlshabers der Wehrmacht bei Heeresgruppe Mitte am 4. August 1941," KTB/OKW, I/2, 1,041–2; Halder, *Halder War Diary*, 4 August 1941, 495–6.

50. Halder, *Halder War Diary*, 5, 8 August 1941, 497–8, 500–4; Engel, *At the Heart of the Reich*, 6 August 1941, 115; Fugate, *Operation Barbarossa*, 219–20; Stahel, *Operation Barbarossa*, 342–3, 368.

51. Halder, *Halder War Diary*, 7, 8 August 1941, 500–4; Hartmann, *Halder*, 281–2; Fugate, *Operation Barbarossa*, 222–3; Stahel, *Operation Barbarossa*, 376–7.

52. Bock, *Diary*, 7, 10, 12 August 1941, 276–81; Halder, *Halder War Diary*, 7, 11 August 1941, 500, 505–6; Fugate, *Operation Barbarossa*, 228–30; Stahel, *Operation Barbarossa*, 343–4, 384.
53. KTB/OKW, I/2, 10 August 1941, 1,043–4; Halder, *Halder War Diary*, 14, 15 August 1941, 508–10; Directive No. 34a, 12 August 1941, in Trevor-Roper, *Blitzkrieg to Defeat*, 93–5; Warlimont, *Inside Hitler's Headquarters*, 187–8; Hartmann, *Halder*, 279–80; Stahel, *Operation Barbarossa*, 393–6.
54. "Vorschlag für Fortführung der Operation der Heeresgruppe Mitte in Zusammenhang mit den Operationen der Heeresgruppe Süd und Nord," KTB/OKW, I/2, 18 August 1941, 1,055–9; Fritz, *Ostkrieg*, 130–1; Fugate, *Operation Barbarossa*, 226–30; Stahel, *Operation Barbarossa*, 405–6.
55. Fritz, *Ostkrieg*, 131; Warlimont, *Inside Hitler's Headquarters*, 188–9; Engel, *At the Heart of the Reich*, 8 August 1941, 116; Stahel, *Operation Barbarossa*, 424; TBJG, 19 August 1941; Neumann and Eberle, *Was Hitler Ill?*, 142–51.
56. Stahel, *Operation Barbarossa*, 338–60, 401–2; Below, *At Hitler's Side*, 110.
57. Fritz, *Ostkrieg*, 131–2; Warlimont, *Inside Hitler's Headquarters*, 189–90; Halder, *Halder War Diary*, 22 August 1941, 514–15; Engel, *At the Heart of the Reich*, 21 August 1941, 117; "Sonderakte," 20 August 1941, "Operative Gedanken des Führers und Weisungen am 21. August 1941," "Studie," 22 August 1941, KTB/OKW, I/2, 1,061–8.
58. Fritz, *Ostkrieg*, 131–2; Engel, *At the Heart of the Reich*, 21 August 1941, 117; "Sonderakte," 20 August 1941, "Operative Gedanken des Führers und Weisungen am 21. August 1941," "Studie," 22 August 1941, KTB/OKW, I/2, 1,061–8.
59. Fritz, *Ostkrieg*, 132–3; Hartmann, *Halder*, 283–4; Engel, *At the Heart of the Reich*, 23 August 1941, 118; Halder, *Halder War Diary*, 22, 24 August 1941, 514–16; Bock, *Diary*, 22, 23, 24 August 1941, 288–93; Guderian, *Panzer Leader*, 198–202; Below, *At Hitler's Side*, 111; Fugate, *Operation Barbarossa*, 236–44; Stahel, *Operation Barbarossa*, 427–36.
60. Hartmann, *Halder*, 284; Fritz, *Ostkrieg*, 133; Müller, "Failure of the Economic Blitzkrieg Strategy," GSWW, IV, 1,124–41; Schüler, "Eastern Campaign as Transportation and Supply Problem," 211–13; Bock, *Diary*, 24 August, 2 September 1941, 292, 301–2; Stahel, *Operation Barbarossa*, 428–30; Creveld, *Supplying War*, 176; Hürter, *Hitlers Heerführer*, 291–2, 295.
61. Pyta, *Hitler*, 369; Hürter, *Hitlers Heerführer*, 292–5; Stahel, *Operation Barbarossa*, 340, 438.
62. Clausewitz, *On War*, 264; Geyer, "German Strategy," 591; Hartmann, *Halder*, 286.
63. Fritz, *Ostkrieg*, 133–4; Stahel, *Operation Barbarossa*, 438, 444–51; Arnold, "Eroberung Kiew," 46.

Chapter 8

1. Domarus, *Speeches*, 2,484–6; for fear of cold, Fritz, *Frontsoldaten*, 109–14.
2. Trevor-Roper, *Table Talk*, 25 September 1941, 40; Stahel, *Kiev*, 165–70; Halder, *Halder War Diary*, 31 August, 2, 4 September 1941, 521–4; Bock, *Diary*, 4 September 1941, 303–4; Guderian, *Panzer Leader*, 210–12.
3. Fritz, *Ostkrieg*, 140–6, quote 144; Fugate, *Operation Barbarossa*, 245–64; Stahel, *Operation Barbarossa*, 439–41; idem, *Kiev*, 99–100, 108, 173, chs 6–7; Bock, *Diary*, 15 September 1941, 313.
4. Stahel, *Kiev*, 346–7; Zhukov, *Memoirs*, 297–9; Fugate, *Operation Barbarossa*, 264–5, 280, 285–9.
5. Hartmann, *Halder*, 287–9; Fugate, *Operation Barbarossa*, 277–9, 309; Fritz, *Ostkrieg*, 183, 190, 192; Stahel, *Kiev*, 173–6; Halder, *Halder War Diary*, 5 September 1941, 524–5; Directive No. 35, 6 September 1941, in Trevor-Roper, *Blitzkrieg to Defeat*, 96–8; Hürter, *Hitlers Heerführer*, 293–7, fn 94 (Halder quote), 302–3; Bock, *Diary*, 7 September 1941, 307.
6. Fritz, *Ostkrieg*, 148–9; Megargee, *Inside Hitler's High Command*, 133, 135; Stahel, *Kiev*, 175–6; Creveld, *Supplying War*, 145–53; Müller, "Failure of Economic Blitzkrieg

Strategy," GSWW, IV, 1,125–32; Klink, "Conduct of Operations," GSWW, IV, 667–70; Reinhardt, *Moscow*, 60–9; Schüler, "Eastern Campaign as a Transportation and Supply Problem," 212.

7. Fritz, *Ostkrieg*, 150–2; Stahel, *Kiev*, 316–31, 338–9; Müller, "Failure of Economic Blitzkrieg Strategy," GSWW, IV, 1,127–32; Klink, "Conduct of Operations," GSWW, IV, 667–70; Reinhardt, *Moscow*, 60–9; Schüler, "Eastern Campaign as Transportation and Supply Problem," 214; Halder, *Halder War Diary*, 26, 28, 29 August 1941, 517, 519, 521; KTB/OKW, I/2, 1,120–1; Overmans, *Deutsche militärische Verluste*, 277–80; Hartmann, *Halder*, 288–9. In early October, Reinhardt replaced Hoth, who was appointed head of the 17th Army in Ukraine, as commander of Panzer Group 3.

8. Hürter, *Hitlers Heerführer*, 297–9; Fritz, *Ostkrieg*, 152–3; Bock, *Diary*, 15 September 1941, 313; Reinhardt, *Moscow*, 57–70; Klink, "Conduct of Operations," GSWW, IV, 664–72; Megargee, *War of Annihilation*, 86–9.

9. Fritz, *Ostkrieg*, 154–6; Hartmann, *Halder*, 289; Hürter, *Hitlers Heerführer*, 298–9; TBJG, 4 October 1941; Bock, *Diary*, 7 October 1941, 325–6; Megargee, *Inside Hitler's High Command*, 135; Klink, "Conduct of Operations," GSWW, IV, 673–4; Reinhardt, *Moscow*, 80–7; Halder, *War Journal*, VII, 8 October 1941, 147; Glantz, *Barbarossa*, 147–53; idem, *When Titans Clashed*, 80–1; Guderian, *Panzer Leader*, 233, 235.

10. Fritz, *Ostkrieg*, 156–7; Hartmann, *Halder*, 289–90; Halder, *Halder War Diary*, 4 October 1941, 546; Kershaw, *Hitler: Nemesis*, 433; Megargee, *War of Annihilation*, 102; Klink, "Conduct of Operations," GSWW, IV, 675–6; Reinhardt, *Moscow*, 87–9, 95–6; Bock, *Diary*, 7, 8, 14 October 1941, 325–6, 332.

11. Hürter, *Hitlers Heerführer*, 299–300; Fritz, *Ostkrieg*, 157–9; Klink, "Conduct of Operations," GSWW, IV, 676–7; Müller, "Failure of Economic Blitzkrieg," GSWW, IV, 1,133; Reinhardt, *Moscow*, 88–9, 92–4, 120, 149, 152; Haupt, *Schlachten der Heeresgruppe Mitte*, 91–2; Hartmann, *Halder*, 290; diary entry of Harald Henry, 20 October 1941, in Bähr, *Kriegsbriefe*, 83; letter of 25 October 1941, in Buchbender and Sterz, *Andere Gesicht*, 85; Fritz, *Frontsoldaten*, 105–7; Ziemke and Bauer, *Moscow to Stalingrad*, 40–1; Kershaw, *War Without Garlands*, 186–91; Bock, *Diary*, 20, 24, 25 October 1941, 337, 340.

12. Fritz, *Ostkrieg*, 160–1; Klink, "Conduct of Operations," GSWW, IV, 678–81; Glantz, *Barbarossa*, 153–5, 157–8; Reinhardt, *Moscow*, 91–5, 148–9, 179; Kershaw, *War Without Garlands*, 166–7, 182–5; Megargee, *War of Annihilation*, 103–4; Bock, *Diary*, 13, 25, 29, 31 October, 1 November 1941, 331, 340, 345–8.

13. Fritz, *Ostkrieg*, 162; Hürter, *Hitlers Heerführer*, 300–1.

14. Hartmann, *Halder*, 290–1; "Beurteilung der Kampfkraft des Ostheeres," 6 November 1941, KTB/OKW, I/2, 1,074–5; Halder, *Halder War Diary*, 7, 19 November 1941, 554–5, 558; Megargee, *Inside Hitler's High Command*, 135–6; Klink, "Conduct of Operations," GSWW, IV, 684–9; Reinhardt, *Moscow*, 170–90.

15. Fritz, *Ostkrieg*, 182; Megargee, *Inside Hitler's High Command*, 135–6; Hürter, *Hitlers Heerführer*, 303–4, 306; Bock, *Diary*, 11, 20, 21 November 1941, 354, 365–6; Halder, *Halder War Diary*, 11 November 1941, 555; Ziemke and Bauer, *Moscow to Stalingrad*, 43.

16. Fritz, *Ostkrieg*, 182–3; Megargee, *Inside Hitler's High Command*, 136; Hartmann, *Halder*, 293–4; Guderian, *Panzer Leader*, 247; Hürter, *Hitlers Heerführer*, 304–6.

17. Fritz, *Ostkrieg*, 182–4; Hürter, *Hitlers Heerführer*, 304–6; Klink, "Conduct of Operations," GSWW, IV, 689–92; Reinhardt, *Moscow*, 173–81, 191–4; Ziemke and Bauer, *Moscow to Stalingrad*, 43–6; Megargee, *War of Annihilation*, 109–10; Bock, *Diary*, 18 November 1941, 362; Ueberschär, "Scheitern," 159; Hartmann, *Halder*, 294–5; Halder, *Halder War Diary*, 22 November 1941, 561–2.

18. Hartmann, *Halder*, 292–3; Engel, *At the Heart of the Reich*, 12, 16, 22 November 1941, 120–2; Halder, *Halder War Diary*, 3, 7, 19, 21, 22, 29, 30 November, 1, 3 December 1941, 552, 554, 557–8, 560–1, 567–8, 570–1, 573–4, 576; Hürter, *Hitlers Heerführer*, 307–10; Fritz, *Ostkrieg*, 164–5.

19. Halder, *Halder War Diary*, 3, 7, 19, 21, 22, 29, 30 November, 1, 3 December 1941, 552, 554, 557–8, 560–1, 567–8, 570–1, 573–4, 576; Hürter, *Hitlers Heerführer*, 307–10; Fritz, *Ostkrieg*, 164–5; Hartmann, *Halder*, 297.

20. Fritz, *Ostkrieg*, 184–6; Reinhardt, *Moscow*, 199–201, 203 n. 19; Klink, "Conduct of Operations," GSWW, IV, 692–3; Bock, *Diary*, 11, 16, 17 November 1941, 355, 359, 361. Halder was informed on 30 November that the Ostheer had a shortage of 340,000 men, but that only 33,000 replacements existed in Germany. See Halder, *Halder War Diary*, 30 November 1941, 571–2.

21. Fritz, *Ostkrieg*, 186–7; Reinhardt, *Moscow*, 214–16; Klink, "Conduct of Operations," GSWW, IV, 693; Ziemke and Bauer, *Moscow to Stalingrad*, 49–54; Megargee, *War of Annihilation*, 113; Kershaw, *War Without Garlands*, 198.

22. Fritz, *Ostkrieg*, 187–8; Hürter, *Hitlers Heerführer*, 310–11; Reinhardt, *Moscow*, 216–17; Klink, "Conduct of Operations," GSWW, IV, 693–6; Hartmann, *Halder*, 296; Halder, *Halder War Diary*, 23 November 1941, 562–3; Guderian, *Panzer Leader*, 251–2; Bock, *Diary*, 21, 23 November 1941, 365–6, 368.

23. Hürter, *Hitlers Heerführer*, 312; Fritz, *Ostkrieg*, 189–90; Halder, *Halder War Diary*, 19, 24 November 1941, 558, 564; Engel, *At the Heart of the Reich*, 25, 30 November 1941, 122–3; DGFP, D, XIII, No. 501 (28 November 1941) and No. 522 (30 November 1941); Kershaw, *Hitler: Nemesis*, 438–41; Ueberschär, "Scheitern des Unternehmens Barbarossa," 160–1; Reinhardt, *Moscow*, 254–5, 262; Tooze, *Wages of Destruction*, 507–8; TBJG, 30 November 1941.

24. Fritz, *Ostkrieg*, 190–1; Halder, *Halder War Diary*, 23 November 1941, 562–4; Reinhardt, *Moscow*, 224–6; Klink, "Conduct of Operations," GSWW, IV, 696–6; Hürter, *Hitlers Heerführer*, 312; Bock, *Diary*, 23 November 1941, 368.

25. Fritz, *Ostkrieg*, 190–2; Reinhardt, *Moscow*, 220–2; Klink, "Conduct of Operations," GSWW, IV, 700–1; Bock, *Diary*, 28 November 1941, 372; Kershaw, *War Without Garlands*, 206–7, 210–11.

26. Bock, *Diary*, 29 November, 1 December 1941, 373, 375–3; Fritz, *Ostkrieg*, 191–2; Ziemke and Bauer, *Moscow to Stalingrad*, 53–4; Reinhardt, *Moscow*, 220–8, 236, 240, 243; Klink, "Conduct of Operations," GSWW, IV, 700–2.

27. Bock, *Diary*, 1, 3 December 1941, 376, 378–9; Hürter, *Hitlers Heerführer*, 312–17; Fritz, *Ostkrieg*, 192–3; Engel, *At the Heart of the Reich*, 12, 16, 22, 24, 25, 30 November, 8 December 1941, 120–4.

28. Fritz, *Ostkrieg*, 199–200.

29. Fritz, *Ostkrieg*, 199–200; Ziemke and Bauer, *Moscow to Stalingrad*, 65–6, 69–76; Reinhardt, *Moscow*, 280–1, 291–3; Hoffmann, "Conduct of the War through Soviet Eyes," GSWW, IV, 898–900; Glantz, *Barbarossa*, 185–204; Megargee, *War of Annihilation*, 130–2; Trevor-Roper, *Blitzkrieg to Defeat*, No. 39, 8 December 1941, 106–10; "Weisung für die Aufgabe des Ostheeres im Winter 1941/42," 8 December 1941, KTB/OKW, I/2, 1,076–82, here 1,078–9.

30. Fritz, *Ostkrieg*, 193–8; KTB/OKW, I/2, no. 45, p. 996; TBJG, 8 December 1941; Trevor-Roper, *Hitler's Table Talk*, 5, 7 January 1942, 181, 186–8; Warlimont, *Inside Hitler's Headquarters*, 207–8; Hillgruber, "Faktor Amerika," 3–21; Wegner, "Hitler's Strategy," GSWW, VI, 112–15, 127; Syring, "Hitlers Kriegserklärung an Amerika," 683, 690; Kershaw, *Hitler: Nemesis*, 442, 456–7; idem, *Fateful Choices*, 382–3, 416–24; Mawdsley, *December 1941*, 22; Rahn, "Atlantic in German Strategy," GSWW, VI, 301–25; Reinhardt, *Moscow*, 257–9.

31. Fritz, *Ostkrieg*, 202; Klink, "Conduct of Operations," GSWW, IV, 702–8; Reinhardt, *Moscow*, 292–3, 299–302; Ziemke and Bauer, *Moscow to Stalingrad*, 69–76; Bock, *Diary*, 8, 10 December 1941, 385–8; Halder, *Halder War Diary*, 8 December 1941, 584; Hartmann, *Halder*, 299.

32. Hürter, *Hitlers Heerführer*, 320–4; Hartmann, *Halder*, 301; Fritz, *Ostkrieg*, 204; Guderian, *Panzer Leader*, 260–1; Bock, *Diary*, 10 December 1941, 387–8.

33. Fritz, *Ostkrieg*, 204; Bock, *Diary*, 10, 11, 13, 16 December 1941, 387–91, 395–6; Reinhardt, *Moscow*, 298.

34. Engel, *At the Heart of the Reich*, 8 December 1941, 124; TBJG, 10, 12, 13 December 1941; Mawdsley, *December 1941*, 221, 250, 263, 271; Fritz, *Ostkrieg*, 178–81; Domarus, *Speeches*, 11, 20 December 1941, 2,539, 2,556.

35. Mawdsley, *December 1941*, 272-3; Domarus, *Speeches*, 19 December 1941, 2,554; Hürter, *Hitlers Heerführer*, 323-6; Fritz, *Ostkrieg*, 204-6; Pyta, *Hitler*, 385; Hartmann, *Halder*, 300-4; TBJG, 20 January 1942.

36. Hürter, *Hitlers Heerführer*, 322, 326-8; Fritz, *Ostkrieg*, 204-5; Bock, *Diary*, 16 December 1941, 395-6; KTB/OKW, I/2, 18 December 1941, 1,084-5; Pyta, *Hitler*, 386, 388-9; Hartmann, *Halder*, 301-3.

37. Hürter, *Hitlers Heerführer*, 327-8, 332-3, 355; Fritz, *Ostkrieg*, 205-6; Megargee, *Inside Hitler's High Command*, 166-9; Pyta, *Hitler*, 389; KTB/OKW, I/2, 18 December 1941, 1,084-5; Balck, *Order in Chaos*, 227; Bock, *Diary*, 16, 18, 19, 22 December 1941, 395, 399-400.

38. Hürter, *Hitlers Heerführer*, 328-30, 335; Fritz, *Ostkrieg*, 207-8; Engel, *At the Heart of the Reich*, 18 December 1941, 125; Reinhardt, *Moscow*, 312; Halder, *Halder War Diary*, 21 December 1941, 594.

39. Hürter, *Hitlers Heerführer*, 331-2; Fritz, *Ostkrieg*, 206-8; Ziemke and Bauer, *Moscow to Stalingrad*, 85-7; Reinhardt, *Moscow*, 311; Klink, "Conduct of Operations," GSWW, IV, 716-20; Kershaw, *Hitler: Nemesis*, 454-5; Guderian, *Panzer Leader*, 264-8.

40. Hürter, *Hitlers Heerführer*, 332-5; Fritz, *Ostkrieg*, 208-9; TBJG, 20 January 1942, 31 March 1945; Pyta, *Hitler*, 395.

41. Hürter, *Hitlers Heerführer*, 332-5; Fritz, *Ostkrieg*, 208-9; Reinhardt, *Moscow*, 314-16; Klink, "Conduct of Operations," GSWW, IV, 722-3; Ziemke and Bauer, *Moscow to Stalingrad*, 100-4.

42. Fritz, *Ostkrieg*, 209-10; Hürter, *Hitlers Heerführer*, 336-7; Ziemke and Bauer, *Moscow to Stalingrad*, 118-34; Reinhardt, *Moscow*, 317-24; Klink, "Conduct of Operations," GSWW, IV, 725-8; Halder, *Halder War Diary*, 2, 3, 5 January 1942, 597-9. On 1 January 1942 both Panzer Groups 3 and 4 were made armies.

43. Hürter, *Hitlers Heerführer*, 337-42; Fritz, *Ostkrieg*, 210-12; Halder, *War Journal*, VII, 11 January 1942, 252; Hartmann, *Halder*, 307-9; "Führerbefehl an die H.Gr. Mitte vom 15. Januar 1942 zum Rückzug auf die 'Winerstellung,'" KTB/OKW, II/4, 15 January 1942, 1,268-9. Halder, on a number of occasions, even considered using gas attacks against the Soviets. See Hartmann, *Halder*, 310, 312.

44. Hürter, *Hitlers Heerführer*, 319, 332ff. and fn 273, 348-50; TBJG, 18 December 1941; Trevor-Roper, *Hitler's Table Talk*, 17, 18 January 1942, 220.

45. Pyta, *Hitler*, 397-9; Heusinger, *Befehl im Widerstreit*, 176-7; Hürter, *Hitlers Heerführer*, 344-9; Heinrici, diary entry of 28 February 1942, in Hürter, *Ein deutscher General*, 147.

46. Hürter, *Hitlers Heerführer*, 344-9; Halder, *Halder War Diary*, 11 March 1942, 609; Fritz, *Ostkrieg*, 216-17; Reinhardt, *Moscow*, 375-8; Schramm, *Hitler*, 161; TBJG, 15 February, 20 March 1942; Kershaw, *Hitler: Nemesis*, 455-7, 500-1, 504-6; Hayward, "Hitler's Quest for Oil," 114.

47. KTB/OKW, 15 May 1945, IV/2, 1,503; Schramm, *Hitler*, 180-1, 204; TBJG, 20 March 1942; KTB/OKW, 21, 24 December 1941, I/2, 1,085-7; Fritz, *Ostkrieg*, 210-17, 230-1.

48. TBJG, 16 December 1941; Heinrici, letter of 16 December 1941, in Hürter, "Sitten und Gebrauche" 392; Pyta, *Hitler*, 399-400.

49. Pyta, *Hitler*, 400-2; Trevor-Roper, *Hitler's Table Talk*, 26, 27 February 1942, 339-40; Lukacs, *Hitler*, 159. His assertion that the Germans had lost a thousand tanks is almost certainly an exaggeration since they barely had that many on the central sector at the beginning of Operation Typhoon. One, admittedly impressionistic, indication of the enormous strain that Hitler was under might be seen in the sheer volume of his nightly monologues. In *Table Talk*, for example, from the beginning of the Soviet offensive until the end of March 1942 they run to almost 250 pages.

50. Megaree, *Inside Hitler's High Command*, 166-9; Zhukov, *Memoirs*, 345; TBJG, 20 March 1942; Stahel, *Kiev*, 351-2.

51. Directive No. 32a, 14 July 1941, in Trevor-Roper, *Blitzkrieg to Defeat*, 82-5; DGFP, D, XIII, No. 242, 384; Hayward, "Too Little, Too Late," 781.

Chapter 9

1. Hitler, "Adolf Hitler Rede am 30. Januar 1942 im Sportpalast in Berlin", http://www. worldfuturefund.org/wffmaster/Reading/Hitler%20Speeches/Hitler%20Rede%20 1942.01.30.htm, (accessed 21 January 2016); Domarus, *Speeches*, 2,570–9; Hitler, "Text of Speech by Chancellor Adolf Hitler at Berlin Sports Palace, January 30, 1942," http:// www.ibiblio.org/pha/policy/1942/420130a.html, trans. by Foreign Broadcast Monitoring Service, FCC, (accessed 21 January 2016). Revealingly, Hitler, who possessed a photographic memory, always incorrectly remembered the date of his "prophecy" against the Jews not as 30 January 1939, but as 1 September 1939, the day Germany invaded Poland.

2. TBJG, 31 January 1942; Domarus, *Speeches*, 15 March 1942, 2,599; KTB/OKW, IV/2, 15 May 1945, 1,503; Schramm, *Hitler*, 161, 204; Hartmann, *Halder*, 312; Wegner, "Hitler's Strategy," 116; Megargee, *Inside Hitler's High Command*, 170.

3. Wegner, "Hitler's Strategy," 116–21; Megargee, *Inside Hitler's High Command*, 170–1.

4. Wegner, "Hitler's Strategy," 126–7; Trevor-Roper, *Hitler's Table- Talk*, 7, 15, 24 January, 2, 6, 27 February 1942, 188, 207, 264–5, 274, 299–300, 346; Jochmann, *Monologe*, 7, 24, 31 January, 2, 6, 27 February 1942, 154–5, 186, 209, 216, 230–1, 263.

5. Wegner, "Hitler's Strategy," 127–9; Hayward, "Hitler's Quest for Oil," 115; "OKW-Weisung vom 14. Dezember 1941 betr. Küstenverteidigung," KTB/OKW, II/4, 1262; Warlimont, *Inside Hitler's Headquarters*, 199–200.

6. Wegner, "Hitler's Strategy," 126–9; Trevor-Roper, *Hitler's Table Talk*, 4 January, 3, 29 July 1942, 177–8, 550–1, 601; Jochmann, *Monologe*, 4 January 1942, 168; Picker, *Hitlers Tischgespräche*, 2 July 1942, 402; Heiber and Glantz, *Hitler and His Generals*, 818 (note 299); TBJG, 20 March, 24 May, 23 June 1942; KTB/OKW, II/3, 23 August 1942, 627–8; Pyta, *Hitler*, 404, 406–7.

7. Trevor-Roper, *Hitler's Table Talk*, 6 February 1942, 301; TBJG, 20 March 1942; Halder, *Halder War Diary*, 28 March 1942, 612; Directive No. 41, 5 April 1942, in Trevor-Roper, *Blizkrieg to Defeat*, 116–21; Fritz, *Ostkrieg*, 231–2; Hayward, "Hitler's Quest for Oil," 125; Ciano, *Diary*, 29 April 1942, 460; Wegner, "Hitler's Strategy," 125.

8. Fritz, *Ostkrieg*, 232; Hartmann, *Halder*, 312–18; Megargee, *Inside Hitler's High Command*, 174–7; Pyta, *Hitler*, 403–4.

9. Fritz, *Ostkrieg*, 232–3; Wegner, "Hitler's Strategy," 126; Eichholtz, *War for Oil*, 82; TBJG, 21 March 1942; Halder, *Halder War Diary*, 28 March, 12 June 1942, 612, 623.

10. Fritz, *Ostkrieg*, 233; TBJG, 21 March 1942; Halder, *Halder War Diary*, 28 March, 12 June 1942, 612, 623; Hartmann, *Halder*, 312–18; Megargee, *Inside Hitler's High Command*, 174–7; Tooze, *Wages of Destruction*, 586–7; Speer, *Inside the Third Reich*, 215.

11. KTB/OKW, II/3, 5 April 1942, 316; Directive No. 41, 5 April 1942, Trevor-Roper, *Blitzkrieg to Defeat*, 118; Citino, *Death of Wehrmacht*, 157–8; Pyta, *Hitler*, 328, 403–6; Hartmann, *Halder*, 312–18.

12. Fritz, *Ostkrieg*, 233–5; Tooze, *Wages of Destruction*, 586–7; Speer, *Inside the Third Reich*, 215; Hayward, "Hitler's Quest for Oil," 108–9; TBJG, 24 May 1942; Jochmann, *Monologe*, 5 August 1942, 283.

13. Fritz, *Ostkrieg*, 236–7; Wegner, "War Against the Soviet Union, 1942–1943," GSWW, VI, 863–82, 895, 904–27; idem, "Vom Lebensraum zum Todesraum," 22–4; Halder, *Halder War Diary*, 21 April 1942, 613–14; Warlimont, *Inside Hitler's Headquarters*, 239–40.

14. Fritz, *Ostkrieg*, 237–8; Wegner, "War Against the Soviet Union, 1942–1943," GSWW, VI, 882–903; idem, "Vom Lebensraum zum Todesraum," 23–4; idem, "Hitlers zweiter Feldzug," 658–9; Kershaw, *Hitler: Nemesis*, 509; Thomas, "Foreign Armies East," 280–2; Tooze, *Wages of Destruction*, 558, 587–9; Harrison, *Soviet Planning*, 63–5, 81–2; Hayward, "Hitler's Quest for Oil," 117–21; TBJG, 23, 26 April 1942.

15. Fritz, *Ostkrieg*, 239; Wegner, "Hitler's Strategy," 131.

16. Fritz, *Ostkrieg*, 241–2; Melvin, *Manstein*, 227–55; Hayward, *Stopped at Stalingrad*, 3–4, 7–9, 27–31; Trevor-Roper, *Hitler's Table Talk*, 5–6 July, 17 October 1941, 4–5, 68–70; Jochmann, *Monologe*, 5–6 July, 17 October 1941, 27, 71–2.

17. Fritz, *Ostkrieg*, 242–7; Melvin, *Manstein*, 255–73.

18. Pyta, *Hitler*, 407–9; Halder, *War Journal*, VII, 20 April 1942, 301; KTB/OKW, II/3, 30 June, 12, 23, 30 August 1942, 460, 574, 627–8, 658–9; KTB/OKW, II/4, 2 September 1942, 1,290; "Midday Situation Report," 5 March 1943, Heiber and Glantz, *Hitler and His Generals*, 89.

19. Fritz, *Ostkrieg*, 247–8.

20. Fritz, *Ostkrieg*, 248–50; Glantz, *To the Gates of Stalingrad*, 37–45, 77–9; Knjazkov, "Die sowjetische Strategie im Jahre 1942," 39–46; Glantz and House, *When Titans Clashed*, 99–101, 111–14; Citino, *Death of the Wehrmacht*, 89–91, 94–7; Wegner, "War Against the Soviet Union, 1942–1943," GSWW, VI, 947; Ziemke and Bauer, *Moscow to Stalingrad*, 269–72; "Beurteilung der Gesamtfeindlage an der Ostfront durch die Abt. Fremde Heere Ost vom 1.5.1942," KTB/OKW, II/V, 1,273–5; Bock, *Diary*, 5 May 1942, 469–70.

21. Fritz, *Ostkrieg*, 250–2, 262; Pyta, *Hitler*, 410–11; Hartmann, *Halder*, 320; Bock, *Diary*, 12, 13, 14, 15, 16, 17, 18 May 1941, 474–81; Halder, *Halder War Diary*, 14, 15, 18 May 1942, 616–18; KTB/OKW, II/3, 19 May 1942, 367; Citino, *Death of the Wehrmacht*, 95–115; Glantz, *To the Gates of Stalingrad*, 77–85; Ziemke and Bauer, *Moscow to Stalingrad*, 273–82; Wegner, "War Against the Soviet Union, 1942–1943," GSWW, VI, 947–50; Hayward, *Stopped at Stalingrad*, 25–126; Mawdsley, *Thunder in the East*, 119.

22. Fritz, *Ostkrieg*, 264–5; Pyta, *Hitler*, 411; Wegner, "War Against the Soviet Union, 1942–1943," GSWW, VI, 966–8; Citino, *Death of the Wehrmacht*, 165–7; Glantz, *To the Gates of Stalingrad*, 122–46; Ziemke and Bauer, *Moscow to Stalingrad*, 333–7; Bock, *Diary*, 28, 29, 30 June, 1, 2, 3, 4 July 1942, 508–15; Halder, *Halder War Diary*, 28, 29 June, 1, 3, 6 July 1942, 629–32, 635.

23. Bock, *Diary*, 28, 30 June, 1, 2, 3 July 1942, 508–13; Halder, *Halder War Diary*, 30 June, 1, 3 July 1942, 630–2; Fritz, *Ostkrieg*, 265; Pyta, *Hitler*, 411.

24. Bock, *Diary*, 3, 4, 5, 6, 7 July 1942, 513–20; Halder, *Halder War Diary*, 3, 5, 6 July 1942, 632–6; Fritz, *Ostkrieg*, 265–6; Hayward, *Stopped at Stalingrad*, 39–140; Citino, *Death of the Wehrmacht*, 172–4; Glantz, *To the Gates of Stalingrad*, 149–63; Ziemke and Bauer, *Moscow to Stalingrad*, 337–44; Wegner, "War Against the Soviet Union, 1942–1943," GSWW, VI, 968–71.

25. Fritz, *Ostkrieg*, 266; Glantz, *To the Gates of Stalingrad*, 149–63; Bock, *Diary*, 7, 8 July 1942, 520.

26. Picker, *Hitlers Tischgespräche*, 26 July 1942, 466; Pyta, *Hitler*, 411; Eichholtz, *War for Oil*, 83–4; Wegner, "Hitler's Strategy," 131–2.

27. Fritz, *Ostkrieg*, 266–7; Wegner, "War Against the Soviet Union, 1942–1943," GSWW, VI, 973–7; Citino, *Death of the Wehrmacht*, 174–5; Glantz, *To the Gates of Stalingrad*, 171–205; Ziemke and Bauer, *Moscow to Stalingrad*, 344–7; Bock, *Diary*, 7, 8, 13 July 1942, 520, 525–6.

28. Fritz, *Ostkrieg*, 267; Bock, *Diary*, 13, 15 July 1942, 526; Halder, *Halder War Diary*, 13 July 1942, 639–40; "Führerbefehl vom 13. Juli 1942 betr. Fortsetzung der Operationen der Heeresgruppen A und B," KTB/OKW, II/4, 1,282–3; Hartmann, *Halder*, 324–5; Wegner, "War Against the Soviet Union, 1942–1943," GSWW, VI, 977–8; Citino, *Death of the Wehrmacht*, 176–80; Glantz, *To the Gates of Stalingrad*, 190–5; Ziemke and Bauer, *Moscow to Stalingrad*, 347–51.

29. Fritz, *Ostkrieg*, 268; Wegner, "Hitler's Strategy," 132–3; idem, "The War Against the Soviet Union, 1942–1943," GSWW, VI, 988–9; Halder, *Halder War Diary*, 6 July 1942, 635; "Führerbefehl vom 9. Juli 1942 betr. Verlegung von Waffen-SS Verbänden in den Bereich des OB West," 9 July 1942, KTB/OKW, II/4, 1,280–1.

30. Fritz, *Ostkrieg*, 269; Wegner, "War Against the Soviet Union, 1942–1943," GSWW, VI, 978–81, 983–4, 989; Glantz, *To the Gates of Stalingrad*, 195–6; Bock, *Diary*, 13 July 1942, 525–6; Halder, *Diary*, 18 July 1942, 642–3; "Richtlinien des Führers vom 17. Juli 1942 für die Fortführung der Operation der Heeresgruppen A und B," KTB/OKW, II/4, 1,284.

31. Fritz, *Ostkrieg*, 269–70; Halder, *Halder War Diary*, 16, 18, 19, 21, 23 July 1942, 641–6; Hartmann, *Halder*, 325–6; Below, *At Hitler's Side*, 149; Wegner, "War Against the Soviet Union, 1942–1943," GSWW, VI, 982–4, 986.

32. Fritz, *Ostkrieg*, 270; Megargee, *Inside Hitler's High Command*, 177–8; Hartmann, *Halder*, 325.
33. Fritz, *Ostkrieg*, 271–2; Hartmann, *Halder*, 326–7; Halder, *Halder War Diary*, 23 July 1942, 646; Directive No. 45, 23 July 1942, Trevor-Roper, *Blitzkrieg to Defeat*, 129–31; Wegner, "War Against the Soviet Union, 1942–1943," GSWW, VI, 984–7.
34. Fritz, *Ostkrieg*, 273; Engel, *At the Heart of the Reich*, 29 July 1942, 129–30.
35. Halder, *Halder War Diary*, 30 July 1942, 649; "Fernschreiben des OKH an die Heeresgruppe A und B – vom 31. Juli 1942 betr. Fortsetzung der Operationen," KTB/OKW, II/4, 1,285; "Besprechung des Führers mit Generalfeldmarschall Keitel am 18. September 1942," in Hürter and Uhl, "Hitler in Vinnica," 607–8, 610–11; Hartmann, *Halder*, 327–9; Fritz, *Ostkrieg*, 273.
36. Eichholtz, *War for Oil*, 76; Hayward, "Too Little, Too Late," 773–4, 779–80; Wegner, "War Against the Soviet Union, 1942–1943," GSWW, VI, 869; Paulus Testimony, 11 February 1946, IMT, VII (Blue Series), 260; KTB/OKW, II/3, 13 August 1942, 581; Tooze, *Wages of Destruction*, 586–7. In his diary as well, Goebbels in August 1942 displayed a generally upbeat tone. See TBJG, August 1942 (especially the first half of the month).
37. Fritz, *Ostkrieg*, 277–8; Engel, *At the Heart of the Reich*, 15, 16 August 1942, 130; TBJG, 20 August 1942; Halder, *Halder War Diary*, 22 August 1942, 660; Below, *Als Hitlers Adjutant*, 313; Speer, *Inside the Third Reich*, 239–40.
38. Halder, *Halder War Diary*, 23, 24 August 1942, 660–1; Warlimont, *Inside Hitler's Headquarters*, 254; Manstein, *Lost Victories*, 261–2; Engel, *At the Heart of the Reich*, 4 September 1942, 131; Fritz, *Ostkrieg*, 279–80; Hartmann, *Halder*, 330–2; Megargee, *Inside Hitler's High Command*, 180–1.
39. Fritz, *Ostkrieg*, 278–9; Hürter and Uhl, "Hitler in Vinnica," 594–6, 605 fn 76; "Besprechung des Führers mit Generalfeldmarschall Keitel am 18. September 1942," in idem, "Hitler in Vinnica," 604–11; Halder, *Halder War Diary*, 30, 31 August 1941, 664–5; KTB/OKW, II/3, 31 August, 8 September 1942, 662, 695–8; Megargee, *Inside Hitler's High Command*, 179–80; Hartmann, *Halder*, 332–3; Engel, *At the Heart of the Reich*, 7, 8 September 1942, 131–2.
40. Fritz, *Ostkrieg*, 279–80; Hürter and Uhl, "Hitler in Vinnica," 588; Warlimont, *Inside Hitler's Headquarters*, 256–8; Hayward, "Too Little, Too Late," 782–3, 788–94.
41. Fritz, *Ostkrieg*, 281; Pyta, *Hitler*, 413–17; Hürter and Uhl, "Hitler in Vinnica," 591; "Führerbefehl vom 8. September 1942 über 'grundsätzliche Aufgaben der Verteidigung,'" "Führerbefehl vom 13. September 1942 betr. Ablösung abgekämpfter Divisionen aus dem Osten," and "Operationsbefehl Nr. 1 vom 14. Oktober 1942 betr. weitere Kampfführung im Osten," KTB/OKW, II/4, 1,292–9, 1,301–4; "Meeting of the Führer with Field Marshal Keitel and General Zeitzler, June 8, 1943," Heiber and Glantz, *Hitler's Generals*, 156–7; Wegner, "Hitler's Strategy," 136; idem, "The War Against the Soviet Union, 1942–1943," GSWW, VI, 1,053–9.
42. Fritz, *Ostkrieg*, 279–80; Hürter and Uhl, "Hitler in Vinnica," 597–8; "Besprechung des Führers mit Generalfeldmarschall Keitel am 18. September 1942," in idem, "Hitler in Vinnica," 606–8, 610–16, 623, 625–6; Engel, *At the Heart of the Reich*, 14, 18 September 1942, 132–3; Halder, *Halder War Diary*, 24 September 1942, 670; Hartmann, *Halder*, 333–4; Megargee, *Inside Hitler's High Command*, 181. Ironically, Hitler also planned to replace Jodl with Paulus, "the only general whom I personally trust," once the battle in Stalingrad had finished. See "Besprechung," 615, 617–18.
43. Megargee, *Inside Hitler's High Command*, 181–4; Hartmann, *Halder*, 337–9; Pyta, *Hitler*, 413–15.
44. Megargee, *Inside Hitler's High Command*, 188–9; Engel, *At the Heart of the Reich*, 2, 3 October 1942, 135; Pyta, *Hitler*, 420.
45. Fritz, *Ostkrieg*, 299–300; Wegner, "War Against the Soviet Union, 1942–1943," GSWW, VI, 1,098–9; Kershaw, *Hitler: Nemesis*, 538–9; Below, *At Hitler's Side*, 157; Engel, *At the Heart of the Reich*, 8 November 1942, 139.
46. Domarus, *Speeches*, 2,694–2,708; TBJG, 9 November 1942; Engel, *At the Heart of the Reich*, 10 November 1942, 139–40; Fritz, *Ostkrieg*, 300–1; Kershaw, *Hitler: Nemesis*,

539-40; "Führerbefehl vom 17. November 1942 betr. Fortführung der Eroberung Stalingrads durch die 6. Armee," in KTB/OKW, II/4, 1,307.

47. "Beurteilung der Feindlage vor Heeresgruppe Mitte vom 6. November 1942 durch Abt. Fremde Heere Ost"; "Kurze Beurteilung der Feindlage vom 12. November 1942 durch Abt. Fremde Heere Ost," KTB/OKW, II/4, 1,305-6; KTB/OKW, II/3, 16, 27 August, 9 September 1942, 597, 646, 703; KTB/OKW, II/4, 26, 27 October 1942, 865, 868; Fritz, *Ostkrieg*, 304-7; Magenheimer, *Hitler's War*, 161; Melvin, *Manstein*, 283-4; Manstein, *Lost Victories*, 268-9.

48. Fritz, *Ostkrieg*, 304-7; Engel, *At the Heart of the Reich*, 10, 22, 24, 27 October 1942, 7 November 1942, 136-9; Melvin, *Manstein*, 283-4; Hayward, "Too Little, Too Late," 792; idem, "Stopped at Stalingrad," 216-18; Below, *At Hitler's Side*, 156-7; Wegner, "War Against the Soviet Union, 1942-1943," GSWW, VI, 1,118, 1,121; Kershaw, *Hitler: Nemesis*, 541-3.

49. Fritz, *Ostkrieg*, 305-8; Engel, *At the Heart of the Reich*, 20 November 1942, 141; Wegner, "War Against the Soviet Union, 1942-1943," GSWW, VI, 1,103-5, 1,111, 1,123-4; Beevor, *Stalingrad*, 226-7, 231, 239-48; Hayward, *Stopped at Stalingrad*, 224-8; Ziemke and Bauer, *Moscow to Stalingrad*, 468-70.

50. Fritz, *Ostkrieg*, 309-11; Engel, *At the Heart of the Reich*, 21 November 1942, 141; Wegner, "War Against the Soviet Union, 1942-1943," GSWW, VI, 1,128-32; Hayward, *Stopped at Stalingrad*, 233-46; Fischer, "Über den Entschluss zur luftversorgung Stalingrads," 51-3; Hümmelchen, "Generaloberst Hans Jeschonnek," in Ueberschär, *Hitlers militärische Elite*, 98-100. Hitler hardly needed any reminders about Demyansk, as he had mentioned the operation just two months earlier. See "Besprechung des Führers mit Generalfeldmarschall Keitel am 18. September 1942," in Hürter and Uhl, "Hitler in Vinnica," 611.

51. Magenheimer, *Hitler's War*, 166; Fritz, *Ostkrieg*, 311; Melvin, *Manstein*, 287-9; Manstein, *Lost Victories*, 318-19; Hayward, *Stopped at Stalingrad*, 233-46; Wegner, "War Against the Soviet Union, 1942-1943," GSWW, VI, 1,132-3.

52. Steinkamp, "Generalfeldmarschall Friedrich Paulus," in Ueberschär, *Hitlers militärische Elite*, 434-5; Hayward, "Stalingrad: Examination of Hitler's Decision," 25-9; Pyta, *Hitler*, 425-6; "Hitler memorandum, 30 June 1938," Domarus, *Speeches*, 1,123.

53. Hayward, "Stalingrad," 29-32; Engel, *At the Heart of the Reich*, 24, 25, 26 November 1942, 142-4; Engel notes the 25th as the date of the discussion, but it was more likely on the 27th.

54. Fritz, *Ostkrieg*, 312; Manstein, *Lost Victories*, 294-7; Melvin, *Manstein*, 287-95; Pyta, *Hitler*, 422-3.

55. Fritz, *Ostkrieg*, 312-13; Manstein, *Lost Victories*, 305; Hayward, "Stalingrad," 33; Pyta, *Hitler*, 422; Hartmann, *Halder*, 304; Wegner, "The War Against the Soviet Union, 1942-1943," GSWW, VI, 137-1,140, 1,148; Hayward, *Stopped at Stalingrad*, 243, 259-60; Beevor, *Stalingrad*, 276-7.

56. Fritz, *Ostkrieg*, 314-18; Engel, *At the Heart of the Reich*, 18, 19, 20, 28 December 1942, 144-6; Melvin, *Manstein*, 287-350; Magenheimer, *Hitler's War*, 163; Citino, *Wehrmacht Retreats*, 55-7.

57. "Führerbefehl vom 27. Dezember 1942 für die weitere Kampfführung auf dem Südflügel der Ostfront," "Operationsbefehl Nr. 2 vom 28. Dezember 1942 betr. weitere Kampfführung auf dem Südflügel der Ostfront," "Ergänzung zum Operationsbefehl Nr. 2 vom 31. Dezember 1942," KTB/OKW, II/4, 1,316-19; "Führerbefehl für die Kampfführung im Südabschnitt der Ostfront von 3.1.1943," "Führerbefehl betr. Befehlsverhältnisse im tunesischen Raum und Aufgaben des Ob. Süd vom 5.1.1943," "Führerbefehl betr. Unterstellungsverhältnisse der 5. Panzer-Armee und Aufgaben des Ob Süd vom 28.1.1943," KTB/OKW, III/6, 1,407-9, 1,414-15; Fritz, *Ostkrieg*, 315-16, 325-6; Manstein, *Lost Victories*, 307-8, 441; Melvin, *Manstein*, 319; Magenheimer, *Hitler's War*, 167-8; Citino, *Wehrmacht Retreats*, 58-63.

58. Pyta, *Hitler*, 438-41; Melvin, *Manstein*, 314-18.

59. TBJG, 23 January 1943; Pyta, *Hitler*, 442-6; Melvin, *Manstein*, 319-20, 325-30; Engel, *At the Heart of the Reich*, 7 February 1943, 147-8; Stahlberg, *Bounden Duty*, 251-4;

Manstein, *Lost Victories*, 365, 406–7; Citino, *Wehrmacht Retreats*, 64–8; Fritz, *Ostkrieg*, 326–7.

60. TBJG, 23 January 1943; Pyta, *Hitler*, 442–6; Melvin, *Manstein*, 319–20, 325–30; Engel, *At the Heart of the Reich*, 7 February 1943, 147–8; Stahlberg, *Bounden Duty*, 251–4; Manstein, *Lost Victories*, 365, 406–7.

61. Manstein, *Lost Victories*, 371–4; Melvin, *Manstein*, 318–20; Fritz, *Ostkrieg*, 323–4; Citino, *Wehrmacht Retreats*, 68–72.

62. Pyta, *Hitler*, 445–8; Domarus, *Speeches*, 2,772–5. Interestingly, just eight days earlier Hitler had survived another attempt by staff from Army Group Center to kill him. A bomb placed on Hitler's aircraft on its return from Army Group headquarters failed to detonate. See Fest, *Plotting Hitler's Death*, 193–6.

63. Citino, *Wehrmacht Retreats*, 72–4, 104–8; Pyta, *Hitler*, 463.

64. Fritz, *Ostkrieg*, 324–6; Wegner, "Hitler's Strategy," 134–44.

Chapter 10

1. Citino, *Wehrmacht Retreats*, 67.

2. Schwarz, *Stabilisierung der Ostfront*, 143–51; "Lagebesprechung vom 18.2.1943 and 19.2.1943, Kriegstagebuch Heeresgruppe Süd," in idem, 254–7; Melvin, *Manstein*, 332–9; Stahlberg, *Bounden Duty*, 248–79; Manstein, *Lost Victories*, 423–6.

3. Schwarz, *Stabilisierung der Ostfront*, 143–51; "Lagebesprechung vom 18.2.1943 and 19.2.1943, Kriegstagebuch Heeresgruppe Süd," in idem, 254–7; Melvin, *Manstein*, 332–9; Stahlberg, *Bounden Duty*, 248–79; Manstein, *Lost Victories*, 423–6.

4. "Lagebesprechung vom 18.2.1943, Kriegstagebuch Heeresgruppe Süd," in Schwarz, *Stabilisierung der Ostfront*, 255; TBJG, 9 March 1943; Speer, *Inside the Third Reich*, 234–5; Pyta, *Hitler*, 449, 454.

5. Manstein, *Lost Victories*, 427; "Lagebesprechung vom 18.2.1943, 19.2.1943, and 10.3.1943, Kriegstagebuch Heeresgruppe Süd," in Schwarz, *Stabilisierung der Ostfront*, 255, 258, 261–2; "Military Situation Report," 5 March 1943, Heiber and Glantz, *Hitler and His Generals*, 93.

6. Pyta, *Hitler*, 450–3; "Military Situation Report," 5 March 1943, Heiber and Glantz, *Hitler and His Generals*, 89; Goebbels, "Speech on the Tenth Anniversary of the Seizure of Power, 30 January 1943," https://archive.org/stream/Dr.Goebbels.SpeechOnTheTenthA nniversaryOfTheSeizureOfPower.30January1943.InGermanToo./Dr.%20Goebbels.%20 Speech%20on%20the%20tenth%20anniversary%20of%20the%20seizure%20of%20 power.%2030%20January,%201943.%20In%20German%20too._djvu.txt (accessed 10 July 2016); Domarus, *Speeches*, 19 February 1943, 2,760.

7. Stahlberg, *Bounden Duty*, 293–4; Manstein, *Lost Victories*, 443; TBJG, 8 May 1943.

8. TBJG, 9 March 1943.

9. Pyta, *Hitler*, 465–7, 487, 497; TBJG, 8 May 1943; Hayward, "Hitler's Quest for Oil," 127–8.

10. Fischer, *Hitler and America*, 202–5.

11. Mastny, "Stalin and Prospects of Separate Peace," 1,365–70; TBJG, 9 March, 8 May 1943; Magenheimer, *Hitler's War*, 191–6; Pyta, *Hitler*, 486. For a skeptical appraisal, see Fleischhauer, *Die Chance des Sonderfriedens*.

12. Mastny, "Stalin and Prospects of Separate Peace," 1,371–6; Magenheimer, *Hitler's War*, 197–9; TBJG, 9 March 1943; Pyta, *Hitler*, 487–9.

13. Fritz, *Ostkrieg*, 338–9; "Operationsbefehl Nr. 6 (Zitadelle) vom 15.4.1943," KTB/OKW, III/6, 1,425.

14. Citino, *Wehrmacht Retreats*, 119–20; Melvin, *Manstein*, 349–51; "Operationsbefehl Nr. 5 (Weisung für die Kampfführung der nächsten Monate an der Ostfront vom 13.3.1943)," "Führerbefehl im Anschluß an die Weisung für die Kampfführung im Osten vom 17.3.1943," KTB/OKW, III/6, 1420–1423; Wegner, "Von Stalingrad nach Kursk," DRZW, VIII, 62, 68–9; idem, "Defensive ohne Strategie," 200–1; TBJG, 25 June, 5 July 1943; Töppel, "Schlacht bei Kursk," 372–3.

15. TBJG, 9, 11, 15, 20 March 1943; Warlimont, *Inside Hitler's Headquarters*, 312; Melvin, *Manstein*, 352; Pyta, *Hitler*, 455; Citino, *Wehrmacht Retreats*, 120–1; Fritz, *Ostkrieg*, 339–40.

16. "Operationsbefehl Nr. 6 (Zitadelle) vom 15.4.1943," KTB/OKW, III/6, 1,425–7; Fritz, *Ostkrieg*, 339–40.

17. Wegner, "Von Stalingrad nach Kursk," DRZW, VIII, 68–76; Töppel, "Schlacht bei Kursk," 376–8; Klink, *Gesetz des Handelns*, 60, 292; Fritz, *Ostkrieg*, 339–40; Citino, *Wehrmacht Retreats*, 121–3; Mitcham and Mueller, "Generalfeldmarschall Walther Model," in Ueberschär, *Hitlers militärische Elite*, 426–9; Frieser, "Schlagen aus der Nachhand," 111–13; Melvin, *Manstein*, 357.

18. Citino, *Wehrmacht Retreats*, 123–4; Guderian, *Panzer Leader*, 306–7.

19. Guderian, *Panzer Leader*, 307; Citino, *Wehrmacht Retreats*, 124–5; Melvin, *Manstein*, 358–9; Manstein, *Lost Victories*, 446–7.

20. Guderian, *Panzer Leader*, 307; Citino, *Wehrmacht Retreats*, 126; Melvin, *Manstein*, 359.

21. Fritz, *Ostkrieg*, 341; TBJG, 7 May 1943; Guderian, *Panzer Leader*, 308–9.

22. Fritz, *Ostkrieg*, 340–2; Citino, *Wehrmacht Retreats*, 127–9; Melvin, *Manstein*, 355–6; Wegner, "Von Stalingrad nach Kursk," DRZW, VIII, 76–7; idem, "Defensive ohne Strategie," 201; Töppel, "Schlacht bei Kursk," 378; Klink, *Gesetz des Handelns*, 163–4; KTB/OKW, III/6, 5 July 1943, 749–50; Frieser, "Schlacht im Kursker Bogen," DRZW, VIII, 139–40.

23. Fritz, *Ostkrieg*, 344–51; Citino, *Wehrmacht Retreats*, 133–4.

24. Fritz, *Ostkrieg*, 344–51; Citino, *Wehrmacht Retreats*, 137; Melvin, *Manstein*, 367–8, 372, 380.

25. Fritz, *Ostkrieg*, 350–1; Frieser, "Schlacht im Kursker Bogen," DRZW, VIII, 139–42; Wegner, "Das Ende der Strategie," 226; idem, "Defensive ohne Strategie," 201; Töppel, "Die Schlacht bei Kursk," 387–9; "Richtlinien des Führers betr. weitere Kampfführung auf Sizilien vom 13.7.1943," KTB/OKW, III/6, 1,446; Manstein, *Lost Victories*, 448–9; Melvin, *Manstein*, 377–8; Stahlberg, *Bounden Duty*, 309–10.

26. TBJG, 19 July 1943; "Denkschrift des Chefs der Seekriegsleitung vom 8.6.1943," "Auszug aus dem Kriegstagebuch der Seekriegsleitung betr. U-Bootskriegführung vom 8.6.1943," KTB/OKW, III/6, 1,435–41; Overy, *Why the Allies Won*, 58; Tooze, *Wages of Destruction*, 597–600.

27. Frieser, "Die Schlacht im Kursker Bogen," DRZW, VIII, 142–7; idem, "Schlage aus der Nachhand," 132; Töppel, "Die Schlacht bei Kursk," 387–97; Fritz, *Ostkrieg*, 351–3; Glantz and House, *Battle of Kursk*, 135, 274; Tooze, *Wages of Destruction*, 597–600; Sokolov, "The Battle for Kursk, Orel, and Char'Kov," in Foerster, *Gezeitenwechsel*, 79–86; Overmans, *Deutsche militärische Verluste*, 278 (on the entire Eastern Front the Germans lost 71,231 men killed in July). See also Sokolov, "Cost of War," 152–93; Zetterling and Frankson, *Kursk 1943*, 111–31, 145–52.

28. Manstein, *Lost Victories*, 443; Citino, *Wehrmacht Retreats*, 142, 212–21, 227–31; Fritz, *Ostkrieg*, 353–7; Melvin, *Manstein*, 385–6.

29. Fritz, *Ostkrieg*, 364–5; Citino, *Wehrmacht Retreats*, 129, 143–4; Pyta, *Hitler*, 486–8.

30. TBJG, 10, 23 September 1943; Domarus, *Speeches*, 2,813, 2,823.

31. TBJG, 27 October 1943; Fleischhauer, *Sonderfrieden*, 168–75, 189–91; Wegner, "Von Stalingrad nach Kursk," DRZW, 8, 55–60; Mastny, "Stalin and Separate Peace," 1,380–1; Pyta, *Hitler*, 487–9.

32. TBJG, 27 October 1943; Pyta, *Hitler*, 504–12.

33. Pyta, *Hitler*, 504–12.

34. Mastny, "Stalin and Separate Peace," 1,382–4; Pyta, *Hitler*, 504–12. Ironically, on the eve of the Normandy invasion Hitler ruled out any separate peace talks with Britain, considering the country finished. See TBJG, 6 June 1944.

35. Melvin, *Manstein*, 382–4; 395–404; Citino, *Wehrmacht Retreats*, 222–5; Fritz, *Ostkrieg*, 369–74, 377–83, 387–98.

36. Fritz, *Ostkrieg*, 367–8; Citino, *Wehrmacht Retreats*, 232–7; 268–9; Melvin, *Manstein*, 392–3; Pyta, *Hitler*, 471–5.

37. Fritz, *Ostkrieg*, 367–8; Citino, *Wehrmacht Retreats*, 232–7; 268–9; Melvin, *Manstein*, 392–3; Pyta, *Hitler*, 471–5.

38. Ziemke, *Stalingrad to Berlin*, 311–12; Wegner, "Kriegführung des 'als ob,'" DRZW, VIII, 1,177–8; Frieser, "Zusammenbruch im Osten," DRZW, VIII, 495, 498; Boog, "Defending German Skies," GSWW, VII, 163; Kershaw, *Hitler: Nemesis*, 632–40; Tooze, *Wages of*

Destruction, 626–34; Weinberg, *A World at Arms*, 656–66; idem, "German Plans for Victory, 1944–1945," 215–28; Citino, *Wehrmacht Retreats*, 275–7.

39. Fritz, *Ostkrieg*, 400–1; Frieser, "Zusammenbruch im Osten," 493–6; Steinert, *Hitler's War and the Germans*, 234–5, 240–1.

40. Pyta, *Hitler*, 534; Hitler Address to Commanders in West, 20 March 1944, in Liddell-Hart, *Rommel Papers*, 465–6.

41. Fritz, *Ostkrieg*, 401; Frieser, "Zusammenbruch im Osten," DRZW, VIII, 493–7; Wegner, "Kriegführung des 'als ob,'" DRZW, VIII, 1,177–8; TBJG, 4, 15 March, 18, 21 April, 6 June 1944; Kershaw, *Hitler: Nemesis*, 636–8; Below, *At Hitler's Side*, 199–200.

42. Directive No. 51, 3 November 1942, in Trevor-Roper, *Hitler's War Directives*, 149–53; "Evening Situation Report, Dec 20, 1943," Heiber and Glantz, *Hitler and His Generals*, 314; Wegner, "Aporie des Krieges," DRZW, VIII, 218–20, 246–50; idem, "Choreographie des Untergangs," DRZW, VIII, 496–506; Frieser, "Rückschlag des Pendels," DRZW, VIII, 361–2; Frieser, "Zusammenbruch im Osten," 499.

43. Directive No. 51, 3 November 1942, in Trevor-Roper, *Blitzkrieg to Defeat*, 149–53; "Evening Situation Report, Dec 20, 1943," and "Midday Situation Report, 28 Jan 1944," Heiber and Glantz, *Hitler and His Generals*, 317, 415; Warlimont, *Inside Hitler's Headquarters*, 409, 428; KTB/OKW, IV/7, 302–3; Magenheimer, *Hitler's War*, 247–8.

44. Vogel, "German and Allied Conduct of the War in the West," GSWW, VII, 508–9; Lieb, *Unternehmen Overlord*, 46–50; Midday Situation Report, 19 November 1943, Heiber and Glantz, *Hitler and His Generals*, 292–3; TBJG, 18 April 1944; Pyta, *Hitler*, 536–9.

45. Vogel, "War in the West," GSWW, VII, 509–10; Lieb, *Unternehmen Overlord*, 50–1; Liddell-Hart, *Rommel Papers*, 466–7; Warlimont, *Inside Hitler's Headquarters*, 409; Pyta, *Hitler*, 540–1.

46. Vogel, "War in the West," GSWW, VII, 509–10; Lieb, *Unternehmen Overlord*, 50–1; Pyta, *Hitler*, 540–1.

47. Vogel, "War in the West," GSWW, VII, 510–33, 582; Lieb, *Unternehmen Overlord*, 51–7; Pyta, *Hitler*, 540–3; Warlimont, *Inside Hitler's Headquarters*, 408, 412–16; Frieser, "Zusammenbruch im Osten," 500.

48. Speer, *Inside the Third Reich*, 346.

49. "Meeting of the Führer with General Jodl and General Zeitzler, December 28, 1943," "Meeting of the Führer with General Zeitzler, December 29, 1943," Heiber and Glantz, *Hitler and His Generals*, 355–7, 375; Pyta, *Hitler*, 525; Melvin, *Manstein*, 408–9; Manstein, *Lost Victories*, 501–4.

50. Melvin, *Manstein*, 410; Manstein, *Lost Victories*, 504–5; Pyta, *Hitler*, 525; TBJG, 3 November 1943, 8 March 1944.

51. Melvin, *Manstein*, 411.

52. Melvin, *Manstein*, 411–12, 417–18; Manstein, *Lost Victories*, 510–12, 538; Pyta, *Hitler*, 481, 513–14, 526; Fritz, *Ostkrieg*, 393, 395–7.

53. Führer Order No. 11, 8 March 1944, in Trevor-Roper, *Hitler's War Directives*, 159–61; Pyta, *Hitler*, 519–23; Jodl, "The Strategic Position in the Beginning of the 5th Year of War," NT, Red Series, VII, Doc. L-172, 928, 974.

54. Lunde, *Hitler's Wave-Breaker Concept*, 34–9; Schramm, *Hitler*, 158–9; Hitler, "Memorandum on the Construction of the West Wall," 28 June 1938, Domarus, *Speeches*, 1,123; Grier, *Hitler, Dönitz, and the Baltic Sea*, XVII–XIX, 145–6; Schreiber, "Ende," DRZW, VIII, 1,131, 1,150–2, 1,161.

55. Pyta, *Hitler*, 532–4; Shepherd, *Hitler's Soldiers*, 400–2, 406–11.

56. Shepherd, *Hitler's Soldiers*, 376–7, 381–2; Lunde, *Hitler's Wave-Breaker Concept*, 39; Warlimont, *Inside Hitler's Headquarters*, 403.

57. Vogel, "War in the West," GSWW, VII, 585–7; Below, *At Hitler's Side*, 202; Lieb, "Rommel in Normandy," 113–36.

58. Vogel, "War in the West," GSWW, VII, 593–4; Kershaw, *Hitler: Nemesis*, 639–40; Weinberg, *A World at Arms*, 686–8; Magenheimer, *Hitler's War*, 248–9; Hastings, *Overlord*, 129.

59. Vogel, "War in the West," GSWW, VII, 593–4; Kershaw, *Hitler: Nemesis*, 639–40; Weinberg, *A World at Arms*, 686–8; Magenheimer, *Hitler's War*, 248–9; Hastings, *Overlord*, 129.

60. TBJG, 7 June 1944; Below, *At Hitler's Side*, 203.
61. Vogel, "War in the West," GSWW, VII, 595; TBJG, 7 June 1944; Kershaw, *Hitler: Nemesis*, 640; Pyta, *Hitler*, 546–7, 552; Lieb, *Unternehmen Overlord*, 91–2; Beevor, *D-Day*, 190.
62. Vogel, "War in the West," GSWW, VII, 598; Lieb, *Unternehmen Overlord*, 95, 112–13, 148; Shepherd, *Hitler's Soldiers*, 436–44.
63. Kershaw, *Hitler: Nemesis*, 642–3; Lieb, *Unternehmen Overlord*, 115; Below, *At Hitler's Side*, 204.
64. Speer, *Inside the Third Reich*, 356; TBJG, 18, 22, 29 June 1944; Heiber and Glantz, *Hitler and His Generals*, 31 July 1944, 457; Kershaw, *Hitler: Nemesis*, 643–6.
65. TBJG, 22, 25 June 1944; Fritz, *Ostkrieg*, 393, 405; Kershaw, *Hitler: Nemesis*, 646; Shepherd, *Hitler's Soldiers*, 445.
66. Fritz, *Ostkrieg*, 411; Frieser, "Zusammenbruch im Osten," DRZW, VIII, 518; Pyta, *Hitler*, 561; Shepherd, *Hitler's Soldiers*, 448; Mawdsley, *Thunder in the East*, 304.
67. Fritz, *Ostkrieg*, 407–9; Frieser, "Zusammenbruch im Osten," DRZW, VIII, 530–5.
68. Fritz, *Ostkrieg*, 407–9; Frieser, "Zusammenbruch im Osten," DRZW, VIII, 530–5; Shepherd, *Hitler's Soldiers*, 248–29, 445–7.
69. Fritz, *Ostkrieg*, 406–7; Frieser, "Zusammenbruch im Osten," DRZW, VIII, 501–5.
70. Fritz, *Ostkrieg*, 407–8, 412–15; Heusinger, *Befehl im Widerstreit*, 330–1; Shepherd, *Hitler's Soldiers*, 448.
71. Fritz, *Ostkrieg*, 415–22; Shepherd, *Hitler's Soldiers*, 448–9; Pyta, *Hitler*, 563, 565; Frieser, "Zusammenbruch im Osten," DRZW, VIII, 556–60, 594; TBJG, 4 August 1944.
72. Shepherd, *Hitler's Soldiers*, 450–3.
73. Shepherd, *Hitler's Soldiers*, 450–3; Fritz, *Frontsoldaten*, 210, 216; Kershaw, *Hitler: Nemesis*, 668–705; Domarus, *Speeches*, 2,931; TBJG, 23 July 1944; Heiber and Glantz, *Hitler and His Generals*, 31 July 1944, 447; Pyta, *Hitler*, 584–6, 589–90.
74. Lieb, *Unternehmen Overlord*, 114–17; Vogel, "War in the West," GSWW, VII, 598–9; Pyta, *Hitler*, 551.
75. TBJG, 29 June 1944; Lieb, *Unternehmen Overlord*, 118; Pyta, *Hitler*, 552.
76. Lieb, *Unternehmen Overlord*, 117–19, 125; Below, *At Hitler's Side*, 212; Vogel, "War in the West," GSWW, VII, 603.
77. Vogel, "War in the West," GSWW, VII, 603; Lieb, *Unternehmen Overlord*, 120–4; "Meeting of the Führer with Colonel General Jodl, July 31, 1944," Heiber and Glantz, *Hitler and His Generals*, 444–5.
78. "Meeting of the Führer with Colonel General Jodl, July 31, 1944," Heiber and Glantz, *Hitler and His Generals*, 444–51; Warlimont, *Inside Hitler's Headquarters*, 444.
79. Vogel, "War in the West," GSWW, VII, 603, 607; Lieb, *Unternehmen Overlord*, 124; Overy, *Why Allies Won*, 167, 171–2; Keegan, *Second World War*, 328; Shepherd, *Hitler's Soldiers*, 457–8.
80. Vogel, "War in the West," GSWW, VII, 607–8; Lieb, *Unternehmen Overlord*, 156.
81. Vogel, "War in the West," GSWW, VII, 608–9; Lieb, *Unternehmen Overlord*, 155–6.
82. Vogel, "War in the West," GSWW, VII, 609–10; Lieb, *Unternehmen Overlord*, 156; Keegan, *Second World War*, 341; Mitcham, "Generaloberst der Waffen-SS Paul Hausser," in Ueberschär, *Hitlers militärische Elite*, 92–4; Blumenson, *Breakout and Pursuit*, 46.
83. Vogel, "War in the West," GSWW, VII, 610–14; Lieb, *Unternehmen Overlord*, 156–70; Shepherd, *Hitler's Soldiers*, 459–62; Pyta, *Hitler*, 558; Mueller, "Generalfeldmarschall Günther von Kluge," in Ueberschär, *Hitler's militärischer Elite*, 134–5.
84. Neitzel, "Der Kampf um die deutschen Atlantik-und Kanalfestungen," 428–30; Warlimont, *Inside Hitler's Headquarters*, 478; Lieb, *Unternehmen Overlord*, 199.

Chapter 11

1. Warlimont, *Inside Hitler's Headquarters*, 486–90; "The Führer's Speech to Division Commanders, December 12, 1944, at Adlerhorst," Heiber and Glantz, *Hitler and his Generals*, 533–41.
2. Magenheimer, *Hitler's War*, 255–7; Warlimont, *Inside Hitler's Headquarters*, 481; Below, *At Hitler's Side*, 222–3; Pyta, *Hitler*, 599–600.

3. KTB/OKW, IV/7, 340–1, 430–1; Balck, *Order in Chaos*, 375; "Meeting of the Führer with Lieutenant-General Westphal and Lieutenant-General Krebs, August 31, 1944," Heiber and Glantz, *Hitler and his Generals*, 466–8; Schramm, *Hitler*, 169; Wilt, *War from the Top*, 274; Warlimont, *Inside Hitler's Headquarters*, 477–8; Vogel, "War in the West," GSWW, VII, 678–9; Lieb, *Unternehmen Overlord*, 205; Magenheimer, *Hitler's War*, 258.

4. Vogel, "War in the West," GSWW, VII, 680; Wilt, *War from the Top*, 274–5; Warlimont, *Inside Hitler's Headquarters*, 480–5; Guderian, *Panzer Leader*, 380; Magenheimer, *Hitler's War*, 258–60.

5. Vogel, "War in the West," GSWW, VII, 680; Wilt, *War from the Top*, 274–5; Warlimont, *Inside Hitler's Headquarters*, 480–5; Guderian, *Panzer Leader*, 380; Magenheimer, *Hitler's War*, 258–60; Jodl to Chief of Staff, OB West, 1 November 1944, KTB/OKW, IV/7, 436.

6. Lieb, *Unternehmen Overlord*, 206; Wilt, *War from the Top*, 276; Vogel, "War in the West," GSWW, VII, 681–2; Magenheimer, *Hitler's War*, 260–1; Dupuy, *Hitler's Last Gamble*, 18.

7. Kershaw, *The End*, 156–9; Vogel, "War in the West," GSWW, VII, 688–94; Lieb, *Unternehmen Overlord*, 207–9; Magenheimer, *Hitler's War*, 261–2; TBJG, 17, 18, 19, 20 December 1944; Speer, *Inside the Third Reich*, 417; Guderian, *Panzer Leader*, 380–1.

8. Vogel, "War in the West," GSWW, VII, 688–94; Lieb, *Unternehmen Overlord*, 207–9; Magenheimer, *Hitler's War*, 261–2; "Meeting of the Führer with Major General Thomale, December 29, 1944, at Adlerhorst," Heiber and Glantz, *Hitler and his Generals*, 568–74, 583; Kershaw, *The End*, 157.

9. Yelton, "Ein Volk steht auf," 1,068–70; Weinberg, "German Plans for Victory, 1944–1945," in idem, *Germany, Hitler, and World War II*, 274–86; Wegner, "Choreographie des Untergangs," 492–518; Geyer, "Endkampf 1918 and 1945," 49–67; Bessel, *Germany 1945*, 38; "The Führer's Speech to Division Commanders, December 28, 1944," Heiber and Glantz, *Hitler and his Generals*, 567.

10. Lieb, *Unternehmen Overlord*, 209–10; Wilt, *War from the Top*, 278; Vogel, "War in the West," GSWW, VII, 696; Geyer, "Insurrectionary Warfare," 492–3; Clausewitz, *On War*, 189; Clausewitz, *War, Politics, and Power*, 301–2; Lunde, *Hitler's Wave-Breaker Concept*, 22; Krüger, "Hitlers Clausewitzkenntnis," 467–71; Wegner, "Choreographie des Untergangs," 493–518; Below, *At Hitler's Side*, 223.

11. Fritz, *Ostkrieg*, 439; Hitler, "Reichstag Speech, 1 September 1939," "Speech in Munich, 8 November 1942," "Proclamation to the German Volk, 1 January 1945," Domarus, *Speeches*, 1,755, 2,696, 2,987–92.

12. Hitler, "Proclamation to the German Volk, 1 January 1945," Domarus, *Speeches*, 2,987–92.

13. Fritz, *Ostkrieg*, 440; idem, *Endkampf*; idem, "This is the Way Wars End," 121–53; Pyta, *Hitler*, 594–6; Overmans, *Deutsche militärische Verluste*, 238, 265–6; Bessel, "The Shadow of Death," 51–2; idem, "Murder amidst Collapse," 255–6; Friedrich, *The Fire*, 144.

14. Fritz, *Ostkrieg*, 441–3; Lakowski, "Zusammenbruch der deutschen Verteidigung," DRZW, X/1, 495–506; Ziemke, *Stalingrad to Berlin*, 418.

15. Fritz, *Ostkrieg*, 441, 443; Guderian, *Panzer Leader*, 382–93; "Evening Situation Report, in Adlerhorst, 9 January 1945," Heiber and Glantz, *Hitler and His Generals*, 593; Lakowski, "Zusammenbruch der deutschen Verteidigung," DRZW, X/1, 496, 502–6; Ziemke, *Stalingrad to Berlin*, 417–18.

16. Fritz, *Ostkrieg*, 441, 443; Lakowski, "Zusammenbruch der deutschen Verteidigung," DRZW, X/1, 496, 502–6; Ziemke, *Stalingrad to Berlin*, 417–18.

17. Fritz, *Ostkrieg*, 443; Kershaw, *The End*, 172–3; Lakowski, "Zusammenbruch der deutschen Verteidigung," DRZW, X/1, 516–18; Glantz and House, *When Titans Clashed*, 242–4; Ziemke, *Stalingrad to Berlin*, 420–2; Le Tissier, *Zhukov at the Oder*, 29–41; TBJG, 5, 21, 28 March 1945; Bessel, *Germany 1945*, 39–40.

18. Fritz, *Ostkrieg*, 443–4; Lakowski, "Zusammenbruch der deutschen Verteidigung," DRZW, X/1, 518–19, 531–7; Glantz and House, *When Titans Clashed*, 242–4; Ziemke, *Stalingrad to Berlin*, 422, 428–9; Le Tissier, *Zhukov at the Oder*, 29–41; Kershaw, *The End*, 173; Guderian, *Panzer Leader*, 393–4.

19. Fritz, *Ostkrieg*, 443–4; Lakowski, "Zusammenbruch der deutschen Verteidigung," DRZW, X/1, 518–19, 531–7; Glantz and House, *When Titans Clashed*, 242–4; Ziemke,

Stalingrad to Berlin, 422, 428–9; Le Tissier, *Zhukov at the Oder*, 29–41; Kershaw, *The End*, 173; Guderian, *Panzer Leader*, 393–4.

20. Fritz, *Ostkrieg*, 433–4, 446–7; Lakowski, "Zusammenbruch der deutschen Verteidigung," DRZW, X/1, 537–50; Ziemke, *Stalingrad to Berlin*, 429–33; Guderian, *Panzer Leader*, 400; Kershaw, *The End*, 196–200; Bessel, *Germany 1945*, 40–1; Frieser, "Zusammenbruch im Osten," 668–78.

21. Fritz, *Ostkrieg*, 433–4, 446–7; Lakowski, "Zusammenbruch der deutschen Verteidigung," DRZW, X/1, 537–50; Ziemke, *Stalingrad to Berlin*, 429–33; Guderian, *Panzer Leader*, 400, 412–13; Speer, *Inside the Third Reich*, 420–1; Kershaw, *The End*, 196–200; Bessel, *Germany 1945*, 40–1; Frieser, "Zusammenbruch im Osten," 668–78; "3rd Situation Report, April 23, 1945," Heiber and Glantz, *Hitler and his Generals*, 719; Pyta, *Hitler*, 606–7; TBJG, 30 January 1945; Grier, *Hitler, Dönitz, and the Baltic Sea*, 131–51, 167–91.

22. Fritz, *Ostkrieg*, 444–5; Lakowski, "Zusammenbruch der deutschen Verteidigung," DRZW, X/1, 520–3; Glantz and House, *When Titans Clashed*, 244–5; Ziemke, *Stalingrad to Berlin*, 421–2; Guderian, *Panzer Leader*, 394–6; Kershaw, *The End*, 174; Le Tissier, *Zhukov at the Oder*, 29–41.

23. Fritz, *Ostkrieg*, 445–6; Kershaw, *The End*, 175; Lakowski, "Zusammenbruch der deutschen Verteidigung," DRZW, X/1, 523–6; Kershaw, *The End*, 202–4; Glantz and House, *When Titans Clashed*, 245–7; Ziemke, *Stalingrad to Berlin*, 423–7.

24. Fritz, *Ostkrieg*, 447–8; Glantz and House, *When Titans Clashed*, 249–50; Mawdsley, *Thunder in the East*, 367–70; Lakowski, "Zusammenbruch der deutschen Verteidigung," DRZW, X/1, 527–31, 550–68; Ziemke, *Stalingrad to Berlin*, 439–44; Glantz and House, *When Titans Clashed*, 251–2, 254–5; Mawdsley, *Thunder in the East*, 370–4.

25. TBJG, 30 January, 2 February 1945; Speer, *Inside the Third Reich*, 424; Kershaw, *The End*, 243–4.

26. TBJG, 1, 2, 6, 12, 18, 19, 20, 28 February 1945; Kershaw, *The End*, 243–6; Speer, *Inside the Third Reich*, 429; Below, *At Hitler's Side*, 227.

27. Zimmermann, "Deutsche militärische Kriegführung im Westen," DRZW, 10/I, 293, 312–15, 321, 409–43; Fritz, *Endkampf*, 3–22, 67–86.

28. Zimmermann, "Deutsche militärische Kriegführung im Westen," DRZW, 10/I, 293, 312–15, 321, 409–43; Fritz, *Endkampf*, 3–22, 67–86.

29. Fritz, *Ostkrieg*, 437–8, 448–9; Guderian, *Panzer Leader*, 412–15; Pyta, *Hitler*, 625–8.

30. Fritz, *Ostkrieg*, 437–8, 448–9; Guderian, *Panzer Leader*, 412–15; Ungvary, "Kriegsschauplatz Ungarn," DRZW, 8, 930–49; Kershaw, *The End*, 252–3; Mawdsley, *Thunder in the East*, 352; Pyta, *Hitler*, 601–2; TBJG, 31 March 1945.

31. Fritz, *Ostkrieg*, 455; Kershaw, *Hitler: Nemesis*, 784; idem, *The End*, 303.

32. Fritz, *Ostkrieg*, 455–6.

33. Fritz, *Ostkrieg*, 455–6; Schwendemann, "Drastic Measures," 599–603, 611–12; Müller, "Zusammenbruch des Wirtschaftslebens," DRZW, X/2, 74–84, 106–19; Speer, *Inside the Third Reich*, 435.

34. Fritz, *Ostkrieg*, 456–8; Schwendemann, "Drastic Measures," 603, 607–8; Müller, "Zusammenbruch des Wirtschaftslebens," DRZW, X/2, 85–8; Speer, *Inside the Third Reich*, 436–9; Below, *At Hitler's Side*, 230; Kershaw, *The End*, 288–90.

35. Fritz, *Ostkrieg*, 456–8; Schwendemann, "Drastic Measures," 603, 607–8; Müller, "Zusammenbruch des Wirtschaftslebens," DRZW, X/2, 85–8; Speer, *Inside the Third Reich*, 436–9; Below, *At Hitler's Side*, 230; Kershaw, *The End*, 288–90.

36. Kershaw, *The End*, 296–300, 303–5; Zimmermann, "Deutsche militärische Kriegführung im Westen," DRZW, 10/I, 332, 443–60; Fritz, *Endkampf*, chs. 3–6.

37. Fritz, *Ostkrieg*, 461–9; Lakowski, "Zusammenbruch der deutschen Verteidigung," DRZW, 10/I, 588–673; Bessel, *Germany 1945*, 104–6, 110–14.

38. Bessel, *Germany 1945*, 99–101; Neumann and Eberle, *Was Hitler Ill?*, 176–85; Pyta, *Hitler*, 608–11; Guderian, *Panzer Leader*, 397, 427–9; TBJG, 1 February, 31 March 1945.

39. TBJG, 22, 28 March 1945; Bessel, *Germany 1945*, 99–101; Kershaw, *Hitler: Nemesis*, 791–2; idem, *The End*, 308–9; "The Führer's Speech to Division Commanders," 28 December 1944, Heiber and Glantz, *Hitler and his Generals*, 554–6; Speer, *Inside the Third Reich*, 433; Pyta, *Hitler*, 634–6.

40. Bessel, *Germany 1945*, 99–101; Kershaw, *Hitler: Nemesis*, 791–2; idem, *The End*, 308–9; Below, *At Hitler's Side*, 234–5, 239; Speer, *Inside the Third Reich*, 463–4; Pyta, *Hitler*, 634, 636–7.
41. Bessel, *Germany 1945*, 101, 106–9; Below, *At Hitler's Side*, 236; Kershaw, *The End*, 339–40; "Wednesday, April 25, 1943," Heiber and Glantz, *Hitler and his Generals*, 722–3.
42. "3rd Situation Report, April 27, 1945," "Wednesday, April 25, 1945," Heiber and Glantz, *Hitler and his Generals*, 722–3, 737; "The Private and Political Testaments of Hitler, April 29, 1945," NT Red Series, VI, Doc. 3569-PS, 261; Neumann and Eberle, *Was Hitler Ill?*, 184; Joachimsthaler, *Hitlers Ende*, 154, 191, 198, 210–11. Part of Hitler's anger and disappointment with Paulus's failure to commit suicide might have stemmed from the high regard in which he held the general. This can clearly be seen in his remarks to Keitel on 18 September 1942. See "Besprechung des Führers mit Generalfeldmarschall Keitel am 18. September 1942," in Hürter and Uhl, "Hitler in Vinnica," 615, 619, 634–5.
43. Bessel, *Germany 1945*, 121, 133; Schramm, *Hitler*, 180–1; Kershaw, *Hitler: Nemesis*, 832–3.
44. Kershaw, *The End*, 272, 312–15, 321–9, 384–5; Fritz, *Endkampf*, ch. 5; idem, *Ostkrieg*, 431, 449–55; Bessel, *Germany 1945*, 115–18, 146–7.
45. Bessel, *Germany 1945*, 146–7; Geyer, "Endkampf," 44–6, 51, 55, 59; Schramm, *Hitler*, 180–1; Lukacs, *Hitler*, 171; Joachimsthaler, *Hitlers Ende*, 191; Hitler, *Testament of Adolf Hitler*, 80. Interestingly, in November 1918 the military high command had supposedly urged Wilhelm II to sacrifice his life in battle in order to save the honor of the nation and give rise to a heroic myth. See Schivelbusch, *Culture of Defeat*, 200.
46. Bessel, *Germany 1945*, 146–7; Geyer, "Endkampf," 44–6, 51, 55, 59; Joachimsthaler, *Hitler's Ende*, 190; "The Private and Political Testaments of Hitler, April 29, 1945," NT Red Series, VI, Doc. 3569-PS, 259–63.

Chapter 12

1. Hitler, *Testament of Adolf Hitler*, 7, 24 February, 2 April 1945, 17, 62–4, 83–4.
2. KTB/OKW, I/1, 9 January 1941, 258; Leach, *German Strategy*, 156; Lukacs, *Hitler*, 151–2; Hitler, *Testament of Adolf Hitler*, 15 February 1945, 37–9.
3. Fritz, *Ostkrieg*, 476.
4. TBJG, 18 August 1941; Halder, *Halder War Diary*, 19 November 1941, 558; Eberle, *Hitlers Weltkriege*, 297.
5. Eberle, *Hitlers Weltkriege*; 292; Lukacs, *Hitler*, 157, 256.
6. Eberle, *Hitlers Weltkriege*, 293–4; "Meeting of the Führer with Lieutenant General Westphal and Lieutenant General Krebs, August 31, 1944," Heiber and Glantz, *Hitler and His Generals*, 468; Clausewitz, *On War*, 189. For Hitler's awareness of Clausewitz's warnings against the shame of "cowardly submission," see *Mein Kampf*, 669.
7. Geyer, "Nazi Pursuit of War," 161–4.

Bibliography

Published Primary Sources

Archiv des Deutschen Auswärtigen Amtes. *26. Mai bis 31. Oktober 1936. Akten zur Deutschen Auswärtigen Politik 1918-1945*. Serie C: 1933–1937, 6 vols. V/2. Göttingen: Vandenhoeck and Ruprecht, 1977.

Bähr, Walter, and Hans Walter Bähr, eds. *Kriegsbriefe gefallener Studenten, 1939-1945*. Tübingen: Wunderlich, 1952.

Balck, Hermann. *Order in Chaos: The Memoirs of General of Panzer Troops Hermann Balck*, ed. and trans. David T. Zabecki and Dieter J. Biedekarken. Lexington, KY: University Press of Kentucky, 2015.

Baumgart, Winfried. "Zur Ansprache Hitlers vor den Führern der Wehrmacht am 22. August 1939," *Vierteljahrshefte für Zeitgeschichte* 16:2 (1968), 120–49.

Beierl, Florian, and Othmar Plöckinger. "Neue Dokumente zu Hitlers Buch 'Mein Kampf,'" *Vierteljahrshefte für Zeitgeschichte* 57:2 (2009), 260–318.

Below, Nicolaus von. *At Hitler's Side: The Memoirs of Hitler's Luftwaffe Adjutant, 1937-1945*. London: Greenhill Books, 2004.

——. *Als Hitlers Adjutant, 1937–45*. Mainz: Hase & Koehler, 1980.

Bock, Fedor von. *Generalfeldmarschall Fedor Von Bock: The War Diary, 1939-1945*, ed. Klaus Gerbet, trans. David Johnston. Atglen, PA: Schiffer Publishing, 1996.

Brandmayer, Balthasar, and Heinz Bayer. *Meldegänger Hitler: Erlebt u. erz*. Munich: Walter, 1933.

Buchbender, Ortwin, and Reinhold Sterz, eds. *Das Andere Gesicht des Krieges: Deutsche Feldpostbriefe, 1939-1945*. Munich: Beck, 1982.

Ciano, Galeazzo. *The Ciano Diaries, 1939-1943: The Complete, Unabridged Diaries of Count Galeazzo Ciano, Italian Minister for Foreign Affairs, 1936-1943*, ed. Hugh Gibson. Garden City, NY: Doubleday, 1946.

Clausewitz, Carl von. *On War*, trans. Michael Howard and Peter Paret, ed. Beatrice Heuser. New York: Oxford University Press, 2007.

——. *On War*, ed. and trans. Michael Howard and Peter Paret. Princeton, N.J.: Princeton University Press, 1976.

——. *Vom Kriege: Hinterlassenes Werk des Generals Carl von Clausewitz. Vollständige Ausgabe im Urtext*, ed. Werner Hahlweg. Available at: https://www.clausewitz.com/readings/VomKriege1832/_VKwholetext.htm (accessed 25 November 2016).

——. *War, Politics, and Power: Selections from* On War, *and* I Believe and Profess, ed. and trans. Edward M. Collins. Chicago, IL: Regnery, 1970.

Delbrück, Hans. *The Dawn of Modern Warfare*, trans. Walter J. Renfroe. Lincoln, NB: University of Nebraska Press, 1990.

——. *Warfare in Antiquity*, trans. Walter J. Renfroe. Lincoln, NB: University of Nebraska Press, 1990.

Deuerlein, Ernst. "Hitlers Eintritt in die Politik und die Reichswehr," *Vierteljahrshefte für Zeitgeschichte* 7:2 (1959), 177–227.

Domarus, Max. *Hitler: Speeches and Proclamations, 1932–1945: The Chronicle of a Dictatorship*, trans. Mary Fran Golbert. Wauconda, IL: Bolchazy-Carducci, 1990.

Dorpalen, Andreas. *The World of General Haushofer: Geopolitics in Action*. New York and Toronto: Farrar & Rinehart, 1942.

Dusik, Bärbel, ed. *Vom Weimarer Parteitag bis zur Reichstagswahl: Juli 1926–Mai 1928* (vol. 2 of *Hitler. Reden, Schriften, Anordnungen. Februar 1925 bis Januar 1933*). Munich: K. G. Saur, 1992.

Engel, Gerhard. *At the Heart of the Reich: The Secret Diary of Hitler's Army Adjutant*, trans. Geoffrey Brooks. London: Greenhill, 2005.

——. *Heeresadjutant bei Hitler, 1938–1943*, ed. Hildegard von Kotze. Stuttgart: Deutsche Verlags-Anstalt, 1974.

Feuersenger, Marianne. *Im Vorzimmer der Macht: Aufzeichnungen aus dem Wehrmachtführungsstab und Führerhauptquartier, 1940–1945*. Munich: Herbig, 1999.

——. *Mein Kriegstagebuch: Zwischen Führerhauptquartier und Berliner Wirklichkeit*. Freiburg im Breisgau: Herder, 1982.

Förster, Jürgen, and Evan Mawdsley. 2004. "Hitler and Stalin in Perspective: Secret Speeches on the Eve of Barbarossa," *War in History* 11:1 (2004), 61–103.

Frisch, Franz A. P. *Condemned to Live: A Panzer Artilleryman's Five-Front War*, trans. Wilbur D. Jones. Shippensburg, PA: Burd Street Press, 2000.

Fröhlich, Elke, ed. *Die Tagebücher von Joseph Goebbels: Sämtliche Fragmente*. 15 vols. Munich: K. G. Saur, 1987.

——. *Die Tagebücher von Joseph Goebbels. Teil I: Aufzeichnungen 1923–1941, Band 1–9; Teil II: Diktate 1941–1945, Band 1–15*. Munich: K. G. Saur, 2005.

Germany, Auswärtiges Amt. *Documents on German Foreign Policy, 1918–1945: From the Archives of the German Foreign Ministry. Series C*. Washington, D.C.: United States Government Printing Office, 1957.

——. *Documents on German Foreign Policy, 1918–1945: From the Archives of the German Foreign Ministry. Series D (1937–45)*. Washington, D.C.: United States Government Printing Office, 1949.

Germany, Nationalversammlung (1919–20). Untersuchungsausschuss über die Weltkriegsverantwortlichkeit. *The Causes of the German Collapse in 1918: Sections of the Officially Authorized Report of the Commission of the German Constituent Assembly and of the German Reichstag, 1919–1928, the Selection and the Translation Officially Approved by the Commission*, ed. and trans. Ralph Haswell Lutz. Stanford, CA: Stanford University Press, 1934.

Gibbons, Robert. "Opposition gegen 'Barbarossa' im Herbst 1940. Eine Denkschrift aus der Deutschen Botschaft in Moskau," *Vierteljahrshefte für Zeitgeschichte* 23:3 (1975), 332–40.

Goebbels, Joseph. *Wesen und Gestalt des Nationalsozialismus*. Berlin: Junker und Dünnhaupt, 1934.

——. "Speech on the Tenth Anniversary of the Seizure of Power, 30 January, 1943." Available at: https://archive.org/stream/Dr.Goebbels.SpeechOnTheTenthAnniversaryOfTheSeizur eOfPower.30January1943.InGermanToo./Dr.%20Goebbels.%20Speech%20on%20 the%20tenth%20anniversary%20of%20the%20seizure%20of%20power.%2030%20 January,%201943.%20In%20German%20too._djvu.txt (accessed 7 October 2016).

Groscurth, Helmuth. *Tagebücher eines Abwehroffiziers 1938–1940; mit Weiteren Dokumenten zur Militäropposition gegen Hitler*, ed. Helmut Krausnick and Harold C. Deutsch. Stuttgart: Deutsches Verlags-Anstalt, 1970.

Guderian, Heinz. *Panzer Leader*. Cambridge, MA: Da Capo Press, 2002.

Halder, Franz. *The Halder War Diary, 1939–1942*, trans. Charles Burdick and Hans Adolf Jacobsen, ed. Charles Burdick and Hans Adolf Jacobsen. Novato, CA: Presidio Press, 1988.

——. *The Private War Journal of Generaloberst Franz Halder, Chief of the General Staff of the Supreme Command of the German Army: 14 August 1939 to 24 September 1942.* 6 vols. Ike Skelton Combined Arms Research Library and Digital Library. Available at: http://cgsc. contentdm.oclc.org/cdm/search/collection/p4013coll8/searchterm/War%20journal% 20of%20Franz%20Halder/field/title/mode/all/conn/and (accessed 18 August 2015).

Hartmann, Christian, and Sergej Slutsch. "Franz Halder und die Kriegsvorbereitungen im Frühjahr 1939. Eine Ansprache des Generalstabschefs des Heeres," *Vierteljahrshefte für Zeitgeschichte* 45:3 (1997), 467–95.

Haushofer, Karl. *Grenzen in ihrer geographischen und politischen Bedeutung.* Berlin: K. Vowinckel, 1927.

Heiber, Helmut, and David M. Glantz, eds. *Hitler and his Generals: Military Conferences 1942–1945,* trans. Roland Winter. New York: Enigma Books, 2003.

Hesse, Kurt. *Der Feldherr Psychologos. Ein Suchen nach dem Führer der deutschen Zukunkt.* Berlin: E. S. Mittler & Son, 1922.

Heusinger, Adolf. *Befehl im Widerstreit: Schicksalsstunden der deutschen Armee, 1923–1945.* Tübingen: R. Wunderlich, 1950.

Hitler, Adolf. "Adolf Hitlers Geheimrede vom 23. November 1937," in *Hitlers Tischgespräche im Führerhauptquartier,* ed. Henry Picker. Berlin: Ullstein, 1999, 691–705.

——. "Adolf Hitlers Geheimrede vom 30. Mai 1942 vor dem 'Militärischen Führernachwuchs,'" in *Hitlers Tischgespräche im Führerhauptquartier,* ed. Henry Picker. Berlin: Ullstein, 1999, 707–23.

——. "Adolf Hitlers Rede an das deutsche Volk, 22. Juni 1941." Available at http://www. worldfuturefund.org/wffmaster/Reading/Hitler%20Speeches/Hitler%20Rede%20 1941.06.22.htm (accessed 5 April 2014).

——. *Hitler Politisches Testament: Die "Bormann Diktate" vom Februar und April 1945,* ed. Martin Bormann. Hamburg: Albrecht Knaus, 1981.

——. *Hitler's Second Book: The Unpublished Sequel to Mein Kampf,* ed. Gerhard L. Weinberg, trans. Krista Smith. New York: Enigma, 2003.

——. "Hitler's Speech to his Generals, 23 November 1939," IMT, *Trial of the Major War Criminals before the International Military Tribunal, Nuremberg, 14 November 1945–1 October 1946.* Nuremberg, Germany, 1947, XXVI, doc. 789-PS.

——. *Hitler's Table Talk, 1941–1944: His Private Conversations,* ed. H. R. Trevor-Roper, trans. Norman Cameron and R. H. Stevens. New York: Enigma Books, 2000.

——. *Hitlers Tischgespräche im Führerhauptquartier, 1941–42,* ed. Henry Picker. Bonn: Athenäum-Verlag, 1951.

——. *Mein Kampf,* trans. Ralph Mannheim. Boston, MA: Houghton Mifflin, 1971.

——. *Monologe im Führer-Hauptquartier 1941–1944,* ed. Heinrich Heim and Werner Jochmann. Hamburg: A. Knaus, 1980.

——. "Rede am 30. Januar 1939 in Berlin." Available at http://www.worldfuturefund.org/ wffmaster/Reading/Hitler%20Speeches/Hitler%20rede%201939.01.30.htm (accessed 4 May 2014).

——. "Rede am 30. Januar 1942 im Sportpalast in Berlin." Available at http://www.world futurefund.org/wffmaster/Reading/Hitler%20Speeches/Hitler%20Rede%201942.01.30. htm (accessed 21 August 2015).

——. "Rede vor den Spitzen der Reichswehr, 3. Februar 1933," Abschrift des kommunis tischen Nachrichtendienstes, Kopie, BArch RY 5/I 6/10/88, Bl. 20–22. Faksimile. Bundesarchiv (BArch), 2010. Available at: http://1000dok.digitale-sammlungen.de/ dok_0109_hrw.pdf (accessed 29 April 2014).

——. "Text of Speech by Chancellor Adolf Hitler at Berlin Sports Palace, January 30, 1942." Available at http://www.ibiblio.org/pha/policy/1942/420130a.html (accessed 21 January 2016).

——. "The Private and Political Testaments of Hitler, April 29, 1945," Office of United States Chief of Counsel for Prosecution of Axis Criminality, *Nazi Conspiracy and Aggression,* vol. VI (Red Series), Doc. No. 3569-PS. Washington, D.C.: United States Government Printing Office, 1946.

——. *The Testament of Adolf Hitler: The Hitler-Bormann Documents, February–April 1945*, ed. Martin Bormann, trans. Craig L. Fraser. Boring, OR: CPA Book Publisher, 2003.

Horn, Wolfgang. "Ein unbekannter Aufsatz Hitlers aus dem Frühjahr 1924," *Vierteljahrshefte für Zeitgeschichte* 16:3 (1968), 280–94.

Hossbach, Friedrich. *Zwischen Wehrmacht und Hitler, 1934–1938*. Göttingen: Vandenhoeck and Ruprecht, 1965.

Hoth, Hermann. *Panzer-Operationen: Die Panzer-Gruppe 3 und der operative Gedanke der deutschen Führung, Sommer 1941*. Heidelberg: K. Vowinckel, 1956.

Hürter, Johannes, ed. *A German General on the Eastern Front: The Letters and Diaries of Gotthard Heinrici, 1941–1942*, trans. Christine Brocks. Barnsley, South Yorkshire: Pen & Sword, 2014.

——. *Ein deutscher General an der Ostfront. Die Briefe und Tagebücher des Gotthard Heinrici 1941/42*. Erfurt: Sutton Verlag, 2001.

——. 'Es herrschen Sitten und Gebräuche, Genauso wie im 30-jährigen Krieg: Das erst Jahr des deutsch-sowjetischen Krieges in Dokumenten des Generals Gotthard Heinrici,' *Vierteljahrshefte für Zeitgeschichte* 48:2 (2000), 329–403.

Hürter, Johannes, and Matthias Uhl. "Hitler in Vinnica: Ein neues Dokument zur Krise im September 1942," *Vierteljahrshefte für Zeitgeschichte* 63:4 (2015), 581–640.

International Military Tribunal. *Trial of the Major War Criminals before the International Military Tribunal, Nuremberg, 14 November 1945–1 October 1946*. 42 vols. Blue Series. Nuremberg, Germany, 1947.

Jäckel, Eberhard, and Axel Kuhn, eds. *Adolf Hitler: Sämtliche Aufzeichnungen: 1905–1924*. Stuttgart: Deutsche Verlags-Anstalt, 1980.

Joachimsthaler, Anton. *Hitlers Ende: Legenden und Dokumente*. Munich: Herbig, 1995.

Jochmann, Werner, ed. *Adolf Hitler: Monologe im Führerhauptquartier 1941–1944. Die Aufzeichnungen Heinrich Heims*. Hamburg: Knaus, 1980.

Jodl, Alfred. "Jodl's Official Diary, Covering the Period from 4 January 1937 to 25 August 1939." Trial of the Major War Criminals before the International Military Tribunal Nuremberg, 14 November 1945–1 October 1946, vol. 28, Doc. 1780-PS. Nuremberg, 1946.

——. "The Strategic Position in the Beginning of the 5th Year of War." NT, Office of United States Chief of Counsel for Prosecution of Axis Criminality. Nazi Conspiracy and Aggression. Nuremberg, Germany, 1947, VII, doc L-172.

Liddell Hart, B. H., ed. *The German Generals Talk*. New York: W. Morrow, 1948.

——. *The Rommel Papers*. New York: Harcourt Brace, 1953.

Lossberg, Bernhard von. *Im Wehrmachtführungsstab. Bericht eines Generalstabsoffiziers*. Hamburg: H. H. Nölke, 1949.

Ludendorff, Erich. *Der totale Krieg*. Munich: Ludendorffs Verlag, 1935.

Mackinder, Halford John. *Democratic Ideals and Reality: A Study in the Politics of Reconstruction*. New York: H. Holt and Company, 1942.

Manstein, Erich von. *Aus einem Soldatenleben, 1887–1939*. Bonn: Athenäum-Verlag, 1958.

——. *Lost Victories*. Novato, CA: Presidio Press, 1982.

——. *Verlorene Siege*. Bonn: Athenäum Verlag, 1955.

Moltke, Helmuth von. "First Debate on the Bill dealing with the Peace Establishment of the German Army, 14 May 1890," in idem, *Essays, Speeches, and Memoirs of Field-Marshal Count Helmuth von Moltke*, trans. Charles Flint McCumpha, Major C. Barter, and Mary Herms, vol. II. New York: Harper and Brothers, 1893.

Moritz, Erhard, ed. *Fall Barbarossa: Dokumente zur Vorbereitung der faschistischen Wehrmacht auf die Aggression gegen die Sowjetunion (1940/41)*. Berlin: Deutscher Militärverlag, 1970.

Müller, Klaus Jürgen, and Ernst Willi Hansen, eds. *Armee und drittes Reich, 1933–1939: Darstellung und Dokumentation*. Paderborn: Schöningh, 1987.

Müller, Rolf-Dieter, and Gerd R. Ueberschär, eds. *Kriegsende 1945: Die Zerstörung des deutschen Reiches*. Frankfurt: Fischer Taschenbuch Verlag, 1994.

Nietzsche, Friedrich. *Thoughts Out of Season*. Project Gutenberg, E-Book #5652. Available at: http://www.gutenberg.org/ebooks/5652 (accessed 3 July 2015).

Office of United States Chief of Counsel for Prosecution of Axis Criminality. *Nazi Conspiracy and Aggression*. 8 vols. 12 books. Red Series. Washington, D.C.: United States Government Printing Office, 1946.

Phelps, Reginald H. "Dokumente aus der 'Kampfzeit' der NSDAP – 1923," Fortsetzung und Schluss. *Deutsche Rundschau* 84:11 (1958), 1,034–44.

——. "Hitler als Parteiredner im Jahre 1920," *Vierteljahrshefte für Zeitgeschichte* 11:3 (1963), 274–330.

——. "Hitlers 'grundlegende' Rede über den Antisemitismus," *Vierteljahrshefte für Zeitgeschichte* 16:4 (1968), 390–420.

Picker, Henry, ed. *Hitlers Tischgespräche im Führerhauptquartier, 1941–42*. Bonn: Athenäum-Verlag, 1951.

Prüller, Wilhelm. *Diary of a German Soldier*, trans. H. C. Robbins Landon. New York: Coward-McCann, 1963.

Reuth, Ralf-Georg, ed. *Joseph Goebbels: Tagebücher, 1924–1945*. 5 vols. Munich: Piper, 1992.

Schramm, Percy Ernst. *Hitler: The Man and the Military Leader*, trans. Donald S. Detwiler. Chicago, IL: Quadrangle Books, 1971.

——. *Kriegstagebuch des Oberkommandos der Wehrmacht 1940–1945*. 8 vols. Munich: Bernard & Graefe, 1961–5; rpt. 1982.

Schroeder, Christa. *Er War Mein Chef. Aus dem Nachlaß der Sekretärin von Adolf Hitler*, ed. Anton Joachimsthaler. Munich: Langen Müller, 1985.

Schwarte, Max von. *Der Krieg der Zukunft*. Leipzig: Reclam, 1931.

Schwarz, Eberhard. *Die Stabilisierung der Ostfront nach Stalingrad: Mansteins Gegenschlag zwischen Donez und Dnjeper im Frühjahr 1943*. Göttingen: Muster-Schmidt, 1985.

Shirer, William L. *Berlin Diary*. New York: Knopf, 1941.

Solleder, Fridolin. *Vier Jahre Westfront: Geschichte des Regiments List R.J.R. 16*. Munich: Schick, 1932.

Speer, Albert. *Inside the Third Reich: Memoirs*, trans. Richard Winston and Clara Winston. New York: Macmillan, 1970.

Stahlberg, Alexander. *Bounden Duty: The Memoirs of a German Officer, 1932–45*, trans. Patricia Crampton. London: Brassey's, 1990.

Treue, Wilhelm. "Hitlers Denkschrift zum Vierjahresplan 1936," *Vierteljahrshefte für Zeitgeschichte* 3 (1955), 184–210.

——. "Rede Hitlers vor der deutsche Presse (10. November 1938)," *Vierteljahrshefte für Zeitgeschichte* 6 (1958), 175–91.

Trevor-Roper, H. R., ed. *Blitzkrieg to Defeat: Hitler's War Directives, 1939–1945*. New York: Holt, Rinehart and Winston, 1965.

——. *Hitler's Table Talk, 1941–1944: His Private Conversations*, trans. Norman Cameron and R. H. Stevens. New York City: Enigma Books, 2000.

Ueberschär, Gerd R., and Wolfram Wette, eds. *Der deutsche Überfall auf die Sowjetunion, 1941: "Unternehmen Barbarossa." Berichte, Analysen, Dokumente*. Frankfurt: Fischer, 1991.

United States Strategic Bombing Survey, *Oil Division Final Report*, 2nd ed. Washington, D.C.: United States Government Printing Office, January 1947, http://hdl.handle.net/2027/mdp.39015011672485 (permanent link; accessed 20 August 2015).

Vogelsang, Thilo. "Hitlers Brief an Reichenau vom 4. Dezember 1932," *Vierteljahrshefte für Zeitgeschichte* 7:4 (1959), 429–37.

——. "Neue Dokumente zur Geschichte der Reichswehr 1930–33," *Vierteljahrshefte für Zeitgeschichte* 2:4 (1954), 397–436.

Völkischer Beobachter. Munich. 8 April 1927.

Völkischer Beobachter. Munich. 2 August 1933.

Vollnhals, Clemens, ed. *Die Wiedergründung des NSDAP Februar 1925–Juni 1926* (vol. 1 of *Hitler: Reden, Schriften, Anordnungen: Februar 1925 bis Januar 1933*). Munich: K. G. Saur, 1992.

Wagner, Eduard. *Der Generalquartiermeister: Briefe und Tagebuchaufzeichnungen des Generalquartiermeisters des Heeres General der Artillerie Eduard Wagner*, ed. Elisabeth Wagner. Munich: G. Olzog, 1963.

Warlimont, Walter. *Inside Hitler's Headquarters, 1939–45*, trans. R. H. Barry. New York: F. A. Praeger, 1964.

Wirsching, Andreas. "'Man kann nur Boden germanisieren.' Eine neue Quelle zu Hitlers Rede vor den Spitzen der Reichswehr am 3. Februar 1933," *Vierteljahrshefte für Zeitgeschichte* 49:3 (2001), 517–50.

Zhukov, Georgii Konstantinovich. *The Memoirs of Marshal Zhukov*. New York: Delacorte Press, 1971.

Secondary Sources

Armbruster, Jan. "Die Behandlung Adolf Hitlers im Lazarett Pasewalk 1918: Historische Mythenbildung durch einseitige bzw. spekulative Pathographie," *Journal für Neurochirurgie und Psychiatrie* 10:4 (2009), 18–23.

Arnold, Klaus Jochen. "Die Eroberung und Behandlung der Stadt Kiew durch die Wehrmacht im September 1941: Zur Radikalisierung der Besatzungspolitik," *Militärgeschichtliche Mitteilungen* 58:1 (1999), 23–63.

Aron, Raymond. *Clausewitz: Philosopher of War*. New York: Simon and Schuster, 1986.

——. "Reason, Passion and Power in the Thought of Clausewitz," *Social Research* 39:4 (1972), 599–621.

Auerbach, Hellmuth. "Hitlers politische Lehrjahre und die Münchener Gesellschaft 1919– 1923. Versuch einer Bilanz anhand der neueren Forschung," *Vierteljahrshefte für Zeitgeschichte* 25:1 (1977), 1–45.

Bahnemann, Jorg. "Der Begriff der Strategie bei Clausewitz, Moltke und Liddell Hart," *Europaeische Sicherheit: Politik – Streitkraefte – Wirtschaft – Technik* 18:1 (1968), 33–57.

Baldwin, P. M. "Clausewitz in Nazi Germany," *Journal of Contemporary History* 16:1 (1981), 5–26.

Bassford, Christopher. *Clausewitz in English: The Reception of Clausewitz in Britain and America, 1815–1945*. New York: Oxford University Press, 1994.

——. "The Character of War in the Real World," in idem, *Clausewitz and His Works*. Available at: http://www.clausewitz.com/readings/Bassford/Cworks/Works.htm#Categories (accessed 3 January 2014).

Bassin, Mark. "Race contra Space: The Conflict between German Geopolitik and National Socialism," *Political Geography Quarterly* 6:2 (1987), 115–34.

Beevor, Antony. *D-Day: The Battle for Normandy*. New York: Viking, 2009.

——. *Stalingrad. The Fateful Siege: 1942–1943*. London: Penguin, 1998.

——. *The Fall of Berlin 1945*. New York: Viking, 2002.

Bessel, Richard. ed. *Fascist Italy and Nazi Germany: Comparisons and Contrasts*. Cambridge: Cambridge University Press, 1996.

——. *Germany 1945: From War to Peace*. New York: HarperCollins, 2009.

——. "Hatred after War," *History & Memory* 17:1 (2005), 195–216.

——. 'Murder amidst Collapse: Explaining the Violence of the Last Months of the Third Reich,' in *Years of Persecution, Years of Extermination: Saul Friedländer and the Future of Holocaust Studies*, ed. Christian Wiese and Paul Betts. London: Continuum, 2010, 255–68.

——. 'The Shadow of Death in Germany at the End of the Second World War,' in *Between Mass Death and Individual Loss: The Place of the Dead in Twentieth-Century Germany*, ed. Alon Confino, Paul Betts, and Dirk Schumann. New York: Berghahn Books, 2008, 51–68.

Blumenson, Martin. *Breakout and Pursuit*. Washington, D.C.: Office of the Chief of Military History, Department of the Army, 1961.

Blumenson, Martin, and James Hodgson. "Hitler versus his Generals in the West," *U.S. Naval Institute Proceedings* 82:12 (1956), 1,281–7.

Boll, Bernd. "Generalfeldmarschall Walter von Reichenau," in *Hitlers militärische Elite. 68 Lebensläufe*, ed. Gerd R. Ueberschär. Darmstadt: Wissenschaftliche Buchgesellschaft, 2011, 195–202.

Bond, Brian. "Liddell Hart and the German Generals," *Military Affairs* 41:1 (1977), 16–22.

Boog, Horst. "Defending German Skies, Part of the Overall Air War Problem: From Early 1943 to the Invasion in 1944," in *The Strategic Air War in Europe and the War in the West and East Asia, 1943–1944/5* (vol. 7 of *Germany and the Second World War*), ed. Horst Boog, Gerhard Krebs, and Detlef Vogel, trans. Derry Cook-Radmore. Oxford: Clarendon Press, 2006, 159–356.

——. "Die strategische Bomberoffensive der Allierten gegen Deutschland und die Reichsluftverteidigung in der Schlußphase des Krieges," in *Der Zusammenbruch des deutschen Reiches, 1945: Die militärische Niederwerfung der Wehrmacht* (vol. 10/1 of *Das deutsche Reich und der Zweite Weltkrieg*), ed. Rolf-Dieter Müller. Munich: Deutsche Verlags-Anstalt, 2008, 777–884.

——. "German Air Intelligence in the Second World War," *Intelligence and National Security* 5:2 (1990), 350–424.

——. "Luftwaffe and Logistics in the Second World War," *Aerospace Historian* 35:2 (1988), 103–10.

——. "The Strategic Air War in Europe and Air Defense of the Reich," in *The Strategic Air War in Europe and the War in the West and East Asia, 1943–1944/5* (vol. 7 of *Germany and the Second World War*), ed. Horst Boog, Gerhard Krebs, and Detlef Vogel, trans. Derry Cook-Radmore. Oxford: Clarendon Press, 2006, 7–458.

Boog, Horst, Gerhard Krebs, and Detlef Vogel, eds. *Das Deutsche Reich in der Defensive: Strategischer Luftkrieg in Europa, Krieg im Westen und in Ostasien 1943–1944/45* (vol. 7 of *Das Deutsche Reich und der Zweite Weltkrieg*). Stuttgart: Deutsche Verlags-Anstalt, 2001.

——. *Der globale Krieg: Die Ausweitung zum Weltkrieg und der Wechsel der Initiative, 1941–1943* (vol. 6 of *Das Deutsche Reich und der Zweite Weltkrieg*). Stuttgart: Deutsche Verlags-Anstalt, 1990.

——. *The Global War: Widening of the Conflict into a World War and the Shift of the Initiative, 1941–1943* (vol. 6 of *Germany and the Second World War*), trans. Ewald Osers. Oxford: Clarendon, Press, 2001.

Boog, Horst, Jürgen Förster, Joachim Hoffmann, Ernst Klink, Rolf-Dieter Müller, and Gerd R. Ueberschär, eds. *Der Angriff auf die Sowjetunion* (vol. 4 of *Das Deutsche Reich und der Zweite Weltkrieg*). Stuttgart: Deutsche Verlags-Anstalt, 1983.

——. *The Attack on the Soviet Union* (vol. 4 of *Germany and the Second World War*), trans. Dean S. McMurry, Ewald Osers, and Louise Willmot. Oxford: Clarendon Press, 1998.

Bullock, Alan. *Hitler: A Study in Tyranny*. New York: Harper & Row, 1962.

——. "Hitler and the Origins of the Second World War," *Proceedings of the British Academy* 5:3 (1967), 259–87.

——. "Personality in History: Hitler and Stalin," *Modern History Review* 5:2 (1993), 2–6.

Carsten, F. L. "Die Reichswehr und Sowjetrussland 1920–1933," *Österreichische Osthefte* 5:6 (1963), 445–63.

——. "Reports by Two German Officers on the Red Army," *Slavonic & East European Review* 41:96 (1962), 217–44.

——. "The Reichswehr and the Red Army, 1920–1933," *Royal United Services Institute Journal* 108:631 (1963), 248–55.

Churchill, Winston. *The Gathering Storm*. Boston, MA: Houghton Mifflin, 1948.

——. *The World Crisis*. London: Thornton Butterworth, 1931.

Citino, Robert M. "Beyond Fire and Movement: Command, Control and Information in the German Blitzkrieg," *Journal of Strategic Studies* 27:2 (2004), 324–44.

——. *Death of the Wehrmacht: The German Campaigns of 1942*. Lawrence, KS: University Press of Kansas, 2007.

——. *Quest for Decisive Victory: From Stalemate to Blitzkrieg in Europe, 1899–1940*. Lawrence, KS: University Press of Kansas, 2002.

——. *The Evolution of Blitzkrieg Tactics: Germany Defends Itself against Poland, 1918–1933*. Westport, CT: Greenwood Press, 1987.

——. *The German Way of War: From the Thirty Years' War to the Third Reich*. Lawrence, KS: University Press of Kansas, 2005.

——. *The Path to Blitzkrieg: Doctrine and Training in the German Army, 1920–1939*. Boulder, CO: Lynne Rienner, 1999.

——. "The Reichswehr Divisional School: Education for Defeat," *Revue d'Allemagne* 30:2 (1998), 137–54.

——. *The Wehrmacht Retreats: Fighting a Lost War, 1943.* Lawrence, KS: University Press of Kansas, 2012.

Cooke, Ronald C., and Roy Conyers Nesbit. *Target: Hitler's Oil: Allied Attacks on German Oil Supplies, 1939–1945.* London: W. Kimber, 1985.

Corum, James S. "From Biplanes to Blitzkrieg: The Development of German Air Doctrine between the Wars," *War in History* 3:1 (1996), 85–101.

——. "The Development of Strategic Air War Concepts in Interwar Germany, 1919–1939," *Air Power History* 44:4 (1997), 18–35.

——. "The German Campaign in Norway 1940 as a Joint Operation," *Journal of Strategic Studies* 21:4 (1998), 50–77.

——. *The Luftwaffe: Creating the Operational Air War, 1918–1940.* Lawrence, KS: University Press of Kansas, 1997.

——. "The Luftwaffe's Army Support Doctrine, 1918–1941," *Journal of Military History* 59:1 (1995), 53–76.

——. *The Roots of Blitzkrieg: Hans von Seeckt and German Military Reform between the World Wars.* Lawrence, KS: University Press of Kansas, 1992.

Corum, James S., and Richard R. Muller. *The Luftwaffe's Way of War: German Air Force Doctrine, 1911–1945.* Mt. Pleasant, SC: Nautical & Aviation Publishing Company of America, 1998.

Creveld, Martin van. "Die deutsche Wehrmacht: Eine militärische Beurteilung," in *Die Wehrmacht: Mythos und Realität,* ed. Rolf-Dieter Müller and Hans-Erich Volkmann, 331–45. Munich: Oldenbourg, 1999.

——. *Fighting Power: German and US Army Performance, 1939–1945.* Westport, CT: Greenwood Press, 1982.

——. "In the Shadow of Barbarossa: Germany and Albania, January–March 1941," *Journal of Contemporary History* 7:3–4 (1972), 221–30.

——. "On Learning from the 'Wehrmacht' and Other Things," *Military Review* 68:1 (1988), 62–71.

——. "Rommel's Supply Problem, 1941–42," *Journal of the Royal United Services Institute for Defence Studies* 119:3 (1974), 67–73.

——. *Supplying War: Logistics from Wallenstein to Patton.* Cambridge: Cambridge University Press, 2004.

——. "The German Attack on the U.S.S.R.: The Destruction of a Legend," *European Studies Review* 2:1 (1972), 69–86.

——. "25 October 1940: A Historical Puzzle," *Journal of Contemporary History* 6:3 (1971), 87–96.

——. "War Lord Hitler: Some Points Reconsidered," *European Studies Review* 4:1 (1974), 57–79.

Crim, Brian E.. "'Our Most Serious Enemy': The Specter of Judeo-Bolshevism in the German Military Community, 1914–1923," *Central European History* 44:4 (2011), 624–41.

Deist, Wilhelm. "Die Reichswehr und der Krieg der Zukunft," *Militärgeschichtliche Zeitschrift* 1:5 (1989), 81–92.

——. *The German Military in the Age of Total War.* Leamington Spa: Berg, 1985.

——. "The Rearmament of the Individual Services, 1933–1939," in *The Build-Up of German Aggression* (vol. 1 of *Germany and the Second World War*), ed. Wilhelm Deist, Manfred Messerschmidt, Hans-Erich Volkmann, and Wolfram Wette, trans. P.S. Falla, Dean S. McMurry, and Ewald Osers, Oxford: Clarendon Press, 1990, 405–504.

——. "The Rearmament of the Wehrmacht," in *The Build-Up of German Aggression* (vol. 1 of *Germany and the Second World War*), ed. Wilhelm Deist, Manfred Messerschmidt, Hans-Erich Volkmann, and Wolfram Wette, trans. P.S. Falla, Dean S. McMurry, and Ewald Osers. Oxford: Clarendon Press, 1990, 375–540.

——. "The Road to Ideological War: Germany 1918–1945," in *The Making of Strategy: Rulers, States, and War,* ed. Williamson Murray, MacGregor Knox, and Alvin Bernstein. Cambridge: Cambridge University Press, 1994, 352–92.

——. "Zum Problem der Deutschen Aufrüstung 1933–1936," *Francia* 5 (1977), 538–65.

Deist, Wilhelm, Manfred Messerschmidt, Hans-Erich Volkmann, and Wolfram Wette, eds. *The Build-Up of German Aggression* (vol. 1 of *Germany and the Second World War*), trans. P. S. Falla, Dean S. McMurry, and Ewald Osers. Oxford: Clarendon Press, 1990.

—— *Ursachen und Vorausetzungen der Deutschen Kriegspolitik* (vol. 1 of *Das Deutsche Reich und der Zweite Weltkrieg*). Stuttgart: Deutsche Verlags-Anstalt, 1979.

DeWeerd, H. A. "Hitler's Plans for Invading Britain," *Military Affairs* 12:3 (1948), 142–8.

DiNardo, R. L. "German Armour Doctrine: Correcting the Myths," *War in History* 3:4 (1996), 384–97.

——. *Mechanized Juggernaut or Military Anachronism? Horses and the German Army of World War II*. Westport, CT: Greenwood Press, 1991.

Diner, Dan. "'Grundbuch des Planeten.' Zur Geopolitik Karl Haushofers," *Vierteljahrshefte für Zeitgeschichte* 32:1 (1984), 1–28.

——. 'Knowledge of Expansion: On the Geopolitics of Karl Haushofer," in *Beyond the Conceivable: Studies in Nazi Germany, Nazism, and the Holocaust*, ed. Dan Diner. Berkeley, CA: University of California Press, 2000, 26–48.

Doenitz, Karl. "Die Schlacht im Atlantik in der Deutschen Strategie des Zweiten Weltkrieges," *Marine-Rundschau* 61:2 (1964), 63–76.

Dülffer, Jost. "Aufrüstung zur Weltmacht. Die Deutsche Marinepolitik 1919/30–1941," *Revue Internationale d'Histoire Militaire* 73 (1991), 101–18.

Dupuy, Trevor N., David L. Bongard, and Richard C. Anderson. *Hitler's Last Gamble: The Battle of the Bulge, December 1944–January 1945*. New York: HarperCollins, 1994.

Eberle, Henrik. *Hitlers Weltkriege: Wie der Gefreite zum Feldherrn wurde*. Hamburg: Hoffmann and Campe, 2014.

Echevarria II, Antulio J. "Borrowing from the Master: Uses of Clausewitz in German Military Literature before the Great War," *War in History* 3:3 (1996), 274–92.

——. "Moltke and the German Military Tradition: His Theories and Legacies," *Parameters: U.S. Army War College* 26:1 (1996), 91–9.

——. "On the Brink of the Abyss: The Warrior Identity and German Military Thought before the Great War," *War & Society* 13:2 (1995), 23–40.

——. "The 'Cult of the Offensive' Revisited: Confronting Technological Change before the Great War," *Journal of Strategic Studies* 25:1 (2002), 199–214.

Eichholtz, Dietrich. *War for Oil: The Nazi Quest for an Oil Empire*, trans. John Broadwin. Washington, D.C.: Potomac Books, 2012.

Fanning Jr., William J. "The Origin of the Term 'Blitzkrieg': Another View," *Journal of Military History* 61:2 (1997), 283–302.

Ferguson, Niall. *The Pity of War*. New York: Basic Books, 1999.

——. *The War of the World: Twentieth-Century Conflict and the Descent of the West*. New York: Penguin Books, 2007.

Fest, Joachim. "Hitlers Krieg," *Vierteljahrshefte für Zeitgeschichte* 38:3 (1990), 359–73.

——. "On Remembering Adolf Hitler," *Encounter* 41:4 (1973), 19–34.

——. *Plotting Hitler's Death: The Story of the German Resistance*, trans. Bruce Little. New York: Metropolitan Books, 1996.

Fischer, Johannes. "Über den Entschluss zur Luftversorgung Stalingrads. Ein Beitrag zur Militärischen Führung im Dritten Reich," *Militärgeschichtliche Mitteilungen* 2 (1969), 7–68.

Fischer, Klaus P. *Hitler and America*. Philadelphia, PA: University of Pennsylvania Press, 2011.

Fleischhauer, Ingeborg. *Die Chance des Sonderfriedens. Deutsch-Sowjetische Geheimgespräche 1941–1945*. Berlin: Siedler, 1986.

Foerster, Roland G., ed. *Gezeitenwechsel im Zweiten Weltkrieg? Die Schlachten von Char'Kov und Kursk in operativer Anlage, Verlauf und politischer Bedeutung*. Hamburg: E. S. Mittler, 1996.

Foerster, Roland G., Karl-Heinz Frieser, and Günter Roth. *Operational Thinking in Clausewitz, Moltke, Schlieffen and Manstein*. Bonn: Verlag E. S. Mittler & Sohn, 1989.

Förster, Jürgen. "Barbarossa Revisited: Strategy and Ideology in the East," *Jewish Social Studies* 50:1 (1988), 21–36.

——. "Das Verhältnis von Wehrmacht und Nationalsozialismus im Entscheidungsjahr 1933," *German Studies Review* 18:3 (1995), 471–80.

——. "Der historische Ort des Unternehmens Barbarossa," in *Der Zweite Weltkrieg: Analysen, Grundzüge, Forschungsbilanz*, ed. Wolfgang Michalka. Munich: Piper, 1989, 626–40.

——. "Hitler's Decision in Favour of War against the Soviet Union," in *The Attack on the Soviet Union* (vol. 4 of *Germany and the Second World War*), ed. Horst Boog, Jürgen Förster, Joachim Hoffmann, Ernst Klink, Rolf-Dieter Müller, and Gerd R. Ueberschär, trans. Dean S. McMurry, Ewald Osers, and Louise Willmot. Oxford: Clarendon Press, 1998, 13–51.

——. "Hitler Turns East – German War Policy in 1940 and 1941," in *From Peace to War: Germany, Soviet Russia, and the World, 1939–1941*, ed. Bernd Wegner. Providence, R.I.: Berghahn, 1997, 115–33.

——. "Ludendorff and Hitler in Perspective: The Battle for the German Soldier's Mind, 1917–1944," *War in History* 10:3 (2003), 321–34.

——. "The Dynamics of Volksgemeinschaft: The Effectiveness of the German Military in the Second World War," in *Military Effectiveness* (3 vols.), ed. Allan R. Millett and Williamson Murray, vol. 3. London: Unwin Hyman, 1988, 180–220.

Förster, Stig. "Facing 'People's War': Moltke the Elder and Germany's Military Options after 1871," *Journal of Strategic Studies* 10:2 (1987), 209–30.

Friedrich, Jörg. *The Fire: The Bombing of Germany, 1940–1945*, trans. Allison Brown. New York: Columbia University Press, 2006.

Frieser, Karl-Heinz, ed. "Der Rückschlag des Pendels: Das Zurückweichen der Ostfront von Sommer 1943 bis Sommer 1944," in *Die Ostfront, 1943/44: Der Krieg im Osten und an den Nebenfronten* (vol. 8 of *Das deutsche Reich und der Zweite Weltkrieg*). Munich: Deutsche Verlags-Anstalt, 2007, 177–450.

——. "Der Zusammenbruch im Osten: Die Rückzugskämpfe seit Sommer 1944," in *Die Ostfront, 1943/44: Der Krieg im Osten und an den Nebenfronten* (vol. 8 of *Das deutsche Reich und der Zweite Weltkrieg*). Munich: Deutsche Verlags-Anstalt, 2007, 493–678.

——. "Die deutschen Blitzkriege: Operativer Triumph – strategische Tragödie," in *Die Wehrmacht: Mythos und Realität*, ed. Rolf-Dieter Müller and Hans-Erich Volkmann. Munich: Oldenbourg, 1999, 182–96.

——. *Die Ostfront, 1943/44: Der Krieg im Osten und an den Nebenfronten* (vol. 8 of *Das deutsche Reich und der Zweite Weltkrieg*). Munich: Deutsche Verlags-Anstalt, 2007.

——. "Die Schlacht im Kursker Bogen," in *Die Ostfront, 1943/44: Der Krieg im Osten und an den Nebenfronten* (vol. 8 of *Das deutsche Reich und der Zweite Weltkrieg*). Munich: Deutsche Verlags-Anstalt, 2007, 83–208.

——. "Die Schlacht um die Seelower Höhen im April 1945," in *Seelower Höhen, 1945*, ed. Roland G. Foerster. Hamburg: E. S. Mittler, 1998, 128–43.

——. "Schlagen aus der Nachhand – Schlagen aus der Vorhand: Die Schlachten von Charkow und Kursk 1943," in *Gezeitenwechsel im Zweiten Weltkrieg? Die Schlachten von Char'kov und Kursk im Frühjahr und Sommer 1943 in operativer Anlage, Verlauf und politischer Bedeutung*, ed. Roland G. Foerster. Hamburg: E. S. Mittler, 1996, 101–35.

——. *The Blitzkrieg Legend: The 1940 Campaign in the West*, trans. John T. Greenwood. Annapolis, MD: Naval Institute Press, 2005.

Fritz, Stephen G. *Endkampf: Soldiers, Civilians, and the Death of the Third Reich*. Lexington, KY: University Press of Kentucky, 2004.

——. *Frontsoldaten: The German Soldier in World War II*. Lexington, KY: University Press of Kentucky, 1995.

——. *Hitlers Frontsoldaten: Der erzählte Krieg*, trans. Klaus Kochman. Berlin: Henschel, 1998.

——. *Ostkrieg: Hitler's War of Extermination in the East*. Lexington, KY: University Press of Kentucky, 2011.

——. "'This is the way wars end, with a bang not a whimper': Middle Franconia in April 1945," *War & Society* 18:2 (2000), 121–53.

——. "'We are trying . . . to change the face of the world': Ideology and Motivation in the Wehrmacht on the Eastern Front. The View from Below," *Journal of Military History* 60:4 (1996), 683–710.

Fugate, Bryan I. *Operation Barbarossa: Strategy and Tactics on the Eastern Front*. Novato, CA: Presidio Press, 1984.

Gat, Azar. "British Influence and the Evolution of the Panzer Arm: Myth or Reality?," *War in History* 4:2 (1997), 150–73.

——. "The Hidden Sources of Liddell Hart's Strategic Ideas," *War in History* 3:3 (1996), 293–308.

Gerwarth, Robert, and Stephan Malinowski. "Der Holocaust als 'kolonialer Genozid'? Europäische Kolonialgewalt und nationalsozialistischer Vernichtungskrieg," *Geschichte und Gesellschaft* 33 (2007), 439–66.

Geyer, Michael. *Aufrüstung oder Sicherheit: Die Reichswehr in der Krise der Machtpolitik 1924–1936.* Wiesbaden: Steiner, 1980.

——. "Das zweite Rüstungsprogramm (1930–1934)," *Militärgeschichtliche Zeitschrift* 17 (1975), 125–72.

——. "Endkampf 1918 and 1945: German Nationalism, Annihilation, and Self-Destruction," in *No Man's Land of Violence: Extreme Wars in the 20th Century*, ed. Alf Lüdtke and Bernd Weisbrod. Göttingen: Wallstein, 2006, 37–67.

——. "German Strategy in the Age of Machine Warfare, 1914–1945," in *Makers of Modern Strategy*, ed. Peter Paret. Princeton, NJ: Princeton University Press, 1996, 527–97.

——. "How the Germans Learned to Wage War: On the Question of Killing in the First and Second World Wars," in *Between Mass Death and Individual Loss: The Place of the Dead in Twentieth-Century Germany*, ed. Alon Confino, Paul Betts, and Dirk Schumann. New York and Oxford: Berghahn Books, 2008, 25–50.

——. "Insurrectionary Warfare: The German Debate about a Levee en Masse in October 1918," *Journal of Modern History* 73:3 (2001), 459.

——. "Restorative Elites, German Society, and the Nazi Pursuit of War," in *Fascist Italy and Nazi Germany: Comparisons and Contrasts*, ed. Richard Bessel. Cambridge: Cambridge University Press, 1996, 134–64.

——. "The Dynamics of Military Revisionism in the Interwar Years," in *The German Military in the Age of Total War*, ed. Wilhelm Deist. Leamington Spa: Berg, 1985, 100–49.

——. "Vom Massenhaften Tötungshandeln, oder: Wie die deutschen das Krieg-machen lernten," in *Massenhaftes Töten: Kriege und Genozid im 20. Jahrhundert*, ed. Peter Gleichmann and Thomas Kühne. Essen: Klartext, 2004, 105–42.

Glantz, David M. *Barbarossa: Hitler's Invasion of Russia.* Stroud, Gloucestershire: Tempus Publishing, 2001.

——. "Prelude to German Operation Blau: Military Operations on Germany's Eastern Front, April–June 1942," *Journal of Slavic Military Studies* 20:2 (2007), 171–234.

——. *To the Gates of Stalingrad: Soviet-German Combat Operations, April–August 1942.* Lawrence, KS: University Press of Kansas, 2009.

Glantz, David M., and Jonathan M. House. *The Battle of Kursk.* Lawrence, KS: University Press of Kansas, 1999.

——. *When Titans Clashed: How the Red Army Stopped Hitler.* Lawrence, KS: University Press of Kansas, 1995.

Goda, Norman J. W. "Black Marks: Hitler's Bribery of His Senior Officers during World War II," *Journal of Modern History* 72:2 (2000), 413–52.

——. "Franco's Bid for Empire: Spain, Germany, and the Western Mediterranean in World War II," *Mediterranean Historical Review* 13:1–2 (1998), 168–94.

——. "The Riddle of the Rock: A Reassessment of German Motives for the Capture of Gibraltar in the Second World War," *Journal of Contemporary History* 28:2 (1993), 297–314.

——. *Tomorrow the World: Hitler, Northwest Africa, and the Path Toward America.* College Station, TX: Texas A&M University Press, 1998.

Grier, Howard D. *Hitler, Dönitz, and the Baltic Sea: The Third Reich's Last Hope, 1944–1945.* Annapolis, MD: Naval Institute Press, 2007.

Groehler, Olaf. "Die Wehrmachtstudie 1936/37," *Revue Internationale d'Histoire Militaire* 71 (1989), 207–25.

——. "Goals and Reason: Hitler and the German Military," in *Operation Barbarossa: The German Attack on the Soviet Union. June 22, 1941*, ed. Joseph L. Wieczynski. Salt Lake City, UT: Charles Schlacks, Jr., 1993, 48–61.

——. "Ziele und Vernunft: Hitler und die Deutschen Militars," *Soviet and Post-Soviet Review* 18:1–3 (1991), 59–77.

Groß, Gerhard P. "Das Dogma der Beweglichkeit: Überlegungen zur Genese der deutschen Heerestaktik im Zeitalter der Weltkrieg," in *Erster Weltkrieg, Zweiter Weltkrieg: Ein Vergleich*, ed. Bruno Thoß and Hans-Erich Volkmann. Paderborn: Schöningh, 2002, 143–66.

——. "Development of Operational Thinking in the German Army in the World War Era," *Journal of Military and Strategic Studies* 13:4 (2011), 1–13.

Gruchmann, Lothar. 1970. "Die 'verpassten strategischen Chancen' der Achsenmächte im Mittelmeerraum 1940/41," *Vierteljahrshefte für Zeitgeschichte* 18:4 (1970), 456–75.

Guettel, Jens-Uwe. "The US Frontier as Rationale for the Nazi East? Settler Colonialism and Genocide in Nazi-Occupied Eastern Europe and the American West," *Journal of Genocide Research* 15:4 (2013), 401–19.

Harris, J. P. "British Military Intelligence and the Rise of German Mechanized Forces, 1929–40," *Intelligence & National Security* 6:2 (1991), 395–417.

——. *Men, Ideas, and Tanks: British Military Thought and Armoured Forces 1903–1939*. Manchester: Manchester University Press, 1995.

——. "The Myth of Blitzkrieg," *War in History* 2:3 (1995), 335–52.

Harrison, Mark. "'Barbarossa': The Soviet Response, 1941," in *From Peace to War: Germany, Soviet Russia and the World, 1939–1941*, ed. Bernd Wegner. Providence, R.I.: Berghahn Books, 1997, 431–8.

——. *Soviet Planning in Peace and War*. Cambridge: Cambridge University Press, 2002.

——. "The USSR and Total War: Why Didn't the Soviet Economy Collapse in 1942?," in *A World at Total War: Global Conflict and the Politics of Destruction, 1937–1945*, ed. Roger Chickering and Stig Förster. Cambridge: Cambridge University Press, 2005, 137–56.

Hartmann, Christian. *Der deutsche Krieg im Osten 1941–1944: Facetten einer Grenzüberschreitung*. Munich: Oldenbourg. 2009.

——. *Halder. Generalstabschef Hitlers 1938–1942*. Paderborn: Schöningh, 1991.

——. *Operation Barbarossa: Nazi Germany's War in the East, 1941–1945*. Oxford: Oxford University Press, 2013.

——. *Von Feldherren und Gefreiten: Zur biographischen Dimension des zweiten Weltkriegs*. Munich: Oldenbourg, 2008.

——. *Wehrmacht im Ostkrieg: Front und Militärisches Hinterland 1941–42*. Munich: Oldenbourg, 2009.

Hastings, Max. *Overlord: D-Day and the Battle for Normandy*. New York: Simon and Schuster, 1984.

Haupt, Werner. *Die Schlachten der Heeresgruppe Mitte 1941–1944*. Dorheim: Podzun-Pallas Verlag, 1983.

Hayward, Joel. "A Case Study in Early Joint Warfare: An Analysis of the 'Wehrmacht's' Crimean Campaign of 1942," *Journal of Strategic Studies* 22:4 (1999), 103–30.

——. "Hitler's Quest for Oil: The Impact of Economic Considerations on Military Strategy, 1941–42," *Journal of Strategic Studies* 18:4 (1995), 94–135.

——. "Stalingrad: An Examination of Hitler's Decision to Airlift," *Airpower Journal* 11 (Spring 1997), 21–37.

——. *Stopped at Stalingrad: The Luftwaffe and Hitler's Defeat in the East, 1942–1943*. Lawrence, KS: University Press of Kansas, 1998.

——. "Too Little, Too Late: An Analysis of Hitler's Failure in August 1942 to Damage Soviet Oil Production," *Journal of Military History* 64:3 (2000), 769–94.

——. "Von Richthofen's 'Giant Fire-Magic': The 'Luftwaffe's' Contribution to the Battle of Kerch, 1942," *Journal of Slavic Military Studies* 10:2 (1997), 97–124.

Herbert, Ulrich. "Was haben die Nationalsozialisten aus dem Ersten Weltkrieg gelernt?," in *Nationalsozialismus und Erster Weltkrieg*, ed. Gerd Krumeich. Essen: Klartext, 2010, 21–32.

Herwig, Holger H. "Geopolitik: Haushofer, Hitler and Lebensraum," *Journal of Strategic Studies* 22:2 (1999), 218–41.

——. *The Daemon of Geopolitics: How Karl Haushofer "Educated" Hitler and Hess*. Lanham, MD: Rowman & Littlefield, 2016.

———. "The Daemon of Geopolitics: Karl Haushofer, Rudolf Hess and Adolf Hitler." Paper presented at the Harmon Memorial Lectures in Military History, United States Air Force Academy, 2010.

Hillgruber, Andreas. "Das Rußland-Bild der führenden deutschen Militärs vor Beginn des Angriffs auf die Sowjetunion," in *Zwei Wege nach Moskau: Vom Hitler-Stalin-Pakt bis Zum "Unternehmen Barbaross"*, ed. Bernd Wegner. Munich: Piper, 1991, 167–84.

———. "Der Hitler-Stalin-Pakt und die Entfesselung des Zweiten Weltkrieges: Situationsanalyse und Machtkalkül der Beiden Paktpartner," *Historische Zeitschrift* 230:2 (1980), 339–61.

———. "Der Zenit des Zweiten Weltkrieges–Juli 1941," in *Die Zerstörung Europas. Beiträge zur Weltkriegsepoche 1914 bis 1945*, ed. Andreas Hillgruber. Frankfurt am Main: Propyläen, 1988, 273–95.

———. "Die Bedeutung der Schlacht von Smolensk in der Zweiten Julihälfte 1941 für den Ausgang des Ostkrieges," in *Die Zerstörung Europas. Beiträge zur Weltkriegsepoche 1914 bis 1945*, ed. Andreas Hillgruber. Frankfurt am Main: Propyläen, 1988, 296–312.

———. "Die Faktor Amerika in Hitlers Strategie 1938–1941," *Aus Politik und Zeitgeschichte* 19:66 (11 May 1966), 3–21.

———. "England in Hitlers Aussenpolitischer Konzeption," *Historische Zeitschrift* 218:1 (1974), 65–84.

———. "England's Place in Hitler's Plans for World Domination," *Journal of Contemporary History* 9:1 (1974), 5–22.

———. "Grundzüge der Nationalsozialistischen Aussenpolitik 1933–45," *Saeculum* 24:4 (1973), 328–45.

———. "Japan und der Fall 'Barbarossa'", *Wehrwissenschaftliche Rundschau* 18:6 (1968), 312–36.

———. "Noch Einmal: Hitlers Wendung gegen die Sowjetunion 1940," *Geschichte in Wissenschaft und Unterricht* 33:4 (1982), 214–26.

———. "The German Military Leaders' View of Russia Prior to the Attack on the Soviet Union," in *From Peace to War: Germany, Soviet Russia and the World, 1939–1941*, ed. Bernd Wegner, 169–85. Providence, R.I.: Berghahn Books, 1997.

Hirschfeld, Gerhard. "Der Führer spricht vom Krieg: Die Erste Weltkrieg in den Reden Adolf Hitlers," in *Nationalsozialismus und Erster Weltkrieg*, ed. Gerd Krumeich. Essen: Klartext, 2010, 35–51.

Hoffmann, Joachim. "Die Sowjetunion bis zum Vorabend des deutschen Angriffs," in *Der Angriff auf die Sowjetunion* (vol. 4 of *Das deutsche Reich und der zweite Weltkrieg*), ed. Horst Boog, Jürgen Förster, Joachim Hoffmann, Ernst Klink, Rolf-Dieter Müller, and Gerd R. Ueberschär. Frankfurt: Fischer Taschenbuch Verlag, 1991, 69–140.

———. "The Conduct of the War through Soviet Eyes," in *The Attack on the Soviet Union* (vol. 4 of *Germany and the Second World War*), ed. Horst Boog, Jürgen Förster, Joachim Hoffmann, Ernst Klink, Rolf-Dieter Müller, and Gerd R. Ueberschär, trans. Dean S. McMurry, Ewald Osers, and Louise Willmot. Oxford: Clarendon Press, 1998, 833–940.

———. "The Soviet Union's Offensive Preparations in 1941," in *From Peace to War: Germany, Soviet Russia and the World, 1939–1941*, ed. Bernd Wegner. Providence, R.I.: Berghahn Books, 1999, 361–80.

Honig, Jan. "The Idea of Total War: From Clausewitz to Ludendorff," in *The Pacific War as Total War: 2011 International Forum on War History: Proceedings: September 14, 2011*. Tokyo: National Institute for Defence Studies, 2012, 29–41.

Housden, Martyn. "Hitler: A Weak Dictator?," *Modern History Review* 14:3 (2002), 11–20.

———. "Lebensraum: Policy or Rhetoric?," *History Today* 51:11 (2001), 23–6.

Hümmelchen, Gerhard. "Generaloberst Hans Jeschonnek," in *Hitlers militärische Elite. 68 Lebensläufe*, ed. Gerd R. Ueberschär. Darmstadt: Wissenschaftliche Buchgesellschaft, 2011, 97–101.

Hürter, Johannes. "Die Wehrmacht vor Leningrad: Krieg und Besatzungspolitik der 18. Armee im Herbst und Winter 1941–1942," *Vierteljahrshefte für Zeitgeschichte* 49:3 (2001), 377–440.

———. "Hitlers Generäle und der Erste Weltkrieg," in *Nationalsozialismus und Erster Weltkrieg*, ed. Gerd Krumeich. Essen: Klartext, 2010, 261–9.

——. *Hitlers Heerführer: Die deutschen Oberbefehlshaber im Krieg gegen die Sowjetunion 1941/42.* Munich: Oldenbourg, 2006.

——. "Konservative Akteure oder totale Krieger? Zum Transformationsprozess einer militärische Elite," in *Verbrechen der Wehrmacht. Bilanz einer Debatte,* ed. Christian Hartmann, Johannes Hürter, and Ulrike Jureit. Munich: Beck, 2005, 50–9.

——. "Kriegserfahrung als Schlüsselerlebnis? Der erste Weltkrieg in der Biographie von Wehrmachtsgeneralen," in *Erster Weltkrieg – Zweiter Weltkrieg. Ein Vergleich,* ed. Bruno Thoß and Hans-Erich Volkmann. Paderborn: Schoningh, 2002, 759–71.

——. "The Military Elite and Volksgemeinschaft," in *Visions of Community in Nazi Germany,* ed. Martina Steber and Bernhard Gotto. Oxford: Oxford University Press, 2014, 257–69.

Jablonsky, David. "Strategy and the Operational Level of War: Part I," *Parameters: U.S. Army War College* 17:1 (1987), 65–76.

——. "The Paradox of Duality: Adolf Hitler and the Concept of Military Surprise," *Intelligence & National Security* 3:3 (1988), 55–117.

Jäckel, Eberhard. *Hitler in History.* Hanover, NH: Brandeis University Press, 1984.

——. *Hitlers Herrschaft: Vollzug einer Weltanschauung.* Stuttgart: Deutsche Verlags-Anstalt, 1986.

Jacobsen, Hans-Adolf. "Kampf um Lebensraum. Zur rolle des Geopolitikers Karl Haushofer im Dritten Reich," *German Studies Review* 4:1 (1981), 79–104.

——. "Motorisierungsprobleme im Winter 1939/40," *Europaeische Sicherheit: Politik – Streitkraefte – Wirtschaft – Technik* 6:9 (1956), 497–518.

——. "Winter 1939–1940: Hitlers Gedanken zur Kriegführung im Westen," *Europaeische Sicherheit: Politik – Streitkraefte – Wirtschaft – Technik* 5:10 (1955), 433–46.

Jersak, Tobias. "Blitzkrieg Revisited: A New Look at Nazi War and Extermination Planning," *Historical Journal* 43:2 (2000), 565–82.

——. "Die Interaktion von Kriegsverlauf und Judenvernichtung: Ein Blick auf Hitlers Strategie im Spätsommer 1941," *Historische Zeitschrift* 268:2 (1999), 311–74.

Jukes, Geoffrey. "Ahead at Half-Time? Hitler's Generals," *NU Historical Journal* 13 (1977), 61–7.

Keegan, John. *The Second World War.* New York: Viking, 1990.

Kellogg, Michael. *The Russian Roots of Nazism: White Emigrés and the Making of National Socialism, 1917–1945.* New York: Cambridge University Press, 2005.

Kershaw, Ian. *Fateful Choices: Ten Decisions that Changed the World, 1940–1941.* New York and London: Penguin, 2007.

——. "Hitler and the Uniqueness of Nazism," *Journal of Contemporary History* 39:2 (2004), 239–54.

——. *Hitler, 1889–1936: Hubris.* New York: Norton, 1999.

——. *Hitler, 1936–1945: Nemesis.* New York: Norton, 2000.

——. "Hitler's Role in the 'Final Solution,'" *Yad Vashem Studies* 34 (2006), 7–43.

——. "Ideologue and Propagandist: Hitler in Light of His Speeches, Writings and Orders, 1925–1928," *Yad Vashem Studies* 23 (1993), 321–34.

——. "Ideologe und Propagandist. Hitler im Lichte seiner Reden, Schriften und Anordnungen 1925–1928," *Vierteljahrshefte für Zeitgeschichte* 40:2 (1992), 263–71.

——. *The End: The Defiance and Destruction of Hitler's Germany, 1944–1945.* New York: Penguin Press, 2011.

——. *The "Hitler Myth": Image and Reality in the Third Reich.* New York and Oxford: Oxford University Press, 1987.

——. "War and Political Violence in Twentieth-Century Europe," *Contemporary European History* 14:1 (2005), 107–23.

——. "Working towards the Führer: Reflections on the Nature of the Hitler Dictatorship," *Contemporary European History* 2:2 (1993), 103–18.

Kershaw, Robert J. *War without Garlands: Operation Barbarossa 1941/42.* Rockville Centre, NY: Sarpedon, 2000.

Killiani, Emanuel. "1914 und 1939: Die Einstellung der obersten Führungsschicht des deutschen Heeres zum Ausbruch beider Kriege (II)," *Wehrkunde: Organ der Gesellschaft für Wehrkunde* 13:12 (1964), 638–44.

Kipp, Jacob. "Barbarossa and the Crisis of Successive Operations: The Smolensk Engagements, July 10–August 7, 1941," *Soviet & Post-Soviet Review* 19:1 (1992), 91–136.

Kitchen, Martin. "Hindenburg, Ludendorff and the Baltic," *East European Quarterly* 11:4 (1977), 429–44.

——. "The Political History of Clausewitz," *Journal of Strategic Studies* 11:1 (1988), 27–50.

——. 'The Traditions of German Strategic Thought,' *The International History Review* 1:2 (April 1979), 163–90.

Klink, Ernst. *Das Gesetz des Handelns. Die Operation "Zitadelle" 1943*. Stuttgart: Deutsche Verlags-Anstalt, 1966.

——. "The Conduct of Operations," in *The Attack on the Soviet Union* (vol. 4 of *Germany and the Second World War*), ed. Horst Boog, Jürgen Förster, Joachim Hoffmann, Ernst Klink, Rolf-Dieter Müller, and Gerd R. Ueberschär, trans. Dean S. McMurry, Ewald Osers, and Louise Willmot, 525–762. Oxford: Clarendon Press, 1998.

——. "The Military Concept of the War Against the Soviet Union," in *The Attack on the Soviet Union* (vol. 4 of *Germany and the Second World War*), ed. Horst Boog, Jürgen Förster, Joachim Hoffmann, Ernst Klink, Rolf-Dieter Müller, and Gerd R. Ueberschär, trans. Dean S. McMurry, Ewald Osers, and Louise Willmot. Oxford: Clarendon Press, 1998, 225–385.

Kluke, Paul. "Deutschland und seine Mitteleuropapolitik," *Bohemia* 6 (1965), 373–89.

——. "Die Beziehungen Deutschlands zu den Nordischen Ländern 1933–1945," *Internationales Jahrbuch für Geschichtsunterricht* 8 (1961), 252–60.

——. "Nationalsozialistische Europaideologie," *Vierteljahrshefte für Zeitgeschichte* 3:3 (1955), 240–75.

Knjazkov, Anatolij S. "Die sowjetische Strategie im Jahre 1942," in *Stalingrad: Ereignis – Wirkung – Symbol*, ed. Jüren Förster. Munich: Piper, 1992, 39–51.

Knox, MacGregor. "1 October 1942: Adolf Hitler, Wehrmacht Officer Policy, and Social Revolution," *Historical Journal* 43:3 (2000), 801.

Koch, H. W. "Hitler and the Origins of the Second World War: Second Thoughts on the Status of Some of the Documents," *Historical Journal* 11:1 (1968), 125–43.

——. "Hitler's 'Programme' and the Genesis of Operation 'Barbarossa,'" *Historical Journal* 26:4 (1983), 891–920.

——. "Operation Barbarossa – the Current State of the Debate," *Historical Journal* 31:2 (1988), 377–90.

——. "The Spectre of a Separate Peace in the East: Russo-German 'Peace Feelers', 1942–1944," *Journal of Contemporary History* 10:3 (1975), 531–49.

Koenen, Gerd. "Hitlers Russland. Ambivalenzen im deutschen 'Drang nach Osten,'" *Kommune. Forum Für Politik, Ökonomie, Kultur* 1 (2003), 1–32.

Kroener, Bernhard. "Squaring the Circle: Blitzkrieg Strategy and Manpower Shortage, 1939–1942," in *The German Military in the Age of Total War*, ed. Wilhelm Deist. Leamington Spa: Berg, 1985, 282–303.

Kroener, Bernhard R., Rolf-Dieter Müller, and Hans Umbreit, eds. *Organisation und Mobilisierung des Deutschen Machtbereichs: Kriegsverwaltung, Wirtschaft und Personelle Ressourcen 1939–1941* (vol. 5/1 of *Das Deutsche Reich und der Zweite Weltkrieg*). Stuttgart: Deutsche Verlags-Anstalt, 1988.

——. *Organisation und Mobilisierung des Deutschen Machtbereichs: Kriegsverwaltung, Wirtschaft und Personelle Ressouren 1942–1945* (vol. 5/2 of *Das Deutsche Reich und der Zweite Weltkrieg*). Stuttgart: Deutsche Verlags-Anstalt, 1999.

——. *Organization and Mobilization of the German Sphere of Power. 1: Wartime Administration, Economy, and Manpower Resources 1939–1941* (vol. 5/1 of *Germany and the Second World War*), trans. Derry Cook-Radmore. Oxford: Clarendon Press, 2000.

Kroll, Frank-Lothar. "Geschichte und Politik im Weltbild Hitlers," *Vierteljahrshefte für Zeitgeschichte* 44:3 (1996), 327–53.

Kroner, Bernhard R. "Auf dem Weg zu einer 'nationalsozialistischen Volksarmee'. Die soziale Öffnung des Heeresoffizierkorps im Zweiten Weltkrieg," in *Von Stalingrad zur Währungsreform. Zur Sozialgeschichte des Umbruchs in Deutschland*, ed. Martin Broszat, Klaus-Dietmar Henke, and Hans Woller. Munich: Oldenbourg, 1988, 651–82.

——. "'Frontochsen' und 'Etappenbullen': Zur Ideologisierung militärischer Organisationsstrukturen im Zweiten Weltkrieg, " in *Die Wehrmacht: Mythos Und Realität*, ed. Rolf-Dieter Müller and Hans-Erich Volkmann. Munich: Oldenbourg, 1999, 371–84.

——. "The 'Frozen Blitzkrieg': German Strategic Planning Against the Soviet Union and the Causes of its Failure," in *From Peace to War: Germany, Soviet Russia and the World, 1939– 1941*, ed. Bernd Wegner. Providence, R.I.: Berghahn Books, 1997, 135–49.

Krüger, Norbert. "Adolf Hitlers Clausewitzkenntnis," *Europaeische Sicherheit: Politik – Streitkraefte – Wirtschaft – Technik* 18:8 (1968), 467–71.

Krumeich, Gerd, ed. *Nationalsozialismus und Erster Weltkrieg*. Essen: Klartext, 2010.

Krumpelt, Ihno. "Die Bedeutung des Rüstungsplanes für den Kriegserfolg," *Europaeische Sicherheit: Politik – Streitkraefte – Wirtschaft – Technik* 20:9 (1970), 494–504.

Kühne, Thomas. *The Rise and Fall of Comradeship: Hitler's Soldiers, Male Bonding, and Mass Violence in the Twentieth Century*. Cambridge: Cambridge University Press, 2017.

Kunz, Andreas. "Die Wehrmacht 1944/45: Eine Armee in Untergang," in *Der Zusammenbruch des Deutschen Reiches 1945: Die Folgen Des Zweiten Weltkrieges* (vol. 10/2 of *Das Deutsche Reich und der Zweite Weltkrieg*), ed. Rolf-Dieter Müller. Munich: Deutsche Verlags-Anstalt, 2008, 3–54.

——. *Wehrmacht und Niederlage: Die Bewaffnete Macht in der Endphase der Nationalsozialistischen Herrschaft, 1944 bis 1945*. Munich: Oldenbourg, 2005.

Lakowski, Richard. "Der Zusammenbruch der deutschen Verteidigung zwischen Ostsee und Karpaten," in *Der Zusammenbruch des Deutschen Reiches 1945: Die Militärische Niederwerfung der Wehrmacht* (vol. 10/1 of *Das Deutsche Reich und der Zweite Weltkrieg*), ed. Rolf-Dieter Müller. Munich: Deutsche Verlags-Anstalt, 2008, 491–680.

Lange, Karl. "Der Terminus 'Lebensraum' in Hitlers Mein Kampf," *Vierteljahrshefte für Zeitgeschichte* 13:4 (1965), 426–37.

Larionov, Valentin. "Why the Wehrmacht Didn't Win in 1941," in *Operation Barbarossa: The German Attack on the Soviet Union, June 22, 1941*, ed. Joseph L. Wieczynski. Salt Lake City, UT: Charles Schlacks, 1993, 206–13.

Le Tissier, Tony. *Zhukov at the Oder: The Decisive Battle for Berlin*. Westport, CT: Praeger, 1996.

Leach, Barry A. *German Strategy against Russia*. Oxford: Clarendon Press, 1973.

Liddell Hart, B. H. "Hitler as War Lord," *Encounter* 30:172 (1968), 69–71.

Lieb, Peter. "Rommel in Normandy," in *Rommel Reconsidered.*, ed. I. F. W. Beckett. Mechanicsburg, PA: Stackpole Books, 2014, 113–36.

——. *Unternehmen Overlord. Die Invasion in der Normandie und die Befreiung Westeuropas*. Munich: C. H. Beck, 2014.

Liulevicius, Vejas Gabriel. *War Land on the Eastern Front: Culture, National Identity, and German Occupation in World War I*. New York: Cambridge University Press, 2000.

Lukacs, John. *The Hitler of History*. New York: A. Knopf, 1997.

Lunde, Henrik. *Hitler's Wave-Breaker Concept: An Analysis of the German End Game in the Baltic*. Philadelphia, PA, and Oxford: Casemate, 2013.

Luvaas, Jay. "Clausewitz, Fuller and Liddell Hart," *Journal of Strategic Studies* 9:2 (1986), 197–212.

Magenheimer, Heinz. *Hitler's War: German Military Strategy, 1940-1945*, trans. Helmut Bögler. London: Arms and Armour, 1998.

Maier, Klaus. "Securing the Northern Flank of Europe. I. German Strategy," in *Germany's Initial Conquests in Europe* (vol. 2 of *Germany in the Second World War*), ed. Klaus Maier, Horst Rohde, Bernd Stegemann, and Hans Umbreit, trans. Dean Scott McMurry, Ewald Osers, and P. S. Falla. Oxford: Oxford University Press, 1991, 181–219.

——. "Total War and German Air Doctrine before the Second World War," in *The German Military in the Age of Total War*, ed. Wilhelm Deist. Leamington Spa: Berg, 1985, 210–19.

Maier, Klaus A., Horst Rohde, Bernd Stegemann, and Hans Umbreit, eds. *Die Errichtung der Hegemonie auf dem europäischen Kontinent* (vol. 2 of *Das deutsche Reich und der zweite Weltkrieg*). Stuttgart: Deutsche Verlags-Anstalt, 1979.

Maier, Klaus A., Horst Rohde, Bernd Stegemann, and Hans Umbreit, eds. *Germany's Initial Conquests in Europe* (vol. 2 of *Germany and the Second World War*), trans. Dean Scott McMurry, Ewald Osers, and P. S. Falla. Oxford: Oxford University Press, 1991.

Maiolo, Joseph A. *Cry Havoc: How the Arms Race Drove the World to War, 1931–1941*. New York: Basic Books, 2010.

Mastny, Vojtech. "Stalin and the Prospects of a Separate Peace in World War II," *American Historical Review* 77:5 (1972), 1, 365–88.

Mauter, Wendell. "The Great War and the Shaping of Adolf Hitler," *European Studies Journal* 18:2 (2001), 39–54.

Mawdsley, Evan. *December 1941: Twelve Days that Began a World War*. New Haven, CT, and London: Yale University Press, 2011.

——. *Thunder in the East: The Nazi-Soviet War, 1941–1945*. London: Hodder Arnold, 2005.

McRandle, James, and James Quirk. "The Blood Test Revisited: A New Look at German Casualty Counts in World War I," *Journal of Military History* 70:3 (2006), 667–701.

Megargee, Geoffrey P. *Inside Hitler's High Command*. Lawrence, KS: University Press of Kansas, 2000.

——. *War of Annihilation: Combat and Genocide on the Eastern Front, 1941*. Lanham, MD: Rowman & Littlefield, 2006.

Melvin, Mungo. *Manstein: Hitler's Greatest General*. New York: Thomas Dunne Books/ St. Martin's Press, 2011.

Messerschmidt, Manfred. "Die Wehrmacht: Vom Realitätsverlust zum Selbstbetrug," in *Ende Des Dritten Reiches – Ende Des Zweiten Weltkriegs*, ed. Hans-Erich Volkmann. Munich: Piper, 1995, 223–57.

——. "June 1941 Seen through German Memoirs and Diaries," *Soviet Union* 18:1–3 (1991), 205–19.

——. "The Road to War, 1936–1938," in *The Build-up of German Aggression* (vol. 1 of *Germany and the Second World War*), ed. Wilhelm Deist, Manfred Messerschmidt, Hans-Erich Volkmann, and Wolfram Wette, trans. P. S. Falla, Dean S. McMurry, and Ewald Osers. Oxford: Oxford University Press, 1981, 615–79.

Michalka, Wolfgang. *Der Zweite Weltkrieg: Analysen, Grundzüge, Forschungsbilanz*. Munich: Piper, 1989.

Mierzejewski, Alfred C. *The Collapse of the German War Economy, 1944–1945: Allied Air Power and the German National Railway*. Chapel Hill, N.C.: University of North Carolina Press, 1988.

——. "When Did Albert Speer Give Up?," *Historical Journal* 31:2 (1988), 391–7.

Millett, Allan R., and Williamson Murray. *Military Effectiveness* (vol. III of *The Second World War*). London: Unwin Hyman, 1988.

Mitcham, Samuel W., Jr. "Generalfeldmarschall Werner von Blomberg," in *Hitlers militärische Elite. 68 Lebensläufe*, ed. Gerd R. Ueberschär, Darmstadt: Wissenschaftliche Buchgesellschaft, 2011, 28–36.

——. "Generaloberst der Waffen-SS Paul Hausser," in *Hitlers militärische Elite. 68 Lebensläufe*, ed. Gerd R. Ueberschär, Darmstadt: Wissenschaftliche Buchgesellschaft, 2011, 89–96.

Mitcham, Samuel W., Jr., and Gene Mueller. "Generalfeldmarschall Walter Model," in *Hitlers militärische Elite. 68 Lebensläufe*, ed. Gerd R. Ueberschär. Darmstadt: Wissenschaftliche Buchgesellschaft, 2011, 424–31.

——. "Generalfeldmarschall Walther von Brauchitsch," in *Hitlers militärische Elite. 68 Lebensläufe*, ed. Gerd R. Ueberschär, Darmstadt: Wissenschaftliche Buchgesellschaft, 2011, 45–52.

——. "Generaloberst Erich Hoepner," in *Hitlers militärische Elite. 68 Lebensläufe*, ed. Gerd R. Ueberschär. Darmstadt: Wissenschaftliche Buchgesellschaft, 2011, 364–70.

Mommsen, Hans. *Der erste Weltkrieg und die europäische Nachkriegsordnung: Sozialer Wandel und Formveränderung der Politik*. Cologne: Böhlau, 2000.

Mueller, Gene. "Generalfeldmarschall Günther von Kluge," in *Hitlers militärische Elite. 68 Lebensläufe*, ed. Gerd R. Ueberschär. Darmstadt: Wissenschaftliche Buchgesellschaft, 2011, 130–7.

Müller, Klaus Jürgen. *Das Heer und Hitler: Armee und nationalsozialistische Regime 1933– 1940*. Stuttgart: Deutsche Verlags-Anstalt, 1969.

Muller, Richard R. "Werner von Blomberg – Hitlers 'idealistischer' Kriegsminister," in *Die Militärelite des drittes Reich*, ed. Ronald M. Smelser and Enrico Syring. Berlin: Ullstein, 1995, 50–65.

Müller, Rolf-Dieter. *Der Feind steht im Osten: Hitlers geheime Pläne für einen Krieg gegen die Sowjetunion im Jahr 1939*. Berlin: Links, 2011.

——. "Die Zusammenbruch des Wirtschaftslebens und die Anfänge," in *Der Zusammenbruch des deutschen Reiches 1945 – Teilband 2: Die Folgen des zweiten Weltkrieges* (vol. 10/2 of *Das Deutsche Reich und der Zweite Weltkrieg*), ed. Rolf Dieter-Müller. Stuttgart: Deutsche Verlags-Anstalt, 2008, 55–200.

——, ed. *Der Zusammenbruch des deutschen Reiches 1945 und die Folgen des zweiten Weltkrieges – Teilband. 1: Die militärische Niederwerfung der Wehrmacht* (vol. 10/1 of *Das Deutsche Reich und der Zweite Weltkrieg*). Stuttgart: Deutsche Verlags-Anstalt, 2008.

——, ed. *Der Zusammenbruch des deutschen Reiches 1945 – Teilband 2: Die Folgen des zweiten Weltkrieges* (vol. 10/2 of *Das Deutsche Reich und der Zweite Weltkrieg*). Stuttgart: Deutsche Verlags-Anstalt, 2008.

——. *Enemy in the East: Hitler's Secret Plans to Invade the Soviet Union*, trans. Alexander Starritt. London: I. B. Taurus, 2015.

——. "From Economic Alliance to a War of Colonial Exploitation," in *The Attack on the Soviet Union* (vol. 4 of *Germany and the Second World War*), ed. Horst Boog, Jürgen Förster, Joachim Hoffmann, Ernst Klink, Rolf-Dieter Müller, and Gerd R. Ueberschär, trans. Dean S. McMurry, Ewald Osers, and Louise Willmot. Oxford: Clarendon Press, 1998, 118–224.

——. "The Failure of the Economic Blitzkrieg Strategy," in *The Attack on the Soviet Union* (vol. 4 of *Germany and the Second World War*), ed. Horst Boog. Jürgen Förster, Joachim Hoffmann, Ernst Klink, Rolf-Dieter Müller, and Gerd R. Ueberschär, trans. Dean S. McMurry, Ewald Osers, and Louise Willmot. Oxford: Clarendon Press, 1998, 1,081–1,188.

——. "The Mobilization of the German Economy for Hitler's War Aims," in *Organization and Mobilization of the German Sphere of Power. 1: Wartime Administration, Economy, and Manpower Resources 1939–1941* (vol. 5/1 of *Germany and the Second World War*), ed. Bernhard R. Kroener, Rolf-Dieter Müller, and Hans Umbreit, trans. Derry Cook-Radmore, 405–786. Oxford: Clarendon Press, 2000.

Müller, Rolf-Dieter, and Hans-Erich Volkmann, eds. *Die Wehrmacht: Mythos und Realitat*. Munich: Oldenbourg, 1999.

Murray, Williamson. "Attrition and the Luftwaffe," *Air University Review* 34:3 (1983), 66–77.

——. "Betrachtungen zur deutschen Strategie im Zweiten Weltkrieg," in *Die Wehrmacht: Mythos und Realität*, ed. Rolf-Dieter Müller and Hans-Erich Volkmann. Munich: Oldenbourg, 1999, 307–30.

——. "British and German Air Doctrine Between the Wars," *Air University Review* 31:3 (1980), 39–58.

——. "Clausewitz: Some Thoughts on What the Germans Got Right," *Journal of Strategic Studies* 9:2 (1986), 267–86.

——. "Force Strategy, Blitzkrieg Strategy and the Economic Difficulties: Nazi Grand Strategy in the 1930s," *Journal of the Royal United Services Institute for Defence Studies* 128:1 (1983), 39–43.

——. "German Army Doctrine, 1918–1939, and the Post-1945 Theory of 'Blitzkrieg Strategy'," in *German Nationalism and the European Response, 1890–1945*, ed. Carole Fink, Isabel V. Hull, and MacGregor Knox, Norman, OK: University of Oklahoma Press, 1985, 71–94.

——. "Munich, 1938: The Military Confrontation," *Journal of Strategic Studies* 2:3 (1979), 282–302.

——. *The Change in the European Balance of Power, 1938–1939: The Path to Ruin*. Princeton, N.J.: Princeton University Press, 1984.

——. "The German Response to Victory in Poland," *Armed Forces & Society* 7:2 (1981), 285–98.

——. "The Luftwaffe Before the Second World War: A Mission, a Strategy?," *Journal of Strategic Studies* 4:3 (1981), 261–70.

——. "The Strategy of the 'Phoney War': A Re-Evaluation," *Military Affairs* 45:1 (1981), 13–17.

Murray, Williamson, MacGregor Knox, and Alvin Bernstein, eds. *The Making of Strategy: Rulers, States, and War*. New York: Cambridge University Press, 1994.

Neitzel, Sönke. "Der Kampf um die deutschen Atlantik-und Kanalfestungen und sein Einfluß auf den alliierten Nachschub während der Befreiung Frankreichs 1944/45," *Militärgeschichtiche Mitteilungen* 55 (1996), 381–430.

Neumann, Hans-Joachim, and Henrik Eberle. *Was Hitler Ill? A Final Diagnosis*, trans. Nick Somers. Malden, MA: Polity Press, 2012.

O'Nell, Robert J. "Doctrine and Training in the German Army, 1919–1939," in *The Theory and Practice of War*, ed. Michael Howard. New York: Praeger, 1966, 143–65.

Ose, Dieter. "Rommel and Rundstedt: The 1944 Panzer Controversy," *Military Affairs* 50:1 (1986), 7–11.

Overmans, Rüdiger. *Deutsche militärische Verluste im Zweiten Weltkrieg*. Munich: Oldenbourg, 1999.

Overy, Richard. "From 'Uralbomber' to 'Amerikabomber': The Luftwaffe and Strategic Bombing," *Journal of Strategic Studies* 1:2 (1978), 154–78.

——. "Germany and the Munich Crisis: A Mutilated Victory?," *Diplomacy & Statecraft* 10:2 (1999), 191–215.

——. "Germany, 'Domestic Crisis' and War in 1939," *Past & Present* 116 (1987), 138–68.

——. "Hitler and Air Strategy," *Journal of Contemporary History* 15:3 (1980), 405–21.

——. "The Bombing of Germany: A Reappraisal," *Modern History Review* 10:4 (1999), 29–33.

——. *War and Economy in the Third Reich*. Oxford: Clarendon Press, 1994.

——. *Why the Allies Won*. New York: Norton, 1995.

Paret, Peter, Gordon Craig, and Felix Gilbert, eds. *Makers of Modern Strategy: From Machiavelli to the Nuclear Age*. Princeton, N.J.: Princeton University Press, 1986.

Phelps, Reginald H. "'Before Hitler Came': Thule Society and German Orden," *Journal of Modern History* 35:3 (1963), 245–61.

——. "Hitler and the 'Deutsche Arbeiterpartei' 1919–1920," *American Historical Review* 68:4 (1963), 974–86.

Pietrow-Ennker, Bianka. "Deutschland im Juni 1941 – Ein Opfer Sowjetischer Aggression? Zur Kontroverse über die Präventivkriegsthese," in *Der zweite Weltkrieg*, ed. Wolfgang Michalka. Munich: Piper, 1989, 586–607.

——. *Präventivkrieg? Der Deutsche Angriff auf die Sowjetunion*. Frankfurt: Fischer Taschenbuch, 2000.

——. "Stalinistische Aussenpolitik 1939–1941: Ein Beitrag zur Vorgeschichte des Deutschen Angriffs auf die Sowjetunion am 22. Juni 1941," *Beitrage zur Geschichte der Arbeiterbewegung* 33:6 (1991), 811–17.

Plöckinger, Othmar. *Geschichte eines Buches: Adolf Hitlers "Mein Kampf", 1922–1945*. Munich: Oldenbourg, 2006.

——. *Unter Soldaten und Agitatoren: Hitlers prägende Jahre im deutschen Militär 1918–1920*. Paderborn: Schöningh, 2013.

Pöhlmann, Markus. "Großer Krieg und nächster Krieg: Der erste Weltkrieg in den Kriegslehren und Planungen von Reichswehr und Wehrmacht," in *Nationalsozialismus und Erster Weltkrieg*, ed. Gerd Krumeich. Essen: Klartext, 2010, 285–97.

Pyta, Wolfram. *Hitler: Der Künstler als Politiker und Feldherr: eine Herrschaftsanalyse*. Munich: Siedler, 2015.

——. "Weltanschauliche und strategische Schicksalsgemeinschaft: Die Bedeutung Japans für das weltpolitische Kalkül Hitlers," in *Naziverbrechen: Täter, Taten, Bewältigungsversuche*, ed. Martin Cüppers, Jürgen Matthäus, and Andrej Angrick. Darmstadt: Wissenschaftliche Buchgesellschaft, 2013, 21–44.

Raack, R. C. "Stalin's Plans for World War Two Told by a High Comintern Source," *Historical Journal* 38:4 (1995), 1,031–6.

——. "Stalin's Plans for World War II," *Journal of Contemporary History* 26:2 (1991), 215–27.

——. "Stalin's Role in the Coming of World War II," *World Affairs* 158:4 (1996), 198–211.

Rahn, Werner. "The Atlantic in German and Allied Strategy," in *The Global War: Widening of the Conflict into a World War and the Shift of the Initiative 1941–1943* (vol. 6 of *Gemany and the Second World War*), ed. Horst Boog, Werner Rahn, and Reinhard Stumpf, trans. Ewald Osers. Oxford: Clarendon Press, 2001, 301–25.

Raphael, Lutz. "Pluralities of National Socialist Ideology: New Perspectives on the Production and Diffusion of National Socialist *Weltanschauung*," in *Visions of Community in Nazi Germany: Social Engineering and Private Lives*, ed. Martina Steber and Bernhard Gotto. Oxford: Oxford University Press, 2014, 73–86.

Raudzens, George. "Blitzkrieg Ambiguities: Doubtful Usage of a Famous Word," *War & Society* 7:2 (1989), 77–94.

Reid, Brian Holden. "J. F. C. Fuller and B. H. Liddell Hart: A Comparison," *Military Review* 70:5 (1990), 64–73.

——. "J. F. C. Fuller's Theory of Mechanized Warfare," *Journal of Strategic Studies* 1:3 (1978), 295–312.

Reinhardt, Klaus. *Die Wende vor Moskau. Das Scheitern der Strategie Hitlers im Winter 1941/42*. Stuttgart: Deutsche Verlags-Anstalt, 1972.

——. *Moscow – The Turning Point: The Failure of Hitler's Strategy in the Winter of 1941–42*, trans. Karl B. Keenan. Oxford: Berg, 1992.

Reynolds, Charles. "Carl von Clausewitz and Strategic Theory," *British Journal of International Studies* 4:2 (1978), 178–90.

Ritchie, David James. "Russo-German War Plans 1941: The Genesis of Barbarossa," *Strategy & Tactics* 108 (1985), 42–56.

Rohde, Horst. "Hitler's First Blitzkrieg and its Consequences for North-Eastern Europe," in *Germany's Initial Conquests in Europe* (vol. 2 of *Germany and the Second World War*), ed. Klaus A. Maier, Horst Rohde, Bernd Stegemann, and Hans Umbreit, trans. Dean Scott McMurry, Ewald Osers, and P. S. Falla. Oxford: Oxford University Press, 1991, 69–150.

Römer, Felix. "Die Wehrmacht und der Kommissarbefehl: Neue Forschungsergebnisse," *Militärgeschichtliche Zeitschrift* 69:2 (2010), 243–74.

——. " 'Im alten Deutschland wäre solcher Befehl nicht möglich gesesen.' Rezeption, Adaption und Umsetzung des Kriegsgerichtsbarkeitserlasses im Ostheer 1941/42," *Vierteljahrshefte für Zeitgeschichte* 56:1 (2008), 53–99.

Rush, Robert S. "A Different Perspective: Cohesion, Morale, and Operational Effectiveness in the German Army, Fall 1944," *Armed Forces & Society* 25:3 (1999), 477–508.

Salewski, Michael. "Die Abwehr der Invasion als Schlüssel zum 'Endsieg'?," in *Die Wehrmacht: Mythos und Realität*, ed. Rolf-Dieter Müller and Hans-Erich Volkmann. Munich: Oldenbourg, 1999, 210–23.

Schivelbusch, Wolfgang. *The Culture of Defeat: On National Trauma, Mourning, and Recovery*, trans. Jefferson Chase. New York: Metropolitan Books, 2003.

Schmider, Klaus. "The Mediterranean in 1940–1941: Crossroads of Lost Opportunities?," *War & Society* 15:2 (2013), 19–41.

Schreiber, Gerhard. "Das Ende des nordafrikanischen Feldzugs und der Krieg in Italien 1943 bis 1945," in *Die Ostfront, 1943/44: Der Krieg im Osten und an den Nebenfronten* (vol. 8 of *Das deutsche Reich und der zweite Weltkrieg*), ed. Karl-Heinz Frieser. Munich: Deutsche Verlags-Anstalt, 2007, 1,100–64.

——. "Der Mittelmeerraum in Hitlers Strategie 1940," *Militargeschichtliche Zeitschrift* 2 (1980), 69–99.

——. "Political and Military Developments in the Mediterranean Area, 1939–1940," in *The Mediterranean, South-East Europe, and North Africa, 1939–1941: From Italy's Declaration of Non-Belligerence to the Entry of the United States into the War* (vol. 3 of *Germany and the Second World War*), ed. Gerhard Schreiber, Bernd Stegemann, and Detlef Vogel, trans. Dean S. McMurry, Ewald Osers, and Louise Willmot. New York: Oxford University Press, 1995, 5–179.

——. "The Mediterranean in Hitler's Strategy in 1940: 'Programme' and Military Planning," in *The German Military in the Age of Total War*, ed. Wilhelm Deist. Leamington Spa: Berg, 1985, 240–81.

Schreiber, Gerhard, Bernd Stegemann, and Detlef Vogel, eds. *Der Mittelmeerraum und Südosteuropa. Von der "Non Belligeranza" Italiens bis zum Kriegseintritt der Vereinigten Staaten* (vol. 3 of *Das deutsche Reich und der zweite Weltkrieg*). Stuttgart: Deutsche Verlags-Anstalt, 1984.

———. *The Mediterranean, South-East Europe, and North Africa, 1939–1941: From Italy's Declaration of Non-Belligerence to the Entry of the United States into the War* (vol. 3 of *Germany and the Second World War*), trans. Dean S. McMurry, Ewald Osers, and Louise Willmot. Oxford: Clarendon Press, 1995.

Schröder, Josef. "Hitlers Weltkriegsstrategie," *Quellen und Forschungen aus Italienischen Archiven und Bibliotheken* 51 (1971), 618–25.

Schröder, Klaus. "Die Gedanken des Oberbefehlshabers der Kriegsmarine zum Kampf gegen England im Atlantik und im Mittelmeer 1939–1940," *Marine-Rundschau* 67:5 (1970), 257–72.

Schüler, Klaus. *Logistik im Rußlandfeldzug. Die Rolle der Eisenbahn bei Planung, Vorbereitung und Durchführung des Deutschen Angriffs auf die Sowjetunion bis zur Krise vor Moskau im Winter 1941/42.* Frankfurt: Peter Lang, 1987.

———. "The Eastern Campaign as a Transportation and Supply Problem," in *From Peace to War: Germany, Soviet Russia and the World, 1939–1941*, ed. Bernd Wegner. Providence, R.I.: Berghahn Books, 1997, 205–22.

Schustereit, Harmut. "Die Mineralöllieferungen der Sowjetunion an das deutsche Reich 1940/41," *Vierteljahrschrift für Sozial und Wirtschaftsgeschichte* 67:3 (1980), 334–53.

———. "Planung und Aufbau der Wirtschaftsorganisation Ost vor dem Russlandfeldzug-Unternehmen 'Barbarossa' 1940/41," *Vierteljahrschrift für Sozial und Wirtschaftsgeschichte* 70:1 (1983), 50–70.

———. *Vabanque: Hitlers Angriff auf die Sowjetunion 1941 als Versuch, durch den Sieg im Osten den Westen zu bezwingen.* Paris: Pour le Mérite, 1988.

Schwarz, Eberhard. *Die Stabilisierung der Ostfront nach Stalingrad: Mansteins Gegenschlag zwischen Donez und Dnjeper im Frühjahr 1943.* Göttingen: Muster-Schmidt, 1985.

———. "Zwischen Stalingrad und Kursk. Die Stabilisierung der Ostfront im Februar/März 1943," in *Stalingrad: Ereignis, Wirkung, Symbol*, ed. Jürgen Förster. Munich: Piper, 1992, 113–29.

Schweller, Randall L. *Deadly Imbalances: Tripolarity and Hitler's Strategy of World Conquest.* New York: Columbia University Press, 1998.

Schwendemann, Heinrich. "Die Deutsche Zusammenbruch im Osten 1944/45," in *Kriegsende 1945. Verbrechen, Katastrophen, Befreiungen in Nationaler und Internationaler Perspektive*, ed. Bernd A. Rusinek. Göttingen: Wallstein, 2004, 125–50.

———. "Drastic Measures to Defend the Reich at the Oder and the Rhine: A Forgotten Memorandum of Albert Speer of 18 March 1945," trans. Helen F. McEwan. *Journal of Contemporary History* 38:4 (2003), 597–614.

———. "German-Soviet Economic Relations at the Time of the Hitler-Stalin Pact 1939–1941," *Cahiers du Monde Russe* 36:1 (1995), 161–78.

———. "Strategie der Selbstvernichtung: Die Wehrmachtführung im 'Endkampf' um das 'Dritte Reich,'" in *Die Wehrmacht: Mythos und Realität*, ed. Rolf-Dieter Müller and Hans-Erich Volkmann. Munich: Oldenbourg, 1999, 224–44.

Shepherd, Ben. *Hitler's Soldiers: The German Army in the Third Reich.* New Haven, CT, and London: Yale University Press, 2016.

Shore, Zach. "Hitler, Intelligence and the Decision to Remilitarize the Rhine," *Journal of Contemporary History* 34:1 (1999), 5–18.

———. "Hitler's Opening Gambit: Intelligence, Encirclement, and the Decision to Ally with Poland," *Intelligence & National Security* 14:3 (1999), 103–22.

Showalter, Dennis E. "A Dubious Heritage: The Military Legacy of the Russo-German War," *Air University Review* 36:3 (1985), 4–23.

———. "Army and Society in Imperial Germany: The Pains of Modernization," *Journal of Contemporary History* 18:4 (1983), 583–618.

———. "From Deterrence to Doomsday Machine: The German Way of War, 1890–1914," *Journal of Military History* 64:3 (2000), 679–710.

——. "German Grand Strategy: A Contradiction in Terms?," *Militärgeschichtliche Zeitschrift* 2 (1990), 65–102.

——. *Hitler's Panzers: The Lightning Attacks that Revolutionized Warfare.* New York: Berkley Caliber, 2009.

——. "Past and Future: The Military Crisis of the Weimar Republic," *War & Society* 14:1 (1996), 49–72.

——. "The Birth of Blitzkrieg," *MHQ: Quarterly Journal of Military History* 7:1 (1994), 82–9.

——. "The Political Soldiers of Bismarck's Germany: Myths and Realities," *German Studies Review* 17:1 (1994), 59–77.

Simms, Brendan. "Against a 'world of enemies': The Impact of the First World War on the Development of Hitler's Ideology," *International Affairs* 90:2 (2014), 317–36.

Smelser, Ronald M., and Enrico Syring, eds. *Die Militärelite des dritten Reiches: 27 biographische Skizzen.* Berlin: Ullstein, 1995.

Smith, Woodruff D. "Friedrich Ratzel and the Origins of Lebensraum," *German Studies Review* 3:1 (1980), 51–68.

——. *The Ideological Origins of Nazi Imperialism.* New York: Oxford University Press, 1986.

Sokolov, Boris V. "The Battle for Kursk, Orel, and Char'Kov," in *Gezeitenwechsel im Zweiten Weltkrieg? Die Schlachten von Char'kov und Kursk in Operativer Anlage, Verlauf und Politischer Bedeutung*, ed. Roland G. Foerster. Hamburg: E. S. Mittler, 1996, 79–86.

——. "The Cost of War: Human Losses for the USSR and Germany, 1939–1945," *The Journal of Slavic Military Studies* 9:1 (1996), 152–93.

Sokolov, Boris V., and David M. Glantz. "The Role of Lend-Lease in Soviet Military Efforts, 1941–1945," *Journal of Slavic Military Studies* 7:3 (1994), 567–86.

Stahel, David. *Kiev 1941: Hitler's Battle for Supremacy in the East.* Cambridge: Cambridge University Press, 2011.

——. *Operation Barbarossa and Germany's Defeat in the East.* Cambridge: Cambridge University Press, 2009.

——. *Operation Typhoon: Hitler's March on Moscow, October 1941.* Cambridge: Cambridge University Press, 2013.

——. *The Battle for Moscow.* Cambridge: Cambridge University Press, 2015.

Stahl, Friedrich-Christian. "Generaloberst Rudolf Schmidt," in *Hitlers militärische Elite. 68 Lebensläufe*, ed. Gerd R. Ueberschär. Darmstadt: Primus Verlag, 1998, 489–96.

Stargardt, Nicholas. *The German War: A Nation Under Arms, 1939–1945: Citizens and Soldiers.* New York: Basic Books, 2015.

Stegemann, Bernd. "Der Entschluss zum Unternehmen Barbarossa: Strategie oder Ideologie?," *Geschichte in Wissenschaft und Unterricht* 33:4 (1982), 205–13.

——. "Geschichte und Politik. Zur Diskussion über den deutschen Angriff auf die Sowjetunion 1941," *Beiträge zur Konfliktforschung* 17:1 (1987), 73–97.

——. "Hitlers Ziele im Ersten Kriegsjahr 1939/40: Ein Beitrag zur Quellenkritik," *Militärgeschichtliche Mitteilungen* 1 (1980), 73–105.

——. "Politics and Warfare in the First Phase of the German Offensive," in *Germany's Initial Conquests in Europe* (vol. 2 of *Germany and the Second World War*), ed. Klaus A. Maier, Horst Rohde, and Hans Umbreit, trans. Dean S. McMurry and Ewald Osers. Oxford: Clarendon Press, 1991, 3–29.

——. "Politik und Kriegführung in der Ersten Phase der Deutschen Initiative," in *Die Errichtung der Hegemonie auf dem Europäischen Kontinent* (vol. 2 of *Das deutsche Reich und der zweite Weltkrieg*), ed. Klaus A. Maier, Horst Rohde, Bernd Stegemann, and Hans Umbreit. Stuttgart: Deutsche Verlags-Anstalt, 1979, 13–39.

Steinert, Marlis. *Hitler.* Munich: C. H. Beck, 1991.

——. *Hitler's War and the Germans: Public Mood and Attitude during the Second World War*, trans. Thomas E. J. de Witt. Athens, OH: Ohio University Press, 1977.

Steinkamp, Peter. "Generalfeldmarschall Friedrich Paulus," in *Hitlers militärische Elite. 68 Lebensläufe*, ed. Gerd R. Ueberschär. Darmstadt: Primus Verlag, 1998, 432–9.

Stevenson, David. *Cataclysm: The First World War as Political Tragedy.* New York: Basic Books, 2005.

Stolfi, R. H. C. "Barbarossa Revisited: A Critical Reappraisal of the Opening Stages of the Russo-German Campaign (June–December 1941)," *Journal of Modern History* 54:1 (1982), 27–46.

——. "Chance in History: The Russian Winter of 1941–1942," *History* 65:214 (1980), 214–28.

——. *Hitler's Panzers East: World War II Reinterpreted.* Norman, OK: University of Oklahoma Press, 1991.

——. "The Greatest Encirclement Battle in History," *RUSI Journal (Royal United Services Institute for Defence Studies)* 12 (1996), 64–72.

Strachan, Hew, "Clausewitz and the First World War," *Journal of Military History* 75 (April 2011), 367–91.

Strawson, John. *Churchill and Hitler: In Victory and Defeat.* London: Constable, 1998.

——. *Hitler as Military Commander.* Barnsley, South Yorkshire: Pen & Sword, 1971.

Strohn, Matthias. "Hans von Seeckt and his Vision of a 'Modern Army'," *War in History* 12:3 (2005), 318–37.

——. *The German Army and the Defence of the Reich: Military Doctrine and the Conduct of the Defensive Battle, 1918–1939.* Cambridge: Cambridge University Press, 2011.

Suvorov, Viktor. "Who was Planning to Attack Whom in June 1941, Hitler or Stalin?," *Journal of the Royal United Services Institute for Defence Studies* 130:2 (1985), 50–5.

Swain, Richard M. "B. H. Liddell Hart and the Creation of a Theory of War, 1919–1933," *Armed Forces & Society* 17:1 (1990), 35–51.

Syring, Enrico. *Hitler: Seine politische Utopie.* Berlin: Propyläen, 1994.

——. "Hitlers Kriegserklärung an Amerika vom 11. Dezember 1941," in *Der Zweite Weltkrieg. Analysen, Grundzüge, Forschungsbilanz,* ed. Wolfgang Michalka. Munich: Piper, 1989, 683–96.

Thies, Jochen. *Hitler's Plans for Global Domination: Nazi Architecture and Ultimate War Aims,* trans. Ian Cooke and Mary-Beth Friedrich. New York: Berghahn Books, 2012.

Thomas, David. "Foreign Armies East and German Military Intelligence in Russia 1941–45," *Journal of Contemporary History* 22:2 (1987), 261–301.

Tooze, Adam. "Hitler's Gamble?," *History Today* 56:11 (2006), 22–8.

——. "No Room for Miracles: German Industrial Output in World War II Reassessed," *Geschichte und Gesellschaft* 31:3 (2005), 439–64.

——. *The Wages of Destruction: The Making and Breaking of the Nazi Economy.* New York: Viking, 2006.

Töppel, Roman. "Legendenbildung in der Geschichtsschreibung – Die Schlacht bei Kursk," *Militärgeschichtliche Zeitschrift* 61:2 (2002), 369–401.

——. " 'Volk und Rasse'. Hitlers Quellen auf der Spur," *Vierteljahrshefte für Zeitgeschichte* 64:1 (2016), 1–35.

Ueberschär, Gerd R. "Das Scheitern des Unternehmen 'Barbarossa': Der deutsch-sowjetische Krieg vom Überfall bis zur Wende vor Moskau im Winter 1941–42," in *"Unternehmen Barbarossa". Der deutsche Überfall auf die Sowjetunion, 1941: Berichte, Analysen, Dokumente,* ed. Gerd R. Ueberschär and Wolfram Wette. Paderborn: Schöningh, 1984, 141–72.

——. "General Halder and the Resistance to Hitler in the German High Command 1938–40," *European History Quarterly* 18:3 (1988), 321–47.

——, ed. "Generaloberst Franz Halder," in *Hitlers militärische Elite. 68 Lebensläufe,* ed. Gerd R. Ueberschär. Darmstadt: Primus Verlag, 1998, 79–88.

——. "Hitlers Entschluß zum 'Lebensraum' Krieg im Osten. Programmatisches Ziel oder militärstrategisches Kalkül?," in *"Unternehmen Barbarossa". Der deutsche Überfall auf die Sowjetunion, 1941: Berichte, Analysen, Dokumente,* ed. Gerd R. Ueberschär and Wolfram Wette. Paderborn: Schoningh, 1984, 13–43.

——. *Hitlers militärische Elite.* Darmstadt: Primus Verlag, 1998.

Ueberschär, Gerd R., and Lev Bezymenski. *Der deutsche Angriff auf die Sowjetunion 1941: Die Kontroverse um die Praventivkriegsthese.* Darmstadt: Primus, 1998.

Ueberschär, Gerd R., and Wolfram Wette, eds. *Der deutsche Überfall auf die Sowjetunion, 1941: "Unternehmen Barbarossa". Berichte, Analysen, Dokumente.* Frankfurt: Fischer, 1991; rpt. 1984.

Ullrich, Volker. *Hitler: Ascent, 1889–1939*, trans. Jefferson Chase. New York: Alfred A. Knopf, 2016.

Umbreit, Hans. "Direct Strategy against Britain. II: Plans and Preparations for a Landing in England," in *Germany's Initial Conquests in Europe* (vol. 2 of *Germany and the Second World War*), ed. Klaus A. Maier, Horst Rohde, and Hans Umbreit, trans. Dean S. McMurry and Ewald Osers. Oxford: Clarendon Press, 1991, 366–73.

———. *Invasion 1944*. Hamburg: E. S. Mittler & Sohn, 1998.

———. "The Battle for Hegemony in Western Europe," in *Germany's Initial Conquests in Europe* (vol. 2 of *Germany and the Second World War*), ed. Klaus A. Maier, Horst Rohde, and Hans Umbreit, trans. Dean S. McMurry and Ewald Osers. Oxford: Clarendon Press, 1991, 229–326.

———. "The Return to an Indirect Strategy against Britain," in *Germany's Initial Conquests in Europe* (vol. 2 of *Germany and the Second World War*), ed. Klaus A. Maier, Horst Rohde, and Hans Umbreit, trans. Dean S. McMurry and Ewald Osers. Oxford: Clarendon Press, 1991, 408–16.

Ungvary, Krisztian. "Kriegsschauplatz Ungarn," in *Die Ostfront 1943/44: Der Krieg im Osten und an den Nebenfronten* (vol. 8 of *Das deutsche Reich und der zweite Weltkrieg*), ed. Karl-Heinz Frieser. Munich: Deutsche Verlags-Anstalt, 2007, 849–960.

Vardi, Gil-li. "Joachim von Stülpnagel's Military Thought and Planning," *War in History* 17:2 (2010), 193–216.

———. "The Enigma of German Operational Theory: The Evolution of Military Thought in Germany, 1919–1938." PhD Thesis. London School of Economics and Political Science (University of London), 2008.

Vego, Milan. "German War Gaming," *Naval War College Review* 65:4 (2012), 106–47.

Vogel, Detlef. "German and Allied Conduct of the War in the West," in *The Strategic Air War in Europe and the War in the West and East Asia, 1943–1944/5* (vol. 7 of *Germany and the Second World War*), ed. Horst Boog, Gerhard Krebs, and Detlef Vogel, trans. Derry Cook-Radmore. Oxford: Clarendon Press, 2006, 459–702.

———. "German Intervention in the Balkans. III: The German Attack on Yugoslavia and Greece," in *The Mediterranean, South-East Europe, and North Africa, 1939–1941: From Italy's Declaration of Non-Belligerence to the Entry of the United States into the War* (vol. 3 of *Germany and the Second World War*), ed. Gerhard Schreiber, Bernd Stegemann, and Detlef Vogel, trans. Dean S. McMurry, Ewald Osers, and Louise Willmot. Oxford: Clarendon Press, 1995, 497–556.

Waddington, Lorna. *Hitler's Crusade: Bolshevism, the Jews, and the Myth of Conspiracy*. London: I. B. Tauris, 2012.

Wallach, Jehuda L. "Adolf Hitlers Privatbibliothek," *Zeitgeschichte* 19 (1992), 29–50.

———. "Feldmarschall Erich von Manstein und die deutsche Judenausrottung in Russland," *Jahrbuch des Instituts für Deutsche Geschichte* 4 (1975), 457–72.

———. "Misperceptions of Clausewitz' 'On War' by the German Military," *Journal of Strategic Studies* 9:2 (1986), 213–39.

———. *The Dogma of the Battle of Annihilation: The Theories of Clausewitz and Schlieffen and Their Impact on the German Conduct of Two World Wars*. Westport, CT: Greenwood, 1986.

Warlimont, Walter. "Die Insel Malta in der Mittelmeerstrategie des zweiten Weltkriegs," *Europaeische Sicherheit: Politik – Streitkraefte – Wirtschaft – Technik* 8:8 (1958), 421–36.

———. *Inside Hitler's Headquarters, 1939–45*, trans. R. H. Barry. New York: F. A. Praeger, 1964.

Watt, Donald Cameron. *How War Came: The Immediate Origins of the Second World War, 1938–1939*. New York: Pantheon Books, 1989.

Weber, Thomas. *Hitler's First War: Adolf Hitler, the Men of the List Regiment, and the First World War*. Oxford: Oxford University Press, 2011.

———. *Wie Adolf Hitler zum Nazi wurde: Vom unpolitischen Soldaten zum Autor von "Mein Kampf,"* trans. Karl Heinz Siber and Heike Schlatterer. Berlin: Propyläen Verlag, 2016.

Wegner, Bernd. 2007. "Das Ende der Strategie. Deutschlands politische und militärische Lage nach Stalingrad," in *Gezeitenwechsel im zweiten Weltkrieg? Die Schlachten von*

Charkov und Kursk in operativer Anlage, Verlauf und politischer Bedeutung, ed. Roland G. Foerster. Hamburg: E. S. Mittler, 1996, 211–28.

——. "Defensive ohne Strategie. Die Wehrmacht und das Jahr 1943," in *Die Wehrmacht: Mythos und Realität*, ed. Rolf-Dieter Müller and Hans-Erich Volkmann. Munich: Oldenbourg, 1999, 197–209.

——. "Die Aporie des Krieges," in *Die Ostfront 1943/44: Der Krieg im Osten und an den Nebenfronten* (vol. 8 of *Das deutsche Reich und der zweite Weltkrieg*), ed. Karl-Heinz Frieser. Munich: Deutsche Verlags-Anstalt, 2007, 211–74.

——. "Die Choreographie des Untergangs," in *Die Ostfront 1943/44: Der Krieg im Osten und an den Nebenfronten* (vol. 8 of *Das deutsche Reich und der zweite Weltkrieg*), ed. Karl-Heinz Frieser. Munich: Deutsche Verlags-Anstalt, 2007, 1,192–1,209.

——. "Die Kriegführung des 'als ob': Deutschlands strategische Lage seit Frühjahr1944," in *Die Ostfront 1943/44: Der Krieg im Osten und an den Nebenfronten* (vol. 8 of *Das deutsche Reich und der zweite Weltkrieg*), ed. Karl-Heinz Frieser. Munich: Deutsche Verlags-Anstalt, 2007, 1,165–91.

——. "Hitler, der zweite Weltkrieg und die Choreographie des Untergangs," *Geschichte und Gesellschaft* 26:3 (2000), 493–518.

——. "Hitler's Grand Strategy between Pearl Harbor and Stalingrad," in *The Global War: Widening of the Conflict into a World War and the Shift of the Initiative 1941–1943* (vol. 6 of *Germany and the Second World War*), ed. Horst Boog, Werner Rahn, Reinhard Stumpf, and Bernd Wegner, trans. Ewald Osers, John Brownjohn, Patricia Crampton, and Louise Willmot. Oxford: Clarendon Press, 2001, 112–60.

——. "'Hitlers Krieg?' Zur Entscheidung, Planung und Umsetzung des 'Unternehmen Barbarossa'," in *Verbrechen der Wehrmacht. Bilanz einer Debatte*, ed. Christian Hartmann, Johannes Hürter, and Ulrike Jureit. Munich: Beck, 2005, 29–39.

——. "Hitlers zweiter Feldzug gegen die Sowjetunion. Strategische Grundlagen und historische Bedeutung," in *Der zweite Weltkrieg: Analysen, Grundzüge, Forschungsbilanz*, ed. Wolfgang Michalka. Munich: Piper, 1989, 652–66.

——. "The War against the Soviet Union, 1942–1943," in *The Global War: Widening of the Conflict into a World War and the Shift of the Initiative 1941–1943* (vol. 6 of *Germany and the Second World War*), ed. Horst Boog, Werner Rahn, Reinhard Stumpf, and Bernd Wegner, trans. Ewald Osers, John Brownjohn, Patricia Crampton, and Louise Willmot. Oxford: Clarendon Press, 2001, 843–1,215.

——. "Vom Lebensraum zum Todesraum. Deutschlands Kriegführung zwischen Moskau und Stalingrad," in *Stalingrad. Ereignis – Wirkung – Symbol*, ed. Jürgen Förster. Munich: Piper, 1992, 17–38.

——. "Von Stalingrad nach Kursk," in *Die Ostfront 1943/44: Der Krieg im Osten und an den Nebenfronten* (vol. 8 of *Das deutsche Reich und der zweite Weltkrieg*), ed. Karl-Heinz Frieser. Munich: Deutsche Verlags-Anstalt, 2007, 3–79.

Weinberg, Gerhard L. "Aspects of World War II German Intelligence," *Journal of Intelligence History* 4:1 (2004), 1–6.

——. *A World at Arms: A Global History of World War II*. Cambridge: Cambridge University Press, 1994.

——. "Die Wehrmacht und Verbrechen im Zweiten Weltkrieg," *Zeitgeschichte* 30:4 (2003), 207–10.

——. "German Diplomacy Towards the Soviet Union," *Soviet Union* 18:1–3 (1991), 317–33.

——. "German Foreign Policy and Poland, 1937–38," *Polish Review* 20:1 (1975), 5–23.

——. "German Plans for Victory, 1944–45," *Central European History* 26:2 (1993), 215–28.

——. *Germany, Hitler, and World War II: Essays in Modern German and World History*. New York: Cambridge University Press, 1995.

——. "Germany's War for World Conquest and the Extermination of the Jews," *Holocaust & Genocide Studies* 10:2 (1996), 119–33.

——. "Hitler and England, 1933–1945: Pretense and Reality," *German Studies Review* 8:2 (1985), 299–309.

——. "Hitler's Image of the United States," *American Historical Review* 69:4 (1964), 1,006–21.

——. "Hitler's Memorandum on the Four-Year Plan: A Note," *German Studies Review* 11:1 (1988), 133–5.

——. *Hitler's Second Book: The Unpublished Sequel to Mein Kampf*, trans. Krista Smith. New York: Enigma Books, 2003.

——. "Some Thoughts on World War II," *Journal of Military History* 56:4 (1992), 659–68.

——. "The Defeat of Germany in 1918 and the European Balance of Power," *Central European History* 2:3 (1969), 248–60.

——. *The Foreign Policy of Hitler's Germany: Starting World War II, 1937–1939.* Chicago, IL: University of Chicago Press, 1980.

——. "The May Crisis, 1938," *The Journal of Modern History* 29:3 (1957), 213–25.

——. "The Nazi-Soviet Pacts: A Half-Century Later," *Foreign Affairs* 68:4 (1989), 175–89.

——. "22 June 1941: The German View," *War in History* 3:2 (1996), 225–33.

——. "Why Hitler Declared War on the United States," *MHQ: The Quarterly Journal of Military History* 4:3 (1992), 18–23.

——. "Who Won World War II and How?," *Journal of Mississippi History* 57:4 (1995), 275–87.

——. *World in the Balance: Behind the Scenes of World War II.* Hanover, N.H.: University Press of New England, 1981.

——. "Zur Frage eines Sonderfriedens im Osten," in *Gezeitenwechsel im zweiten Weltkrieg? Die Schlachten von Charkov und Kursk im Frühjahr und Sommer 1943 in Operativer Anlage, Verlauf und politischer Bedeutung*, ed. Roland G. Foerster. Hamburg: E. S. Mittler, 1996, 173–83.

Westermann, Edward. *Hitler's Ostkrieg and the Indian Wars: Comparing Genocide and Conquest.* Norman, OK: University of Oklahoma Press, 2016.

Wette, Wolfram. *Die Wehrmacht: Feindbilder, Vernichtungskrieg, Legenden.* Frankfurt: Fischer Taschenbuch Verlag, 2005.

——. *The Wehrmacht: History, Myth, Reality*, trans. Deborah Lucas Schneider. Cambridge, MA: Harvard University Press, 2007.

Wieczynski, Joseph L., ed. *Operation Barbarossa: The German Attack on the Soviet Union, June 22, 1941.* Salt Lake City, UT: C. Schlacks, 1993.

Wildt, Michael. *Generation des Unbedingten: Das Führungskorps des Reichssicherheitshauptamtes.* Hamburg: Hamburger Edition, 2002.

Williams, John Frank. *Corporal Hitler and the Great War 1914–1918: The List Regiment.* London: Frank Cass, 2005.

Wilt, Alan F. "Hitler's Late Summer Pause in 1941," *Military Affairs* 45:4 (1981), 187–91.

——. *War from the Top: German and British Military Decision Making during World War II.* Bloomington, IN: Indiana University Press, 1990.

Wright, Jonathan, and Paul Stafford. "Hitler, Britain and the Hossbach Memorandum," *Militärgeschichtliche Zeitschrift* 2 (1987), 77–123.

Yelton, David K. "'Ein volk steht auf': The German Volkssturm and Nazi Strategy, 1944–45," *Journal of Military History* 64:4 (2000), 1,061–83.

——. *Hitler's Volkssturm: The Nazi Militia and the Fall of Germany, 1944–1945.* Lawrence, KS: University Press of Kansas, 2002.

Zeidler, Manfred. "Die Rote Armee auf Deutschem Boden," in *Der Zusammenbruch des Deutschen Reiches 1945: Die Militärische Niederwerfung der Wehrmacht* (vol. 10/1 of *Das deutsche Reich und der zweite Weltkrieg*), ed. Rolf-Dieter Müller. Munich: Deutsche Verlags-Anstalt, 2008, 681–776.

——. *Kriegsende im Osten. Die Rote Armee und die Besetzung Deutschlands Östlich von Oder und Neiße 1944/45.* Munich: Oldenbourg, 1996.

Zetterling, Niklas. "Loss Rates on the Eastern Front during World War II," *Journal of Slavic Military Studies* 9 (1996), 895–906.

Zetterling, Niklas, and Anders Frankson. "Analyzing World War II Eastern Front Battles," *The Journal of Slavic Military Studies* 11:1 (1998), 176–203.

——. *Kursk 1943: A Statistical Analysis.* London: Frank Cass, 2000.

Zhukov, Georgii Konstantinovich. *The Memoirs of Marshal Zhukov.* New York: Delacorte Press, 1971.

Ziemke, Earl. "Franz Halder at Orsha: The German General Staff Seeks a Consensus," *Military Affairs* 39:4 (1975), 173–6.

——. *Stalingrad to Berlin: The German Defeat in the East.* Washington, D.C.: Office of the Chief of Military History, U.S. Army, 1968.

Ziemke, Earl, and Magna E. Bauer. *Moscow to Stalingrad: Decision in the East.* Washington, D.C.: Center of Military History, United States Army, 1987.

Zimmerer, Jürgen. "Holocaust und Kolonialismus: Beitrag zu einer Archäologie des Genozidalen Gedankens," *Zeitschrift für Geschichtswissenschaft* 51:12 (2003), 1,098–119.

——. "The Birth of the 'Ostland' out of the Spirit of Colonialism: A Postcolonial Perspective on the Nazi Policy of Conquest and Extermination," *Patterns of Prejudice* 39:2 (2005), 197–219.

Zimmermann, John. "Die deutsche militärische Kriegführung im Westen 1944/45," in *Der Zusammenbruch des deutschen Reiches 1945: Die militärische Niederwerfung der Wehrmacht* (vol. 10/1 of *Das deutsche Reich und der zweite Weltkrieg*), ed. Horst Boog, Richard Lakowski, Werner Rahn, Manfred Zeidler, and John Zimmermann. Munich: Deutsche Verlags-Anstalt, 2008, 277–490.

Zitelmann, Rainer. *Hitler. Selbstverständnis eines Revolutionärs.* Hamburg: Berg, 1987.

——. "Zur Begründung des 'Lebensraum' Motivs in Hitlers Weltanschauung," in *Der Zweite Weltkrieg: Analysen, Grundzüge, Forschungsbilanz,* ed. Wolfgang Michalka. Munich: Piper, 1989, 551–67.

Index